Red Hat® Linux® Security and Optimization

Mohammed J. Kabir

Hungry Minds, Inc.

New York, NY • Indianapolis, IN • Cleveland, OH

Red Hat® Linux® Security and Optimization

Published by
Hungry Minds, Inc.
909 Third Avenue
New York, NY 10022
www.hungryminds.com

Library of Congress Control Number: 2001092938

ISBN: 0-7645-4754-2

Printed in the United States of America

10 9 8 7 6 5 4 3 2 1

1B/SX/RR/QR/IN

Distributed in the United States by Hungry Minds, Inc.

Distributed by CDG Books Canada Inc. for Canada; by Transworld Publishers Limited in the United Kingdom; by IDG Norge Books for Norway; by IDG Sweden Books for Sweden; by IDG Books Australia Publishing Corporation Pty. Ltd. for Australia and New Zealand; by TransQuest Publishers Pte Ltd. for Singapore, Malaysia, Thailand, Indonesia, and Hong Kong; by Gotop Information Inc. for Taiwan; by ICG Muse, Inc. for Japan; by Intersoft for South Africa; by Eyrolles for France; by International Thomson Publishing for Germany, Austria, and Switzerland; by Distribuidora Cuspide for Argentina; by LR International for Brazil; by Galileo Libros for Chile; by Ediciones ZETA S.C.R. Ltda. for Peru; by WS Computer Publishing Corporation, Inc., for the Philippines; by Contemporanea de Ediciones for Venezuela; by Express Computer Distributors for the Caribbean and West Indies; by Micronesia Media Distributor, Inc. for Micronesia; by Chips Computadoras S.A. de C.V. for Mexico; by Editorial Norma de Panama S.A. for Panama; by American Bookshops for Finland.

For general information on Hungry Minds' products and services please contact our Customer Care department within the U.S. at 800-762-2974, outside the U.S. at 317-572-3993 or fax 317-572-4002.

For sales inquiries and reseller information, including discounts, premium and bulk quantity sales, and foreign-language translations, please contact our Customer Care department at 800-434-3422, fax 317-572-4002 or write to Hungry Minds, Inc., Attn: Customer Care Department, 10475 Crosspoint Boulevard, Indianapolis, IN 46256.

For information on licensing foreign or domestic rights, please contact our Sub-Rights Customer Care department at 212-884-5000.

For information on using Hungry Minds' products and services in the classroom or for ordering examination copies, please contact our Educational Sales department at 800-434-2086 or fax 317-572-4005.

For press review copies, author interviews, or other publicity information, please contact our Public Relations department at 317-572-3168 or fax 317-572-4168.

For authorization to photocopy items for corporate, personal, or educational use, please contact Copyright Clearance Center, 222 Rosewood Drive, Danvers, MA 01923, or fax 978-750-4470.

Credits

ACQUISITIONS EDITOR
Debra Williams Cauley

PROJECT EDITOR
Pat O'Brien

TECHNICAL EDITORS
Matthew Hayden
Sandra "Sam" Moore

COPY EDITORS
Barry Childs-Helton
Stephanie Provines

EDITORIAL MANAGER
Kyle Looper

RED HAT PRESS LIAISON
Lorien Golaski, Red Hat
Communications Manager

SENIOR VICE PRESIDENT, TECHNICAL
PUBLISHING
Richard Swadley

VICE PRESIDENT AND PUBLISHER
Mary Bednarek

PROJECT COORDINATOR
Maridee Ennis

GRAPHICS AND PRODUCTION
SPECIALISTS
Karl Brandt
Stephanie Jumper
Laurie Petrone
Brian Torwelle
Erin Zeltner

QUALITY CONTROL TECHNICIANS
Laura Albert
Andy Hollandbeck
Carl Pierce

PERMISSIONS EDITOR
Carmen Krikorian

MEDIA DEVELOPMENT SPECIALIST
Marisa Pearman

PROOFREADING AND INDEXING
TECHBOOKS Production Services

About the Author

Mohammed Kabir is the founder and CEO of Evoknow, Inc. His company specializes in open-source solutions and customer relationship management software development. When he is not busy managing software projects or writing books, he enjoys traveling around the world. Kabir studied computer engineering at California State University, Sacramento. He is also the author of *Red Hat Linux Server* and *Apache Server Bible*. He can be reached at kabir@evoknow.com.

This book is dedicated to my wife, who proofs my writing, checks my facts, and writes my dedications.

Preface

This book is focused on two major aspects of Red Hat Linux system administration: performance tuning and security. The tuning solutions discussed in this book will help your Red Hat Linux system to have better performance. At the same time, the practical security solutions discussed in the second half of the book will allow you to enhance your system security a great deal. If you are looking for time saving, practical solutions to performance and security issues, read on!

How This Book is Organized

The book has five parts, plus several appendixes.

Part 1: System Performance

This part of the book explains the basics of measuring system performance, customizing your Red Hat Linux kernel to tune the operating system, tuning your hard disks, and journaling your filesystem to increase file system reliability and robustness.

Part II: Network and Service Performance

This part of the book explains how to tune your important network services, including Apache Web server, Sendmail and postfix mail servers, and Samba and NFS file and printer sharing services.

Part III: System Security

This part of the book covers how to secure your system using kernel-based Linux Intrusion Detection System (LIDS) and Libsafe buffer overflow protection mechanisms. Once you have learned to secure your Red Hat Linux kernel, you can secure your file system using various tools. After securing the kernel and the file system, you can secure user access to your system using such tools as Pluggable Authentication Module (PAM), Open Source Secure Socket Layer (OpenSSL), Secure Remote Password (SRP), and xinetd.

Part IV: Network Service Security

This part of the book shows how to secure your Apache Web server, BIND DNS server, Sendmail and postfix SMTP server, POP3 mail server, Wu-FTPD and ProFTPD FTP servers, and Samba and NFS servers.

Part V: Firewalls

This part of the book shows to create packet filtering firewall using iptables, how to create virtual private networks, and how to use SSL based tunnels to secure access to system and services. Finally, you will be introduced to an wide array of security tools such as security assessment (audit) tools, port scanners, log monitoring and analysis tools, CGI scanners, password crackers, intrusion detection tools, packet filter tools, and various other security administration utilities.

Appendixes

These elements include important references for Linux network users, plus an explanation of the attached CD-ROM.

Conventions of This Book

You don't have to learn any new conventions to read this book. Just remember the usual rules:

♦ When you are asked to enter a command, you need press the Enter or the Return key after you type the command at your command prompt.

♦ A `monospaced` font is used to denote configuration or code segment.

♦ Text in `italic` needs to be replaced with relevant information.

Watch for these icons that occasionally highlight paragraphs.

The Note icon indicates that something needs a bit more explanation.

The Tip icon tells you something that is likely to save you some time and effort.

The Caution icon makes you aware of a potential danger.

The cross-reference icon tells you that you can find additional information in another chapter.

Tell Us What You Think of This Book

Both Hungry Minds and I want to know what you think of this book. Give us your feedback. If you are interested in communicating with me directly, send e-mail messages to kabir@evoknow.com. I will do my best to respond promptly.

Acknowledgments

While writing this book, I often needed to consult with many developers whose tools I covered in this book. I want to specially thank a few such developers who have generously helped me present some of their great work.

Huagang Xie is the creator and chief developer of the LIDS project. Special thanks to him for responding to my email queries and also providing me with a great deal of information on the topic.

Timothy K. Tsai, Navjot Singh, and Arash Baratloo are the three members of the Libsafe team who greatly helped in presenting the Libsafe information. Very special thanks to Tim for taking the time to promptly respond to my emails and providing me with a great deal of information on the topic.

I thank both the Red Hat Press and Hungry Minds teams who made this book a reality. It is impossible to list everyone involved but I must mention the following kind individuals.

Debra Williams Cauley provided me with this book opportunity and made sure I saw it through to the end. Thanks, Debra.

Terri Varveris, the acquisitions editor, took over in Debra's absence. She made sure I had all the help needed to get this done. Thanks, Terri.

Pat O'Brien, the project development editor, kept this project going. I don't know how I could have done this book without his generous help and suggestions every step of the way. Thanks, Pat.

Matt Hayden, the technical reviewer, provided numerous technical suggestions, tips, and tricks — many of which have been incorporated in the book. Thanks, Matt.

Sheila Kabir, my wife, had to put up with many long work hours during the few months it took to write this book. Thank you, sweetheart.

Contents at a Glance

Contents

Part I

System Performance

Chapter 1

Performance Basics

IN THIS CHAPTER

- ◆ Assessing system performance accurately
- ◆ Taking your system's pulse with `ps`
- ◆ Measuring system activity with `top`
- ◆ Checking memory, input, and output with `vmstat`
- ◆ Analyzing with `Vtad`

RED HAT LINUX is a great operating system for extracting the last bit of performance from your computer system, whether it's a desktop unit or a massive corporate network. In a networked environment, optimal performance takes on a whole new dimension – the efficient delivery of security services – and the system administrator is the person expected to deliver. If you're like most system administrators, you're probably itching to start tweaking – but before you do, you may want to take a critical look at the whole concept of "high performance."

Today's hardware and bandwidth – fast and relatively cheap – has spoiled many of us. The long-running craze to buy the latest computer "toy" has lowered hardware pricing; the push to browse the Web faster has lowered bandwidth pricing while increasing its carrying capacity. Today, you can buy 1.5GHz systems with 4GB of RAM and hundreds of GB of disk space (ultra-wide SCSI 160, at that) without taking a second mortgage on your house. Similarly, about $50 to $300 per month can buy you a huge amount of bandwidth in the U.S. – even in most metropolitan homes.

Hardware and bandwidth have become commodities in the last few years – but are we all happy with the performance of our systems? Most users are likely to agree that even with phenomenal hardware and bandwidth, their computers just don't seem that fast anymore – but how many people distinguish between two systems that seem exactly the same except for processor speed? Unless you play demanding computer games, you probably wouldn't notice much difference between 300MHz and 500MHz when you run your favorite word processor or Web browser.

Actually, much of what most people accept as "high performance" is based on their human *perception* of how fast the downloads take place or how crisp the video on-screen looks. Real measurement of performance requires accurate tools and repeated sampling of system activity. In a networked environment, the need for such measurement increases dramatically; for a network administrator, it's indispensable.

Accordingly, this chapter introduces a few simple but useful tools that measure and monitor system performance. Using their data, you can build a more sophisticated perception of how well your hardware actually performs. When you've established a reliable baseline for your system's performance, you can tune it to do just what you want done—starting with the flexibility of the Red Hat Linux operating system, and using its advantages as you configure your network to be fast, efficient, and secure.

Measuring System Performance

A good introduction to the use of Linux tools to measure and monitor system performance is to start with ps, top, vmstat, and Vtad. These programs are easy to find, easy to use, and illustrate the kinds of information an administrator needs to keep an eye on.

Monitoring system performance with ps

Having a realistic idea of what's running is always the first step in monitoring system performance. The ps Linux utility monitors the processes that are running on your system; you can tell the utility how many (or how few) to monitor.

The ps utility shows not only each process, but also how much memory it's using—as well as how much CPU time, which user owns the process, and many other handy bits of data. A sample of the ps command's output looks like this:

```
PID TTY          TIME CMD
4406 pts/1    00:00:00 su
4407 pts/1    00:00:00 bash
4480 pts/1    00:00:00 ps
```

Here ps reports that three programs are running under the current user ID: su, bash, and ps itself. If you want a list of all the processes running on your system, you can run ps aux to get one. A sample of the ps aux command's output (abbreviated, of course) looks like this:

```
USER    PID %CPU %MEM   VSZ  RSS TTY STAT START   TIME COMMAND
root      1  0.1  0.1  1324  532 ?   S    10:58   0:06 init [3]
root      2  0.0  0.0     0    0 ?   SW   10:58   0:00 [kflushd]
root      3  0.0  0.0     0    0 ?   SW   10:58   0:00 [kupdate]
root      4  0.0  0.0     0    0 ?   SW   10:58   0:00 [kpiod]
root      5  0.0  0.0     0    0 ?   SW   10:58   0:00 [kswapd]
root      6  0.0  0.0     0    0 ?   SW<  10:58   0:00 [mdrecoveryd]
root     45  0.0  0.0     0    0 ?   SW   10:58   0:00 [khubd]
root    349  0.0  0.1  1384  612 ?   S    10:58   0:00 syslogd -m 0
root    359  0.0  0.1  1340  480 ?   S    10:58   0:00 klogd
rpc     374  0.0  0.1  1468  576 ?   S    10:58   0:00 portmap
[Remaining lines omitted]
```

Sometimes you may want to run ps to monitor a specific process for a certain length of time. For example, say you installed a new Sendmail mail-server patch and want to make sure the server is up and running – and you also want to know whether it uses more than its share of system resources. In such a case, you can combine a few Linux commands to get your answers – like this:

```
watch --interval=n  "ps auxw | grep process_you_want_to_monitor"
```

For example, you run watch --interval=30 "ps auxw | grep sendmail. By running the ps program every 30 seconds you can see how much resource sendmail is using.

Combining ps with the tree command, you can run pstree, which displays a tree structure of all processes running on your system. A sample output of pstree looks like this:

```
init-+-apmd
     |-atd
     |-crond
     |-identd---identd---3*[identd]
     |-kflushd
     |-khubd
     |-klogd
     |-kpiod
     |-kswapd
     |-kupdate
     |-lockd---rpciod
     |-lpd
     |-mdrecoveryd
     |-6*[mingetty]
     |-named
     |-nmbd
     |-portmap
     |-rhnsd
     |-rpc.statd
     |-safe_mysqld---mysqld---mysqld---mysqld
     |-sendmail
     |-smbd---smbd
     |-sshd-+-sshd---bash---su---bash---man---sh---sh-+-groff---grotty
     |      |                                         `-less
     |       `-sshd---bash---su---bash---pstree
     |-syslogd
     |-xfs
      `-xinetd
```

You can see that the parent of all processes is init. One branch of the tree is created by safe_mysqld, spawning three mysqld daemon processes. The sshd branch shows that the sshd daemon has forked two child daemon processes — which have open bash shells and launched still other processes. The pstree output was generated by one of the sub-branches of the sshd daemon.

Tracking system activity with top

This utility monitors system activity interactively. When you run top from a shell window or an xterm, it displays all the active processes and updates the screen (using a user-configurable interval). A sample top session is shown here:

```
12:13pm  up  1:15,  2 users,  load average: 0.05, 0.07, 0.01
48 processes: 47 sleeping, 1 running, 0 zombie, 0 stopped
CPU states:  1.1% user,  2.1% system,  0.0% nice, 96.7% idle
Mem:    387312K av,   96876K used,  290436K free,   27192K shrd,   36040K buff
Swap: 265064K av,       OK used,  265064K free                   34236K cached
PID USER      PRI  NI  SIZE  RSS SHARE STAT %CPU %MEM   TIME COMMAND
 6748 kabir    15   0  1032 1032   832 R    0.9  0.2  0:00 top
    1 root      0   0   532  532   468 S    0.0  0.1  0:06 init
    2 root      0   0     0    0     0 SW   0.0  0.0  0:00 kflushd
    3 root      0   0     0    0     0 SW   0.0  0.0  0:00 kupdate
    4 root      0   0     0    0     0 SW   0.0  0.0  0:00 kpiod
    5 root      0   0     0    0     0 SW   0.0  0.0  0:00 kswapd
    6 root    -20 -20     0    0     0 SW<  0.0  0.0  0:00 mdrecoveryd
   45 root      0   0     0    0     0 SW   0.0  0.0  0:00 khubd
  349 root      0   0   612  612   512 S    0.0  0.1  0:00 syslogd
  359 root      0   0   480  480   408 S    0.0  0.1  0:00 klogd
  374 rpc       0   0   576  576   484 S    0.0  0.1  0:00 portmap
  390 root      0   0     0    0     0 SW   0.0  0.0  0:00 lockd
  391 root      0   0     0    0     0 SW   0.0  0.0  0:00 rpciod
  401 rpcuser   0   0   768  768   656 S    0.0  0.1  0:00 rpc.statd
  416 root      0   0   524  524   460 S    0.0  0.1  0:00 apmd
  470 nobody    0   0   720  720   608 S    0.0  0.1  0:00 identd
  477 nobody    0   0   720  720   608 S    0.0  0.1  0:00 identd
  478 nobody    0   0   720  720   608 S    0.0  0.1  0:00 identd
  480 nobody    0   0   720  720   608 S    0.0  0.1  0:00 identd
  482 nobody    0   0   720  720   608 S    0.0  0.1  0:00 identd
  489 daemon    0   0   576  576   500 S    0.0  0.1  0:00 atd
  504 named     0   0  1928 1928  1152 S    0.0  0.4  0:00 named
  535 root      0   0  1040 1040   832 S    0.0  0.2  0:00 xinetd
  550 root      0   0  1168 1168  1040 S    0.0  0.3  0:00 sshd
  571 lp        0   0   888  888   764 S    0.0  0.2  0:00 lpd
  615 root      0   0  1480 1480  1084 S    0.0  0.3  0:00 sendmail
  650 root      0   0   744  744   640 S    0.0  0.1  0:00 crond
```

```
657 root        0   0   912  912   756 S     0.0  0.2   0:00 safe_mysqld
683 mysql       0   0  1376 1376  1008 S     0.0  0.3   0:00 mysqld
696 xfs         0   0  2528 2528   808 S     0.0  0.6   0:00 xfs
704 mysql       0   0  1376 1376  1008 S     0.0  0.3   0:00 mysqld
```

By default, top updates its screen every second — an interval you can change by using the d *seconds* option. For example, to update the screen every 5 seconds, run the top d 5 command. A 5- or 10-second interval is, in fact, more useful than the default setting. (If you let top update the screen every second, it lists itself in its own output as the main resource consumer.) Properly configured, top can perform interactive tasks on processes.

If you press the *h* key while top is running, you will see the following output screen:

```
Proc-Top Revision 1.2
Secure mode off; cumulative mode off; noidle mode off
Interactive commands are:
space    Update display
^L       Redraw the screen
fF       add and remove fields
oO       Change order of displayed fields
h or ?   Print this list
S        Toggle cumulative mode
i        Toggle display of idle processes
I        Toggle between Irix and Solaris views (SMP-only)
c        Toggle display of command name/line
l        Toggle display of load average
m        Toggle display of memory information
t        Toggle display of summary information
k        Kill a task (with any signal)
r        Renice a task
N        Sort by pid (Numerically)
A        Sort by age
P        Sort by CPU usage
M        Sort by resident memory usage
T        Sort by time / cumulative time
u        Show only a specific user
n or #   Set the number of process to show
s        Set the delay in seconds between updates
W        Write configuration file ~/.toprc
q        Quit
Press any key to continue
```

Using the keyboard options listed in the output shown here, you can

◆ Control how top displays its output

◆ Kill a process or task (if you have the permission)

Checking memory and I/O with vmstat

The vmstat utility also provides interesting information about processes, memory, I/O, and CPU activity. When you run this utility without any arguments, the output looks similar to the following:

```
procs         memory          swap    io system      cpu
r b w  swpd free  buff cache si so bi bo in  cs us sy id
0 0 0     8 8412 45956 52820  0  0  0  0 104 11 66  0 33
```

◆ The procs fields show the number of processes

  ■ Waiting for run time (r)

  ■ Blocked (b)

  ■ Swapped out (w)

◆ The memory fields show the kilobytes of

  ■ Swap memory

  ■ Free memory

  ■ Buffered memory

  ■ Cached memory

◆ The swap fields show the kilobytes per second of memory

  ■ Swapped in from disk (si)

  ■ Swapped out to disk (so)

◆ The io fields show the number of blocks per second

  ■ Sent to block devices (bi)

  ■ Received from block devices (bo)

◆ The system field shows the number of

  ■ Interrupts per second (in)

  ■ Context switches per second (cs)

- The cpu field shows the percentage of total CPU time as

  - User time (us)

  - System time (sy)

  - Idle (id) time

If you want vmstat to update information automatically, you can run it as vmstat nsec, where nsec is the number of seconds you want it to wait before another update.

Running Vtad to analyze your system

Vtad is a Perl-based system-analysis tool that uses the /proc filesystem to determine system configuration. You can download Vtad from the following Web address:

www.blakeley.com/resources/vtad

Vtad periodically checks your system performance and prescribes remedies. It uses a default ruleset that provides the following analysis:

- Compare /proc/sys/kernel/shmmax with /proc/meminfo/Mem (physical memory)

  If the shared memory takes up less than 10 percent of physical memory, Vtad recommends that you increase your system's shared memory — usually to 25 percent for a typical system. Doing so helps Web servers like Apache perform file caching.

- Compare the /proc/sys/fs/file-max value against /proc/sys/fs/inode-max

  You're warned if the current values are not ideal. Typically, the Linux kernel allows three to four times as many open inodes as open files.

- Check the /proc/sys/net/ipv4/ip_local_port_range file to confirm that the system has 10,000 to 28,000 local ports available.

  This can boost performance if you have many proxy server connections to your server.

  The default ruleset also checks for free memory limits, fork rates, disk I/O rates, and IP packet rates. Once you have downloaded Vtad, you can run it quite easily on a shell or xterm window by using perl vtad.pl command. Here is a sample output of the script.

```
Checking recommendations for /proc/sys/fs/file-max /proc/sys/kernel/osrelease
/proc/sys/kernel/shmmax /proc/sys/net/ipv4/ip_local_port_range
apache/conf/httpd.conf/MaxRequestsPerChild
Sun May 20 11:15:14 2001 RED (/proc/sys/kernel/shmmax)
        shmmax-to-physical-memory ratio here 0.1
        REMEDY: raise shmmax (echo 8030208 > /proc/kernel/shmmax)
VTad 1.0b2 running on Linux 2.2
Sun May 20 11:15:14 2001 RED (/proc/sys/net/ipv4/ip_local_port_range)
        range of local IP port numbers here 28000
        REMEDY: echo 32768 61000 > /proc/sys/net/ip_local_port_range
Checking /proc/meminfo/MemFree /proc/meminfo/SwapFree /proc/net/snmp/Ip
/proc/stat/cpu /proc/stat/disk /proc/stat/processes /proc/sys/fs/file-nr
/proc/sys/fs/inode-nr every 30 seconds.
```

Summary

Knowing how to measure system performance is critical in understanding bottle-necks and performance issues. Using standard Red Hat Linux tools, you can measure many aspects of your system's performance. Tools such as ps, top, and vmstat tell you a lot of how a system is performing. Mastering these tools is an important step for anyone interested in higher performance.

Chapter 2

Kernel Tuning

IN THIS CHAPTER

- ◆ Configuring kernel source
- ◆ Compiling a new kernel
- ◆ Configuring LILO to load the new kernel
- ◆ Allocating file handles for demanding applications

IF YOU HAVE INSTALLED THE BASIC Linux kernel that Red Hat supplied, probably it isn't optimized for your system. Usually the vendor-provided kernel of any OS is a "generalist" rather than a "specialist" – it has to support most installation scenarios. For example, a run-of-the-mill kernel may support both EIDE and SCSI disks (when you need only SCSI *or* EIDE support). Granted, using a vendor-provided kernel is the straightforward way to boot up your system – you can custom-compile your own kernel and tweak the installation process when you find the time. When you do reach that point, however, the topics discussed in this chapter come in handy.

Compiling and Installing a Custom Kernel

Thanks to the Linux kernel developers, creating a custom kernel in Linux is a piece of cake. A Linux kernel is *modular* – the features and functions you want can be installed individually (as modules). Before you pick and choose the functionality of your OS, however, you build a kernel from source code.

Downloading kernel source code (latest distribution)

The first step to a customized kernel is to obtain a firm foundation – the stable source code contained in the Linux kernel.

1. Download the source code from www.kernel.org or one of its mirror sites (listed at the main site itself).

2. Extract the source in the `/usr/src` directory.

   Kernel source distributions are named `linux-version.tar.gz`, where `version` is the version number of the kernel (for example, `linux-2.4.1.tar.gz`).

 In this chapter, I assume that you have downloaded and extracted (using the `tar xvzf linux-2.4.1.tar.gz` command) the kernel 2.4.1 source distribution from the `www.kernel.org` site.

Creating the /usr/src/linux symbolic link

When you extract the kernel source (as discussed in the previous section), a new directory is created. This new directory must be symbolically linked to /usr/src/linux. (A symbolic link is a directory entry that points another directory entry to another existing directory.) The source code expects the /usr/src/linux symbolic link entry to point to the real, top-level source code directory. Here is how you create this symbolic link:

1. Run the `ls -l` command.

   The result shows where `/usr/src/linux` currently points. The `->` in the `ls` output points to linux-2.4.0. Typically, `/usr/src/linux` is a symbolic link to the current source distribution of the kernel. For example, on my system, `ls -l` reports this:

   ```
   lrwxrwxrwx    1 root  root   11 Feb 13 16:21 linux -> linux-
   2.4.0
   ```

Distribution versus kernel — what's the "real" version?

New Linux users often get confused when the version numbers of the distribution and the kernel mismatch. Why (they ask) do I keep talking about Linux *2.4* when what they see on the market is (apparently) *7.x?* The answer lies in the nature of the open-source concept: Working independently, various programmers have developed the basic kernel of Linux code in diverse directions — like variations on a theme. Each variation has a series of distributions and a body of users to whom it is distributed. Thanks to popular, easy-to-recognize distributions like Red Hat Linux, many newcomers think *distribution 7.x* of Linux is the "only" — or the "latest" — *version* (and that everything in it is uniformly "version 7.*x*" as if it were marketed by Microsoft or Apple). These days (and in this book) I try to overturn that mistaken notion; when I refer to Linux 2.4, I say "Linux *kernel* 2.4, in *distribution 7.x*" to be as clear as possible.

drwxrwxrwx — not rwxrwxrwx — is in the `ls -l` output.

2. Run one of these commands:

   - If `/usr/src/linux` is a symbolic link, run the `rm -f linux` command.

     This removes the symbolic link.

   - If `/usr/src/linux` is a directory, run the command `mv linux linux.oldversion` (*oldversion* is the version number of the current kernel).

     This renames the old kernel source directory, clearing the way for the installation of the new kernel source.

3. Run the command `ln -s /usr/src/linux-2.4.1 linux`.

   This creates a new symbolic link, `linux`, that points to the `/usr/src/linux-2.4.1` directory.

4. Change your directory path to `/usr/src/linux`.

At this point you have the kernel source distribution ready for configuration. Now you are ready to select a kernel configuration method.

Selecting a kernel-configuration method

You can configure a Linux kernel by using one of three commands:

- `make config`. This method uses the bash shell; you configure the kernel by answering a series of questions prompted on the screen. (This approach may be too slow for advanced users; you can't go back or skip forward.)

- `make menuconfig`. You use a screen-based menu system (a much more flexible method) to configure the kernel. (This chapter assumes that you use this method.)

- `make xconfig`. This method, which uses the X Window system (a Linux graphical interface), is geared to the individual user's desktop environment. I do not recommend it for server administrators; the X Window system is too resource-intensive to use on servers (which already have enough to do).

If this isn't the first time you are configuring the kernel, run `make mrproper` from the `/usr/src/linux` directory to remove all the existing object files and clean up the source distribution. Then, from the `/usr/src/linux` directory — which is a symbolic link to the Linux kernel (in this example, `/usr/src/linux-2.4.1`) — run the `make menuconfig` command to configure Linux.

Using menuconfig

When you run the `make menuconfig` command, it displays a list of submenus in a main menu screen. The result looks like this:

```
Code maturity level options  --->
 Loadable module support  --->
 Processor type and features  --->
 General setup  --->
 Memory Technology Devices (MTD)  --->
 Parallel port support  --->
 Plug and Play configuration  --->
 Block devices  --->
 Multi-device support (RAID and LVM)  --->
 Networking options  --->
 Telephony Support  --->
 ATA/IDE/MFM/RLL support  --->
 SCSI support  --->
 I20 device support  --->
 Network device support  --->
 Amateur Radio support  --->
 IrDA (infrared) support  --->
 ISDN subsystem  --->
 Old CD-ROM drivers (not SCSI, not IDE)  --->
 Input core support  --->
 Character devices  --->
 Multimedia devices  --->
 File systems  --->
 Console drivers  --->
 Sound  --->
 USB support  --->
 Kernel hacking  --->
 ---
 Load an Alternate Configuration File
 Save Configuration to an Alternate File
```

In the preceding list, `--->` indicates a submenu, which you may also find within a top-level submenu (such as `Network device support` menu).

♦ Use Up and Down arrow keys on your keyboard to navigate the sub-menus. Press the Enter key to select a menu.

♦ Press the space bar to toggle a highlighted option on or off.

CODE MATURITY LEVEL OPTIONS

The very first submenu, `Code maturity level options`, is the first one to set. This option instructs the `menuconfig` program to hide or display experimental kernel features. Though often interesting to the programmer, experimental features are not yet considered *mature* (stable) code.

Selecting *Prompt for development and/or incomplete code/drivers* (by pressing the spacebar to put an asterisk between the square brackets next to the option) displays many experimental — potentially unreliable — features of the latest kernel. Then they show up in other submenu options. If you don't plan to implement these risky options, why display them?

Making this call is harder than it may seem. Experimental features could offer interesting new capabilities; at the same time, you don't want to put anything unreliable on your system. So here's the rule that I use:

♦ *Don't* select this option if the system is

■ A production server

■ The only system in your home or organization

TIP Use only *mature* code if a system must be reliable.

♦ If the machine you're configuring isn't critical to your home or business, you can enable this option to experiment with new kernel features.

TIP Any organization that depends on Linux should have at least one separate experimental Linux system so administrators can try new Linux features without fearing data losses or downtime.

LOADABLE MODULE SUPPORT

Loadable module support should have all options selected by default, because you will take advantage of Linux kernel's modular design.

In this chapter, I show you how you can build certain features in two forms:

◆ Modules

   When you compile a feature as a kernel module, it is only loaded when needed.

 The make menuconfig based kernel configuration interface shows this option as [M] next to a feature when you use the space bar to select the option.

◆ Within the kernel binary

   When you choose to compile a feature part of the kernel, it becomes part of the kernel image. This means that this feature is always loaded in the kernel.

 The make menuconfig based kernel configuration interface shows this option as [*] next to a feature when you use the space bar to select the option.

HARDWARE

Think of kernel as the interface to your hardware. The better it is tuned to your hardware, the better your system works. The following hardware-specific options provide optimal configuration for your system.

 Because most Linux users run Intel hardware, I focus on Intel-specific options throughout the chapter. I also assume that you use fairly modern hardware (less than two years old).

CPU SUPPORT   Linux kernel can be configured for the Intel x86 instruction set on these CPUs:

- ◆ "386" for

    - ■   AMD/Cyrix/Intel 386DX/DXL/SL/SLC/SX

    - ■   Cyrix/TI486DLC/DLC2

    - ■   UMC 486SX-S

    - ■   NexGen Nx586

 Only "386" kernels run on a 386-class machine.

- ◆ "486" for

    - ■ AMD/Cyrix/IBM/Intel 486DX/DX2/DX4

    - ■ AMD/Cyrix/IBM/Intel SL/SLC/SLC2/SLC3/SX/SX2

    - ■ UMC U5D or U5S

- ◆ "586" for generic Pentium CPUs, possibly lacking the TSC (time stamp counter) register.

- ◆ "Pentium-Classic" for the Intel Pentium.

- ◆ "Pentium-MMX" for the Intel Pentium MMX.

- ◆ "Pentium-Pro" for the Intel Pentium Pro/Celeron/Pentium II.

- ◆ "Pentium-III" for the Intel Pentium III.

- ◆ "Pentium-4" for the Intel Pentium 4.

- ◆ "K6" for the AMD K6, K6-II and K6-III (also known as K6-3D).

- ◆ "Athlon" for the AMD Athlon (K7).

- ◆ "Crusoe" for the Transmeta Crusoe series.

- ◆ "Winchip-C6" for original IDT Winchip.

- ◆ "Winchip-2" for IDT Winchip 2.

- ◆ "Winchip-2A" for IDT Winchips with 3dNow! capabilities.

You can find your processor by running the command `cat /proc/cpuinfo` in another window. The following code is a sample output from this command.

```
processor       : 0
vendor_id       : GenuineIntel
cpu family      : 6
model           : 8
model name      : Pentium III (Coppermine)
stepping        : 1
cpu MHz         : 548.742
cache size      : 256 KB
fdiv_bug        : no
hlt_bug         : no
f00f_bug        : no
coma_bug        : no
fpu             : yes
fpu_exception   : yes
cpuid level     : 2
wp              : yes
flags           : fpu vme de pse tsc msr pae mce cx8 sep mtrr pge mca cmov pat
pse36 mmx fxsr sse
bogomips        : 1094.45
```

The first line in the preceding code shows how many processors you have in the system. (0 represents a single processor, 1 is two processors, and so on.) "Model name" is the processor name that should be selected for the kernel.

 Choosing a specific processor prevents this kernel from running on an x86 system without the same processor. If you compile the kernel to support the default x386 processor, just about any modern x86 machine (386 or higher) can run the kernel but not necessarily as efficiently as possible. Unless you are compiling the kernel for wide use, choosing a particular CPU is best.

Follow these steps to select the appropriate CPU support:

1. Select the Processor type and features submenu from the main menu.

   The first option in the submenu is the currently chosen processor for your system. If the chosen processor isn't your exact CPU model, press the enter key to see the list of supported processors.

2. Select the math emulation support.

   If you use a Pentium-class machine, math emulation is unnecessary. Your system has a math co-processor.

TIP If you don't know whether your system has a math co-processor, run the cat /proc/cpuinfo and find the fpu column. If you see 'yes' next to fpu, you have a math coprocessor (also known as an fpu, or *floating-point unit*).

TIP If you have a Pentium Pro; Pentium II or later model Intel CPU; or an Intel clone such as Cyrix 6x86, 6x86MX AMD K6-2 (stepping 8 and above), and K6-3, enable the Memory Type Range Register (MTRR) support by choosing the Enable MTRR for PentiumPro/II/III and newer AMD K6-2/3 systems option. MTRR support can enhance your video performance.

3. If you have a system with multiple CPUs and want to use multiple CPUs using the symmetric multiprocessing support in the kernel, enable the Symmetric multi-processing (SMP) support option.

NOTE When you use SMP support, you can't use the advanced power management option.

MEMORY MODEL   This tells the new kernel how much RAM you have or plan on adding in the future.

The Intel 32-bit address space enables a maximum of 4GB of memory to be used. However, Linux can use up to 64GB by turning on Intel Physical Address Extension (PAE) mode on Intel Architecture 32-bit (IA32) processors such as Pentium Pro, Pentium II, and Pentium III. In Linux terms, memory above 4GB is *high memory*.

To enable appropriate memory support, follow these steps:

1. From the main menu, select Processor type and features submenu

2. Select High Memory Support option.

NOTE To determine which option is right for your system, you must know the amount of physical RAM you currently have and will add (if any).

You have three choices:

- If you never plan on getting more than 1GB for your machine, you don't need high memory support. Choose the off option.

- If the machine will have a maximum of 4GB of RAM and currently has 1GB or more, choose the 4GB option.

- If the machine has more than 4GB of RAM now and you plan on adding more in the future, choose the 64GB option.

When the new kernel is built, memory should be auto-detected. To find how much RAM is seen by the kernel, run `cat /proc/meminfo`, which displays output as shown below.

```
Mem:  393277440 308809728 84467712       0 64643072 111517696
Swap: 271392768         0 271392768
MemTotal:       384060 kB
MemFree:         82488 kB
MemShared:           0 kB
Buffers:         63128 kB
Cached:         108904 kB
Active:           5516 kB
Inact_dirty:    166516 kB
Inact_clean:         0 kB
Inact_target:       16 kB
HighTotal:           0 kB
HighFree:            0 kB
LowTotal:       384060 kB
LowFree:         82488 kB
SwapTotal:      265032 kB
SwapFree:       265032 kB
```

In the preceding list, MemTotal shows the total memory seen by kernel. In this case, it's 384060 kilobytes (384MB). Make sure your new kernel reports the amount of memory you have installed. If you see a very different number, try rebooting the kernel and supplying mem="nnnMB" at the boot prompt (nnn is the amount of memory in MB). For example, if you have 2GB of RAM, you can enter mem="2048MB" at the LILO prompt. Here's an example of such a prompt:

```
Lilo: linux mem="2048MB"
```

DISK SUPPORT   Hard disks are generally the limiting factor in a system's performance. Therefore, choosing the right disk for your system is quite important. Generally, there are three disk technologies to consider:

◆ EIDE/IDE/ATA

EIDE/IDE/ATA are the most common disk drives.

- They're cheaper than the other two types.

- They're slower than the other two types, so they're usually used in home or desktop environments where massive disk I/O isn't common. Fortunately, EIDE disks are becoming faster.

◆ SCSI

SCSI rules in the server market. A server system without SCSI disks is unthinkable to me and many other server administrators.

◆ Fiber Channel

Fiber Channel disk is the hottest, youngest disk technology and not widely used for reasons such as extremely high price and interconnectivity issues associated with fiver technology. However, Fiber Channel disks are taking market share from SCSI in the enterprise or high-end storage area networks. If you need Fiber Channel disks, you need to consider a very high-end disk subsystem such as a storage area network (SAN) or a storage appliance.

Choosing a disk for a system (desktop or server) becomes harder due to the buzzwords in the disk technology market. Table 2-1 explains common acronyms.

TABLE 2-1: COMMON DISK TECHNOLOGY

Common Terms	Meaning	Standard Name
IDE	Integrated Disk Electronics.	ATA -1
ATA	AT Attachment.	ATA is the superset of the IDE specifications.
Fast-IDE or Fast-ATA	Second generation IDE.	ATA-2
EIDE	Enhanced IDE. It provides support for larger disks, more disks (4 instead of 2), and for other mass storage units such as tapes and CDs.	ATA-3
UltraDMA/33 or UDMA/33	Using fast direct memory access (DMA) controller, this type of disk provides faster and more CPU non-intensive transfer rates.	ATA-4

Continued

TABLE 2-1: COMMON DISK TECHNOLOGY *(Continued)*

Common Terms	Meaning	Standard Name
ATAPI	ATA Packet Interface. It's a protocol used by EIDE tape and CD-ROM drives, similar in many respects to the SCSI protocol.	
SCSI or narrow SCSI	Small Computer System Interface. The initial implementation of SCSI was designed primarily for narrow (8-bit), single-ended, synchronous or asynchronous disk drives and was very limited relative to today's SCSI. It includes synchronous and asynchronous data transfers at speeds up to 5MB per second.	SCSI-1
Fast SCSI or Fast-10	Fast SCSI uses 10 MHz bus instead of 5 MHz bus used in narrow SCSI. On an 8-bit (narrow) SCSI-bus, this increases the theoretical maximum speed from 5MB per second to 10MB per second. A 16-bit (wide) bus can have a transfer rate up to 20MB per second.	SCSI-2
Ultra or Fast-20 SCSI	Synchronous data transfer option, which enables up to 20 MHz data clocking on the bus. 40MB per second for 16-bit (wide) bus (Ultra Wide SCSI).	SCSI-3
Ultra 2 or Fast-40 SCSI	Synchronous data transfer option, which enables up to 40 MHz data clocking on the bus. 80MB per second for 16-bit (wide) bus (Ultra2 Wide SCSI)	SCSI-3
Ultra 3 or Ultra160 or Fast-80	160MB per second for wide bus.	SCSI-3

Most people either use IDE/EIDE hard disks or SCSI disks. Only a few keep both types in the same machine, which isn't a problem. If you only have one of these two in your system, enable support for only the type you need unless you plan on adding the other type in the future.

If you use at least one EIDE/IDE/ATA hard disk, follow these steps:

1. Select the ATA/IDE/MFM/RLL support option from the main menu and enable the ATA/IDE/MFM/RLL support option by including it as a module.

2. Select the IDE, ATA, and ATAPI Block devices submenu and enable the Generic PCI IDE chipset support option.

3. If your disk has direct memory access (DMA) capability, then:

   ■ Select the Generic PCI bus-master DMA support option.

   ■ Select the Use PCI DMA by default when available option to make use of the direct memory access automatically.

Chapter 3 details how to tune EIDE/IDE/ATA disks with hdparam.

You see a lot of options for chipset support. Unless you know your chipset and find it in the list, ignore these options.

If you use at least one SCSI disk, follow these steps:

1. Select the SCSI support submenu and choose SCSI support from the submenu as a module.

2. Select the SCSI disk support option as a module.

3. Select support for any other type of other SCSI device you have, such as tape drive or CD.

4. Select the SCSI low-level drivers submenu, and then select the appropriate driver for your SCSI host adapter.

5. Disable Probe all LUNs because it can hang the kernel with some SCSI hardware.

6. Disable Verbose SCSI error reporting.

7. Disable SCSI logging facility.

TIP If you will use only one type of disks (either EIDE/IDE/ATA or SCSI), disabling support in the kernel for the other disk type saves memory.

PLUG AND PLAY DEVICE SUPPORT If you have Plug and Play (PNP) devices in your system, follow these steps to enable PNP support in the kernel:

1. Select the Plug and Play configuration submenu.
2. Select all options in the submenu to enable Plug and Play hardware support.

BLOCK DEVICE SUPPORT To enable support for block devices in the kernel, follow these steps:

1. Select the Block devices submenu.
2. Select the appropriate block devices you have.

   For most systems, the Normal PC floppy disk support is sufficient.

TIP If you want to use RAM as a filesystem, RAM disk support isn't best. Instead, enable Simple RAM-based filesystem support under File systems submenu.

3. If a regular file will be a filesystem, enable the loopback device support.

TIP A loopback device, such as loop0, enables you to mount an ISO 9660 image file (CD filesystem), then explore it from a normal filesystem (such as ext2).

NETWORK DEVICE SUPPORT To enable network device support in the kernel, select the Network device support submenu and choose the Network device support option for your network.

- ◆ If you connect your system to an Ethernet (10 or 100 Mbps), select the Ethernet (10 or 100 Mbps) submenu, choose Ethernet (10 or 100 Mbps) support, and implement one of these options:

  - If your network interface card vendor is listed in the Ethernet (10 or 100 Mbps) support menu, select the vendor from that menu.

  - If your PCI-based NIC vendor isn't listed in the Ethernet (10 or 100 Mbps) support menu, select your vendor in the EISA, VLB, PCI and on-board controllers option list.

TIP   If you don't find your PCI NIC vendor in the Ethernet (10 or 100 Mbps) support menu or the EISA, VLB, PCI and on-board controllers option list, choose the PCI NE2000 and clones support option.

  - If your ISA NIC vendor isn't listed in the Ethernet (10 or 100 Mbps) support menu, select your vendor in the Other ISA cards option.

TIP   If you don't find your ISA NIC vendor in the Ethernet (10 or 100 Mbps) support menu or the Other ISA cards option list, choose the NE2000/NE1000 support option.

- ◆ If you have at least one gigabit (1000 Mbps) adapter, choose the Ethernet (1000 Mbps) submenu and select your gigabit NIC vendor.

- ◆ If you have the hardware to create a wireless LAN, select the Wireless LAN support and choose appropriate wireless hardware.

USB SUPPORT   If you have at least one USB device to connect to your Linux system, select the USB support and choose the appropriate options for such features as USB audio/multimedia, modem, and imaging devices.

UNIVERSAL SYSTEM OPTIONS
These configuration options apply for servers, desktops, and laptops.

NETWORKING SUPPORT   Even if you don't want to network the system, you must configure the networking support from the General setup submenu using the Networking support option. (Some programs assume that kernel has networking support. By default, networking support is built into the kernel.)

Check the Networking options submenu to confirm that these options are enabled; enable them if they aren't already enabled:

◆ TCP/IP networking

◆ Unix domain socket support

PCI SUPPORT Most modern systems use PCI bus to connect to many devices. If PCI support isn't enabled on the General setup submenu, enable it.

SYSTEM V IPC AND SYSCTL SUPPORT Inter Process Communication (IPC) is a mechanism that many Linux applications use to communicate with one another. If the System V IPC option isn't enabled on the General setup submenu, enable it.

The sysctl interface is used to dynamically manipulate many kernel parameters. If the Sysctl support option isn't enabled on the General setup menu, enable it.

CONSOLE SUPPORT The system console is necessary for a Linux system that needs to be managed by a human, whether the system is a server, desktop, or laptop. The system console

◆ Receives all kernel messages and warnings

◆ Enables logins in single-user mode

To customize console support, apply these options:

◆ Choose the Console drivers submenu, then select the VGA text console option.

◆ If you want to choose video mode during boot up, apply these steps:

  ■ Select Video mode selection support option

  ■ Enter vga=ask option to the LILO prompt during the boot up process

  You can add this option to the /etc/lilo.conf file and rerun LILO using the /sbin/lilo command.

CHARACTER DEVICE SUPPORT You need virtual terminals on the console to access your system via shell programs. Select virtual terminal support from the character devices submenu.

◆ Select the character devices submenu and enable Virtual terminals option.

TIP Most users want to enable the Support for console on virtual terminal option.

◆ If you have serial devices (such as mouse or external terminal devices) to attach to a serial port, enable serial port support using the Standard/generic (8250/16550 and compatible UARTs) serial support option.

FILESYSTEM SUPPORT   It is generally a good idea to enable only the following filesystems support in the kernel:

◆ Second Extended Filesystem (ext2)

This is the default filesystem for Linux.

◆ ISO 9660 CD

This is the filesystem for most CD-ROMs.

◆ /proc

This is the pseudo filesystem used by the kernel and other programs.

These should be enabled by default. To ensure that these filesystems are supported, select the File systems submenu and choose these filesystem types from the list.

DESKTOP/LAPTOP SYSTEM OPTIONS
If you are running Linux on desktop or a laptop system, you want such capabilities as printing, playing music, and using the The X Window System. Hence, the settings discussed here enable the kernel level options needed for such goals.

MOUSE SUPPORT   If you have a non-serial, non-USB mouse such as bus-mouse or a PS/2 mouse or another non-standard mouse, follow these steps:

1. Select the Character devices submenu, followed by the Mice submenu.

2. Select the appropriate mouse support.

PARALLEL PORT SUPPORT   To use a parallel port printer or other parallel port devices, you must enable parallel port support from the Parallel port support submenu from the main menu. Follow these steps:

1. Choose the parallel port support.

2. Choose Use FIFO/DMA if available from the PC-style hardware option.

MULTIMEDIA SUPPORT   Most multimedia include sound. To enable sound from your Linux system:

1. Select the Sound submenu.

2. Choose the appropriate sound card for your system.

If you have audio/video capture hardware or radio cards, follow these steps to enable support:

1. Select the Multimedia devices submenu.

2. Choose Video For Linux to locate video adapter(s) or FM radio tuner(s) you have on your system.

JOYSTICK SUPPORT   Joystick support depends on the Input core support. Follow these steps for joystick support:

1. Select Input core support submenu, then enable input core support.

2. Choose Joystick support, then select the Character devices menu.

3. On the the Joysticks submenu, choose the appropriate joystick controller for your joystick vendor.

POWER MANAGEMENT SUPPORT   Laptop users need to enable power management for maximum battery life. For power management, select these options:

◆ Select the General setup submenu and choose the Power Management support option.

◆ If your system has Advanced Power Management BIOS, choose Advanced Power Management BIOS support.

DIRECT RENDERING INFRASTRUCTURE (DRI) FOR THE X WINDOW SYSTEM   If you have a high-end video card (16 MB or more video memory and chip-level support of direct rendering), find whether it can take advantage of the DRI support now available in the X Window System.

1. Choose the Character devices submenu and select Direct Rendering Manager (XFree86 DRI support) option.

2. If you see your video card listed, select it to enable the DRI support.

PCMCIA/CARDBUS SUPPORT   To enable PCMCIA/CardBus support, follow these steps:

1. Select the PCMCIA/CardBus support submenu from the General setup submenu.

2. Select the CardBus support option.

To use PCMCIA serial devices, follow these steps:

1. Enable PCMCIA device support from the Character devices submenu.

2. Select either

   ■ PCMCIA serial device support

   ■ CardBus serial device support

If you have PCMCIA network devices, follow these steps to support them:

1. Select the PCMCIA network device support option from the Network device support submenu.

2. Select appropriate vendor from the list.

PPP SUPPORT   Most desktop or laptop systems use the Point-to-Point Protocol (PPP) for dialup network communication.

To enable PPP support, select the PPP (point-to-point protocol) support option from the Network device support submenu.

SERVER OPTIONS

Usually, a server system doesn't need support for such features as sound, power management, multimedia, and infrared connectivity, so you shouldn't enable any of these features in the kernel.

A few very important kernel configuration options can turn your system into a highly reliable server. These options are discussed in the following sections.

LOGICAL VOLUME MANAGEMENT SUPPORT   Logical volume is a new feature to Linux and can be very useful for a server system with multiple disks. Follow these steps to enable LVM support:

1. Select the Multi-device support (RAID and LVM) submenu.

2. Choose the Logical volume manager (LVM) support option.

Chapter 3 explains how to use logical volume management.

SOFTWARE RAID SUPPORT   If you will use software RAID for your server, follow these steps to enable it:

1. Select the Multi-device support (RAID) submenu.

2. Choose the RAID support option.

3. Choose the type of RAID you want to use:

   - Linear (append) mode
   - RAID-0 (striping)
   - RAID-1 (mirroring of similar size disks)
   - RAID 4/5

PSEUDO TERMINAL (PTY) SUPPORT   If you use the server to enable many users to connect via SSH or telnet, you need pseudo terminal (PTY) support. Follow these steps:

1. Enable PTY support from the Character device submenu by selecting the Maximum number of Unix98 PTYs in use (0-2048) option.

   By default, the system has 256 PTYs. Each login requires a single PTY.

2. If you expect more than 256 simultaneous login sessions, set a value between 257 and 2048.

Each PTY uses at least 2 MB of RAM. Make sure you have plenty of RAM for the number of simultaneous login sessions you select.

REAL-TIME CLOCK SUPPORT FOR SMP SYSTEM   If you use multiple CPU (enabled Symmetric Multi Processing support), enable the enhanced Real Time Clock (RTC) so that it's set in an SMP-compatible fashion. To enable RTC, enable Enhanced Real Time Clock Support option from the Character devices submenu.

IP PACKET FILTERING (FIREWALL) OPTIONS

Although there are many other options that you can configure in the kernel, the options discussed so far should be a good start for a lean, mean custom kernel for your system. Save the configuration you have created and proceed to compile the kernel as discussed in the following sections.

If you your server will use the firewall features of Linux, see Chapter 20.

Compiling the kernel

Compiling a configured kernel requires checking source code dependencies, then compiling the kernel and module images. The source dependency checks make sure that all source code files are available for the features that you choose. The image creation process compiles the source code and builds binaries for the kernel and the modules.

CHECKING SOURCE DEPENDENCIES

Before you can compile the kernel, you need to ensure that all the source dependencies are in good shape.

To do that, you can run the `make depend` command from /usr/src/linux as root. This command

◆ Performs dependency checks

◆ Prepares the source for image compilation

If you get any error messages from the preceding command, you might have a source distribution integrity problem. In such cases, you must download a new copy of the latest stable kernel source and reconfigure it from the beginning.

After you have run this command, you are ready to compile the kernel and its modules.

COMPILING IMAGES AND MODULES

The kernel compilation involves building an image (binary) file of

◆ The kernel itself

◆ The necessary kernel modules images

The following sections explain how to compile both the kernel image and the modules images.

COMPILING THE KERNEL IMAGE To create the kernel image file, run the `make bzImage` command from /usr/src/linux as root.

Depending on your processor speed, the compile time can vary from a few minutes to hours. On my Pentium III 500 MHz system with 384MB of RAM, the kernel compiles in less than five minutes.

Once the `make bzImage` command is finished, a kernel image file called bzImage is created in a directory specific to your system architecture. For example, an x86 system's new kernel bzImage file is in `/usr/src/linux/arch/i386/boot`.

COMPILING AND INSTALLING THE MODULES In the process of the kernel configuration, you have set up at least one feature as kernel modules and, therefore, you need to compile and install the modules.

Use the following commands to compile and install the kernel modules.

```
make modules
make modules_install
```

If you are compiling the same version of the kernel that is currently running on your system, first back up your modules from `/lib/modules/x.y.z` (where x.y.z is the version number of the current kernel). You can simply run `cp -r /lib/modules/x.y.z  /lib/modules/x.y.z.current` (by replacing x.y.z with appropriate version number) to create a backup module directory with current modules.

Once the preceding commands are done, all new modules will be installed in a new subdirectory in the `/lib` directory.

Booting the new kernel

Before you can boot the new kernel, it must be installed.

This is a very important step. You must take great care so you can still boot the old kernel if something goes wrong with the new kernel.

Now you can install the new kernel and configure LILO to boot either kernel.

INSTALLING THE NEW KERNEL

The Linux kernel is kept in /boot directory. If you open your /etc/lilo.conf file and look for a line like image=/path/to/kernel, then you see that this usually is something like image=/boot/vmlinuz-x.y.z (where x.y.z is the version number). Copy the new kernel using the cp /usr/src/linux/arch/i386/boot/bzImage /boot/vmlinuz-x.y.z (don't forget to replace x.y.z. with the version number). For example, to install a new 2.4.1 kernel, the copy command is

```
cp /usr/src/linux/arch/i386/boot/bzImage /boot/vmlinuz-2.4.1
```

CONFIGURING LILO

LILO is the boot loader program and it must be configured before you can boot the new kernel.

Edit the LILO configuration file called /etc/lilo.conf as follows:

1. Copy the current lilo section that defines the current image and its settings.

   For example, Listing 2-1 shows a sample /etc/lilo.conf file with a single kernel definition. As it stand right now, lilo boots the kernel labeled linux (because default = linux is set).

Listing 2-1: /etc/lilo.conf

```
boot=/dev/hda
map=/boot/map
install=/boot/boot.b
prompt
timeout=50
message=/boot/message
linear
default=linux
image=/boot/vmlinuz-2.4.0-0.99.11
        label=linux
        read-only
        root=/dev/hda1
```

2. Copy the following lines and append to the end of the current /etc/lilo.conf file.

```
image=/boot/vmlinuz-2.4.0-0.99.11
        label=linux
        read-only
        root=/dev/hda1
```

3. Change the image path to the new kernel image you copied. For example, if you copied the new kernel image `/usr/src/linux/arch/i386/boot/bzImage` to the `/boot/vmlinuz-2.4.1` directory, then set **image=/boot/vmlinuz-2.4.1**.

4. Change the label for this new segment to **linux2**. The resulting file is shown in Listing 2-2.

Listing 2-2: /etc/lilo.conf (updated)

```
boot=/dev/hda
map=/boot/map
install=/boot/boot.b
prompt
timeout=50
message=/boot/message
linear
default=linux
image=/boot/vmlinuz-2.4.0-0.99.11
        label=linux
        read-only
        root=/dev/hda1
image=/boot/vmlinuz-2.4.1
        label=linux2
        read-only
        root=/dev/hda1
```

5. Run **/sbin/lilo** to reconfigure `lilo` using the updated `/etc/lilo.conf` file.

Never experiment with new kernel from a remote location. Always restart the system from the system console to load a new kernel for the first time.

REBOOTING NEW KERNEL

After installing the new kernel, follow these steps to reboot for the first time:

1. Reboot the system from the console, using the `/sbin/shutdown -r now` command.

   During the reboot process, you see the `lilo` prompt.

2. At the `lilo` prompt, enter **linux2**.

The default, `linux`, would load the old kernel.

With the new label `linux2` associated with the new kernel, your system attempts to load the new kernel. Assuming everything goes well, it should boot up normally and the login prompt should appear.

3. At the login prompt, log in as `root` from the console.

4. When you are logged in, run the **uname -a** command, which should display the kernel version number along with other information.

Here's a sample output:

```
Linux rhat.nitec.com 2.4.1 #2 SMP Wed Feb 14 17:14:02 PST
2001 i686 unknown
```

I marked the version number in bold. The #2 reflects the number of times I built this kernel.

Run the new kernel for several days before making it the default for your system. If the kernel runs for that period without problems — provided you are ready to make this your default kernel — simply edit the /etc/lilo.conf file, change `default=linux` to **default=linux2**, and rerun **/sbin/lilo** to reconfigure `lilo`.

To keep `default=linux`, simply switch `label=linux2` to **label=linux,** then remove the old kernel image-definition from the /etc/lilo.conf file or change the label of the old kernel's image-definition file to something else. You must run **/sbin/lilo** after you modify /etc/lilo.conf file.

Running Demanding Applications

A lean kernel is a candidate for demanding applications that make heavy use of your resources. Such applications are often not suitable for resource configurations.

Multi-threaded mail servers have a couple of common problems. Follow these steps to fix them:

◆ Running out of filehandles.

Thousands of files can be opened from the message queue. These steps allow extra filehandles to accomodate them:

1. Determine the number of filehandles for the entire system.

   To find the number of filehandles, run the `cat /proc/sys/fs/file-max` command. You should see a number like 4096 or 8192.

2. To increase the number of filehandles (often called file descriptors), add the following lines in your /etc/rc.d/rc.local script (replace nnnn with the number of filehandles you need):

   ```
   echo  nnnn > /proc/sys/fs/file-max
   ```

   The following line makes the system-wide filehandles total 10240 (10K):

   ```
   echo  10240 > /proc/sys/fs/file-max
   ```

◆ Starting too many threads

   Using too many threads will reach the system's simultaneous process capacity. To set per process filehandle limit, follow these steps:

   1. Edit the /etc/security/limits.conf file and add the following lines:

      ```
      *        soft     nofile  1024
      *        hard     nofile  8192
      ```

      The preceding code makes the filehandle limit 8192.

   2. Make sure that /etc/pam.d/system-auth has a line like the following:

      ```
      session  required  /lib/security/pam_limits.so
      ```

      This ensures that a user can open up to 8,192 files simultaneously when she logs in. To see what kind of system resources a user can consume, run `ulimit -a` (assuming you use the bash shell). Here's a sample output:

      ```
      core file size (blocks)          1000000
      data seg size (kbytes)           unlimited
      file size (blocks)               unlimited
      max locked memory (kbytes)       unlimited
      max memory size (kbytes)         unlimited
      open files                       1024
      pipe size (512 bytes)            8
      stack size (kbytes)              8192
      cpu time (seconds)               unlimited
      max user processes               12287
      virtual memory (kbytes)          unlimited
      ```

      In the preceding code, the open files (filehandles) and max user processes line are bold. To enable users to run fewer processes, (about 8192 at most), add the following lines in /etc/security/limits.conf file.

```
*        soft     nproc    4096
*        hard     nproc    8192
```

This setting applies to both processes and the child threads that each process opens.

 You can also configure how much memory a user can consume by using soft and hard limits settings in the same file. The memory consumption is controlled using such directives as data, memlock, rss, and stack. You can also control the CPU usage of a user. Comments in the file provide details on how to configure such limits.

Summary

Configuring a custom kernel suits your system needs. A custom kernel is a great way to keep your system lean and mean, because it won't have unnecessary kernel modules or potential crashes due to untested code in the kernel.

Chapter 3

Filesystem Tuning

IN THIS CHAPTER

- ◆ Tuning your hard disks

- ◆ Tuning your ext2 filesystem

- ◆ Using a ReiserFS journaling filesystem

- ◆ Using logical volume management

- ◆ Using a RAM-based filesystem for high-speed access

A WISE ENGINEER ONCE TOLD ME that anyone you can see moving with your naked eye isn't fast enough. I like to spin that around and say that anything in your computer system that has moving parts isn't fast enough. Disks, with moving platters, are the slowest devices, even today. The filesystems that provide a civilized interface to your disks are, therefore, inherently slow. Most of the time, the disk is the bottleneck of a system.

In this chapter, you tune disks and filesystems for speed, reliability, and easy administration.

Tuning your hard disks

SCSI and IDE are the most common types of hard disk today. SCSI disks and the SCSI controllers are much more expensive because they provide more performance and flexibility. IDE or the enhanced version of IDE called EIDE drives are more commonplace in the personal and disk I/O non-intensive computing.

SCSI PERFORMANCE

If you have a modern, ultra-wide SCSI disk set up for your Red Hat Linux system, you are already ahead of the curve and should be getting good performance from your disks. If not (even if so), the difference between SCSI and IDE is useful to explore:

- ◆ SCSI disk controllers handle most of the work of transferring data to and from the disks; IDE disks are controlled directly by the CPU itself. On a busy system, SCSI disks don't put as much load on the CPU as IDE drives add.

◆ SCSI disks have wider data transfer capabilities, whereas IDE disks are still connected to the system via 16-bit bus.

 If you need high performance, SCSI is the way to go. Buy brandname SCSI adapters and ultra-wide, 10K-RPM or larger SCSI disks and you have done pretty much all you can do to improve your disk subsystem.

Whether you choose SCSI or IDE disks, multiple disks are a must if you are serious about performance.

◆ At minimum, use two disks — one for operating systems and software, the other for data.

◆ For Web servers, I generally recommend a minimum of three disks. The third disk is for the logs generated by the Web sites hosted on the machine. Keeping disk I/O spread across multiple devices minimizes wait time.

 Of course, if you have the budget for it, you can use fiber channel disks or a storage-area network (SAN) solution. Enterprises with high data-storage demands often use SANs. A less expensive option is a hardware/software RAID solution, which is also discussed in this chapter.

EIDE PERFORMANCE

You can get better performance from your modern EIDE drive. Before doing any tinkering and tuning, however, you must determine how well your drive is performing. You need a tool to measure the performance of your disk subsystem. The hdparam tool is just right for the job; you can download the source distribution of this tool from metalab.unc.edu/pub/Linux/system/hardware/ and compile and install it as follows:

1. Use su to navigate to root.

2. Extract the source distribution in a suitable directory such as /usr/local/src.

   For example, I ran the tar xvzf hdparm-3.9.tar.gz command in /usr/local/src to extract the hdparam version 3.9 source distribution.

3. Change to the newly created subdirectory and run the `make install` command to compile and install the `hdparam` binary and the manual page.

The binary is by default installed in `/usr/local/sbin` directory. It's called `hdparam`.

 Back up your data before using `hdparam`. Because `hdparam` enables you to change the behavior of your IDE/EIDE disk subsystem — and Murphy's Law always lurks in the details of any human undertaking — a misconfiguration could cause your system to hang. Also, to make such an event less likely, experiment with `hdparam` in single-user mode before you use it. You can reboot your system and force it into single-user mode by entering **linux single** at the `lilo` prompt during bootup.

After you have installed the `hdparam` tool, you are ready to investigate the performance of your disk subsystem. Assuming your IDE or EIDE hard disk is `/dev/hda`, run the following command to see the state of your hard disk configuration:

```
hdparam /dev/hda
```

You should see output like the following:

```
/dev/hda:
multcount    =  0 (off)
I/O support  =  0 (default 16-bit)
unmaskirq    =  0 (off)
using_dma    =  0 (off)
keepsettings =  0 (off)
nowerr       =  0 (off)
readonly     =  0 (off)
readahead    =  8 (on)
geometry     =  2494/255/63, sectors = 40079088, start = 0
```

As you can see, almost everything in this default mode is turned off; changing some defaults may enhance your disk performance. Before proceeding, however, we need more information from the hard disk. Run the following command:

```
hdparm -i /dev/hda
```

This command returns information like the following:

```
/dev/hda:
Model=WDC WD205AA, FwRev=05.05B05, SerialNo=WD-WMAOW1516037
 Config={ HardSect NotMFM HdSw>15uSec SpinMotCtl Fixed DTR>5Mbs FmtGapReq }
 RawCHS=16383/16/63, TrkSize=57600, SectSize=600, ECCbytes=40
 BuffType=DualPortCache, BuffSize=2048kB, MaxMultSect=16, MultSect=16
 CurCHS=16383/16/63, CurSects=16514064, LBA=yes, LBAsects=40079088
 IORDY=on/off, tPIO={min:120,w/IORDY:120}, tDMA={min:120,rec:120}
 PIO modes: pio0 pio1 pio2 pio3 pio4
 DMA modes: mdma0 mdma1 *mdma2 udma0 udma1 udma2 udma3 udma4
```

The preceding command displays the drive identification information (if any) that was available the last time you booted the system – for example, the model, configuration, drive geometry (cylinders, heads, sectors), track size, sector size, buffer size, supported DMA mode, and PIO mode. Some of this information will come in handy later; you may want to print this screen so you have it in hard copy. For now, test the disk subsystem by using the following command:

```
/usr/local/sbin/hdparm -Tt /dev/hda
```

You see results like the following:

```
/dev/hda:
 Timing buffer-cache reads:   128 MB in  1.01 seconds = 126.73 MB/sec
 Timing buffered disk reads:  64 MB in 17.27 seconds = 3.71 MB/sec
```

These actual numbers you see reflect the untuned state of your disk subsystem.

The -T option tells hdparam to test the cache subsystem (that is, the memory, CPU, and buffer cache). The -t tells hdparam to report stats on the disk (/dev/hda), reading data not in the cache. Run this command a few times and figure an average of the MB per second reported for your disk. This is roughly the performance state of your disk subsystem. In this example, the 3.71MB per second is the read performance, which is low.

Now improve the performance of your disk. Go back to the hdparam -i /dev/hda command output and look for MaxMultSect value. In this example, it's 16. Remember that the hdparam /dev/hda command showed that multcount value to be 0 (off). This means that multiple-sector mode (that is, IDE block mode) is turned off.

The multiple sector mode is a feature of most modern IDE hard drives. It enables the drive to transfer multiple disk sectors per I/O interrupt. By default, it's turned off. However, most modern drives can perform 2, 4, 8, or 16 sector transfers per I/O interrupt. If you set this mode to the maximum possible value for your drive (the MaxMultiSect value), you should see your system's throughput increase from 5 to 50 percent (or more) – while reducing the operating system overhead by 30 to 50 percent. In this example, the `MaxMultiSect` value is 16, so the `-m` option of the hdparam tool to set this and see how performance increases. Run the following command:

```
/usr/local/sbin/hdparm -m16 /dev/hda
```

Running the performance test using the `hdparam -tT /dev/hda` command demonstrates the change. For the example system, the change looks like this:

```
/dev/hda:
 Timing buffer-cache reads:    128 MB in  1.01 seconds = 126.73 MB/sec
 Timing buffered disk reads:   64 MB in 16.53 seconds =  3.87 MB/sec
```

The performance of the drive has gone up from 3.71MB per second to 3.87MB per second. Not much, but not bad. Probably your drive can do better than that if your disk and controller are fairly new. You can probably achieve 20 to 30MB per second.

If hdparam reported that your system's I/O support setting is 16-bit, and you have a fairly new (one or two years old) disk subsystem, try enabling 32-bit I/O support. You can do so by using the `-c` option for hdparam and selecting one of its three values:

- 0 enables default 16-bit I/O support

- 1 enables 32-bit support

- 3 enables 32-bit support with a special synchronization sequence required by many IDE/EIDE processors. (This value works well with most systems.)

Set the options as follows:

```
/usr/local/sbin/hdparm -m16 -c3 /dev/hda
```

The command uses the `-m16` option (mentioned earlier) and adds `-c3` to enable 32-bit I/O support. Now running the program with the `-t` option shows the following results:

```
/dev/hda:
 Timing buffered disk reads:   64 MB in  8.96 seconds =  7.14 MB/sec
```

The performance of the disk subsystem has improved – practically doubled – and you should be able to get even more.

- If your drive supports direct memory access (DMA), you may be able to use the `-d` option, which enables DMA mode.

◆ Typically, -d1 -X32 options or -d1 -X66 options are used together to apply the DMA capabilities of your disk subsystem.

   ■ The first set of options (-d1 -X32) enables the multiword DMA mode2 for the drive.

   ■ The next set of options (-d1 -X66) enables UltraDMA mode2 for drives that support UltraDMA burst timing feature.

   These options can dramatically increase your disk performance. (I have seen 20MB per second transfer rate with these options on various new EIDE/ATA drives.)

◆ -u1 can boost overall system performance by enabling the disk driver to unmask other interrupts during the processing of a disk interrupt. That means the operating system can attend to other interrupts (such as the network I/O and serial I/O) while waiting for a disk-based data transfer to finish.

hdparam offers many other options — but be careful with them. Most of them can corrupt data if used incorrectly. Always back up your data before playing with the hdparam tool. Also, after you have found a set of options to work well, you should put the hdparam command with options in the /etc/rc.d/rc.local script so that they are set every time you boot the system. For example, I have added the following line in the /etc/rc.d/rc.local file in one of my newer Red Hat Linux systems.

```
hdparm -m16 -c3 -u1 -d1 -X66   /dev/hda
```

Tuning ext2 Filesystem

For years the ext2 filesystem has been the *de facto* filesystem for Linux. It isn't the greatest filesystem in the world but it works reasonably well. One of the ways you can improve its performance is by changing the default block size from 1024 to a multiple of 1024 (usually no more than 4096) for servers with mostly large files. Here's how you can change the block size.

Changing the block size of the ext2 filesystem

To find out what kind of files you have on an ext2 partition, do the following:

1. Use su to navigate to root; change to the top directory of the ext2 partition.

2. Run the following command (actually a small, command-line script using find and the awk utility). The script displays all files, their sizes, and the size of the entire partition — both total and average.

```
find . -type f -exec ls -l {} \; | \
awk 'BEGIN {tsize=0;fcnt=1;} \
{ printf("%03d File: %-060s size: %d bytes\n",fcnt++, $9,
$5); \
tsize += $5; } \
END { printf("Total size = %d\nAverage file size = %.02f\n",
\
tsize, tsize/fcnt); }'
```

3. After you know the average size of the filesystem, you can determine whether to change the block size. Say you find out your average file size is 8192, which is 2 × 4096. You can change the block size to 4096, providing smaller, more manageable files for the ext2 filesystem.

4. Unfortunately, you can't alter the block size of an existing ext2 filesystem without rebuilding it. So you must back up all your files from the filesystem and then rebuild it using the following command:

```
/sbin/mke2fs /dev/partition -b 4096
```

For example, if you have backed up the /dev/hda7 partition and want to change the block size to 4096, the command would look like this:

```
/sbin/mke2fs /dev/hda7 -b 4096 command.
```

Changing the block size to a higher number than the default (1024) may yield significant performance in raw reading speed by reducing number of seeks, potentially faster fsck session during boot, and less file fragmentation.

However, increasing the block size blindly (that is, without knowing the average file size) can result in wasted space. For example, if the average file size is 2010 bytes on a system with 4096 byte blocks, each file wastes on an average 4096 – 2010 = 2086 bytes! Know your file size before you alter the block size.

Using e2fsprogs to tune ext2 filesystem

To tune the ext2 filesystem, install the e2fsprogs utility package as follows:

1. Download the e2fsprogs-version.src.rpm (replace version with the latest version number) source distribution from www.rpmfind.net. I downloaded the e2fsprogs-1.19-0.src.rpm package. You can also get the source from the e2fsprogs project site at e2fsprogs.sourceforge.net.

When the download is complete, su to root.

2. Run the `rpm -ivh e2fsprogs-version.src.rpm` command to extract the source into a `/usr/src/redhat/SOURCES/` directory. The source RPM drops an `e2fsprogs-version.tar.gz` file.

   Use the `tar xvzf e2fsprogs-version.tar.gz` command to extract the file and create a subdirectory called `e2fsprogs-version`.

3. Change to the new subdirectory `e2fsprogs-version`.

4. Run `mkdir build` to create a new subdirectory and then change to that directory.

5. Run `../configure` script to configure the source tree.

6. Run the `make` utility to create the binaries.

7. Run `make check` to ensure that everything is built correctly.

8. Run the `make install` command to install the binaries.

After you have installed the `e2fsprogs` utilities you can start using them as discussed in the following section.

USING THE TUNE2FS UTILITY FOR FILESYSTEM TUNING

You can use the `tune2fs` utility to tune various aspects of an ext2 filesystem. However, never apply the ext2 utilities on a mounted ext2 and always back up your data whenever you are modifying anything belonging to a filesystem. In the following section I discuss the `tune2fs` utility (part of the `e2fsprogs` package) to tune an unmounted ext2 filesystem called /dev/hda7. If you at least one of the settings discussed below, don't forget to change the partition name (/dev/hda7) with an appropriate name. First let's take a look at what `tune2fs` shows as the current settings for the unmounted /dev/hda7. Run the following command:

```
/sbin/tune2fs -l /dev/hda7
```

The output should be like the following:

```
tune2fs 1.19, 13-Jul-2000 for EXT2 FS 0.5b, 95/08/09
Filesystem volume name:    <none>
Last mounted on:           <not available>
Filesystem UUID:           5d06c65b-dd11-4df4-9230-a10f2da783f8
Filesystem magic number:   0xEF53
Filesystem revision #:     1 (dynamic)
Filesystem features:       filetype sparse_super
Filesystem state:          clean
Errors behavior:           Continue
Filesystem OS type:        Linux
Inode count:               1684480
Block count:               13470471
```

```
Reserved block count:      673523
Free blocks:               13225778
Free inodes:               1674469
First block:               1
Block size:                1024
Fragment size:             1024
Blocks per group:          8192
Fragments per group:       8192
Inodes per group:          1024
Inode blocks per group:    128
Last mount time:           Thu Feb 15 17:51:19 2001
Last write time:           Thu Feb 15 17:51:51 2001
Mount count:               1
Maximum mount count:       20
Last checked:              Thu Feb 15 17:50:23 2001
Check interval:            15552000 (6 months)
Next check after:          Tue Aug 14 18:50:23 2001
Reserved blocks uid:       0 (user root)
Reserved blocks gid:       0 (group root)
First inode:               11
Inode size:                128
```

The very first setting I would like for you to understand is the *error behavior.*
This setting dictates how kernel behaves when errors are detected on the filesystem.
There are three possible values for this setting:

◆ Continue

   The default setting is to continue even if there is an error.

◆ Remount-ro (readonly)

◆ Panic

The next setting, mount count, is the number of time you have mounted this
filesystem.

The next setting shows the maximum mount count (20), which means that after
the maximum number of read/write mode mounts the filesystem is subject to a fsck
checking session during the next boot cycle.

The last checked setting shows the last date at which an fsck check was performed.
The check interval for two consecutive fsck sessions. The check interval is only used if
the maximum read/write mount count isn't reached during the interval. If you don't
unmount the filesystem for 6 months, then although the mount count is only 2, the
fsck check is forced because the filesystem exceeded the check interval. The next fsck
check date is shown in next check after setting. The reserved block UID and GID settings show which user and group has ownership of the reserved portion of this filesystem. By default, the reserved portion is to be used by super user (UID = 0, GID = 0).

On an unmounted filesystem such as /dev/hda7, you can change the maximum read/write mount count setting to be more suitable for your needs using the -c option with tune2fs. For example, /sbin/tune2fs -c 1 /dev/hda7 forces fsck check on the filesystem every time you boot the system. You can also use the -i option to change the time-based fsck check enforcement schedule. For example, the /sbin/tune2fs --i7d /dev/hda7 command ensures that fsck checks are enforced if the filesystem is remounted in read/write mode after a week. Similarly, the /sbin/tune2fs --i0 /dev/hda7 command disables the time-based fsck checks.

USING THE E2FSCK UTILITY FOR CHECKING AND REPAIRING FILESYSTEM

If you have a corrupt ext2 filesystem, you can use the e2fsck utility to fix it. To check a partition using e2fsck, you must unmount it first and run the /sbin/e2fsck /dev/device command where /dev/*device* is your disk drive. For example, to force fsck check on a device called /dev/hda7, I can use the /sbin/e2fsck -f /dev/hda7 command. Such as check may display output as shown below.

```
e2fsck 1.19, 13-Jul-2000 for EXT2 FS 0.5b, 95/08/09
Pass 1: Checking inodes, blocks, and sizes
Pass 2: Checking directory structure
Pass 3: Checking directory connectivity
Pass 4: Checking reference counts
Pass 5: Checking group summary information
/dev/hda7: 12/1684256 files (0.0% non-contiguous), 52897/3367617 blocks
```

The e2fsck utility asks you repair questions, which you can avoid by using the -p option.

Using a Journaling Filesystem

A journaling filesystem is simply a transaction-based filesystem. Each filesystem activity that changes the filesystem is recorded in a transaction log. In the event of a crash, the filesystem can replay the necessary transactions to get back to a stable state in a very short time. This is a technique that many database engines such as IBM DB2 and Oracle use to ensure that system is always in a known and recoverable state.

The problem with ext2 filesystem is that in the unfortunate event of a crash, the filesystem can be in such an unclean state that it may be corrupt beyond any meaningful recovery. The fsck program used to check and potentially repair the filesystem often can't do much to fix such problems. With a journaling filesystem, such a nightmare is a thing of the past! Because the transaction log records all the activities in the filesystem, a crash recovery is fast and data loss is minimum.

A journaling filesystem doesn't log data in the log; it simply logs meta-data related to disk operations so replaying the log only makes the filesystem consistent from the structural relationship and resource allocation point of view. Some small data loss is possible. Also, logging is subject to the media errors like all other activity. So if the media is bad, journaling won't help much.

Journaling filesystem is new to Linux but has been around for other platforms. There are several flavors of experimental journaling filesystem available today:

♦ IBM developed JFS open source for Linux.

JFS has been ported from AIX, IBM's own operating system platform, and still not ready for production use. You can find more information on JFS at http://oss.software.ibm.com/developerworks/opensource/jfs.

♦ Red Hat's own ext3 filesystem which is ext2 + journaling capabilities.

It's also not ready for prime time. You can download the alpha release of ext3 ftp site at ftp://ftp.linux.org.uk/pub/linux/sct/fs/jfs/.

♦ ReiserFS developed by Namesys is currently included in the Linux kernel source distribution. It has been used more widely than the other journaling filesystems for Linux. So far, it is leading the journaling filesystem arena for Linux.

♦ I discuss how you can use ReiserFS today in a later section. ReiserFS was developed by Hans Reiser who has secured funding from commercial companies such as MP3, BigStorage.com, SuSe, and Ecila.com. These companies all need better, more flexible filesystems, and can immediately channel early beta user experience back to the developers. You can find more information on ReiserFS at http://www.namesys.com.

♦ XFS journaling filesystem developed by Silicon Graphics, Inc. (SGI).

You can find more information on XFS at http://oss.sgi.com/projects/xfs/. XFS is a fast, solid 64-bit filesystem, which means that it can support large files (9 million terabytes) and even larger filesystems (18 million terabytes).

Because ReiserFS is included with Linux kernel 2.4.1 (or above), I discuss how you can use it in the following section.

As of this writing the ReiserFS filesystem can't be used with NFS without patches, which aren't officially available for the kernel 2.4.1 o above yet.

Compiling and installing ReiserFS

Here's how you can compile and install ReiserFS (reiserfs) support in Linux kernel 2.4.1 or above.

1. Get the latest Linux kernel source from `http://www.kernel.org` and extract it in `/usr/src/linux-version` directory as root, where *version* is the current version of the kernel. Here I assume this to be 2.4.1.

2. Run `make menuconfig` from the `/usr/src/linux-2.4.1`.

3. Select the Code maturity level options submenu and using spacebar select the Prompt for development and/or incomplete code/drivers option. Exit the submenu.

4. Select the File systems submenu. Using spacebar, select Reiserfs support to be included as a kernel module and exit the submenu.

Don't choose the Have reiserfs do extra internal checking option under ReiserFS support option. If you set this to yes, then reiserfs performs extensive checks for internal consistency throughout its operation, which makes it very slow.

5. Ensure that all other kernel features that you use are also selected as usual (see Tuning kernel for details).

6. Exit the main menu and save the kernel configuration.

7. Run the `make dep` command to as suggested by the menuconfig program.

8. Run `make bzImage` to create the new kernel. Then run make modules and make modules_install to install the new modules in appropriate location.

9. Change directory to `arch/i386/boot` directory. Note, if your hardware architecture is Intel, you must replace i386 and possibly need further instructions from a kernel HOW-TO documentation to compile and install your flavor of the kernel. I assume that most readers are i386-based.

10. Copy the bzImage to `/boot/vmlinuz-2.4.1` and edit the `/etc/lilo.conf` file to include a new configuration such as the following:

```
image=/boot/vmlinuz-2.4.1
        label=linux2
        read-only
        root=/dev/hda1
```

11. Run the `/sbin/lilo` command to reconfigure LILO and reboot your system. At the lilo prompt enter linux2 and boot the new kernel. If you have any problem, you should be able to reboot to your standard linux kernel, which should be default automatically.

12. After you have booted the new kernel, you are ready to use ReiserFS (reiserfs).

Using ReiserFS

Because ReiserFS (reiserfs) is still under the "experimental" category, I highly recommend restricting it to a non-critical aspect of your system. Ideally, you want to dedicate an entire disk or at least one partition for ReiserFS and use it and see how you like it.

To use ReiserFS with a new partition called `/dev/hda7`, simply do the following:

1. As `root`, ensure that the partition is set as Linux native (83) by using `fdisk` or another disk-partitioning tool.

2. Create a ReiserFS (reiserfs) filesystem on the new partition, using the `/sbin/mkreiserfs /dev/hda7` command.

3. Create a mount point for the new filesystem. For example, I can create a mount point called /jfs, using the `mkdir /jfs` command.

4. Mount the filesystem, using the `mount -t reiserfs /dev/hda7 /jfs` command. Now you can access it from /jfs mount point.

Benchmarking ReiserFS

To see how a journaling filesystem stacks up against the `ext2` filesystem, here's a little benchmark you can do on your own.

 TIP   I assume that you have created a brand new ReiserFS filesystem on `/dev/hda7` and can mount it on `/jfs`. To do this benchmark, you must not store any data in this partition. So back up everything you have in `/jfs` because you erase everything on `/jfs` in this process.

Create a shell script called `reiserfs_vs_ext2.bash` in your /tmp directory, as shown in Listing 3-1.

Listing 3-1: /tmp/reiserfs_vs_ext2.bash

```
#!/bin/bash
#
# This script is created based on the file_test script
# found in the home-grown benchmark found at http://www.namesys.com
#
if [ $# -lt 6 ]
then
        echo Usage: file_test dir_name device nfiles size1 size2 log_name
        exit
fi
TESTDIR=$1
DEVICE=$2
LOGFILE=$6
/bin/umount $TESTDIR
/sbin/mkreiserfs $DEVICE
mount -t reiserfs $DEVICE $TESTDIR
echo 1. reiserfs 4KB creating files ...
echo "reiserfs 4KB create" $3 "files of size: from " $4 "to" $5  > $LOGFILE
(time -p ./mkfile $TESTDIR $3 $4 $5)>> $LOGFILE 2>&1
echo done.
sync
df >> $LOGFILE
/bin/umount $TESTDIR
/sbin/mke2fs $DEVICE -b 4096
mount -t ext2 $DEVICE $TESTDIR
echo 2. ext2fs 4KB creating files ...
echo "ext2fs 4KB create" $3 "files of size: from " $4 "to" $5  >> $LOGFILE
(time -p ./mkfile $TESTDIR $3 $4 $5)>> $LOGFILE 2>&1
echo done.
sync
df >> $LOGFILE
/bin/umount $TESTDIR
```

Download a small C program called `mkfile.c` in /tmp. This program, developed by the ReiserFS team, is available at www.namesys.com/filetest/mkfile.c. From the /tmp directory, compile this program using the `gcc -o mkfile mkfile.c` command. Change the permission of the `reiserfs_vs_ext2.bash` and `mkfile` program, using the `chimed 755 reiserfs_vs_ext2.bash mkfile` command.

Now you are ready to run the benchmark test. Run the following command from the /tmp directory as root:

```
./reiserfs_vs_ext2.bash  /jfs /dev/hda7 100000 1024 4096 log
```

You are asked to confirm that you want to lose all data in /dev/hda7. Because you have already emptied this partition for testing, specify yes and continue. This test creates 100,000 files that range in size from 1K to 4K, in both the ReiserFS (reiserfs) and ext2 filesystems by creating each of these two filesystem in /dev/hda7 in turn. The results are recorded in the /tmp/log file. Here is a sample /tmp/log file:

```
reiserfs 4KB create 100000 files of size: from  1024 to 4096
real 338.68
user 2.83
sys 227.83
Filesystem            1k-blocks      Used Available Use% Mounted on
/dev/hda1             1035660      135600    847452  14% /
/dev/hda5             4134868     2318896   1605928  60% /usr
/dev/hda7            13470048      332940  13137108   3% /jfs
ext2fs 4KB create 100000 files of size: from  1024 to 4096
real 3230.40
user 2.87
sys 3119.12
Filesystem            1k-blocks      Used Available Use% Mounted on
/dev/hda1             1035660      135608    847444  14% /
/dev/hda5             4134868     2318896   1605928  60% /usr
/dev/hda7            13259032      401584  12183928   4% /jfs
```

The report shows that to create 100K files of size 1K–4K, Reiserfs (reiserfs) took 338.68 real-time seconds while ext2 took 3230.40 real-time seconds. So the performance is nice.

Although journaling filesystem support is very new to Linux, it's gotten a lot of attention from the industry interested in using Linux in the enterprise, so journaling filesystems will mature in a fast track. I recommend that you use this flavor of the journaling filesystem on an experimental level and become accustomed to its sins and fancies.

Now lets look at another enterprising effort in the Linux disk management called Logical Volume Management or LVM for short. LVM with journaling filesystems will ensures Linux's stake in the enterprise-computing world. Good news is that you don't have to have a budget of the size of a large enterprise to get the high reliability and flexibility of a LVM based disk subsystem. Lets see how you can use LVM today.

Managing Logical Volumes

Logical Volume Management (LVM) and its journaling filesystems ensure Linux a significant place in the enterprise-computing world. You don't need the budget of a large enterprise to get the high reliability and flexibility of an LVM-based disk subsystem. Here's how you can use LVM today.

Traditionally, installing Linux meant partitioning the hard drive(s) into / (root), /usr, /home, and swap space. Problems cropped up if you ran out of disk space in one of these partitions. In most cases, the system administrator would then create a /usr2 (or /home2) partition and tweak the scripts – or create symbolic links to fool the programs into using the new space. Although this practice creates unnecessary busy work and makes the system more "customized," it has been acceptable in the administrative scenarios of small-to-mid-size systems. However, a larger, enterprise-class environment sets a different standard; such disk administration wastes too many resources, which dictatces a different solution: Grow the needed partitions (such as /usr and /home) by adding new disk media without changing the mount points. This is possible by means of a concept called *logical volumes,* now available to anyone using Linux.

Think of logical volumes as a high-level storage layer that encapsulates the underlying physical storage layer. A *logical volume* can consist of at least one physical disk – sometimes several – made available as a single mount point such as /usr, /home, or /whatever. The benefit is easier administration. Adding storage to a logical volume means simply adding physical disks to the definition of the volume; reducing the storage area is a matter of removing physical disks from the logical volume.

 You can find out more about LVM at http://sistina.com/lvm/.

Compiling and installing the LVM module for kernel

The latest Linux kernel 2.4.1 (or above) source distribution ships with the LVM source code. Enabling LVM support is a simple matter of compiling and installing a new kernel, as follows:

1. su to root and change directory to the top-level kernel source directory (for example, /usr/src/linux-2.4.1). Run make menuconfig to configure the kernel.

2. Select the Multi-device support (RAID and LVM) support submenu. Press the spacebar once to include Multiple devices driver support (RAID and LVM) support in the kernel; then select Logical volume manager (LVM) support as a kernel module. Save the kernel configuration as usual.

3. Compile and install the kernel as usual (see Kernel Tuning chapter for details).

4. Run /sbin/modprobe lvm-mod to load the LVM kernel module. To verify that this module is loaded properly, run the /sbin/lsmod command and you should see the module listed as one of the loaded kernel modules. Add the following lines in /etc/modules.conf to automatically load the lvm-mod module when needed in the future.

```
alias block-major-58        lvm-mod
alias char-major-109        lvm-mod
```

5. Create a script called /etc/rc.d/init.d/lvm (as shown in Listing 3-2), to start and stop LVM support automatically (during the boot and shutdown cycles respectively).

Listing 3-2: /etc/rc.d/init.d/lvm

```
!/bin/bash
#
# lvm    This shell script takes care of
#        starting and stopping LVM-managed
#        volumes.
#
# chkconfig: - 25 2
# description: LVM is Logical Volume Management
# Source function library.
. /etc/rc.d/init.d/functions
[ -f /sbin/vgscan ] || exit 0
[ -f /sbin/vgchange ] || exit 0
RETVAL=0
start() {
        # Start LVM.
        gprintf "Starting LVM: "
        /sbin/vgscan;
        /sbin/vgchange -ay
}
stop() {
        # Stop LVM.
```

Continued

Listing 3-2 *(Continued)*

```
            gprintf "Shutting down LVM: "
            /sbin/vgchange -an
}
restart() {
        stop
        start
}
# See how we were called.
case "$1" in
        start)
                  start
                  ;;
        stop)
                  stop
                  ;;
        restart)
                  restart
                  ;;
        *)
                  echo "Usage: lvm {start|stop|restart}"
                  exit 1
esac
exit $?
```

6. Create two symblock links to the /etc/rc.d/init.d/lvm script, using the following commands:

```
ln -s /etc/rc.d/init.d/lvm /etc/rc.d/rc3.d/S25lvm
ln -s /etc/rc.d/init.d/lvm /etc/rc.d/rc3.d/K25lvm
```

Creating a logical volume

In this example, assume that you have two hard disks called /dev/hda and /dev/hdc — and that each one has a free partition: /dev/hda7 (for /dev/hda) and /dev/hdc1 (for /dev/hdb). You want to create an LVM using these two partitions.

1. Run the /sbin/fdisk /dev/hda command. Using fdisk commands, toggle the appropriate partition's ID to 8e (Linux LVM). The following listing shows the example (edited for brevity) fdisk session to change the ID for a partition called /dev/hda7. The necessary user input is shown in bold letters.

```
Command (m for help): p
Disk /dev/hda: 255 heads, 63 sectors, 2494 cylinders
Units = cylinders of 16065 * 512 bytes
```

```
     Device Boot Start    End    Blocks   Id  System
/dev/hda1    *      1    131   1052226   83  Linux
/dev/hda2         262   2494  17936572+  f  Win95
/dev/hda5         262    784   4200934+ 83  Linux
/dev/hda6         785    817    265041   82  Linux swap
/dev/hda7         818   2494  13470471   83  Linux
Command (m for help): t
Partition number (1-7): 7
Hex code (type L to list codes): 8e
Changed system type of partition 7 to 8e (Linux LVM)
Command (m for help): p
Disk /dev/hda: 255 heads, 63 sectors, 2494 cylinders
Units = cylinders of 16065 * 512 bytes
     Device Boot Start    End    Blocks   Id  System
/dev/hda1    *      1    131   1052226   83  Linux
/dev/hda2         262   2494  17936572+  f  Win95
/dev/hda5         262    784   4200934+ 83  Linux
/dev/hda6         785    817    265041   82  Linux swap
/dev/hda7         818   2494  13470471   8e  Linux LVM
Command (m for help): w
The partition table has been altered!
```

Do this step for the /dev/hdc1 partition.

2. Run the `/sbin/pvcreate /dev/hda7 /dev/hdc1` command to create two physical volumes.

3. Run the `/sbin/vgcreate big_disk /dev/hda7 /dev/hdc1` command to create a new volume group called big_disk. The command shows the following output:

```
vgcreate -- INFO: using default physical extent size 4 MB
vgcreate -- INFO: maximum logical volume size is 255.99
Gigabyte
vgcreate -- doing automatic backup of volume group "big_disk"
vgcreate -- volume group "big_disk" successfully created and
activated
```

4. To confirm that the volume group is created using the /dev/hda7 physical volume, run the `/sbin/pvdisplay /dev/hda7` command to display stats as shown below:

```
--- Physical volume ---
PV Name                 /dev/hda7
VG Name                 big_disk
PV Size                 12.85 GB / NOT usable 2.76 MB [LVM: 133
KB]
PV#                     1
```

```
PV Status              available
Allocatable            yes
Cur LV                 0
PE Size (KByte)        4096
Total PE               3288
Free PE                3288
Allocated PE           0
PV UUID                2IKjJh-MBys-FI6R-JZgl-80ul-uLrc-PTahOa
```

As you can see, the VG Name (volume group name) for /dev/hda7 is
big_disk, which is exactly what we want. You can run the same command
for /dev/hdc1 as shown below:

```
--- Physical volume ---
PV Name                /dev/hdc1
VG Name                big_disk
PV Size                3.91 GB / NOT usable 543 KB [LVM: 124
KB]
PV#                    2
PV Status              available
Allocatable            yes
Cur LV                 0
PE Size (KByte)        4096
Total PE               1000
Free PE                1000
Allocated PE           0
PV UUID                RmxH4b-BSfX-ypN1-cfwO-pZHg-obMz-JKkNK5
```

5. You can also display the volume group information by using the
/sbin/vgdisplay command, which shows output as follows:

```
--- Volume group ---
VG Name                big_disk
VG Access              read/write
VG Status              available/resizable
VG #                   0
MAX LV                 256
Cur LV                 0
Open LV                0
MAX LV Size            255.99 GB
Max PV                 256
Cur PV                 2
Act PV                 2
VG Size                16.75 GB
PE Size                4 MB
Total PE               4288
Alloc PE / Size        0 / 0
```

```
Free  PE / Size        4288 / 16.75 GB
VG UUID                VMttR1-T10e-I4js-oXmi-uEle-hprD-iqhCIX
```

In the preceding report, the total volume group size (VG Size) is roughly the sum of the two physical volumes we added to it.

6. Run the `/sbin/lvcreate --L10G -nvol1` big_disk command to create a 10GB logical volume called /dev/big_disk/vol1, using the big_disk volume group.

TIP

You use disk striping and then use `-i` option to specify the number of physical volumes to scatter the logical volume and `-I` option to specify the number of kilobytes for the granularity of the stripes. Stripe size must be 2^n (n = 0 to 7). For example, to create a striped version of the logical volume(using the two physical volumes you added in the volume group earlier), you can run the `/sbin/lvcreate -i2 -I4 -L10G -nvol1 big_disk` command. I don't recommend striping because currently you can't add new physical volumes to a striped logical volume, which sort of defeats the purpose of LVM.

7. Decide whether to use a journaling filesystem (such as reiserfs) or ext2 for the newly created logical volume called vol1. To create a reiserfs filesystem, run the `/sbin/mkreiserfs /dev/big_disk/vol1` command, or to create an ext2 filesystem run the `/sbin/mke2fs -b 4096 /dev/big_disk/vol1` command. If you want to use a different block size, change 4096 to be 1024, or 2048, or your custom block size as needed. I prefer to create the reiserfs filesystem when using logical volumes.

8. Create a mount point called /vol1, using the `mkdir /vol1` command. Then mount the filesystem, using the `mount /dev/big_disk/vol1 /vol1` command. You may have to add `-t reiserfs` option when mounting a reiserfs filesystem. Run `df` to see the volume listed in the output. Here's a sample output:

```
Filesystem           1k-blocks       Used Available Use% Mounted on
/dev/hda1            1035660       243792    739260  25% /
/dev/hda5            4134868      2574004   1350820  66% /usr
/dev/big_disk/vol1   10485436       32840  10452596   1% /vol1
```

You are all set with a new logical volume called vol1. The LVM package includes a set of tools to help you manage your volumes.

USING PHYSICAL VOLUME MANAGEMENT UTILITIES

Several utilities can manage physical volumes used for your logical volumes.

◆ The /sbin/pvscan utility enables you to list all physical volumes in your system.

◆ The /sbin/pvchange utility enables you to change attributes of a physical volume.

◆ The /sbin/pvcreate utility enables you to create a new physical volume.

◆ /sbin/pvdata displays debugging information for a physical volume.

◆ /sbin/pvdisplay displays attribute information for a physical volume.

◆ The /sbin/pvmove utility enables you to move data from one physical volume to another within a volume group.

For example, say that you have a logical volume group called vol1 consisting of a single volume group called big_disk, which has two physical volumes /dev/hda7 and /dev/hdc1. You want to move data from /dev/hda7 to /dev/hdc1 and remove /dev/hda7 with a new disk (or partition). In such case, first ensure that /dev/hdc1 has enough space to hold all the data from /dev/hda7. Then run the /sbin/pvmove /dev/hda8 /dev/hdc1 command.

This operation takes a considerable amount of time (depending on data) and also shouldn't be interrupted.

USING VOLUME GROUP MANAGEMENT UTILITIES

To manage a volume group, which consists of at least one physical volume, you can use the following utilities:

◆ The vgscan utility enables you to list all the volume groups in your system.

◆ The /sbin/vgcfgbackup utility backs up a volume group descriptor area.

◆ The /sbin/vgcfgrestore utility restores a volume group descriptor area.

◆ The /sbin/vgchange utility changes attributes of a volume group. For example, you can activate a volume group by using -a y option and use the -a n option to deactivate it.

◆ The /sbin/vgck utility checks a volume group descriptor area consistency.

◆ The /sbin/vgcreate utility enables you to create a new volume group.

- The /sbin/vgdisplay utility displays volume group information.

- The /sbin/vgexport utility makes an inactive volume group unknown to the system so that you can remove physical volumes from it.

- The /sbin/vgextend utility enables you to add physical volumes to a volume group.

- The /sbin/vgimport utility enables you to import a volume group that has been previously exported using the vgexport utility.

- The /sbin/vgmerge utility enables you to merge two volume groups.

- The /sbin/vgmknodes utility enables you to create volume group directories and special files.

- The /sbin/vgreduce utility enables you to reduce a volume group by removing at least one unused physical volume from the group.

- The /sbin/vgremove utility enables you to remove a volume group that doesn't have any logical volume and also is inactive. If you have a volume group that has at least one logical volume, you must deactivate and remove it first.

- The /sbin/vgrename utility enables you to rename a volume group.

- The /sbin/vgscan utility scans all disks for volume groups and also builds the /etc/lvmtab and other files in /etc/lvmtab.d directory, which are used by the LVM module.

- The /sbin/vgsplit utility enables you to split a volume group.

USING LOGICAL VOLUME MANAGEMENT UTILITIES
The following utilities enable you to manage logical volumes:

- The /sbin/lvchange utility enables you to change attributes of a logical volume. For example, you can activate a logical volume group using -a y option and deactivate it using -a n option. Once it's deactivated, you may have to use the vmchange command before you can activate the volume group.

- The /sbin/lvcreate utility enables you to create a new logical volume using an existing volume group.

- The /sbin/lvdisplay utility enables you display attributes of a logical volume.

- The /sbin/lvextend utility enables you to extend the size of a logical volume.

- The /sbin/lvreduce utility enables you to change the size of an existing, active logical volume.

- The /sbin/lvremove utility enables you to remove an inactive logical volume.

- The /sbin/lvrename utility enables you to rename an existing logical volume.

- The /sbin/lvscan utility enables you to locate all logical volumes on your system.

USING LOGICAL VOLUME MANAGER UTILITIES

The following utilities give you control of the logical volume management module itself.

- The /sbin/lvmchange utility enables you to change the attribute of the logical volume manager. You shouldn't need to use this utility in normal operation.

- The /sbin/lvmcreate_initrd utility enables you to a bootable initial RAM disk using a logical volume.

- The /sbin/lvmdiskscan utility enables you to scan all storage devices in your system that can be used in logical volumes.

- The /sbin/lvmsadc utility enables you to collect read/write statistics of a logical volume.

- The /sbin/lvmsar utility enables you to report read/write statistics to a log file.

Adding a new disk or partition to a logical volume

After a logical volume has been in use for a while, eventually you have to add new disks to it as your system needs more space. Here I add a new disk partition /dev/hdc2 to the already created logical volume called /dev/big_disk/vol1.

1. su to root and run /sbin/pvscan to view the state of all your physical volumes. Here's a sample output.

```
pvscan -- reading all physical volumes (this may take a
while...)
pvscan -- ACTIVE   PV "/dev/hda7" of VG "big_disk" [12.84 GB
/ 2.84 GB free]
pvscan -- ACTIVE   PV "/dev/hdc1" of VG "big_disk" [3.91 GB /
3.91 GB free]
pvscan -- total: 2 [16.75 GB] / in use: 2 [16.75 GB] / in no
VG: 0 [0]
```

2. Run `/sbin/vgdisplay big_disk` to learn the current settings for the big_disk volume group. Here's a sample output:

```
--- Volume group ---
VG Name                 big_disk
VG Access               read/write
VG Status               available/resizable
VG #                    0
MAX LV                  256
Cur LV                  0
Open LV                 0
MAX LV Size             255.99 GB
Max PV                  256
Cur PV                  2
Act PV                  2
VG Size                 16.75 GB
PE Size                 4 MB
Total PE                4288
Alloc PE / Size         0 / 0
Free  PE / Size         4288 / 16.75 GB
VG UUID                 p3N102-z7nM-xH86-DWw8-yn2J-Mw3Y-1shq62
```

As you can see here, the total volume group size is about 16 GB.

3. Using the `fdisk` utility, change the new partition's system ID to 8e (Linux LVM). Here's a sample `/sbin/fdisk /dev/hdc` session on my system.

```
Command (m for help): p
Disk /dev/hdc: 255 heads, 63 sectors, 1583 cylinders
Units = cylinders of 16065 * 512 bytes
    Device Boot     Start       End     Blocks    Id  System
/dev/hdc1               1       510    4096543+   8e  Linux LVM
/dev/hdc2             511      1583    8618872+   83  Linux
Command (m for help): t
Partition number (1-4): 2
Hex code (type L to list codes): 8e
Changed system type of partition 2 to 8e (Linux LVM)
Command (m for help): p
Disk /dev/hdc: 255 heads, 63 sectors, 1583 cylinders
Units = cylinders of 16065 * 512 bytes
    Device Boot     Start       End     Blocks    Id  System
/dev/hdc1               1       510    4096543+   8e  Linux LVM
/dev/hdc2             511      1583    8618872+   8e  Linux LVM
Command (m for help): v
62 unallocated sectors
Command (m for help): w
The partition table has been altered!
```

4. Run `/sbin/mkreiserfs /dev/hdc2` to create a reiserfs filesystem, but if you have been using `ext2` filesystems for the logical volume, use the `/sbin/mke2fs /dev/hdc2` command instead.

5. Run `/sbin/pvcreate /dev/hdc2` to create a new physical volume using the `/dev/hdc2` partition.

6. Run `/sbin/vgextend big_disk /dev/hdc2` to add the partition to the `big_disk` volume group. To verify that the disk partition has been added to the volume group, run the `/sbin/vgdisplay /dev/big_disk` command. You should see output like the following:

```
--- Volume group ---
VG Name                big_disk
VG Access              read/write
VG Status              available/resizable
VG #                   0
MAX LV                 256
Cur LV                 1
Open LV                0
MAX LV Size            255.99 GB
Max PV                 256
Cur PV                 3
Act PV                 3
VG Size                24.97 GB
PE Size                4 MB
Total PE               6392
Alloc PE / Size        4608 / 18 GB
Free  PE / Size        1784 / 6.97 GB
VG UUID                VMttR1-T10e-I4js-oXmi-uE1e-hprD-iqhCIX
```

In this report, the volume group size has increased to about 25GB because we added approximately 8GB to 16GB of existing volume space.

7. You must unmount the logical volumes that use the volume group. In my example, I can run `umount /dev/big_disk/vol1` to unmount the logical volume that uses the `big_disk` volume group.

TIP   If you get a `device busy` error message when you try to unmount the filesystem, you are either inside the filesystem mount point or you have at least one user (or program) currently using the filesystem. The best way to solve such a scenario is to take the system down to single-user mode from the system console, using the `/etc/rc.d/rc 1` command and staying out of the mount point you are trying to unmount.

8. Increase the size of the logical volume. If the new disk partition is (say) 8GB and you want to extend the logical volume by that amount, do so using the `/sbin/lvextend -L +8G /dev/big_disk/vol1` command. You should see output like the following:

```
lvextend -- extending logical volume "/dev/big_disk/vol1" to
18 GB
lvextend -- doing automatic backup of volume group "big_disk"
lvextend -- logical volume "/dev/big_disk/vol1" successfully
extended
```

9. After the logical volume has been successfully extended, resize the filesystem accordingly:

   ◆ If you use a `reiserfs` filesystem, you can run

   ```
   /sbin/resize_reiserfs -f /dev/big_disk/vol1
   ```

   If the filesytem is already mounted, run the same command without the `-f` option.

   ◆ If you use the `ext2` filesystem, you can use the following command to resize both the filesystem and the volume itself.:

   ```
   /sbin/e2fsadm -L +8G /dev/big_disk/vol1
   ```

10. You can mount the logical volume as usual.

   For example, (if you use `reiserfs` filesystems for the disks, the following command mounts the logical volume as a `reiserfs` filesystem:

   ```
   mount /dev/big_disk/vol1 /vol1 -t reiserfs
   ```

   If you use an `ext2` filesystem, use `-t ext2` instead.

Removing a disk or partition from a volume group

Before you remove a disk from a logical volume, back up all the files. Now say that you have a logical volume called `/dev/big_disk/vol1` which is made up of `/dev/hda7`, `/dev/hdc1`, and `/dev/hdc2`. Now you want to remove `/dev/hda7` because it's too slow (or for some other reason). Here's how you can do so.

Every time I reduced a logical volume to a smaller size, I had to recreate the filesystem. All data was lost. The lesson? Always back up the logical volume first.

1. Move the data on the physical volume /dev/hda7 to another disk or partition in the same volume group. If /dev/hdc1 has enough space to keep the data, you can simply run the /sbin/pvmove /dev/hda7 /dev/hdc1 command to move the data. If you don't have the space in either you must add a disk to replace /dev/hda7 if you want to save the data.

2. Remove the physical volume /dev/hda7 from the volume group, using the following command:

   ```
   /sbin/vgreduce big_disk /dev/hda7
   ```

3. Reduce the size of the logical volume /dev/big_disk/vol1. To reduce it by 2GB, first reduce the filesystem size:

   ◆ If you use reiserfs filesystem, run the following commands:

     ```
     /sbin/resize_reiserfs -s -2G /dev/big_disk/vol1
     /sbin/lvreduce -L -1G /dev/big_disk/vol1
     ```

   ◆ If you use ext2 filesystem for the logical volume, run the following command:

     ```
     /sbin/e2fsadm -L -2G /dev/big_disk/vol1 .
     ```

LVM when matured and supported as a mainstream disk management solution under Linux, increases storage reliability and eases storage administration under Linux's belt of capabilities; thus, making good inroads towards enterprise computing. Because the enterprise IT managers are already looking at Linux, the technologies that are required by them are likely to be fast tracked automatically because of commercial interests. Supporting Linux for the enterprise is going to be a big business in the future, so technologies like LVM will mature quickly. Being on the front with such technology today, ensures that your skill set is high on demand. So don't put off LVM if it isn't yet mainstream in Linux; it's simply coming to a job near you.

Using RAID, SAN, or Storage Appliances

No storage-management discussion can be complete with talking about Redundant Array of Independent Disks (RAID), Storage-Area Networks (SANs), or the storage appliance solutions available today. Most of these solutions involve vendor-specific hardware that isn't Linux-specific, so I won't go in-depth on those issues.

Using Linux Software RAID

I have never got around to using the software RAID capabilities of Linux because something about a software RAID bothers me. I just can't convince myself to play with software RAID because I have used hardware RAID devices extensively and found them to be very suitable solutions. In almost all situations where RAID is a solution, someone is willing to pay for the hardware. Therefore, I can't recommend software RAID as a tested solution with anywhere near the confidence I have in hardware RAID.

Using Hardware RAID

Hardware RAID has been around long enough to become very reliable and many hardware raid solutions exist for Linux. One of my favorite solutions is IBM's ServerRAID controller that can interface with IBM's external disk storage devices such as EXP 15 and EXP 200. Similar solutions are available from other vendors.

A hardware RAID solution typically uses ultra-wide SCSI disks and an internal RAID controller card for Linux. (Most RAID vendors now support native Linux drivers.)

No matter which RAID (hardware or software) you use, you must pick a RAID level that is suitable for your needs. Most common RAID levels are 1 and 5. RAID 1 is purely disk mirroring. To use disk mirroring RAID 1 with 100 GB of total space, you need 200 GB of disk space.

RAID 5 is almost always the best choice. If you use N devices where the smallest has size S, the size of the entire array is (N-1)*S. This "missing" space is used for parity (redundancy) information. (Use same-size media to ensure that your disk space isn't wasted.)

Using Storage-Area Networks (SANs)

Storage-Area Networking (SAN) is the new Holy Grail of storage solutions. Companies like EMC, IBM, Compaq, and Storage Networks are the SAN experts. Typically, a SAN solution consists of dedicated storage devices that you place in a fiver channel network and the storage is made available to your Linux systems via dedicated switching hardware and fiber channel interface cards. Generally speaking, SAN is for the enterprise world and not yet ready for the small- to mid-range organizations.

If you co-locate your Linux systems in a well known data center such as those provided by large ISPs like Exodus, Global Center, and Globix, chances are you will find SAN as a value-added service. This may be one way to avoid paying for the expensive SAN hardware and still have access to it. I know of Storage Networks who provide such services in major ISP locations. They also have fiber rings throughout the US, which means you can make your disks in New York appear in California with negligible latency.

Using Storage Appliances

Storage appliances are no strangers to network/system administrators. Today, you can buy dedicated storage appliances that hook up to your 10 or 100 or 1000 Mb Ethernet and provide RAIDed storage services. These devices are usually remote managed using Web. They are good for small- to mid-range organizations and often very easy to configure and manage.

Using a RAM-Based Filesystem

If you are creating storage space for a small system, a temporary, small filesystem in RAM – a *ramfs* for short – can provide high-speed access. This filesystem is relatively small because (by default) the maximum RAM that a ramfs can use is one-half the total RAM on your system. So if you have 2GB RAM, a ramfs can use only 1GB. Because I haven't yet seen systems with more than 4GB of RAM, even 2GB ramfs is really small compared to today's large disk-based filesystems. The ramfs is perfect for many small files that must be accessed fast. For example, I use a ramfs for a set of small images used in a heavily accessed Web site.

To use a ramfs, you must enable ramfs support in the kernel:

1. Get the latest Linux kernel source from `www.kernel.org` and then (as `root`) extract it into the `/usr/src/linux-version` directory, (where *version* is the current version of the kernel). Here I assume this to be 2.4.1.

2. Select the `File systems` submenu. Using the spacebar, select `Simple RAM-based file system support` to be included as a kernel module and exit the submenu.

3. Ensure that all other kernel features that you use are also selected as usual (see "Tuning the kernel" for details).

4. Exit the main menu and save the kernel configuration.

5. Run the `make dep` command to as suggested by the `menuconfig` program.

6. Run `make bzImage` to create the new kernel. Then run `make modules` and `make modules_install` to install the new modules in appropriate locations.

7. Change directory to `arch/i386/boot` directory. Note, if your hardware architecture is Intel, you must replace i386 and possibly need further instructions from a kernel HOW-TO documentation to compile and install your flavor of the kernel. I assume that most readers are i386-based.

8. Copy the `bzImage` to `/boot/vmlinuz-2.4.1` and edit the `/etc/lilo.conf` file to include a new configuration such as the following:

```
image=/boot/vmlinuz-2.4.1
        label=linux3
        read-only
        root=/dev/hda1
```

9. Run the `/sbin/lilo` command to reconfigure LILO and reboot your system. At the `lilo` prompt, enter `linux3` and boot the new kernel. If you have any problem, you should be able to reboot to your standard Linux kernel, which should be default automatically.

10. After you have booted the new kernel, you are now ready to use the ramfs capability. Create a directory called `ramdrive` by using the `mkdir /ramdrive` command.

11. Mount the ramfs filesystem by using the `mount -t ramfs none /ramdrive` command.

You are all set to write files to `/ramdrive` as usual.

When the system is rebooted or you unmount the filesystem, all contents are lost. This is why it should be a temporary space for high-speed access. Because ramfs is really not a block device, such programs as `df` and `du` can't see it. You can verify that you are really using RAM by running the `cat /proc/mounts` command and look for an entry such as the following:

`none /ram ramfs rw 0 0`

TIP You can specify options using `-o` option when mounting the filesystem just like mounting a regular disk-based filesystem. For example, to mount the ramfs filesystem as read-only, you can use `-o ro` option. You can also specify special options such as `maxsize=n` where *n* is the number of kilobytes to allocate for the filesystem in RAM; `maxfiles=n` where *n* is the number of all files allowed in the filesystem; `maxinodes=n` where *n* is the maximum number of inodes (default is 0 = no limits).

If you run a Web server, you should find many uses for a RAM-based filesystem. Elements such as common images and files of your Web site that aren't too big can be kept in the ramfs filesystem. You can write a simple shell script to copy the contents from their original location on each reboot. Listing 3-3 creates a simple script for that.

Listing 3-3: make_ramfs.sh

```sh
#!/bin/sh
#
# Simply script to create a ramfs filesystem
# on $MOUNTPOINT (which must exists).
#
# It copies files from $ORIG_DIR to $MOUNTPOINT
# and changes ownership of $MOUTPOINT to
# $USER and $GROUP
#
# Change values for these variables to suit
# your needs.
MOUNTPOINT=/ram
ORIG_DIR=/www/commonfiles
USER=httpd
GROUP=httpd
MOUNTCMD=/bin/mount
CHOWN=/bin/chown
CP=/bin/cp
echo -n "Creating ramfs filesytem in $MOUNTPOINT ";
$MOUNTCMD -t ramfs none $MOUNTPOINT
echo "done.";
echo -n "Copying $ORIG_DIR to $MOUNTPOINT ... ";
$CP -r $ORIG_DIR $MOUNTPOINT
echo "done.";
echo -n "Changing ownership to $USER:$GROUP for $MOUNTPOINT ...";
$CHOWN -R $USER:$GROUP $MOUNTPOINT
echo "done.";
```

To use this script on your system, do the following:

1. Create this script, `make_ramfs.sh` in `/usr/local/scripts` directory. Create the `/usr/local/scripts` directory if you don't have one.

2. Edit `/etc/rc.d/rc.local` file and append the following line to it:

   `/usr/local/scripts/make_ramfs.sh`

3. Create a directory called `ram` using the `mkdir /ram` command. If you keep the files you want to load in RAM in any other location than `/www/commonfiles`, then modify the value for the `ORIG_DIR` variable in the script. For example, if your files are in the `/www/mydomain/htdocs/common` directory, then set this variable to this directory.

4. If you run your Web server using any other username and group than httpd, then change the USER and GROUP variable values accordingly. For example, if you run Apache as nobody (user and group), then set USER=nobody and GROUP=nobody.

5. Assuming you use Apache Web server, create an alias in your httpd.conf file such as the following:

```
Alias /commonfiles/  "/ram/commonfiles/"
```

Whenever Apache Web server needs to access /commonfiles/*, it now uses the version in the RAM, which should be substantially faster than the files stored in the original location. Remember, the RAM-based version disappears whenever you reboot or unmount the filesystem. So never update anything there unless you also copy the contents back to a disk-based directory.

If you have mounted a ramfs filesystem using a command such as mount -t ramfs none /ram and copied contents to it and later reran the same mount command, it wipes out the contents and remounts it. The /proc/mounts file shows multiple entries for the same mount point, which causes problem in unmounting the device. If you must regain the memory for other use, you must reboot. Watch for this problem to be fixed in later Linux releases.

Summary

In this chapter you learned about how to tune your disks and filesystems. You learned to tune your IDE/EIDE drives for better performance; you learned to enhance ext2 performance along with using journaling filesystems like ReiserFS, logical volume management, and RAM-based filesystems.

Part II

Network and Service Performance

Chapter 4

Network Performance

IN THIS CHAPTER

◆ Tuning your network

◆ Segmenting your network

◆ Balancing the traffic load using round-robin DNS

◆ Using IP accounting

THE NETWORK DEVICES (such as network interface cards, hubs, switches, and routers) that you choose for your network have a big effect on the performance of your network so it's important to choose appropriate network hardware. Because network hardware is cheap today, using high performance PCI-based NIC or 100Mb switches is no longer a pipe dream for network administrators. Like the hardware, the high-speed bandwidth is also reasonably cheap. Having T1 connection at the office is no longer a status symbol for network administrators. Today, burstable T3 lines are even available in many places. So what is left for network tuning? Well, the very design of the network of course! In this chapter I discuss how you can design high-performance networks for both office and public use. However, the Ethernet Local Area Network (LAN) tuning discussion is limited to small- to mid-range offices where the maximum number of users is fewer than a thousand or so. For larger-scale networks you should consult books that are dedicated to large networking concepts and implementations. This chapter also covers a Web network design that is scalable and can perform well under heavy load.

Tuning an Ethernet LAN or WAN

Most Ethernet LANs start with at least one hub. Figure 4-1 shows a typical, small Ethernet LAN.

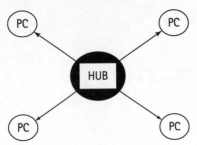

Figure 4-1: A small Ethernet LAN

As the company grows bigger, the small LAN started to look like the one shown in Figure 4-2.

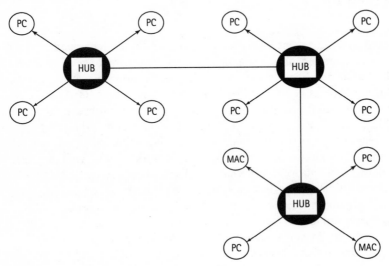

Figure 4-2: A small but growing Ethernet LAN

As the company prospers, the number of people and the computers grow and eventually you have a network that looks as shown in Figure 4-3.

In my experience, when a network of cascading Ethernet hubs reaches about 25 or more users, typically it has enough diverse users and tasks that performance starts to degrade. For example, I have been called in many times to analyze networks that started degrading after adding only a few more machines. Often those "few more machines" were run by "network-heavy" users such as graphic artists who shared or downloaded huge art and graphics files throughout the day as part of their work or research. Today it's even easier to saturate a 10Mb Ethernet with live audio/video feeds (or other apps that kill network bandwidth) that office users sometimes run on their desktops. So it's very important to design a LAN that can perform well under a heavy load so everyone's work gets done fast.

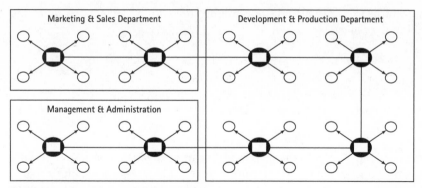

Figure 4-3: A not-so-small Ethernet LAN

Although commonly used, Ethernet hubs are not the best way to expand a LAN to support users. Network expansions should be well planned and implemented, using appropriate hardware; the following sections discuss how you can do that.

Using network segmentation technique for performance

The network shown in Figure 4-3 has a major problem. It's a single Ethernet segment that has been put together by placing a group of hubs in a cascading fashion, which means that all the computers in the network see all the traffic. So when a user from the production department copies a large file from another user next to her in the same department, a computer in the marketing department is deprived of the bandwidth to do something else. Figure 4-4 shows a better version of the same network.

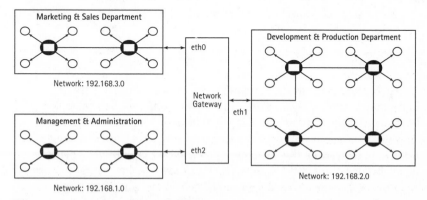

Figure 4-4: A segmented Ethernet LAN

Here the departments are segmented in the different IP networks and interconnected by a network gateway. This gateway can be a Red Hat Linux system with IP forwarding turned on and a few static routing rules to implement the following standard routing policy:

```
IF source and destination of a packet is within the same network THEN
    DO NOT FORWARD the network traffic to any other attached networks
ELSE IF
    FORWARD the network traffic to the appropriate attached network only
END
```

Here's an example: John at the marketing department wants to access a file from Jennifer, who works in the same department. When John accesses Jennifer's shared drive, the IP packets his system transmits and receives aren't to be seen by anyone in the management/administration or development/production departments. So if the file is huge, requiring three minutes to transfer, no one in the other department suffers network degradation. Of course marketing personnel who are accessing the network at the time of the transfer *do* see performance degrade. But you can reduce such degradation by using switching Ethernet hardware instead of simple Ethernet hubs (I cover switches in a later section).

The network gateway computer in Figure 4-4 has three Ethernet interface (NIC) cards; each of these cards is connected to a different department (that is, network). The marketing and sales department is on a Class C (192.168.3.0) network, which means this department can have 254 host computers for their use. Similarly, the other departments have their own Class C networks. Here are the steps needed to create such a setup.

There are many ways to do this configuration. For example, instead of using different Class C networks to create departmental segments, you can use a set of Class B subnets (or even a set of Class C subnets, depending on the size of your departments). In this example, I use different Class C networks to make the example a bit simpler to understand.

1. For each department in your organization, create a Class C network. Remember that a Class C network gives you a total of 254 usable IP addresses. If your department size is larger than 254, then you should consider breaking up the department into multiple networks or use a Class B network instead. In this example, I assume that each of your departments has fewer than 254 computers; I also assume that you have three departmental segments as shown in Figure 4-4 and you have used 192.168.1.0, 192.168.2.0, and 192.168.3.0 networks.

2. On your Red Hat Linux system designated to be the network gateway, turn on IP forwarding.

- **Run** `/sbin/sysctl -w net.ipv4.ip_forward=1` command as root

- Add this command at the end of your `/etc/rc.d/rc.local` script so that IP forwarding is turned on whenever you reboot your system.

TIP

You may already have IP forwarding turned on; to check, run the `cat /proc/sys/net/ipv4/ip_forward` command. 1 means that IP forwarding is on and 0 means that IP forwarding is turned off.

3. **Create** `/etc/sysconfig/network-scripts/ifcfg-eth0`, `/etc/sysconfig/network-scripts/ifcfg-eth1`, and `/etc/sysconfig/network-scripts/ifcfg-eth2` **files, as shown here:**

```
# Contents of ifcfg-eth0 file
DEVICE=eth0
BROADCAST=192.168.1.255
IPADDR=192.168.1.254
NETMASK=255.255.255.0
NETWORK=192.168.1.0
ONBOOT=yes


# Contents of ifcfg-eth1 file
DEVICE=eth1
BROADCAST=192.168.2.255
IPADDR=192.168.2.254
NETMASK=255.255.255.0
NETWORK=192.168.2.0
ONBOOT=yes


# Contents of ifcfg-eth2 file
DEVICE=eth2
BROADCAST=192.168.3.255
IPADDR=192.168.3.254
NETMASK=255.255.255.0
NETWORK=192.168.3.0
ONBOOT=yes
```

4. Connect the appropriate network to the proper Ethernet NIC on the gateway computer. The `192.168.1.0` network should be connected to the `eth0`, `192.168.2.0` should be connected to `eth1`, and `192.168.3.0` should be connected to `eth2`. Once connected, you can simply restart the machine — or bring up the interfaces, using the following commands from the console.

```
/sbin/ifconfig eth0 up
/sbin/ifconfig eth1 up
/sbin/ifconfig eth2 up
```

5. Set the default gateway for each of the networks. For example, all the computers in the `192.168.1.0` network should set their default route to be `192.168.1.254`, which is the IP address associated with the `eth0` device of the gateway computer.

That's all there is to isolating each department into its own network. Now traffic from one network only flows to the other when needed. This enables the bandwidth on each department to be available for its own use most of the time.

Using switches in place of hubs

When a large LAN is constructed with a set of cascading hubs to support many computers, the bandwidth is shared by all of the computers. If the total bandwidth is 10 Mbps, the entire network is limited to that amount. However, this can easily become a serious bottleneck in a busy network where large files are often accessed or audio/video streams are common. In such a case an Ethernet switch can work like magic.

The major difference between an Ethernet hub and switch is that each port on a switch is its own logical segment. A computer connected to a port on an Ethernet switch has a full bandwidth to it and need not contend with other computers for collisions. One of the main reasons you purchase a switch over a hub is for its address-handling capabilities. Whereas a hub doesn't look at the address of a data packet and just forwards data to all devices on the network, a switch should read the address of each data packet and correctly forward the data to the intended recipients. If the switch doesn't correctly read the packet address and correctly forward the data, it has no advantage over a hub. Table 4-1 lists the major differences between hub and switch.

TABLE 4-1: DIFFERENCES BETWEEN AN ETHERNET HUB AND A SWITCH

Hub	Switch
Total network bandwidth is limited to the speed of the hub; that is, A 10Base-T hub provides 10Mb bandwidth, no matter how many ports.	Total network bandwidth is determined by the number of ports on the switch; that is, a 12 port 100Mb switch can support up to 1200 Mbps bandwidth — this is referred to as the switch's maximum aggregate bandwidth.

Hub	Switch
Supports half duplex communications limiting the connection to the speed of the port; that is, 10Mb port provides a 10Mb link.	Switches that support full duplex communications offer the capability to double the speed of each link; that is, from 100Mb to 200Mb.
Hop count rules limit the number of hubs that can be interconnected between two computers.	Enables users to greatly expand networks; there are no limits to the number of switches that can be interconnected between two computers.
Cheaper than switches	Slightly more expensive than hubs.

No special hardware is needed on the devices that connect to an Ethernet switch. The same network interface used for shared media 10Base-T hubs works with an Ethernet switch. From that device's perspective, connecting to a switched port is just like being the only computer on the network segment.

 One common use for an Ethernet switch is to break a large network into segments. While it's possible to attach a single computer to each port on an Ethernet switch, it's also possible to connect other devices such as a hub. If your network is large enough to require multiple hubs, you could connect each of those hubs to a switch port so that each hub is a separate segment. Remember that if you simply cascade the hubs directly, the combined network is a single logical Ethernet segment.

Using fast Ethernet

The traditional Ethernet is 10 Mbps, which simply isn't enough in a modern business environment where e-mail-based communication, Internet access, video conferencing, and other bandwidth-intensive operations are more commonplace. The 100 Mbps Ethernet is the way to go. However, 100 Mbps or "fast" Ethernet is still expensive if you decide to use fast switches, too. I highly recommend that you move towards a switched fast Ethernet. The migration path from 10 Mbps to 100 Mbps can be expensive if you have a lot of computers in your network. Each computer in your network must have 100 Mbps-capable NIC installed, which can be expensive in cost, staff, and time. For a large LAN with hundreds of users, upgrade one segment at a time. You can start by buying 10 (ten) 100 Mbps dual-speed NIC for machines and, thus, support your existing 10 Mbps and upcoming 100 Mbps infrastructure seamlessly.

The fast Ethernet with switching hardware can bring a high degree of performance to your LAN. Consider this option if possible. If you have multiple departments to interconnect, consider an even faster solution between the departments. The emerging gigabit Ethernet is very suitable for connecting local area networks to form a wide area network (WAN).

Using a network backbone

If you are dealing with a mid-size network environment where hundreds of computers and multiple physical locations are involved, design the network backbone that carries network traffic between locations. Figure 4-5 shows one such network.

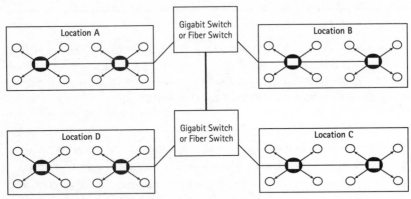

Figure 4-5: A WAN with a gigabit/fiber switched backbone

Here the four locations A, B, C, and D are interconnected using either a gigabit or fiver switched backbone. A large bandwidth capacity in the backbone has two benefits:

◆ **It accommodates worst-case scenarios.** A typical example is when the entire WAN is busy because most of the computers are transmitting and receiving data to and from the network. If the backbone is 10 Mb (or even 100 Mb), performance can degrade – and user perception of the slowdown varies widely.

◆ **It makes your network amenable to expansion.** For example, if location A decides to increase its load, the high bandwidth available at the backbone can handle the load.

Fiber optics work very well in enterprise networks as a backbone infrastructure. Fiber offers exceptional performance for high-bandwidth applications, and is extremely reliable and secure. Fiber isn't susceptible to many of the sources of interference that can play havoc with copper-based cabling systems. Fiber is also considered to be more secure because it can't be tapped unless you cut and splice the fiber strands — a task that is virtually impossible without detection. If you need to connect a set of buildings within a corporate complex or academic campus, then fiber optics offers the very best solution. While it's possible to use fiber optics to connect PCs and printers in a LAN, only organizations with serious security concerns and extremely data-intensive applications regularly do so. Fiber-optic networks are expensive to implement, and their installation and maintenance demand a higher level of expertise. At a time when we can achieve 100 Mbps speed over copper cabling, it's seldom cost-effective to use fiber optics for a small office network.

 If you have mission-critical applications in your network that are accessed via the backbone, you must consider adding redundancy in your backbone so that if one route goes down because of an equipment failure or any other problem, an alternative path is available. Adding redundancy doesn't come cheap, but it's a must for those needing a high uptime percentage.

Understanding and controlling network traffic flow

Understanding how your network traffic flows is the primary key in determining how you can tune it for better performance. Take a look at the network segment shown in Figure 4-6.

Here three Web servers are providing Web services to the Internet and they share a network with an NFS server and a database server. What's wrong with this picture? Well, several things are wrong. First of all, these machines are still using dumb hub instead of a switch. Second of all, the NFS and database traffic is competing with the incoming and outgoing Web traffic. If a Web application needs database access, it generates database requests, in response to a Web request from the Internet, which in turn reduces from the bandwidth available for other incoming or outgoing Web requests, thus, effectively making the network unnecessarily busy or less responsive. How can you solve such a problem? Using a traffic control mechanism, of course! First determine what traffic can be isolated in this network. Naturally, the database and NFS traffic is only needed to service the Web servers. In such a case, NFS and database traffic should be isolated so that they don't compete with Web traffic. Figure 4-7 shows a modified network diagram for the same network.

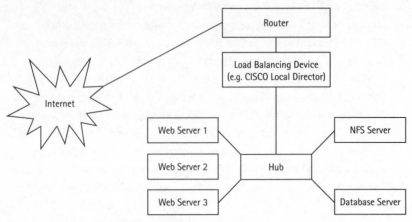

Figure 4–6: An inefficient Web network

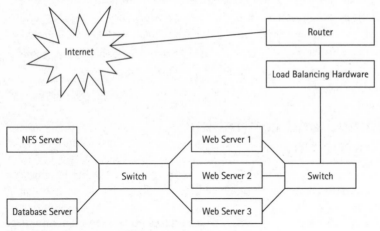

Figure 4–7: An improved Web network

Here the database and the NFS server are connected to a switch that is connected to the second NIC of each Web server. The other NIC of each Web server is connected to a switch that is in turn connected to the load balancing hardware. Now, when a Web request comes to a Web server, it's serviced by the server without taking away from the bandwidth of other Web servers. The result is a tremendous increase in network efficiency, which trickles down to more positive user experience.

After you have a good network design, your tuning focus should be shifted to applications and services that you provide. In many cases, depending on your network load, you may have to consider deploying multiple servers of the same kind to implement a more responsive service. This is certainly true for the Web. In the following section I show you a simple-to-use load-balancing scheme using a DNS trick.

Balancing the traffic load using the DNS server

The idea is to share the load among multiple servers of a kind. This typically is used for balancing the Web load over multiple Web servers. This trick is called *round-robin Domain Name Service*.

Suppose you have two Web servers, www1.yourdomain.com (192.168.1.10) and www2.yourdomain.com (192.168.1.20), and you want to balance the load for www.yourdomain.com on these two servers by using the round-robin DNS trick. Add the following lines to your yourdomain.com zone file:

```
www1   IN   A 192.168.1.10
www2   IN   A 192.168.1.20
www    IN   CNAME   www1
www    IN   CNAME   www2
```

Restart your name server and ping the www.yourdomain.com host. You see the 192.168.1.10 address in the ping output. Stop and restart pinging the same host, and you'll see the second IP address being pinged, because the preceding configuration tells the name server to cycle through the CNAME records for www. The www.yourdomain.com host is both www1.yourdomain.com and www2.yourdomain.com.

Now, when someone enters www.yourdomain.com, the name server sends the first address once, then sends the second address for the next request, and keeps cycling between these addresses.

One of the disadvantages of the round-robin DNS trick is that the name server can't know which system is heavily loaded and which isn't — it just blindly cycles. If a server crashes or becomes unavailable for some reason, the round-robin DNS trick still returns the broken server's IP on a regular basis. This could be chaotic, because some people get to the sites and some won't.

If your load demands better management and your server's health is essential to your operation, then your best choice is to get a hardware solution that uses the new director products such as Web Director (www.radware.com/), Ace Director (www.alteon.com/), or Local Director (www.cisco.com/). I have used both Local Director and Web Director with great success.

IP Accounting

As you make headway in tuning your network, you also have a greater need to determine how your bandwidth is used. Under Linux, you can use the IP accounting scheme to get that information.

IP accounting on a Linux system that isn't a network gateway?

Yes, technically you can do it. If your system is not a gateway— it doesn't do IP forwarding and `/proc/sys/net/ipv4/ip_forward` is set to 0 — you can run IP accounting if you place the NIC in promiscuous mode, use the `/sbin/ifconfig eth0 up promisc` command, and then apply IP accounting rules. For the sake of network efficiency (and your sanity), however, I highly recommend that you try IP accounting on a Linux network gateway system instead.

Knowing how your IP bandwidth is used helps you determine how to make changes in your network to make it more efficient. For example, if you discover that one segment of your network has 70 percent of its traffic going to a different segment on average, you may find a way to isolate that traffic by providing a direct link between the two networks. IP accounting helps you determine how IP packets are passed around in your network.

To use IP accounting, you must configure and compile the kernel with network packet-filtering support. If you use the `make menuconfig` command to configure the kernel, you can find the `Network packet filtering (replaces ipchains)` feature under the `Networking options` submenu. Build and install the new kernel with packet filtering support (See the Tuning Kernel chapter for details on compiling and installing a custom kernel).

IP accounting on a Linux network gateway

Here I assume that you want to have a network gateway among three networks — `192.168.1.0` (eth0), `192.168.2.0` (eth1), and `207.183.15.0` (eth2). Here, the first two networks are your internal department and the third one is the uplink network to your Internet service provider.

Now you want to set up IP accounting rules that tell you how many packets travel between the `192.168.1.0` network and the Internet. The IP accounting rules that you need are as follows:

```
/sbin/iptables -A FORWARD -i eth2 -d 192.168.1.0/24
/sbin/iptables -A FORWARD -o eth2 -s 192.168.1.0/24
```

Here the first states that a new rule be appended (`-A`) to the FORWARD chain such that all packets destined for the `192.168.1.0` network be counted when the packets travel via the eth2 interface of the gateway machine. Remember, the eth2 interface is connected to the ISP network (possibly via a router, DSL device, or Cable modem). The second rule states that another rule be appended to the FORWARD chain such that any IP packet originated from the `192.168.1.0` network and passing through the eth2 interface be counted. These two rules effectively count all IP packets (whether incoming or outgoing) that move between the 192.168.1.0 network and the Internet. To do the same for the 192.168.2.0 network, use the following rules:

```
/sbin/iptables -A FORWARD -i eth2 -d 192.168.2.0/24
/sbin/iptables -A FORWARD -o eth2 -s 192.168.2.0/24
```

After you have set up the preceding rules, you can view the results from time to time by using the /sbin/iptables -L -v -n command. I usually open an SSH session to the network gateway and run /usr/bin/watch -n 3600 /sbin/iptables -L -v -n to monitor the traffic on an hourly basis.

If you are interested in finding out what type of network services are requested by the departments that interact with the Internet, you can do accounting on that, too. For example, if you want to know how much of the traffic passing through the eth2 interface is Web traffic, you can implement a rule such as the following:

```
/sbin/iptables -A FORWARD -o eth0 -m tcp -p tcp --dport www
```

This records traffic meant for port 80 (www port in /etc/services). You can add similar rules for other network services found in the /etc/services files.

Summary

The state of your network performance is the combined effect of your operating system, network devices, bandwidth, and the overall network design you choose to implement.

Chapter 5

Web Server Performance

IN THIS CHAPTER

- ◆ Controlling Apache
- ◆ Accelerating Web performance

THE DEFAULT WEB SERVER software for Red Hat Linux is Apache — the most popular Web server in the world. According to Apache Group (its makers), the primary mission for Apache is accuracy as an HTTP protocol server first; performance (per se) is second. Even so, Apache offers good performance in real-world situations — and it continues to get better. As with many items of technology, proper tuning can give an Apache Web server excellent performance and flexibility. In this chapter, I focus on Apache tuning issues — and introduce you to the new kernel-level HTTP daemon (available for the 2.4 and later kernels) that can speed the process of Web design.

Apache architecture makes the product extremely flexible. Almost all of its processing — except for core functionality that handles requests and responses — happens in individual modules. This approach makes Apache easy to compile and customize.

 In this book (as in my other books), a common thread running through all of the advice that bears repeating: *Always compile your server software if you have access to the source code.* I believe that the best way to run Apache is to compile and install it yourself. Therefore my other recommendations in this section assume that you have the latest distribution of the Apache source code on your system.

Compiling a Lean and Mean Apache

Compiling an efficient server means removing everything you don't need and retaining only the functions you want Apache to perform. Fortunately, the module-based Apache architecture makes an efficient — and highly customized — installation relatively easy. Here's how:

1. Know what Apache modules you currently have; decide whether you really need them all. To find out what modules you currently have installed in Apache binary code (httpd), run the following command while logged in as root:

```
/usr/local/apache/bin/httpd -l
```

Change the path (/usr/local/apache) if you have installed Apache in another location. This command displays all the Apache modules currently compiled in the httpd binary. For example, the default Apache installation compiles the following modules:

```
Compiled-in modules:
  http_core.c
  mod_env.c
  mod_log_config.c
  mod_mime.c
  mod_negotiation.c
  mod_status.c
  mod_include.c
  mod_autoindex.c
  mod_dir.c
  mod_cgi.c
  mod_asis.c
  mod_imap.c
  mod_actions.c
  mod_userdir.c
  mod_alias.c
  mod_access.c
  mod_auth.c
  mod_setenvif.c
suexec: disabled; invalid wrapper /workspace/h1/bin/suexec
```

If you installed a default Apache binary, you can also find out what modules are installed by default by running the configuration script using the following command:

```
./configure --help
```

This command displays command-line help, which are explained in Table 5-1.

TABLE 5-1: THE OPTIONS FOR THE CONFIGURE SCRIPT

Option	Meaning
--cache-file=*FILE*	Cache test results in *FILE*
--help	Print this message

Option	Meaning
--no-create	Do not create output files
--quiet or --silent	Do not print 'checking...' messages
--version	Print the version of autoconf that created configure Directory and filenames:
--prefix=PREFIX	Install architecture-independent files in PREFIX [/usr/local/apache2]
--exec-prefix=EPREFIX	Install architecture-dependent files in EPREFIX [same as prefix]
--bindir=DIR	User executables in DIR [EPREFIX/bin]
--sbindir=DIR	System admin executables in DIR [EPREFIX/sbin]
--libexecdir=DIR	Program executables in DIR [EPREFIX/libexec]
--datadir=DIR	Read-only architecture-independent data in DIR [PREFIX/share]
--sysconfdir=DIR	Read-only single-machine data in DIR [PREFIX/etc]
--sharedstatedir=DIR	Modifiable architecture-independent data in DIR [PREFIX/com]
--localstatedir=DIR	Modifiable single-machine data in DIR [PREFIX/var]
--libdir=DIR	Object code libraries in DIR [EPREFIX/lib]
--includedir=DIR	C header files in DIR [PREFIX/include]
--oldincludedir=DIR	C header files for non-GCC in DIR [/usr/include]
--infodir=DIR	Info documentation in DIR [PREFIX/info]
--mandir=DIR	man documentation in DIR [PREFIX/man]
--srcdir=DIR	Find the sources in DIR [configure dir or ...]
--program-prefix=PREFIX	Prepend PREFIX to installed program names
--program-suffix=SUFFIX	Append SUFFIX to installed program names
--program-transform-name=PROGRAM	Run sed PROGRAM on installed program names
--build=BUILD	Configure for building on BUILD [BUILD=HOST]
--host=HOST	Configure for HOST
--target=TARGET	Configure for TARGET [TARGET=HOST]
--disable-FEATURE	Do not include FEATURE (same as --enable-FEATURE=no)
--enable-FEATURE[=ARG]	Include FEATURE [ARG=yes]

Continued

TABLE 5-1: THE OPTIONS FOR THE CONFIGURE SCRIPT *(Continued)*

Option	Meaning
`--with-`*PACKAGE*`[=`*ARG*`]`	Use *PACKAGE* [*ARG*=yes]
`--without-`*PACKAGE*	Do not use *PACKAGE* (same as `--with-PACKAGE=no`)
`--x-includes=`*DIR*	X include files are in *DIR*
`--x-libraries=`*DIR*	X library files are in *DIR*
`--with-optim=`*FLAG*	Obsolete (use OPTIM environment variable)
`--with-port=`*PORT*	Port on which to listen (default is 80)
`--enable-debug`	Turn on debugging and compile-time warnings
`--enable-maintainer-mode`	Turn on debugging and compile-time warnings
`--enable-layout=`*LAYOUT*	Use the select directory layout
`--enable-modules=`*MODULE-LIST*	Enable the list of modules specified
`--enable-mods-shared=MODULE-LIST`	Enable the list of modules as shared objects
`--disable-access`	Host-based access control
`--disable-auth`	User-based access control
`--enable-auth-anon`	Anonymous user access
`--enable-auth-dbm`	DBM-based access databases
`--enable-auth-db`	DB-based access databases
`--enable-auth-digest`	RFC2617 Digest authentication
`--enable-file-cache`	File cache
`--enable-dav-fs`	DAV provider for the filesystem
`--enable-dav`	WebDAV protocol handling
`--enable-echo`	ECHO server
`--enable-charset-lite`	Character set translation
`--enable-cache`	Dynamic file caching
`--enable-disk-cache`	Disk caching module
`--enable-ext-filter`	External filter module
`--enable-case-filter`	Example uppercase conversion filter
`--enable-generic-hook-export`	Example of hook exporter
`--enable-generic-hook-import`	Example of hook importer

Option	Meaning
`--enable-optional-fn-import`	Example of optional function importer
`--enable-optional-fn-export`	Example of optional function exporter
`--disable-include`	Server-Side Includes
`--disable-http`	HTTP protocol handling
`--disable-mime`	Mapping of file-extension to MIME
`--disable-log-config`	Logging configuration
`--enable-vhost-alias`	Mass -hosting module
`--disable-negotiation`	Content negotiation
`--disable-dir`	Directory request handling
`--disable-imap`	Internal imagemaps
`--disable-actions`	Action triggering on requests
`--enable-speling`	Correct common URL misspellings
`--disable-userdir`	Mapping of user requests
`--disable-alias`	Translation of requests
`--enable-rewrite`	Regex URL translation
`--disable-so`	DSO capability
`--enable-so`	DSO capability
`--disable-env`	Clearing/setting of ENV vars
`--enable-mime-magic`	Automatically determine MIME type
`--enable-cern-meta`	CERN-type meta files
`--enable-expires`	Expires header control
`--enable-headers`	HTTP header control
`--enable-usertrack`	User-session tracking
`--enable-unique-id`	Per-request unique IDs
`--disable-setenvif`	Base ENV vars on headers
`--enable-tls`	TLS/SSL support
`--with-ssl`	Use a specific SSL library installation
`--with-mpm=`*MPM*	Choose the process model for Apache to use: *MPM*=`{beos threaded prefork spmt_os2 perchild}`

Continued

TABLE 5-1: THE OPTIONS FOR THE CONFIGURE SCRIPT *(Continued)*

Option	Meaning
`--disable-status`	Process/thread monitoring
`--disable-autoindex`	Directory listing
`--disable-asis`	As-is filetypes
`--enable-info`	Server information
`--enable-suexec`	Set UID and GID for spawned processes
`--disable-cgid`	CGI scripts
`--enable-cgi`	CGI scripts
`--disable-cgi`	CGI scripts
`--enable-cgid`	CGI scripts
`--enable-shared[=PKGS]`	Build shared libraries [default=no]
`--enable-static[=PKGS]`	Build static libraries [default=yes]
`--enable-fast-install[=PKGS]`	Optimize for fast installation [default=yes]
`--with-gnu-ld`	Assume the C compiler uses GNU ID [default=no]
`--disable-libtool-lock`	Avoid locking (might break parallel builds)
`--with-program-name`	Alternate executable name
`--with-suexec-caller`	User allowed to call SuExec
`--with-suexec-userdir`	User subdirectory
`--with-suexec-docroot`	SuExec root directory
`--with-suexec-uidmin`	Minimal allowed UID
`--with-suexec-gidmin`	Minimal allowed GID
`--with-suexec-logfile`	Set the logfile
`--with-suexec-safepath`	Set the safepath
`--with-suexec-umask`	Amask for `suexec`'d process

2. Determine whether you need the modules that you have compiled in Apache binary (httpd). By removing unnecessary modules, you achieve a performance boost (because of the reduced size of the binary code file) and – potentially, at least – greater security.

TIP

For example, if you plan never to run CGI programs or scripts, you can remove the `mod_cgi` module — which reduces the size of the binary file and also shuts out potential CGI attacks, making a more secure Apache environment. If can't service CGI requests, all CGI risk goes to zero. To know which modules to keep and which ones to remove, know how each module functions; you can obtain this information at the `www.apache.org` Web site. Reading the Apache documentation for each module can help you determine whether you have any use for a moduleot.

Make a list of modules that you can do without and continue to the next step.

3. After you decide which default modules you don't want to keep, simply run the configuration script from the top Apache directory, specifying the `--disable-`*`module`* option for each module you want to remove. Here's an example:

```
./configure --prefix=/usr/local/apache \
            --disable-cgi \
            --disable-imap \
            --disable-userdir \
            --disable-autoindex \
            --disable-status
```

In this list, the `configure` script must install Apache in `/usr/local/apache`, using the `--prefix` option; it's also told to disable the CGI module (`mod_cgi`), the server-side image-mapping module (`mod_imap`), the module that supports the `user/public_html` directory (`mod_userdir`), the automatic directory-indexing module (`mod_autoindex`), and the server-status module (`mod_status`).

4. After you have run the appropriate configuration command in the previous step, you can run the `make; make install` commands to build and install the lean and mean Apache server.

Tuning Apache Configuration

When you configure an Apache source using the `configure` script with the `-- prefix` option, this process specifies the primary configuration file as the `httpd.conf` file (stored in the `conf` directory of your Apache installation directory). The `httpd.conf` file consists of a set of Apache directives, some of which are designed to help you fine-tune Apache performance. This section covers those Apache directives.

Controlling Apache processes

Use the following directives to control how Apache executes in your system. Using these directives also gives you control of how Apache uses resources on your system. For example, you can decide how many child server processes to run on your system, or how many threads you should enable Apache to use on a Windows platform.

A few things to remember when configuring these directives:

♦ The more processes you run, the more load your CPUs must handle.

♦ The more processes you run, the more RAM you need.

♦ The more processes you run, the more operating-system resources (such as file descriptors and shared buffers) you use.

Of course, more processes could also mean more requests serviced – hence more hits for your site. So set these directives by balancing experimentation, requirements, and available resources.

StartServers

StartServers is set to 3 by default, which tells Apache to start three child servers as it starts.

Syntax: StartServers number

Default setting: StartServers 3

Context: Server config

You can start more servers if you want, but Apache is pretty good at increasing the number of child processes as needed based on load. So, changing this is not required.

SENDBUFFERSIZE
This directive sets the size of the TCP send buffer to the number of bytes specified.

Syntax: SendBufferSize bytes

Context: Server config

On a high-performance network, you may increase server performance if you set this directive to a higher value than the operating-system defaults.

LISTENBACKLOG

This directive defends against a known type of security attack called *denial of service* (*DoS*) by enabling you to set the maximum length of the queue that handles pending connections.

Syntax: `ListenBacklog backlog`

Default setting: `ListenBacklog 511`

Context: Server config

 Increase this value if you detect that you are under a TCP SYN flood attack (a type of DoS attack); otherwise you can leave it alone.

TIMEOUT

In effect, the Web is really a big client/server system in which the Apache server responds to requests. The requests and responses are transmitted via packets of data. Apache must know how long to wait for a certain packet. This directive configures the time in seconds.

Syntax: `TimeOut number`

Default setting: `TimeOut 300`

Context: Server config

The time you specify here is the maximum time Apache waits before it breaks a connection. The default setting enables Apache to wait for 300 seconds before it disconnects itself from the client. If you are on a slow network, you may want to increase the time-out value to decrease the number of disconnects.

Currently, this time out setting applies to:

◆ The total amount of time it takes to receive a `GET` request

◆ The amount of time between receipt of TCP packets on a `POST` or `PUT` request

◆ The amount of time between `ACK`s on transmissions of TCP packets in responses

MAXCLIENTS

This directive limits the number of simultaneous requests that Apache can service.

Syntax: `MaxClients number`

Default setting: `MaxClients 256`

Context: Server config

When you use the default MPM module (threaded) the number of simultaneous request is equal to the value of this directive multiplied by the value of the ThreadsPerChild directive. For example, if you have MaxClients set to default (256) and ThreadsPerChild set to default (50) the Apache server can service a total of 12800 (256 x 50) requests. When using the perfork MPM the maximum number of requests is limited by only the value of MaxClients. The default value (256) is the maximum setting for this directive. If you wish to change this to a higher number, you will have to modify the HARD_SERVER_LIMIT constant in mpm_default.h file in the source distribution of Apache and recompile and reinstall it.

MAXREQUESTSPERCHILD

This directive sets the number of requests a child process can serve before getting killed.

Syntax: `MaxRequestsPerChild number`

Default setting: `MaxRequestsPerChild 0`

Context: Server config

The default value of 0 makes the child process serve requests forever. I do not like the default value because it allows Apache processes to slowly consume large amounts of memory when a faulty `mod_perl` script or even a faulty third-party Apache module leaks memory. If you do not plan to run any third-party Apache modules or `mod_perl` scripts, you can keep the default setting or else set it to a reasonable number. A setting of 30 ensures that the child process is killed after processing 30 requests. Of course, new child processes are created as needed.

MAXSPARESERVERS

This directive lets you set the number of idle Apache child processes that you want on your server.

Syntax: `MaxSpareServers number`

Default setting: `MaxSpareServers 10`

Context: Server config

If the number of idle Apache child processes exceeds the maximum number specified by the `MaxSpareServers` directive, then the parent process kills off the excess processes. Tuning of this parameter should only be necessary for very busy sites. Unless you know what you are doing, do not change the default.

MINSPARESERVERS

The `MinSpareServers` directive sets the desired minimum number of idle child server processes. An idle process is one that is not handling a request. If there are fewer idle Apache processes than the number specified by the `MinSpareServers` directive, then the parent process creates new children at a maximum rate of 1 per second. Tuning of this parameter should only be necessary on very busy sites. Unless you know what you are doing, do not change the default.

Syntax: `MinSpareServers` *number*

Default setting: `MinSpareServers 5`

Context: Server config

KEEPALIVE

The `KeepAlive` directive enables you to activate/deactivate persistent use of TCP connections in Apache.

Syntax: `KeepAlive On | Off`

Default setting: `KeepAlive On`

Context: Server config

Older Apache servers (prior to version 1.2) may require a numeric value instead of `On/Off` when using `KeepAlive` This value corresponds to the maximum number of requests you want Apache to entertain per request. A limit is imposed to prevent a client from taking over all your server resources. To disable `KeepAlive` in the older Apache versions, use 0 (zero) as the value.

KEEPALIVETIMEOUT

If you have the `KeepAlive` directive set to on, you can use the `KeepAliveTimeout` directive to limit the number of seconds Apache will wait for a subsequent request before closing a connection. After a request is received, the timeout value specified by the `Timeout` directive applies.

Syntax: `KeepAliveTimeout` *seconds*

Default setting: `KeepAliveTimeout 15`

Context: Server config

KEEPALIVETIMEOUT

If you have the `KeepAlive` directive set to on, you can use the `KeepAliveTimeout` directive to limit the number of seconds Apache will wait for a subsequent request before closing a connection. After a request is received, the timeout value specified by the `Timeout` directive applies.

Syntax: `KeepAliveTimeout seconds`

Default setting: `KeepAliveTimeout 15`

Context: Server config

Controlling system resources

Apache is flexible in enabling you to control the amount of system resources (such as CPU time and memory) it consumes. These control features come in handy for making your Web server system more reliable and responsive. Often a typical hack attempts to make a Web server consume all available system resources until the system becomes unresponsive – in effect, halted. Apache provides a set of directives to combat such a situation.

RLIMITCPU

The `RLimitCPU` directive enables you to control the CPU usage of Apache children-spawned processes such as CGI scripts. The limit does not apply to Apache children themselves or to any process created by the parent Apache server.

Syntax: `RLimitCPU  n | 'max' [ n | 'max']`

Default setting: Not set; uses operating system defaults

Context: Server config, virtual host

The `RLimitCPU` directive takes the following two parameters:The first parameter sets a soft resource limit for all processes and the second parameter, which is optional, sets the maximum resource limit. Note that raising the maximum resource limit requires that the server be running as `root` or in the initial startup phase.For each of these parameters, there are two possible values:

- ◆ *n* is the number of seconds per process.

- ◆ and *max* is the maximum resource limit allowed by the operating system.

RLIMITMEM

The RLimitMEM directive limits the memory (RAM) usage of Apache children-spawned processes such as CGI scripts. The limit does not apply to Apache chidren themselves or to any process created by the parent Apache server.

Syntax: RLimitMEM *n* | *'max'* [*n* | *'max'*]

Default setting: Not set; uses operating system defaults

Context: Server config, virtual host

The RLimitMEM directive takes two parameters. The first parameter sets a soft resource limit for all processes, and the second parameter, which is optional, sets the maximum resource limit. Note that raising the maximum resource limit requires that the server be started by the root user. For each of these parameters, there are two possible values:

- ◆ n is the number of bytes per process
- ◆ max is the maximum resource limit allowed by the operating system

RLIMITNPROC

The RLimitNPROC directive sets the maximum number of simultaneous Apache children-spawned processes per user ID.

Syntax: RLimitNPROC *n* | *'max'* [*n* | *'max'*]

Default setting: Unset; uses operating system defaults

Context: Server config, virtual host

The RLimitNPROC directive takes two parameters. The first parameter sets the soft resource limit for all processes, and the second parameter, which is optional, sets the maximum resource limit. Raising the maximum resource limit requires that the server be running as root or in the initial startup phase. For each of these parameters, there are two possible values:

- ◆ n is the number of bytes per process
- ◆ max is the maximum resource limit allowed by the operating system

If your CGI processes are run under the same user ID as the server process, use of RLimitNPROC limits the number of processes the server can launch (or "fork"). If the limit is too low, you will receive a "Cannot fork process" type of message in the error log file. In such a case, you should increase the limit or just leave it as the default.

LIMITREQUESTBODY

The `LimitRequestBody` directive enables you to set a limit on the size of the HTTP request that Apache will service. The default limit is 0, which means unlimited. You can set this limit from 0 to 2147483647 (2GB).

Syntax: `LimitRequestBody bytes`

Default setting: `LimitRequestBody 0`

Context: Server, virtual host, directory, .htaccess

Setting a limit is recommended only if you have experienced HTTP-based denial of service attacks that try to overwhelm the server with large HTTP requests. This is a useful directive to enhance server security.

LIMITREQUESTFIELDS

The `LimitRequestFields` directive allows you to limit number of request header fields allowed in a single HTTP request. This limit can be 0 to 32767 (32K). This directive can help you implement a security measure against large request based denial of service attacks.

Syntax: `LimitRequestFields number`

Default setting: `LimitRequestFields 100`

Context: Server config

LIMITREQUESTFIELDSIZE

The `LimitRequestFieldsize` directive enables you to limit the size (in bytes) of a request header field. The default size of 8190 (8K) is more than enough for most situations. However, if you experience a large HTTP request-based denial of service attack, you can change this to a smaller number to deny requests that exceed the limit. A value of 0 sets the limit to unlimited.

Syntax: `LimitRequestFieldsize bytes`

Default setting: `LimitRequestFieldsize 8190`

Context: Server config

LIMITREQUESTLINE

The `LimitRequestLine` directive sets the limit on the size of the request line. This effectively limits the size of the URL that can be sent to the server. The default limit should be sufficient for most situations. If you experience a denial of service attack that uses long URLs designed to waste resources on your server, you can reduce the limit to reject such requests.

Syntax: `LimitRequestLine` *bytes*

Default setting: `LimitRequestLine 8190`

Context: Server config

Using dynamic modules

Apache loads all the precompiled modules when it starts up; however, it also provides a dynamic module-loading and -unloading feature that may be useful on certain occasions. When you use the following dynamic module directives, you can change the list of active modules without recompiling the server.

CLEARMODULELIST

You can use the `ClearModuleList` directive to clear the list of active modules and to enable the dynamic module-loading feature. Then use the `AddModule` directive to add modules that you want to activate.

Syntax: `ClearModuleList`

Default setting: None

Context: Server config

ADDMODULE

The `AddModule` directive can be used to enable a precompiled module that is currently not active. The server can have modules compiled that are not actively in use. This directive can be used to enable these modules. The server comes with a preloaded list of active modules; this list can be cleared with the `ClearModuleList` directive. Then new modules can be added using the `AddModule` directive.

Syntax: `AddModule` *module module* ...

Default setting: None

Context: Server config

After you have configured Apache using a combination of the mentioned directives, you can focus on tuning your static and dynamic contents delivery mechanisms. In the following sections I show just that.

Speeding Up Static Web Pages

Although everyone is screaming about dynamic Web contents that are database-driven or served by fancy application servers, the static Web pages still are there. In fact, static Web pages aren't likely to be completely replaced by dynamic content in

the near future. Some dynamic contents systems even create dynamically and periodically generated static Web pages as cache contents for faster delivery. Because
serving a static page usually is faster than serving a dynamic page, the static page
is not going away soon. In this section I improve the speed of static page delivery
using Apache and the new kernel HTTP module.

Reducing disk I/O for faster static page delivery

When Apache gets a request for a static Web page, it performs a directory tree
search for .htaccess files to ensure that the requested page can be delivered to the
Web browser. For example, say that an Apache server running on www.nitec.com
receives a request such as http://www.nitec.com/training/linux/sysad/
intro.html. Apache performs the following checks:

```
/.htaccess
%DocRoot%/.htaccess
%DocRoot%/training/.htaccess
%DocRoot%/training/linux/.htaccess
%DocRoot%/training/linux/sysad/.htaccess
```

where %DocRoot% is the document root directory set by the DocumentRoot directive in the httpd.conf file. So if this directory is /www/nitec/htdocs, then the
following checks are made:

```
/.htaccess
/www/.htaccess
/www/nitec/.htaccess
/www/nitec/htdocs/.htaccess
/www/nitec/htdocs/training/.htaccess
/www/nitec/htdocs/training/linux/.htaccess
/www/nitec/htdocs/training/linux/sysad/.htaccess
```

Apache looks for the .htaccess file in each directory of the translated (from the
requested URL) path of the requested file (intro.html). As you can see, a URL that
requests a single file can result in multiple disk I/O requests to read multiple files.
This can be a performance drain for high-volume sites. In such case, your best
choice is to disable .htaccess file checks altogether. For example, when the following configuration directives are placed within the main server section (that is, not
within a VirtualHost directive) of the httpd.conf file, it disables checking for
.htaccess for every URL request.

```
<Directory />
  AllowOverride None
</Directory>
```

When the preceding configuration is used, Apache simply performs a single disk I/O to read the requested static file and therefore gain performance in high-volume access scenarios.

Using Kernel HTTP daemon

The new Linux 2.4 kernel ships with a kernel module called `khttpd`, which is a kernel-space HTTP server. This kernel module can serve static contents, such as an HTML file or an image, faster than Apache. This is because the module operates in kernel space and directly accesses the network without needing to operating in user-space like other Web servers, such as Apache. However, this module isn't a replacement for Apache or any other Web server, because it can only serve static contents. It can intercept the request for static contents and pass through requests that it can't service to a Web server such as Apache running on the same machine. You can learn more about this module at `www.fenrus.demon.nl`. I only recommend this module for those who need a dedicated static contents server such as an image server.

Speeding Up Web Applications

Dynamic contents for the Web are typically generated three ways: server-side scripts/applications, client-side scripts, or a combination of both server-side scripts/applications and client-side scripts. The client-side scripts have nothing to do with your Linux server and therefore are not covered in this chapter. However, the server-side scripts/applications run on the Linux server, so their performance problems are addressed in this section.

Typically, Perl and Java are the primary languages for Web contents development under the Linux platform. Perl is more common than Java because the Java run-time environment has had a lot of performance problems in Linux platforms (although these are likely to be resolved in the near future). In this section I focus primarily on Perl-based Web application performance.

Perl-based Common Gateway Interface (CGI) script is the granddaddy of server-side Web scripting. However, as Web matured, the number of people browsing the Web grew, the shortcomings of CGI scripts became evident. Here are the primary reasons CGI scripts don't cut it any more:

- ◆ **A CGI script is started every time a request is made,** which means that if the Apache server receives 100 requests for the same script, there are 100 copies of the same script running on the server, which makes CGI a very unscalable solution.

- ◆ **A CGI script can't maintain persistent connection to a back-end database,** which means a connection needs to be established every time a script needs to access a database server. This effectively makes CGI scripts slow and resource hungry.

◆ **CGI scripts are often hacks** that are quickly put together by a system-inexperienced developer and therefore poses great security risks.

Unfortunately, many Web sites still use CGI scripts because they are easy to develop and often freely available. Stay away from CGI scripts and use more scalable and robust solutions such as the mod_perl, mod_fastcgi, or even Java servlets (discussed in the following sections).

Using mod_perl

The Apache mod_perl module alone keeps Perl in the mainstream of Web development. This module for Apache enables you to create highly scalable, Perl-based Web applications that can apply the following facts:

◆ **A scalable Web application isn't a CGI script.** A mod_perl-based script isn't a CGI script. A mod_perl-based script isn't invoked for every URL request for that script. A new process isn't created every time a mod_perl script is requested, which enables the platform to be scalable and robust.

◆ **A scalable Web application can apply persistent store and database connections.** A mod_perl-based script can apply shared memory or keep persistent connections opened to local or remote database servers.

Fortunately, switching your Perl-based CGI scripts to mod_perl isn't hard at all. In the following section I show how you can install mod_perl for Apache and also develop performance-friendly mod_perl scripts.

INSTALLING MOD_PERL

1. Extract mod_perl-$x.y\_z$.tar.gz (where $x.y\_z$ is the latest version number for mod_perl source distribution) using the tar xvzf mod_perl-$x.y\_z$.tar.gz command in the parent directory of your Apache source distribution. If you have extracted the Apache source distribution in /usr/src/redhat/SOURCES/apache_$x.y.z$ directory, then you must extract the mod_perl source distribution in the /usr/src/redhat/SOURCES directory.

2. Change directory to mod_perl-$x.y\_z$ and run

```
perl Makefile.PL
    APACHE_SRC=../apache_x.y.z/src \
    DO_HTTPD=1 \
    USE_APACI=1 \
    PREP_HTTPD=1 \
    EVERYTHING=1
```

3. Run the `make; make install` commands to build `mod_perl` binaries and Perl modules.

4. Change directory to `../apache_x.y.z` and run:

```
./configure -prefix=/usr/local/apache \
--activate-module=src/modules/perl/libperl.a
```

If you want to enable or disable other Apache modules, make sure you add the appropriate `--enable-module` and `--disable-module` options in the preceding command line. For example, the following configuration creates a very lean and mean Apache server with `mod_perl` support:

```
./configure --prefix=/usr/local/apache \
            --disable-module=cgi \
            --disable-module=imap \
            --disable-module=userdir \
            --disable-module=autoindex \
        --disable-module=status \
        --activate-module=src/modules/perl/libperl.a
```

5. Run the `make; make install` commands to build and install the Apache Web server.

CONFIGURING MOD_PERL

Here's how you can configure `mod_perl` for Apache:

1. First determine where you want to keep your `mod_perl` scripts.

   Keep your `mod_perl` scripts outside your document root tree (that is, the directory pointed by `DocumentRoot` directive). This ensures that the `mod_perl` script source isn't accidentally exposed to the world. Also ensure that the file permissions for the `mod_perl` script directory is set only for the Apache Web server user. For example, for a Web site whose `DocumentRoot` is set to `/www/mysite/htdocs`, the ideal `mod_perl` script directory can be `/www/mysite/perl-bin`. After you have determined what this directory is, create a file in this directory called `startup.pl` (or use any other name) that contains the following lines:

```
#!/usr/bin/perl
# If you installed perl in another location
# make sure you change /usr/bin/perl to appropriate
# path.

use strict;

# extend @INC to include the new mod_perl script
# location(s)
```

```
use lib qw(/www/mysite/perl-bin);
```

```
# Following line is required.
1;
```

To keep your `mod_perl` scripts in multiple locations, simply type in the additional path in the `use lib` line. For example, to add another `mod_perl` script location called `/www/mysite/stable/perl-bin`, you can simply change the last line in the preceding script so it reads as follows:

```
use lib qw(/www/mysite/perl-bin /www/mysite/stable/perl-bin);
```

2. Tell Apache to execute the startup script (called `startup.pl` in the previous step) when it starts. You can do that by adding the following directive in the `httpd.conf` file.

```
PerlRequire /www/mysite/perl-bin/startup.pl
```

3. If you know that you are using a set of Perl modules often, you can preload them by adding `use modulename ()` line in the `startup.pl` script before the `1;` line. For example, if you use the `CGI.pm` module (yes, it works with both CGI and `mod_perl` scripts) in many of your `mod_perl` scripts, you can simply preload it in the `startup.pl` script, as follows:

```
use CGI ();
```

Here's an example of my `startup.pl` script.

```
#!/usr/bin/perl

# CVS ID: $Id$

use strict;

# extend @INC if needed
use lib qw(/www/release/perl-bin
           /www/beta/perl-bin
           /www/alpha/perl-bin);

use CGI ();
CGI->compile(':all');

use Apache ();
use Apache::DBI ();

1;
```

I have added `CGI->compile(':all');` line after `use CGI ();` line because `CGI.pm` doesn't automatically load all its methods by default; instead, it provides the `compile()` function to force loading of all methods.

4. Determine how you want to make your mod_perl scripts available in your Web site. I prefer specifying a <Location> directive for each script, as in the following example:

```
<Location /cart>
   SetHandler perl-script
   PerlHandler ShoppingCart
</Location>
```

Here a mod_perl script called ShoppingCart.pm is set up as the request handler for the /cart URL segment. For example, if a Web site called www.domain.com uses the preceding configuration, all requests for www.domain.com/cert are serviced by the ShoppingCart.pm script. This script must reside in a standard Perl path (that is, be part of @INC) or it must be in the path specified in the startup.pl using the use lib line. For example, suppose your startup.pl script has the following line:

```
use lib qw(/www/mysite/perl-bin);
```

Then the ShoppingCart.pm script can reside in /www/mysite/perl-bin directory. As mentioned before, all requests to /cart are serviced by this script. For example, /cart/abc or /cart/whatever are serviced by this script. If you want to run a different script, say Calc.pm, for a sublocation of this URL such as /car/calc, then you must specify another <Location> directive as follows:

```
<Location /cart/calc>
   SetHandler perl-script
   PerlHandler Calc
</Location>
```

Now all requests such as www.domain.com/cart/calc or www.domain.com/cart/calc/whatever, and so on, are serviced by the Calc.pm script.

Use of the <Location> directive to associate a mod_perl script with a URL has the added side effect of enabling you to hide the actual script name so it never appears in the URL. For example, when someone accesses www.domain.com/cart in the current example, s/he has no idea that the Apache server is actually executing a script called ShoppingCart.pm in the /www/mysite/perl-bin directory. This is nice in the sense that it enables you to hide details of your system from prying eyes.

Also, if you wanted to keep a sublocation called /cart/static to be serviced by the default Apache handler, you can simply use the following configuration:

```
<Location /cart/static>
    SetHandler default-handler
</Location>
```

This setting makes sure that any request to www.domain.com/cart/static (or to a sublocation) is serviced by the default Apache handler.

Now all you need is mod_perl scripts to try out your new mod_perl-enabled Apache server. Because mod_perl script development is largely beyond the scope of this book, I provide a basic a test script called HelloWorld.pm (shown in Listing 5-1).

Listing 5-1: HelloWorld.pm

```
#!/usr/bin/perl -w
# CVS ID: $Id$Id:
package HelloWorld;
# A simple mod_perl script that says "Hello World"
# and displays the process ID of the Apache child
# process and a count of (similar) requests served by it.
#
use strict;
use Apache::Constants qw(:common :response);
use CGI;
my $counter = 0;
sub handler{
    my $r = shift;
    my $query = new CGI;
    print $query->header(-type => 'text/html');
    print "Hello World <br>";
    print "Apache child server PID : $$ <br>";
    print "Similar requests processed by this server is: ",
        $counter++, "<br>";
    return DONE;
}
1;
```

You can put the HelloWorld.pm in a location specified by the use lib line your startup.pl script and create a configuration such as the following in httpd.conf.

```
<Location /test>
    SetHandler perl-script
    PerlHandler HelloWorld
</Location>
```

After you have the preceding configuration, start or restart the Apache server and access the `HelloWorld.pm` script using `http://your.server.com/test`. You should see the "Hello World" message, the PID of the Apache child server, and a count of how many similar requests this child server has served so far.

If you run this test (that is, access the `/test` URL) with the default values for the `MinSpareServers`, `MaxSpareServers`, `StartServers`, `MaxRequestsPerChild`, `MaxClients` directives, you may get confused. Because your default settings are likely to cause Apache to run many child servers and because Apache chooses the child server per `/test` request, you may find the count to go up and down as your subsequent `/test` requests are serviced by any of the many child servers. If you keep making requests for the `/test` URL, eventually you see that all child servers are reporting upwards count until it dies because of the `MaxRequestsPerChild` setting. This is why it's a good idea to set these directives as follows for testing purposes:

```
MinSpareServers 1
MaxSpareServers 1
StartServers 1
MaxRequestsPerChild 10
MaxClients 1
```

Restart the Apache server and access /test and you see that Apache services each 10 of your requests using a single child server whose count only increases.

Use of `mod_perl` scripts within your Apache server ensures that your response time is much better than CGI equivalent. However, heavy use of `mod_perl` scripts also creates some side-effects that can be viewed as performance problems, which I cover in the next section.

SOLVING PERFORMANCE PROBLEMS RELATED TO A HEAVY MOD_PERL ENVIRONMENT

When you start using many `mod_perl` scripts, you see that your Apache child server processes become larger in size. You can view this using the `top` command. As long as you have plenty of RAM you should be fine. However, no one ever has too much RAM. So it's a good idea to avoid relying on having lots of memory as the solution. Instead, Here's how you can address this problem more effectively.

If you find that Apache child processes are larger due to many `mod_perl` scripts that are getting loaded in them, consider having a dedicated script server that only serves dynamic contents. Figure 5-1 shows how this can work.

When a user requests the home page of a site called `www.domain.com`, the Apache server responsible for static pages returns the `index.html` page to the client. The page contains embedded links for both static and dynamic contents. The figure shows two such links: `login` and `privacy`. When the end-user clicks on the `login` link it requests `http://myapps.domain.com/login`, which is a different Apache server than the `www.domain.com` server. In fact these two should be two different Linux systems in the ideal world. However, not everyone can afford to split the dynamic and static contents like this, so it isn't appropriate for everyone.

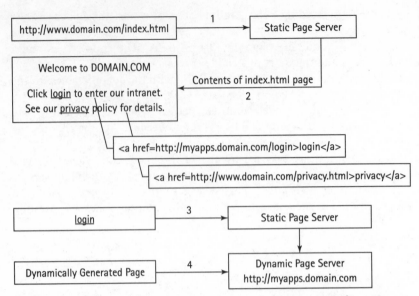

Figure 5-1: Separating static and dynamic (mod_perl script-generated) contents

If you must keep the `mod_perl` and static contents on the same Linux system running Apache, you still can ensure that fat Apache child processes aren't serving static pages. Here's a solution that I like:

1. Compile and install the `mod_proxy` module for your Apache Web server

2. Copy your existing `httpd.conf` file to `httpd-8080.conf` and modify the Port directive to be `Port 8080` instead of `Port 80`. Remove all `mod_perl`-specific configurations from `httpd.conf` so that all your `mod_perl` configurations are in `httpd-8080.conf` file.

3. Modify the `httpd.conf` file to have the following proxy directives:

   ```
   ProxyPass /myapps http://127.0.0.1:8080/myapps
   ```

   You can change *myapps* to whatever you like. If you do change this, make sure you change it in every other location that mentions it. Here we are telling the Apache server serving static pages that all requests to `/myapps` URL are to be serviced via the proxy module, which should get the response from the Apache server running on the same Linux system (`127.0.0.1` is the local host) but on port `8080`.

4. Add the following configuration in `httpd-8080.conf` to create a `mod_perl` script location.

   ```
   <Location /myapps>
       SetHandler perl-script
   ```

```
PerlHandler MyApp1
</Location>
```

Don't forget to change *MyApp1* to whatever your script name is.

Now start (or restart) the Apache server (listening on port 80) as usual using the `apachectl` command. However, you must start the Apache on port 8080 using the `/usr/local/apache/bin/httpd  -f  /usr/local/apache/conf/httpd-8080.conf` command. This assumes that you have installed /usr/local/apache directory; if that isn't so, make sure you change the path. Now you have two Apache parent daemons (which run as `root`) running two sets of children — where one set services the static pages and uses the proxy module to fetch the dynamic, `mod_perl` script pages using the `ProxyPass` directive. This enables you to service the static pages using a set of child servers that aren't running any Perl code whatsoever. On the other hand, the server on port 8080 services only dynamic requests so you effectively have a configuration that is very performance-friendly.

Scripts running under `mod_perl` run fast because they are loaded within each child server's code space. Unlike its CGI counterpart, a `mod_perl` script can keep persistent connection to an external database server — thus speeding up the generation of database-driven dynamic content. However, a new problem introduces itself if you run a very large Web server. When you run 50 or 100 or more Apache server processes to service many simultaneous requests, it's possible for Apache to eventually open up that many database connections and keep each connection persist for the duration of each child. Say that you run a Web server system where you run 50 Apache child processes so that you can service about 50 requests per second and you happen to have a `mod_perl`-based script that opens a database connection in the initialization stage. As requests come to your database script, eventually Apache manages to service such requests using each of its child processes and thus opening up 50 database connections. Because many database servers allocate expensive resources on a per-connection basis, this could be a major problem on the database side. For example, when making such connections to an IBM Universal Database Server (UDB) Enterprise Edition running on a remote Linux system, each Apache child has a counter-part connection related process on the database server. If such environment uses load balancing hardware to balance incoming requests among a set of `mod_perl`-enabled Apache Web server there is likely to be a scenario when each Web server system running 50 Apache child processes have all opened up connection to the database server. For example, if such an environment consists of 10 Web servers under the load-balancing hardware, then the total possible connections to the database server is 10 x 50 or 500, which may create an extensive resource load on the database server.

One possible solution for such a scenario is to find a way to have the database time-out any idle connections, make the `mod_perl` script code detect a stale connection, and have it reinitiate connection. Another solution is to create a persistent database proxy daemon that each Web server uses to fetch data from the database.

Fortunately, FastCGI or Java Servlets have more native solution for such problems and should be considered for heavily used database-driven applications. Here's another performance-boosting Web technology called FastCGI.

Using FastCGI

Like mod_perl scripts, FastCGI applications run all the time (after the initial loading) and therefore provide a significant performance advantage over CGI scripts. Table 5-2 summarizes the differences between a FastCGI application and mod_perl script.

TABLE 5-2: DIFFERENCE BETWEEN A FASTCGI APPLICATION AND MOD_PERL SCRIPTS

Topic	FastCGI Applications	Mod_perl Scripts
Apache platform dependent	No. FastCGI applications can run on non-Apache Web servers, such as IIS and Netscape Web Server.	Yes. Only Apache supports mod_perl module
Perl-only solution	No. FastCGI applications can be developed in many languages, such as C, C++, and Perl.	Yes
Runs as external process	Yes	No
Can run on remote machine	Yes	No
Multiple instances of the application/script are run	Typically a single FastCGI application is run to respond to many requests that are queued. However, if the load is high, multiple instances of the same application are run	Number of instances of mod_perl script equal to the number of child Apache server processes.
Wide support available	Yes. However, at times I get the impression that FastCGI development is slowing down, but I can't verify this or back this up	Yes. There are many mod_perl sites on the Internet and support via Usenet or Web is available.

Topic	FastCGI Applications	Mod_perl Scripts
Database connectivity	Because all requests are sent to a single FastCGI application, you only need to maintain a single database connection with the back-end database server. However, this can change when Apache FastCGI process manager spawns additional FastCGI application instances due to heavy load. Still, the number of FastCGI instances of an application is likely to be less than the number of Apache child processes.	Because each Apache child process runs the mod_perl script, each child can potentially have a database connection to the back-end database. This means you can potentially end up with hundreds of database connections from even a single Apache server system.

Like mod_perl, the Apache module for FastCGI, mod_fastcgi, doesn't come with the standard Apache distribution. You can download it from www.fastcgi. com. Here's how you can install it.

Installing and configuring FastCGI module for Apache

I assume that you have installed the Apache source distribution in /usr/src/ redhat/SOURCES/apache_x.y.z (where x.y.z is the latest version of Apache). To install the mod_fastcgi module for Apache, do the following:

1. Su to root.

2. Extract the mod_fastcgi source distribution using the tar xvzf mod_fastcgi.x.y.z.tar.gz command. Then copy the mod_fastcgi source directory to the /usr/src/redhat/SOURCES/apache_x.y.z/ src/modules/fastcgi directory.

3. Configure Apache using the configuration script (configure) with the following option:

   --active-module=src/modules/fastcgi/libfastcgi.a

If you already compiled Apache with many other options and would like to retain them, simply run the following command from the /usr/src/redhat/SOURCES/apache_x.y.z directory.

```
./config.status --activate-
module=src/modules/fastcgi/libfastcgi.a
```

4. Run the make; make install command from the same directory to compile and install the new Apache with mod_fastcgi support.

5. You are ready to configure Apache to run FastCGI applications. First determine where you want to keep the FastCGI applications and scripts. Ideally, you want to keep this directory outside the directory specified in the DocumentRoot directive. For example, if your set DocumentRoot to /www/mysite/htdocs, consider using /www/mysite/fast-bin as the FastCGI application/script directory. I assume that you will use my advice and do so. To tell Apache that you have created a new FastCGI application/script directory, simply use the following configuration:

```
Alias /apps/ "/www/mysite/fast-bin/"
<Directory "/www/mysite/fast-bin">
    Options ExecCGI
    SetHandler fastcgi-script
</Directory>
```

This tells Apache that the alias /apps/ points to the /www/mysite/fast-bin directory – and that this directory contains applications (or scripts) that must run via the fastcgi-script handler.

6. Restart the Apache server and you can access your FastCGI applications/scripts using the http://www.yourdomain.com/fast-bin/appname URL where www.yourdomain.com should be replaced with your own Web server hostname and appname should be replaced with the FastCGI application that you have placed in the /www/mysite/fast-bin directory. To test your FastCGI setup, you can simply place the following test script (shown in Listing 5-2) in your fast-bin directory and then access it.

Listing 5-2: testfcgi.pl

```
#!/usr/bin/perl -w
#
# CVS ID: $Id$Id:
use strict;
use CGI::Fast qw(:standard);
# Do any startup/initialization steps here.
my $counter = 0;
```

```
#
# Start the FastCGI request loop
#
while (new CGI::Fast) {
   print header;
   print "This is a FastCGI test script" . br;
   print "The request is serviced by script PID: $$"  . br;
   print "Your request number is : ", $counter++, br;
}
exit 0;
```

When you run the script in Listing 5-2, using a URL request such as http://www.yourserver.com/fast-bin/testfcgi.pl, you see that the PID doesn't change and the counter changes as you refresh the request again and again. If you run ps auxww | grep testfcgi on the Web server running this FastCGI script, you see that there is only a single instance of the script running and it's serving all the client requests. If the load goes really high, Apache launches another instance of the script.

FastCGI is a great solution for scaling your Web applications. It even enables you to run the FastCGI applications/scripts on a remote application server. This means you can separate your Web server from your applications and thus gain better management and performance potentials. Also, unlike with mod_perl, you aren't limited to Perl-based scripts for performance; with FastCGI, you can write your application in a variety of application programming languages, such as C, C++, and Perl.

Quite interestingly, Java has begun to take the lead in high-performance Web application development. Java used to be considered slow and too formal to write Web applications, even only a few years ago. As Java has matured, it has become a very powerful Web development platform. With Java you have Java Servlets, Java Server Pages, and many other up and coming Java technologies that can be utilized to gain high scalability and robustness. Java also gives you the power to create distributed Web applications easily.

Using Java servlets

For some unknown reason, Java on Linux platform did not get a great start. It's slowly coming around and the Java run-time environment and development tools are more stable. Even so, complex multithreaded Java servlets still don't always work well under Linux when the same code works just fine under other Java-friendly operating systems (such as Solaris or Windows 2000).

Using Java Servlets with back-end database applications is really ideal. You can implement a master Java servlet that acts as a database connection pool and keeps a given set of connections to the back-end database server. When another servlet needs a connection to the database, it can get it from the connection pool server and return it after it has finished using the connection. This provides a much more managed database pooling than both mod_perl or mod_fastcgi approach discussed earlier. If you are thinking about why I keep referring to database connectivity, then you have not developed major Web software yet. Just about every major Web software development requires back-end database connectivity, so I often consider a platform good or bad according to how well (and easily) it allows management of such resources. Java servlets definitely win this one over mod_perl or mod_fastcgi.

To find more information on Java servlets on Apache, check the http://java. apache.org/ Web site.

Now that you know many ways to speed up your static and dynamic Web contents, consider speeding up your access to someone else's contents. This is typically done by setting up a proxy server with caching capability. In the following section I cover Squid, which is just that.

Using Squid proxy-caching server

Squid is an open-source HTTP 1.1-compliant, proxy-caching server that can enhance your users' Web-browsing experience. You can download the latest, stable Squid source distribution from www.squid-cache.org.

Ideally, you want to run the proxy-caching server with two network interfaces.

◆ One interface connects it to the Internet gateway or the router

◆ One interface connects it to the internal network.

 TIP   Disabling IP forwarding on the proxy-caching system ensures that no one can bypass the proxy server and access the Internet directly.

Here's how you can install and configure it for your system.

COMPILING AND INSTALLING SQUID PROXY-CACHING SERVER

1. Su to root and extract the source distribution using the tar xvzf suid-version.tar.gz (where version is the latest version number of the Squid software).

2. Run the ./configure --prefix=/usr/local/squid command to configure Squid source code for your system.

3. Run make all; make install to install Squid in the /usr/local/squid directory.

CONFIGURING SQUID PROXY-CACHING SERVER

After you have installed Squid, you have to configure it.
Here's how you can configure Squid.

1. Create a group called `nogroup`, using the `groupadd nogroup` command. This group is used by Squid.

2. Run the `chown -R nobody:nogroup /usr/local/squid` command to give the ownership of the `/usr/local/squid` directory and all its subdirectories to nobody user and the group called nogroup.

   This enables Squid (running as nobody user) to create cache directories and files and write logs.

3. Decide which port you want to run the proxy-cache on. Most sites run proxy-cache on 8080, so I use that value here.

4. Add the following line in the `squid.conf` file:

   `http_port 8080`

   This tells Squid to listen to port 8080 for proxy requests.

   If you prefer a different port, use it here. Don't use a port that is already in use by another server. Ideally, you want to use port numbers above 1024 to avoid collision with standard services, but if you know you aren't running a Web server on port 80 and want to run your proxy-cache on that port you can do so. A quick way to check whether a port is available is to run `telnet localhost` *portnumber* command (where *portnumber* is the port number you want to use for proxy-cache). If you get a connection failure message, the port is currently not in use.

5. Define where you want to keep the cache data. Define the following line in the `squid.conf`.

   `cache_dir ufs /usr/local/squid/cache 100 16 256`

   This tells Squid to store the cache data in `/usr/local/squid/cache`. If you have a very large user base that is going to use this proxy-cache, it's a very good idea to have multiple cache directories spanning over different disks. This reduces disk I/O-related wait because multiple, independent disks are always faster than a single disk.

5. Create an *access control list (ACL)* that enables your network access to the proxy-cache selectively.

   By default, Squid doesn't allow any connection from anywhere; this security feature uses a simple approach: Deny everyone, allow only those who should have access. For example, if your network address is `192.168.1.0` with subnet 255.255.255.0, then you can define the following line in squid.conf to create an ACL for your network.

```
acl local_net src 192.168.1.0/255.255.255.0
```

6. Add the following line just before the http_access deny all line.

```
http_access allow local_net
```

This tells Squid to enable machines in local_net ACL access to the proxy-cache using the following line in squid.conf.

7. Tell Squid the username of the cache-manager user. If you want to use webmaster@*yourdomain.com* as the cache-manager user account, define the following line in the squid.conf file:

```
cache_mgr webmaster
```

8. Tell Squid which user and group it should run as. Add the following lines in squid.conf

```
cache_effective_user nobody
cache_effective_group nogroup
```

Here, Squid is told to run as the nobody user and use permissions for the group called nogroup.

Save the squid.conf file and run the following command to create the cache directories.

```
/usr/local/squid/squid -z
```

Now you can run the /usr/local/squid/bin/squid & command to start Squid for the first time. You can verify it's working in a number of ways:

- ◆ Squid shows up in a ps -x listing.

- ◆ Running client www.nitec.com dumps Web-page text to your terminal.

- ◆ The files cache.log and store.log in the directory /usr/local/squid/logs show Squid to be working.

- ◆ Running squid -k check && echo "Squid is running" tells you when Squid is active.

Now for the real test: If you configure the Web browser on a client machine to use the Squid proxy, you should see results. In Netscape Navigator, select Edit → Preferences and then select Proxies from within the Advanced category. By selecting Manual Proxy Configuration and then clicking View, you can specify the IP address of the Squid server as the http, FTP, and Gopher proxy server. The default proxy port is 3128; unless you have changed it in the squid.conf file, place that number in the port field.

You should be able to browse any Web site as if you don't use a proxy. You can double-check that Squid is working correctly by checking the log file /usr/local/squid/logs/access.log from the proxy server and making sure the Web site you were viewing is in there.

TWEAKING SQUID TO FIT YOUR NEEDS

Now that you have Squid up and running, you can customize it to fit your needs. At this point it isn't restricting your users from accessing any sites. You can define rules in your squid.conf file to set access control lists and allow or deny visitors according to these lists.

```
acl BadWords url_regex foo bar
```

By adding the preceding line, you have defined an ACL rule called BadWords that matches any URL containing the words foo or bar. This applies to http://foo.deepwell.com/pictures and http://www.thekennedycompound.com/ourbar.jpg because they both contain words that are members of BadWords.

You can block your users from accessing any URLs that match this rule by adding the following command to the squid.conf file:

```
http_access deny BadWords
```

Almost every administrator using word-based ACLs has a story about not examining all the ways a word can be used. Realize that if you ban your users from accessing sites containing the word "sex," you are also banning them from accessing www.buildersexchange.com and any others that may have a combination of letters matching the forbidden word.

Because all aspects of how Squid functions are controlled within the squid.conf file, you can tune it to fit your needs. For example, you can enable Squid to use 16MB of RAM to hold Web pages in memory by adding the following line:

```
cache_mem  16 MB
```

By trial and error, you may find you need a different amount.

The cache_mem isn't the amount of memory Squid consumes; it only sets the maximum amount of memory Squid uses for holding Web pages, pictures, and so forth. The Squid documentation says you can expect Squid to consume up to three times this amount.

By using the line:

```
emulate_httpd_log on
```

you arrange that the files in /var/log/squid are written in a form like the Web server log files. This arrangement enables you to use a Web statistics program such as Analog or Webtrends to analyze your logs and examine the sites your users are viewing.

Some FTP servers require that an e-mail address be used when one is logging in anonymously. By setting ftp_user to a valid e-mail address, as shown here, you give the server at the other end of an FTP session the data it wants to see:

```
ftp_user squid@deepwell.com
```

TIP You may want to use the address of your proxy firewall administrator. This would give the foreign FTP administrator someone to contact in case of a problem.

If you type in a URL and find that the page doesn't exist, probably that page won't exist anytime in the near future. By setting negative_ttl to a desired number of minutes, as shown in the next example, you can control how long Squid remembers that a page was not found in an earlier attempt. This is called *negative caching.*

```
negative_ttl 2 minutes
```

This isn't always a good thing. The default is five minutes, but I suggest reducing this to two minutes or possibly one minute, if not disabling it all together. Why would you do such a thing? You want your proxy to be as transparent as possible. If a user is looking for a page she knows exists, you don't want a short lag time between the URL coming into the world and your user's capability to access it.

Ultimately, a tool like Squid should be completely transparent to your users. This "invisibility" removes them from the complexity of administration and enables them to browse the Web as if there were no Web proxy server. Although I don't detail that here, you may refer to the Squid Frequently Asked Questions at http://squid.nlanr.net/Squid/FAQ/FAQ.html. Section 17 of this site details using Squid as a transparent proxy.

Also, if you find yourself managing a large list of "blacklisted" sites in the squid.conf file, think of using a program called a *redirector.* Large lists of ACL rules can begin to slow a heavily used Squid proxy. By using a redirector to do this same job, you can improve on Squid's efficiency of allowing or denying URLs according to filter rules. You can get more information on Squirm – a full-featured redirector made to work with Squid – from http://www.senet.com.au/squirm/.

The `cachemgr.cgi` file comes in the Squid distribution. It's a CGI program that displays statistics of your proxy and stops and restarts Squid. It requires only a few minutes of your time to install, but it gives you explicit details about how your proxy is performing. If you'd like to tune your Web cache, this tool can help.

If you are interested in making Squid function beyond the basics shown in this chapter, check the Squid Web page at `http://squid.nlanr.net/`.

Summary

In this chapter, you explored tuning Apache for performance. You examined the configuration directives that enable you to control Apache's resource usage so it works just right for your needs. You also encountered the new HTTP kernel module called `khttpd`, along with techniques for speeding up both dynamic and static Web-site contents. Finally, the chapter profiled the Squid proxy-cache server and the ways it can help you enhance the Web-browsing experience of your network users

Chapter 6

E-Mail Server Performance

SENDMAIL IS THE DEFAULT Mail Transport Agent (MTA) for not only Red Hat Linux but also many other Unix-like operating systems. Therefore, Sendmail is the most widely deployed mail server solution in the world. In recent years, e-mail has taken center stage in modern business and personal communication – which has increased the demand for reliable, scalable solutions for e-mail servers. This demand helped make the MTA market attractive to both open-source and commercial software makers; Sendmail now has many competitors. In this chapter, I show you how to tune Sendmail and a few worthy competing MTA solutions for higher performance.

Choosing Your MTA

A default open-source Sendmail installation works for most small-to-midsize organizations. Unless you plan to deal with a very high volume of e-mails per day, you are most likely fine with the open-source version of Sendmail.

Choosing the right MTA may be dependent on another factor: administration. Although Sendmail has been around for decades, it's still not well understood by many system administrators. The configuration files, the M4 macros, the rule sets are a lot for a beginning or even an intermediate-level system administrator. There is no great Web-based management tool for the open-source version; there are no Apache-like, directive-oriented configuration options. The complexity of managing Sendmail often forces system administrators to leave it in its out-of-the-box state. As a result, many Sendmail sites simply run the default options – which are often minimal and not well suited to any specific organization's needs. The complexity of Sendmail also made it the ideal target for many security attacks over the years.

Left to itself, Sendmail also has performance problems. If it's running as root, a master Sendmail process forks its child processes so they service incoming or outgoing mail requests individually. Creating a new process for each request is an expensive – and old – methodology, though it's only a big problem for sites with heavy e-mail load.

So consider the administrative complexity, potential security risks, and performance problems associated with Sendmail before you select it as your MTA. Even so, system administrators who have taken the time to learn to work with Sendmail should stick with it because Sendmail is about as flexible as it is complex. If you can beat the learning curve, go for it.

These days, open-source Sendmail has major competitors: commercial Sendmail, qmail, and Postfix. Commercial Sendmail is ideal for people who love Sendmail and want to pay for added benefits such as commercial-grade technical support, other derivative products, and services. Postfix and qmail are both open-source products.

A LOOK AT QMAIL

The qmail solution has momentum. Its security and performance are very good. However, it also suffers from administration complexity problems. It isn't an easy solution to manage. I am also not fond of qmail license, which seems to be a bit more restrictive than most well known open-source projects. I feel that the qmail author wants to control the core development a bit more tightly than he probably should. However, I do respect his decisions, especially because he has placed a reward for finding genuine bugs in the core code. I have played with qmail a short time and found the performance to be not all that exciting, especially because a separate process is needed to handle each connection. My requirements for high performance were very high. I wanted to be able to send about a half million e-mails per hour. My experiments with qmail did not result in such a high number. Because most sites aren't likely to need such a high performance, I think qmail is suitable for many sites but it didn't meet either my performance or administration simplicity requirements. So I have taken a wait-and-see approach with qmail.

A LOOK AT POSTFIX

Postfix is a newcomer MTA. The Postfix author had the luxury of knowing all the problems related to Sendmail and qmail. So he was able to solve the administration problem well. Postfix administration is much easier than both Sendmail and qmail, which is a big deal for me because I believe software that can be managed well can be run well to increase productivity.

Some commercial MTA solutions have great strength in administration – and even in performance. My favorite commercial outbound MTA is PowerMTA from Port25.

In this chapter, I tune Sendmail, Postfix, and PowerMTA for performance.

Tuning Sendmail

The primary configuration file for Sendmail is /etc/mail/sendmail.cf, which appears very cryptic to beginners. This file is generated by running a command such as m4 < /path/to/chosen.mc > /etc/mail/sendmail.cf, where

`/path/to/chosen.mc` file is your chosen M4 macro file for the system. For example, I run the following command from the `/usr/src/redhat/SOURCES/sendmail-8.11.0/cf/cf` directory to generate the `/etc/mail/sendmail.cf` for my system:

```
m4 < linux-dnsbl.mc > /etc/mail/sendmail.cf
```

The `linux-dnsbl.mc` macro file instructs m4 to load other macro files such as `cf.m4`, `cfhead.m4`, `proto.m4`, `version.m4` from the `/usr/src/redhat/SOURCES/sendmail-8.11.0/cf/m4` subdirectory. Many of the options discussed here are loaded from these macro files. If you want to generate a new `/etc/mail/sendmail.cf` file so that your changes aren't lost in the future, you must change the macro files in `cf/m4` subdirectory of your Sendmail source installation.

If you don't have these macro files because you installed a binary RPM distribution of Sendmail, you must modify the `/etc/mail/sendmail.cf` file directly.

In any case, always back up your working version of `/etc/mail/sendmail.cf` before replacing it completely using the `m4` command as shown in the preceding example or modifying it directly using a text editor.

Now, here's what you can tune to increase Sendmail performance.

Controlling the maximum size of messages

To control the size of e-mails that you can send or receive via Sendmail, use the MaxMessageSize option in your `mc` file as follows:

```
# maximum message size
define('confMAX_MESSAGE_SIZE','1000000')dnl
```

After regenerating the `/etc/mail/sendmail.cf` file using the `m4` command, you will have the following line in the `/etc/mail/sendmail.cf` file

```
O MaxMessageSize=1000000
```

This tells Sendmail to set the maximum message size to 1,000,000 bytes (approx. 1MB). Of course, you can choose a different number to suit your needs. Any message larger than the set value of the MaxMessageSize option will be rejected.

Caching Connections

Sendmail controls connection caches for IPC connections when processing the queue using ConnectionCacheSize and ConnectionCacheTimeout options.

It searches the cache for a pre-existing, active connection first. The ConnectionCacheSize defines the number of simultaneous open connections that are permitted. The default is two, which is set in `/etc/mail/sendmail.cf` as follows:

```
O ConnectionCacheSize=2
```

You can set it in your mc file using the following:

```
define('confMCI_CACHE_SIZE', 4)dnl
```

Here, the maximum number of simultaneous connections is four. Note that setting this too high will create resource problems on your system, so don't abuse it.

 Setting the cache size to 0 will disable the connection cache.

The ConnectionCacheTimeout option specifies the maximum time that any cached connection is permitted to remain idle. The default is

```
O ConnectionCacheTimeout=5m
```

Which means that maximum idle time is five minutes. I don't recommend changing this option.

CONTROLLING FREQUENCY OF THE MESSAGE QUEUE

Typically, when Sendmail is run as a standalone service (that is, not as a xinetd-run service), the -q option is used to specify the frequency at which the queue is processed. For example, the /etc/sysconfig/sendmail file has a line such as the following:

```
QUEUE=1h
```

This line is used by the /etc/rc.d/init.d/sendmail script to supply the value for the -q command line option for the Sendmail binary (/usr/sbin/sendmail).

The default value of 1h (one hour) is suitable for most sites, but if you frequently find that the mailq | wc -l command shows hundreds of mails in the queue, you may want to adjust the value to a smaller number, such as 30m (30 minutes).

CONTROLLING MESSAGE BOUNCE INTERVALS

When a message can't be delivered to the recipient due to a remote failure such as "recipient's disk quota is full" or "server is temporarily unavailable," the message is queued and retried and finally bounced after a timeout period. The bounce timeout can be adjusted by defining the following options in your mc file:

```
define('confTO_QUEUERETURN', '5d')dnl
define('confTO_QUEUERETURN_NORMAL', '5d')dnl
define('confTO_QUEUERETURN_URGENT', '2d')dnl
define('confTO_QUEUERETURN_NONURGENT', '7d')dnl
```

These options result in the following configuration lines in /etc/mail/ sendmail.cf:

```
O Timeout.queuereturn=5d
O Timeout.queuereturn.normal=5d
O Timeout.queuereturn.urgent=2d
O Timeout.queuereturn.non-urgent=7d
```

Here, the default bounce message is sent to the sender after five days, which is set by the Timeout.queuereturn (that is, the confTO_QUEUERETURN option line in your mc file). If the message was sent with a normal priority, the sender receives this bounce message within five days, which is set by Timeout.queuereturn.normal option (that is, the confTO_QUEUERETURN_NORMAL in your mc file).

If the message was sent as urgent, the bounce message is sent in two days, which is set by Timeout.queuereturn.urgent (that is, the confTO_QUEUERETURN_URGENT option in the mc file).

If the message is sent with low priority level, it's bounced after seven days, which is set by the Timeout.queuereturn.non-urgent option (that is, the confTO_QUEUERETURN_NONURGENT option in the mc file).

If you would like the sender to be warned prior to the actual bounce, you can use the following settings in your mc file:

```
define('confTO_QUEUEWARN', '4h')dnl
define('confTO_QUEUEWARN_NORMAL', '4h')dnl
define('confTO_QUEUEWARN_URGENT', '1h')dnl
define('confTO_QUEUEWARN_NONURGENT', '12h')dnl
```

When you regenerate your /etc/mail/sendmail.cf file with the preceding options in your mc file, you will get lines such as the following:

```
O Timeout.queuewarn=4h
O Timeout.queuewarn.normal=4h
O Timeout.queuewarn.urgent=1h
O Timeout.queuewarn.non-urgent=12h
```

Here, the default warning (stating that a message could not be delivered) message is sent to the sender after four hours. Similarly, senders who use priority settings when sending mail can get a warning after four hours, one hour, and 12 hours for normal-, urgent-, and low-priority messages respectively.

CONTROLLING THE RESOURCES USED FOR BOUNCED MESSAGES

As mentioned before, a message is tried again and again for days before it is removed from the queue. Retrying a failed message takes resources away from the new messages that the system needs to process. Probably a failed message will fail for a while, so trying to resend it too quickly is really a waste of resources.

You can control the minimum time a failed message must stay in the queue before it's retried using the following line in your mc file:

```
define('confMIN_QUEUE_AGE', '30m')dnl
```

This results in the following line in your /etc/mail/sendmail.cf file after it's regenerated.

```
O MinQueueAge=30m
```

This option states that the failed message should sit in the queue for 30 minutes before it's retried.

Also, you may want to reduce the priority of a failed message by setting the following option in your mc file:

```
define('confWORK_TIME_FACTOR', '90000')
```

This will result in the following option in your /etc/mail/sendmail.cf file after it's regenerated.

```
O RetryFactor=90000
```

This option sets a retry factor that is used in the calculation of a message's priority in the queue. The larger the retry factor number, the lower the priority of the failed message becomes.

Controlling simultaneous connections

By default, Sendmail enables an unlimited number of connections per second. It accepts as many connections as possible under Linux. If you run Sendmail in a system that isn't just a mail server, this unlimited connection capability may not be suitable, because it takes system resources away from your other services. For example, if you run a Web server on the same machine you run Sendmail on, you may want to limit the SMTP connections to an appropriate value using the following option line in your mc file:

```
define(confCONNECTION_RATE_THROTTLE', '5')dnl
```

This command creates the following configuration option in /etc/mail/sendmail.cf file after you regenerate it.

```
O ConnectionRateThrottle=5
```

Now Sendmail will accept only five connections per second. Because Sendmail doesn't pre-fork child processes, it starts five child processes per second at peak load. This can be dangerous if you don't put a cap in the maximum number of children that Sendmail can start. Luckily, you can use the following configuration option in your mc file to limit that:

```
define('confMAX_DAEMON_CHILDREN', '15')dnl
```

This command creates the following configuration option in /etc/mail/ sendmail.cf file after you regenerate it.

```
O MaxDaemonChildren=15
```

This limits the maximum number of child processes to 15. This throttles your server back to a degree that will make it unattractive to spammers, since it really can't relay that much mail (if you've left relaying on).

Limiting the load placed by Sendmail

You can instruct Sendmail to stop delivering mail and simply queue it if the system load average gets too high. You can define the following option in your mc file:

```
define('confQUEUE_LA', '5')dnl
```

This command creates the following configuration option in /etc/mail/ sendmail.cf file after you regenerate it.

```
O QueueLA=5
```

Here, Sendmail will stop delivery attempts and simply queue mail when system load average is above five. You can also refuse connection if the load average goes above a certain threshold by defining the following option in your mc file:

```
define('confREFUSE_LA', '8')dnl
```

This command creates the following configuration option in /etc/mail/ sendmail.cf file after you regenerate it.

```
O RefuseLA=8
```

Here, Sendmail will refuse connection after load average goes to eight or above. Note that locally produced mail isn't still accepted for delivery.

Saving memory when processing the mail queue

When Sendmail processes the mail queue, the program's internal data structure demands more RAM – which can be a problem for a system with not much memory to spare. In such a case, you can define the following option in your mc file:

```
define('confSEPARATE_PROC', 'True')dnl
```

This command creates the following configuration option in /etc/mail/ sendmail.cf file after you regenerate it.

```
O ForkEachJob=True
```

This command forces Sendmail to fork a child process to handle each message in the queue – which reduces the amount of memory consumed because queued messages won't have a chance to pile up data in memory.

However, all those individual child processes impose a significant performance penalty – so this option isn't recommended for sites with high mail volume.

 If the ForkEachJob option is set, Sendmail can't use connection caching.

Controlling number of messages in a queue run

If you want to limit the number of messages that Sendmail reads from the mail queue, define the following option in your mc file:

```
define('confMAX_QUEUE_RUN_SIZE','10000')
```

This command creates the following configuration option in the /etc/mail/ sendmail.cf file after you regenerate it.

```
O MaxQueueRunSize=10000
```

Here, Sendmail will stop reading mail from the queue after reading 10,000 messages. Note that when you use this option, message prioritization is disabled.

Handling the full queue situation

The Sendmail queue directory (specified by the QueueDirectory option in /etc/mail/sendmail.cf file or the QUEUE_DIR option in your mc file) is at its best if you keep it in a disk partition of its own. This is especially true for a large mail site. The default path for the queue is /var/spool/mqueue. A dedicated queue disk partition (or even a full disk) will enhance performance by itself.

To avoid running out of queue space in a high e-mail volume site, set a limit so Sendmail refuses mail until room is available in the queue. You can define the following option in your mc file for this purpose:

```
define('confMIN_FREE_BLOCKS', '100')dnl
```

This command creates the following configuration option in /etc/mail/
sendmail.cf file after you regenerate it:

```
O MinFreeBlocks=100
```

This setting tells Sendmail to refuse e-mail when fewer than 100 1K blocks of
space are available in the queue directory.

Tuning Postfix

Postfix is the new MTA on the block. There is no RPM version of the Postfix distribution yet, but installing it is simple. I show the installation procedure in the
following section.

Installing Postfix

Download the source distribution from www.postfix.org site. As of this writing
the source distribution was postfix-19991231-pl13.tar.gz. When you get the
source, the version number may be different; always use the current version number when following the instructions given in this book.

1. Su to root.

2. Extract the source distribution in /usr/src/redhat/SOURCES directory
   using the tar xvzf postfix-19991231-pl13.tar.gz command. This
   will create a subdirectory called postfix-19991231-pl13. Change to the
   postfix-19991231-pl13 directory.

> If you don't have the latest Berkeley DB installed, install it before continuing.
> You can download the latest Berkeley DB source from ww.sleepycat.com.

3. Run the make command to compile the source.

4. Create a user called postfix using the useradd postfix -s /bin/true
   -d /dev/null command.

5. Create a file called /etc/aliases with the following line:

   ```
   postfix: root
   ```

6. Run the `sh INSTALL.sh to` installation command to configure and install the Postfix binaries. Simply accept the default values.

7. Browse the `/etc/postfix/main.cf` and modify any configuration option that needs to be changed.

TIP   You can skip Step 8 to get started quickly.

8. Decide whether to keep the Posfix spool directory (`/var/spool/postfix/maildrop`).configured in one of the following ways:

   a **World-writeable**

   This is the default.

   b **Sticky (1733)**

   c **More restricted (mode 1730)**

   Because the `maildrop` directory is world-writeable, there is no need to run any program with special privileges (set-UID or set-GID), and the spool files themselves aren't world-writeable or otherwise accessible to other users. I recommend that you keep the defaults.

Now you can start your Postfix as follows:

```
postfix start
```

The first time you start the application, you will see warning messages as it creates its various directories. If you make any changes to configuration files, reload Postfix:

```
postfix reload
```

Limiting number of processes used

You can control the total number of concurrent processes used by Postfix using the following parameter in the `/etc/postfix/main.cf` file.
```
default_process_limit = 50
```

Here, Postfix is enabled to run a total of 50 concurrent processes (such as smtp client, smtp server, and local delivery). You can override this setting in the `/etc/postfix/master.cf` file by changing the maxproc column for a service. For example, to receive 100 messages at a time, you can modify the `/etc/postfix/`

`master.cf` file to have the maxproc column set to 100 for smtp service as shown below.

```
# ========================================================================
# service type  private unpriv  chroot  wakeup  maxproc command + args
#               (yes)   (yes)   (yes)   (never) (50)
# ========================================================================
smtp      inet n       -       n       -       100     smtpd
```

Limiting maximum message size

You can set the maximum message size to using the following parameter in the `/etc/postfix/main.cf` file.

```
message_size_limit = 1048576
```

Here, the maximum message size is set to 1048576 bytes (1MB).

Limiting number of messages in queue

To control the number of active messages in the queue, use the following parameter in the `/etc/postfix/main.cf` file:

```
qmgr_message_active_limit = 1000
```

This sets the active message limit to 1000.

Limiting number of simultaneous delivery to a single site

It is impolite and possibly illegal to flood too many concurrent SMTP connections to any remote server. Some sites such as AOL, Yahoo!, and Hotmail may require you to sign an agreement before you can use a high number of connections to these sites. Postfix enables you to limit the number of concurrent connections that it makes to a single destination using the following parameter:

```
default_destination_concurrency_limit = 10
```

This tells Postfix to set a limit of to 10 on concurrent connections to a single site.

Controlling queue full situation

If your server handles lots of mail and you often find that the queue space is nearly full, consider adding the following parameter in the `/etc/postfix/main.cf` file:

```
queue_minfree = 1048576
```

Here, Postfix will refuse mail when the queue directory (that is, the disk partition the queue directory is in) is 1048576 bytes (1MB) in size.

Controlling the length a message stays in the queue

You need to bounce a message after repeated attempts at delivery. The length of time a failed message remains in the queue can be set in the /etc/postfix/main.cf file using the following parameter:

```
maximal_queue_lifetime = 5
```

Here, Postfix will return the undelivered message to the sender after five days of retries. If you would like to limit the size of the undelivered (bounce) message sent to the sender, use the following parameter:

```
bounce_size_limit = 10240
```

Here, Posfix returns 10240 bytes (10K) of the original message to the sender.

Controlling the frequency of the queue

To control the frequency of the queue runs, use the following parameter in the /etc/postfix/main.cf file:

```
queue_run_delay = 600
```

Here the parameter specifies that queues may run every 600 seconds (10 minutes).

Using PowerMTA for High-Volume Outbound Mail

PowerMTA from Port25 is a multithreaded, highly scalable commercial MTA designed for high-volume, outbound mail delivery. You can download an RPM binary package from their Web site at www.port25.com. However, you do need to fill out their evaluation request form to get the license key needed to start the evaluation process. They send the evaluation license key via e-mail within a reasonable timeframe (usually in the same day).

After you have the binary RPM package and the license key, you can install it using the rpm -ivh pmta-package.rpm command, replacing pmta-package.rpm with the name of the RPM file you downloaded from the Port25 Web site. The RPM package that I downloaded, for example, was called PowerMTA-1.0rel-200010112024.rpm.

After RPM is installed, configure it by following these steps:

1. Edit the /etc/pmta/license file and insert the evaluation license data you received from Port25 via e-mail.

2. Edit the /etc/pmta/config file and set the postmaster directive to an appropriate e-mail address.

   For example, replace #postmaster you@your.domain with something like postmaster root@yourdomain.com.

3. If you use Port25's Perl submission API to submit mail to the PowerMTA (pmta) daemon, then change directory to /opt/pmta/api and extract the Submitter-1.02.tar.gz (or a later version) by using the tar xvzf Submitter-1.02.tar.gz command.

4. Change to the new subdirectory called Submitter-1.02 and run the following Perl commands — perl Makefile.PL; make; make test; make install — in exactly that sequence. Doing so installs the Perl submitter API module.

To start the PowerMTA (pmta) server, run the /etc/rc.d/init.d/pmta start command to start the service. Thereafter, whenever you reconfigure the server by modifying the /etc/pmta/config file, make sure you run the /usr/sbin/pmta reload command.

Because PowerMTA is a multithreaded application, many threads are listed as processes if you run commands such as ps auxww | grep pmta. Don't be alarmed if you see a lot of threads; PowerMTA can launch up to 800 threads under the Linux platform.

Using multiple spool directories for speed

Power MTA can take advantage of multiple spool directories using the spool directive in /etc/pmta/config file. For example, you can have

```
spool /spooldisk1
spool /spooldisk2
spool /spooldisk3
```

Here, PowerMTA is told to manage spooling among three directories. Three different fast (ultra-wide SCSI) disks are recommended for spooling. Because spooling on different disks reduces the I/O-related wait for each disk, it yields higher performance in the long run.

Setting the maximum number of file descriptors

PowerMTA uses many file descriptors to open many files in the spool directories; to accommodate it, you need a higher descriptor limit than the default set by Linux.

You can view the current file-descriptor limits for your system by using the `cat /proc/sys/fs/file-max` command.

 TIP Use the `ulimit -Hn 4096` command to set the file descriptor limit to 4096 when you start PowerMTA from the `/etc/rc.d/init.d/pmta` script.

Setting a maximum number of user processes

PowerMTA also launches many threads, so you must increase the maximum number of processes that can run under a single user account. You can set that limit in the `/etc/rc.d/init.d/pmta` script by adding a line such as the following:

```
ulimit -Hu 1024
```

Here, PowerMTA is enabled to launch 1,024 threads.

Setting maximum concurrent SMTP connections

PowerMTA enables you to limit how many concurrent SMTP connections can access a specific domain; you do so in the `/etc/pmta/config` file. The default maximum is set by a wildcard domain-container directive that looks like this:

```
<domain *>
    max-smtp-out     20  # max. connections *per domain*
    bounce-after     4d12h   # 4 days, 12 hours
    retry-after      60m      # 60 minutes
    log-resolution   no
    log-connections  no
    log-commands     no
    log-data         no
</domain>
```

Here the `max-smtp-out` directive is set to 20 for all (*) domains. At this setting, PowerMTA opens no more than 20 connections to any one domain. If, however, you have an agreement with a particular domain that allows you to make more connections, you can create a domain-specific configuration to handle that exception. For example, to connect 100 simultaneous PowerMTA threads to your friend's domain (myfriendsdomain.com), you can add the following lines to the `/etc/pmta/config` file:

```
<domain myfriendsdomain.com>
  max-smtp-out     100
</domain>
```

Don't create such a configuration without getting permission from the other side. If the other domain is unprepared for the swarm of connecitons, you may find your mail servers blacklisted. You may even get into legal problems with the remote party if you abuse this feature.

Monitoring performance

Because PowerMTA is a high-performance delivery engine, checking on how it's working is a good idea. You can run the /usr/sbin/pmta show status command to view currently available status information. Listing 6-1 shows a sample status output.

Listing 6-1: Sample output of /usr/sbin/pmta status

```
PowerMTA v1.0rel status on andre.intevo.com on 2001-01-07 00:30:30


Traffic    ------------inbound------------   ------------outbound-----------
              rcpts      msgs      kbytes      rcpts      msgs      kbytes
     Total   221594    221594   5230009.5     221174    221174   4884289.7
 Last Hour        0         0         0.0          0         0         0.0
  Top/Hour   138252    138252   3278106.9     131527    131527   3339707.1
 Last Min.        0         0         0.0          0         0         0.0
  Top/Min.     7133      7133     69948.1       3002      3002     62914.8


Connections   active       top    maximum  Domain       cached     pending
   Inbound         0         3         30  Names          4844           0
  Outbound         1       698        800

                                           Spool        in use    recycled
SMTP queue     rcpts   domains     kbytes  Files           659        1000
                 340        11     9629.0  Init.                  complete


    Status   running   Started  2001-01-05 13:48:50   Uptime   1 10:41:40
```

Here, in the Top/Hour row, PowerMTA reports that it has sent 131,527 messages in an hour. Not bad. But PowerMTA can do even better. After a few experiments, I have found it can achieve 300-500K messages per hour easily – on a single PIII Red Hat Linux system with 1GB of RAM.

PowerMTA is designed for high performance and high volume. Its multithreaded architecture efficiently delivers a large number of individual e-mail messages to many destinations.

Summary

Sendmail, Postfix, and PowerMTA are common Mail Transport Agents (MTAs). They can be fine-tuned for better resource management and higher performance.

Chapter 7

NFS and Samba Server Performance

IN THIS CHAPTER

◆ Tuning Samba

◆ Tuning NFS server

A HIGHLY TUNED SAMBA or NFS server has the following characteristics:

◆ **Its hardware is optimal.** A typical client/server system falls short of optimal because of three hardware bottlenecks:

■ **Disk drives.** Any component with moving parts always moves too slow compared to information, which moves at the speed of electric impulses. Fortunately, fast, modern hardware is relatively cheap. You can buy 10,000-RPM ultra-wide SCSI disk drives without paying an arm and a leg.

■ **CPU.** As with single-user systems, the basic principle that governs CPU selection is *the faster the better* — and thanks to Intel and friends, 1GHz CPUs are available in the PC market.

◆ **Network cabling.** Unfortunately, now-obsolescent 10MB Ethernet is still the norm in most organizations. 100MB Ethernet is still not deployed everywhere. I have used a PIII 500 MHz Samba system with 10 local, ultra-wide, 10K RPM drives on three disk controllers on a 100MB Ethernet to service over 100 users who included office administrators (small file and infrequent access users), engineers (frequent file access users), and graphics artists (large file users). My biggest worry was controlling the temparature of the server because the 10K RPM drives heated up fast. I had to use many small fans as disk bay covers to cool the server.

◆ **Its server configuration is optimal.** And that means a lot of careful attention to settings, usually on the part of the system administrator. Unfortunately, there is no easy way to formulate the ideal configuration for your Samba or NFS server. Each implementation has its own needs; the best method is trial and error. This chapter shows many configuration options that can help make your trial-and-error experiments effective.

Tuning Samba Server

This section shows how you can tune the Samba server for best performance.

Controlling TCP socket options

The Samba server uses TCP packets to communicate with the clients. You can enhance the performance by adding the following parameter in the /etc/samba/ smb.conf file.

```
socket options = TCP_NODELAY SO_RCVBUF=8192 SO_SNDBUF=8192
```

The TCP_NODELAY option tells the Samba server to send as many packets as necessary to keep the delay low. The SO_RCVBUF and SO_SNDBUF options set the send and receive window (buffer) size to 8K (8192 bytes), which should result in good performance. Here we are instructing the Samba server to read/write 8K data before requesting an acknowledgement (ACK) from the client side.

USING OPPORTUNISTIC LOCKS (OPLOCKS)

When a client accesses a file from a Samba server, it doesn't know whether the file is accessed by others who may change the file contents. However, if the Samba server somehow could tell the client that it has exclusive access to a file, the client can then cache the file contents and thus increase performance. To enable a client to locally cache a file, the server uses opportunistic locks (*oplocks*). If you have the following parameter set in the /etc/samba/smb.conf file for a share, the server can grant an oplock for clients, which should result in about 30 percent or more performance gain.

```
oplocks = true
```

Newer versions of Samba (2.0.5 or later) support a new type of opportunistic lock parameter called level2 oplocks. This type of oplock is used for read-only access. When this parameter is set to true, you should see a major performance gain in concurrent access to files that are usually just read. For example, executable applications that are read from a Samba share can be accessed faster due to this option.

Samba also has a fake oplocks parameter that can be set to true to grant oplocks to any client that asks for one. However, fake oplocks are depreciated and should never be used in shares that enable writes. If you enable fake oplocks for shares that clients can write to, you risk data corruption.

Note that when you enable oplocks for a share such as the following:

```
[pcshare]
comment   = PC Share
path      = /pcshare
public    = yes
```

```
writable  = yes
printable = no
write list = @pcusers
oplocks   = true
```

you may want to tell Samba to ignore oplock requests by clients for files that are writeable. You can use the veto oplock files parameter to exclude such files. For example, to exclude all files with doc extension from being oplocked, you can use

```
veto oplock files = /*.doc/
```

CONTROLLING THE WRITE-AHEAD BEHAVIOR

If you run the Samba server on a system where disk access is comparable to network access speed, you can use the read size parameter. For example,

```
read size = 16384
```

When the amount of data transferred is larger than the specified read size parameter, the server either begins to write data to disk before it receives the whole packet from the network or to write to the network before all data has been read from the disks.

CONTROLLING THE WRITE SIZE

The maximum size of a single packet is controlled by a network option called Maximum Transport Unit (MTU), which is set in network configuration. The default value is 1500; you can check the MTU value set for a network interface by running the ifconfig command. Now, if Samba transmits data in a smaller size than the MTU, throughput is reduced. The max xmit parameter controls the write size that Samba uses when writing data to the network. The default value of this parameter is set to 65,536, which is the maximum value. You can set it to anything between 2048 to 65,536. However, on slow networks this value may not be optimal. On slow networks, use a small value like 2048 for better performance; on high-speed networks, leave the default as is.

CONTROLLING RAW READS

When the read raw parameter is set, the Samba server reads a maximum of 65,536 bytes in a single packet. However, in some instances setting this parameter may actually reduce performance. The only sure way to tell whether read raw = yes helps your Server or not is to try using Samba while setting read raw = no. If you see a performance drop, enable it again.

CONTROLLING RAW WRITES

When the write raw parameter is set, the Samba server writes a maximum of 65,536 bytes in a single packet. However, in some instances setting this parameter may actually reduce performance. The only sure way to tell whether `write raw = yes` helps your Server or not is to try using Samba while setting `write raw = no`. If you see a performance drop, enable it again.

SETTING THE LOG LEVEL APPROPRIATELY

Setting the `log level` parameter to anything above two will reduce performance greatly because each log entry is flushed to disk. I recommend that you set `log level` to one.

CACHE CURRENT DIRECTORY PATH

Setting the `getwd cache = yes` parameter enables caching of current directory path which avoids time-consuming tree traversal by the server.

AVOIDING STRICT LOCKING AND SYNCHRONIZATION FOR FILES

There are a few strict parameters that are best avoided.

◆ If you set the `strick locking` parameter to `yes`, then Samba server will perform lock checks on each read/write operation, which will severely decrease performance. So don't use this option; especially on Samba shares that are really remote NFS-mounted filesystems.

◆ If you set the `strict sync` parameter to `yes`, the Samba server will write each packet to disk and wait for the write to complete whenever the client sets the sync bit in a packet. This will cause severe performance problems when working with Windows clients running MS explorer or other programs like it, which set the sync bit for every packet.

AUTOMATICALLY CREATING USER ACCOUNTS

Although this isn't a performance option, it saves you a lot of administrative hassle, so it is included here. When you want Windows users or other Linux-based Samba clients to access your Samba server, you need user accounts for each client. If the Samba resource you want to offer to these clients can be shared using a single account, you can simply create a user account called `myguest` using the `useradd myguest` command and set `guest account = myguest` in the global section of the `/etc/samba/smb.conf` file. Then you can use the `guest ok = yes` parameter in the appropriate resource section to enable guest access for that resource. For example:

```
[printers]
    comment = All Printers
    path = /var/spool/samba
    browseable = no
    guest ok = no
    printable = yes
```

Here, all the printers managed by Samba are accessible via guest accounts. However, it isn't often desirable to use guest accounts to access shares. For example, enabling guest access to a user's home directory isn't desirable for the obvious reasons.

Unfortunately, maintaining Linux user accounts for all your Windows users can be a tough task, especially because you must manually synchronize the addition and removal of such users. Fortunately, if you use domain-level security you can automate this process using the following parameters in the global section:

```
add user script = /usr/sbin/useradd %u -g smbusers
delete user script = /usr/sbin/userdel %u
```

Whenever a Windows user (or a remote Samba client) attempts to access your Samba server (using domain level security), it creates a new user account if the password server (typically the Primary Domain Controller) authenticates the user. Also, the user account is removed if the password server fails to authenticate the user.

This means that if you add a new user account in your Windows 2000/NT domain and your Samba server uses a Windows 2000/NT server for domain-level security, the corresponding Linux account on the Samba server is automatically managed.

Tuning Samba Client

If you use Windows clients such as Windows 9x and Windows 2000/NT to access the Samba server, consult your operating system guide to determine if you can increase the performance of the TCP/IP stack used.

Tuning NFS Server

The primary bottleneck in an NFS environment is the disk I/O speed of the NFS server. The disk I/O speed is dependent on what kind of disk subsystem you use with your NFS server. For example, running an NFS server using IDE disks doesn't yield great performance versus running a server with ultra-wide, SCSI disks that have high RPM rates. The maximum number of I/O operations per second will dictate how well your NFS server performs. I have used an Intel Xeon 500 system with 10 ultra-wide SCSI disks in RAID 5 as an NFS server for about 50 users with great success.

After you have decided on a good disk subsystem, such as a RAID 5 using an array of 10K RPM ultra-wide SCSI disks with a disk controller that has a large built-in disk cache, your next hardware bottleneck is the network itself. Isolating high-bandwidth traffic into its own network is a good way to reduce performance loss. So I recommend that you connect your NFS servers to your NFS clients using a dedicated 100 Mb Ethernet of its own. Create an NFS backbone, which only moves NFS packets. This will result in a high-performance NFS network.

Optimizing read/write block size

The default read and write block size for NFS is 4096 bytes (4KB), which may not be optimal for all situations. You can perform a test to determine whether changing the block size will help you or not. Here's how you perform such a test.

This test assumes that you have an NFS server running on a Linux system and also have a Linux-based NFS client system. The test also assumes that the client mounts a filesystem called /mnt/nfs1 from the NFS server.

1. Su to root on the NFS client machine.

2. You need to know the total amount of memory your system has. You should know this by default because it's your system, but if you don't remember too well, you can run the cat /proc/meminfo command to view the memory information for your system. This will display similar to what is shown below:

```
         total:     used:     free: shared: buffers: cached:
Mem: 263720960 260456448  3264512 30531584 228245504
6463488
Swap: 271392768  6209536 265183232
MemTotal:    257540 kB
MemFree:       3188 kB
MemShared:    29816 kB
Buffers:     222896 kB
Cached:        6312 kB
BigTotal:         0 kB
BigFree:          0 kB
SwapTotal:   265032 kB
SwapFree:    258968 kB
```

3. The total amount of system memory is shown under the column heading total:; divide this number by 1,048,576 (1024x1024) to get the total (approximate) memory size in megabytes. In the preceding example, this number is 251MB.

   Interestingly, total memory is never reported accurately by most PC system BIOS, so you must round the number based on what you know about the total memory. In my example, I know that the system should have 256MB of RAM, so I use 256MB as the memory size in this test.

 If you have RAM > 1GB, I recommend using 512MB as the RAM size for this experiment. Although you may have 1GB+ RAM, pretend that you have 512MB for this experiment.

4. Change directory to a currently mounted /mnt/nfs1 NFS file directory. Run the du command to see whether you have at least 512MB (2 x total RAM) of free space available on the NFS directory. If you don't, you can't continue with this experiment. I assume that you do have such space available.

5. We want to measure the write performance of your current NFS setup. So we will write a 512MB (16KB/block x 32,768 blocks) file called 512MB.dat in the /mnt/nfs1 directory using the following command:

```
time dd if=/dev/zero \
        of=/mnt/nfs1/512MB.dat \
        bs=16k count=32768
```

This command runs the time command, which records execution time of the program named as the first argument. In this case, the dd command is timed. The dd command is given an input file (using if option) called /dev/zero. This file is a special device that returns a 0 (zero) character when read. If you open this file for reading, it keeps returning a 0 character until you close the file. This gives us an easy source to fill out an output file (specified using the of option) called /mnt/nfs1/512MB.dat; the dd command is told to use a block size (specified using bs option) of 16KB and write a total of 32,768 blocks (specified using the count option). Because 16KB/block times 32,768 blocks equal 512MB, we will create the file we intended. After this command is executed, it prints a few lines such as the following:

```
32768+0 records in
32768+0 records out
1.610u 71.800s 1:58.91 61.7% 0+0k 0+0io 202pf+0w
```

Here the dd command read 32,768 records from the /dev/zero device and also wrote back the same number of records to the /mnt/nfs1/512MB.dat file. The third line states that the copy operation took one minute and 58.91 seconds. Write this line in a text file as follows:

```
Write, 1, 1.610u, 71.800s, 1:58.91, 61.7%
```

Here, you are noting that this was the first (1st) write experiment.

6. We need to measure the read performance of your current NFS setup. We can simply read the 512MB file we created earlier and see how long it takes to read it back. To read it back and time the read access, you can run the following command:

```
time dd if=/mnt/nfs1/512MB.dat \
        of=/dev/null \
        bs=16k count=32768
```

Here the dd command is timed again to read the /mnt/nfs1/512MB.dat file as input, then output the file contents to /dev/null, which is the official bottomless bit bucket for Linux. Like before, record the time used in the same file you wrote the read performance record. For example, the read test using the preceding command displayed the following output on my system.

Record the third line as follows:

```
Read, 1, 1.970u, 38.970s, 2:10.44, 31.3%
```

Here, you are noting that this was the first (1st) read experiment.

7. Remove the 512MB.dat file from /mnt/nfs1 and umount the partition using the umount /mnt/nfs1 command. The unmounting of the NFS directory ensures that disk caching doesn't influence your next set of tests.

8. Repeat the write and read back test (Steps 5 - 7) at least five times. You should have a set of notes as follows:

```
Read,   1, 1.971u, 38.970s, 2:10.44, 31.3%
Read,   2, 1.973u, 38.970s, 2:10.49, 31.3%
Read,   3, 1.978u, 38.971s, 2:10.49, 31.3%
Read,   4, 1.978u, 38.971s, 2:10.49, 31.3%
Read,   5, 1.978u, 38.971s, 2:10.49, 31.3%

Write, 1, 1.610u, 71.800s, 1:58.91, 61.7%
Write, 2, 1.610u, 71.801s, 1:58.92, 61.7%
Write, 3, 1.610u, 71.801s, 1:58.92, 61.7%
Write, 4, 1.610u, 71.801s, 1:58.92, 61.7%
Write, 5, 1.611u, 71.809s, 1:58.92, 61.7%
```

9. Calculate the average read and write time from the fifth column (shown in bold).

You have completed the first phase of this test. You have discovered the average read and write access time for a 512MB file. Now you can start the second phase of the test as follows:

1. Unmount the /mnt/nfs1 directory on the NFS client system using the umount /mnt/nfs1 command.

2. Modify the /etc/fstab file on the NFS client system such that the /mnt/nfs1 filesystem is mounted with the rsize=8192, wsize=8192 options as shown below:

```
nfs-server-host:/nfs1 /mnt/nfs1 nfs \
rsize=8192, wsize=8192 0 0
```

3. Mount the `/mnt/nfs1` directory back using the `mount /mnt/nfs1` command.

4. Perform Steps 4 to 9 of the previous experiment.

5. Compare the read and write access averages between phase 1 and phase 2 of the test. If the results in phase 2 (this part) of the test looks better, the changing of the read and write blocks have increased your NFS performance. If not, remove the `rsize=8192, wsize=8192` options from the line in `/etc/fstab`. Most likely, the read and write block size change will increase NFS performance. You can also experiment with other block sizes. It's advisable that you use multiples of 1024 in block size because 1024 is the actual filesystem block size. Also, don't use larger numbers above 8192 bytes.

If the block size change works for you, keep the `rsize=8192, wsize=8192` (or whatever you find optimal via further experiment) in the `/etc/fstab` line for the `/mnt/nfs1` definition.

Setting the appropriate Maximum Transmission Unit

The Maximum Transmission Unit (MTU) value determines how large a single packet transmission can be. If the MTU is set too small, NFS performance will suffer greatly. To discover the appropriate MTU setting, do the following:

1. `su` to `root` on the NFS client system.

2. Run the `tracepath` *nfsserver*`/2049` command where `nfsserver` is your NFS server's hostname. The command will report the MTU for the path.

3. Check out the current MTU that the network interface uses to access the NFS server. You can simply run the `ifconfig` command list information about all your up and running network interfaces.

4. If you see that your MTU setting for the appropriate network interface is not the same as the one reported by the `tracepath` command, use `ifconfig` to set it using the `mtu` option. For example, the `ifconfig eth0 mtu 512` command sets the MTU for network interface `eth0` to 512 bytes.

Running optimal number of NFS daemons

By default, you run eight NFS daemons. To see how heavily each `nfsd` thread is used, run the `cat /proc/net/rpc/nfsd` command. The last ten numbers on the line in that file indicate the number of seconds that the `nfsd` thread usage was at that percentage of the maximum allowable. If you have a large number in the top

three deciles, you may want to increase the number of nfsd instances. To change
the number of NFS daemons started when your server boots up, do the following:

1. su to root.

2. Stop nfsd using the /etc/rc.d/init.d/nfs stop command if you run it
   currently.

3. Modify the /etc/rc.d/init.d/nfs script so that RPCNFSDCOUNT=8 is set
   to an appropriate number of NFS daemons.

4. Start nfsd using the /etc/rc.d/init.d/nfs start command.

CONTROLLING SOCKET INPUT QUEUE SIZE

By default, Linux uses a socket input queue of 65,535 bytes (64KB). If you run 8
NFS daemons (nfsd) on your system, each daemon gets 8K buffer to store data in
the input queue. Increase the queue size to at least 256KB as follows:

1. su to root.

2. Stop nfsd using the /etc/rc.d/init.d/nfs stop command if you run it
   currently.

3. Modify the /etc/rc.d/init.d/nfs script so that just before the NFS daemon (nfsd) is started using the daemon rpc.nfsd $RPCNFSDCOUNT line,
   the following lines are added:

   ```
   echo 262144 > /proc/sys/net/core/rmem_default
   echo 262144 > /proc/sys/net/core/rmem_max
   ```

4. Right after the daemon rpc.nfsd $RPCNFSDCOUNT line, add the following
   lines:

   ```
   echo 65536 > /proc/sys/net/core/rmem_default
   echo 65536 > /proc/sys/net/core/rmem_max
   ```

5. Restart NFS daemon using the /etc/rc.d/init.d/nfs start command.

Now each NFS daemon started by the /etc/rc.d/init.d/nfs script uses 32K
buffer space in the socket input queue.

Monitoring packet fragments

The Linux kernel controls the number of unprocessed UDP packet fragments it can
handle using a high to low range. When unprocessed UDP packet fragment size
reaches the high mark (usually 262,144 bytes or 256KB), the kernel throws away the
incoming packet fragments. In other words, when UDP packet fragments reach the
high mark, packet loss starts. The loss of packet fragments continues until the total
unprocessed fragment size reaches a low threshold (usually 196,608 bytes or 192KB).

Because NFS protocol uses fragmented UDP packets, the preceding high to low threshold used by Linux matters in NFS performance.

◆ You can view the current value of your high threshold size; run

```
cat /proc/sys/net/ipv4/ipfrag_high_thresh
```

◆ You can change the high values by running

```
echo high-number > /proc/sys/net/ipv4/ipfrag_high_thresh
```

◆ You can view the low threshold value by running

```
cat /proc/sys/net/ipv4/ipfrag_low_thresh
```

◆ To change the low number, run

```
echo low-number > /proc/sys/net/ipv4/ipfrag_low_thresh
```

Summary

In this chapter you learned to tune the Samba and NFS servers.

Part III

System Security

## Chapter 8

Kernel Security

IN THIS CHAPTER

- ◆ Using Linux Intrusion Detection System (LIDS)
- ◆ Libsafe
- ◆ Protecting stack elements

THIS CHAPTER PRESENTS kernel- or system-level techniques that enhance your overall system security. I cover the Linux Intrusion Detection System (LIDS) and Libsafe, which transparently protect your Linux programs against common stack attacks.

Using Linux Intrusion Detection System (LIDS)

The root is the source of all evil. Probably this statement only makes sense to Unix/Linux system administrators. After an unauthorized `root` access is confirmed, damage control seems very hopeless, or at least is at the intruder's mercy.

In a default Red Hat Linux system, several subsystems are typically unprotected.

- ◆ **Filesystem.** The system has many important files, such as `/bin/login`, that hackers exploit frequently because they aren't protected. If a hacker breaks in, he can access the system in the future by uploading a modified login program such as `/bin/login`. In fact, files (that is, programs) such as `/bin/login` shouldn't change frequently (if at all) — therefore, they must not be left unprotected.

- ◆ **Running processes.** Many processes run with the `root` privileges, which means that when they are exploited using tricks such as buffer overflow (explained in the "Using libsafe to Protect Program Stacks" section), the intruder gains full `root` access to the system.

LIDS enhances system security by reducing the root user's power. LIDS also implements a low-level security model – in the kernel – for the following purposes:

- Security protection

- Incident detection

- Incident-response capabilities

For example, LIDS can provide the following protection:

- Protect important files and directories from unauthorized access on your hard disk, no matter what local filesystem they reside on.

- Protect chosen files and directories from modifications by the root user, so an unauthorized root access doesn't turn an intruder into a supervillain.

- Protect important processes from being terminated by anyone, including the root user. (Again, this reduces root user capabilities.)

- Prevent raw I/O operations from access by unauthorized programs.

- Protect a hard disk's master boot record (MBR).

LIDS can detect when someone scans your system using port scanners – and inform the system administrator via e-mail. LIDS can also notify the system administrator whenever it notices any violation of imposed rules – and log detailed messages about the violations (in LIDS-protected, tamper-proof log files). LIDS can not only log and send e-mail about detected violations, it can even shut down an intruder's interactive session

Building a LIDS-based Linux system

The Linux Intrusion Detection System (LIDS) is a kernel patch and a suite of administrative tools that enhances security from within the Linux operating system's kernel. LIDS uses a *reference monitor* security model, putting everything it refers to – the subject, the object, and the access type – in the kernel. If you want more information about this approach, the LIDS project Web site is www.lids.org/about.html.

A LIDS-enabled Linux system runs a customized kernel, so you must have the latest kernel source from a reliable kernel site, such as www.kernel.org. After you have downloaded and extracted the kernel in /usr/src/linux, download the LIDS patch for the specific kernel you need. For example, if you use kernel 2.4.1, make sure you download the LIDS patch from the LIDS project Web site. Typically, the LIDS patch and administrative tool package is called lids-$x.x.x.y.y.y$.tar.gz, where $x.x.x$ represents the LIDS version number and $y.y.y$ represents the kernel version (for example, lids-1.0.5-2.4.1).

TIP

I use LIDS 1.0.5 for kernel 2.4.1 in the instructions that follow. Make sure you change the version numbers as needed. Extract the LIDS source distribution in the `/usr/local/src` directory using the `tar xvzf lids-1.0.5-2.4.1.tar.gz` command from the `/usr/local/src` directory. Now you can patch the kernel.

NOTE

Make sure that `/usr/src/linux` points to the latest kernel source distribution that you downloaded. You can simply run `ls -l /usr/src/linux` to see which directory the symbolic link points to. If it points to an older kernel source, remove the link using `rm -f /usr/src/linux` and re-link it using `ln -s /usr/src/linux-`*version* `/usr/src/linux`, where *version* is the kernel version you downloaded. For example, `ln -s /usr/src/linux-2.4.1 /usr/src/linux` links the latest kernel 2.4.1 source to `/usr/src/linux`.

Patching, compiling, and installing the kernel with LIDS. Before you can use LIDS in your system you need to patch the kernel source, then compile and install the updated kernel. Here is how you can do that:

1. As `root`, extract the LIDS patch package in a suitable directory of your choice.

   I usually keep source code for locally compiled software in the `/usr/local/src` directory. I assume that you will do the same. So from the `/usr/local/src` directory, run the `tar xvzf lids-1.0.5-2.4.1.tar.gz` command. Doing so creates a new subdirectory called `lids-1.0.5-2.4.1`.

2. Change directory to `/usr/src/linux` and run the `patch -p < /usr/local/src/lids-1.0.5-2.4.1.patch` command to patch the kernel source distribution.

3. Run the `make menuconfig` command from the `/usr/src/linux` directory to start the menu-based kernel configuration program.

NOTE

Instead of using `make menuconfig` command, you can also use the `make config` command to configure the kernel.

4. From the main menu, select the `Code maturity level options` submenu and choose the `Prompt for development and/or incomplete code/drivers` option by pressing the spacebar key; then exit this submenu.

5. Select the `Sysctl support` from the `General setup` submenu; then exit the submenu.

6. From the main menu, select the `Linux Intrusion Detection System` submenu.

This submenu appears only if you have completed Steps 4 and 5, at the bottom of the main menu; you may have to scroll down a bit.

7. From the LIDS submenu, select the `Linux Intrusion Detection System support (EXPERIMENTAL) (NEW)` option.

You see a list of options:

```
(1024)    Maximum protected objects to manage (NEW)
(1024)    Maximum ACL subjects to manage (NEW)
(1024)    Maximum ACL objects to manage (NEW)
(1024)    Maximum protected proceeds (NEW)
[ ]    Hang up console when raising a security alert (NEW)
[ ]    Security alert when executing unprotected programs
before sealing LIDS (NEW)
[ ]    Try not to flood logs (NEW)
[ ]    Allow switching LIDS protections (NEW)
[ ]    Port Scanner Detector in kernel (NEW)
[ ]    Send security alerts through network (NEW)
[ ]     LIDS Debug  (NEW)
```

The default limits for managed, protected objects, ACL subjects/objects, and protected processes should be fine for most systems. You can leave them as is.

- If you want LIDS to disconnect the console when a user violates a security rule, select the `Hang up console when raising a security alert` option.

- If you want to issue a security alert when a program is executed before LIDS protection is enabled, select the `Security alert when executing unprotected programs before sealing LIDS` option.

 LIDS is enabled during bootup (as described later in the chapter), so it's likely that you will run other programs before running LIDS. When you select this option, however, you can also disable execution of unprotected programs altogether using the `Do not execute unprotected programs before sealing LIDS` option. I don't recommend that you disable unprotected programs completely during bootup unless you are absolutely sure that everything you want to run during boot (such as the utilities and daemons) is protected and doesn't stop the normal boot process.

8. Enable the `Try not to flood logs (NEW)` option.

 Leave the default 60-second delay between logging of two identical entries. Doing so helps preserve your sanity by limiting the size of the log file. The delay will ensure too many log entries are not written too fast.

9. Select `Allow switching LIDS protections` option if you want to enable switching of LIDS protection. If you do, you can customize this further by selecting the value for the following options:

- `Number of attempts to submit password`

- `Time to wait after a fail (seconds)`

- `Allow remote users to switch LIDS protections`

- `Allow any program to switch LIDS protections`

- `Allow reloading config. file`

These are my preferences:

```
[*]     Allow switching LIDS protections (NEW)
(3)     Number of attempts to submit password (NEW)
(3)     Time to wait after a fail (seconds) (NEW)
[*]     Allow remote users to switch LIDS protections (NEW)
[ ]     Allow any program to switch LIDS protections (NEW)
[*]     Allow reloading config. file (NEW)
```

10. Select the `Port Scanner Detector in kernel` option and the `Send security alerts through network` option. Don't change the default values for the second option.

11. Save your kernel configuration and run the following commands to compile the new kernel and its modules (if any).

```
make depend
make bzImage
make modules
make modules_install
```

 If you aren't compiling a newer kernel version than what is running on the system, back up the `/bin/modules/current-version` directory (where `current-version` is the current kernel version). For example, if you are compiling 2.4.1 and you already have 2.4.1 running, then run the `cp -r /lib/modules/2.4.1 /lib/modules/2.4.1.bak` command to back-up the current modules. In case of a problem with the new kernel, you can delete the broken kernel's modules and rename this directory with its original name.

12. Copy the newly created `/usr/src/linux/arch/i386/boot/bzImage` kernel image to `/boot/vmlinuz-lids-1.0.5-2.4.1` using the `cp /usr/src/linux/arch/i386/boot/bzImage /boot/vmlinuz-lids-1.0.5-2.4.1` command.

13. In the `/etc/lilo.conf` file, add the following:

```
image=/boot/vmlinuz-lids-1.0.5-2.4.1
      label=lids
      read-only
      root=/dev/hda1
```

If `/dev/hda1` isn't the `root` device, make sure you change it as appropriate.

14. Run `/sbin/lilo` to reconfigure LILO.

When the LILO is reconfigured, the kernel configuration is complete.

COMPILING, INSTALLING, AND CONFIGURING LIDS

After configuring the kernel, you can proceed with the rest of your LIDS configuration.

Here's how to compile and install the LIDS administrative program `lidsadm`.

1. Assuming that you have installed the LIDS source in the `/usr/local/src` directory, change to `/usr/local/src/lids-1.0.5-2.4.1/lidsadm-1.0.5`.

2. Run the `make` command, followed by the `make install` command.

   These commands perform the following actions:

   - Install the `lidsadm` program in `/sbin`.

   - Create the necessary configuration files (`lids.cap`, `lids.conf`, `lids.net`, `lids.pw`) in `/etc/lids`.

3. Run the `/sbin/lidsadm -P` command and enter a password for the LIDS system.

   This password is stored in the `/etc/lids/lids.pw` file, in RipeMD-160 encrypted format.

4. Run the `/sbin/lidsadm -U` command to update the `inode/dev` numbers.

5. Configure the `/etc/lids/lids.net` file. A simplified default `/etc/lids/lids.net` file is shown in Listing 8-1.

Listing 8-1: /etc/lids/lids.net

```
MAIL_SWITCH= 1
MAIL_RELAY=127.0.0.1:25
MAIL_SOURCE=lids.sinocluster.com
MAIL_FROM= LIDS_ALERT@lids.sinocluster.com
MAIL_TO= root@localhost
MAIL_SUBJECT= LIDS Alert
```

- The `MAIL_SWITCH` option can be 1 or 0 (1 turns on the e-mail alert function, 0 turns it off). Leave the default (1) as is.

- Set the `MAIL_RELAY` option to the IP address of the mail server that LIDS should use to send the alert message.

  If you run the mail server on the same machine you are configuring LIDS for, leave the default as is. The port number, 25, is the default SMTP port and should be left alone unless you are running your mail server on a different port.

- Set the `MAIL_SOURCE` option to the hostname of the machine being configured. Change the default to the appropriate hostname of your system.

- Set the `MAIL_FROM` option to an address that tells you which system the alert is coming from. Change the default to reflect the hostname of your system.

TIP

You don't need a real mail account for the *from* address. The `MAIL_TO` option should be set to the e-mail address of the administrator of the system being configured. Because the `root` address, `root@localhost`, is the default administrative account, you can leave it as is. The `MAIL_SUBJECT` option is obvious and should be changed as needed.

6. Run the `/sbin/lidsadm -L` command, which should show output like the following:

```
LIST
        Subject                 ACCESS TYPE   Object
        --------------------------------------------------------
        Any File                READ          /sbin
        Any File                READ          /bin
        Any File                READ          /boot
        Any File                READ          /lib
        Any File                READ          /usr
        Any File                DENY          /etc/shadow
        /bin/login              READ          /etc/shadow
        /bin/su                 READ          /etc/shadow
        Any File                APPEND        /var/log
        Any File                WRITE         /var/log/wtmp
        /sbin/fsck.ext2         WRITE         /etc/mtab
        Any File                WRITE         /etc/mtab
        Any File                WRITE         /etc
        /usr/sbin/sendmail      WRITE         /var/log/sendmail.st
        /bin/login              WRITE         /var/log/lastlog
        /bin/cat                READ          /home/xhg
        Any File                DENY          /home/httpd
        /usr/sbin/httpd         READ          /home/httpd
        Any File                DENY          /etc/httpd/conf
        /usr/sbin/httpd         READ          /etc/httpd/conf
        /usr/sbin/sendmail      WRITE         /var/log/sendmail.st
        /usr/X11R6/bin/XF86_SVGA NO_INHERIT   RAWIO
        /usr/sbin/in.ftpd       READ          /etc/shadow
        /usr/sbin/httpd         NO_INHERIT    HIDDEN
```

This step reveals what's protected by default.

Because you aren't likely to have `/home/xhg` (the home directory of the author of LIDS), you can remove the configuration for it using the `/sbin/lidsadm -D -s /bin/cat -o /home/xhg` command. You can leave everything else as is, making changes later as needed.

7. Add the following line to the /etc/rc.d/rc.local file to seal the kernel during the end of the boot cycle:

   /sbin/lidsadm -I

8. Enter lids at the LILO prompt.

   This step reboots the system and chooses the LIDS-enabled kernel.

When the system boots and runs the /sbin/lidsadm -I command from the /etc/rc.d/rc.local script, it seals the kernel and the system is protected by LIDS.

Administering LIDS

After you have your LIDS-enabled Linux system in place, you can modify your initial settings as the needs of your organization change. Except for the /etc/lids/lids.net file, you must use the /sbin/lidsadm program to modify the LIDS configuration files: /etc/lids/lids.conf, /etc/lids/lids.pw, and /etc/lids/lids.cap.

- ◆ The /etc/lids/lids.conf file stores the Access Control List (ACL) information.

- ◆ The /etc/lids/lids.cap file contains all the capability rules for the system.

  You can enable or disable a specific capability on the system by editing this file, using the /sbin/lidsadm command. Put a plus sign (+) in front of a capability's name to enable it; use a minus sign (-) to disable.

- ◆ The /etc/lids/lids.net file configures the mail setup needed for e-mailing security alerts. You can use a regular text editor such as vi, emacs, or pico to edit this file.

When LIDS must stop for system-administration tasks, do the following:

- ◆ Use the /sbin/lidsadm -S -- -LIDS or the /sbin/lidsadm -S -- -LIDS_GLOBAL command.

- ◆ Provide the LIDS password to switch off LIDS.

After you make changes in a LIDS configuration file (using the lidsadm command), reload the updated configuration into the kernel by running the /sbin/lidsadm -S -- + RELOAD_CONF command.

To add a new ACL in the /etc/lids/lids.conf file, use the /sbin/lidsadm command like this:

/sbin/lidsadm -A [-s *subject*] [-t | -d | -i] -o *object* -j TARGET

In the preceding line of code

◆ The -A option tells the /sbin/lidsadm program to add a new ACL.

◆ The -s *subject* option specifies a subject of the ACL.

A subject can be any program (for example, /bin/cat).

 TIP When you don't specify a subject, the ACL applies to everything.

◆ The -t, -d, and -i options aren't typically needed.

◆ The -o *object* option specifies the name of the object, which can be one of the following:

- File
- Directory
- Capability

Each ACL requires a named object.

◆ The -j *TARGET* option specifies the target of the ACL.

- When the new ACL has a file or directory as the object, the target can be READ, WRITE, APPEND, DENY, or IGNORE.
- If the object is a Linux capability, the target must be either INHERIT or NO_INHERIT. This defines whether the object's children can have the same capability.

PROTECTING FILES AND DIRECTORIES

You can use lidsadm to protect important files and directories. LIDS provides the following types of protection for files and directories

◆ READ: Makes a file or directory read-only

◆ WRITE: Allows modifications of the file or directory

◆ IGNORE: Ignores all other protections that may be set for a file or directory

◆ APPEND: Allows adding to the file

◆ DENY: Denies all access to the file or directory

MAKING FILES OR DIRECTORIES READ-ONLY To make a file called /path/
filename read-only so that no one can change it, run the following command:

```
/sbin/lids -A -o /path/filename -j READ
```

To make a directory called /mypath read-only, run the following command:

```
/sbin/lids -A -o /mypath -j READ
```

 No program can write to the file or directory. Because you don't specify a
subject in any of the preceding commands, the ACL applies to all programs.

DENYING ACCESS TO A FILE OR DIRECTORY To deny access to a file called
/etc/shadow, run the following command:

```
/sbin/lids -A -o /etc/shadow -j DENY
```

After you run the preceding command and the LIDS configuration is reloaded,
you can run commands such as ls -l /etc/shadow and cat /etc/shadow to
check whether you can access the file. None of these programs can see the file
because we implicitly specified the subject as all the programs in the system.
However, if a program such as /bin/login should access the /etc/shadow file,
you can allow it to have read access by creating a new ACL, as in the following
command:

```
/sbin/lids -A -s /bin/login -o /etc/shadow -j READ
```

ENABLING APPEND-ONLY ACCESS Typically, programs need append-only access
only to critical system logs such as /var/log/messages or /var/log/secure. You
can enable append-only mode for these two files using the following commands:

```
/sbin/lids -A -o /var/log/messages -j APPEND
/sbin/lids -A -o /var/log/secure -j APPEND
```

ALLOWING WRITE-ONLY ACCESS To allow a program called /usr/local/
apache/bin/httpd to write to a protected directory called /home/httpd, run the
following commands:

```
/sbin/lids -A -o /home/httpd -j DENY
/sbin/lids -A -s /usr/local/apache/bin/httpd -o /home/httpd -j READ
```

DELETING AN ACL   To delete all the ACL rules, run the /sbin/lidsadm -Z command. To delete an individual ACL rule, simply specify the subject (if any) and/or the object of the ACL. For example, if you run /sbin/lidsadm -D -o /bin command, all the ACL rules with /bin as the object are deleted. However, if you run /sbin/lidsadm -D -s /bin/login -o /bin, then only the ACL that specifies /bin/login as the subject and /bin as the object is deleted.

 Specifying the -Z option or the -D option without any argument deletes all your ACL rules.

USING MY PREFERRED FILE AND DIRECTORY PROTECTION SCHEME   Here's my preferred file and directory protection scheme.

```
# Make the /boot directory or partition read-only
/sbin/lidsadm -A -o /boot -j READ
# Make the system library directory read-only
# This protects the lib/modules as well
/sbin/lidsadm -A -o /lib -j READ
# Make the root user's home directory read-only
/sbin/lidsadm -A -o /root -j READ
# Make the system configuration directory read-only
/sbin/lidsadm -A -o /etc -j READ
# Make the daemon binary directory read-only
/sbin/lidsadm -A -o /sbin -j READ
# Make the other daemon binary directory read-only
/sbin/lidsadm -A -o /usr/sbin -j READ
# Make the general binary directory read-only
/sbin/lidsadm -A -o /bin -j READ
# Make the other general binary directory read-only
/sbin/lidsadm -A -o /usr/bin -j READ
# Make the general library directory read-only
/sbin/lidsadm -A -o /usr/lib -j READ
# Make the system log directory append-only
/sbin/lidsadm -A -o /var/log -j APPEND
# Make the X Windows binary directory read-only
/sbin/lidsadm -A -o /usr/X11R6/bin -j READ
```

Apart from protecting your files and directories using the preceding technique, LIDS can use the Linux Capabilities to limit the capabilities of a running program (that is, process). In a traditional Linux system, the root user (that is, a user with UID and GID set to 0) has all the "Capabilities" or ability to perform any task by running any process. LIDS uses Linux Capabilities to break down all the power of the `root` (or processes run by `root` user) into pieces so that you can fine-tune the capabilities of a specific process. To find more about the available Linux Capabilities, see the `/usr/include/linux/capability.h header` file. Table 8-1 lists all Linux Capabilities and their status (on or off) in the default LIDS Capabilities configuration file `/etc/lids/lids.cap`.

TABLE 8-1: LIST OF LINUX CAPABILITIES

#	Capability Name	Meaning	Status in /etc/lids/lids.cap
0	CAP_CHOWN	Allow/disallow the changing of file ownership	Allow
1	CAP_DAC_OVERRIDE	Allow/disallow override of all DAC access restrictions	Allow
2	CAP_DAC_READ_SEARCH	Allow/disallow override of all DAC restrictions regarding read and search	Allow
3	CAP_FOWNER	Allow/disallow the following restrictions: (1) that the effective user ID shall match the file owner ID when setting the S_ISUID and S_ISGID bits on a file; (2) that the effective group ID shall match the file owner ID when setting that bit on a file	Allow
4	CAP_FSETID	Allow/disallow access when the effective user ID does not equal owner ID	Allow
5	CAP_KILL	Allow/disallow the sending of signals to processes belonging to others	Allow
6	CAP_SETGID	Allow/disallow changing of the GID	Allow
7	CAP_SETUID	Allow/disallow changing of the UID	Allow
8	CAP_SETPCAP	Allow/disallow the transferring and removal of current set to any PID	Allow

Continued

TABLE 8-1: LIST OF LINUX CAPABILITIES *(Continued)*

#	Capability Name	Meaning	Status in /etc/lids/lids.cap
9	CAP_LINUX_IMMUTABLE	Allow/disallow the modification of immutable and append-only files	Disallow
10	CAP_NET_BIND_SERVICE	Allow/disallow binding to ports below 1024	Disallow
11	CAP_NET_BROADCAST	Allow/disallow broadcasting/ listening to multicast	Allow
12	CAP_NET_ADMIN	Allow/disallow network administration of the following tasks: (1) interface configuration; (2) administration of IP firewall; (3)masquerading and accounting; (4) setting debug option on sockets; (5) modification of routing tables; (6) setting arbitrary process / process group ownership on sockets; (7) binding to any address for transparent proxying; (8) setting Type Of Service (TOS); (9) setting promiscuous mode; (10) clearing driver statistics; (11) multicasting; (12) read/write of device-specific registers	Disallow
13	CAP_NET_RAW	Allow/disallow use of raw sockets	Disallow
14	CAP_IPC_LOCK	Allow/disallow locking of shared memory segments	Allow
15	CAP_IPC_OWNER	Allow/disallow IPC ownership checks	Allow
16	CAP_SYS_MODULE	Allow/disallow insertion and removal of kernel modules	Disallow
17	CAP_SYS_RAWIO	Allow ioperm(2)/iopl (2) to access CAP_SYS_CHROOT chroot(2)	Disallow
18	CAP_SYS_CHROOT	Allow/disallow chroot system call	Disallow
19	CAP_SYS_PTRACE	Allow/disallow ptrace	Allow

#	Capability Name	Meaning	Status in /etc/lids/lids.cap
20	CAP_SYS_PACCT	Allow/disallow configuration of process accounting	Allow
21	CAP_SYS_ADMIN	Allow/disallow various system administration tasks	Allow
22	CAP_SYS_BOOT	Allow/disallow reboot	Allow
23	CAP_SYS_NICE	Allow/disallow changing of process priority using the nice command	Allow
24	CAP_SYS_RESOURCE	Allow/disallow setting of system resource limit	Allow
25	CAP_SYS_TIME	Allow/disallow setting of system time	Allow
26	CAP_SYS_TTY_CONFIG	Allow/disallow pseudo terminal (TTY) configuration	Allow
27	CAP_MKNOD	Allow/disallow the privileged aspects of mknod() system call	Allow
28	CAP_LEASE	Allow/disallow taking of leases on files	Allow
29	CAP_HIDDEN	Allow/disallow hiding of a process to rest of the system	Allow
30	CAP_INIT_KILL	Allow/disallow programs the capability of killing children of the init process (PID = 1)	Allow

The default settings for the Linux Capabilities that appear in Table 8-1 are stored in the /etc/lids/lids.cap file, as shown in Listing 8-2.

Listing 8-2: /etc/lids/lids.cap

```
+0:CAP_CHOWN
+1:CAP_DAC_OVERRIDE
+2:CAP_DAC_READ_SEARCH
+3:CAP_FOWNER
+4:CAP_FSETID
+5:CAP_KILL
+6:CAP_SETGID
+7:CAP_SETUID
```

Continued

Listing 8-2 *(Continued)*

```
+8:CAP_SETPCAP
-9:CAP_LINUX_IMMUTABLE
-10:CAP_NET_BIND_SERVICE
+11:CAP_NET_BROADCAST
-12:CAP_NET_ADMIN
-13:CAP_NET_RAW
+14:CAP_IPC_LOCK
+15:CAP_IPC_OWNER
-16:CAP_SYS_MODULE
-17:CAP_SYS_RAWIO
-18:CAP_SYS_CHROOT
+19:CAP_SYS_PTRACE
+20:CAP_SYS_PACCT
-21:CAP_SYS_ADMIN
+22:CAP_SYS_BOOT
+23:CAP_SYS_NICE
+24:CAP_SYS_RESOURCE
+25:CAP_SYS_TIME
+26:CAP_SYS_TTY_CONFIG
+27:CAP_MKNOD
+28:CAP_LEASE
+29:CAP_HIDDEN
+30:CAP_INIT_KILL
```

The + sign enables the capability; the - sign disables it. For example, in the preceding listing, the last Linux Capability called `CAP_INIT_KILL` is enabled, which means that a `root`-owned process could kill any child process (typically daemons) created by the `init` process. Using a text editor, enable or disable the Linux Capabilities you want.

PROTECTING YOUR SYSTEM USING LIDS-MANAGED LINUX CAPABILITIES

You can use LIDS-provided capabilities to protect your system. Here you learn how to use the Linux Capabilities managed by LIDS.

PROTECTING DAEMONS FROM BEING KILLED BY ROOT Typically, the `init` process starts daemon processes such as the Sendmail mail transport agent and Apache Web server. If you want to protect them from being killed by the `root` user, modify the `CAP_INIT_KILL` settings in `/etc/lids/lids.cap` to the following:

```
-30:CAP_INIT_KILL
```

After you have reloaded the LIDS configuration (using the `/sbin/lidsadm -S --+ RELOAD_CONF` command) or rebooted the system and sealed the kernel (using the

/sbin/lidsadm -I command in the /etc/rc.d/rc.local script) you (as root) can't kill the init children. This ensures that even if your system is compromised and an intruder has gained root privileges, he can't kill the daemons and replace them with his Trojan versions.

HIDING PROCESSES FROM EVERYONE By default, the CAP_HIDDEN capability is turned on in the /etc/lids/lids.cap configuration file. This can hide a process from everyone using the following command (*/path/to/binary* is the fully quali-fied path to the executable that you want to hide when running):

```
lidsadm -A -s /path/to/binary -t -o CAP_HIDDEN -j INHERIT
```

For example, to hide the Apache server process /usr/local/apache/bin/httpd when running, simply run the following command:

```
lidsadm -A -s /usr/local/apache/bin/httpd -t -o CAP_HIDDEN -j INHERIT
```

This labels the process as hidden in the kernel and it can't be found using any user-land tools such as ps, top, or even by exploring files in the /proc filesystem.

DISABLING RAW DEVICE ACCESS BY PROCESSES Normally, only special processes need access to raw devices. So it's a good idea to disable accesses to raw devices and enable as needed, which conforms to the overall security concept of *close all, open only what you need.*

The raw device access is controlled using the CAP_SYS_RAWIO capability, which is disabled by default in the /etc/lids/lids.cap configuration file. If the capa-bility were enabled, processes could access such raw block devices as

- ♦ ioperm/iopi
- ♦ /dev/port
- ♦ /dev/mem
- ♦ /dev/kmem

For example, when this capability is off (as in the default) the /sbin/lilo program can't function properly because it needs raw device-level access to the hard disk.

But some special programs may want this capability to run properly, such as XF86_SVGA. In this case, we can add the program in the exception list like this:

```
lidsadm -A -s /usr/X11R6/bin/XF86_SVGA -t -o CAP_SYS_RAWIO -j INHERIT
```

This makes XF86_SVGA have the capability of CA_SYS_RAWIO while other programs are unable to obtain CAP_SYS_RAWIO.

DISABLING NETWORK-ADMINISTRATION TASKS   By default, the CAP_NET_ADMIN capability is turned off, which means that a network administrator (typically the root user) can no longer do the following network administration tasks:

◆ Configuring Ethernet interface

◆ Administering IP firewall, masquerading, and accounting

◆ Setting debug option on sockets

◆ Modifying routing tables

◆ Setting arbitrary process or process group ownership on sockets

◆ Binding to any address for transparent proxying

◆ Setting Type Of Service (TOS)

◆ Setting promiscuous mode

◆ Clearing driver statistics

◆ Multicasting

◆ Reading/writing device-specific registers

The default setting (this capability is turned off) is highly recommended. For one of the preceding tasks, simply take down LIDS temporarily using the /sbin/ lidsadm -S -- -LIDS command.

PROTECTING THE LINUX IMMUTABLE FLAG FOR FILES   The ext2 filesystem has an extended feature that can flag a file as immutable. This is done using the chattr command. For example, the chattr +i /path/to/myfile turns /path/to/myfile into an immutable file. A file with the immutable attribute can't be modified or deleted or renamed, nor can it be symbolically linked. However, the root user can change the flag by using the chattr -i /path/to/myfile command. Now, you can protect immutable files even from the super user (root) by disabling the CAP_LINUX_IMMUTABLE capability.

   The CAP_LINUX_IMMUTABLE capability is disabled by default in /etc/lids/lids.cap.

DETECTING SCANNERS   If you have enabled the built-in port scanner during kernel compilation as recommended in the Patching, compiling, and installing the

kernel with LIDS section, you can detect port scanners. This scanner can detect half-open scan, SYN stealth port scan, Stealth FIN, Xmas, Null scan, and so on. The detector can spot such tools as Nmap and Satan – and it's useful when the raw socket (CAP_NET_RAW) is disabled.

When CAP_NET_RAW is turned off, some common scanners available to users (most of which are based on sniffing) don't work properly. But the kernel-based scanner provided by LIDS is more secure to begin with — it doesn't use any socket. You may want to consider using the LIDS-supplied scanner in tandem with (or instead of) turning off the raw socket.

RESPONDING TO AN INTRUDER

When LIDS detects a violation of any ACL rule, it can respond to the action by the following methods:

♦ **Logging the message.** When someone violates an ACL rule, LIDS logs a message using the kernel log daemon (klogd).

♦ **Sending e-mail to appropriate authority.** LIDS can send e-mail when a violation occurs. This feature is controlled by the /etc/lids/lids.net file.

♦ **Hanging up the console.** If you have enabled this option during kernel patching for LIDS (as discussed in Step 9 in the section called "Patching, compiling, and installing the kernel with LIDS"), the console is dropped when a user violates an ACL rule.

Another similar system to LIDS is the OpenWall project (www.openwall.com/linux/). The OpenWall project has some security features that differ from those of LIDS – one of the OpenWall patches (for example) makes the stack area of a process nonexecutable. Take a look at this work-in-progress project.

Using libsafe to Protect Program Stacks

Process stacks are vulnerable to buffer overflow – and you can bet that hackers know it. Exploitation of that vulnerability makes up a significant portion of security attacks in recent years.

You can address this problem by including a dynamically loadable library called libsafe in the kernel. The libsafe program has distinctive advantages:

◆ libsafe works with existing binary programs.

◆ libsafe doesn't require special measures such as:

■ Operating-system modifications

■ Access to the source code of defective programs

■ Recompilation or offline processing of binaries

◆ libsafe can be implemented system-wide and remain transparent to users.

The libsafe solution is based on a middleware software layer that intercepts all function calls made to library functions that are known to be vulnerable. In response to such calls, libsafe creates a substitute version of the corresponding function to carry out the original task — but in a manner that contains any buffer overflow within the current stack frame. This strategy prevents attackers from "smashing" (overwriting) the return address and hijacking the control flow of a running program.

libsafe can detect and prevent several known attacks, but its real benefit is that it can prevent yet unknown attacks — and do it all with negligible performance overhead.

That said, most network-security professionals accept that fixing defective (vulnerable) programs is the best solution to buffer-overflow attacks — *if* you know that a particular program is defective. The true benefit of using libsafe and other alternative security measures is protection against future buffer overflow attacks on programs that aren't known to be vulnerable.

libsafe doesn't support programs linked with libc5. If a process protected by libsafe experiences a segmentation fault, use the ldd utility to determine whether the process is linked with libc5. If that is the case, then either recompile/re-link the application with libc6 (that is, glibc) or download a newer version that has been linked with libc6. Most applications are offered with a libc6 version.

One known source of vulnerability in some programs is their use of easily exploited functions in the C programming language. libsafe currently monitors the unsafe C functions listed in Table 8-2.

TABLE 8-2: LIST OF UNSAFE C FUNCTIONS MONITORED BY LIBSAFE

C Function	Potential Damage
strcpy(char *dest, const char *src)	May overflow the dest buffer
strcat(char *dest, const char *src)	May overflow the dest buffer
getwd(char *buf)	May overflow the buf buffer
gets(char *s)	May overflow the s buffer
[vf]scanf(const char *format, ...)	May overflow its arguments
realpath(char *path, char resolved_path[])	May overflow the path buffer
[v]sprintf(char *str, const char *format, ...)	May overflow the str buffer

Compiling and installing libsafe

The source code for libsafe is available for download at the following Web address:

www.research.avayalabs.com/project/libsafe

To use libsafe, download the latest version (presently 2.0) and extract it into the /usr/local/src directory. Then follow these steps:

1. As root, change directory to /usr/local/src/libsafe and run make to compile libsafe.

   If you get error messages, consult the INSTALL file for help.

2. After you have compiled libsafe, install the library using the make install command.

3. Before you can use libsafe, you must set the LD_PRELOAD environment variable for each of the processes you want to protect with libsafe. Simply add the following lines to your /etc/bashrc script:

   LD_PRELOAD=/lib/libsafe.so.1
   export LD_PRELOAD

4. Modify the /etc/cshrc script to include the following line:

   setenv LD_PRELOAD /lib/libsafe.so.1

After adding libsafe protection for your processes, use your programs as you would normally. libsafe transparently checks the parameters for supported unsafe functions. If such a violation is detected, libsafe takes the following measures:

◆ The entire process group receives a SIGKILL signal.

◆ An entry is added to /var/log/secure. The following is an example of such an entry:

```
Feb 26 13:57:40 k2 libsafe[15704]: Detected an attempt to
write across stack boundary.
Feb 26 13:57:40 k2 libsafe[15704]: Terminating
/users/ttsai/work/security.DO_2/test/t91
Feb 26 13:57:40 k2 libsafe[15704]: scanf()
```

For greater security, the dynamic loader disregards environmental variables such as LD_PRELOAD when it executes set-UID programs. However, you can still use libsafe with set-UID programs if you use one of the following two methods:

◆ Append the path to libsafe.so.1 to /etc/ld.so.preload instead of using the LD_PRELOAD environment variable.

If you use /etc/ld.so.preload, install libsafe.so.1 on your root filesystem, for instance in /lib, as is done by the default installation. Using a directory that isn't available at boot time, such as /usr/local/lib causes trouble at the next reboot. You should also remove libsafe from /etc/ld.so.preload when installing a new version. First test it using LD_PRELOAD. Then — and only if everything is okay — you can put it back into /etc/ld.so.preload.

◆ If you have a version of ld.so that's more recent than 1.9.0, you can set LD_PRELOAD to contain only the base name libsafe.so.1 without having to include the directory.

If you use this approach, the file is found if it's in the shared library path (which usually contains /lib and /usr/lib).

Because the search is restricted to the library search path, this also works for set-UID programs.

Add the following lines to the `/etc/bashrc` script:

```
LD_PRELOAD=libsafe.so.1
export LD_PRELOAD
```

Add the following line to the `/etc/csh.cshrc` script.

```
setenv LD_PRELOAD libsafe.so.1
```

 This line makes `libsafe` easier to turn off if something goes wrong.

After you have installed libsafe and appropriately configured either `LD_PRELOAD` or `/etc/ld.so.preload`, `libsafe` is ready to run. You can monitor processes with no changes.

If a process attempts to use one of the monitored functions to overflow a buffer on the stack, the following actions happen immediately:

♦ A violation is declared.

♦ A message is output to the standard error stream.

♦ An entry is made in `/var/log/secure`.

♦ A core dump and a stack dump are produced (provided the corresponding options are enabled) during compilation. (See the `libsafe/INSTALL` file.)

Programs written in C have always been plagued with buffer overflows. Two reasons contribute to this:

♦ Many functions provided by the standard C library (such as those listed in the introduction) are unsafe.

♦ The C programming language doesn't automatically check the bounds of references to arrays and pointers.

 Many programs experience buffer overflows — which makes them vulnerable, without exception, to security attacks. Programmers should check explicitly to ensure that these functions can't overflow any buffers — but too often they omit such checks.

libsafe in action

libsafe uses a novel method to detect and handle buffer-overflow attacks. Without requiring source code, it can transparently protect processes against stack-smashing attacks — even on a system-wide basis — by intercepting calls to vulnerable library functions, substituting overflow-resistant versions of such functions, and restricting any buffer overflow to the current stack frame.

The key to using libsafe effectively is to estimate a safe upper limit on the size of buffers — and to instruct libsafe to impose it automatically. This estimation can't be performed at compile time; the size of the buffer may not yet be known then. For the most realistic estimate of a safe upper limit, calculate the buffer size *after* the start of the function that makes use of the buffer. This method can help you determine the maximum buffer size by preventing such local buffers from extending beyond the end of the current stack frame — thus enabling the substitute version of the function to limit how many times a process may write to the buffer without exceeding the estimated buffer size. When the return address from that function (which is located on the stack) can't be overwritten, control of the process can't be commandeered.

Summary

LIDS is a great tool to protect your Linux system from intruders. Since LIDS is a kernel level intrusion protection scheme, it is hard to defeat using traditional hacking tricks. In fact, a sealed LIDS system is very difficult to hack. Similarly, a system with Libsafe support can protect your programs against buffer overflow attacks, which are the most common exploitations of weak server software. By implementing LIDS and Libsafe on your system, you are taking significant preventive measures against attacks. These two tools significantly enhance overall system security.

Chapter 9

Securing Files and Filesystems

IN THIS CHAPTER

- ◆ Managing files, directories, and permissions
- ◆ Using groups for file security
- ◆ Using `ext2` security features
- ◆ Checking file integrity

FILES are at the heart of modern computing. Virtually everything you do with a computer these days creates, accesses, updates, or deletes files in your computer or on a remote server. When you access the Web via your PC, you access files. It doesn't matter if you access a static HTML page over the Web or run a Java Servlet on the server, everything you do is about files. A file is the most valuable object in computing.

Unfortunately, most computer users don't know how to take care of their files. For example, hardly anyone takes a systematic, process-oriented approach to storing files by creating a manageable directory hierarchy. Often over the past decade I have felt that high schools or and colleges should offer courses to teach everyone to manage computer files.

Although lack of organization in file management impedes productivity, it isn't the only problem with files. Thanks to many popular personal operating systems from one vendor, hardly anyone with a PC knows anything about file security. When users migrate from operating systems such as MS-DOS and Windows 9*x*, they are 100 percent unprepared to understand how files work on Linux or other Unix/Unix-like operating systems. This lack of understanding can became a serious security liability, so this chapter introduces file and directory permissions in terms of their security implications. I also examine technology that helps reduce the security risks associated with files and filesystems.

Managing Files, Directories, and User Group Permissions

If a user creates, modifies, or deletes a file that doesn't have appropriate file permissions and a malicious user from inside (or a hacker from outside) can get hold

179

of the file, the result is a probable security problem for the user or the system. It's very important that everyone – both user and system administrator – understand file permissions in depth. (If you already do, you may want to skim or skip the next few sections.)

Understanding file ownership & permissions

Every file on a Linux system is associated with a user and a group. Consider an example:

```
-rw-rw-r— 1 sheila  intranet  512 Feb 6 21:11 milkyweb.txt
```

The preceding line is produced by the `ls -l milkyweb.txt` command on my Red Hat Linux system. (You may already know that the `ls` program lists files and directories.) The `-l` option shows the complete listing for the `milkyweb.txt` file. Now consider the same information in a tabular format in Table 9-1.

TABLE 9-1: OUTPUT OF AN EXAMPLE LS –1 COMMAND

Information Type	ls Output
File access permission	`-rw-rw-r—`
Number of links	1
User (file owner)	`Sheila`
Group	`Intranet`
File size (in bytes)	512
Last modification date	`Feb 6`
Last modification time	`21:11`
Filename	`milkyweb.txt`

Here the `milkyweb.txt` file is owned by a user called `sheila`. She is the only regular user who can change the access permissions of this file. The only other user who can change the permissions is the superuser (that is, the `root` account). The group for this file is `intranet`. Any user who belongs to the `intranet` group can access (read, write, or execute) the file under current group permission settings (established by the owner).

To become a file owner, a user must create the file. Under Red Hat Linux, when a user creates a file or directory, its group is also set to the default group of the user (which is the private group with the same name as the user). For example, say that I log in to my Red Hat Linux system as `kabir` and (using a text editor such as `vi`) create a file called `todo.txt`. If I do an `ls -l todo.txt` command, the following output appears:

```
-rw-rw-r- 1 kabir    kabir    4848 Feb 6 21:37 todo.txt
```

As you can see, the file owner and the group name are the same; under Red Hat Linux, user `kabir`'s default (private) group is also called `kabir`. This may be confusing, but it's done to save you some worries, and of course you can change this behavior quite easily. Under Red Hat Linux, when a user creates a new file, the following attributes apply:

◆ The file owner is the file creator.

◆ The group is the owner's default group.

As a regular user, you can't reassign a file or directory's ownership to someone else. For example, I can't create a file as user Kabir and reassign its ownership to a user called Sheila. Wonder why this is so? Security, of course. If a regular user can reassign file ownership to others, someone could create a nasty program that deletes files, changes the program's ownership to the superuser, and wipes out the entire filesystem. Only the superuser can reassign file or directory ownership.

Changing ownership of files and directories using chown

As a superuser, you can change the ownership of a file or directory using the `chown` command:

```
chown  newuser file or directory
```

For example:

```
chown  sheila kabirs_plans.txt
```

This command makes user `sheila` the new owner of the file `kabirs_plans.txt`.

If the superuser would also like to change the group for a file or directory, she can use the `chown` command like this:

```
chown  newuser.newgroup file or directory
```

For example:

```
chown  sheila.admin kabirs_plans.txt
```

The preceding command not only makes `sheila` the new owner, but also resets the group of the file to `admin`.

If the superuser wants to change the user and/or the group ownership of all the files or directories under a given directory, she can use the `-R` option to run the `chown` command in recursive mode. For example:

```
chown  -R sheila.admin /home/kabir/plans/
```

The preceding command changes the user and group ownership of the `/home/kabir/plans/` directory — and all the files and subdirectories within it.

Although you must be the superuser to change the ownership of a file, you can still change a file or directory's group as a regular user using the `chgrp` command.

Changing group ownership of files and directories with chgrp

The `chgrp` command enables you to change the group ownership of a file or directory if you are also part of the new group. This means you can change groups only if you belong to both the old *and* new groups, as in this example:

```
chgrp httpd  *.html
```

If I run the preceding command to change the group for all the HTML files in a directory, I must also be part of the `httpd` group. You can find what groups you are in using the `groups` command without any argument. Like the `chown` command, `chgrp` uses `-R` to recursively change group names of files or directories.

Using octal numbers to set file and directory permissions

Although octal numbers are my favorite method for understanding file and directory access permissions, I must warn you that this approach involves converting octal digits to binary bits. If you feel mathematically challenged, you can skip this section; the next section explains the same permissions using a somewhat simpler concept: the access string.

Since octal numbers are useful in an accurate explanation of access permissions, a small memory refresher is in order. The octal number system uses eight digits in the same way the decimal system uses ten; the familiar decimal digits are 0-9, the corresponding octal digits are 0-7. This difference has a practical use: In the binary system of ones and zeros that underlies computer code, each octal digit can represent *three* binary bits. Table 9-2 shows the binary equivalent for each octal digit.

TABLE 9-2: OCTAL DIGITS AND THEIR BINARY EQUIVALENTS

Octal	Binary
0	000
1	001
2	010
3	011
4	100
5	101
6	110
7	111

This table demonstrates the relative efficiency of the octal system. An administrator has to set permissions for many different files and directories; this compact numeric system puts a practical limit on the number of bits required in a representation of any one file/directory permission.

 When any of these digits is omitted, the space next to the leftmost digit is considered a zero.

Table 9-3 shows a few example permission values that use octal digits.

TABLE 9-3: EXAMPLE PERMISSION VALUES USING OCTAL DIGITS

Permission Value	Explanation
0400	Only read (r) permission for the file owner. This is equivalent to 400, where the missing octal digit is treated as a leading zero.
0440	Read (r) permission for both the file owner and the users in the group. This is equivalent to 440.

Continued

TABLE 9-3: EXAMPLE PERMISSION VALUES USING OCTAL DIGITS *(Continued)*

Permission Value	Explanation
0444	Read (r) permission for everyone. This is equivalent to 444.
0644	Read (r) and write (w) permissions for the file owner. Everyone else has read-only access to the file. This is equivalent to 644; the number 6 is derived by adding 4 (r) and 2 (w).
0755	Read (r), write (w), and execute (x) permissions for the file owner and read (r) and execute (x) permissions to the file for everyone else. This is equivalent to 755; the number 7 is derived by adding 4 (r) + 2 (w) + 1 (x).
4755	Same as 755 in the previous example, except this file is set-UID. When an executable file with set-UID permission is run, the process runs as the owner of the file. In other words, if a file is set-UID and owned by the user gunchy, any time it's run, the running program enjoys the privileges of the user gunchy. So if a file is owned by root and the file is also set to set-UID, anyone who can run the file essentially has the privileges of the superuser. If anyone but root can alter a set-UID root file, it's a major security hole. Be very careful when setting the set-UID bit.
2755	Like 755 but also sets the set-GID bit. When such a file is executed, it essentially has all the privileges of the group to which the file belongs.
1755	Like 755 but also sets the sticky bit. The sticky bit is formally known as the *save text mode*. This infrequently used feature tells the operating system to keep an executable program's image in memory even after it exits. This should reduce the startup time of a large program. Instead of setting the sticky bit, recode the application for better performance when possible.

To come up with a suitable permission setting, first determine what access the user, the group, and everyone else should have and consider if the set-UID, set-GID, or sticky bit is necessary. After you have determined the need, you can construct each octal digit using 4 (read), 2 (write), and 1 (execute), or construct a custom value by adding any of these three values. Although using octal numbers to set permissions may seem awkward at the beginning, with practice their use can become second nature.

Using permission strings to set access permissions

One alternative to using octal digits for setting permissions is a method (supposedly simpler) that uses a special version of an access string called a *permission string*. To create a permission string, specify each permission type with one character (shown in parentheses), as in the following example:

- ◆ Whom does the permission affect? You have the following choices:

    - ■ u (user)

    - ■ g (group)

    - ■ o (others)

    - ■ a (all)

- ◆ What permission type should you set? You have the following choices:

    - ■ r (read)

    - ■ w (write)

    - ■ x (execute)

    - ■ s (set-UID or set-GID)

    - ■ t (sticky bit)

- ◆ What is the action type? Are you setting the permission or removing it? When setting the permissions, + specifies an addition and - specifies a removal.

    For example, a permission string such as u+r allows the file owner read access to the file. A permission string such as a+rx allows everyone to read and execute a file. Similarly, u+s makes a file set-UID; g+s makes it set-GID.

Changing access privileges of files and directories using chmod

The chmod (*change mode*) utility can change permission modes. Both the octal and the string method work with this nifty utility, as in this example:

```
chmod 755 *.pl
```

The preceding command changes permissions for files ending with the extension .pl. It sets write and execute permissions for each .pl file (7 = 4 [read] + 2 [write] + 1 [execute]) and grants them to the file's owner. The command also sets the files as readable and executable (5 = 4 [read] + 1 [execute]) by the group and others.

You can accomplish the same using the string method, like this:

```
chmod a+rx,u+w *.pl
```

Here a+rx allows read (r) and execute (x) permissions for all (a), and u+w allows the file owner (u) to write (w) to the file.

Remember these rules for multiple access strings:

◆ Separate each pair of values by a comma.

◆ No space is allowed between the permissions strings.

If you want to change permissions for all the files and subdirectories within a directory, you can use the -R option to perform a recursive permission operation. For example:

```
chmod -R 750 /www/mysite
```

Here the 750 octal permission is applied to all the files and subdirectories of the /www/mysite directory.

The permission settings for a directory are like those for regular files, but not identical. Here are some special notes on directory permissions:

◆ Read-only access to a directory doesn't allow you to cd into that directory; to do that, you need execute permission.

◆ Execute-only permission can access the files inside a directory if the following conditions exist:

■ You know their names.

■ You can read the files.

◆ To list the contents of a directory (using a program such as ls) and also cd into a directory, you need both read and execute permissions.

◆ If you have write permission for a directory, you can create, delete, or modify any files or subdirectories within that directory — even if someone else owns the file or subdirectory.

Managing symbolic links

Apart from the regular files and directories, you encounter another type of file quite frequently — *links* (files that point to other files). A link allows one file or directory to have multiple names. Two types of links exist:

◆ Hard

◆ Soft (symbolic)

Here I discuss the special permission issues that arise from links.

CHANGING PERMISSIONS OR OWNERSHIP OF A HARD LINK

If you change the permission or the ownership of a hard link, it also changes the original file's permission. For example, take a look at the following ls -l output:

```
-rw-r—r—  1 root              21 Feb  7 11:41 todo.txt
```

Now, if the root user creates a hard link (using the command line Len todo.txt plan) called plan for todo.txt, the ls -l output looks like this:

```
-rw-r—r—  2 root              21 Feb  7 11:41 plan
-rw-r—r—  2 root              21 Feb  7 11:41 todo.txt
```

As you can see, the hard link, plan, and the original file (todo.txt) have the same file size (as shown in the fourth column) and also share the same permission and ownership settings. Now, if the root user runs the following command:

```
chown  sheila plan
```

It gives the ownership of the hard link to a user called sheila; will it work as usual? Take a look at the ls -l output after the preceding command:

```
-rw-r—r—  2 sheila   root     21 Feb  7 11:41 plan
-rw-r—r—  2 sheila   root     21 Feb  7 11:41 todo.txt
```

As you can see, the chown command changed the ownership of plan, but the ownership of todo.txt (the original file) has also changed. So when you change the ownership or permissions of a hard link, the effect also applies to the original file.

CHANGING PERMISSIONS OR OWNERSHIP OF A SOFT LINK

Changing the ownership of a symbolic link or soft link doesn't work the same way. For example, take a look at the following ls -l output:

```
lrwxrwxrwx  1 sheila   root      8 Feb  7 11:49 plan -> todo.txt
-rw-r—r—  1 sheila   root     21 Feb  7 11:41 todo.txt
```

Here you can see that the plan file is a symbolic (soft) link for todo.txt. Now, suppose the root user changes the symbolic link's ownership, like this:

```
chown kabir plan
```

The ls -l output shows the following:

```
lrwxrwxrwx   1 kabir    root       8 Feb  7 11:49 plan -> todo.txt
-rw-r—r—  1 sheila   root      21 Feb  7 11:41 todo.txt
```

The question is, can user kabir write to todo.txt using the symbolic link (plan)? The answer is no, unless the directory in which these files are stored is owned by kabir. So changing a soft link's ownership doesn't work in the same way as with hard links. If you change the permission settings of a soft link, however, the file it points to gets the new settings, as in this example:

```
chmod 666 plan
```

This changes the todo.txt file's permission as shown here in the ls -l listing:

```
-rw-rw-rw-   1 kabir    kabir     25 Feb  7 11:52 plan
-rw-r—r—  1 sheila   root      21 Feb  7 11:41 todo.txt
```

So be cautious with links; the permission and ownership settings on these special files are *not* intuitive.

Managing user group permission

Linux user groups are defined in the /etc/group file. A *user group* is a comma-separated user list that has a unique group ID (GID) number. For example:

```
lazyppl:x:666:netrat,mkabir,mrfrog
```

Here the user group called lazyppl has three users (netrat, mkabir, mrfrog) as members.

By default, Red Hat Linux supplies a number of user groups, many of which don't even have a user as a member. These default groups are there for backward compatibility with some programs that you may or may not install. For example, the Unix-to-Unix Copy (uucp) program can use the uucp group in /etc/group, but probably you aren't going to use uucp to copy files over the Internet. You are more likely to use the FTP program instead.

Don't delete these unused groups. The likelihood of breaking a program is high if you do.

USING RED HAT'S PRIVATE USER GROUPS

When you create a new user using the `useradd` command, Red Hat Linux automatically creates a group in the `/etc/group` file. This group has the exact same name as the user and the only member in that group is the user herself. For example, if you create a user called `mrfrog` using the `useradd mrfrog` command, you see this entry in the `/etc/group` file:

```
mrfrog:x:505:
```

This group is used whenever `mrfrog` creates files or directories. But you may wonder why `mrfrog` needs a private user group like that when he already owns everything he creates. The answer, again, has security ramifications: The group prevents anyone else from reading `mrfrog`'s files. Because all files and directories created by the `mrfrog` user allow access only to their owner (`mrfrog`) and the group (again `mrfrog`), no one else can access his files.

CREATING USER GROUPS TO DEPARTMENTALIZE USERS

If several people need access to a set of files or directories, a user group can control access. For example, say that you have three users: `mrfrog`, `kabir`, `sheila` who need read, write, and execute access to a directory called `/www/public/htdocs` directory. You can create a user group called `webmaster` using `groupadd webmaster`, which creates the following entry in the `/etc/group` file:

```
webmaster:x:508:
```

You can modify this line so it looks like this:

```
webmaster:x:508:mrfrog,kabir,sheila
```

Now you can change the `/www/public/htdocs` directory permission, using the `chown :webmaster /www/public/htdocs`.

If you want to change the group ownership for all subdirectories under the named directory, use the `-R` option with the `chown` command.

Now the three users can access files in that directory only if the file-and-directory permissions allow the group users to view, edit, and delete files and directories. To make sure they can, run the `chmod 770 /www/public/htdocs` command. Doing so allows them read, write, and execute permission for this directory. However, when any one of them creates a new file in this directory, it is accessible only by that person; Red Hat Linux automatically sets the file's ownership to the user and group ownership to the user's private group. For example, if the user `kabir` runs the `touch myfile.txt` command to create an empty file, the permission setting for this file is as shown in the following line:

```
-rw-rw-r--   1 kabir    kabir           0 Dec 17 17:41 myfile.txt
```

This means that the other two users in the `webmaster` group can read this file because of the world-readable settings of the file, but they can't modify it or remove it. Because `kabir` wants to allow them to modify or delete this file, he can run the `chgrp webmaster myfile.txt` command to change the file's group permission as shown in the following line:

```
-rw-rw-r--   1 kabir    webmaster       0 Dec 17 17:42 myfile.txt
```

Now everyone in the `webmaster` group can do anything with this file. Because the `chgrp` command is cumbersome to run every time someone creates a new file, you can simply set the `SGID` bit for the directory by using the `chmod 2770 /www/public/htdocs` command. This setting appears as the following when the `ls -l` command is run from the `/www/public` directory.

```
drwxrws---   2 bin      webmaster    4096 Dec 17 17:47 htdocs
```

If any of the `webmaster` members creates a file in the `htdocs` directory, the command gives the group read and write permissions to the file by default.

 When you work with users and groups, back up original files before making any changes. This saves you a lot of time if something goes wrong with the new configuration. You can simply return to the old configurations by replacing the new files with old ones. If you modify the `/etc/group` file manually, make sure you have a way to check for the consistency of information between the `/etc/group` and `/etc/passwd` files.

Checking Consistency of Users and Groups

Many busy and daring system administrators manage the `/etc/group` and `/etc/passwd` file virtually using an editor such as `vi` or `emacs`. This practice is very common and quite dangerous. I recommend that you use `useradd`, `usermod`, and `userdel` commands to create, modify, and delete users and `groupadd`, `groupmod`, and `groupdel` to create, modify, and delete user groups.

When you use these tools to manage your user and group files, you should end up with a consistent environment where all user groups and users are accounted for. However, if you ever end up modifying these files by hand, watch for inconsistencies that can become security risks or at least create a lot of confusion. Also, many system administrators get in the habit of pruning these files every so often to ensure that no unaccounted user group or user is in the system. Doing this manually every time is very unreliable. Unfortunately, no Red Hat-supplied tool exists that can ensure that you don't break something when you try to enhance your system security. This bugged me enough times that I wrote a Perl script called chk_pwd_grp.pl, shown in Listing 9-1, that performs the following consistency checks:

◆ Check for duplicate username and UID in the /etc/passwd file.

◆ Check for invalid GID in the /etc/passwd file.

◆ Check for duplicate group and GID in the /etc/group file.

◆ Check for unused, non-standard groups in the /etc/group file.

◆ Check for nonexistent users in /etc/group who don't exist in /etc/passwd.

Listing 9-1: The chk_pwd_grp.pl script

```perl
#!/usr/bin/perl
#  Purpose: checks /etc/passwd and /etc/group for inconsistencies
#           and produces report
#  Features
#       - checks for duplicate username and UID in /etc/passwd file.
#       - checks for invalid GID in /etc/passwd file.
#       - checks for duplicate group and GID in /etc/group file.
#       - checks for unused, non-standard groups in /etc/group file.
#       - checks for non-existent users in /etc/group who don't exist
#         in /etc/passwd
#
#  Written by: Mohammed J. Kabir (kabir@nitec.com)
#  CVS Id:  $id$
#
use strict;
use constant DEBUG => 0;
my $PASSWD_FILE = '/etc/passwd';
my $GROUP_FILE  = '/etc/group';
# Groups that are supplied by Red Hat by default are considered
# okay even if they don't get used in /etc/passwd
my %DEFAULT_GROUP = (
              root     => 1,  bin      => 1,
```

Continued

Listing 9-1 *(Continued)*

```
              adm     => 1, tty     => 1,
              kmem    => 1, wheel   => 1,
              man     => 1, games   => 1,
              nobody  => 1, users   => 1,
              pppusers => 1, popusers => 1,
              daemon  => 1, sys     => 1,  rpc     => 1,
              disk    => 1, lp      => 1,  mem     => 1,
              mail    => 1, news    => 1,  uucp    => 1,
              gopher  => 1, dip     => 1,  ftp     => 1,
              utmp    => 1, xfs     => 1,  floppy  => 1,
              slipusers => 1, rpcuser => 1,
              slocate => 1
              );
# Get information from the passwd file
my (    $userByUIDRef,
        $uidByGIDRef,
        $uidByUsernameRef)                   = get_user_info($PASSWD_FILE);
# Get information from the group file
my (    $groupByGIDRef,
        $groupByUsernameRef,
        $groupByUserListRef,
        $groupBySizeRef) = get_group_info($GROUP_FILE,
                                          $userByUIDRef,
                                          $uidByGIDRef,
                                          $uidByUsernameRef);
# Make report using information from both passwd and group files
my $report = make_group_report(
                $userByUIDRef,
                $uidByGIDRef,
                $groupByGIDRef,
                $groupByUsernameRef,
                $groupByUserListRef,
                $groupBySizeRef);
# Print report
print $report;
# Exit program
exit 0;
# subroutine blocks
sub get_user_info {
    #
    # Read the passwd file and create multiple hashes needed
    # for analysis
    #
    my $passwdFile = shift;
```

```perl
   # Open file
   open(PWD, $passwdFile) || die "Can't read $passwdFile $!\n";
   # Declare variables
   my (%userByUIDHash, %uidByGIDHash,
       %uidByUsernameHash, $user,$uid,$gid);
   # Set line count
   my $lineCnt = 0;
   # Parse the file and stuff hashes
   while(<PWD>){
     chomp;
     $lineCnt++;
     # Parse the current line
     ($user,undef,$uid,$gid) = split(/:/);
     # Detect duplicate usernames
     if (defined $userByUIDHash{$uid} &&
         $user eq $userByUIDHash{$uid}) {
       warn("Warning! $passwdFile [Line: $lineCnt] : " .
            "multiple  occurance of username $user detected\n");
     # Detect
     } elsif (defined $userByUIDHash{$uid}) {
       warn("Warning! $passwdFile [Line: $lineCnt] : " .
            "UID ($uid) has been used for user $user " .
            "and $userByUIDHash{$uid}\n");
     }
     $userByUIDHash{$uid} = $user;
     $uidByGIDHash{$gid} = $uid;
     $uidByUsernameHash{$user} = $uid;
   }
   close(PWD);
   return(\%userByUIDHash, \%uidByGIDHash, \%uidByUsernameHash);
}
sub get_group_info {
   my ($groupFile, $userByUIDRef, $uidByGIDRef, $uidByUsernameRef) = @_;
   open(GROUP, $groupFile) || die "Can't read $groupFile $!\n";
   my (%groupByGIDHash,
       %groupByUsernameHash,
       %groupByUserListHash,
       %groupBySizeHash,
       %gidByGroupHash,
       $group,$gid,
       $userList);
   my $lineCnt = 0;
   while(<GROUP>){
     chomp;
     $lineCnt++;
```

Continued

Listing 9-1 *(Continued)*

```perl
    # Parse the current line
    ($group,undef,$gid,$userList) = split(/:/);
    # Detect duplicate GID
    if (defined $groupByGIDHash{$gid}) {
        warn("Warning! $GROUP_FILE [Line: $lineCnt] : " .
            "duplicate GID ($gid) found! Group: $group\n");
    } elsif (defined $gidByGroupHash{$group}){
        warn("Warning! $GROUP_FILE [Line: $lineCnt] : " .
            "duplicate group name ($group) detected.\n");
    }
    $groupByGIDHash{$gid} = $group;
    $gidByGroupHash{$group} = $gid;
    foreach my $user (split(/,/,$userList)) {
        # If user doesn't exist in /etc/passwd file
        if (! defined $uidByUsernameRef->{$user}) {
            warn("Warning! $GROUP_FILE [Line: $lineCnt] : user $user " .
                "does not exist in $PASSWD_FILE\n");
        }
        $groupByUsernameHash{$user} = $gid;
        $groupByUserListHash{$gid} = $userList;
        DEBUG and print "Total members for $group = ",
                        scalar (split(/,/,$userList)), "\n";
        $groupBySizeHash{$group} =
                    scalar (split(/,/,$userList))
    }
}
close(PWD);
return(\%groupByGIDHash,
        \%groupByUsernameHash,
        \%groupByUserListHash,
        \%groupBySizeHash);
}
sub make_group_report {
    my ($userByUIDRef,
        $uidByGIDRef,
        $groupByGIDRef,
        $groupByUsernameRef,
        $groupByUserListRef,
        $groupBySizeRef) = @_;
    my $report = '';
    my ($totalGroups,
        $groupName,
        $totalPrivateGroups,
        $totalPublicGroups);
```

```perl
    # Get total user count in /etc/passwd
    my $totalUsers = scalar keys %$userByUIDRef;
    foreach my $gid (sort keys %$groupByGIDRef) {
      $totalGroups++;
      $groupName = $groupByGIDRef->{$gid};
      DEBUG and print "Group: $groupName\n";
      # If group has members listed in the /etc/group file
      # then list them
      if ($groupByUserListRef->{$gid} ne '') {
         $totalPublicGroups++;
      # Maybe this is a private user group?
      } elsif (defined $uidByGIDRef->{$gid}) {
         $totalPrivateGroups++;
      # This is a default user group or an empty group
      } elsif (! defined $DEFAULT_GROUP{$groupName}) {
        warn("Warning! $GROUP_FILE : Non-standard user group " .
             "$groupByGIDRef->{$gid} does not have " .
             "any member.\n");
      }
    }

    # Now check to see if /etc/passwd has any user with
    # invalid group
    foreach my $gid (keys %$uidByGIDRef){
       if (! defined $groupByGIDRef->{$gid}) {
          warn("Warning! $PASSWD_FILE : user " .
               "$userByUIDRef->{$uidByGIDRef->{$gid}} ".
               "belongs to an invalid group (GID=$gid)\n" );
       }
    }

    # Create report
    $report .=<<REPORT;
        Total users  : $totalUsers
        Total groups : $totalGroups
 Private user groups : $totalPrivateGroups
  Public user groups : $totalPublicGroups
GROUP\t\tTOTAL
=====\t\t=====
REPORT
    foreach my $group (reverse
       sort {$groupBySizeRef->{$a} <=> $groupBySizeRef->{$b}}
       keys %$groupBySizeRef) {
       $report .= sprintf("%s\t\t%2d\n",
                    $group,
                    $groupBySizeRef->{$group});
```

Continued

Listing 9-1 *(Continued)*

```
    }
    $report .= "\n";
    return $report;
}
# End of chk_pwd_grp.pl script
```

Before I modify /etc/passwd or /etc/group using the Red Hat-supplied utilities or manually (yes, I am guilty of this habit myself), I simply run the preceding script to check for warning messages. Here is a sample output of the perl chk_pwd_grp.pl command:

```
Warning! /etc/passwd [Line: 2] : UID (0) has been used for user hacker and root
Warning! /etc/group [Line: 3] : user xyz does not exist in /etc/passwd
Warning! /etc/group : Non-standard user group testuser does not have any member.
Warning! /etc/passwd : user hacker belongs to an invalid group (GID=666)
        Total users   : 27
        Total groups  : 40
   Private user groups : 14
    Public user groups : 11
GROUP           TOTAL
=====           =====
daemon          4
bin             3
adm             3
sys             3
lp              2
disk            1
wheel           1
root            1
news            1
mail            1
uucp            1
```

I have many warnings as shown in the first few lines of the above output. Most of these warnings need immediate action:

♦ The /etc/passwd file (line #2) has a user called hacker who uses the same UID (0) as root.

This is definitely very suspicious, because UID (0) grants root privilege! This should be checked immediately.

◆ A user called xyz (found in /etc/group line #3) doesn't even exist in the /etc/passwd file.

This means there is a group reference to a user who no longer exists. This is definitely something that has potential security implications so it also should be checked immediately.

◆ A non-standard user group called testuser exists that doesn't have any members.

A non-standard user group is a group that isn't one of the following:

■ /etc/group by default

■ a private user group

◆ User hacker belongs to an invalid group whose GID is 666.

◆ The script also reports the current group and account information in a simple text report, which can be very useful to watch periodically.

I recommend that you create a small script called cron_chk_pwd_grp.sh, as shown in Listing 9-2, in the /etc/cron.weekly directory.

Listing 9-2: The cron_chk_pwd_grp.sh script

```
#!/bin/sh
# Standard binaries
MAIL=/bin/mail
RM=/bin/rm
PERL=/usr/bin/perl
# Change the path
SCRIPT=/path/to/chk_pwd_grp.pl
TMP_FILE=/tmp/$$
# Change the username
ADMIN=root@localhost
# Get the date and week number
DATE=`/bin/date "+%m-%d-%Y [Week: %U]"`
# Run the script and redirect output
#(STDOUT and STDERR) to $TMP_FILE
$PERL $SCRIPT > $TMP_FILE 2>&1;
# Send the script report via email to ADMIN user
$MAIL -s "User and Group Consistency Report $DATE " \
$ADMIN < $TMP_FILE;
# Delete the temporary file
$RM -f $TMP_FILE;
# Exit
exit 0;
```

◆ Change the SCRIPT=/path/to/chk_pwd_grp.pl line to point to the appropriate, fully qualified path of the chk_pwd_grp.pl script.

◆ Change the ADMIN=root@localhost to the appropriate e-mail address.

Now you receive an e-mail report from the user and group consistency checker script, chk_pwd_grp.pl, on a weekly basis to the e-mail address used for ADMIN.

Securing Files and Directories

A few steps can ensure the security of files and directories on your system. The very first step is to define a system-wide permission setting; next step is to identify the world-accessible files and dealing with them as appropriate; the third step is to locate set-UID and set-GID and dealing with them as appropriate. All of these steps are discussed in the following sections.

Before you can enhance file and directory security, establish the directory scheme Red Hat Linux follows. This helps you plan and manage files and directories.

Understanding filesystem hierarchy structure

Red Hat follows the Filesystem Hierarchy Standard (FHS) maintained at the www.pathname.com/fhs/ Web site. According to the FHS Web site, the FHS defines a common arrangement of the many files and directories in Unix-like systems that many different developers and groups such as Red Hat have agreed to use. Listing 9-3 shows the FHS that Red Hat Linux uses.

Listing 9-3: FHS used in Red Hat Linux

```
/              (root partition)
|
|---dev        (device files)
|---etc        (system configuration files)
|   |---X11    (X Window specific)
|   +---skel   (Template files for user shells)
|
|---lib        (library files)
|---proc       (kernel proc Filesystem)
|---sbin       (system binaries)
|---usr        (userland programs)
|   |---X11R6
|   |---bin    (user executables)
```

```
|   |---dict   (dictionary data files)
|   |---doc    (documentation for binaries)
|   |---etc    (configuration for binaries)
|   |---games  (useless, boring games)
|   |---include  (c header files)
|   |---info     (documentation for binaries)
|   |---lib      (library files for binaries)
|   |---libexec  (library files)
|   |---local    (locally installed software directory)
|   |   |---bin
|   |   |---doc
|   |   |---etc
|   |   |---games
|   |   |---info
|   |   |---lib
|   |   |---man
|   |   |---sbin
|   |   +---src
|   |
|   |---man   (manual pages)
|   |---share (shared files such as documentation)
|   +- src    (linux source code)
|
|---var
|   |---catman
|   |---lib
|   |---local
|   |---lock   (lock directory)
|   |---log    (log directory)
|   |---named
|   |---nis
|   |---preserve
|   |---run
|   +--spool   (spool directory)
|   |   |---anacron
|   |   |---at
|   |   |---cron
|   |   |---fax
|   |   |---lpd
|   |   |---mail    (received mail directory)
|   |   |---mqueue  (mail queue)
|   |   |- news
|   |   |---rwho
|   |   |---samba
```

Continued

Listing 9-3 *(Continued)*

```
|   |   |---slrnpull
|   |   |---squid
|   |   |---up2date
|   |   |---uucp
|   |   |---uucppublic
|   |   |---vbox
|   |   +---voice
|   +---tmp
|
+---tmp  (temporary files)
```

The FHS-based directory structure is reasonably simple. I have provided a brief explanation of what the important directories are all about in the preceding listing. FHS requires that the /usr directory (usually a disk partition by itself) be mounted as read-only, which isn't the case with Red Hat Linux. If /usr is read-only, it enhances system security greatly because no one can modify any binaries in /usr/bin or /usr/local/bin directories (if /usr/local is a subdirectory of /usr and not a separate partition itself).

However, mounting /usr as read-only has one major inconvenience: If you plan to add new software to your system, you probably will write to /usr or one of its subdirectories to install most software. This is probably why the Red Hat-supplied default /etc/fstab file doesn't mount /usr as read-only. Here's what I recommend:

◆ If you make your system available on the Internet, seriously consider making the /usr partition read-only.

◆ Because it's an industry standard not to modify production systems, you can enforce the read-only /usr rule for yourself and others. Fully config-ure your system with all necessary software and test it for a suitable period of time; reconfigure if necessary. Then run the system for another test period with /usr set to read-only. If you don't see any problem with any of your software or services, you should be able to enforce a read-only /usr in your production system.

◆ To make the /usr read-only, modify the /etc/fstab file. Edit the file and comment out the line that mounts /usr using default mount options. This line in my /etc/fstab looks like this:

```
LABEL=/usr  /usr  ext2 defaults  1 2
```

◆ After you have commented this line out by placing a # character in front of the line, you can create a new line like this:

```
LABEL=/usr /usr  ext2 ro,suid,dev,auto,nouser,async  1 2
```

◆ The new fstab line for /usr simply tells mount to load the filesystem using ro,suid,dev,auto,nouser, and async mount options. The defaults option in the commented-out version expanded to rw,suid,dev,auto, nouser, and async. Here you are simply replacing rw (read-write) with ro (read-only).

◆ Reboot your system from the console and log in as root.

◆ Change directory to /usr and try to create a new file using a command such as touch mynewfile.txt in this directory. You should get an error message such as the following:

```
touch: mynewfile.txt: Read-only filesystem
```

◆ As you can see, you can no longer write to the /usr partition even with a root account, which means it isn't possible for a hacker to write there either.

Whenever you need to install some software in a directory within /usr, you can comment out the new /usr line and uncomment the old one and reboot the system. Then you can install the new software and simply go back to read-only configuration.

 TIP If you don't like to modify /etc/fstab every time you write to /usr, you can simply make two versions of /etc/fstab called /etc/fstab.usr-ro (this one has the read-only, ro, flag for /usr line) and /etc/fstab/usr-rw (this one has the read-write, rw, flag for the /usr line) and use a symbolic link (using the ln command) to link one of them to /etc/fstab as desired.

Setting system-wide default permission model using umask

When a user creates a new file or directory, Linux uses a mask value to determine the permission setting for the new file or directory. The mask value is set using a command called umask. If you run the umask command by itself, you see the current creation mask value. The mask value is stored as an octal number; it's the complement of the desired permission mode. For example, a mask value of 002 makes Linux create files and directories with permission settings of 775. Similarly, a mask value of 777 would result in a permission setting of 000, which means no access.

You can set the default umask value for all the users in /etc/profile. For example, the default /etc/profile includes the following line, which determines umask settings for users.

```
if [ `id -gn` = `id -un` -a `id -u` -gt 14 ]; then
        umask 002
else
        umask 022
fi
```

This script segment ensures that all users with UID > 14 get a umask setting of 002 and users with UID < 14, which includes root and the default system accounts such as ftp and operator, get a umask setting of 022. Because ordinary user UID starts at 500 (set in /etc/login.defs; see UID_MIN) they all get 002, which translates into 775 permission setting. This means that when an ordinary user creates a file or directory, she has read, write, and execute for herself and her user group (which typically is herself, too, if Red Hat private user groups are used) and the rest of the world can read and execute her new file or change to her new directory. This isn't a good idea because files should never be world-readable by default. So I recommend that you do the following:

◆ Modify /etc/profile and change the umask 002 line to umask 007, so that ordinary user files and directories have 770 as the default permission settings. This file gets processed by the default shell /bin/bash. The default umask for root is 022, which translates into a 755 permission mode. This is a really bad default value for all the users whose UID is less then 14. . Change the umask to 077, which translates a restrictive (that is, only file owner access) 700 permission mode. The modified code segment in /etc/profile looks like this:

```
if [ `id -gn` = `id -un` -a `id -u` -gt 14 ]; then
        umask 077
else
        umask 007
fi
```

backwards

◆ Modify the /etc/csh.login file and perform the preceding change. This file is processed by users who use /bin/csh or /bin/tcsh login shells.

TIP If you use the su command to become root, make sure you use the su - command instead of su without any argument. The - ensures that the new shell acts like a login shell of the new user's (that is, root.) In other words, using the - option, you can instruct the target shell (by default it's bin/bash unless you changed the shell using the chsh command) to load appropriate configuration files such as /etc/profile or /etc/csh.login.

Dealing with world-accessible files

After you have made sure that the default permission mode for new files and directories is properly configured as discussed in the preceding text, you can remove problematic files and directories. Any user on the system can access a world-accessible file or directory. The best way to handle world-readable, world-writeable, and world-executable files or directories is to not have any of them.

Unfortunately, you may need some world-readable files and world-executables directories when creating public directories for user Web sites or other shared disk concepts. However, world-writeable files and directories and world-executable files should be avoided completely. You can regularly find these files and directories by using a script, as shown in Listing 9-4.

Listing 9-4: The find_worldwx.sh

```
!/bin/sh
# Purpose: to locate world-writable files/dir and
#          world-executable files# Written by Mohammed J. Kabir
# Standard binaries
FIND=/usr/bin/find
CAT=/bin/cat
RM=/bin/rm
MAIL=/bin/mail
# Get the date and week number
DATE=`/bin/date "+%m-%d-%Y [Week: %U]"`
# Starting path
ROOT_DIR=/
ADMIN=root@localhost
# Temp directory
TMP_DIR=/tmp
WORLD_WRITABLE=-2
WORLD_EXEC=-1
TYPE_FILE=f
TYPE_DIR=d
TYPE_LINK=l
RUN_CMD=-ls
OUT_FILE=$$.out
# Find all world-writable files/directories (that is, not
# symbolic links
echo "List of all world-writable files or directories" > $OUT_FILE;
$FIND $ROOT_DIR -perm $WORLD_WRITABLE ! -type $TYPE_LINK \
$RUN_CMD  >> $OUT_FILE;
echo >> $OUT_FILE;
echo "List of all world-executable files" >> $OUT_FILE;
$FIND $ROOT_DIR -perm $WORLD_EXEC -type $TYPE_FILE \
```

Continued

Listing 9-4 *(Continued)*

```
$RUN_CMD >> $OUT_FILE;
# Send the script report via email to ADMIN user
$MAIL -s "World-wx Report $DATE " $ADMIN < $OUT_FILE;
$RM -f $OUT_FILE;
exit 0;
```

When you run this script as a `cron` job from `/etc/cron.weekly`, it sends e-mail to `ADMIN` every week (so don't forget to change `root@localhost` to a suitable e-mail address), listing all world-writeable files and directories, as well as all world-executable files. An example of such an e-mail report (slightly modified to fit the page) is shown in the following listing:

```
From root  sun Dec 17 21:27:56 2000
Date: sun, 17 Dec 2000 21:27:56 -0500
From: root <root@k2.intevo.com>
To: kabir@k2.intevo.com
subject: World-wx Report 12-17-2000 [Week: 51]
List of all world-writable files or directories
 14625  4 drwxrwxrwt 11 root  root   4096 Dec 17 21:24 /tmp
 17422  0 -rw-rw-rw-  1 root  root      0 Dec 17 20:53 /tmp/deadletter
 44648  4 drwxrwxrwx  2 root  root   4096 Dec 17 20:53 /tmp/rootkit
List of all world-executable files
104581  8 -rwxr-xr-x  1 root  root      7151 Oct 17 11:50 /tmp/hack.o
4554    4 -rwxr-xr-x  1 root  webmaste  1716 Dec 12 22:50 /tmp/x86.asm
```

When you receive such e-mails, look closely; spot and investigate the files and directories that seem fishy (that is, out of the ordinary). In the preceding example, the `rootkit` directory and the `hack.o` in `/tmp` would raise a red flag for me; I would investigate those files immediately. Unfortunately, there's no surefire way to spot suspects — you learn to suspect everything at the beginning and slowly get a working sense of where to look. (May the force be with you.)

In addition to world-writeables, two other risky types of files exist that you should keep an eye open for: SUID and SGID files.

Dealing with set–UID and set–GID programs

An ordinary user can run a set-UID (SUID) program with the privileges of another user. Typically, SUID programs run applications that *should* be run as `root` — which poses a great security risk. Listing 9-5 shows an example that illustrates this risk: a simple Perl script called `setuid.pl`.

Listing 9-5: The setuid.pl script

```
#!/usr/bin/perl
# Purpose: demonstrate set-uid risk
```

```
#
use strict;
# Log file path
my $LOG_FILE = "/var/log/custom.log";
# Open log file
open(LOG,">>$LOG_FILE") || die "Can't open $LOG_FILE $!\n";
# Write an entry
print LOG "PID $$ $0 script was run by $ENV{USER}\n";
# Close log file
close(LOG);
# Exit program
exit 0;
This script simply writes a log entry in /var/log/custom.log file and exits.
When an ordinary user runs this script she gets the following error message:
Can't open /var/log/custom.log Permission denied
```

The final line of Listing 9-5 shows that the /var/log/custom.log cannot be opened, which is not surprising. Because the /var/log directory isn't writeable by an ordinary user; only root can write in that directory. But suppose the powers-that-be require ordinary users to run this script. The system administrator has two dicey alternatives:

◆ Opening the /var/log directory for ordinary users

◆ Setting the UID of the script to root and allowing ordinary users to run it

Because opening the /var/log to ordinary users is the greater of the two evils, the system administrator (forced to support setuid.pl) goes for the set-UID approach. She runs the chmod 5755 setuid.pl command to set the set-uid bit for the script and allow everyone to run the script. When run by a user called kabir, the script writes the following entry in /var/log/custom.log:

```
PID 2616 ./setuid.pl script was run by kabir
```

As shown, the script is now enabling the ordinary user to write to /var/log/custom.log file. A malicious user (typically not someone from inside your organization, but an outsider who managed to break into an ordinary user account) looks for set-UID programs and checks for a way to exploit them.

Going back to the simple example, if the user account called kabir is hacked by one such bad guy, he can run a command such as find / -type f -perm -04000 -ls to locate set-UID programs such as setuid.pl. Upon finding such a program, the hacker can look for a way to gain root access.

You may be thinking (correctly) that because setuid.pl is a Perl script, the hacker could easily study the source code, find out why a set-UID script was required, and plan an attack. But don't trust your C programs either; Listing 9-6 shows the source code of a small C program called write2var.c.

Listing 9-6: The write2var.c source file

```
/*
  Purpose: to demonstrate set-uid issue
  Written by Mohammed J. Kabir
*/
#include <stdio.h>
#include <string.h>
#include <stdlib.h>
int main(void)
{
    FILE *out;
    char *str;
    // Try to allocate 128 bytes of memory to store fqpn of log
    if ( (str = malloc(128)) == NULL)
    {
        fprintf(stderr,
                "Cannot allocate memory to store filename.\n");
        return 0;
    }
    // Assign filename to allocated memory (string)
    strcpy(str, "/var/log/test.log");
    // Try to open the log file for writing
    if (( out = fopen(str, "a+")) == NULL )
    {
        fprintf(stderr, "Cannot open the log file.\n");
        return 1;
    }
    // Write to log
    fputs("Wrote this line\n",out);
    fclose(out);
    // Done
    return 0;
}
```

When this C program is compiled (using the `gcc -o test write2var.c` command), it can run as `./go` from the command-line. This program writes to `/var/log/test.log` if it's run as `root`, but must run as a set-UID program if an ordinary user is to run it. If this program is set-UID and its source code isn't available, the hacker can simply run the `strings ./go` command — or run the `strace ./go` command to investigate why a set-UID program was necessary — and try to exploit any weakness that shows up. For example, the `strings go` command shows the following output:

```
/lib/ld-linux.so.2
__gmon_start__
```

```
libc.so.6
strcpy
__cxa_finalize
malloc
fprintf
__deregister_frame_info
fclose
stderr
fopen
_IO_stdin_used
__libc_start_main
fputs
__register_frame_info
GLIBC_2.1.3
GLIBC_2.1
GLIBC_2.0
PTRh
Cannot allocate memory to store filename.
/var/log/test.log
Cannot open the log file.
Wrote this line
```

Notice the line in bold; even a not-so-smart hacker can figure that this program reads or writes to /var/log/test.log. Because this is a simple example, the hacker may not be able to do much with this program, but at the least he can corrupt entries in the /var/log/test.log file by manually editing it. Similarly, a set-GID (SGID) program can run using its group privilege. The example ls -l output in the following listing shows a setuid and setgid file.

```
-rwsr-x---  1 root    root         0 Dec 18 00:58 /tmp/setuid
-rwxr-s---  1 root    root         0 Dec 18 00:57 /tmp/setgid
```

Both the set-UID and the set-GID fields are represented using the *s* character (shown in bold for emphasis). Listing 9-7 shows a script called find_suid_sgid.sh that you can run from /etc/cron.weekly; it e-mails you an SUID/SGID report every week.

Listing 9-7: The find_suid_sgid.sh script

```
#!/bin/sh
# Purpose: to locate world-writable files/dir and
#          world-executable files
# Written by Mohammed J. Kabir
# Standard binaries
FIND=/usr/bin/find
```

Continued

Listing 9-7 *(Continued)*

```
CAT=/bin/cat
RM=/bin/rm
MAIL=/bin/mail
# Get the date and week number
DATE=`/bin/date "+%m-%d-%Y [Week: %U]"`
# Starting path
ROOT_DIR=/
ADMIN=root@localhost
# Temp directory
TMP_DIR=/tmp
WORLD_WRITABLE=-2
WORLD_EXEC=-1
TYPE_FILE=f
TYPE_DIR=d
TYPE_LINK=l
RUN_CMD=-ls
OUT_FILE=$$.out
# Find all world-writable files/directories (that is, not
# symbolic links
echo "List of all world-writable files or directories" > $OUT_FILE;
$FIND $ROOT_DIR -perm $WORLD_WRITABLE ! -type $TYPE_LINK \
$RUN_CMD  >> $OUT_FILE;
echo >> $OUT_FILE;
echo "List of all world-executable files" >> $OUT_FILE;
$FIND $ROOT_DIR -perm $WORLD_EXEC -type $TYPE_FILE \
$RUN_CMD  >> $OUT_FILE;
# Send the script report via email to ADMIN user
$MAIL -s "World-wx Report $DATE " $ADMIN < $OUT_FILE;
cat $OUT_FILE;
$RM -f $OUT_FILE;
```

Remember to change ADMIN=root@localhost to a suitable e-mail address for you.

Using ext2 Filesystem Security Features

So far I have been discussing various risky system features such as world-writeable files, set-UID and set-GID files, and some directories of the Linux filesystem that get in the way of system security. Fortunately, an ext2 filesystem also has some built-in security measures you can use to your advantage.

The Linux ext2 filesystem supports a set of extended attributes (listed in Table 9-4) that can help you tighten security.

TABLE 9-4: EXT2 FILESYSTEM EXTENDED ATTRIBUTES WITH SECURITY USES

Extended Attribute	Description
A	When the A attribute is set, file-access time isn't updated. This can benefit computers that have power-consumption problems because it makes some disk I/O is unnecessary.
S	When the S attribute is set, the file is synchronized with the physical storage, which in the long run provides a higher level of data integrity at the expense of performance.
a	File becomes append-only — files can be created or modified within a particular directory but can't be removed.
i	Files can't be changed. In a particular directory, files can be modified but new files can't be created or deleted.
d	The dump program ignores the file.
c	Setting this attribute means that a write request coming to the file is compressed and a read request is automatically uncompressed. This attribute isn't yet available in the 2.2 or 2.4 kernel.
s	When a file with this attribute is deleted, the file data is overwritten with zeros. This attribute isn't yet available in the 2.2 or 2.4 kernel.
U	When a file with this attribute is deleted, the data is moved away so it can be undeleted. This attribute isn't yet available in the 2.2 or 2.4 kernel.

Using chattr

The ext2 filesystem used for Red Hat Linux provides some unique features. One of these features makes files immutable by even the root user. For example:

```
chattr +i filename
```

This command sets the i attribute of a file in an ext2 filesystem. This attribute can be set or cleared only by the root user. So this attribute can protect against file accidents. When this attribute is set, the following conditions apply:

◆ No one can modify, delete, or rename the file.

◆ New links can't point to this file.

When you need to clear the attribute, you can run the following command:

```
chattr -i filename
```

Using lsattr

If you start using the `chattr` command, sometimes you notice that you can't modify or delete a file, although you have the necessary permission to do so. This happens if you forget that earlier you set the `immutable` attribute of the file by using `chattr` — and because this attribute doesn't show up in the `ls` output, the sudden "freezing" of the file content can be confusing. To see which files have which `ext2` attributes, use the `lsattr` program.

Unfortunately, what you know now about file and filesystem security may be old news to informed bad guys with lots of free time to search the Web. Use of tools such as `chattr` may make breaking in harder for the bad guy, but they don't make your files or filesystems impossible to damage. In fact, if the bad guy gets `root`-level privileges, `ext2` attributes provide just a simple hide-and-seek game.

Using a File Integrity Checker

Determining whether you can trust your files is a major problem after a break-in. You may wonder whether the bad guy has installed a Trojan application or embedded a virus to infect new files (and possibly provide access to other computers that you access). None of the methods examined so far in this chapter can handle this aspect of a security problem. The solution? Run a file integrity checker program; the upcoming section shows how.

A *file integrity checker* is a tool that allows checksum-like values to use hashing functions. These values are stored in a safe place that is guaranteed unalterable (for example, read-only media like CD-ROM). The file integrity checker then can check the current files against the checksum database and detect whether files have been altered.

Using a home-grown file integrity checker

Listing 9-8 shows a simple MD5 digest-based file integrity checker script with the `Digest::MD5` module in Perl.

Listing 9-8: The md5_fic.pl script

```perl
#!/usr/bin/perl
#  Purpose: creates and verifies MD5 checksum for files.
#  1st time:
#  md5_fic.pl /dir/filename creates and stores a MD5 checksum
#  2nd time:
#  md5_fic.pl /dir/filename verifies the integrity of the file
```

```perl
#              using the stored MD5 checksum
# If the /dir/filename has changed, the script reports '*FAILED*'
# else it reports 'PASSED'
# Limited wildcard supported. Example: md5_fic.pl /dir/*.conf
#
# Written by: Mohammed J. Kabir
# CVS ID: $Id$
use strict;
use File::Basename;
use Digest::MD5;
use constant DEBUG => 0;
use constant UMASK => 0777;
# Change this directory to an appropriate path on your system
my $SAFE_DIR = '/usr/local/md5';
# Cycle through each file given in the command-line
foreach my $filename (@ARGV) {
   # If the given filename does not exist, show syntax msg
   syntax() if (! -R $filename);
   # Create path to the checksum file
   my $chksumFile = get_chksum_file($filename);
   # Create intermediate directory names for the checksum path
   my $dir2 = dirname($chksumFile);
   my $dir1 = dirname($dir2);
   # Create intermediate directories if they don't exist
   mkdir $dir1, UMASK if (! -e $dir1);
   mkdir $dir2, UMASK if (! -e $dir2);
   DEBUG and print "Checksum File $chksumFile\n";
   # Get data from the input file
   my $data = get_data_from_file($filename);
   # If MD5 checksum exists for this file
   if (! -e $chksumFile ) {
     DEBUG and print "Writing MD5 fingerprint for $filename to $chksumFile\n";

     # Create a MD5 digest for the data we read from the file
     my $newDigest = get_digest($data);

     # Write the digest to the checksum file for this input file
     write_data_to_file($chksumFile, $newDigest);

     # Show status message
     printf("%-40s ... MD5 finger-print created\n", $filename);
   } else {

     DEBUG and print "Verifying $filename with $chksumFile\n";
```

Continued

Listing 9-8 *(Continued)*

```perl
CAT=/bin/cat
    # Read the old digest from the checksum file we created
    # earlier for this input file.
    my $oldDigest = get_data_from_file($chksumFile);

    # Create a new digest for the data read from the current
    # version of the file
    my $newDigest = get_digest($data);

    # Compare the old and the current checksum and see if
    # data has been altered or not; report accordingly
    my $status = ($oldDigest eq $newDigest) ? 'PASSED' :  '*FAILED*';

    # Show status message
    printf("%-40s ... %s\n", $filename,$status);
    }
}
exit 0;
sub write_data_to_file {
# Write data to file

   my ($filename, $data) = @_;
   open(DATA, ">$filename") || die "Can't write $filename $!\n";
   print DATA $data;
   close(DATA);
}


sub get_data_from_file {
# Load data from a given file
#
   my $filename = shift;
   local $/ = undef;
   open(FILE, $filename) || die "Can't read $filename $!\n";
   my $data = <FILE>;
   close(FILE);
   return $data;
}
sub get_digest {
# Calculate a MD5 digest for the given data
#
   my $data = shift;
   my $ctx = Digest::MD5->new;
   $ctx->add($data);
   my $digest;
```

```
    $digest = $ctx->digest;
    #$digest = $ctx->hexdigest;
    #$digest = $ctx->b64digest;
    return $digest;
}
sub syntax {
# Print syntax
#
    die "Syntax: $0 /dir/files\nLimited wild card supported.\n";
}
sub get_chksum_file {
#  Create the path (based on the given filename) for the checksum file
#
    my $filename = shift;
    my $chksumFile = sprintf("%s/%s/%s/%s.md5",
                             $SAFE_DIR,
                             lc substr(basename($filename),0,1),
                             lc substr(basename($filename),1,1),
                             basename($filename) );
    return $chksumFile;
}
# END OF SCRIPT
```

The md5_fic.pl script takes filenames as command-line arguments. For example, if you run the ./md5_fic.pl /etc/pam.d/* command, the script generates the following output:

```
/etc/pam.d/chfn                   ... MD5 finger-print created
/etc/pam.d/chsh                   ... MD5 finger-print created
/etc/pam.d/ftp                    ... MD5 finger-print created
/etc/pam.d/kbdrate                ... MD5 finger-print created
/etc/pam.d/linuxconf              ... MD5 finger-print created
/etc/pam.d/linuxconf-auth         ... MD5 finger-print created
/etc/pam.d/linuxconf-pair         ... MD5 fincer-print created
/etc/pam.d/login                  ... MD5 finger-print created
/etc/pam.d/other                  ... MD5 finger-print created
/etc/pam.d/passwd                 ... MD5 finger-print created
/etc/pam.d/ppp                    ... MD5 finger-print created
/etc/pam.d/rexec                  ... MD5 finger-print created
/etc/pam.d/rlogin                 ... MD5 finger-print created
/etc/pam.d/rsh                    ... MD5 finger-print created
/etc/pam.d/samba                  ... MD5 finger-print created
/etc/pam.d/su                     ... MD5 finger-print created
/etc/pam.d/sudo                   ... MD5 finger-print created
/etc/pam.d/system-auth            ... MD5 finger-print created
```

The script simply reads all the files in /etc/pam.d directory and creates MD5 checksums for each file. The checksum files are stored in a directory pointed by the $SAFE_DIR variable in the script. By default, it stores all checksum files in /usr/local/md5. Make sure you change the $SAFE_DIR from /usr/local/md5 to an appropriate path the you can later write-protect. For example, use /mnt/floppy to write the checksums to a floppy disk (which you can later write-protect).

After the checksum files are created, every time you run the script with the same arguments, it compares the old checksum against one it creates from the current contents of the file. If the checksums match, then your file is still authentic, because you created the checksum file for it last time. For example, running the ./md5_fic.pl /etc/pam.d/* command again generates the following output:

```
/etc/pam.d/chfn                 ... PASSED
/etc/pam.d/chsh                 ... PASSED
/etc/pam.d/ftp                  ... PASSED
/etc/pam.d/kbdrate              ... PASSED
/etc/pam.d/linuxconf            ... PASSED
/etc/pam.d/linuxconf-auth       ... PASSED
/etc/pam.d/linuxconf-pair       ... PASSED
/etc/pam.d/login                ... PASSED
/etc/pam.d/other                ... PASSED
/etc/pam.d/passwd               ... PASSED
/etc/pam.d/ppp                  ... PASSED
/etc/pam.d/rexec                ... PASSED
/etc/pam.d/rlogin               ... PASSED
/etc/pam.d/rsh                  ... PASSED
/etc/pam.d/samba                ... PASSED
/etc/pam.d/su                   ... PASSED
/etc/pam.d/sudo                 ... PASSED
/etc/pam.d/system-auth          ... PASSED
```

Because the files have not changed between the times you executed these two commands, the checksums still match; therefore each of the files passed.

Now if you change a file in the /etc/pam.d directory and run the same command again, you see a *FAILED* message for that file because the stored MD5 digest does not match the newly computed digest. Here's the output after I modified the /etc/pam.d/su file.

```
/etc/pam.d/chfn                 ... PASSED
/etc/pam.d/chsh                 ... PASSED
/etc/pam.d/ftp                  ... PASSED
/etc/pam.d/kbdrate              ... PASSED
/etc/pam.d/linuxconf            ... PASSED
```

```
/etc/pam.d/linuxconf-auth            ... PASSED
/etc/pam.d/linuxconf-pair            ... PASSED
/etc/pam.d/login                     ... PASSED
/etc/pam.d/other                     ... PASSED
/etc/pam.d/passwd                    ... PASSED
/etc/pam.d/ppp                       ... PASSED
/etc/pam.d/rexec                     ... PASSED
/etc/pam.d/rlogin                    ... PASSED
/etc/pam.d/rsh                       ... PASSED
/etc/pam.d/samba                     ... PASSED
/etc/pam.d/su                        ... *FAILED*
/etc/pam.d/sudo                      ... PASSED
/etc/pam.d/system-auth               ... PASSED
```

You can also run the script for a single file. For example, the ./md5_fic.pl /etc/pam.d/su command produces the following output:

```
/etc/pam.d/su                        ... *FAILED*
```

A file integrity checker relies solely on the pristine checksum data. The data mustn't be altered in any way. Therefore, it's extremely important that you don't keep the checksum data in a writeable location. I recommend using a floppy disk (if you have only a few files to run the checksum against), a CD-ROM, or a read-only disk partition.

Write-protect the floppy, or mount a partition read-only after you check the checksum files.

This little script is no match for a commercial-grade file integrity checker such as Tripwire.

Using Tripwire Open Source, Linux Edition

In a great move towards open-source software, Tripwire released Tripwire Open Source, Linux Edition, under the General Public License (GPL). Simply speaking, Tripwire is a file-and-directory integrity checker; it creates a database of signatures for all files and directories and stores them in one file. When Tripwire is run again, it computes new signatures for current files and directories and compares them with the original signatures stored in the database. If it finds a discrepancy, it reports the file or directory name along with information about the discrepancy.

You can see why Tripwire can be a great tool for helping you determine which files were modified in a break-in. Of course, for that you must ensure the security of the database that the application uses. When creating a new server system, many experienced system administrators do the following things:

1. Ensure that the new system isn't attached to any network to guarantee that no one has already installed a Trojan program, virus program, or other danger to your system security.

2. Run Tripwire to create a signature database of all the important system files, including all system binaries and configuration files.

3. Write the database in a recordable CD-ROM.

   This ensures that an advanced bad guy can't modify the Tripwire database to hide Trojans and modified files from being noticed by the application. Administrators who have a small number of files to monitor often use a floppy disk to store the database. After writing the database to the floppy disk, the administrator write-protects the disk and, if the BIOS permits, configures the disk drive as a read-only device.

4. Set up a cron job to run Tripwire periodically (daily, weekly, monthly) such that the application uses the CD-ROM database version.

GETTING TRIPWIRE

Red Hat Linux includes the binary Tripwire RPM file. However, you can download the free (LGPL) version of Tripwire from an RPM mirror site such as http://fr.rpmfind.net. I downloaded the Tripwire source code and binaries from this site by using http://fr.rpmfind.net/linux/rpm2html/search.php?query=Tripwire.

The source RPM that I downloaded was missing some installation scripts, so I downloaded the source again from the Tripwire Open Source development site at the http://sourceforge.net/projects/tripwire/ site. The source code I downloaded was called tripwire-2.3.0-src.tar.gz. You may find a later version there when you read this. In the spirit of compiling open-source software from the source code, I show compiling, configuring, and installing Tripwire from the tripwire-2.3.0-src.tar.gz file.

When following the instructions given in the following section, replace the version number with the version of Tripwire you have downloaded.

TIP If you want to install Tripwire from the binary RPM package, simply run the `rpm -ivh tripwire-version.rpm` command. You still must configure Tripwire by running `twinstall.sh`. Run this script from the `/etc/trip-wire` directory and skip to Step 7 in the following section.

COMPILING TRIPWIRE

To compile from the source distribution, do the following:

1. `su` to `root`.

2. Extract the tar ball, using the `tar xvzf tripwire-2.3.0-src.tar.gz` command. This creates a subdirectory called `/usr/src/redhat/SOURCES/tripwire-2.3.0-src`.

   Change your current directory to `/usr/src/redhat/SOURCES/tripwire-2.3.0-src/src`.

3. Run the `make release` command to compile all the necessary Tripwire binaries. (This takes a little time, so do it just before a coffee break.)

   After it is compiled, install the binaries: Change directory to `/usr/src/redhat/SOURCES/tripwire-2.3.0-src/install`. Copy the `install.cfg` and `install.sh` files to the parent directory using the `cp install.* ..` command.

4. Before you run the installation script, you may need to edit the `install.cfg` file, which is shown in Listing 9-9. For example, if you aren't a `vi` editor fan, but rather camp in the `emacs` world, you change the `TWEDITOR` field in this file to point to `emacs` instead of `/usr/bin/vi`. I wouldn't recommend changing the values for CLOBBER, TWBIN, TWPOLICY, TWMAN, TWDB, TWDOCS, TWSITEKEYDIR, TWLOCALKEYDIR settings. However, you may want to change the values for TWLATEPROMPTING, TWLOOSEDIRCHK, TWMAILNOVIOLATIONS, TWEMAILREPORTLEVEL, TWREPORTLEVEL, TWSYSLOG, TWMAILMETHOD, TWMAILPROGRAM, and so on. The meaning of these settings are given in the comment lines above each setting in the install.cfg file.

Listing 9-9: The install.cfg file

```
# install.cfg
# default install.cfg for:
# Tripwire(R) 2.3 Open Source for Linux
# NOTE:  This is a Bourne shell script that stores installation
#        parameters for your installation.  The installer will
```

Continued

Listing 9-9 *(Continued)*

```
#        execute this file to generate your config file and also to
#        locate any special configuration needs for your install.
#        Protect this file, because it is possible for
#        malicious code to be inserted here
# This version of Tripwire has been modified to conform to the FHS
# standard for Unix-like operating systems.
# To change the install directory for any tripwire files, modify
# the paths below as necessary.
#=========================================================
# If CLOBBER is true, then existing files are overwritten.
# If CLOBBER is false, existing files are not overwritten.
CLOBBER=false
# Tripwire binaries are stored in TWBIN.
TWBIN="/usr/sbin"
# Tripwire policy files are stored in TWPOLICY.
TWPOLICY="/etc/tripwire"
# Tripwire manual pages are stored in TWMAN.
TWMAN="/usr/man"
# Tripwire database files are stored in TWDB.
TWDB="/var/lib/tripwire"
# Tripwire documents directory
TWDOCS="/usr/doc/tripwire"
# The Tripwire site key files are stored in TWSITEKEYDIR.
TWSITEKEYDIR="${TWPOLICY}"
# The Tripwire local key files are stored in TWLOCALKEYDIR.
TWLOCALKEYDIR="${TWPOLICY}"
# Tripwire report files are stored in TWREPORT.
TWREPORT="${TWDB}/report"
# This sets the default text editor for Tripwire.
TWEDITOR="/bin/vi"
# TWLATEPROMTING controls the point when tripwire asks for a password.
TWLATEPROMPTING=false
# TWLOOSEDIRCHK selects whether the directory should be monitored for
# properties that change when files in the directory are monitored.
TWLOOSEDIRCHK=false
# TWMAILNOVIOLATIONS determines whether Tripwire sends a no violation
# report when integrity check is run with --email-report but no rule
# violations are found.  This lets the admin know that the integrity
# was run, as opposed to having failed for some reason.
TWMAILNOVIOLATIONS=true
# TWEMAILREPORTLEVEL determines the verbosity of e-mail reports.
TWEMAILREPORTLEVEL=3
```

```
# TWREPORTLEVEL determines the verbosity of report printouts.
TWREPORTLEVEL=3
# TWSYSLOG determines whether Tripwire will log events to the system log
TWSYSLOG=false
####################################
# Mail Options - Choose the appropriate
# method and comment the other section
####################################
####################################
# SENDMAIL options - DEFAULT
# Either SENDMAIL or SMTP can be used to send reports via TWMAILMETHOD.
# Specifies which sendmail program to use.
####################################
TWMAILMETHOD=SENDMAIL
TWMAILPROGRAM="/usr/lib/sendmail -oi -t"
####################################
# SMTP options
# TWSMTPHOST selects the SMTP host to be used to send reports.
# SMTPPORT selects the SMTP port for the SMTP mail program to use.
####################################
# TWMAILMETHOD=SMTP
# TWSMTPHOST="mail.domain.com"
# TWSMTPPORT=25
#########################################################################
# Copyright (C) 1998-2000 Tripwire (R) Security Systems, Inc. Tripwire (R) is a
# registered trademark of the Purdue Research Foundation and is licensed
# exclusively to Tripwire (R) Security Systems, Inc.
        ###########################################################
```

5. Run the ./install.sh command. This walks you through the installation process. You are asked to press Enter, accept the GPL licensing agreement, and (finally) to agree to the locations to which files copy.

6. After the files are copied, you are asked for a site pass phrase.

   This pass phrase encrypts the Tripwire configuration and policy files. Enter a strong pass phrase (that is, not easily guessable and at least eight characters long) to ensure that these files aren't modified by any unknown party.

7. Choose a local pass phrase. This pass phrase encrypts the Tripwire database and report files.

   Choose a strong pass phrase..

8. You are asked for the site pass phrase.

   The installation program signs the configuration file using your pass phrase. A clear-text version of the Tripwire configuration file is created in /etc/tripwire/twcfg.txt. The encrypted, binary version of the configuration file – which is what Tripwire uses – is stored in /etc/tripwire/tw.cfg. The clear-text version is created for your inspection. The installation program recommends that you delete this file manually after you have examined it.

9. You are asked for the site pass phrase so the installation program can use it for signing the policy file.

   The installation program creates a clear-text policy file in /etc/tripwire/twpol.txt and the encrypted version is kept in /etc/tripwire/tw.pol. (You learn to modify the text version of the policy file later – and to create the binary, encrypted version that Tripwire uses.)

CONFIGURING TRIPWIRE POLICY

The *policy file* defines rules that Tripwire uses to perform integrity checks. Each rule defines which files and directories to check – and what types of checks to perform. Additionally, each rule can include information such as name and severity. Syntax for a typicalrule is shown in the following example:

```
(attribute=value attribute=value ...)
{
   /path/to/a/file/or/directory      -> mask;

}
```

Table 9-5 lists available attributes and their meanings.

TABLE 9-5 LIST OF AVAILABLE ATTRIBUTES

Attribute	Meaning
rulename=name	This attribute associates a name to the rule. This attribute makes Tripwire reports more readable and easy to sort by named rules.
emailto=emailaddr	When a rule is violated, the e-mail address given as value for this attribute receives a violation report.

Attribute	Meaning
severity=*number*	This attribute can associate a severity level (that is, importance) to a rule. This makes Tripwire reports easier to manage.
recurse=true | false	This attribute determines whether a directory is automatically recursed. If it's set to true (or -1), all subdirectories are recursed; if it's set to false (or 0), the subdirectories aren't traversed. Any numeric value in the range of -1 to 1000000 (excluding -1 and 0) dictates the depth to which the subdirectories are recursed. For example recurse=3 means that subdirectories up to level-3 depth are recursed.

Look at the following example rule:

```
(Rulename= "OS Utilities", severity=100)
{
  /bin/ls        -> +pinugtsdrbamcCMSH-1;

}
```

Here the rule being defined is called the OS Utilities rule; it has a severity rating of 100 — which means violation of this rule is considered a major problem; the +pinugtsdrbamcCMSH-1 properties of /bin/ls is checked. Table 9-6 describes each of these property/mask characters.

TABLE 9-6 PROPERTY/MASKS CHARACTERS USED IN TRIPWIRE POLICY FILE

Property or Mask	Description
a	Access timestamp of the file or directory
b	Number of blocks allocated to the file
c	Inode timestamp
d	ID of the disk where the inode resides
g	Owner's group

Continued

TABLE 9-6 PROPERTY/MASKS CHARACTERS USED IN TRIPWIRE POLICY FILE
(Continued)

Property or Mask	Description
i	Inode number
l	File is increasing in size
m	Modification timestamp
n	Inode reference count or number of links
p	Permission bits of file or directory
r	ID of the device pointed to by an inode belonging to a device file
s	Size of a file
t	Type of file
u	Owner's user ID
C	CRC-32 value
H	Haval value
M	MD5 value
S	SHA value
+	Record and check the property followed by this character
-	Ignore the property followed by this character

Another way to write the previous rule is shown in the following line:

```
/bin/ls -> +pinugtsdrbamcCMSH-l (Rulename= "OS Utilities", severity=100);
```

The first method is preferable because it can group many files and directories under one rule. For example, all the listed utilities in the following code fall under the same policy:

```
SEC_CRIT  = +pinugtsdrbamcCMSH-l;
(Rulename= "OS Utilities", severity=100)
{
  /bin/ls        -> $(SEC_CRIT);
  /bin/login     -> $(SEC_CRIT);
```

```
/bin/ls          -> $(SEC_CRIT);
/bin/mail        -> $(SEC_CRIT);
/bin/more        -> $(SEC_CRIT);
/bin/mt          -> $(SEC_CRIT);
/bin/mv          -> $(SEC_CRIT);
/bin/netstat     -> $(SEC_CRIT);
}
```

 The preceding code uses the SEC_CRIT variable, which is defined before it's used in the rule. This variable is set to +pinugtsdrbamcCMSH-1 and substituted in the rule statements using $(SEC_CRIT). This can define one variable with a set of properties that can be applied to a large group of files and/or directories. When you want to add or remove properties, you simply change the mask value of the variable; the change is reflected everywhere the variable is used. Some built-in variables are shown in Table 9-7.

TABLE 9-7: A SELECTION OF BUILT-IN VARIABLES FOR THE TRIPWIRE POLICY FILE

Variable	Meaning
ReadOnly	+pinugtsdbmCM-rlacSH. Good for files that should remain read-only.
Dynamic	+pinugtd-srlbamcCMSH. Good for user directories and files that are dynamic and sub of changes.
Growing	+pinugtdl-srbamcCMSH. Good for files that grow in size.
Device	+pugsdr-intlbamcCMSH. Good for device files.
IgnoreAll	-pinugtsdrlbamcCMSH. Checks if the file exists or not but doesn't check anything else.
IgnoreNone	+pinugtsdrbamcCMSH-1. Opposite of IgnoreAll. Checks all properties.

When creating a rule, consider the following:

◆ Don't create multiple rules that apply to the same file or directory, as in this example:

```
/usr                 -> $(ReadOnly);
/usr                 -> $(Growing);
```

Tripwire complains about such a policy.

♦ More specific rules are honored, as in this example:

```
/usr                    -> $(ReadOnly);
/usr/local/home         -> $(Dynamic);
```

In the second line of the example, when you check a file with the path /usr/local/home/*filename*, Tripwire checks the properties substituted by the variable $(Dynamic).

If you want to create or modify rules, run the following command:

```
/usr/sbin/twadmin --create-polfile /etc/twpol.txt
```

The command generates the encrypted /etc/tripwire/tw.pol policy file. You are asked for the site pass phrase needed to sign (that is, encrypt) the policy file.

CREATING THE TRIPWIRE DATABASE
Before you initialize the Tripwire database file, be absolutely certain that bad guys have not already modified the files on your current system. This is why the best time for creating this database is when your new system hasn't yet been connected to the Internet or any other network. After you are certain that your files are untouched, run the following command:

```
/usr/sbin/tripwire --init
```

This command applies the policies listed in the /etc/tripwire/tw.pol file and creates a database in var/lib/tripwire/k2.intevo.com.

After you have created the database, move it to a read-only medium such as a CD-ROM or a floppy disk (write-protected after copying) if possible.

PROTECTING TRIPWIRE ITSELF
Bad guys can modify the Tripwire binary (/usr/sbin/tripwire) or the /etc/tripwire/tw.pol policy file to hide traces of their work. For this reason, you can run the /usr/sbin/siggen utility to create a set of signatures for these files. To generate a signature for the /usr/sbin/tripwire binary, you can run the /usr/sbin/siggen -a /usr/sbin/tripwire command.

You see something like the following on-screen:

```
-------------------------------------------------------------------
Signatures for file: /usr/sbin/tripwire
CRC32       BmL3O1
MD5         BrP2IBO3uAzdbRc67CI16i
SHA         F1IH/HvV3pb+tDhK5weOnKvFUxa
HAVAL       CBLgPptUYq2HurQ+sTa5tV
-------------------------------------------------------------------
```

You can keep the signature in a file by redirecting it to that file. (Print the signature too.) Don't forget to generate a signature for the `siggen` utility itself, also. If you ever get suspicious about Tripwire not working right, run the `siggen` utility on each of these files and compare the signatures. If any of them don't match, then you shouldn't trust those files; replace them with fresh new copies and launch an investigation into how the discrepancy happened.

RUNNING TRIPWIRE TO DETECT INTEGRITY IN INTERACTIVE MODE

You can run Tripwire in the interactive mode using the `/usr/sbin/tripwire --check --interactive` command. In this mode, a report file is generated and loaded in the preferred editor. The summary part of an example Tripwire report generated by this command is shown in the following listing:

```
Tripwire(R) 2.3.0 Integrity Check Report
Report generated by:         root
Report created on:           Fri Dec 22 02:31:25 2000
Database last updated on:    Fri Dec 22 02:13:44 2000
================================================================================
Report summary:
================================================================================
Host name:                   k2.intevo.com
Host IP address:             172.20.15.1
Host ID:                     None
Policy file used:            /etc/tripwire/tw.pol
Configuration file used:     /etc/tripwire/tw.cfg
Database file used:          /var/lib/tripwire/k2.intevo.com.twd
Command line used:           /usr/sbin/tripwire --check --interactive
================================================================================
Rule summary:
--------------------------------------------------------------------------------
  Section: Unix Filesystem
--------------------------------------------------------------------------------
  Rule Name                  Severity Level  Added   Removed Modified
  ---------                  --------------  -----   ------- --------
    Invariant Directories    66              0       0       0
    Temporary directories    33              0       0       0
  * Tripwire Data Files      100             0       0       1
    Critical devices         100             0       0       0
    User binaries            66              0       0       0
    Tripwire Binaries        100             0       0       0
  * Critical configuration files 100         0       0       1
    Libraries                66              0       0       0
    Shell Binaries           100             0       0       0
```

```
Filesystem and Disk Administration Programs
                                  100            0        0        0
Kernel Administration Programs    100            0        0        0
Networking Programs               100            0        0        0
System Administration Programs    100            0        0        0
Hardware and Device Control Programs
                                  100            0        0        0
System Information Programs        100           0        0        0
Application Information Programs
                                  100            0        0        0
Shell Related Programs            100            0        0        0
Critical Utility Sym-Links        100            0        0        0
Critical system boot files        100            0        0        0
System boot changes               100            0        0        0
OS executables and libraries      100            0        0        0
Security Control                  100            0        0        0
Login Scripts                     100            0        0        0
Operating System Utilities        100            0        0        0
Root config files                 100            0        0        0
Total objects scanned:   14862
Total violations found:   2
```

Two rules violations exist, which are marked using the "*" sign on the very left of the lines.

♦ The "Tripwire Data Files" rule. The report also states that there's another violation for the "Critical configuration files" rule. In both cases, a file has been modified that was supposed to be. Now, the Object summary section of the report shows the following lines:

```
==============================================================================
Object summary:
==============================================================================
------------------------------------------------------------------------------

# Section: Unix Filesystem
------------------------------------------------------------------------------

------------------------------------------------------------------------------
Rule Name: Tripwire Data Files (/etc/tripwire/tw.pol)
Severity Level: 100
------------------------------------------------------------------------------
Remove the "x" from the adjacent box to prevent updating the database
with the new values for this object.
Modified:
[x] "/etc/tripwire/tw.pol"
------------------------------------------------------------------------------
```

```
Rule Name: Critical configuration files (/etc/cron.daily)
Severity Level: 100
--------------------------------------------------------------------------------
Remove the "x" from the adjacent box to prevent updating the database
with the new values for this object.
Modified:
[x] "/etc/cron.daily"
```

As shown, Tripwire shows exactly which files were modified and what rules these files fall under. If these modifications are okay, I can simply leave the 'x' marks in the appropriate sections of the report and exit the editor. Tripwire updates the database per my decision. For example, if I leave the 'x' marks on for both files, next time when the integrity checker is run, it doesn't find these violations any more because the modified files are taken into account in the Tripwire database. However, if one of the preceding modifications was not expected and looks suspicious, Tripwire has done its job!

TIP If you want to view a report from the /var/lib/tripwire/report directory at any time, you can run the /usr/sbin/twprint -m r -- twrfile *reportfilename* command.

RUNNING TRIPWIRE TO DETECT INTEGRITY AUTOMATICALLY

You can also run Tripwire as a cron job by creating a small script such as the one shown in Listing 9-10.

Listing 9-10: The /etc/cron.daily/tripwire-check file

```
#!/bin/sh
HOST_NAME=`uname -n`
if [ ! -e /var/lib/tripwire/${HOST_NAME}.twd ] ; then
    echo "***    Error: Tripwire database for ${HOST_NAME} not found.    ***"
    echo "*** Run "/etc/tripwire/twinstall.sh" and/or "tripwire --init". ***"
else
    test -f /etc/tripwire/tw.cfg &&  /usr/sbin/tripwire --check
fi
```

This script checks whether the Tripwire database file exists or not. If it exists, the script then looks for the configuration file. When both files are found, it runs the /usr/sbin/tripwire command in a non-interactive mode. This results in a report file; if you have configured rules using the emailto attribute, e-mails are sent to the appropriate person(s).

UPDATING THE TRIPWIRE DATABASE

Update the Tripwire database whenever you have a change in the filesystem that generates a false warning. For example, if you modify a configuration file or remove a program that Tripwire is "watching" for you, it generates a violation report. Therefore, whenever you change something intentionally, you must update the database. You can do it two ways:

- ◆ Reinitialize the database using the /usr/sbin/tripwire --init command.

- ◆ Update the database using the /usr/sbin/tripwire --update command.

> The update method should save you a little time because it doesn't create the entire database again.

Similarly, when you change the Tripwire policy file, /etc/tripwire/twpol.txt, update the database. Again, instead of reinitializing the entire database using the --init option, you can instruct the program to apply policy changes and update the database using the /usr/sbin/tripwire --update-policy /etc/tripwire/twpol.txt command.

After you create a Tripwire database, it should be updated every time you update your policy file. Instead of reinitializing the database every time you change (or experiment) with your policy file, you can run the tripwire --update-policy /etc/tripwire/twpol.txt command to update the database. This saves a significant amount of time.

GETTING THE TRIPWIRE REPORT BY E-MAIL

If you use the emailto attribute in rules, you can receive violation (or even non-violation) reports from Tripwire. This is especially useful if you are running Tripwire checks as a cron job. (See the preceding section, "Running Tripwire to detect integrity automatically.")

Before you can get e-mail from Tripwire, you must configure the e-mail settings in the /etc/tripwire/twcfg.txt file and rebuild the configuration file using the /usr/sbin/twadmin --create-cfgfile /etc/tripwire/twcfg.txt command. The settings that control e-mail are explained in Table 9-8.

TABLE 9-8: E-MAIL SETTINGS FOR TRIPWIRE CONFIGURATION FILE

Attribute	Meaning
`MAILMETHOD = SMTP	SENDMAIL`	Default: `MAILMETHOD = SENDMAIL` This attribute sets the mail delivery method Tripwire uses. The default allows Tripwire to use the Sendmail daemon, which must be specified using the `MAILPROGRAM` attribute discussed later. Because most popular Sendmail-alternative mail daemons (such as qmail and postoffice), work very much like Sendmail, you can still set this to `SENDMAIL` and specify the path to your alternative daemon using the `MAILPROGRAM`. However, if you don't run a Sendmail or a Sendmail-like daemon on the machine on which you run Tripwire, you can set this attribute to `SMTP` and specify the `SMTPHOST` and `SMTPPORT` number attributes. Assuming the `SMTPHOST` allows your system to relay messages, Tripwire connects to the host via the SMTP port and delivers messages that are later delivered to the appropriate destination by the host.
`SMTPHOST = hostname	IP Address`	Default: none This attribute can specify the hostname of a mail server. Use this only if you don't have mail capabilities in the same system where Tripwire runs. You can look up the mail server IP or hostname using the `nslookup -q=mx yourdomain` command.
`SMTPPORT = port number`	Default: none This attribute specifies the TCP port number of the remote mail server. Typically, this should be set to 25. You only need this if you set `MAILMETHOD` to `SMTP`.

Continued

TABLE 9-8: E-MAIL SETTINGS FOR TRIPWIRE CONFIGURATION FILE *(Continued)*

Attribute	Meaning
MAILPROGRAM = */path/to/mail/program*	Default: `MAILPROGRAM = /usr/sbin/sendmail -oi -t` This attribute specifies the mail daemon path and any arguments to run it. This attribute only makes sense if you use `MAILMETHOD = SENDMAIL`.
EMAILREPORTLEVEL = 0 - 4	Default: `EMAILREPORTLEVEL = 3` This attribute specifies the level of information reported via e-mail. Leave the default as is.
MAILNOVIOLATIONS = true | false	Default: `MAILNOVIOLATIONS = true` If you don't want to receive e-mail when no violation is found, set this to `false`.

To test your e-mail settings, you can run Tripwire using the `/usr/sbin/tripwire -m t -email your@emailaddr` command. Remember to change the `you@emailaddr` to your own e-mail address.

Setting up Integrity-Checkers

When you have many Linux systems to manage, it isn't always possible to go from one machine to another to perform security checks — in fact, it isn't recommended. When you manage a cluster of machines, it's a good idea to centralize security as much as possible. As mentioned before, Tripwire can be installed and set up as a `cron` job on each Linux node on a network, but that becomes a lot of work (especially on larger networks). Here I discuss a new integrity checker called Advanced Intrusion Detection Environment (AIDE), along with a Perl-based utility called Integrity Checking Utility (ICU) that can automate integrity checking on a Linux network.

Setting up AIDE

AIDE is really a Tripwire alternative. The author of AIDE liked Tripwire but wanted to create a free replacement of Tripwire with added functionality. Because Tripwire Open Source exists, the "free aspect" of the AIDE goal no longer makes any difference, but the AIDE tool is easy to deploy in a network environment with the help of ICU.

You can get Tripwire company to sell you a shrink-wrapped, integrity checking solution that works in a cluster of Linux hosts. So inquire about this with Tripwire.

Downloading and extracting the latest source distribution from `ftp://ftp.linux.hr/pub/aide/` is the very first step in establishing AIDE. As of this writing the latest version is 0.7 (`aide-0.7.tar.gz`). When following these instructions, make sure you replace the version number with the version you are currently installing. Here's how you can compile AIDE:

1. `su` to `root`.

2. Extract the source tar ball.

   For version 0.7, use the `tar xvzf aide-0.7.tar.gz` command in the `/usr/src/redhat/SOURCES` directory. You see a new subdirectory called `aide-0.7`.

3. Change your current directory to `aide-0.7` and run the `./configure` command.

4. Run `make; make install` to compile and install the software.

   The AIDE binary, `aide`, is installed in `/usr/local/bin` and the `man` pages are installed in the `/usr/local/man` directory.

Now you can set up ICU.

ICU requires that you have SSH1 support available in both the ICU server and ICU client systems. You must install OpenSSH (which also requires OpenSSL) to make ICU work. See Chapter 12 and Chapter 11 for information on how to meet these prerequisites.

Setting up ICU

To use the Perl-based utility called Integrity Checking Utility (ICU) you have to set up the ICU server and client software.

ESTABLISHING AN ICU SERVER

Start the setup process by downloading the latest version of ICU from the `http://nitzer.dhs.org/ICU/ICU.html` site. I downloaded version 0.2 (`ICU-0.2.tar.gz`) for these instructions. As always, make sure you replace the version number mentioned here with your current version of ICU.

Here's how you can compile ICU on the server that manages the ICU checks on other remote Linux systems:

1. su to root on the system where you want to run the ICU service.

   This is the server that launches ICU on remote Linux systems and performs remote integrity checking and also hosts the AIDE databases for each host.

2. Extract the source in /usr/src/redhat/SOURCES.

   A new subdirectory called ICU-0.2 is created.

3. Run the cp -r /usr/src/redhat/SOURCES/ICU-0.2 /usr/local/ICU command to copy the source in /usr/local/ICU, which makes setup quite easy because the author of the program uses this directory in the default configuration file.

4. Create a new user account called icu, using the adduser icu command.

   - Change the ownership of the /usr/local/ICU directory to the new user by running the chown -R icu /usr/local/ICU command.

   - Change the permission settings using the chmod -R 700 /usr/local/ICU command so that only the new user can access files in that directory.

5. Edit the ICU configuration file (ICU.conf) using your favorite text editor.

   - Modify the icu_server_name setting to point to the ICU server that launches and runs ICU on remote Linux machines.

     This is the machine you are currently configuring.

   - Change the admin_e-mail setting to point to your e-mail address.

     If you don't use Sendmail as your mail server, change the sendmail setting to point to your Sendmail-equivalent mail daemon.

6. The default configuration file has settings that aren't compatible with OpenSSH utilities. Change these settings as shown here:

OpenSSH-incompatible setting	Change to
ssh = /usr/local/bin/ssh1	ssh = /usr/local/bin/ssh
scp = /usr/local/bin/scp1	scp = /usr/local/bin/scp
ssh_keygen = /usr/local/bin/ssh-keygen1	ssh_keygen = /usr/local/bin/ssh-keygen

7. Remove the -l option from the following lines of the scp (secure copy) command settings in the ICU.conf file:

```
get_bin_cmd = %scp% -l -P %port% -i %key_get_bin_priv% \
root@%hostname%:%host_basedir%/aide.bin %tmp_dir%/ 2>&1
get_conf_cmd = %scp% -l -P %port% -i %key_get_conf_priv% \
root@%hostname%:%host_basedir%/aide.conf %tmp_dir%/ 2>&1
get_db_cmd = %scp% -l -P %port% -i %key_get_db_priv% \
root@%hostname%:%host_basedir%/aide.db %tmp_dir%/ 2>&1
```

8. su to the icu user using the su icu command. Run the ./ICU.pl -G command to generate five pairs of keys in the keys directory.

9. Run the ./ICU.pl -s to perform a sanity check, which ensures that everything is set up as needed.

   If you get error messages from this step, fix the problem according to the messages displayed.

10. Copy and rename the AIDE binary file from /usr/local/bin to /usr/local/ICU/binaries/aide.bin-i386-linux, using the following command:

```
cp /usr/local/bin/aide /usr/local/ICU/binaries/aide.
bin-i386-linux
```

I recommend that you read the man page for AIDE configuration (using the man aide.conf command) before you modify this file. For now, you can leave the configuration as is.

Now you can set up a remote Linux system as an ICU client.

ESTABLISHING AN ICU CLIENT

The ICU server runs AIDE on this remote host via the SSH1 protocol. Here's how you add a host that the ICU server manages:

1. Modify the /usr/local/ICU/ICU.hosts file to add a line using the following syntax:

```
hostname:email:OS:architecture:SSH1 port
```

An example is shown here:

```
k2.intevo.com:admin@id10t.intevo.com:linux:i386:22
```

2. Perform a sanity check for the host using the ./ICU.pl -s -r *hostname* command. For the preceding example, this command is ./ICU.pl -s -r

k2.intevo.com. Remember to replace the hostname with the actual host-name of the Linux computer that you want to bring under ICU control.

3. Create a tar ball containing all the necessary files for the host, using the ./ICU.pl -n -r hostname command. This creates a .tar file called /usr/local/ICU/databases/hostname.icu-install.tar.

4. FTP the .tar file to the desired remote Linux system whose files you want to bring under integrity control. Log in to the remote Linux system and su to root.

5. Run the tar xvf *hostname*.icu-install.tar command to extract it in a temporary directory. This creates a new subdirectory within the extraction directory called *hostname-icu-install*.

6. From the new directory, run the ./icu-install.sh command to install a copy of aide.conf and aide.db to the /var/adm/.icu directory

7. Append five public keys to ~/.ssh/authorized_keys - key_init_db.pub to initialize the database, key_check.pub to run an AIDE check, key_get_bin.pub to send aide.bin (the AIDE binary), key_get_conf.pub to send aide.conf (configuration) and key_get_db.pub to send aide.db (the integrity database).

The keys don't use any pass phrase because they are used via cron to run automatic checks.

Now you can start ICU checks from the ICU server.

INITIALIZING THE REMOTE HOST'S INTEGRITY DATABASE
Before you can perform the actual integrity checks on any of the remote systems, you have to create the initial integrity database.

1. Log in as icu user and change directory to /usr/local/ICU.

2. Run the ./ICU.pl -i -r *hostname* command, where *hostname* should be replaced with the name of the remote Linux system (the name of your new ICU client).

3. Because this is the first time you are connecting to the remote system using the icu account, you are prompted as follows:

```
The authenticity of host 'k2.intevo.com' can't be
established.
RSA key fingerprint is
1d:4e:b3:d1:c2:94:f5:44:e9:ae:02:65:68:4f:07:57.
Are you sure you want to continue connecting (yes/no)? yes
```

4. Enter **yes** to continue. You see a warning message as shown here:

```
Warning: Permanently added 'k2.intevo.com,172.20.15.1' (RSA)
to the list of known hosts.
```

5. Wait until the database is initialized. Ignore the `traverse_tree()` warning messages from AIDE. Your screen displays output similar to the following example:

```
Verbose mode activated.
Initializing sanity check.
Sanity check passed.
Database initialization started
Checking if port 22 is open.
Executing init command: '/usr/local/bin/ssh -x -l root -p 22 -i
/usr/local/ICU/keys/key_init_db k2.intevo.com "/var/adm/.icu/aide.bin -i -c
/var/adm/.icu/aide.conf -V5 -A gzip_dbout=no -B gzip_dbout=no -B
database_out=file:/var/adm/.icu/aide.db.new -B
database=file:/var/adm/.icu/aide.db -B report_url=stdout; mv
/var/adm/.icu/aide.db.new /var/adm/.icu/aide.db" 2>&1'
This may take a while.
traverse_tree():No such file or directory: /root/.ssh2
traverse_tree():No such file or directory: /usr/heimdal
traverse_tree():No such file or directory: /usr/krb4
traverse_tree():No such file or directory: /usr/krb5
traverse_tree():No such file or directory: /usr/arla
mv: overwrite `/var/adm/.icu/aide.db'? y
aide.conf              100%
|*****************************************************|  5787     00:00
aide.db                100%
|*****************************************************|  3267 KB  00:03
All files successfully received.
Sending mail to kabir@k2.intevo.com with subject: [ICU - k2.intevo.com]  Welcome
to ICU!
Database initialization ended.
```

When initializing a new host, the first integrity database and configuration are saved as `/usr/localICU/databases/hostname/archive/aide.db-first-TIMESTAMP.gz` and `/usr/localICU/databases/hostname/archive/aide.conf-first-.TIMESTAMP`. For example, `/usr/localICU/databases/k2.intevo.com/archive/aide.db-first-Sat Dec 23 11:30:50 2000.gz` and `/usr/localICU/databases/k2.intevo.com/archive/aide.conf-first-Sat Dec 23 11:30:50 2000` are the initial database and configuration files created when the preceding steps were followed by a host called `k2.intevo.com`.

After the database of the remote host is initialized, you can run file-system integrity checks on the host.

CHECKING REMOTE HOST'S INTEGRITY DATABASE

To perform a file-system integrity check on a remote Linux system (in this case, your new ICU client), you can do the following:

1. Become the `icu` user on the ICU server.

2. Change directory to `/usr/local/ICU`.

3. Run the `./ICU.pl -v -c -r` *hostname* command, where *hostname* is the name of the ICU client system. For example, the `./ICU.pl -v -c -r r2d2.intevo.com` command performs filesystem integrity checks on the `r2d2.intevo.com` site from the ICU server. An example output of this command is shown in the following listing:

```
Verbose mode activated.
Initializing sanity check.
Sanity check passed.
Check started.
Checking if port 22 is open.
Getting files from r2d2.intevo.com: aide.bin aide.conf aide.db
All files successfully received.
Verifying MD5 fingerprint of the AIDE database...match.
Verifying MD5 fingerprint of the AIDE configuration...match.
Verifying MD5 fingerprint of the AIDE binary...match.
Executing AIDE check command on the remote host. This may take a while.
Getting files from r2d2.intevo.com: aide.db
All files successfully received.
A change in the filesystem was found, updating
/usr/local/ICU/databases/r2d2.intevo.com/aide.db.current.
Saving copy as /usr/local/ICU/databases/ r2d2.intevo.com/archive/aide.db-sun Dec
24 09:56:26 2000.
Sending mail to kabir@r2d2.intevo.com with subject: [ICU - r2d2.intevo.com]
Warning: Filesystem has changed (Added=2,Removed=0,Changed=11)
Check ended.
You have new mail in /var/mail/kabir
```

 TIP If you don't use the `-v` option in the preceding command, `ICU.pl` is less verbose. The `-v` option is primarily useful when you run the command from an interactive shell. Also, you can add the `-d` option to view debugging information if something isn't working right.

If the filesystems on the remote machine have changed, the administrator is notified via e-mail. As shown in the preceding sample output, two new files have been added and eleven files were modified. The e-mail sent to the administrator (kabir@ r2d2.intevo.com) looks like this:

```
From icu  sun Dec 24 09:56:30 2000
Date: sun, 24 Dec 2000 09:56:30 -0500
From: The ICU server <kabir@intevo.com>
To: kabir@r2d2.intevo.com
subject: [ICU - r2d2.intevo.com]  Warning: Filesystem has changed
(Added=2,Removed=0,Changed=11)
X-ICU-version: ICU v0.2 By Andreas Ÿstling, andreaso@it.su.se.
*** Warning ***
The filesystem on r2d2.intevo.com has changed.
This could mean that authorized changes were made, but it could
also mean that the host has been compromised. The database has been
updated with these changes and will now be regarded as safe.
Consider updating your /var/adm/.icu/aide.conf if you get warnings
about these changes all the time but think that the changes are legal.
Below is the output from AIDE. Read it carefully.
 AIDE found differences between database and filesystem!!
 Start timestamp: 2000-12-24 09:50:34
 summary:
 Total number of files=35619,added files=2,removed files=0,changed files=11
 Added files:
 added:/etc/rc.d/rc3.d/S65named
 added:/var/lib/tripwire/report/r2d2.intevo.com-20001224-091546.twr
 Changed files:
 changed:/etc/rc.d/rc3.d
 changed:/etc/mail/virtusertable.db
 changed:/etc/mail/access.db
 changed:/etc/mail/domaintable.db
 changed:/etc/mail/mailertable.db
 changed:/etc/aliases.db
 changed:/etc/ioctl.save
 changed:/etc/issue
 changed:/etc/issue.net
 changed:/boot
 changed:/boot/System.map
[Information on change details are not shown here]
```

With the AIDE and ICU combo, you can detect filesystem changes quite easily. You can, in fact, automate this entire process by running the ICU checks on remote machines as a `cron` job on the ICU server. Here's how:

1. Become the `icu` user on the ICU server.

2. Run the `crontab -e` command to enter new `cron` entries for the `icu` user.

3. Enter the following line (remember to replace *hostname* with appropriate remote host name).

```
15 1 * * * cd /usr/local/ICU; ./ICU.pl -c -r hostname
```

4. Save and exit the `crontab` file.

This runs filesystem integrity checks on the named host at 01:15 AM every morning. After you create a `cron` job for a host, monitor the `log` file (`/usr/local/ICU/logs/hostname.log`) for this host on the ICU server next morning to ensure that `ICU.pl` ran as intended.

 If you have a lot of remote Linux systems to check, add a new entry in the `/var/spool/cron/icu` file (using the `crontab -e` command), as shown in the preceding example. However, don't schedule the jobs too close to each other. If you check five machines, don't start all the `ICU.pl` processes at the same time. Spread out the load on the ICU server by scheduling the checks at 15- to 30-minute intervals. This ensures the health of your ICU server.

When `ICU.pl` finds integrity mismatches, it reports it via e-mail to the administrator. It's very important that the administrator reads her e-mail or else she won't know about a potential break-in.Doing Routine Backups

Protecting your system is more than keeping bad guys out. Other disasters threaten your data. Good, periodic backup gives you that protection.

The most important security advice anyone can give you is *back up regularly*. Create a maintainable backup schedule for your system. For example, you can perform incremental backups on weekdays and schedule a full backup over the weekend. I prefer removable media-based backup equipment such as 8mm tape drives or DAT drives. A removable backup medium enables you to store the information in a secure offsite location. Periodically check that your backup mechanism is functioning as expected. Make sure you can restore files from randomly selected backup media. You may recycle backup media, but know the usage limits that the media manufacturer claims.

Another type of "backup" you should do is backtracking your work as a system administrator. Document everything you do, especially work that you do as a superuser. This documentation enables you to trace problems that often arise while you are solving another.

 I keep a large history setting (a shell feature that remembers *N* number last commands), and I often print the history in a file or on paper. The `script` command also can record everything you do while using privileged accounts.

Using the dump and restore utilities

The dump and restore utilities can back up files onto tape drives, backup disks, or other removable media. The dump command can perform incremental backups, which makes the backup process much more manageable than simply copying all files on a routine basis. The restore command can restore the files backed up by the dump command. To learn more about these utilities, visit http://dump.sourceforge.net.

You need ext2 file-system utilities to compile the dump/restore suite. The ext2 file-system utilities (e2fsprogs) contain all of the standard utilities for creating, fixing, configuring, and debugging ext2 filesystems. Visit http://sourceforge.net/projects/e2fsprogs for information on these utilities.

Creating a Permission Policy

Most user problems on Unix and Unix-like systems are caused by file permissions. If something that was working yesterday and the day before yesterday all of a sudden stops working today, first suspect a permission problem. One of the most common causes of permission problems is the root account. Inexperienced system administrators often access files and programs via a superuser (root) account. The problem is that when the root user account runs a program, the files created can often be set with root ownership — in effect, that's an immediate and unintended gap in your security.

Setting configuration file permissions for users

Each user's home directory houses some semi-hidden files that start with a period (or dot). These files often execute commands at user login. For example, shells (csh, tcsh, bash, and so on) read their settings from a file such as .cshrc or .bashrc. If a user doesn't maintain file permissions properly, another not-so-friendly user can cause problems for the naive user. For example, if one user's .cshrc file is writeable by a second user, the latter can play a silly trick such as putting a logout command at the beginning of the .cshrc file so that the first user is logged out as soon as she logs in. Of course, the silly trick could develop into other tricks that violate a user's file privacy in the system. Therefore, you may want to watch for such situations on a multiuser system. If you only have a few users, you can also quickly perform simple checks like the following:

```
find /home -type f -name ".*rc" -exec ls -l {} \;
```

This command displays permissions for all the dot files ending in "rc" in the /home directory hierarchy. If your users' home directories are kept in /home, this shows you which users may have a permission problem.

Setting default file permissions for users

As a system administrator, you can define the default permission settings for all the user files that get on your system. The umask command sets the default permissions for new files.

Setting executable file permissions

Only the owner should have write permission for program files run by regular users. For example, the program files in /usr/bin should have permission settings such that only root can read, write, and execute; the settings for everyone else should include only read and execute. When others besides the owner can write to a program file, serious security holes are possible. For example, if someone other than the root user can write to a program such as /usr/bin/zip, a malicious user can replace the real zip program with a Trojan horse program that compromises system security, damaging files and directories anywhere it goes. So, always check the program files on your systems for proper permissions. Run COPS frequently to detect permission-related problems.

Summary

Improper file and directory permissions are often the cause of many user support incidents and also the source of many security problems. Understanding of file and directory permissions is critical to system administration of a Linux system. By setting default permissions for files, dealing with world-accessible and set-UID and set-GID files, taking advantage of advanced ext2 filesystem security features, using file integrity checkers such as Tripwire, AIDE, ICU, etc. you can enhance your system security.

Chapter 10

PAM

PLUGGABLE AUTHENTICATION MODULES (PAM) were originally developed for the Solaris operating system by Sun Microsystems. The Linux-PAM project made PAM available for the Linux platform. PAM is a suite of shared libraries that grants privileges to PAM-aware applications.

What is PAM?

You may wonder how programs such as `chsh`, `chfn`, `ftp`, `imap`, `linuxconf`, `rlogin`, `rexec`, `rsh`, `su`, `login`, and `passwd` suddenly understand the shadow password scheme (see Chapter 12) and use the `/etc/shadow` password file instead of the `/etc/passwd` file for authentication. They can do so because Red Hat distributes these programs with shadow password capabilities. Actually, Red Hat ships these programs with the much grander authentication scheme — PAM. These PAM-aware programs can enhance your system security by using both the shadow password scheme and virtually any other authentication scheme.

Traditionally, authentication schemes are built into programs that grant privileges to users. Programs such as `login` or `passwd` have the necessary code for authentication. Over time, this approach proved virtually unscaleable, because incorporating a new authentication scheme required you to update and recompile privilege-granting programs. To relieve the privilege-granting software developer from writing secure authentication code, PAM was developed. Figure 10-1 shows how PAM works with privilege-granting applications.

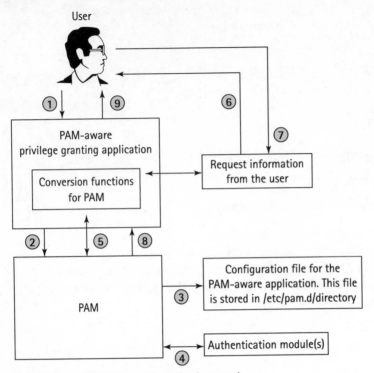

Figure 10-1: How PAM-aware applications work

When a privilege-granting application such as /bin/login is made into a PAM-aware application, it typically works in the manner shown in Figure 10-1 and described in the following list:

1. A user invokes such an application to access the service it offers.

2. The PAM-aware application calls the underlying PAM library to perform the authentication.

3. The PAM library looks up an application-specific configuration file in the /etc/pam.d/ directory. This file tells PAM what type of authentication is required for this application. (In case of a missing configuration file, the configuration in the /etc/pam.d/other file is used.)

4. The PAM library loads the required authentication module(s).

5. These modules make PAM communicate with the conversation functions available in the application.

6. The conversation functions request information from the user. For example, they ask the user for a password or a retina scan.

7. The user responds to the request by providing the requested information.

8. The PAM authentication modules supply the application with an authentication status message via the PAM library.

9. If the authentication process is successful, the application does one of the following:

   - Grants the requested privileges to the user

   - Informs the user that the process failed

Think of PAM as a facility that takes the burden of authentication away from the applications and stacks multiple authentication schemes for one application. For example, the PAM configuration file for the rlogin application is shown in Listing 10-1.

Listing 10-1: The /etc/pam.d/rlogin file

```
#%PAM-1.0
auth       required    /lib/security/pam_securetty.so
auth       sufficient  /lib/security/pam_rhosts_auth.so
auth       required    /lib/security/pam_stack.so service=system-auth
auth       required    /lib/security/pam_nologin.so
account    required    /lib/security/pam_stack.so service=system-auth
password   required    /lib/security/pam_stack.so service=system-auth
session    required    /lib/security/pam_stack.so service=system-auth
```

In this file, multiple pluggable authentication modules from /lib/security authenticate the user.

Working with a PAM configuration file

Listing 10-1 shows what a PAM configuration file for an application looks like. Blank lines and lines starting with a leading # character are ignored. A configuration line has the following fields:

```
module-type control-flag module-path module-args
```

Currently, four module types exist, which are described in Table 10-1.

TABLE 10-1: PAM MODULE TYPES

Module Type	Description
auth	Does the actual authentication. Typically, an auth module requires a password or other proof of identity from a user.
account	Handles all the accounting aspects of an authentication request. Typically, an account module checks whether the user access meets all the access guidelines. For example, it can check whether the user is accessing the service from a secure host and during a specific time.
password	Sets password.
session	Handles session management tasks, such as refreshing session tokens.

The control flag defines how the PAM library handles a module's response. Four control flags, described in Table 10-2, are currently allowed.

TABLE 10-2: PAM MODULE CONTROL FLAGS

Control Flag	Description
required	This control flag tells the PAM library to require the success of the module specified in the same line. When a module returns a response indicating a failure, the authentication definitely fails, but PAM continues with other modules (if any). This prevents users from detecting which part of the authentication process failed, because knowing that information may aid a potential attacker.
requisite	This control flag tells the PAM library to abort the authentication process as soon as the PAM library receives a failure response.
sufficient	This control flag tells the PAM library to consider the authentication process complete if it receives a success response. Proceeding with other modules in the configuration file is unnecessary.
optional	This control flag is hardly used. It removes the emphasis on the success or failure response of the module.

The control-flag field also permits conditional flags. The conditional flags take the following form:

```
[key1=value1 key2=value2 ...]
```

The key in this key value list, can be one of the following:

```
open_err, symbol_err, service_err, system_err, buf_err,
perm_denied, auth_err, cred_insufficient,
authinfo_unavail, user_unknown, maxtries,
new_authtok_reqd, acct_expired, session_err,
cred_unavail, cred_expired, cred_err, no_module_data,
conv_err, authtok_err, authtok_recover_err,
authtok_lock_busy, authtok_disable_aging, try_again,
ignore, abort, authtok_expired, module_unknown,
bad_item, and default.
```

The value in this key value list can be one of the following:

```
ignore, ok, done, bad, die, reset, or a positive
integer
```

If a positive integer is used, PAM skips that many records of the same type.

The module path is the path of a pluggable authentication module. Red Hat Linux stores all the PAM modules in the /lib/security directory. You can supply each module with optional arguments, as well.

In Listing 10-1, the PAM library calls the pam_securetty.so module, which must return a response indicating success for successful authentication. If the module's response indicates failure, PAM continues processing the other modules so that the user (who could be a potential attacker) doesn't know where the failure occurred. If the next module (pam_rhosts_auth.so) returns a success response, the authentication process is complete, because the control flag is set to sufficient. However, if the previous module (pam_securetty.so) doesn't fail but this one fails, the authentication process continues and the failure doesn't affect the final result. In the same fashion, the PAM library processes the rest of the modules.

The order of execution exactly follows the way the modules appear in the configuration. However, each type of module (auth, account, password, and session) is processed in stacks. In other words, in Listing 10-1, all the auth modules are stacked and processed in the order of appearance in the configuration file. The rest of the modules are processed in a similar fashion.

Establishing a PAM-aware Application

Every program that requires user authentication under Red Hat Linux can use PAM. In fact, virtually all such programs include their own PAM configuration file in

/etc/pam.d directory. Because each application has its own configuration file, custom authentication requirements are easily established for them. However, too many custom authentication requirements are probably not a good thing for management. This configuration management issue has been addressed with the recent introduction of a PAM module called the pam_stack.so. This module simply can jump to another PAM configuration while in the middle of one. This can be better explained with an example. Listing 10-2 shows /etc/pam.d/login, the PAM configuration file for the login application.

Listing 10-2: The /etc/pam.d/login file

```
#%PAM-1.0
auth       required     /lib/security/pam_securetty.so
auth       required     /lib/security/pam_stack.so service=system-auth
auth       required     /lib/security/pam_nologin.so
account    required     /lib/security/pam_stack.so service=system-auth
password   required     /lib/security/pam_stack.so service=system-auth
session    required     /lib/security/pam_stack.so service=system-auth
session    optional     /lib/security/pam_console.so
```

When the PAM layer is invoked by the login application, it looks up this file and organizes four different stacks:

◆ Auth stack

◆ Account stack

◆ Password stack

◆ Session stack

In this example, the auth stack consists of the pam_securetty, pam_stack, and pam_nologin modules. PAM applies each of the modules in a stack in the order they appear in the configuration file. In this case, the pam_securetty module must (because of the "required" control flag) respond with a failure for the auth processing to continue. After the pam securetty module is satisfied, the auth processing moves to the pam_stack module. This module makes PAM read a configuration file specified in the service=*configuration* argument. Here, the system-auth configuration is provided as the argument; therefore, it's loaded. The default version of this configuration file is shown in Listing 10-3.

Listing 10-3: The /etc/pam.d/system-auth file

```
#%PAM-1.0
# This file is auto-generated.
# User changes are destroyed the next time authconfig is run.
auth        sufficient    /lib/security/pam_unix.so likeauth nullok md5 shadow
```

```
auth         required      /lib/security/pam_deny.so
account      sufficient    /lib/security/pam_unix.so
account      required      /lib/security/pam_deny.so
password     required      /lib/security/pam_cracklib.so retry=3
password     sufficient    /lib/security/pam_unix.so nullok use_authtok md5
shadow
password     required      /lib/security/pam_deny.so
session      required      /lib/security/pam_limits.so
session      required      /lib/security/pam_unix.so
```

As shown, this configuration has its own set of auth, account, password, and session stacks. Because the pam_stack module can jump to a central configuration file like this one, it enables a centralized authentication configuration, which leads to better management of the entire process. You can simply change the system-auth file and affect all the services that use the pam_stack module to jump to it. For example, you can enforce time-based access control using a module called pam_time (the *Controlling access by time* section explains this module) for every type of user access that understands PAM. Simply add the necessary pam_time configuration line in the appropriate stack in the system-auth configuration file.

Typically, when you are establishing a new PAM-aware application on Red Hat Linux, it should include the PAM configuration file. If it doesn't include one or it includes one that appears to not use this centralized configuration discussed, you can try the following:

1. If you have a PAM configuration file for this application, rename it to /etc/pam.d/*myapp*.old, where *myapp* is the name of your current PAM configuration file.

2. Create a new file called /etc/pam.d/*myapp* so that it has the following lines:

```
auth        required   /lib/security/pam_stack.so
service=system-auth
auth        required   /lib/security/pam_nologin.so
account     required   /lib/security/pam_stack.so
service=system-auth
password    required   /lib/security/pam_stack.so
service=system-auth
session     required   /lib/security/pam_stack.so
service=system-auth
```

3. The preceding PAM configuration delegates actual configuration to the /etc/pam.d/system-auth file.

4. Access the application as usual. If you have no problem accessing it, you just created a centrally managed PAM configuration file for *myapp* application.

5. If you run into a problem, run the `tail -f /var/log/messages` command on a shell or xterm and try *myapp* as usual. Watch the log messages that PAM generates.

PAM-generated log messages usually have PAM_*modulename* strings in them where *modulename* is the name of the PAM module that is attempting a task. The log information should show why the application isn't working as usual. If you still can't fix it and have an old configuration, simply rename the old configuration file back to *myapp* so that you can use the application. In such a case, your application doesn't work with the `system-auth` configuration and you can't do much to change that.

Most PAM-aware applications are shipped with their own PAM configuration files. But even if you find one that is not, it's still using PAM. By default, when PAM can't find a specific configuration file for an application, it uses the default `/etc/pam.d/other` configuration. This configuration file is shown in Listing 10-4.

Listing 10-4: The /etc/pam.d/other file

```
#%PAM-1.0
auth      required      /lib/security/pam_deny.so
account   required      /lib/security/pam_deny.so
password  required      /lib/security/pam_deny.so
session   required      /lib/security/pam_deny.so
```

This configuration simply denies access using the `pam_deny` module, which always returns failure status. I recommend that you keep this file the way it is so that you have a "deny everyone access unless access is permitted by configuration" type of security policy.

Using Various PAM Modules to Enhance Security

Red Hat Linux ships with many PAM modules.

♦ `pam_access.so`

This module uses the `/etc/security/access.conf` configuration file. This configuration file has the following configuration format:

```
< + or - > : <username list> : <tty list | host list]
```

The positive sign in the first field indicates a grant permission; the negative sign indicates a deny permission. The user list consists of at least one comma-separated username or group. The third field can either be a list of tty devices or host/domain names.

When you want to restrict a certain user from logging in via the physical console, use the tty list. To restrict login access by hostname or domain names (prefixed with a leading period), specify the host or domain names in a comma-separated list. Use ALL to represent everything; use EXCEPT to exclude list on the right side of this keyword; use LOCAL to match anything without a period in it. For example:

```
-:sysadmin:ALL EXCEPT LOCAL
```

Here, users in the `sysadmin` group are denied login access unless they log in locally using the console.

- pam_console.so

- This module controls which PAM-aware, privileged commands such as `/sbin/shutdown`, `/sbin/halt`, and `/sbin/reboot` an ordinary user can run.

See the *Securing console access using mod_console* section.

◆ `pam_cracklib.so`

This module checks the strength of a password using the crack library.

◆ `pam_deny.so`

This module always returns false. For example, it's used in the `/etc/pam.d/other` configuration to deny access to any user who is trying to access a PAM-aware program without a PAM configuration file.

◆ `pam_env.so`

This module sets environment variables.

See `/etc/security/pam_env.conf` for details.

◆ `pam_filter.so`

This module accesses STDIN and STDOUT data that passes between the user and the application. It's currently not used in any default configuration shipped with Red Hat Linux.

◆ `pam_ftp.so`

This is a simple FTP authentication module that currently is not used.

◆ `pam_group.so`

This is the group access module that uses the `/etc/security/group.conf` file to provide (or remove) group access to services.

Using this module you can give a group (in /etc/group) access to PAM-aware programs.

◆ pam_issue.so

This module displays the contents of the /etc/issue file during login process.

This module isn't recommended because displaying unnecessary information before a user can be authenticated can give clues to a potential intruder.

◆ pam_lastlog.so

This module displays information about a user's last login.

This module isn't recommended because displaying unnecessary information before a user can be authenticated can give clues to a potential intruder.

◆ pam_limits.so

This module sets resource limits using the /etc/security/limits.conf file for an ordinary user session.

See the *Managing System Resources Among Users* section for details.

◆ pam_listfile.so

This module reads a file and performs an action (that is, it enables or denies access) based on the existence or non-existence of an item such as username, tty, host, groups, or shell.

See the *Restricting FTP access by username* section in Chapter 18 for an example of this module.

◆ pam_localuser.so

This module returns success when the user being authenticated is found in the /etc/passwd file of the server. Optionally, you can specify a different file for the file argument, as in the following example:

```
auth  required /lib/security/pam_localuser.so \
               file=/etc/myusers
```

If you add the preceding line in a PAM-aware application configuration file, the authentication is successful if the user being authenticated is listed in /etc/myusers file.

 TIP The functionally of this module is like the pam_listfile.so module.

◆ pam_mail.so

This module checks whether the user has new or unread e-mail and displays a message.

◆ pam_mkhomedir.so

This module creates a user's home directory upon the first successful login. It's very useful if you use a central user information repository (using LDAP orNIS) to manage a large number of users. For example, after you create the user account on the LDAP server, the home directories aren't needed on all the machines the user has access privileges to if these machines use the following line in the configuration of access control application such as login and sshd:

```
session required /lib/security/pam_mkhomedir.so \
skel=/etc/skel/ umask=0022
```

This line assumes that you want to get the user resource files (such as dot files for shell) from the /etc/skel directory and also set a umask of 0022 for the new home directory and dot files.

◆ pam_motd.so

Displays the /etc/motd (message of the day) file when a user successfully logs in. You can also display a different file using the mod=/path/to/filename option.

This module isn't recommended because displaying unnecessary information before a user can be authenticated can give clues to a potential
intruder.

◆ pam_nologin.so

This module can restrict all users but root from logging into the system.

See the *Restricting access to everyone but root* section.

◆ pam_permit.so

This module works as an auth, account, password, or session module
and always returns success. This should be used only for very low-risk
authentication or authorization tasks. For example, enabling any user to
use the kbdrate command to reset the keyboard repeat rate and delay
time isn't risky. Therefore, it's acceptable for the /etc/pam.d/kbdrate
configuration file to look like this:

```
auth       sufficient   /lib/security/pam_rootok.so
auth       required     /lib/security/pam_console.so
account    required     /lib/security/pam_permit.so
```

◆ pam_pwdb.so

This is the old password database module.

Use pam_unix instead.

◆ pam_radius.so

This module provides session services for users authenticated via a
RADIUS server.

◆ pam_rhosts_auth.so

This is the rhosts module.

Stay away from rhosts enabled services such as rlogin and rsh. These
were considered major security holes for years.

◆ `pam_rootok.so`

This is the root access module. When you are logged in as root and run programs such as `shutdown`, `reboot`, `halt`, or any other privileged command, normally you should be authenticated.

> If this module is used in the PAM configuration of such commands, the root user is excused from entering her password. The most useful place for this module is in `/etc/pam.d/su` because root shouldn't need a password to `su` to an ordinary user.

◆ `pam_securetty.so`

This module reads the `/etc/securetty` file and checks to ensure that root user can't log in from any tty device not mentioned in this file.

◆ `pam_shells.so`

This module authenticates a user if her login shell is listed in the `/etc/shells` file.

◆ `pam_stack.so`

This module can jump out of the current configuration file in `/etc/pam.d` to another one. For example, does `/etc/pam.d/sshd` have the following line?

```
auth        required       /lib/security/pam_stack.so \
service=system-auth
```

If so, when PAM is authenticating an SSH request on behalf of the `sshd` daemon, it jumps to `/etc/pam.d/system-auth` file and performs the `auth` process found in that file.

> This module enables a highly manageable authentication scheme by centralizing authentication requirements in one or multiple configuration files that can be used by many programs. For example, if you decide that the authentication process for `sshd` and `login` are the same, without `pam_stack` you must create duplicate configuration in the `/etc/pam.d/sshd` and `/etc/pam.d/login` files. That means if you later decide to add another `pam_module` for more control, you must then change both of these configuration files. Using `pam_stack`, you can centralize the authentication rules to one file and only change this file to reflect your requirements change to every program that should use the new module.

◆ `pam_stress.so`

This module enables you to stress test your applications. I have never used this module and don't know of any good application for it.

◆ `pam_tally.so`

This module tracks access attempts for a user account. It can deny access after a specified number of failures.

◆ `pam_time.so`

See the *Controlling access by time* section for details.

◆ `pam_unix_acct.so`

This module no longer exists. It's now a symbolic link for the `pam_unix.so` module.

◆ `pam_unix_auth.so`

This module no longer exists. It's now a symbolic link for the `pam_unix.so` module.

◆ `pam_unix_passwd.so`

This module no longer exists. It's now a symbolic link for the `pam_unix.so` module.

◆ `pam_unix_session.so`

This module no longer exists. It's now a symbolic link for the `pam_unix.so` module.

◆ `pam_unix.so`

This is the standard password module that can work with both `/etc/passwd` and the `/etc/shadow` files.

◆ `pam_warn.so`

This module logs warning messages about requested authentication and authorization process.

The `pam_warn.so` module doesn't perform any authentication step itself.

◆ `pam_wheel.so`

This module restricts root access to users belonging to the wheel group. For example, the `/etc/pam.d/su` configuration includes a line such as the following:

```
auth        required       /lib/security/pam_wheel.so use_uid
```

This makes PAM confirm that the person trying to `su` to root (that is, not trying to `su` to a non-root user) belongs to the wheel group in `/etc/group` file.

◆ `pam_xauth.so`

This module works as a session module for forwarding `xauth` keys when programs such as `su` and `linuxconf` are used under X Window.

A few of these modules can enhance and enforce your system security policy.

Controlling access by time

To restrict access to services by time, you need an accounting module called `pam_time` (`/lib/security/pam_time.so`). This module can be configured to deny access to users based on the following criteria:

◆ Their name

◆ Time of day

◆ Day of the week

◆ Service they are applying for

◆ The terminal from which they are making their request

Its actions are determined with the `/etc/security/time.conf` configuration file. Follow these steps:

1. For control of all user access, modify the `/etc/pam.d/system-auth` PAM configuration file by adding the following line:

```
account  required  /lib/security/pam_time.so
```

2. Devise an access policy for login service. This example assumes that users should log in after 6 a.m. and no later than 8 p.m.

3. Configure the `/etc/security/time.conf` file. The configuration lines in this file have the following syntax:

```
services;ttys;users;times
```

You can use some special characters in the fields. Table 10-3 describes the special characters.

TABLE 10-3: SPECIAL CHARACTERS FOR CONFIGURATION FIELDS IN /ETC/SECURITY/TIME.CONF

Character	Meaning
!	NOT. For example, !login means "not login" or "except login."
|	OR. For example, kabir|ronak means "either kabir or ronak."
&	AND. For example, login&su means "both login and su."
*	Wildcard. For example, foo* means "everything that starts with foo."

Table 10-4 describes the fields in such a configuration line.

TABLE 10-4: FIELDS OF THE /ETC/SECURITY/TIME.CONF FILE

Field	Description
services	A list of services that are affected by the time restriction. For example, for control of login and su using one rule, specify the service to be login&su in a configuration line.
ttys	A list of terminals that are affected by the time restriction. For example, for control of only pseudoterminals and not the console terminals, specify ttyp*!tty*, where ttyp* lists all the pseudoterminals used in remote login via services such as Telnet, and tty* lists all the console terminals.
users	A list of users who are affected by the time restriction. For example, to specify all the users, use the wildcard character * in a configuration line.
time	A list of times when the restrictions apply. You can specify time as a range in a 24-hour clock format. For example, to specify a range from 8 p.m. to 6 a.m., specify 2000-0600 (that is, *HHMM* format, where *HH* is 00-23 and *MM* is 00-59). You can also specify days by using a two-character code, such as Mo (Monday), Tu (Tuesday), We (Wednesday), Th (Thursday), Fr (Friday), Sa (Saturday), and Su (Sunday). You can also use special codes, such as Wk for all weekdays, Wd for weekends, and Al for all seven days. For example, to restrict access to a service from 8 p.m. to 6 a.m. every day, specify a time range as !Al2000-0600.

For the ongoing example, you can create a time-based rule that prohibits login access from 8 p.m. to 6 a.m. for all users who access the system via remote means (such as Telnet) by adding the following line to the /etc/security/time.conf file:

```
login;ttyp*;*;!Al2000-0600
```

This line can be interpreted this way:

```
If (requested service is login) and
    (access is made from a pseudo ttyp type device) and
    (current time is between 8PM to 6AM) then
     Access to the requested service is not allowed.
Else
     Access to the requested service is permitted.
End
```

To enable a user called kabir access to the system at any time, but make all other users follow the preceding rule, modify the rule this way:

```
login;ttyp*;*!kabir;!Al2000-0600
```

Restricting access to everyone but root

The pam_nologin module can restrict all users but root from accessing the system. The module is used this way:

```
auth required /lib/security/pam_nologin.so
```

This module checks for the existence of the /etc/nologin file. If this file exits, the module returns failure but displays the contents of this file on screen so users see the reason for the restriction.

Typically, the /etc/nologin file is created when the system administrator (root) should perform maintenance tasks such as the following:

◆ Rebooting the server

◆ Installing special software

◆ Configuring disk drives

To disable user login, create the file by running the touch /etc/nologin command. If you want to write a note to the users, modify this file and tell the users why they can't access your system at this time. After you are done, remove the /etc/nologin file so that users can log in again.

If you enable multiple login methods such as ssh or telnet (not recommended), make sure each of the PAM configuration files for these services requires the pam_nologin configuration as shown in the beginning of this section. Also, if you use multiple auth lines in a PAM configuration such as the /etc/pam.d/login, make sure the nologin line appears before any auth line with the sufficient control flag. Otherwise, the /etc/nologin isn't displayed because the module may not be used.

Managing system resources among users

By restricting a user account's capability to hog system resources, you can keep your system safe from user abuses. The pam_limits module can manage system resources for an individual user or a group of users. The following list shows the major resources that you can manage with this module:

◆ Maximum number of processes (nproc)

◆ Maximum number of logs (maxlogins)

◆ Process priority for user run commands (priority)

◆ Maximum CPU time (cpu) in minutes

◆ Maximum stack size in user programs (stack)

◆ Maximum number of opened files (nofile)

◆ Maximum data size (data)

◆ Maximum file size (fsize)

◆ Maximum resident memory size of a user process (rss)

◆ Maximum size of the core file (core)

◆ Maximum memory address space (as)

Each configuration line in the /etc/security/limits.conf file has the following format:

```
username | @group | *   hard | soft  resourcename value
```

The following list defines the codes used in the preceding format:

◆ The @ symbol denotes a user group.

◆ Thard is the maximum limit.

- ◆ `Tsoft` is the default limit.

- ◆ The `resourcename` is the name of the resource, such as the following:

  - ■ `nproc`

  - ■ `maxlogins`

  - ■ `nofiles`

  - ■ `rss`

  - ■ `fsize`

  - ■ `stack`

- ◆ `Tvalue` is the limit you want to set.

For example:

```
kabir    hard    nproc    5
```

Here, the user `kabir` has a hard limit of five (5) on the number of processes he can run. In other words, if this user tries to run more than five processes, the system refuses to run more than five. For example, after logging in, the user runs the `ps auxww | grep ^ kabir` command to see the number of processes owned by him. The command returns the following lines:

```
kabir    1626  0.0  0.5  2368 1324 pts/2    S    14:36   0:00 -tcsh
kabir    1652  0.0  0.2  2552  752 pts/2    R    14:40   0:00 ps auxww
kabir    1653  0.0  0.2  1520  596 pts/2    R    14:40   0:00 grep ^kabir
```

User `kabir` shows one shell process (`tcsh`) and two other processes (`ps` and `grep`) that are part of the preceding command. Now, running the `man perl` command shows the following message:

```
sh: fork: Resource temporarily unavailable
sh: fork: Resource temporarily unavailable
Error executing formatting or display command.
System command (cd /usr/share/man ; (echo -e ".ll 11.3i\n.pl 1100i"; /bin/gunzip
-c /usr/share/man/man1/perl.1.gz; echo ".pl \n(nlu+10") | /usr/bin/gtbl |
/usr/bin/groff -Tlatin1 -mandoc | /usr/bin/less -isr) exited with status 128.
No manual entry for perl
```

The command failed because it tried to fork more than five processes. Such control over the number of processes that a user can run could have a great impact on overall system reliability, which translates well for security. A reliable system is predictable and predictable systems are more secure than the ones that aren't.

Securing console access using mod_console

This module typically controls device permissions and privileged command settings for users who log in via the physical console. When an ordinary user logs in to a Red Hat Linux system via the console, she has full access to many attached devices, such as the floppy drive, the CD drive, and the Zip drive. The permission settings that enable an ordinary console user access to such devices are configured in the /etc/security/console.perms file.

To limit ordinary console users from accessing a particular device, comment out the appropriate device permission line in this file. For example, if you don't want an ordinary console user to access the floppy and the CD drives on the system, you must comment out the following lines in the /etc/security/console.perms file.

```
<console>  0660 <floppy>    0660 root.floppy
<console>  0600 <cdrom>     0600 root.disk
```

Also the <console>, <floppy>, and <cdrom> aliases (also known as classes) must point to the desired devices. The default values for these aliases are also found in the same file. They are shown below:

```
<console>=tty[0-9][0-9]* :[0-9]\.[0-9] :[0-9]
<floppy>=/dev/fd[0-1]*
<cdrom>=/dev/cdrom* /dev/cdwriter*
```

As shown, the values contain wildcards and simple, regular expressions. The default values should cover most typical situations.

As mentioned before, the pam_console module also controls which PAM-aware, privileged commands such as /sbin/shutdown, /sbin/halt, and /sbin/reboot an ordinary user can run. Let's take a look at what happens when an ordinary user runs the shutdown command.

♦ The user enters the shutdown -r now command at the console prompt to reboot the system.

♦ The /usr/bin/shutdown script, which is what the user runs, runs a program called consolehelper. This program in turn uses a program called userhelper that runs the /sbin/reboot program. In this process, the PAM configuration for the reboot program (stored in /etc/pam.d/reboot) is applied.

♦ In the /etc/pam.d/reboot file you will see that the pam_console module is used as an auth module, which then checks for the existence of a file called /etc/security/console.apps/reboot. If this file exists and the user meets the authentication and authorization requirements of the /etc/pam.d/reboot configuration, the reboot command is executed.

If the user runs the `shutdown` command using the -h option, the `/usr/bin/shutdown` script uses the `/sbin/halt` program in place of `/sbin/reboot` and uses halt-specific PAM configuration files.

Consider these security scenarios:

♦ Prevent an ordinary console user from rebooting or halting by removing the `/etc/security/console.apps/reboot` or `/etc/security/console.apps/halt` file accordingly. However, console users are typically trusted unless the console is located in an unsecured place.

♦ If you house your system in an ISP co-location facility or other unsecured places, consider restricting access to the `shutdown`, `reboot`, and `halt` commands by modifying the `/etc/pam.d/reboot`, `/etc/pam.d/halt`, and `/etc/pam.d/shutdown` files to the following line:

```
auth   required   /lib/security/pam_stack.so service=system-auth
```

♦ This makes sure that even if someone can access a user account or opened shell (perhaps you didn't log out when you walked away from the system), he must know the user's password to shut down, reboot, or halt the machine. In my recent security analysis experience, I found instances where many organizations housed their Web servers in ISP co-location facilities, which are very secured from outside. However, many of the servers had physical consoles attached to them and often had opened shell running simple stats programs such as `top` and `vmstat`. Anyone could stop these programs and simply pull a prank by typing shutdown, reboot, or, even worse – halt! It is essential in these situations to require the password, using the configuration line discussed in the preceding text.

It's a big step towards security management that Red Hat Linux ships with PAM and PAM-aware applications. To follow the PAM happenings, visit the primary PAM distribution site at `www.us.kernel.org/pub/linux/libs/pam/` frequently.

Summary

PAM is a highly configurable authentication technology that introduces a layer of middleware between the application and the actual authentication mechanism. In addition to this, PAM can handle account and session data, which is something that normal authentication mechanisms don't do very well. Using various PAM modules, you can customize authentication processes for users, restrict user access to console and applications based on such properties as username, time, and terminal location.

Chapter 11

OpenSSL

IN THIS CHAPTER

◆ Understanding how SSL works

◆ Installing and configuring OpenSSL

◆ Understanding server certificates

◆ Getting a server certificate from a commercial CA

◆ Creating a private certificate authority

ONLY A FEW YEARS AGO, the Internet was still what it was initially intended to be — a worldwide network for scientists and engineers. By virtue of the Web, however, the Internet is now a network for everyone. These days, it seems as though everyone and everything is on the Internet. It's also the "new economy" frontier; thousands of businesses, large and small, for better or worse, have set up e-commerce sites for customers around the world. Customers are cautious, however, because they know that not all parts of the Internet are secured.

To eliminate this sense of insecurity in the new frontier, the Netscape Corporation invented a security protocol that ensures secured transactions between the customer's Web browser and the Web server. Netscape named this protocol Secured Sockets Layer (SSL). Quickly SSL found its place in many other Internet applications, such as e-mail and remote access. Because SSL is now part of the foundation of the modern computer security infrastructure, it's important to know how to incorporate SSL in your Linux system. This chapter shows you how.

Understanding How SSL Works

The foundation of SSL is encryption. When data travels from one point of the Internet to another, it goes through a number of computers such as routers, gateways, and other network devices.

As you can see, the data must travel through many nodes. Although data packets travel at a high speed (usually reaching their destination in milliseconds), interception is still a possibility at one of these nodes — which is why we need a secured mechanism for exchanging sensitive information. This security is achieved through encryption.

Technically speaking, *encryption* is the mathematical encoding scheme that ensures that only the intended recipient can access the data; it hides the data from eavesdroppers by sending it in a deliberately garbled form. Encryption schemes often restrict access to resources. For example, if you log on to a Unix or Windows NT system, the passwords or keys you use are typically stored in the server computer in an encrypted format. On most Unix systems, a user's password is encrypted and matched with the encrypted password stored in an /etc/passwd file. If this comparison is successful, the user is given access to the requested resource. Two kinds of encryption schemes are available.

Symmetric encryption

Symmetric encryption is like the physical keys and locks you probably use every day. Just as you would lock and unlock your car with the same key, *symmetric encryption* uses one key to lock and unlock an encrypted message.

Because this scheme uses one key, all involved parties must know this key for the scheme to work.

Asymmetric encryption

Asymmetric encryption works differently from symmetric encryption. This scheme has two keys:

◆ A public key

◆ A private key

The extra key is the *public* key (so this scheme is also known as *public key encryption*).

When data is encrypted with the public key, it can only be decrypted using the private key, and vice versa. Unlike symmetric encryption, this scheme doesn't require that the sender know the receiver's private key to unlock the data. The public key is widely distributed, so anyone who needs a secure data communication can use it. The private key is never distributed; it's always kept secret.

SSL as a protocol for data encryption

Using both symmetric and asymmetric encryption schemes, Netscape developed the open, nonproprietary protocol called Secured Socket Layer (SSL) for data encryption, server authentication, data integrity, and client authentication for TCP/IP-based communication.

The SSL protocol runs above TCP/IP and below higher-level, application-layer protocols such as HTTP, FTP, and IMAP. It uses TCP/IP on behalf of the application-layer protocols. Doing so accomplishes the following:

◆ Allows an SSL-enabled server to authenticate itself to an SSL-enabled client

♦ Allows the client to authenticate itself to the server

♦ Allows both machines to establish an encrypted connection

HOW DOES SSL WORK?

In an SSL-based transaction, the server sends a *certificate* (defined later in this chapter) to the client system.

1. A certificate is typically issued by a well-known digital certificate issuing company known as a Certificate Authority (CA).

   The Certificate Authority encrypts the certificate using its private key. The client decrypts the certificate using the public key provided by the Certificate Authority.

   Because the certificate contains the CA server's public key, the client can now decrypt any encrypted data sent by the server.

2. The server sends a piece of data identifying itself as the entity mentioned in the certificate. It then creates a digest message of the same data it sent to identify itself earlier.

   The digest is then encrypted using the server's private key. The client now has the following information:

   ■ The certificate from a known CA stating what the server's public key should be

   ■ An identity message from the server

   ■ An encrypted digest version of the identity message

3. Using the server's public key, the client can decrypt the digest message. The client then creates a digest of the identity message and compares it with the digest sent by the server.

   A match between the digest and the original message confirms the identity of the server. Why? The server initially sent a certificate signed by a known CA, so the client is absolutely sure to whom this public key belongs. However, the client needed proof that the server that sent the certificate is the entity that it claims to be, so the server sent a simple identification message along with a public-key-encrypted digest of the same message. If the sending server hadn't had the appropriate private key, it would have been unable to produce the same digest that the client computed from the identification message.

If this seems complex , it is — intentionally so — and it doesn't end here. The client can now send a symmetric encryption key to the server, using the server's public key to encrypt the new message. The server can then use this new key to encrypt data and transmit it to the client. Why do that all over again? Largely because symmetric encryption is much faster than asymmetric encryption.

 Asymmetric encryption (using private and public keys) safely transmits a randomly generated symmetric key from the client to the server; this key is later used for a fast, secured communication channel.

If an impostor sits between the client and the server system, and is capable of intercepting the transmitted data, what damage can it do? It doesn't know the secret symmetric key that the client and the server use, so it can't determine the content of the data; at most, it can introduce garbage in the data by injecting its own data into the data packets.

To avoid this, the SSL protocol allows for a *message-authentication code (MAC)*. A MAC is simply a piece of data computed by using the symmetric key and the transmitted data. Because the impostor doesn't know the symmetric key, it can't compute the correct value for the MAC. For example, a well-known cryptographic digest algorithm called MD5 (developed by RSA Data Security, Inc.) can generate 128-bit MAC values for each transmitted data packet. The computing power and time required to successfully guess the correct MAC value this way is almost nonexistent. SSL makes secure commerce possible on the Internet.

OBTAINING SSL

For many years, SSL was available mainly in commercial Linux software such as Stronghold, an Apache-based, commercial Web server. Because of patent and US export restrictions, no open-source versions of SSL for Linux were available for a long time. Recently, the OpenSSL Project has changed all that.

Understanding OpenSSL

The OpenSSL Project is an open-source community collaboration to develop commercial-grade SSL, Transport Layer Security (TLS), and full-strength, general-purpose cryptography library packages. The current implementation of SSL is also called OpenSSL. OpenSSL is based on SSLeay library, which has been developed by Eric A. Young and Tim J. Hudson. The OpenSSL software package license allows both commercial and noncommercial use of the software.

Uses of OpenSSL

SSL can be used in many applications to enhance and ensure transactional data security: OpenSSL simply makes that capability more widely available. This section examines using OpenSSL for the following security tasks:

- ◆ Securing transactions on the Web using Apache-SSL (see Chapter 15 for details)

- ◆ Securing user access for remote access to your Linux computer

- ◆ Securing Virtual Private Network (VPN) connections via PPP, using OpenSSL-based tunneling software (see Chapter 20 for details)

- ◆ Securing e-mail services (IMAP, PO3) via tunneling software that uses OpenSSL (see Chapter 20 for details).

Getting OpenSSL

OpenSSL binaries are currently shipped with the Red Hat Linux distribution in RPM packages. So you can either use the RPM version supplied by Red Hat or you can simply download the source code from the official OpenSSL Web site at www.openssl.org/source.

As mentioned throughout the book, I prefer that security software be installed from source distribution downloaded from authentic Web or FTP sites. So, in the following section I discuss the details of compiling and installing OpenSSL from the official source distribution downloaded from the OpenSSL Web site.

 If you must install OpenSSL from the RPM, use a trustworthy, binary RPM distribution, such as the one found on the official Red Hat CD-ROM. To install OpenSSL binaries from an RPM package, simply run the rpm -ivh openssl-packagename.rpm command.

Installing and Configuring OpenSSL

The OpenSSL Web site offers the OpenSSL source in a gzip compressed tar file. The latest version as of this writing is openssl-0.9.6.tar.gz. Before you can start with the compilation process, you must ensure that your system meets the prerequisites.

OpenSSL prerequisites

The OpenSSL source distribution requires that you have Perl 5 and an ANSI C compiler. I assume that you installed both Perl 5 and gcc (C compiler) when you set up your Linux system.

Compiling and installing OpenSSL

Compiling OpenSSL is a simple task. Follow the steps given below.

1. Log in to your Linux system as `root` from the console.

2. Copy the OpenSSL source tar ball into the `/usr/src/redhat/SOURCES` directory.

3. Extract the source distribution by running the `tar xvzf openssl-version.tar.gz` command.

   For example, to extract the `openssl-0.9.6.tar.gz` file, I can run the `tar xvzf openssl-0.9.6.tar.gz` command. The `tar` command creates a directory called `openssl-version`, which in my example is `openssl-0.9.6`.

 TIP You can delete the tar ball at this point if disk space is an issue for you. First, however, make sure you have successfully compiled and installed OpenSSL.

---

4. Make the newly created directory your current directory.

At this point, feel free to read the `README` or `INSTALL` files included in the distribution. The next step is to configure the installation options; certain settings are needed before you can compile the software.

To install OpenSSL in the default `/usr/local/ssl` directory, run the following command:

```
./config
```

However, if you must install it in a different directory, append `--prefix` and `--openssldir` flags to the preceding command. For example, to install OpenSSL in `/opt/security/ssl` directory, the preceding command line looks like this:

```
./config --prefix=/opt/security
```

You can use many other options with the `config` or `Configure` script to prepare the source distribution for compilation. These options are listed and explained in Table 11-1.

TABLE 11-1: CONFIGURATION OPTIONS FOR COMPILING OPENSSL

Configuration Options	Purpose
`--prefix=DIR`	This option installs OpenSSL in the `DIR` directory. It creates subdirectories such as `DIR/lib`, `DIR/bin`, `DIR/include/openssl`. The configuration files are stored in `DIR/ssl` unless you use the `--openssldir` option to specify this directory.
`--openssldir=DIR`	This option specifies the configuration files directory. If the `--prefix` option isn't used, all files are stored in this directory.
`Rsaref`	This option forces building of the RSAREF toolkit. To use the RSAREF toolkit, make sure you have the RSAREF library (`librsaref.a`) in your default library search path.
`no-threads`	This option disables support for multithreaded applications.
`threads`	This option enables support for multithreaded applications.
`no-shared`	This option disables the creation of a shared library.
`Shared`	This option enables the creation of a shared library.
`no-asm`	This option disables the use of assembly code in the source tree. Use this option only if you are experiencing problems in compiling OpenSSL.
`386`	Use this only if you are compiling OpenSSL on an Intel 386 machine. (Not recommended for newer Intel machines.)
`no-<cipher>`	OpenSSL uses many cryptographic ciphers such as `bf`, `cast`, `des`, `dh`, `dsa`, `hmac`, `md2`, `md5`, `mdc2`, `rc2`, `rc4`, `rc5`, `rsa`, and `sha`. If you want to exclude a particular cipher from the compiled binaries, use this option.
`-Dxxx`, `-lxxx`, `-Lxxx`, `-fxxx`, `-Kxxx`	These options enable you to specify various system-dependent options. For example, Dynamic Shared Objects (DSO) flags, such as `-fpic`, `-fPIC`, and `-KPIC` can be specified on the command line. This way one can compile OpenSSL libraries with Position Independent Code (PIC), which is needed for linking it into DSOs. Most likely you won't need any of these options to compile OpenSSL. However, if you have problems compiling it, you can try some of these options with appropriate values. For example, if you can't compile because OpenSSL complains about missing library files, try specifying the system library path using the `-L` option.

After you have run the `config` script without any errors, run the `make` utility. If the `make` command is successful, run `make test` to test the newly built binaries. Finally, run `make install` to install OpenSSL in your system.

TIP

If you have problems compiling OpenSSL, one source of the difficulty may be a library-file mismatch — not unusual if the latest version of software like OpenSSL is being installed on an old Linux system. Or the problem may be caused by an option, specified in the command line, that's missing an essential component. For example, if you don't have the RSAREF library (not included in Red Hat Linux) installed on your system and you are trying to use the `rsaref` option, the compilation fails when it tries to build the binaries. Here some traditional programming wisdom comes in handy: Make sure you know exactly what you're doing when you use specific options. If neither of these approaches resolves the problem, try searching the OpenSSL FAQ page at `www.openssl.org/support/faq.html`. Or simply install the binary RPM package for OpenSSL.

Understanding Server Certificates

Before you can use OpenSSL with many SSL-capable applications (such as OpenSSH and Apache-SSL), you must create appropriate server certificates.

What is a certificate?

In an SSL transaction, a *certificate* is a body of data placed in a message to serve as proof of the sender's authenticity. It consists of encrypted information that associates a public key with the true identity of an individual, server, or other entity, known as the *subject*. It also includes the identification and electronic signature of the issuer of the certificate. The issuer is known as a Certificate Authority (CA).

A certificate may contain other information that helps the CA manage certificates (such as a serial number and period of time when the certificate is valid). Using an SSL-enabled Web browser (such as Netscape Navigator or Microsoft Internet Explorer), you can view a server's certificate easily.

The identified entity in a certificate is represented by distinguished name fields (as defined in the X509 standard). Table 11-2 lists common distinguished name fields.

TABLE 11–2: DISTINGUISHED NAME FIELDS

DN Field:	Abbreviation	Meaning
Common Name	CN	Certified entity is known by this name.
Organization or Company	O	Entity is associated with this organization.
Organizational Unit	OU	Entity is associated with this organization unit.
City/Locality	L	Entity is located in this city.
State/Province	ST	Entity is located in this state or province.
Country	C	Name is located in this country (2-digit ISO country code).

The certificate is usually transmitted in binary code or as encrypted text.

What is a Certificate Authority (CA)?

A Certificate Authority (CA) is a trusted organization that issues certificates for both servers and clients (that is, users.) To understand the need for such an organization, consider the following scenario.

One of your clients wants secure access to a Web application on your extranet Web server. She uses the HTTPS protocol to access your extranet server, say

```
https://extranet.domain.com/login.servlet
```

Her Web browser initiates the SSL connection request. Your extranet Web server uses its private key to encrypt data it sends to her Web browser – which decrypts the data using your Web server's public key.

Because the Web server also sends the public key to the Web browser, there's no way to know whether the public key is authentic. What stops a malicious hacker from intercepting the information from your extranet server and sending his own public key to your client? That's where the CA comes in to play. After verifying information regarding your company in the offline world, a CA has issued you a server certificate – signed by the CA's own public key (which is well known). Genuine messages from your server carry this certificate. When the Web browser receives the server certificate, it can decrypt the certificate information using the well-known CA's public key. This ensures that the server certificate is authentic. The Web browser can then verify that the domain name used in the authentic certificate is the same as the name of the server it's communicating with.

Similarly, if you want to ensure that a client is really who she says she is, you could enforce a client-side certificate restriction, creating a closed-loop secured process for the entire transaction.

 If each party has a certificate that validates the other's identity, confirms the public key, and is signed by a trusted agency, then they both are assured that they are communicating with whom they think they are.

Two types of Certificate Authority exist:

♦ Commercial CA

♦ Self-certified private CA

Commercial CA

A commercial Certificate Authority's primary job is to verify the authenticity of other companies' messages on the Internet. After a CA verifies the offline authenticity of a company by checking various legal records (such as official company registration documents and letters from top management of the company), one of its appropriately empowered officers can sign the certificate. Only a few commercial CAs exist; the two best known are

♦ Verisign (www.verisign.com)

♦ Thawte (www.thawte.com)

 Verisign recently acquired Thawte Consulting, which created an overwhelming monopoly in the digital-certificate marketplace.

Self-certified, private CA

A private CA is much like a root-level commercial CA: It's self-certified. However, a private CA is typically used in a LAN or WAN environment (or in experimenting with SSL). For example, a university with a WAN that interconnects departments may decide on a private CA instead of a commercial one. If you don't expect an unknown user to trust your private CA, you can still use it for such specific purposes.

Getting a Server Certificate from a Commercial CA

You can get a certificate from a commercial CA or create your own CA to certify your servers and clients. To get a signed certificate from a commercial CA, you must meet its requirements. Commercial CAs have two requirements:

◆ Prove that you are the entity you claim to be.

 To meet this requirement, usually you follow the CA's guidelines for verifying individuals or organizations. Consult with your chosen CA to find out how to proceed.

◆ Submit a Certificate Signing Request (CSR) in electronic form.

Typically, if you plan to get your Web server certified, be prepared to submit copies of legal documents such as business registration or incorporation papers. Here, I show you how you can create a CSR using OpenSSL.

GENERATING A PRIVATE KEY

The very first step to creating a CSR is creating a private key for your server.

To generate an encrypted private key for a Web server host called www.domain.com, for example, you would run the following command:

```
openssl genrsa -des3 -out www.domain.com.key 1024 -rand /dev/urandom.
```

After running this command, you are asked for a *pass phrase* (that is, password) for use in encrypting the private key. Because the private key is encrypted using the des3 cipher, you are asked for the pass phrase every time your server is started. If this is undesirable, you can create an unencrypted version of the private key by removing the -des3 option in the preceding command line.

 To ensure a high level of security, use an encrypted private key. You don't want someone else who has access to your server to see (and, possibly, later use) your private key.

The content of the www.domain.com.key file is shown in Listing 11-1.

Listing 11-1: The content of www.domain.com.key file

```
-----BEGIN RSA PRIVATE KEY-----
Proc-Type: 4,ENCRYPTED
DEK-Info: DES-EDE3-CBC,C48E9F2F597AF968
```

Continued

Listing 11-1 *(Continued)*

```
47f4qGkVrfFfTNEygEs/uyaPOeAqksOnALtKUvADHKL7BhaB+8BrT/Haa7MHwEzU
jjaRd1XF1k1Ej3qH6d/Z1OAwVfYiAYvO1H3wQB2p11Suxui2sm7ZRkYUOpRMjxZI
/srHn/DU+dUq11pH3vJRw2hHNVjHUBOcuCszZ8GOhICa5MFGsZxDR+cKPOT2Uvf5
j1GyiMroBzNOQFOv8sqwZoSOsuKHU9ZKdA/Pcbu+fwyDWFzNfr8HPNTImlaMjGEt
i9LWZikzBW2mmaw79Pq6xSyqL+7dKXmiQL6d/bYiHOZUYHjMkJtqUp1fNXxJd4T6
kB8xVbvjPivo1AyvYKOqmmVQp7WDnEyrrYUZVyRuOa+1O5OaTG2GnfSy32YGuNTY
1MB3PH5BuocSRp+9SsKKTVoWOaO1nORtgVk/EZTO2Eo94qPcsZes6YyAwY4fFVAw
gG/G3ZJCPdjBI2YLmvhua3bvp9duc5CXmKDxOO49VvjbEB/yvi9pLbuj8KuAt4ht
fZcZB94wxrR/EMGODs2xgNhH+SwEf5Pc/bPUMRCq/Ot6F/HJ47jVnUf17tdtoTT7
UbQQVyAsr9tKSFzsRKMOGBO4VoenkD5CzUUF3iO/NaXSs/EFu9HG1ctWRKZEVIp/
MSJBe3jYDXbmeGdQGNJUExpY64hv1XoNdOpAJkOE622o2a11raFus12PotNvWYdI
TShgoIHSmNgQQLCfssJH5TABKyLejsgQy5Rz/Vp3kDzkWhwECOhI42pOS8sr4GhM
6YEdASb51uP3ftn2ivKshueZHpFOvS1pCGjnEYAEdY4QLJkreznM8w==
-----END RSA PRIVATE KEY-----
```

GENERATING A CERTIFICATE SIGNING REQUEST

You generate the Certificate Signing Request as follows:

1. Run the following command:

   ```
   openssl req -new -key www.domain.com.key -out
   www.domain.com.csr
   ```

   Don't forget to change www.domain.com with your server's hostname.

2. If you encrypted the private key earlier, you are asked for the pass phrase for the private key. Enter the appropriate pass phrase. Then you are asked for country name, state, city, organization name, organization unit/department name, common name (that is, your name if the certificate request is for yourself) or your server's hostname, as well as e-mail address and some optional information (such as a challenge password and an optional company name).

3. When you have filled in the necessary information, you submit your CSR to a Certificate Authority such as Thawte. The certification process then turns to verifying your individual or business-identity documents; such verification may take from a few days to a few weeks or even months. (In the upcoming section, I use Thawte as the chosen CA in the examples.)

4. If you are in a rush to get the certificate so you can start testing your system and its online security — or have other reasons to get a temporary certificate fast — ask the officers of your CA. They may have a way for you to get a temporary, *untrusted* certificate. For example, Thawte allows you to submit your CSR via the Web for a temporary certificate, which you receive in minutes via e-mail.

Creating a Private Certificate Authority

If you aren't interested in getting a signed certificate from a commercial CA, you can create your own CA — and certify entities such as your servers or users — at any time.

It may be possible to get a cross-linked certificate for your private CA from a commercial CA. In such a case, your private CA is chained to the commercial CA — and everyone should trust any certificate you issue. However, the commercial CA may limit your certificate-granting authority to your own organization to ensure that you don't become a competitor.

It is quite easy to create a private, self-certified CA using OpenSSL. Simply download the latest `ssl.ca-version.tar.gz` script distribution version from the user-contributed software section (`www.openssl.org/contrib`) of the OpenSSL Web site. Extract this file to a directory of your choice. A subdirectory called `ssl.ca-version` is created. You find a set of `sh` scripts in the directory.

Here is how you can create server and client certificates using your own CA:

◆ Run the `new-root-ca.sh` script to create a self-signed root certificate for your private CA. You are asked for a pass phrase. This pass phrase is required to sign future certificates.

◆ Creating a server certificate

Run the `new-server-cert.sh www.domain.com` script to create a server's private and public keys. You are asked for distinguished name fields for the new server certificate. The script also generates a CSR, which you can send to a commercial CA later if you so choose.

◆ Signing a server certificate

Run the `sign-server-cert.sh` script to approve and sign the server certificate you created using the `new-server-cert.sh` script.

◆ Creating a user or client certificate

Run the `new-user-cert.sh` script to create a user certificate. User certificates when signed by a commercial certificate authority can be used with Web browsers to authenticate users to remote services. However, user certificates have not yet become common because of lack of understanding and availability of both client and server software.

◆ Signing a user or client certificate

Run the `sign-user-cert.sh` script to sign a user certificate. Also, run the `p12.sh` script to package the private key, the signed key, and the CA's Public key into a file with a `.p12` extension. This file can then be imported into applications such as e-mail clients for use.

Now you can use OpenSSL with various applications.

Summary

OpenSSL is an integral part of security. The more you get used to OpenSSL, the more easily you can incorporate it in many services. You learn about using OpenSSL with Apache and other applications to enhance security, in many chapters in this book.

Chapter 12

Shadow Passwords and OpenSSH

IN THIS CHAPTER

- ◆ Understanding user-access risks
- ◆ Using shadow passwords
- ◆ Exploring OpenSSH
- ◆ Securing user access
- ◆ Creating a user-access policy
- ◆ Monitoring user access

MOST SECURITY BREAK-INS VIA the Internet follow this sequence:

- ◆ A hacker launches a program to exploit a known bug in an Internet service daemon process.
- ◆ The exploit program tricks the buggy daemon to change system files for root access.
- ◆ The hacker logs on to the system using an ordinary user account, which he or she either created or stole using the exploit program.
- ◆ The hacker changes more system files and installs trojan programs, which ensure back-door access for a later time.

Ever wonder what would it be like if you could remove all nonconsole user access from your Internet server — or from the Linux system in your LAN? If a user had only one way to gain shell access to your Linux system — via the console — perhaps the number of break-ins would drop substantially. Of course, that would turn Linux into Windows NT! Or would it?

Actually, removing user access altogether isn't quite practical for most Linux installations. So you must understand the risks involving user accounts and reduce the risks as much as you can. In this chapter you learn exactly that. Typically, a user accesses a Linux system via many means such as Web, Telnet, FTP, rlogin, rsh, or rexec. Here I discuss only the non-anonymous types of user access that require Linux user accounts.

Understanding User Account Risks

Typically, a user gains non-anonymous access to a Linux system via a username and a password. She enters the username and password at the prompt of a communication program and gains access. Unfortunately (in most cases), the client machine transmits both the username and password to the Linux server without any encryption, in clear text. A malicious hacker could use network packet-sniffing hardware/software to sniff out the username and password — with no special effort required beyond being part of the same network. For example, let's say that joel is a user of a large ISP called DummyISP and connects to his Linux server (which is colocated at the ISP facility). A hacker who hacked into another colocated server on the same ISP network can now sniff IP packets on their way in and out of their network — and find Joe's username and password if he uses services such as Telnet or FTP to connect to his system. Clear-text passwords are indeed a big risk, especially when the password travels over an untrusted public network: the Internet.

If you run a Linux system that allows shell access to many users, make sure the /var/log directory and its files aren't readable by ordinary users. I know of many incidents when ordinary "unfriendly" users gained access to other user accounts by simply browsing the /var/log/messages log file. Every time login fails because of a username and/or password mismatch, the incident is recorded in the /var/log/messages file. Because many users who get frustrated with the login process after a few failed attempts often type their passwords in the login: prompt instead of the password: prompt, there may be entries in the messages file that show their passwords. For example, log entries may show that user mrfrog failed to log in a few times, then got in via Telnet, but one entry (in bold) reveals the user's password when he mistakenly entered the password as a response to the login: prompt.

```
login: FAILED LOGIN 2 FROM neno FOR mrfrog,
Authentication failure
PAM_unix: Authentication failure; (uid=0) ->
mysecretpwd for system-auth service
login: FAILED LOGIN 3 FROM neno FOR mysecretpwd,
Authentication failure
PAM_unix: (system-auth) session opened for user mrfrog
by (uid=0)
```

Now if anyone but the root user can access such a log file, disaster may result. Never let anyone but the root account access your logs!

Although passing clear-text usernames and passwords over a network is a big concern, many more security issues are tied to user access. For example, a great security risk arises in systems that allow users to pick or change their passwords; most users tend to choose easy passwords that they can remember. If you survey your user base, hardly anyone has passwords like "x86n0op916". In most cases you find that people choose passwords from dictionary words, names, and numbers that they use every day.

In addition, as a result of a long-lasting Unix tradition, Linux systems store the password in a world-readable /etc/passwd file. Although the password entries aren't stored in clear text, the file has been the primary target of many security exploits, decade after decade. A typical hacker simply tries to retrieve this file in order to run a password-guessing program like crack to find weak passwords.

If you combine easy-to-guess, clear-text passwords with a world-readable /etc/passwd storage location, the result is a major security risk in your user-authentication process.

Securing User Accounts

To manage your accounts to reduce risks in your user-authentication process, give each entry in the /etc/passwd file the following format:

```
username:password:uid:gid:fullname:homedir:shell
```

Table 12-1 describes each of these fields.

TABLE 12-1: /ETC/PASSWD FIELDS

Field Name	Function
Username	Login name of the account
Password	Encoded password
UID	Unique user ID
GID	Group ID
Fullname	Typically used to store a user's real-world full name but can store short comments
Homedir	User's home directory path
Shell	User's login shell

As mentioned before, /etc/passwd is a world readable text file that holds all user passwords in an encoded form. The password file *should* be world-readable; after all, many applications depend on user information such as user ID, group ID, full name, or shell for their services. To improve the security of your user-authentication process, however, you can take several measures immediately. The upcoming sections describe them.

Using shadow passwords and groups

Ensure that /etc/passwd can't give away your user secrets. For this you need *shadow passwords*. Luckily, by default Red Hat Linux uses a shadow-password scheme — and it begins by storing the user passwords someplace other than the /etc/passwd file. Instead, the passwords are stored in the /etc/shadow file, which has the following format:

```
username:password:last:may:must:warn:expire:disable:reserved
```

Table 12-2 describes each of these fields.

TABLE 12-2: /ETC/SHADOW FIELDS

Field Name	Function
username	The username
password	The encoded password
last	Days since January 1, 1970 that password was last changed
may	Minimum days a user must wait before she can change the password since her last change
must	Maximum number of days that the user can go on without changing her password
warn	Number of days when the password change reminder starts
expire	Days after password expires that account is disabled
disable	Days since Jan. 1, 1970 that account is disabled
reserved	A reserved field

The /etc/passwd file format remains exactly the same as it was — except the password field is always set to 'x' instead of the encoded user password.

An example entry of the /etc/shadow password file looks like this:

```
mrfrog:$1$ar/xabcl$XKfp.T6gFb6xHxol4xHrk.:11285:0:99999:7:::
```

This line defines the account settings for a user called mrfrog. Here mrfrog has last changed his password 11285 days since January 1, 1970. Because the minimum number of days he must wait before he can change the password is set to 0, he can change it at any time. At the same time, this user can go on for 99,999 days without changing the password.

AGING YOUR USER ACCOUNTS

Although a shadow-password file *could* allow users to go on without changing their passwords, good security demands otherwise. Therefore, the shadow-password mechanism can incorporate the concept of password aging so the users must change passwords at a set interval.

Under a shadow-password scheme, when you create a new user account, the user entry in /etc/shadow is created using the default values stored in the /etc/login.defs configuration file. The default version of this file contains the following entries:

```
PASS_MAX_DAYS    99999
PASS_MIN_DAYS    0
PASS_MIN_LEN     5
PASS_WARN_AGE    7
```

The PASS_MAX_DAYS entry dictates how long a user can go on without changing her password. The default value is 99999, which means that a user can go for approximately 274 years before changing the password. I recommend changing this to a more realistic value. An appropriate value probably is anywhere from 30 to 150 days for most organizations. If your organization frequently faces password security problems, use a more restrictive number in the 15- to 30-day range.

The PASS_MIN_DAYS entry dictates how long the user must wait before she can change her password since her last change. The default value of 0 lets the user change the password at any time. This user flexibility can be good if you can ensure that your users choose hard-to-guess passwords. The PASS_MIN_LEN entry sets the minimum password length. The default value reflects the frequently used minimum size of 5. The PASS_WARN_AGE entry sets the reminder for the password change. I use the following settings in many systems that I manage:

```
PASS_MAX_DAYS    150
PASS_MIN_DAYS    0
PASS_MIN_LEN     5
PASS_WARN_AGE    7
```

TIP   Before changing a system configuration file such as `/etc/login.defs`, `/etc/passwd`, or `/etc/shadow`, back up the file.

After you modify the `/etc/login.defs` file, make sure your aging policy works as expected.

TESTING YOUR NEW ACCOUNT AGING POLICY IN ACTION

Create a test user account using the `useradd` *testuser* command and set the password using the `passwd` *testuser* command. Then verify that the default values from `/etc/login.defs` are used in the `/etc/shadow` file. To simulate aging, you can simply modify the last password change day count. This shows an entry in my `/etc/shadow` file for `testuser`.

```
testuser:$1$/f0dEYFo$qcxNCerBbSE6unDn2uaCb1:11294:0:150:7:::
```

Here the last password change was on Sunday, December 3, 2000, which makes 11,294 days since January 1, 1970. Now, if I want to see what happens after 150 days have elapsed since the last change, I can simply subtract 150+1 from 11,295 and set the last change value like this:

```
testuser:$1$/f0dEYFo$qcxNCerBbSE6unDn2uaCb1:11143:0:150:7:::
```

Now, if I try to log in to the system using this account, I must change the password because it has aged. Once you have tested your settings by changing appropriate values in the `/etc/shadow` file, you have a working password-aging policy.

 CAUTION   Remove the test user account using the `userdel` *testuser* command.

Checking password consistency

When you work with password files like `/etc/passwd` and `/etc/shadow`, be very careful:

◆ Back up these files before modification.

◆ Confirm the validity of your files by running a consistency checker.

The `pwck` command can do exactly that. This command performs integrity checking for both of the password files and the /etc/group file, too.

Although shadow passwords and password aging are great ways to fight user security risks, the clear-text password risk still remains. To eliminate that risk, stop using shell access that requires clear-text passwords.

TIP Normally you should have only one superuser (that is, `root`) account in your /etc/passwd and /etc/shadow files. For security, periodically scan these files so you know there's only one `root` entry. The `grep ':x:0:' /etc/passwd` command displays all users who have `root` access.

Eliminating risky shell services

Telnet, which uses clear-text passwords, is the primary culprit of all shell-related security incidents. Unfortunately, Red Hat Linux comes with Telnet service turned on. Don't use Telnet for accessing your Linux system. To disable Telnet do the following:

CAUTION Don't continue if you are currently using Telnet to access the server. You must follow the steps below from the console.

◆ Log in to your Linux system as `root` from the console.

◆ Using **vi** or another text editor, open the /etc/services file. Search for the string **telnet**, and you should see a line such as the following:

```
telnet          23/tcp
```

◆ Insert a **#** character before the word `telnet`, which should make the line look like this:

```
#telnet         23/tcp
```

◆ Save the /etc/services file.

◆ Modify the /etc/xinetd.conf file by adding `disabled = telnet` line in the defaults section.

XREF For more about configuring `xinetd`, see Chapter 14.

◆ If you have a file called /etc/xinetd.d/telnet, modify this file by adding a new line, disabled = yes, so that the Telnet service definition looks like the following:

```
service telnet
{
        disable          = yes
        flags            = REUSE
        socket_type      = stream
        wait             = no
        user             = root
        server           = /usr/sbin/in.telnetd
        log_on_failure   += USERID
        disabled          = yes

}
```

◆ Restart xinetd using the killall -USR1 xinetd command.

This command disables the Telnet service immediately. Verify that Telnet service is no longer available by running the telnet localhost 23 command; you should get the following error message:

```
Trying 127.0.0.1...
telnet: Unable to connect to remote host: Connection refused
```

If you don't get this error message, xinetd hasn't been restarted properly in the last step of the example. Retry that command and return to verifying.

As an added security precaution, remove the /usr/sbin/in.telnetd Telnet daemon.

Although Telnet is the most frequently used method for accessing a remote system, you may also have rlogin, rsh, or rexec services turned on. Check the following directory carefully:

```
/etc/xinetd.d/<each of the mentioned r* service>
```

If you don't see a disabled = yes line in the service definition, add one in each of these files and then restart xinetd.

If it isn't practical to access the system via the console, use Secure Shell (SSH) for remote access. SSH encrypts all your traffic, including your passwords, when you connect to another machine over the network, effectively eliminating risks associated with eavesdropping in a network connection.

Using OpenSSH for Secured Remote Access

The OpenSSH suite of tools implements the SSH1 and SSH2 protocols. These protocols allow a cryptographically secure connection between the server running the OpenSSH daemon and the client machine.

Getting and installing OpenSSH

You can download OpenSSH from `http://www.openssh.com`; the latest version is 2.3.0. Download the following RPM packages:

```
openssh-version.rpm
openssh-clients-version.rpm
openssh-server-version.rpm
openssh-version.src.rpm
```

You need only the first three RPM if you want to install the OpenSSH binaries.

OpenSSH uses OpenSSL (See Using OpenSSL chapter) and the general-purpose, in-memory compression/decompression library called Zlib. Red Hat supplies Zlib RPMs, which should be already installed on your system. You can check this using the `rpm -qa | grep zlib` command. If you don't already have Zlib installed, download and install the Zlib RPM packages (`zlib-version.rpm`, `zlib-devel-version.rpm`) from a Red Hat RPM site. You can also download the Zlib source code from `ftp://ftp.freesoftware.com/pub/infozip/zlib/`, then compile and install it. Once your system meets all the OpenSSH prerequisites, you can install OpenSSH.

I downloaded the following RPM packages:

```
openssh-2.3.0p1-1.i386.rpm
openssh-clients-2.3.0p1-1.i386.rpm
openssh-server-2.3.0p1-1.i386.rpm
openssh-2.3.0p1-1.src.rpm
```

To avoid or reduce future debugging time, it's better to install the client software on the server and thus remove the issues that occur because of remote access. Running the client from the server ensures that you aren't likely to face DNS issues or other network issues. Once you get the client working on the server, you can try a remote client knowing that the software works and any problem probably is related to network configuration and availability.

I like to have source code available — so I installed all the preceding packages using the `rpm -ivh openssh*.rpm` command. If you decide to compile the source code (`openssh-version.src.rpm`), see the following instructions after you run the `rpm -ivh openssh-version.src.rpm` command:

 Because the source distribution doesn't install all the necessary configuration files, be sure to install all the binary RPMs *first* — and then compile and install the source on top of them.

1. Make `/usr/src/redhat/SOURCES` your current directory.

2. Extract the OpenSSH tar ball by using the **tar xvzf openssh-version.tar.gz** command. This extracts the source code and creates a new directory called `openssh-version`. Make `openssh-version` your current directory.

3. Run `./configure`, then `make`, and finally `make install` to install the OpenSSH software.

4. Replace the binary RPM installed lines in the `/etc/pam.d/sshd` file with the lines shown in the listing that follows. The new file tells the SSH daemon to use the system-wide authentication configuration (found in the `/etc/pam.d/system-auth` file).

```
#%PAM-1.0
auth        required        /lib/security/pam_stack.so service=system-auth
auth        required        /lib/security/pam_nologin.so
account     required        /lib/security/pam_stack.so service=system-auth
password    required        /lib/security/pam_stack.so service=system-auth
session     required        /lib/security/pam_stack.so service=system-auth
```

Now you can configure OpenSSH.

Configuring OpenSSH service

The RPM version of the OpenSSH distribution creates a directory called `/etc/ssh`. This directory contains the following files:

```
ssh_host_dsa_key
ssh_host_dsa_key.pub
ssh_host_key
ssh_host_key.pub
sshd_config
```

Files ending with a .pub extension store the public keys for the OpenSSH server. The files with the .key extension store the private keys. The private keys shouldn't be readable by anyone but the root user. The very last file, sshd_config, is the configuration file. Listing 12-1 shows the default version of this file (slightly modified for brevity).

Listing 12-1: /etc/ssh/ssh_config

```
# /etc/ssh/ssh_config file
# This is ssh server systemwide configuration file.
Port 22
ListenAddress 0.0.0.0
HostKey /etc/ssh/ssh_host_key
ServerKeyBits 768
LoginGraceTime 600
KeyRegenerationInterval 3600
PermitRootLogin yes
IgnoreRhosts yes
StrictModes yes
X11Forwarding no
X11DisplayOffset 10
PrintMotd yes
KeepAlive yes
SyslogFacility AUTH
LogLevel INFO
RhostsAuthentication no
RhostsRSAAuthentication no
RSAAuthentication yes
PasswordAuthentication yes
PermitEmptyPasswords no
    CheckMail no
```

These directives may require changes:

- ◆ Port specifies the port number that sshd binds to listen for connections.

  - The default value of 22 is standard.

  - You can add multiple Port directives to make sshd listen to multiple ports.

 TIP A non-standard port for SSH (a port other than 22) can stop some port scans.

- ◆ ListenAddress specifies the IP address to listen on.

  - ■ By default, sshd listens to all the IP addresses bound to the server.

  - ■ The Port directive must come before the ListenAddress directive.

- ◆ HostKey specifies the fully qualified path of the private RSA host key file.

- ◆ ServerKeyBits specifies the number of bits in the server key.

- ◆ LoginGraceTime specifies the grace period for login request to complete.

- ◆ KeyRegenerationInterval specifies the time interval for generating the key.

- ◆ PermitRootLogin, when set to yes, enables sshd to log in as the root user. Set this to no unless you have used the /etc/hosts.allow and /etc/hosts.deny files (discussed in a later section) to restrict sshd access.

- ◆ IgnoreRhostshas, when set to yes, enables sshd to ignore the .rhosts file found in a user's home directory. Leave the default as is.

- ◆ StrictModes, when set to yes, has sshd enable a strict mode of operation. Normally sshd doesn't allow connection to users whose home directory (or other important files such as .rhosts) are world-readable. Leave the default as is.

- ◆ X11Forwarding, if set to yes, allows X Window System forwarding. I typically don't use the X Window System, so I set this to no.

- ◆ X11DisplayOffset specifies the first X Window System display available to SSH for forwarding. Leave the default as is.

- ◆ PrintMotd, when set to yes, has sshd print the /etc/motd file when a user logs in. This is a relatively minor option.

- ◆ KeepAlive, when set to yes, has sshd use the KeepAlive protocol for reducing connection overhead. Leave the default as is.

- ◆ SyslogFacility specifies which syslog facility is used by sshd. Leave the default as is.

- ◆ LogLevel specifies which log level is used for syslog. Leave the default as is.

- ◆ RhostsAuthentication, when set to no, has sshd disable any authentication based on .rhosts- or /etc/hosts.equiv. Leave the default as is.

◆ RhostsRSAAuthentication, when set to no, has sshd disable .rhosts-based authentication even if RSA host authentication is successful. Leave the default as is.

◆ RSAAuthentication specifies whether RSA-based authentication is allowed. Leave the default as is.

◆ PasswordAuthentication specifies whether password-based authentication is allowed. Leave the default as is.

◆ PermitEmptyPasswords specifies whether empty passwords are okay. Leave the default as is.

◆ CheckMail, upon successful login, has sshd check whether the user has e-mail. Leave the default as is.

Once you've made all the necessary changes to the /etc/ssh/ssh_config file, you can start sshd. The next subsections discuss the two ways you can run sshd:

◆ standalone service

◆ xinetd service

STANDALONE SERVICE

The standalone method is the default method for running sshd. In this method, the daemon is started at server startup, using the /etc/rc.d/init.d/sshd script. This script is called from the appropriate run-level directory. For example, if you boot your Linux system in run-level 3 (default for Red Hat Linux), you can call the script by using the /etc/rc.d/rc3.d/S55sshd link, which points to the /etc/rc.d/init.d/sshd script.

To run sshd in standalone mode, you must install the openssh-server-version.rpm package. If you have installed sshd only by compiling the source code, follow these steps:

1. Create a script named /etc/rc.d/init.d/sshd, as shown in Listing 12-2. This script is supplied by Red Hat in the binary RPM package for the sshd server.

Listing 12-2: /etc/rc.d/init.d/sshd

```
#!/bin/bash
# Init file for OpenSSH server daemon
# chkconfig: 2345 55 25
# description: OpenSSH server daemon
# processname: sshd
# config: /etc/ssh/ssh_host_key
# config: /etc/ssh/ssh_host_key.pub
```

Continued

Listing 12-2 *(Continued)*

```
# config: /etc/ssh/ssh_random_seed
# config: /etc/ssh/sshd_config
# pidfile: /var/run/sshd.pid
# source function library
. /etc/rc.d/init.d/functions
RETVAL=0
# Some functions to make the below more readable
KEYGEN=/usr/bin/ssh-keygen
RSA_KEY=/etc/ssh/ssh_host_key
DSA_KEY=/etc/ssh/ssh_host_dsa_key
PID_FILE=/var/run/sshd.pid
do_rsa_keygen() {
        if $KEYGEN -R && ! test -f $RSA_KEY ; then
                echo -n "Generating SSH RSA host key: "
                if $KEYGEN -q -b 1024 -f $RSA_KEY -C '' -N '' >&/dev/null; then
                        success "RSA key generation"
                        echo
                else
                        failure "RSA key generation"
                        echo
                        exit 1
                fi
        fi
}
do_dsa_keygen() {
        if ! test -f $DSA_KEY ; then
                echo -n "Generating SSH DSA host key: "
                if $KEYGEN -q -d -b 1024 -f $DSA_KEY -C '' -N '' >&/dev/null;
then
                        success "DSA key generation"
                        echo
                else
                        failure "DSA key generation"
                        echo
                        exit 1
                fi
        fi
}
case "$1" in
        start)
                # Create keys if necessary
                do_rsa_keygen;
                do_dsa_keygen;
```

```
                echo -n "Starting sshd: "
                if [ ! -f $PID_FILE ] ; then
                        sshd
                        RETVAL=$?
                        if [ "$RETVAL" = "0" ] ; then
                                success "sshd startup"
                                touch /var/lock/subsys/sshd
                        else
                                failure "sshd startup"
                        fi
                fi
                echo
                ;;
        stop)
                echo -n "Shutting down sshd: "
                if [ -f $PID_FILE ] ; then
                        killproc sshd
                        [ $RETVAL -eq 0 ] && rm -f /var/lock/subsys/sshd
                fi
                echo
                ;;
        restart)
                $0 stop
                $0 start
                RETVAL=$?
                ;;
        condrestart)
                if [ -f /var/lock/subsys/sshd ] ; then
                        $0 stop
                        $0 start
                        RETVAL=$?
                fi
                ;;
        status)
                status sshd
                RETVAL=$?
                ;;
        *)
                echo "Usage: sshd {start|stop|restart|status|condrestart}"
                exit 1
                ;;
esac
exit $RETVAL
```

2. Link this script to your run-level directory, using the following command:

```
ln -s /etc/rc.d/init.d/sshd /etc/rc.d/rc3.d/S55sshd
```

This form of the command assumes that your run level is 3, which is typical.

The `openssh-server-version.rpm` package contains the preceding script along with other files, making it easy to administer the SSH daemon. If you installed this package earlier, you can start the daemon this way:

```
/etc/rc.d/init.d/sshd start
```

When you run the preceding command for the very first time, you see output like this:

```
Generating SSH RSA host key: [  OK  ]
Generating SSH DSA host key: [  OK  ]
Starting sshd: [  OK  ]
```

Before the SSH daemon starts for the very first time, it creates both public and private RSA and DSA keys — and stores them in the `/etc/ssh` directory. Make sure that the key files have the permission settings shown here:

```
-rw-------   1 root     root          668 Dec  6 09:42 ssh_host_dsa_key
-rw-rw-r--   1 root     root          590 Dec  6 09:42 ssh_host_dsa_key.pub
-rw-------   1 root     root          515 Dec  6 09:42 ssh_host_key
-rw-rw-r--   1 root     root          319 Dec  6 09:42 ssh_host_key.pub
-rw-------   1 root     root         1282 Dec  3 16:44 sshd_config
```

The files ending in _key are the private key files for the server and must not be readable by anyone but the `root` user. To verify that the SSH daemon started, run `ps aux | grep sshd`, and you should see a line like this one:

```
root      857  0.0  0.6  3300 1736 ?          S    09:29   0:00 sshd
```

Once the SSH daemon starts, SSH clients can connect to the server. Now, if you make configuration changes and want to restart the server, simply run the `/etc/rc.d/init.d/sshd restart` command. If you want to shut down the `sshd` server for some reason, run the `/etc/rc.d/init.d/sshd stop` command.

You can safely run the `/etc/rc.d/init.d/sshd stop` command, even if you are currently connected to your OpenSSH server via an SSH client. You aren't disconnected.

RUNNING SSHD AS XINETD SERVICE

Every time sshd runs, it generates the server key — which is why sshd is typically run only once (in standalone mode) during server startup. However, to use xinetd's access control features for the ssh service, you can run it as xinetd service. Here's how:

1. Create a service file for xinetd called /etc/xinetd.d/sshd, as shown in the following listing:

```
service ssh
{
        socket_type             = stream
        wait                    = no
        user                    = root
        server                  = /usr/local/sbin/sshd
        server_args             = -i
        log_on_success          += DURATION USERID
        log_on_failure          += USERID
        nice                    = 10
}
```

2. Run the ps auxw | grep sshd command to check whether sshd is already running. If it's running, stop it by using the /etc/rc.d/init.d/ sshd stop command.

3. Force xinetd to load its configuration using the killall -USR1 xinetd command.

Now you can set up SSH clients. Typically, most people who access a Linux server are running sshd from another Linux system (or from a PC running Windows or some other operating system).

Connecting to an OpenSSH server

A Linux system can connect to an OpenSSH server. To run the OpenSSH client on a Linux system install OpenSSL (see Using OpenSSL chapter) and the following OpenSSH packages.

```
openssh-version.rpm
openssh-clients-version.rpm
```

Try the client software on the server itself so that you know the entire client/server environment is working before attempting to connect from a remote client system.

If you are following my recommendations, then you already have these two packages installed on your server. If that is the case, go forward with the configuration as follows:

1. Log on to your system as an ordinary user.

2. Generate a public and private key for yourself, which the client uses on your behalf.

   To generate such keys run the `/usr/bin/ssh-keygen` command.

   This command generates a pair of public and private RSA keys, which are needed for default RSA authentication. The keys are stored in a subdirectory called `.ssh` within your home directory.

   - `identity.pub` is the public key.

   - `identity` is the private key.

3. To log in to the OpenSSH server, run the `ssh -l username hostname` command, where *username* is your username on the server and the *hostname* is the name of the server.

   For example, to connect to a server called `k2.nitec.com`, I can run the `ssh -l kabir k2.nitec.com` command.

4. The first time you try to connect to the OpenSSH server, you see a message that warns you that `ssh`, the client program, can't establish the authenticity of the server. An example of this message is shown here:

   `The authenticity of host 'k2.nitec.com' can't be established.`

   You are asked whether you want to continue. Because you must trust your own server, enter yes to continue. You are warned that this host is permanently added to your known host list file. This file, `known_hosts`, is created in the `.ssh` directory.

5. You are asked for the password for the given username. Enter appropriate password.

 To log in without entering the password, copy the `identity.pub` file from your workstation to a subdirectory called `.ssh` in the home directory on the OpenSSH server. On the server, rename this `identity.pub` file to `authorized_keys`, using the `mv identity.pub authorized_keys` command. Change the permission settings of the file to 644, using the `chmod 644 authorized_keys` command. Doing so ensures that only you can change your public key and everyone else can only read it. This allows the server to authenticate you by using the your public key, which is now available on both sides.

6. Once you enter the correct password, you are logged in to your OpenSSH server using the default SSH1 protocol. To use the SSH2 protocol:

   - Use the -2 option

   - Create RSA keys using the ssh-keygen command.

If you enter a pass phrase when you generate the keys using ssh-keygen program, you are asked for the pass phrase every time ssh accesses your private key (~/.ssh/identity) file. To save yourself from repetitively typing the pass phrase, you can run the script shown in Listing 12-3.

Listing 12-3: ssh-agent.sh script

```
#!/bin/sh
# Simple script to run ssh-agent only once.
# Useful in a multi-session environment (like X),
# or if connected to a machine more than once.
# Written by: Danny Sung <dannys@mail.com>
# Released under the GPL
# Sat May 22 23:04:19 PDT 1999
# $Log: ssh-agent.sh,v $
# Revision 1.4  1999/05/23 07:52:11  dannys
# Use script to print, not ssh-agent.
# Revision 1.3  1999/05/23 07:44:59  dannys
# Added email address to comments.
# Added GPL license.
# Revision 1.2  1999/05/23 07:43:04  dannys
# Added ability to kill agent.
# Added csh/sh printouts for kill statement.
# Revision 1.1.1.1  1999/05/23 06:05:46  dannys
# SSH utilities/scripts
#
SSHDIR="${HOME}/.ssh"
HOSTNAME="`hostname`"
LOCKFILE="${SSHDIR}/agent/${HOSTNAME}"
SHELL_TYPE="sh"
RUNNING=0
parse_params()
{
```

Continued

Listing 12-3 *(Continued)*

```
    while [ $# -ge 1 ]; do
      case "$1" in
         -s)
             SHELL_TYPE="sh"
             ;;
         -c)
             SHELL_TYPE="csh"
             ;;
         -k)
             kill_agent
             ;;
         *)
             echo "[-cs] [-k]"
             exit 0
             ;;
      esac
      shift
    done
}
setup_dir()
{
    if [ ! -e "${SSHDIR}/agent" ]; then
       mkdir "${SSHDIR}/agent"
    fi
}
get_pid()
{
    if [ -e "${LOCKFILE}" ]; then
       PID=`cat "${LOCKFILE}" | grep "echo" | sed 's/[^0-9]*//g'`
    else
       PID=""
    fi
}
check_stale_lock()
{
    RUNNING="0"
    if [ ! -z "$PID" ]; then
       ps_str=`ps auxw | grep $PID | grep -v grep`
       if [ -z "$ps_str" ]; then
          rm -f "${LOCKFILE}"
       else
          # agent already running
          RUNNING="1"
       fi
    fi
```

```
}
start_agent()
{
   if [ "$RUNNING" = "1" ]; then
      . "${LOCKFILE}" > /dev/null
   else
      ssh-agent -s > "${LOCKFILE}"
      . "${LOCKFILE}" > /dev/null
   fi
}
kill_agent()
{
   check_stale_lock
   if [ -e "${LOCKFILE}" ]; then
      . "${LOCKFILE}" > /dev/null
      case "$SHELL_TYPE" in
         sh)
            PARAMS="-s"
            ;;
         csh)
            PARAMS="-c"
            ;;
         *)
            PARAMS=""
            ;;
      esac
      ssh-agent ${PARAMS} -k > /dev/null
      rm -f "${LOCKFILE}"
   fi
   print_kill
   exit 0
}
print_agent()
{
   case "$SHELL_TYPE" in
      csh)
         echo "setenv SSH_AUTH_SOCK $SSH_AUTH_SOCK;"
         echo "setenv SSH_AGENT_PID $SSH_AGENT_PID;"
         ;;
      sh)
         echo "SSH_AUTH_SOCK=$SSH_AUTH_SOCK; export SSH_AUTH_SOCK;"
         echo "SSH_AGENT_PID=$SSH_AGENT_PID; export SSH_AGENT_PID;"
         ;;
   esac
   echo "echo Agent pid $PID"
```

Continued

Listing 12-3 *(Continued)*

```
}
print_kill()
{
    case "$SHELL_TYPE" in
        csh)
            echo "unsetenv SSH_AUTH_SOCK;"
            echo "unsetenv SSH_AGENT_PID;"
            ;;
        sh)
            echo "unset SSH_AUTH_SOCK;"
            echo "unset SSH_AGENT_PID;"
            ;;
    esac
    echo "echo Agent pid $PID killed"
}
setup_dir
get_pid
parse_params $*
check_stale_lock
start_agent
get_pid
print_agent
```

When you run this script once, you can use ssh multiple times without entering the pass phrase every time. For example, after you run this script you can start the X Window System as usual using startx or other means you use. If you run ssh for remote system access from xterm, the pass phrase isn't required after the very first time. This can also be timesaving for those who use ssh a lot.

Managing the root Account

In most cases, an intruder with a compromised user account tries for root access as soon as possible. This is why it's very important to know how to manage your root account.

Typically, the root account is the Holy Grail of all break-in attempts. Once the root account is compromised, the system is at the mercy of an intruder. By simply running a command such as rm -rf /, an intruder can wipe out everything on the root filesystem or even steal business secrets. So if you have root access to your system, be very careful how you use it. Simple mistakes or carelessness can create serious security holes that can cause great harm. Each person with root privileges must follow a set of guidelines. Here are the primary guidelines that I learned from experienced system administrators:

◆ **Be root only if you must.** Having `root` access doesn't mean you should log in to your Linux system as the `root` user to read e-mail or edit a text file. Such behavior is a recipe for disaster! Use a `root` account only to

   ▪ Modify a system file that can't be edited by an ordinary user account

   ▪ Enable a service or to do maintenance work, such as shutting down the server

◆ **Choose a very difficult password for root.**

`root` is the Holy Grail for security break-ins. Use an unusual combination of characters, pun\ctuation marks, and numbers.

◆ **Cycle the `root` password frequently.** Don't use the same `root` password more than a month. Make a mental or written schedule to change the `root` password every month.

◆ **Never write down the `root` password.** In a real business, usually the `root` password is shared among several people. So make sure you notify appropriate coworkers of your change, or change passwords in their presence. Never e-mail the password to your boss or colleagues.

Limiting root access

Fortunately, the default Red Hat Linux system doesn't allow login as `root` via Telnet or any other remote-access procedure. This magic is done using the `/etc/securetty` file. This file lists a set of TTY devices that are considered secure for `root` access. The default list contains only `vc/1` through `vc/11` and `tty1` through `tty11`; that is, virtual consoles 1 through 11, which are tied to `tty1` through `tty11`. This is why you can log in directly as `root` only from the physical console screen using a virtual console session. The big idea here is that if you are at the system console, you are okay to be the `root` user.

If you look at the `/etc/inittab` file, you notice that it has lines such as the following:

```
# Run gettys in standard runlevels
1:2345:respawn:/sbin/mingetty tty1
2:2345:respawn:/sbin/mingetty tty2
3:2345:respawn:/sbin/mingetty tty3
4:2345:respawn:/sbin/mingetty tty4
```

```
5:2345:respawn:/sbin/mingetty tty5
6:2345:respawn:/sbin/mingetty tty6
```

These lines tie `vc/1` through `vc/6` to `tty1` through `tty6`. You can remove the rest of the unused virtual consoles and TTYs from the `/etc/securetty` file (the lines for `vc/7` through `vc/11` and `tty7` through `tty11`).

The `/etc/securetty` file must not be readable by anyone other than the `root` user account itself. Because login-related processes run as `root`, they can access the file to verify that `root`-account access is authorized for a certain `tty` device. If pseudo-terminal devices such as `pts/0`, `pts/1`, and `pts/3` are placed in this file, you can log in as the `root` user — which means that anyone else can try brute-force hacks to break in, simply by trying to log in as `root`. To ensure that this file has the appropriate permission settings that don't allow others to change the file, run the `chown root /etc/securetty` and `chmod 600 /etc/securetty` commands.

The OpenSSH daemon, `sshd`, doesn't use the `/etc/securetty` file to restrict access to the root account. It uses a directive called `PermitRootLogin` in the `/etc/ssh/sshd_config` file to control root logins. If this directive is set to `yes` then direct `root` login from remote systems is allowed. Disable this option by setting it to `no` and restarting the daemon (using the `/etc/rc.d/init.d/sshd restart` command).

You can't log in as `root` because of `/etc/securetty` (or the `PermitRootLogin = no` line in the `/etc/ssh/sshd_config` file). So if you need to be the `root` user and can't access the machine from the physical console, you can use the `su` command.

Using su to become root or another user

The `su` command can run a shell with a user and group ID other than those you used to log in. For example, if you are logged in as user `kabirmj` and want to become user `gunchy`, simply run `su gunchy`.

To run the `su` session as a login session of the new user, use the `-` option. For example, `su - gunchy` switches to the user `gunchy` and runs such files as `.login`, `.profile`, and `.bashrc` files as if the user had logged in directly.

Similarly, to become the `root` user from an ordinary user account, run the `su root` command. You are asked for the `root` password. Once you enter the appropriate password, you are in.

TIP   A common shortcut switch to `root` is to run the `su` command without any username.

You can switch back and forth between your `root` session and the original session by using the `suspend` and `fg` commands. For example, you can `su` to `root` from an ordinary user account and then if you must return to the original user shell, simply run the `suspend` command to temporarily stop the `su` session. To return to the `su` session run the `fg` command.

The `su` command is a PAM-aware application and uses the `/etc/pam.d/su` configuration file as shown in Listing 12-4.

Listing 12-4: /etc/pam.d/su

```
#%PAM-1.0
auth        sufficient    /lib/security/pam_rootok.so
# Uncomment the following line to implicitly trust users in the "wheel" group.
#auth        sufficient    /lib/security/pam_wheel.so trust use_uid
# Uncomment the following line to require a user to be in the "wheel" group.
#auth        required       /lib/security/pam_wheel.so use_uid
auth        required       /lib/security/pam_stack.so service=system-auth
account     required       /lib/security/pam_stack.so service=system-auth
password    required       /lib/security/pam_stack.so service=system-auth
session     required       /lib/security/pam_stack.so service=system-auth
session     optional       /lib/security/pam_xauth.so
```

The preceding configuration file allows the `root` user to `su` to any other user without a password, which makes sense because going from high privilege to low privilege isn't insecure by design. However, the default version of this file also permits any ordinary user who knows the `root` password to `su` to `root`. No one but the `root` user should know his or her password; making the `root` account harder to access for unauthorized users who may have obtained the password makes good security sense. Simply *uncomment* (that is, remove the # character from) the following line:

```
#auth    required    /lib/security/pam_wheel.so use_uid
```

Now the users who are listed in the `wheel` group in the `/etc/group` file can use the `su` command to become `root`.

An ordinary user can su to other ordinary user accounts without being a member of the wheel group. The wheel group restrictions apply only to root account access.

Now, if you want to enable a user to become root via the su facility, simply add the user into the wheel group in the /etc/group file. For example, the following line from my /etc/group file shows that only root and kabir are part of the wheel group.

```
wheel:x:10:root,kabir
```

 Don't use a text editor to modify the /etc/group file. Chances of making human mistakes such as typos or syntax errors are too great and too risky. Simply issue the usermod command to modify a user's group privileges. For example, to add kabir to the wheel group, run the usermod -G wheel kabir command.

The su command is great to switch over from an ordinary user to root but it's an all-or-nothing type of operation. In other words, an ordinary user who can su to root gains access to all that root can do. This is often not desirable. For example, say you want a coworker to be able to start and stop the Web server if needed. If you give her the root password so that she can su to root to start and stop the Web server, nothing stops her from doing anything else root can do. Thankfully, there are ways to delegate selected root tasks to ordinary users without giving them full root access.

Using sudo to delegate root access

There are two common ways to delegate root tasks. You can change file permissions for programs that normally can only be run by root. Typically, you use set-UID for this so that an ordinary user can act as the root user. Using set-UID is discussed in a later chapter (see Securing Filesystems.) This method, though, is very unsafe and cumbersome to manage. The other option is called *sudo*, which is short for *superuser do*.

The sudo suite of programs can let users (or user groups) run selected commands as root. When an ordinary user uses sudo to execute a privileged command, sudo logs the command and the arguments so that a clear audit trail is established.

Because the sudo package isn't in the standard Red Hat Linux distribution, you must install it yourself.

COMPILING AND INSTALLING SUDO

The official Web site for the sudo package is http://www.courtesan.com/sudo/. You can download the sudo source distribution from there. Or, you can download the RPM version of sudo from the very useful RPM Finder Web site at http://rpmfind.net. Search for *sudo* to locate the sudo RPMs at this site.

Because I prefer to compile and install software, I recommend that you download the sudo source RPM package. As of this writing the latest source sudo RPM is sudo-1.6.3-4.src.rpm. The version that you download may be different, so make sure you replace the version number (1.6.3-4) wherever I refer to it in the following section.

To install the latest sudo binary RPM package suitable for your Red Hat Linux architecture (such as i386, i686, or alpha), download it from the RPM Finder Web site and install it using the rpm command. For example, the latest binary RPM distribution for i386 (Intel) architecture is sudo-1.6.3-4.i386.rpm. Run the rpm -ivh *sudo-1.6.3-4.i386.rpm* command to install the package.

After downloading the source RPM package, complete the following steps to compile and install sudo on your system.

1. su to root.

2. Run rpm -ivh sudo-1.6.3-4.src.rpm command to extract the sudo tar ball in /usr/src/redhat/SOURCES directory.

   Change your current directory to /usr/src/redhat/SOURCES. If you run ls -l sudo* you see a file such as the following:

   ```
   -rw-r--r--    1 root      root        285126 Apr 10  2000 sudo-
   1.6.3.tar.gz
   ```

3. Extract the sudo-1.6.3.tar.gz file using the tar xvzf sudo-1.6.3.tar.gz command. This creates a subdirectory called sudo-1.6.3. Change your current directory to sudo-1.6.3.

4. Run the ./configure --with-pam script to configure sudo source code for your system. The --with-pam option specifies that you want to build sudo with PAM support.

5. Run make to compile. If you don't get any compilation errors, you can run make install to install the software.

6. Run cp sample.pam /etc/pam.d/sudo to rename the sample PAM configuration file; then copy it to the /etc/pam.d directory.

Modify the /etc/pam.d/sudo file to have the following lines:

```
#%PAM-1.0
auth      required    /lib/security/pam_stack.so
service=system-auth
account   required    /lib/security/pam_stack.so
service=system-auth
password  required    /lib/security/pam_stack.so
service=system-auth
session   required    /lib/security/pam_stack.so
service=system-auth
```

7. Run the make clean command to remove unnecessary object files.

CONFIGURING AND RUNNING SUDO

The sudo configuration file is called /etc/sudoers. Use the visudo program as root to edit this file. The visudo command

◆ Locks the /etc/sudoers file to prevent simultaneous changes by multiple root sessions.

◆ Checks for configuration syntax.

TIP

By default, the visudo command uses the vi editor. If you aren't a vi fan and prefer emacs or pico, you can set the EDITOR environment variable to point to your favorite editor, which makes visudo run the editor of your choice. For example, if you use the pico editor, run export EDITOR=/usr/bin/pico for a bash shell, or run setenv EDITOR /usr/bin/pico editor for csh, tcsh shells. Then run the visudo command to edit the /etc/sudoers contents in the preferred editor.

The default /etc/sudoers file has one configuration entry as shown below:

```
root    ALL=(ALL) ALL
```

This default setting means that the root user can run any command on any host as any user. The /etc/sudoers configuration is quite extensive and often confusing. The following section discusses a simplified approach to configuring sudo for practical use.

Two types of configuration are possible for sudo:

♦ **Aliases.** An alias is a simple name for things of the same kind. There are four types of aliases supported by `sudo` configuration.

- `Host_Alias` = *list of one or more hostnames*. For example, `WEB-SERVERS = k2.nitec.com, everest.nitec.com` defines a host alias called `WEBSERVERS`, which is a list of two hostnames.

- `User_Alias` = *list of one or more users*. For example, `JRADMINS = dilbert, catbert` defines a user alias called `JRADMIN`, which is a list of two users.

- `Cmnd_Alias` = *list of one or more commands*. For example, `COMMANDS = /bin/kill, /usr/bin/killall` defines a command alias called `COMMANDS`, which is a list of two commands.

♦ **User specifications.** A user specification defines *who* can run *what* command as *which* user.

For example:

```
JRADMINS  WEBSERVER=(root) COMMANDS
```

This user specification says `sudo` allows the users in `JRADMINS` to run programs in `COMMANDS` on `WEBSERVER` systems as `root`. In other words, it specifies that user `dlibert` and `catbert` can run `/bin/kill` or `/usr/bin/killall` command on `k2.nitec.om`, `everest.nitec.com` as `root`. Listing 12-5 is an example configuration.

Listing 12-5: /etc/sudoers sample configuration file

```
Host_Alias WEBSERVER = www.nitec.com
User_Alias WEBMASTERS = sheila, kabir
Cmnd_Alias KILL = /bin/kill, /usr/bin/killall
WEBMASTERS  WEBSERVER=(root) KILL
```

The preceding configuration authorizes user `sheila` and `kabir` to run (via `sudo`) the kill commands (`/bin/kill` and `/usr/bin/killall`) as `root` on `www.nitec.com`. In other words, these two users can kill any process on `www.nitec.com`. How is this useful? Let's say that user `sheila` discovered that a program called `oops.pl` that the system administrator (`root`) ran before going to lunch has gone nuts and is crawling the Web server. She can `kill` the process without waiting for the sysadmin to return. User `sheila` can run the `ps auxww | grep oops.pl` command to check whether the `oops.pl` program is still running. The output of the command is:

```
root  11681 80.0 0.4 2568 1104 pts/0 S 11:01 0:20 perl /tmp/oops.pl
```

She tries to `kill` it using the `kill -9 11681` command, but the system returns `11681: Operation not permitted` error message. She realizes that the process is owned by root (as shown in the ps output) and runs sudo kill -9 11681 to kill it. Because she is running the sudo command for the very first time, she receives the following message from the sudo command.

```
We trust you have received the usual lecture from the local System
Administrator. It usually boils down to these two things:
        #1) Respect the privacy of others.
        #2) Think before you type.
Password:
```

At this point she is asked for her own password (not the root password) and once she successfully provides the password, sudo runs the requested command, which kills the culprit process immediately. She then verifies that the process is no longer running by rerunning the ps auxww | grep oops.pl command. As shown sudo can safely delegate system tasks to junior-level administrators or coworkers. After all, who likes calls during the lunch?. Listing 12-6 presents a practical sudo configuration that I use to delegate some of the Web server administration tasks to junior administrators.

Listing 12-6: Kabir's /etc/sudoers for a Web server

```
# sudoers file.
# This file MUST be edited with the 'visudo'
# command as root.
# See the sudoers man page for the details on how
# to write a sudoers file.
# Host alias specification
Host_Alias WEBSERVER = www.intevo.com
# User alias specification
User_Alias WEBMASTERS = wsajr1, wsajr2
# Cmnd alias specification
Cmnd_Alias APACHE = /usr/local/apache/bin/apachectl
Cmnd_Alias KILL   = /bin/kill, /usr/bin/killall
Cmnd_Alias REBOOT = /usr/sbin/shutdown
Cmnd_Alias HALT   = /usr/sbin/halt
# User privilege specification
WEBMASTERS  WEBSERVER=(root) APACHE, KILL, REBOOT, HALT
```

This configuration allows two junior Web administrators (wsajr1 and wsajr2) to start, restart, stop the Apache Web server using the /usr/local/apache/bin/apachectl command. They can also kill any process on the server and even reboot or halt the server if need be. All this can happen without having the full root access.

Commands that allow shell access (such as editors like vi or programs like less) shouldn't run via the sudo facility, because a user can run any command via the shell and gain full root access intentionally or unintentionally.

The configuration I use is quite simple compared to what is possible with sudo. (Read the sudoers man pages for details.) However, it's a good idea to keep your /etc/sudoers configuration as simple as possible. If the program you want to give access to others is complex or has too many options, consider denying it completely. Don't give out sudo access to users you don't trust. Also, get in the habit of auditing sudo-capable users frequently using the logs.

AUDITING SUDO USERS

By default, sudo logs all attempts to run any command (successfully or unsuccessfully) via the syslog. You can run sudo -V to find which syslog facility sudo uses to log information. You can also override the default syslog facility configuration in /etc/sudoers. For example, adding the following line in /etc/sudoers forces sudo to use the auth facility of syslog.

```
Defaults               syslog=auth
```

To keep a separate sudo log besides syslog managed log files, you can add a line such as the following to /etc/sudoers:

```
Defaults               log_year, logfile=/var/log/sudo.log
```

This forces sudo to write a log entry to the /var/log/sudo.log file every time it's run.

Monitoring Users

There are some simple tools that you can use every day to keep yourself informed about who is accessing your system. These tools aren't exactly monitoring tools by design, but you can certainly use them to query your system about user activity. Often I have discovered (as have many other system administrators) unusual activity with these tools, perhaps even by luck, but why quibble? The tools have these capabilities; an administrator should be aware of them. In this section I introduce some of them.

Finding who is on the system

You can use the who or w commands to get a list of users who are currently on your system. Here is some sample output from who:

```
swang     pts/1    Dec 10 11:02
jasont    pts/2    Dec 10 12:01
zippy     pts/3    Dec 10 12:58
mimi      pts/0    Dec 10  8:46
```

If you simply want a count of the users, run who -q. The w command provides more information than who does. Here's an example output of the w command.

```
USER      TTY      FROM            LOGIN@   IDLE   JCPU    PCPU    WHAT
swang     pts/1    reboot.nitec.co 11:02am 12.00s  0.29s   0.15s   pine
jasont    pts/2       k2.nitec.co  12:01pm  2.00s  0.12s   0.02s   vi .plan
zippy     pts/3    reboot.nitec.co 12:58pm 17:45   0.04s   0.04s   -tcsh
mimi      pts/0 gatekeeper.nitec.co 8:46am  0.00s  1.02s   0.02s   lynx
```

Here user swang appears to read e-mail using pine, user jasont is modifying his .plan file, user zippy seems to be running nothing other than the tcsh shell, and user mimi is running the text-based Web browser Lynx.

When you have a lot of users (in the hundreds or more), running w or who can generate more output than you want to deal with. Instead of running the who or w commands in such cases, you can run the following script from Listing 12-7 to check how many unique and total users are logged in.

Listing 12-7: The who.sh script

```
#!/bin/sh
# Purpose: this simple script uses the common Linux
# utilities to determine the total and unique number
# of users logged on the system
# Version: 1.0
#
WHO=/usr/bin/who
GREP=/bin/grep
AWK=/bin/awk
SORT=/bin/sort
WC=/usr/bin/wc
SED=/bin/sed
echo -n "Total unique users:";
# Filter the output of the who command using awk to
# extract the first column and then uniquely sort the
# columns using sort. Pipe the sorted output to wc for
# line count. Finally remove unnecessary white spaces
```

```
# from the output of wc using sed
$WHO | $AWK '{print $1}' | $SORT -u | $WC -l | $SED 's/ */ /g';
# Use grep to filter the output of the who command to
# find the line containing user count.
# Then print out the user count using awk.
$WHO -q | $GREP users | $AWK 'BEGIN{FS="=";} {printf("\nTotal user sessions:
%d\n\n", $2);}';
# Exit
exit 0;
```

You can run this script from the command line as sh who.sh at any time to check how many total and unique users are logged in. Also, if you want to run the command every minute, use the watch -n 60 sh /path/to/who.sh command. This command runs the who.sh script every 60 seconds. Of course, if you want to run it at a different interval, change the number accordingly.

Finding who was on the system

You can run the last command to find users who have already logged out. Last uses the /var/log/wtmp file to display a list of users logged in (and out) since that file was created. You specify a username, and it displays information only for the given user. You can also use the finger username command to see when someone last logged in.

To use the finger command on the local users; you don't need the finger daemon.

All the commands (who, w, last, finger) discussed in this section depend on system files such as /var/log/wtmp and /var/run/utmp files. Make sure that these files aren't world-writeable; otherwise a hacker disguised as an ordinary user can remove his tracks.

Creating a User-Access Security Policy

System and network administrators are often busy beyond belief. Any administrator that manages ten or more users know that there's always something new to take care of every day. I often hear that user administration is a thankless job, but it doesn't have to be. With a little planning and documentation, an administrator can make life easier for herself and everyone else involved. If every administrator would craft a tight security policy and help users understand and apply it, user-access-related security incidents would subside dramatically. Follow these guidelines for creating a user security policy.

◆ **Access to a system is a privilege.** This privilege comes with responsibility; one must take all precautions possible to ensure the access privilege can't be easily exploited by potential vandals. Simply knowing who may be watching over your shoulder when you enter a password can increase user-access security.

◆ **Passwords aren't a personal preference.** A user must not consider her password as something that she has a lot of control over when it comes to choosing one.

◆ **Passwords expire.** A user must accept that passwords aren't forever.

◆ **Passwords are organizational secrets.** A user must never share or display passwords. A user must not store passwords in a handheld PC, which can get lost and fall in wrong hands. Never give passwords to anyone over the phone.

◆ **Not all passwords are created equal.** Just having a password isn't good enough. A good password is hard to guess and often hard to remember. A user must make great efforts to memorize the password.

Creating a User-Termination Security Policy

It is absolutely crucial that your organization create a user-termination security policy to ensure that people who leave the organization can't become potential security liabilities. By enforcing a policy upon user termination, you can make sure your systems remain safe from any ill-conceived action taken by an unhappy employee.

When a user leaves your organization, you have two alternatives for a first response:

◆ Remove the person's account by using the `userdel` *username* command.

◆ Disable the user account so it can't log in to the system, using the `usermod -s /bin/true` *username* command.

The command modifies the user account called *username* in `/etc/password` file and changes the login shell to `/bin/true`, which doesn't allow the user to log in interactively.

To display a message such as `Sorry, you are no longer allowed to access our systems`, you can create a file called `/bin/nologin` this way:

```
#!/bin/sh
echo "Sorry, you are no longer allowed to access our systems.";
exit 0;
```

Set the `nologin` script's ownership to `root` with the `chown root /bin/nologin` command. Make it executable for everyone by using the `chmod 755 /bin/nologin` command. Run the `usermod -s /bin/nologin` *username* command. When a terminated user tries to log in, the script runs and displays the intended message.

Summary

This chapter examined the risks associated with user access and some responses to the risks — such as using shadow passwords, securing a user-authentication process by using an OpenSSH service, restricting the access granted to the `root` user account, and delegating `root` tasks to ordinary users in a secure manner.

Chapter 13

Secure Remote Passwords

IN THIS CHAPTER

- ◆ Setting up Secure Remote Password (SRP)
- ◆ Securing Telnet using SRP

SECURE REMOTE PASSWORD (SRP) is an open source password-based authentication protocol. SRP-enabled client/server suites don't transmit passwords (encrypted or in clear text) over the network. This entirely removes the possibility of password spoofing. SRP also doesn't use encryption to perform authentication, which makes it faster than the public/private key–based authentication schemes currently available. To learn more about this protocol visit the official SRP Web site at `http://srp.standford.edu`.

Setting Up Secure Remote Password Support

As of this writing there's no RPM package available for SRP. You need to download the source distribution from `http://srp.stanford.edu`, then compile and install it. In this section I discuss how you can do that.

1. Download the latest SRP source distribution from the preceding Web site.

   As of this writing the source distribution is called srp-1.7.1.tar.gz. As usual, make sure that you replace the version number (1.7.1) with the appropriate version number of the distribution you are about to install.

2. Once downloaded, `su` to `root` and copy the `.tar` file in the `/usr/src/redhat/SOURCES` directory.

3. Extract the source distribution in the `/usr/src/redhat/SOURCES` directory using the `tar xvzf srp-1.7.1.tar.gz` command. This creates a subdirectory called `srp-1.7.1`. Change your current directory to this new subdirectory.

4. Run the `configure` script with these options:

```
--with-openssl
--with-pam
```

I assume that you have extracted and compiled OpenSSL source in the `/usr/src/redhat/SOURCES/openssl-0.9.6` directory. Run the `config-ure` script as shown below:

```
./configure --with-openssl=/usr/src/redhat/SOURCES/openssl-0.9.6 \
            --with-pam
```

5. Once the SRP source is configured for OpenSSL and PAM support by the options used in the preceding command, run the `make` and `make install` commands to install the software.

At this point you have compiled and installed SRP, but you still need the Exponential Password System (EPS) support for SRP applications.

Establishing Exponential Password System (EPS)

The SRP source distribution includes the EPS source, which makes installation easy. However, the default installation procedure didn't work for me, so I suggest that you follow my instructions below.

1. `su` to `root`.

2. Change the directory to `/usr/src/redhat/SOURCES/srp-1.7.1/base/pam_eps`.

3. Install the PAM modules for EPS in the `/lib/security` directory with the following command:

```
install -m 644 pam_eps_auth.so pam_eps_passwd.so
/lib/security
```

4. Run the `/usr/local/bin/tconf` command. You can also run it from the `base/src` subdirectory of the SRP source distribution.

The `tconf` command generates a set of parameters for the EPS password file.

5. Choose the predefined field option.

The `tconf` utility also creates `/etc/tpasswd` and `/etc/tpasswd.conf` files.

Select the predefined field number 6 or above. The number 6 option is 1,024 bits. If you choose a larger field size, the computation time to verify the parameters used by EPS increases.

The more bits that you require for security, the more verification time costs you.

At this point, you have the EPS support installed but not in use. Thanks to the PAM technology used by Linux, upgrading your entire (default) password authentication to EPS is quite easy. You modify a single PAM configuration file.

Using the EPS PAM module for password authentication

To use the EPS PAM module for password authentication, do the following:

1. As root, create a backup copy of your /etc/pam.d/system-auth file. (You'll need this if you run into problems with the EPS.) You can simply switch back to your old PAM authentication by overwriting the modified system-auth file with the backed-up version.

2. Modify the system-auth file as shown in Listing 13-1.

Listing 13-1: /etc/pam.d/system-auth

```
#%PAM-1.0
# This file is auto-generated.
# User changes are destroyed the next time authconfig is run.
# DON'T USE authconfig!
auth        required      /lib/security/pam_unix.so likeauth nullok md5 shadow
auth        sufficient    /lib/security/pam_eps_auth.so
auth        required      /lib/security/pam_deny.so
account     sufficient    /lib/security/pam_unix.so
account     required      /lib/security/pam_deny.so
password    required      /lib/security/pam_cracklib.so retry=3
password    required      /lib/security/pam_eps_passwd.so
```

Continued

Listing 13-1 *(Continued)*

```
password    sufficient    /lib/security/pam_unix.so nullok use_authtok md5
shadow
password    required      /lib/security/pam_deny.so
session     required      /lib/security/pam_limits.so

        session       required        /lib/security/pam_unix.so
```

3. Notice the lines in bold. The first bold line indicates that the ESP auth module for PAM can satisfy authentication requirements. The second bold line specifies that the `pam_eps_passwd.so` PAM module for EPS is used for password management. The placement of these lines (in bold) is very important. No line with `sufficient` control fag can come before the `pam_eps_auth.so` or `pam_eps_passwd.so` lines.

Now you can convert the passwords in `/etc/passwd` (or in `/etc/shadow`) to EPS format.

Converting standard passwords to EPS format

User passwords are never stored in `/etc/passwd` or in `/etc/shadow`, so there is no easy way to convert all of your existing user passwords to the new EPS format. These two files store only encrypted versions of password verification strings generated by a one-way hash algorithm used in the crypt() function.

So the best way for converting to ESP passwords is by making users change their passwords using the `passwd` command as usual. If your `/etc/pam.d/passwd` file still uses the default settings, as shown in Listing 13-2, the pam_eps_passwd.so module used in `/etc/pam.d/system-auth` configuration writes an EPS version of the password verification string (not the user's actual password) in the `/etc/tpasswd` file.

Listing 13-2: /etc/pam.d/passwd

```
#%PAM-1.0
auth        required      /lib/security/pam_stack.so service=system-auth
account     required      /lib/security/pam_stack.so service=system-auth
password    required      /lib/security/pam_stack.so service=system-auth
```

 Ordinary user passwords may need to be changed by using the root account once before `map_eps_passwd.so` will write to the `/etc/tpasswd` file. This bug or configuration problem may be already corrected for you if you are using a newer version.

Once you have converted user passwords in this manner you can start using the SRP version of applications such as Telnet.

Using SRP-Enabled Telnet Service

The SRP distribution includes SRP-enabled Telnet server and client software. To install the SRP-enabled Telnet client/server suite, do the following:

1. su to root and change the directory to the Telnet subdirectory of your SRP source distribution, which for my version is /usr/src/redhat/SOURCES/srp-1.7.1/telnet.

2. Run make and make install to the Telnet server (telnetd) software in /usr/local/sbin and the Telnet client (telnet) in /usr/local/bin.

3. Change the directory to /etc/xinetd.conf. Move your current Telnet configuration file for xinetd to a different directory if you have one.

4. Create a Telnet configuration file called /etc/xinetd.d/srp-telnetd, as shown in Listing 13-3.

Listing 13-3: /etc/xinetd.d/srp-telnetd

```
# default: on
# description: The SRP Telnet server serves Telnet connections.
# It uses SRP for authentication.
service telnet
{
        socket_type             = stream
        wait                    = no
        user                    = root
        server                  =  /usr/local/sbin/telnetd
        log_on_success          += DURATION USERID
        log_on_failure          += USERID
        nice                    = 10
        disable                 = no
}
```

5. Restart xinetd using the killall -USR1 xinetd command.

6. Create or modify the /etc/pam.d/telnet file as shown in Listing 13-4.

Listing 13-4: /etc/pam.d/telnet

```
#%PAM-1.0
auth        required      /lib/security/pam_listfile.so item=user \
                          sense=deny file=/etc/telnetusers onerr=succeed
auth        required      /lib/security/pam_stack.so service=srp-telnet
auth        required      /lib/security/pam_shells.so
account     required      /lib/security/pam_stack.so service=srp-telnet
session     required      /lib/security/pam_stack.so service=srp-telnet
```

 If you have modified the /etc/pam.d/system-auth file as shown in Listing 13-1, you can replace the service=srp-telnet option in the preceding listing to service=system-auth. This can keep one systemwide PAM configuration file, which eases your authentication administration. Also, you can skip step 7.

7. Create a file called /etc/pam.d/srp-telnet as shown in Listing 13-5.

Listing 13-5: /etc/pam.d/srp-telnet

```
#%PAM-1.0
auth        required      /lib/security/pam_unix.so likeauth nullok md5 shadow
auth        sufficient     /lib/security/ pam_eps_auth.so
auth        required      /lib/security/pam_deny.so
account     sufficient     /lib/security/pam_unix.so
account     required      /lib/security/pam_deny.so
password    required      /lib/security/pam_cracklib.so retry=3
password    required      /lib/security/pam_eps_passwd.so
password    sufficient     /lib/security/pam_unix.so nullok use_authtok md5
shadow
password    required      /lib/security/pam_deny.so
session     required      /lib/security/pam_limits.so
session     required      /lib/security/pam_unix.so
```

Now you have an SRP-enabled Telnet server. Try the service by running the SRP-enabled Telnet client (found in the /usr/local/bin directory) using the /usr/local/bin/telnet localhost command. When prompted for the username and password, use an already SRP-converted account. The username you use to connect to the SRP-enabled Telnet server via this client must have an entry in /etc/tpasswd, or the client automatically fails over to non-SRP (clear-text password) mode. Here's a sample session:

```
$ telnet localhost 23
Trying 127.0.0.1...
Connected to localhost.intevo.com (127.0.0.1).
Escape character is '^]'.
[ Trying SRP ... ]
SRP Username (root): kabir
[ Using 1024-bit modulus for 'kabir' ]
SRP Password:
[ SRP authentication successful ]
[ Input is now decrypted with type CAST128_CFB64 ]
[ Output is now encrypted with type CAST128_CFB64 ]
Last login: Tue Dec 26 19:30:08 from reboot.intevo.com
```

To connect to your SRP-enabled Telnet server from other Linux workstations, you must install SRP support and the SRP Telnet client software on them. Also, there are many SRP-enabled non-Linux versions of Telnet clients available, which may come in handy if you have a heterogeneous network using multiple operating systems.

Using SRP-enabled Telnet clients from non-Linux platforms

Many SRP-enabled Telnet clients exist for the other popular operating systems. You can find a list of these at `http://srp.stanford.edu`. One SRP-enabled Telnet client works on any system that supports Java, which covers just about every modern operating system.

Using SRP-Enabled FTP Service

The SRP distribution includes an SRP-enabled FTP server and FTP client software. To install the SRP-enabled FTP service do the following:

1. `su` to `root` and change the directory to the FTP subdirectory of your SRP source distribution, which for my version is `/usr/src/redhat/SOURCES/srp-1.7.1/ftp`.

2. Run `make` and `make install` to the FTP server (ftpd) software in `/usr/local/sbin` and the FTP client (ftp) in `/usr/local/bin`.

3. Change the directory to `/etc/xinetd.conf`. Move your current FTP configuration file for `xinetd` to a different directory if you have one.

4. Create an FTP configuration file called `/etc/xinetd.d/srp-ftpd`, as shown in Listing 13-6.

Listing 13-6: /etc/xinetd.d/srp-ftpd

```
# default: on
# description: The SRP FTP server serves FTP connections.
# It uses SRP for authentication.
service ftp
{
        socket_type             = stream
        wait                    = no
        user                    = root
        server                  = /usr/local/sbin/ftpd
        log_on_success          += DURATION USERID
        log_on_failure          += USERID
        nice                    = 10
        disable                 = no
}
```

If you don't want to fall back to regular FTP authentication (using a clear-text password) when SRP authentication fails, add `server_args = -a` line after the `socket_type` line in the preceding configuration file.

5. Restart xinetd using the `killall -USR1 xinetd` **command.**

6. Create or modify the `/etc/pam.d/ftp` **file as shown in Listing 13-7.**

Listing 13-7: /etc/pam.d/ftp

```
#%PAM-1.0
auth       required      /lib/security/pam_listfile.so item=user \
                         sense=deny file=/etc/ftpusers onerr=succeed
auth       required      /lib/security/pam_stack.so service=srp-ftp
auth       required      /lib/security/pam_shells.so
account    required      /lib/security/pam_stack.so service=srp-ftp
session    required      /lib/security/pam_stack.so service=srp-ftp
```

If you have modified the `/etc/pam.d/system-auth` file as shown in Listing 13-1 you can replace the `service=srp-ftp` option in the listing to `service=system-auth`. This keeps one systemwide PAM configuration file, which eases your authentication administration. Also, you can skip step 7.

7. Create a file called /etc/pam.d/srp-ftp as shown in Listing 13-8.

Listing 13-8: /etc/pam.d/srp-ftp

```
#%PAM-1.0
auth        required     /lib/security/pam_unix.so likeauth nullok md5 shadow
auth        sufficient    /lib/security/pam_eps_auth.so
auth        required     /lib/security/pam_deny.so
account     sufficient   /lib/security/pam_unix.so
account     required     /lib/security/pam_deny.so
password    required     /lib/security/pam_cracklib.so retry=3
password    required     /lib/security/pam_eps_passwd.so
password    sufficient   /lib/security/pam_unix.so nullok use_authtok md5
shadow
password    required     /lib/security/pam_deny.so
session     required     /lib/security/pam_limits.so
session     required     /lib/security/pam_unix.so
```

Now you have an SRP-enabled FTP server. Try the service by running the SRP-enabled FTP client (found in the /usr/local/bin directory) using the /usr/local/bin/ftp localhost command. When prompted for the username and password, use an already SRP-converted account. The username you use to connect to the SRP-enabled FTP server via this client must have an entry in /etc/tpasswd, or the client automatically fails over to non-SRP (clear-text password) mode. Here's a sample session:

```
$ /usr/local/bin/ftp localhost
Connected to localhost.intevo.com.
220 k2.intevo.com FTP server (SRPftp 1.3) ready.
SRP accepted as authentication type.
Name (localhost:kabir): kabir
SRP Password:
SRP authentication succeeded.
Using cipher CAST5_CBC and hash function SHA.
200 Protection level set to Private.
232 user kabir authorized by SRP.
230 User kabir logged in.
Remote system type is UNIX.
Using binary mode to transfer files.
```

The SRP-enabled FTP service supports the following cryptographic ciphers:

```
NONE (1)
BLOWFISH_ECB (2)
BLOWFISH_CBC (3)
```

```
BLOWFISH_CFB64 (4)
BLOWFISH_OFB64 (5)
CAST5_ECB (6)
CAST5_CBC (7)
CAST5_CFB64 (8)
CAST5_OFB64 (9)
DES_ECB (10)
DES_CBC (11)
DES_CFB64 (12)
DES_OFB64 (13)
DES3_ECB (14)
DES3_CBC (15)
DES3_CFB64 (16)
DES3_OFB64 (17)
```

Also, MD5 and SHA hash functions are supported. By default, the CAST5_CBC cipher and SHA hash function are used. To specify a different cipher, use the -c option. For example, the /usr/local/bin/ftp -c blowfish_cfb64 localhost command uses the BLOWFISH_CFB64 cipher, not CAST5_CBC. To use the MD5 hash function, use the -h option. The /usr/local/bin/ftp -h md5 localhost command uses the MD5 hash function, not SHA.

Details of these ciphers or hash functions are beyond the scope of this book. You can learn about these ciphers at security-related Web sites. See Appendix C for online resources.

To connect to your SRP-enabled FTP server from other Linux workstations, install SRP support along with the SRP-enabled FTP client on them. There are also SRP-enabled FTP clients for non-Linux systems.

Using SRP-enabled FTP clients from non-Linux platforms

Kermit 95 — available for Windows 95, 98, ME, NT, and 2000, and OS/2 — is SRP enabled and has a built-in FTP client. Visit http://www.columbia.edu/kermit/k95.html for details.

Summary

Transmitting plain-text passwords over a network such as Internet is very risky. Secure Remote Password (SRP) protocol provides you with an alternative to sending plain-text passwords over the network. Using SRP you can secure the authentication aspect of such protocols as Telnet and FTP.

Chapter 14

xinetd

IN THIS CHAPTER

◆ What is `xinetd`?

◆ Compiling and installing `xinetd`

◆ Restricting access to common Internet services

◆ Preventing denial-of-service attacks

◆ Redirecting services

AS A SECURE REPLACEMENT for the `inetd` daemon, `xinetd` offers greater flexibility and control. The `xinetd` daemon has the same functionality as `inetd`, but adds access control, port binding, and protection from denial-of-service attacks.

One drawback is its poor support for Remote Procedure Call (RPC)-based services (listed in `/etc/rpc`). Because most people don't run RPC-based services, this doesn't matter too much. If you need RPC-based services, you can use inetd to run those services while running `xinetd` to manage your Internet services in a secure, controlled manner. In this chapter I dicuss how you can set up xinetd and manage various services using it in a secure manner.

What Is xinetd?

Typically, Internet services on Linux are run either in stand-alone or `xinetd`-run mode. Figure 14-1 shows a diagram of what the stand-alone mode looks like.

As shown in stand-alone mode, a parent or master server is run at all times. This master server

◆ Listens to ports on network interfaces.

◆ Preforks multiple child servers that wait for requests from the master server.

When the master server receives a request from a client system, it simply passes the request information to one of its ready-to-run child server processes. The child server interacts with the client system and provides necessary service.

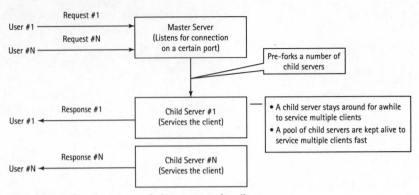

Figure 14–1: Stand-alone mode Internet service diagram

Apache Web Server is typically stand-alone, though it can run as a `xinetd`-run server.

Figure 14-2 shows a diagram of how a `xinetd`-run service works.

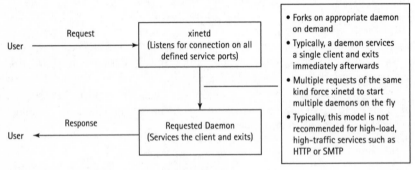

Figure 14–2: xinetd–run Internet service diagram

There is no master server other than the `xinetd` server itself. The server is responsible for listening to all necessary ports for all the services it manages. Once a connection for a particular service arrives, it forks the appropriate server program, which in turn services the client and exits. If the load is high, `xinetd` services multiple requests by running multiple servers.

However, because `xinetd` must fork a server as requests arrive, the penalty is too great for anything that receives or can receive heavy traffic. For example, running Apache as a `xinetd` service is practical only for experimentation and internal purposes. It isn't feasible or run Apache as a `xinetd`-run service for a high-profile Web site. The overhead of forking and establishing a new process for each request is too much of a load and a waste of resources.

Because load is usually not an issue, plenty of services can use `xinetd`. FTP service and POP3 service by using `xinetd`, for example, are quite feasible for even large organizations.

Setting Up xinetd

By default, `xinetd` gets installed on your Red Hat Linux 7.*x* system. Make sure, though, that you always have the latest version installed. In the following section I show installation of and configuration for the latest version of `xinetd`.

Getting xinetd

As with all open-source Linux software, you have two choices for sources of `xinetd`:

◆ Install a binary RPM distribution of `xinetd` from the Red Hat CD-ROM or download it from a Red Hat RPM site such as `http://rpmfind.net`.

◆ Download the source RPM distribution, then compile and install it yourself.

I prefer the source distribution, so I recommend that you try this approach, too. However, if you must install the binary RPM, download it and run the `rpm -ivh` `xinetd-version-architecture.rpm` file to install. In the following section, I show how you can compile and install `xinetd`.

Compiling and installing xinetd

After downloading the source RPM distribution, follow the steps below to compile `xinetd`.

1. Run `rpm -ivh xinet-version.src.rpm`, where xinet-*version*.src.rpm is the name of the source RPM distribution file.

   This places a tar archive called `xinetd-version.tar.gz` in the `/usr/sr324c/redhat/SOURCES` directory.

2. Go to the `/usr/src/redhat/SOURCES` directory and run the `tar xvzf` `xinetd-version.tar.gz` command to extract the source tree.

   The tar program extracts the source in a subdirectory called `xinetd-version`.

3. Go to `xinetd-version` and run the `./configure` script.

   To control maximum load placed on the system by any particular `xinetd`-managed service, use the `--with-loadavg` option with the script.

To configure the TCP wrapper (tcpd) for xinetd, run the `configure` script with the `--with-libwrap=/usr/lib/libwrap.a` option. This controls access by using `/etc/hosts.allow` and `/etc/hosts.deny` files. Choose this option only if you invest a great deal of time creating these two files.

4. Run `make` and `make install` if you don't receive an error during step 3.

   If you get an error message and can't resolve it, use the binary RPM installation.

5. Create a directory called `/etc/xinetd.d`.

   This directory stores the `xinetd` configuration files for each service you want to run via `xinetd`.

6. Create the primary `xinetd` configuration file called `/etc/xinetd.conf` as shown in Listing 14-1.

   The binary RPM `xinetd` package comes with this file.

Listing 14-1: The /etc/xinetd.conf file

```
# Simple configuration file for xinetd
# Some defaults, and include /etc/xinetd.d/
defaults
{
        instances               = 60
        log_type                = SYSLOG authpriv
        log_on_success          = HOST PID
        log_on_failure          = HOST RECORD
}
includedir /etc/xinetd.d
```

At startup, `xinetd` reads this file, which accordingly should be modified for greater security. (See "Strengthening the Defaults in `/etc/xinetd.conf`," later in this chapter, for details.)

7. Create a script called `/etc/rc.d/init.d/xinetd` as shown in Listing 14-2.

   This script — needed to start `xinetd` from an appropriate run level — is supplied by Red Hat in the binary distribution only.

Listing 14-2: The /etc/rc.d/init.d/xinetd file

```
#! /bin/sh
# xinetd          This starts and stops xinetd.
# chkconfig: 345 56 50
# description: xinetd is a powerful replacement
# for inetd. xinetd has access control mechanisms,
# extensive logging capabilities, the ability to
# make services available based on time, and can
# place limits on the number of servers that can
# be started,among other things.
# processname: /usr/sbin/xinetd
# config: /etc/sysconfig/network
# config: /etc/xinetd.conf
# pidfile: /var/run/xinetd.pid
PATH=/sbin:/bin:/usr/bin:/usr/sbin
# Source function library.
. /etc/init.d/functions
# Get config.
test -f /etc/sysconfig/network && . /etc/sysconfig/network
# Check that networking is up.
[ ${NETWORKING} = "yes" ] || exit 0
[ -f /usr/sbin/xinetd ] || exit 1
[ -f /etc/xinetd.conf ] || exit 1
RETVAL=0
start(){
    echo -n "Starting xinetd: "
    daemon xinetd -reuse -pidfile /var/run/xinetd.pid
    RETVAL=$?
    echo
    touch /var/lock/subsys/xinetd
    return $RETVAL
}
stop(){
    echo -n "Stopping xinetd: "
    killproc xinetd
    RETVAL=$?
    echo
    rm -f /var/lock/subsys/xinetd
    return $RETVAL
}
reload(){
    echo -n "Reloading configuration: "
    killproc xinetd -USR2
    RETVAL=$?
    echo
```

Continued

Listing 14-2 *(Continued)*

```
    return $RETVAL
}
restart(){
    stop
    start
}
condrestart(){
    [ -e /var/lock/subsys/xinetd ] && restart
    return 0
}
# See how we were called.
case "$1" in
    start)
        start
        ;;
    stop)
        stop
        ;;
    status)
        status xinetd
        ;;
    restart)
        restart
        ;;
    reload)
        reload
        ;;
    condrestart)
        condrestart
        ;;
    *)
        echo "Usage: xinetd
{start|stop|status|restart|condrestart|reload}"
        RETVAL=1
esac
exit $RETVAL
```

8. Change the directory to /etc/rc.d/rc[1-5].d where [1-5] should be replaced with the run-level number between 1 and 5. In most cases, your default run level is 3, so you would change directory to /etc/rc.d/rc3.d.

 If you don't know your run level, run the run level command and the number returned is your current run level.

9. Create a symbolic link called S50xinetd that points to /etc/rc.d/ init.d/xinetd script. Run the ln -s /etc/rc.d/init.d/xinetd S50xinetd command to create this link.

TIP To automatically run xinetd in other run levels you may choose to use, create a similar link in the appropriate run-level directory.

Configuring xinetd for services

After compiling and installing xinetd, configure each service that you want to manage via xinetd. When xinetd is started, the /etc/xinetd.conf file, shown in Listing 14-1, is loaded. This file sets some defaults and instructs xinetd to load additional service configuration files from the /etc/xinetd.d directory. The xinetd daemon parses each file in this directory and loads all the services that are configured properly.

TIP If you have an inetd.conf file that you want to convert to xinetd.conf, run xinetd/xconv.pl < /etc/inetd.conf > /tmp/xinetd.conf command from the directory where you extracted xinetd source RPM. In my example, this directory is /usr/src/redhat/SOURCES/xinetd-2.1.8.9pre11/xinetd.

The default values section enclosed within the curly braces {} have the following syntax:

<attribute> <assignment operator> <value> <value> ...

The following are common xinetd service attributes and their options.

   ◆ bind IP Address

     See "Creating an Access-Discriminative Service" in this chapter.

   ◆ cps sec [wait sec]

     See "Limiting the number of servers" in this chapter.

   ◆ flags keyword

     This attribute can specify seven flags:

       ■ REUSE — Sets the SO_REUSEADDR flag on the service socket.

- IDONLY — This flag accepts connections from only those clients that have an identification (identd) server.

- NORETRY — This flag instructs the server not to fork a new service process again if the server fails.

- NAMEINARGS — This flag specifies that the first value in the server_args attribute is used as the first argument when starting the service specified. This is most useful when using tcpd; you would specify tcpd in the server attribute (and ftpd -l as the service) in the server_args attribute.

- INTERCEPT — This flag tells the server to intercept packets to verify that a source's IP is acceptable. (It is not applicable to all situations.)

- NODELAY — This option sets the TCP_NODELAY flag for the socket.

- DISABLE — This option sets the TCP_NODELAY flag for the socket.

- KEEPALIVE — This option sets the SO_KEEPALIVE flag in the socket for TCP-based services.

◆ id

Identifies the service. By default, the service's name is the same as the id attribute.

◆ instances *number*

Specifies the maximum number of servers that can run concurrently.

◆ log type

This takes one of two forms:

- log_type syslog *facility*

- log_type file [soft_limit [hard_limit]] [path]

When xinetd starts a service, it writes a log entry in the log_type specified file or syslog facility. See "Limiting log file size" in this chapter.

◆ log_on_success *keyword*

Specifies the information that needs to be logged upon successful start of a service. This attribute can take five optional values:

- PID — This value is the server's PID (if it's an internal xinetd service, the PID is 0)

- HOST — This value is the client's IP address.

- USERID — This value is the identity of the remote user.

- EXIT — This value is the exit status code of the service.

- DURATION — This value is the session duration of the service.

◆ log_on_failure *keyword*

As with log_on_success, xinetd logs an entry when a service can't be started. This attribute can take four values as arguments:

- HOST – This value is the client's IP address.

- USERID – This value is the identity of the remote user.

- ATTEMPT – Records the access attempt.

- RECORD – Logs everything that xinetd knows about the client.

◆ max_load number

See "Limiting load" in this chapter.

◆ nice number

Sets the process priority of the service run by xinetd.

◆ no_access [IP address] [hostname] [network/netmask]

Defines a list of IP addresses, hostnames, networks, and/or netmask that are denied access to the service. (For details, see Appendix A.)

◆ only_from [ip address] [hostname] [network/netmask]

Specifies a list of IP addresses, hostnames, network(s), and/or netmask(s) allowed to access the service (see Appendix A). If you don't supply a value for this attribute, the service is denied to everyone.

◆ per_source number

See "Limiting the number of servers" in this chapter.

◆ UNLIMITED

See "Limiting the number of servers" in this chapter.

◆ port number

Specifies the port number for a service. Use this only if your service port isn't defined in /etc/services.

◆ protocol *keyword*

Specifies the protocol name that must exist in /etc/protocols. Normally a service's default protocol is used.

◆ Redirect IP address

See "Redirecting and Forwarding Clients" in this chapter.

◆ Redirect hostname port

See "Redirecting and Forwarding Clients" in this chapter.

- ◆ `server path`

  Specifies the path to the server executable file.

- ◆ `server_args [arg1] [arg2] [arg3]...`

  Specifies the list of arguments that are passed on to the server.

- ◆ `socket_type` *keyword*

  Specifies any of four socket types:

  - ▪ `Stream` (TCP)

  - ▪ `dgram` (UDP)

  - ▪ `raw`

  - ▪ `seqpacket`.

- ◆ `type` *keyword*

- ◆ `xinetd`

  Specifies service type. Can manage three different types of services:

  - ▪ INTERNAL – These services are directly managed by `xinetd`.

  - ▪ RPC – `xinetd` isn't (yet) good at handling RPC services that are defined in `/etc/rpc`. Use `inetd` instead with RPC-based services.

  - ▪ UNLISTED – Services that aren't listed in `/etc/services` or in `/etc/rpc`.

- ◆ `wait yes | no`

  If the service you want to manage by using `xinetd` is multithreaded, set this attribute to `yes`; otherwise set it to `no`.

  - ▪ When wait is set to `yes`, only one server is started by `xinetd`.

  - ▪ When `wait` is set to `no`, `xinetd` starts a new server process for each request.

The following table lists the three possible assignment operators.

Assignment Operator	Description
=	Assigns a value to the attribute
+=	Adds a value to the list of values assigned to a given attribute
-=	Removes a value from the list of values for a given attribute

The default attributes found in the /etc/xinetd.conf file applies to each managed service. As shown in Listing 14-1, the defaults section:

♦ Tells xinetd to allow 60 instances of the same service to run.

This means that when xinetd is in charge of managing the FTP service, it allows 60 FTP sessions to go on simultaneously.

♦ Tells xinetd to use the syslog (the authpriv facility) to log information.

♦ Instructs xinetd to log

- hostname (HOST) and process ID (PID) upon successful start of a service,

- hostname and all available information (RECORD) when a service doesn't start.

As mentioned earlier, each service has its own configuration file (found in the /etc/xinetd.d directory), and that's what you normally use to configure it. For example, a service called myservice would be managed by creating a file called /etc/xinetd.d/myservice, which has lines such as the following:

```
service myservice
{
    attribute1 operator value1, value2, ...
    attribute2 operator value1, value2, ...
    . . .
    attributeN operator value1, value2, ...
}
```

You can start quickly with only the default configuration found in the /etc/xinetd.conf file. However, there is a lot of per-service configuration that should be done (discussed in later sections) before your xinetd configuration is complete.

Starting, Reloading, and Stopping xinetd

If you followed the installation instructions in the previous section, your xinetd should automatically start when you reboot the system. You can also start it manually without rebooting the system. To start xinetd, run the /etc/rc.d/init.d/ xinetd start command.

Any time you add, modify, or delete /etc/xinetd.conf (or any other files in the /etc/xinet.d directory), tell xinetd to reload the configuration. To do so, use the /etc/rc.d/init.d/xinetd reload command.

TIP If you prefer the `kill` command, you can use `kill -USR1 xinetd PID` or `killall -USR1 xinetd` to soft-reconfigure `xinetd`. A soft reconfiguration using the `SIGUSR1` signal makes `xinetd` reload the configuration files and adjust accordingly. To do a hard reconfiguration of the `xinetd` process, simply replace `USR1` with `USR2` (`SIGUSR2` signal). This forces `xinetd` to reload the configuration and remove currently running services.

To stop `xinetd`, run the `/etc/rc.d/init.d/xinetd stop` command.

Strengthening the Defaults in /etc/xinetd.conf

The `defaults` section, shown in Listing 14-1, isn't ideal for strong security. It doesn't obey the prime directive of a secured access configuration: "Deny everyone; allow only those who should have access." So add an attribute that fixes this insecurity:

```
no_access = 0.0.0.0/0
```

The `0.0.0.0/0 IP` address range covers the entire IP address space. The `no_access` attribute set to such an IP range disables access from all possible IP addresses — that is, everyone. You must open access on a per-service basis.

Here is how you can fine tune the default configuration:

- ◆ The default configuration allows 60 instances of a service to run if necessary because of load. This number seems high. I recommend that this number be scaled back to 15 or 20. You can change it later as needed. For example, if you find that your server gets more than 20 FTP requests simultaneously, you can change the `/etc/xinetd/ftp` service file to set instances to a number greater than 20.

- ◆ The default configuration doesn't restrict how many connections one remote host can make to a service. Set this to 10, using the `per_source` attribute.

- ◆ Disable all the `r*` services (such as `rlogin`, `rsh`, and `rexec`); they are considered insecure and shouldn't be used. You can disable them in the `defaults` section by using the `disabled` attribute.

Now the `defaults` section looks like this:

```
defaults
{
    instances       = 20
    log_type        = SYSLOG authpriv
    log_on_success  = HOST PID
    log_on_failure  = HOST RECORD
    # Maximum number of connections allowed from
    # a single remote host.
    per_source      = 10
            # Deny access to all possible IP addresses. You MUST
    # open access using only_from attribute in each service
    # configuration file in /etc/xinetd.d directory.
    no_access       = 0.0.0.0/0
    # Disable services that are not to be used
    disabled        = rlogin rsh rexec
}
```

After you create the `defaults` section as shown here, you can start `xinetd`. You can then create service-specific configuration files and simply reload your `xinetd` configuration as needed.

Running an Internet Daemon Using xinetd

An Internet service that runs via `xinetd` is defined using an `/etc/xinetd.d/`*service* file where the filename is the name of the service. Listing 14-3 shows a simple configuration for an Internet service called `myinetservice`.

Listing 14-3: /etc/xinetd.d/myinetservice

```
service myinetservice
{
    socket_type = stream
    wait        = no
    user        = root
    server      = /path/to/myinetserviced
    server_args = arg1 arg2
}
```

To set up services such as FTP, Telnet, and `finger`, all you need is a skeleton configuration as in the preceding listing; change the values as needed. For example, Listing 14-4 shows `/etc/xinetd.d/ftp`, the FTP configuration file.

Listing 14-4: /etc/xinetd.d/ftpd

```
service ftp
{
    socket_type      = stream
    wait             = no
    user             = root
    server           = /usr/sbin/in.ftpd
    server_args      = -l -a
}
```

Here the server attribute points to /usr/sbin/in.ftpd, the server_args attribute is set to -l and -a, and everything else is the same as in the skeleton configuration. You can enhance such configuration to add more attributes as needed. For example, say you want to log more than what the defaults section provides for the FTP service, such that a successful login (log_on_success) then logs not only the HOST and PID, but also the DURATION and USERID. You can simply use the += operator to add these log options:

```
log_on_success    += DURATION USERID
```

When reloaded, the xinetd daemon sees this line as

```
log_on_success    = HOST PID DURATION USERID
```

You are adding values to the list already specified in the log_on_success attribute in the defaults section in /etc/xinetd.conf. Similarly, you can override a default value for your service configuration. Say you don't want to log via syslog, and prefer to log by using a file in the /var/log directory. You can override the default log_type setting this way:

```
log_type          = FILE /var/log/myinetdservice.log
```

Also, you can add new attributes as needed. For example, to control the FTP server's priority by using the nice attribute, you can add it into your configuration. The completed example configuration is shown in Listing 14-5.

Listing 14-5: /etc/xinetd.d/ftpd

```
service ftp
{
    socket_type      = stream
    wait             = no
    user             = root
    server           = /usr/sbin/in.ftpd
```

```
    server_args        = -l -a
    log_on_success     += DURATION USERID
    nice               = 10
}
```

Controlling Access by Name or IP Address

It is common practice to control access to certain services via name (that is, hostname) or IP address. Previously (in the inetd days) this was possible only by using the TCP wrapper program called tcpd, which uses the /etc/hosts.allow and /etc/hosts.deny files to control access. Now xinetd comes with this feature built in.

If you want your Telnet server accessible only within your organization's LAN, use the only_from attribute. For example, if your network address and netmask in (CIDR) format is 192.168.0.0/24, you can add the following line in the /etc/xinetd.d/telnet configuration file.

```
# Only allow access from the 192.168.0.0/24 subnet
only_from      = 192.168.0.0/24
```

This makes sure that only the computers in the 192.168.0.0 network can access the Telnet service.

If you want to limit access to one or a few IP addresses instead of a full network, you can list the IP addresses as values for the only_from attribute as shown in this example:

```
# Only allow access from two known IP addresses
only_from      = 192.168.0.100 172.20.15.1
```

Here, access to the Telnet service is limited to two IP addresses.

If you want to allow connections from a network such as 192.168.0.0/24 but don't want a subnet 192.168.0.128/27 to access the service, add the following lines to the configuration file:

```
# Only allow access from the 192.168.0.0/24 subnet
only_from      = 192.168.0.0/24
# Don't allow access from the 192.168.0.128/27 subnet
no_access   = 192.168.0.128/27
```

Although only_from makes the service available to all usable IP addresses ranging from 192.168.0.1 to 192.168.0.254, the noaccess attribute disables the IP addresses that fall under the 192.168.0.128 network.

If you want to allow access to the service from a network 192.168.0.0/24 but also want to block three hosts (with IP addresses 192.168.0.100, 192.168.0.101, and 192.168.0.102), the configuration that does the job is as follows:

```
# Only allow access from the 192.168.0.0/24 subnet
only_from     = 192.168.0.0/24
# Don't allow access from the 192.168.0.128/27 subnet
no_access   = 192.168.0.100 192.168.0.101 192.168.0.102
```

Controlling Access by Time of Day

Sooner or later, most security administrators have to restrict access to a service for a certain period of time. Typically, the need for such restriction comes from services that must be restarted (or go into maintenance mode) during a 24-hour cycle. For example, if you're running a database server, you may find that performing a backup requires taking all database access offline because of the locks. Luckily, if such a service is managed by xinetd, you can control access by using the access_times attribute – and may not have to deny access while you're creating the backup. For example, you can control access to your FTP server during office hours if you add the following configuration:

```
# Allow access only during office hours
access_times = 08:00-17:00
```

When a user tries connecting to the service before or after these hours, access is denied.

Reducing Risks of Denial-of-Service Attacks

Denial-of-Service (DoS) attacks are very common these days. A typical DoS attacker diminishes your system resources in such a way that your system denies responses to valid user requests. Although it's hard to foolproof a server from such attacks, precautionary measures help you fight DoS attacks effectively. In this section, I discuss how xinetd can reduce the risk of DoS attacks for services it manages.

Limiting the number of servers

To control how many servers are started by xinetd use the instances attribute. This attribute allows you to specify the maximum number of server instances that xinetd can start when multiple requests are received as shown in this example:

```
#Only 10 connections at a time
instances     = 10
```

Here, xinetd starts a maximum of ten servers to service multiple requests. If the number of connection requests exceeds ten, the requests exceeding ten are refused until at least one server exits.

Limiting log file size

Many attackers know that most services write access log entries. They often send many requests to daemons that write lots of log entries and try to fill disk space in /var or other partitions. Therefore, a maximum log size for services is a good idea.

By default, xinetd writes log entries using the daemon.info facility of syslog (syslogd). You can use this attribute to change the syslog facility this way:

```
log_type SYSLOG facility
```

To use the authpriv.info facility of syslog, use:

```
log_type SYSLOG authpriv.info
```

Also, xinetd can write logs to a file of your choice. The log_type syntax for writing logs is:

```
log_type FILE /path/to/logfile [soft_limit [hard_limit]]
```

For example, to limit the log file /var/log/myservice.log for a service to be 10,485,760 bytes (10MB) at the most and receive warning in syslog when the limit approaches 8,388,608 bytes (8MB) then use the log_type attribute this way:

```
log_type FILE /var/log/myservice.log 8388608 10485760
```

When the log file reaches 8MB, you see an alert entry in syslog and when the log file reaches the 10MB limit, xinetd stops any service that uses the log file.

Limiting load

You can use the maxload attribute to specify the system load at which xinetd stops accepting connection for a service. This attribute has the following syntax:

```
max_load number
```

This number specifies the load at which the server stops accepting connections; the value for the load is based on a one-minute CPU load average, as in this example:

```
#Not under load
max_load     = 2.9
```

When the system load average goes above 2.9, this service is temporarily disabled until the load average lowers.

To use the `max_load` attribute, compile `xinetd` with the `-with-load-avrg` option.

The `nice` attribute sets the process priority of the server started by `xinetd` as shown in this example:

```
#Be low priority
nice         = 15
```

This ensures that the service started by `xinetd` has a low priority.

To set a high priority use a smaller number. Highest priority is `-20`.

Limiting the rate of connections

This attribute controls how many servers for a custom service `xinetd` starts per second. The first number (in seconds) specifies the frequency (connections per second). The second number (also in seconds) specifies how long `xinetd` waits after reaching the `server/sec` limit, as in this example:

```
#Only 5 connections per second
cps          = 10 60
```

Here `xinetd` starts a maximum of 10 servers and waits 60 seconds if this limit is reached. During the wait period, the service isn't available to any new client. Requests for service are denied.

Creating an Access–Discriminative Service

Occasionally, a service like HTTP or FTP has to run on a server in a way that discriminates according to where the access request came from. This access discrimination allows for tight control of how the service is available to the end user.

For example, if you have a system with two interfaces (eth0 connected to the local LAN and eth1 connected to an Internet router), you can provide FTP service with a different set of restrictions on each interface. You can limit the FTP service on the public (that is, eth1), Internet-bound interface to allow FTP connections only during office hours when a system administrator is on duty and let the FTP service run unrestrictedly when requested by users in the office LAN. Of course, you don't want to let Internet users access your FTP site after office hours, but you want hardworking employees who are working late to access the server via the office LAN at any time.

You can accomplish this using the `bind` attribute to bind an IP address to a specific service. Because systems with multiple network interfaces have multiple IP addresses, this attribute can offer different functionality on a different interface (that is, IP address) on the same machine.

Listing 14-6 shows the `/etc/xinetd.d/ftp-worldwide` configuration file used for the public FTP service.

Listing 14-6: /etc/xinetd.d/ftp-worldwide

```
service ftp
{
  id            = ftp-worldwide
  wait          = no
  user          = root
  server        = /usr/sbin/in.ftpd
  server_args   = -l
  instances     = 10
  cps           = 5
  nice          = 10
  only_from     = 0.0.0.0/0
  bind          = 169.132.226.215
  access_times  = 08:00-17:00
}
```

The proceeding configuration does the following

◆ The `id` field sets a name ("ftp-worldwide") for the FTP service that is available to the entire world (the Internet).

◆ This service is bound to the IP address on the eth1 interface (169.132.226.215). It's open to everyone because the `only_from` attribute allows any IP address in the entire IP address space (0.0.0.0/0) to access it.

◆ Access is restricted to the hours 08:00-17:00 using the `access_times` attribute.

◆ Only ten instances of the FTP server can run at a time.

◆ Only five instances of the server can be started per second.

◆ The service runs with a low process-priority level (10), using the `nice` attribute.

Listing 14-7 shows the private (that is, office LAN access only) FTP service configuration file called `/etc/xinetd.d/ftp-office`.

Listing 14-7: /etc/xinetd.d/ftp-office

```
service ftp
{
  id            = ftp-office
  socket_type   = stream
  wait          = no
  user          = root
  server        = /usr/sbin/in.ftpd
  server_args   = -l
  only_from     = 192.168.1.0/24
  bind          = 192.168.1.215
}
```

Here the private FTP service is named ftp-office — using the id attribute — and it's bound to the 192.168.1.0 network. Every host on this Class C network can access this FTP server. But no external server (for example, one on the Internet) has access to this server.

Redirecting and Forwarding Clients

Using port redirection you can point clients to a different port on the server or even forward them to a different system. The redirect attribute can redirect or forward client requests to a different system or a different port on the local system. The redirect attribute has the following syntax:

```
redirect  IP address or hostname   port
```

When `xinetd` receives a connection for the service with the redirect attribute, it spawns a process and connects to the port on the IP or hostname specified as the value of the redirect attribute. Here's how you can use this attribute.

Say that you want to redirect all Telnet traffic destined for the Telnet server (running on IP address 169.132.226.215) to 169.132.226.232. The machine with the 169.132.226.215 IP address needs the following /etc/xinetd.d/telnet configuration:

```
service telnet
{
    flags       = REUSE
    socket_type = stream
    protocol    = tcp
    wait        = no
    user        = root
    bind        = 169.132.226.215
    redirect    = 169.132.226.232
}
```

Here the `redirect` attribute redirects Telnet requests to 169.132.226.215 to another host with IP address 169.132.226.232. Any time you run Telnet 169.132.226.215 from a machine, the request forces xinetd to launch a process and act as a Telnet proxy between 169.132.226.215 and 169.132.226.232. You don't need a `server` or server_args attribute here.

The 169.132.226.232 machine doesn't even have to be a Linux system. However, if the destination of the redirect (169.132.226.232) is a Linux system – and you want to run Telnet on a nonstandard port such as 2323 on that machine – you can create a configuration file for xinetd called /etc/xinetd.d/telnet2323. It would look like this:

```
service telnet2323
{
    id          = telnet2323
    flags       = REUSE
    socket_type = stream
    protocol    = tcp
    wait        = no
    user        = root
    bind        = 169.132.226.232
    port        = 2323
    server      = /usr/sbin/in.telnetd
}
```

Here the `id` field distinguishes the special service and port attribute lets `xinetd` know that you want to run the Telnet daemon on port 2323 on 169.132.226.232. In such a case change redirect 169.132.226.232 23 to redirect 169.132.226.232 2323 in /etc/xinetd.d/telnet on the machine with the IP address 169.132.226.215.

Figure 14-3 illustrates how you can use this redirection feature to access a private network from the Internet.

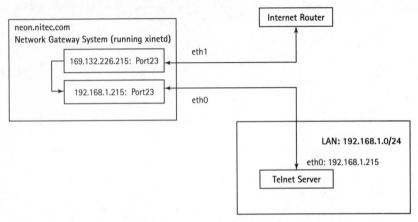

Figure 14-3: Using redirection to access a private network

As shown in the figure, the neon.nitec.com system is a Linux gateway between the Internet and a private network 192.168.1.0/24. The gateway implements the redirect this way:

```
service telnet
{
    flags       = REUSE
    socket_type = stream
    protocol    = tcp
    wait        = no
    user        = root
    bind        = 169.132.226.215
    redirect    = 192.168.1.215 23
}
```

When a Telnet request such as telnet 169.132.226.215 is received by the xinetd daemon on 169.132.226.215, it launches a process to proxy all data between 169.132.226.215 and 192.168.1.215.

Using TCP Wrapper with xinetd

When `xinetd` is compiled with TCP wrapper support (using the `-with-libwrap` configuration option), all services can use the `/etc/hosts.allow` and `/etc/hosts.deny` files. For example, say you want to run the `finger` server via `xinetd` and control it via the TCP wrapper. Here's what you do:

1. Modify the `/etc/xinetd.d/finger` file as shown below:

   ```
   service finger
   {
   flags        = REUSE NAMEINARGS
   protocol     = tcp
   socket_type  = stream
   wait         = no
   user         = nobody
   server       = /usr/sbin/tcpd
   server_args  = /usr/sbin/in.fingerd
   }
   ```

2. To control access to the `finger` daemon, modify `/etc/hosts.allow` and `/etc/hosts.deny` as needed. For example, to deny everyone access to the `finger` daemon except hostname `192.168.1.123`, you can create an entry in `/etc/hosts.allow` this way:

   ```
   in.fingerd: 192.168.1.123
   ```

3. Modify `/etc/hosts.deny` this way:

   ```
   in.fingerd: ALL
   ```

This makes `xinetd` run the TCP wrapper (`/usr/sbin/tcpd`) with the command-line argument `/usr/sbin/in.fingerd` (which is the `finger` daemon).

Running sshd as xinetd

Every time `sshd` runs, it generates a server key. This is why `sshd` is typically a stand-alone server (that is, started once during server start-up). However, to use `xinetd`'s access control features for SSH service, you can run it as a `xinetd` service. Here's how:

1. Create a `xinetd` service file called `/etc/xinetd.d/sshd` as shown in the following listing.

   ```
   service ssh
   {
   ```

```
        socket_type                 = stream
        wait                        = no
        user                        = root
        server                      = /usr/local/sbin/sshd
        server_args                 = -i
        log_on_success              += DURATION USERID
        log_on_failure              += USERID
        nice                        = 10
    }
```

2. Run `ps auxw | grep sshd` to check whether `sshd` is already running. If it's running, stop it by using `/etc/rc.d/init.d/sshd stop`.

3. Force `xinetd` to load its configuration, using `killall -USR1 xinetd`.

You can use an SSH client to access the server as usual.

Using xadmin

The `xinetd` daemon provides an internal administrative service called `xadmin`. This service provides information about the `xinetd`-run services. You can set up this service configuration file, `/etc/xinetd.d/xadmin`, this way:

```
service xadmin
{
    type         = INTERNAL UNLISTED
    port         = 9100
    protocol     = tcp
    socket_type  = stream
    wait         = no
    instances    = 1
    only_from    = localhost
    cps          = 1
}
```

The configuration tells `xinetd` to run only one instance of the `xadmin` service on the nonstandard (that is, not listed in `/etc/services`) port, 9100, using TCP. Because `xadmin` shows information about the `xinetd`-run services, it isn't advisable to make this service available to the public. That's why the configuration makes this service available only on `localhost` (that is, `127.0.0.1`). You must log on to the system locally to access this service. Only one connection per second is allowed for this service.

To run this service from `localhost`, run the `telnet localhost 9100` command. Listing 14-8 shows a sample session when connected to this service.

Listing 14–8: Sample xadmin session

```
Trying 127.0.0.1...
Connected to localhost.intevo.com.
Escape character is '^]'.
> help
xinetd admin help:
show run  :   shows information about running services
show avail:   shows what services are currently available
bye, exit :   exits the admin shell
> show run
Running services:
service  run retry attempts descriptor
ftp server
pid = 2232
start_time = Thu Dec 14 21:56:47 2000
Connection info:
        state = CLOSED
        service = ftp
        descriptor = 11
        flags = 9
        remote_address = 172.20.15.100,2120
        Alternative services =
log_remote_user = YES
writes_to_log = YES
xadmin server
pid = 0
start_time = Fri Dec 15 19:00:00 2000
Connection info:
        state = OPEN
        service = xadmin
        descriptor = 11
        flags = 0x9
        remote_address = 127.0.0.1,1534
        Alternative services =
log_remote_user = YES
writes_to_log = NO
> show avail
Available services:
service   port   bound address    uid redir addr redir port
xadmin    9100   0.0.0.0          0
ftp       21     0.0.0.0          0
telnet    23     0.0.0.0          0
shell     514    0.0.0.0          0
login     513    0.0.0.0          0
```

Continued

Listing 14–8 *(Continued)*

```
finger    79    0.0.0.0         99
> bye
bye bye
Connection closed by foreign host.
```

The `xadmin` commands entered at the > prompt are shown in boldface. The `help` command lists available `xadmin` commands. The `show run` command shows information about currently running services that `xinetd` started. In the example, `ftp` and `xadmin` are the only services run by `xadmin`. The `show avail` command shows the configured services.

Summary

The `xinetd` daemon is a secure replacement for the traditional `inetd` daemon. It allows each service to have its own configuration file and provides a greater flexibility in controlling access to the services it manages. It offers good support for handling many denial of service attacks as well.

Part IV

Network Service Security

Chapter 15

Web Server Security

APACHE, THE DEFAULT WEB-SERVER program for Red Hat Linux, is the most widely used Web server in the world. Apache developers pay close attention to Web security issues, which keeps Apache in good shape for keeping security holes to a minimum in server code. However, most security issues surrounding Web sites exist because of software misconfiguration or misunderstanding of underlying server technology. This chapter examines some common Web security risks – and some ways to reduce or eliminate them.

Understanding Web Risks

The very first step in protecting your Web server from vandals is understanding and identifying security risks. Not long ago, Web sites served only static HTML pages, which made them less prone to security risks. The only way a vandal could hack into such Web sites was to break into the server by gaining illegal access. This was typically done by using weak passwords (passwords that are easily guessed or dictionary words) or by tricking another server program.

These days most Web sites no longer serve static HTML pages; typically they serve dynamic content, personalized for a rich user experience. Many Web sites tie in applications for valuable customer service or perform e-commerce activities – and that's where they also take some (usually inadvertent) risks.

Most Web sites that have been hacked by vandals are not vandalized because of the Web server software; they are hacked because holes in their applications or scripts are exploited.

Most Web-security experts agree that scripts or applications running on a Web server are the biggest risk factors. Because CGI scripts are generally responsible for creating dynamic content, they often cause the most damage. This chapter examines security risks associated with CGI scripts and shows how you can reduce such risks. First – appropriately for the most-used Web server – is a look at how you can configure Apache for enhanced security.

Configuring Sensible Security for Apache

Sensible security configuration for Apache includes creating dedicated user and group accounts, using a security-friendly directory structure, establishing permissions and index files, and disabling risky defaults. The following sections provide a closer look.

Using a dedicated user and group for Apache

Apache can be run as a standalone or an inetd-run service. If you run Apache as an inetd service, don't worry about the User and Group directives. If you run Apache as a standalone server, however, make sure you create a dedicated user and group for Apache. Don't use the nobody user or the nogroup group, especially if your system has already defined these. Likely there are other services or other places where your system uses them. Instead, create a new user and group for Apache.

 For clarity, this chapter refers to the Apache-dedicated user and group accounts as the httpd user and the httpd group; you may want to use a different name for these accounts.

When you use a dedicated user and group for Apache, permission-specific administration of your Web content becomes simpler to do: Just ensure that only the Apache user has read access to your Web content. If you want to create a directory to which some CGI scripts may write data, enable write permissions for only the Apache user.

Using a safe directory structure

Most Apache installations have four main directories:

- ♦ ServerRoot stores server configuration (conf subdirectory), binary (bin subdirectory), and other server-specific files.

◆ DocumentRoot stores Web site content such as HTML, JavaScript, and images.

◆ ScriptAlias stores CGI scripts.

◆ CustomLog and ErrorLog store access and error log files. You can specify two different directories for each of these directives, but keeping one log directory for all the log files is usually more manageable in the long run.

I recommend using a directory structure where all four primary directories are independent of each other — meaning no primary directory is a subdirectory of any other.

◆ ServerRoot should point to a directory that can be accessed only by the root user.

◆ The DocumentRoot directory needs access permission for

   ■ Users who maintain your Web site

   ■ The Apache user or group (specified using the User and Group directives in the httpd.conf file)

◆ The ScriptAlias directory should be accessible only to script developers and an Apache user or group.

◆ The CustomLog or ErrorLog directory should be accessible only by the root user.

Not even the Apache user or group should have access to the log directory. The following example shows such a directory structure:

```
/
+---home
|   +---httpd     (ServerRoot)
+---www
|   +---htdocs    (DocumentRoot)
|   +---cgi-bin   (ScriptAlias)
|   +---logs      (CustomLog and ErrorLog)
.
```

This directory structure is quite safe in many ways. To understand why, first look at the following Apache configuration in httpd.conf.

```
ServerRoot      /home/httpd
DocumentRoot    /www/htdocs
ScriptAlias     /cgi-bin/      "/www/cgi-bin/"
CustomLog       /www/logs/access.log common
ErrorLog        /www/logs/error.log
```

Because all these major directories are independent (not one is a subdirectory of another) they are safe. A permissions mistake in one directory doesn't affect the others.

Using appropriate file and directory permissions

ServerRoot should be accessible only by the root user, because no one but the root should configure or run Apache. DocumentRoot should be accessible to users who manage the contents of your Web site and the Apache user (specified using the User directive) or the Apache group (specified using Group directive).

For example, if you want a user called html guru to publish content on your Web site and you run Apache as httpd user, here's how you make both Apache and the named user access the DocumentRoot directory:

1. Create a new group called webteam with this command:

   ```
   groupadd webteam
   ```

2. Add html guru as a user to the webteam group with this command:

   ```
   usermod -G webteam htmlguru
   ```

3. Change the ownership of the DocumentRoot directory (and all the subdirectories below it) with this command:

   ```
   chown -R httpd.webteam /www/htdocs
   ```

   This command sets the directory ownership to Apache (that is, the httpd user) and sets the group ownership to webteam, which includes the html-guru user. This means both the Apache and html guru accounts can access the document tree.

4. Change the permission of the DocumentRoot directory (and all the subdirectories below it) this way:

   ```
   chmod -R 2570 /www/htdocs
   ```

   This command makes sure that the files and subdirectories under the DocumentRoot are readable and executable by the Apache user and that the webteam group can read, write, and execute everything. It also ensures that whenever a new file or directory is created in the document tree, the webteam group has access to it.

   One great advantage of this method is that adding new users to the webteam is as simple as running the following command:

   ```
   usermod -G webteam <new username>
   ```

5. To remove an existing user from the webteam group, simply run:

   ```
   usermod -G <username> [group1,group2,group3,...]
   ```

In this configuration, group1, group2, group3, and so on are groups (excluding the webteam group) that this user currently belongs to.

 TIP You can find which group(s) a user belongs to by running the group <username> command.

ScriptAlias should be accessible only to the CGI developers and the Apache user. I recommend that you create a new group called webdev for the developer(s). Although the developer group (webdev) needs read, write, and execute access for the directory, the Apache user requires only read and execute access. Don't allow the Apache user to write files in this directory. For example, say you have the following ScriptAlias in httpd.conf:

```
ScriptAlias   /cgi-bin/      "/www/cgi-bin/"
```

If httpd is your Apache user and webdev is your developer group, set the permissions for /www/cgi-bin like this:

```
chown -R httpd.webdev /www/cgi-bin
chmod -R 2570 /www/cgi-bin
```

Alternatively, if you want only one user (say, cgiguru) to develop CGI scripts, you can set the file and directory permission this way:

```
chown -R cgiguru.httpd /www/cgi-bin
chmod -R 750 /www/cgi-bin
```

Here the user cgiguru owns the directory and the group (specified by the Group directive) used for Apache server and is the group owner of the directory and its files.

The log directory used in CustomLog and ErrorLog directives should be writable only by the root user. The recommended permissions setting for such a directory (say, /www/logs) is:

```
chown -R root.root /www/logs
chmod -R 700 /www/logs
```

 CAUTION Don't allow anyone (including the Apache user or group) to read, write, or execute files in the log directory specified in CustomLog and ErrorLog directives.

Whenever implementing an access policy for a Web directory remember:

◆ Take a conservative approach to allowing access to new directories that are accessible via Web.

◆ Don't allow Web visitors to view any directory listings. You can hide your directory listings using the methods discussed below.

Using directory index file

Whenever a user requests access to a directory via Web, Apache does the following:

1. Apache checks whether the directory is accessible.

   If it is accessible, Apache continues; if it is not, Apache displays an error message.

2. If the directory is accessible, Apache looks for a directory index file specified using the `DirectoryIndex` directive. By default, this file is `index.html`.

   ■ If it can read this file in the requested directory, the contents of the file are displayed.

   ■ If such a file doesn't exist, Apache checks whether it can create a dynamic listing for the directory. If that action is allowed, then Apache creates dynamic listings and displays the contents of the directory to the user.

Any directory listings dynamically generated by Apache provide potential bad guys with clues about your directory structure; you shouldn't allow such listings. The simplest way to avoid creating a dynamic directory listing is by specifying the filenames of your directory listings in the `DirectoryIndex` directive. For example, Apache first looks for `index.html` in the requested directory of the URL; then it looks for `index.htm` if `index.html` is missing — provided you set `DirectoryIndex` with this command:

```
DirectoryIndex index.html index.htm
```

One common reason that many Web sites have an exposed directory or two is that someone creates a new directory and forgets to create the index file — or uploads an index file in the wrong case (`INDEX.HTML` or `INDEX.HTM`, for example). If this happens frequently, a CGI script can automatically redirect users to your home page or perhaps to an internal search engine interface. Simply modify the `DirectoryIndex` directive so it looks like this:

```
DirectoryIndex index.html index.htm /cgi-bin/index.pl
```

Now add a CGI script such as the one shown in Listing 15-1 in the ScriptAlias-specified directory.

Listing 15-1: index.pl

```
#!/usr/bin/perl
# Purpose: this script is used to redirect
#          users who enter URL that points to
#          directories without index.html page.
#
# Set the automatically redirect URL
my $AUTO_REDIRECT_URL = '/';
# Get the current URL path
my $curDir = $ENV{REQUEST_URI};
# if the current URL path isn't home page (/) then
# redirect user to home page
if ($curDir ne '/'){
   print redirect($AUTO_REDIRECT_URL);
# If the home page is also missing the index page,
# we can't redirect back to home page (to avoid
# recursive redirection) so display an error message.
} else {
   print header;
   print "HOME PAGE NOT FOUND!";
}
exit 0;
```

This script runs if Apache doesn't find the directory index files (index.html or index.htm). The script simply redirects a user, whose URL points to a directory with no index file, to the home page of the Web site.

Change /cgi-bin/ from the path of the directive if you use another alias name.

If you want to not display any directory listings, you can simply disable directory listings by setting the following configuration:

```
<Directory />
  Options -Indexes
</Directory >
```

The Options directive tells Apache to disable all directory-index processing.

You may also want to tell Apache not to allow symbolic links; they can expose part of the disk space that you don't want to make public. To do so, use the minus sign when you set the `Options` directive so it looks like this: `-FollowSymLinks`.

Disabling default access

A good security model dictates that no access exists by default; get into the habit of permitting no access at first. Permit specific access only to specific directories. To implement no-default access, use the following configuration segment in `httpd.conf`:

```
<Directory />
   Order deny,allow
   Deny from all
</Directory>
```

This segment disables all access first. For access to a particular directory, use the `<Directory...>` container again to open that directory. For example, if you want to permit access to `/www/htdocs`, add the following configuration:

```
<Directory "/www/htdocs">
   Order deny,allow
   Allow from all
</Directory>
```

This method — opening only what you need — is highly recommended as a preventive security measure.

Don't allow users to change any directorywide configuration options using a per-directory configuration file (`.htaccess`) in directories that are open for access.

Disabling user overrides

To disable users' override capability for configuration settings that use the per-directory configuration file (`.htaccess`) in any directory, do the following :

```
<Directory />
   AllowOverride None
</Directory>
```

This disallows user overrides and speeds up processing (because the server no longer looks for the per-directory access control files (.htaccess) for each request).

Using Paranoid Configuration

Want to go a few steps further into the land of paranoia in search of security? Here's what I consider a "paranoid" configuration for Apache.

◆ No CGI script support.

  CGI scripts are typically the cause of most Web security incidents.

◆ No SSI support.

  SSI pages are often problematic since some SSI directives that can be incorporated in a page can allow running CGI programs

◆ No standard World Wide Web URLs.

  Allowing Web sites to use the www.domain.com/~username URL scheme for individual users introduces many security issues such as

  ■ Users may not take appropriate cautions to reduce the risk of exposing filesystem information to the rest of the world.

  ■ Users can make mistakes that make nonpublic disk areas of the server publicly accessible.

◆ Don't provide status information via the Web.

  Apache provides a status module that offers valuable status information about the server via the Web. This information can give clues to vandals. Not installing the module in the first place is the paranoid way of making sure the vandals can't access such information.

The preceding paranoid configuration can be achieved using the following configuration command:

```
./configure --prefix=/home/apache \
        --disable-module=include \
        --disable-module=cgi \
        --disable-module=userdir \
        --disable-module=status
```

Once you have run the preceding configuration command from the src directory of the Apache source distribution, you can make and install Apache (in /home/apache) using the preceding paranoid configuration.

Many "paranoid" administrators run Apache on nonstandard ports such as 8080 or 9000. To run Apache on such ports, change the `Port` directive in `httpd.conf`. Vandals typically use port-scanner software to detect `HTTP` ports. However, using nonstandard ports also makes legitimate users work harder to reach the benefits of your site, because they must know and type the port number (`www.domain.com:port`) at the end of the URL used to enter your Web site.

Reducing CGI Risks

CGI isn't inherently insecure, but poorly written CGI scripts are a major source of Web security holes. The simplicity of the CGI specification makes it easy for many inexperienced programmers to write CGI scripts. These inexperienced programmers, unaware of the security aspects of internetworking, may create applications or scripts that work but may also create unintentional back doors and holes on the system.

I consider CGI *applications* and CGI *scripts* to be interchangeable terms.

Information leaks

Vandals can make many CGI scripts leak information about users or the resources available on a Web server. Such a leak helps vandals break into a system. The more information a vandal knows about a system, the better informed the break-in attempt, as in the following example:

```
http://unsafe-site.com/cgi-bin/showpage.cgi?pg=/doc/article1.html
```

Say this URL displays `/doc/article1.html` using the `showpage.cgi` script. A vandal may try something like

```
http://unsafe-site.com/cgi-bin/showpage.cgi?pg=/etc/passwd
```

This displays the user password file for the entire system if the `showpage.cgi` author does not protect the script from such leaks.

Consumption of system resources

A poorly written CGI script can also consume system resources such that the server becomes virtually unresponsive, as shown in this example:

```
http://unsafe-site.com/cgi-bin/showlist.pl?start=1&stop=15
```

Say that this URL allows a site visitor to view a list of classifieds advertisements in a Web site. The `start=1` and `stop=15` parameters control the number of records displayed. If the `showlist.pl` script relies only on the supplied start and stop values, then a vandal can edit the URL and supply a larger number for the stop parameter to make `showlist.pl` display a larger list then usual. The vandal's modification can overload the Web server with requests that take longer to process, making real users wait (and, in the case of e-commerce, possibly move on to a competitor's site).

Spoofing of system commands via CGI scripts

Vandals can trick an HTML form-based mailer script to run a system command or give out confidential system information. For example, say you have a Web form that visitors use to sign up for your services or provide you with feedback. Most of these Web forms use CGI scripts to process the visitors' reqests and send thank-you notes via e-mail. The script may perform a process like the following to send the e-mail:

```
system("/bin/mail  -s $subject $emailAddress < $thankYouMsg");
```

In this case, the system call runs the `/bin/mail` program and supplies it the value of variable `$subject` as the subject header and the value of variable `$emailAddress` as the e-mail address of the user and redirects the contents of the file named by the `$thankYouMsg` variable. This works, and no one should normally know that your application uses such a system call. However, a vandal interested in breaking into your Web site may examine everything she has access to, and try entering irregular values for your Web form. For example, if a vandal enters `vandal@emailaddr < /etc/passwd;` as the e-mail address, it fools the script into sending the `/etc/passwd` file to the vandal-specified e-mail address.

 TIP   If you use the `system()` function in your CGI script, use the `-T` option in your `#!/path/to/perl` line to enable Perl's taint-checking mode and also set the `PATH` (environment variable) using set `$ENV{PATH} = '/path/to/commands/you/call/via/system'` to increase security.

Keeping user input from making system calls unsafe

Most security holes created by CGI scripts are caused by inappropriate user input. Use of certain system calls in CGI script is quite unsafe. For example, in Perl (a widely used CGI programming language) such a call could be made using `system()`, exec(), piped open(), and eval() functions. Similarly, in C the popen() and system() functions are potential security hazards. All these functions/commands typically invoke a subshell (such as /bin/sh) to process the user command.

Even shell scripts that use system(), exec() calls can open a port of entry for vandals. *Backtick quotes* (features available in shell interpreters and Perl that capture program output as text strings) are also dangerous.

To illustrate the importance of careful use of system calls, take a look this innocent-looking Perl code segment:

```perl
#!/usr/bin/perl
# Purpose: to demonstrate security risks in
# poorly written CGI script.
# Get the domain name from query string
# environment variable.
#
# Print the appropriate content type.
# Since whois output is in plain text
# we choose to use text/plain as the content-type here.
print "Content-type: text/plain\n\n";
# Here is the bad system call
system("/usr/bin/whois $domain");
# Here is another bad system call using backticks.
# my $output = `/usr/bin/whois $domain`;
# print $output;
exit 0;
```

This little Perl script should be a Web-based whois gateway. If this script is called whois.pl, and it's kept in the cgi-bin directory of a Web site called unsafe-site.com, a user can call this script this way:

```
http://unsafe-site.com/cgi-bin/script.pl?domain=anydomain.com
```

The script takes anydomain.com as the $domain variable via the QUERY_STRING variable and launches the /usr/bin/whois program with the $domain value as the argument. This returns the data from the whois database that InterNIC maintains. This is all very innocent, but the script is a disaster waiting to happen. Consider the following line:

```
http://unsafe-site.com/cgi-bin/script.pl?domain=nitec.com;ps
```

This does a whois lookup on a domain called nitec.com and provides the output of the Unix ps utility that shows process status. This reveals information about the system that shouldn't be available to the requesting party. Using this technique, anyone can find out a great deal about your system. For example, replacing the ps command with df (a common Unix utility that prints a summary of disk space) enables anyone to determine what partitions you have and how full they are. I leave to your imagination the real dangers this security hole could pose.

Don't trust any input. Don't make system calls an easy target for abuse.

Two overall approaches are possible if you want to make sure your user input is safe:

◆ **Define a list of acceptable characters.** Replace or remove any character that isn't acceptable.

The list of valid input values is typically a predictable, well-defined set of manageable size.

This approach is less likely to let unaccepable characters through. A programmer must ensure that only acceptable characters are identified.

Building on this philosophy, the Perl program presented earlier could be sanitized to contain *only* those characters allowed, for example:

```perl
#!/usr/bin/perl -w
# Purpose: This is a better version of the previous
# whois.pl script.
# Assign a variable the acceptable character
# set for domain names.
my $DOMAIN_CHAR_SET='-a-zA-Z0-9_.';
# Get the domain name from query string
# environment variable.
my $domain = $ENV{'QUERY_STRING'};
# Now remove any character that doesn't
# belong to the acceptable character set.
$domain =~ s/[^$DOMAIN_CHAR_SET]//g;
# Print the appropriate content type.
# Since whois output is in plain text we
# choose to use text/plain as the content-type here.
print "Content-type: text/plain\n\n";
# Here is the system call
system("/usr/bin/whois $domain");
# Here is another system call using backticks.
```

```
# my $output = `/usr/bin/whois $domain`;
# print $output;
exit 0;
```

The `$DOMAIN_CHAR_SET` variable holds the acceptable character set, and the user input variable `$domain` is searched for anything that doesn't fall in the set. The unacceptable character is removed.

◆ **Scan the input for illegal characters and replace or remove them.**

For example, for the preceding `whois.pl` script, you can add the following line:

```
$domain =~ s/[\/ ;\[\]\<\>&\t]//g;
```

 This is an inadvisable approach. Programmers must know all possible combinations of characters that could cause trouble. If the user creates input not predicted by the programmer, there's the possibility that the program may be used in a manner not intended by the programmer.

The best way to handle user input is by establishing rules to govern it, clarifying

◆ What you expect

◆ How you can determine if what you have received is acceptable

If (for example) you are expecting an e-mail address as input (rather than just scanning it blindly for shell metacharacters), use a regular expression such as the following to detect the validity of the input as a possible e-mail address:

```
$email = param('email-addr');
if ($email=~ /^[\w-\.]+\@[\w-\.]+$/) {
 print "Possibly valid address."
 }
else {
 print "Invalid email address.";
 }
```

Just sanitizing user input isn't enough. Be careful about how you invoke external programs; there are many ways you can invoke external programs in Perl. Some of these methods include:

◆ **Backtick.** You can capture the output of an external program:

```
$list = '/bin/ls -l /etc';
```

This command captures the `/etc` directory listing.

◆ **Pipe.** A typical pipe looks like this:

```
open (FP, " | /usr/bin/sort");
```

◆ **Invoking an external program.** You have a couple of options with external programs:

- `system()` — wait for it to return:

```
system "/usr/bin/lpr data.dat";
```

- `exec()` — don't wait for it to return:

```
exec "/usr/bin/sort < data.dat";
```

TIP

All these constructions can be risky if they involve user input that may contain shell metacharacters. For `system()` and `exec()`, there's a somewhat obscure syntactical feature that calls external programs directly rather than through a shell. If you pass the arguments to the external program (not in one long string, but as separate elements in a list), Perl doesn't go through the shell, and shell metacharacters have no unwanted side effects, as follows:

```
system "/usr/bin/sort","data.dat";
```

You can use this feature to open a pipe without using a shell. By calling open the character sequence `-|` , you fork a copy of Perl and open a pipe to the copy. Then, the child copy immediately forks another program, using the first argument of the `exec` function call.

To read from a pipe without opening a shell, you can use the `-|` character sequence:

```
open(GREP,"-|") || exec "/usr/bin/grep",$userpattern,$filename;
while (<GREP>) {
  print "match: $_";
  }
close GREP;
```

These forms of `open()`s are more secure than the piped `open()`s. Use these whenever applicable.

Many other obscure features in Perl can call an external program and lie to it about its name. This is useful for calling programs that behave differently depending on the name by which they were invoked. The syntax is

```
system $real_name "fake_name","argument1","argument2"
```

Vandals sometimes alter the PATH environment variable so it points to the program they want your script to execute — rather than the program you're expecting. Invoke programs using full pathnames rather than relying on the PATH environment variable. That is, instead of the following fragment of Perl code

```
system("cat /tmp/shopping.cart.txt");
```

use this:

```
system "/bin/cat" , "/tmp/shopping.cart.txt ";
```

If you must rely on the path, set it yourself at the beginning of your CGI script, like this:

```
$ENV{'PATH'}="bin:/usr/bin:/usr/local/bin";
```

Remember these guidelines:

♦ Include the previous line toward the top of your script whenever you use taint checks.

Even if you don't rely on the path when you invoke an external program, there's a chance that the invoked program does.

♦ You must adjust the line as necessary for the list of directories you want searched.

♦ It's not a good idea to put the current directory into the path.

User modification of hidden data in HTML pages

HTTP is a stateless protocol. Many Web developers keep state information or other important data in cookies or in hidden tags. Because users can turn off cookies and creating unique temporary files per user is cumbersome, hidden tags are frequently used. A *hidden tag* looks like the following:

```
<input type=hidden name="datakey" value="dataValue">
```

For example:

```
<input type=hidden name="state" value="CA">
```

Here the hidden tag stores state=CA, which can be retrieved by the same application in a subsequent call. Hidden tags are common in multiscreen Web applications. Because users can manually change hidden tags, they shouldn't be trusted at all. A developer can use two ways of protecting against altered data:

♦ Verify the hidden data before each use.

♦ Use a security scheme to ensure that data hasn't been altered by the user.

In the following example CGI script, shown in Listing 15-2, I demonstrate the MD5 message digest algorithm to protect hidden data.

 The details of the MD5 algorithm are defined in RFC 1321.

Listing 15–2: hidden–md5.eg

```perl
#!/usr/bin/perl -w
# Purpose: this script demonstrates the use of
#          MD5 message digest in a multiscreen
#          Web application.
# CVS: $Id$
############################################################
use strict;
use CGI qw(:standard);
my $query = new CGI;
# Call the handler subroutine to process user data
&handler;
# Terminate
exit 0;
sub handler{
    #
    # Purpose: determine which screen to display
    #          and call the appropriate subroutine to
    #          display it.
    #
    # Get user-entered name (if any) and email address
    # (if any) and initialize two variables using given
    # name and e-mail values. Note, first time we will
    # not have values for these variables.
    my $name   = param('name');
    my $email  = param('email');
    # Print the appropriate Content-Type header and
    # also print HTML page tags
    print header,
        start_html(-title => 'Multiscreen Web Application Demo');
    # If we don't have value for the $name variable,
```

Continued

Listing 15-2 *(Continued)*

```perl
    # we have not yet displayed screen one so show it.
    if ($name eq ''){
       &screen1;
    # if we have value for the $name variable but the
    # $email variable is empty then we need to show
    # screen 2.
    } elsif($email eq '') {
       &screen2($name);
    # We have value for both $name and $email so
    # show screen 3.
    } else {
       &screen3($name, $email);
    }
    # Print closing HTML tag for the page
    print end_html;
}
sub screen1{
    #
    # Purpose: print an HTML form that asks the
    # user to enter her name.
    #
    print h2("Screen 1"),
        hr({-size=>0,-color=>'black'}),
            start_form,
          'Enter name: ',
            textfield(-name => 'name', -size=>30),
          submit(-value => ' Next '),
          end_form;
}
sub screen2{
    #
    # Purpose: print an HTML form that asks the
    # user to enter her email address. It also
    # stores the name entered in the previous screen.
    #
    # Get the name
    my $name  = shift;
    # Create an MD5 message disgest for the name
    my $digest = &create_message_digest($name);
    # Insert the digest as a new CGI parameter so
    # that we can store it using CGI.pm's hidden()
    # subroutine.
    param('digest', $digest);
    # Now print the second screen and insert
    # the $name and the $digest values as hidden data.
```

```
        print h2("Screen 2"),
            hr({-size=>0,-color=>'black'}),
            start_form,
            'Enter email: ',
            textfield(-name => 'email', -size=>30),
            hidden('name'),
            hidden('digest'),
            submit(-value => ' Next '),
            end_form;
}
sub screen3{
    #
    # Purpose: print a message based on the data gathered
    #          in screen 1 and 2. However, print the message
    #          only if the entered data has not been altered.
    #
    # Get name and email address
    my ($name, $email) = @_;
    # Get the digest of the $name value
    my $oldDigest = param('digest');
    # Create a new digest of the value of the $name variable
    my $newDigest = &create_message_digest($name);
    # If both digests are not same then (name) data has been altered
    # in screen 2. Display an alert message and stop processing
    #in such a case.
    if ($oldDigest ne $newDigest){
        return (0, alert('Data altered. Aborted!'));
    }
    # Since data is good, process as usual.
    print h2("Screen 3"),
    hr({-size=>0,-color=>'black'}),
    p('Your name is '. b($name) .
        ' and your email address is '. b($email) . '.'),
    a({-href=>"$ENV{SCRIPT_NAME}"},'Restart');
}
sub create_message_digest{
    #
    # Purpose: create a message digest for the
    #          given data. To make the digest hard
    #          to reproduce by a vandal, this subroutine
    #          uses a secret key.
    #
    my $data = shift;
    my $secret = 'ID10t' ;  # Change this key if you like.
    # We need the following line to tell Perl that
```

Continued

Listing 15-2 *(Continued)*

```
    # we want to use the Digest::MD5 module.
    use Digest::MD5;
    # Create a new MD5 object
    my $ctx = Digest::MD5->new;
    # Add data
    $ctx->add($data);
    # Add secret key
    $ctx->add($secret);
    # Create a Base64 digest
    my $digest = $ctx->b64digest;
    # Return the digest
    return $digest;
}
sub alert{
  #
  # Purpose: display an alert dialog box
  #          using JavaScript
  #
  # Get the message that we need to display
  my $msg = shift;
  # Create JavaScript that uses the alert()
  # dialog box function to display a message
  # and then return the browser to previous screen
  print <<JAVASCRIPT;
  <script language="JavaScript">
  alert("$msg");
  history.back();
  </script>
JAVASCRIPT
}
```

This is a simple multiscreen CGI script that asks the user for a name in the first screen and an e-mail address in the following screen and finally prints out a message. When the user moves from one screen to another, the data from the previous screen is carried to the next screen through hidden tags. Here's how this script works.

The first screen asks the user for her name. Once the user enters her name, the following screen asks for the user's e-mail address. The HTML source of this screen is shown in Listing 15-3.

Listing 15-3: HTML source for screen 2 of hidden-md5.eg

```
<!DOCTYPE HTML PUBLIC "-//IETF//DTD HTML//EN">
<HTML>
  <HEAD>
    <TITLE>Multiscreen Web Application Demo</TITLE>
```

```
 </HEAD>
 <BODY>
 <H2>Screen 2</H2>
 <HR SIZE="0" COLOR="black">
 <FORM METHOD="POST"
        ENCTYPE="application/x-www-form-urlencoded">
 Enter email:
 <INPUT TYPE="text"
        NAME="email"
        SIZE=30>
 <INPUT TYPE="hidden"
        NAME="name"
        VALUE="Cynthia">
 <INPUT TYPE="hidden"
        NAME="digest"
        VALUE="IzrSJlLrsWlYHNfshrKw/A">
 <INPUT TYPE="submit"
        NAME=".submit"
        VALUE=" Next ">
 </FORM>
 </BODY>
</HTML>
```

Notice that the hidden data is stored using the following lines:

```
<INPUT TYPE="hidden"
       NAME="name"
       VALUE="Cynthia">
<INPUT TYPE="hidden"
       NAME="digest"
       VALUE="IzrSJlLrsWlYHNfshrKw/A">
```

The first hidden data tag line stores name=Cynthia and the second one stores digest=IzrSJlLrsWlYHNfshrKw/A. The second piece of data is the message digest generated for the name entered in screen 1. When the user enters her e-mail address in the second screen and continues, the final screen is displayed.

However, before the final screen is produced, a message digest is computed for the name field entered in screen 1. This digest is compared against the digest created earlier to verify that the value entered for the name field in screen 1 hasn't been altered in screen 2. Because the MD5 algorithm creates the same message digest for a given data set, any differences between the new and old digests raise a red flag, and the script displays an alert message and refuses to complete processing. Thus, if a vandal decides to alter the data stored in screen 2 (shown in Listing 15-3) and submits the data for final processing, the digest mismatch allows the script to detect the alteration and take appropriate action. In your real-world CGI scripts (written in Perl) you can use the create_message_digest() subroutine to create a message digest for anything.

TIP You can download and install the latest version of `Digest::MD5` from CPAN by using the `perl -MCPAN -e shell` command, followed by the `install Digest::MD5` command at the CPAN shell prompt.

Wrapping CGI Scripts

The best way to reduce CGI-related risks is to not run any CGI scripts – but in these days of dynamic Web content, that's unrealistic. Perhaps you can centralize all CGI scripts in one location and closely monitor their development to ensure that they are well written.

In many cases, especially on ISP systems, all users with Web sites want CGI access. In this situation, it may be a good idea to run CGI scripts under the UID of the user who owns the CGI script. By default, CGI scripts that Apache runs use the Apache UID. If you run these applications using the owner's UID, all possible damage is limited to what the UID is permitted to access. This way, a bad CGI script run with a UID other than the Apache server UID can damage only the user's files. The user responsible for the CGI script will now be more careful, because the possible damage affects his or her content solely. In one shot, you get increased user responsibility and awareness and (simultaneously) a limit on the area that could suffer potential damage. To run a CGI script using a UID other than that of the Apache server, you need a special type of program called a *wrapper,* which can run a CGI script as the user who owns the file rather than as the Apache server user. Some CGI wrappers do other security checks before they run the requested CGI scripts.

suEXEC

Apache includes a support application called suEXEC that lets Apache users run CGI and SSI programs under UIDs that are different from the UID of Apache. suEXEC is a `setuid` wrapper program that is called when an HTTP request is made for a CGI or SSI program that the administrator designates to run as a UID other than that of the Apache server. In response to such a request, Apache provides the suEXEC wrapper with the program's name and the UID and GID. suEXEC runs the program using the given UID and GID.

Before running the CGI or SSI command, the suEXEC wrapper performs a set of tests to ensure that the request is valid.

- ◆ This testing procedure ensures that the CGI script is owned by a user who can run the wrapper and that the CGI directory or the CGI script isn't writable by anyone but the owner.

- ◆ After the security checks are successful, the suEXEC wrapper changes the UID and the GID to the target UID and GID via `setuid` and `setgid` calls, respectively.

◆ The group-access list is also initialized with all groups in which the user is a member. suEXEC cleans the process's environment by

■ Establishing a safe execution path (defined during configuration).

■ Passing through only those variables whose names are listed in the safe environment list (also created during configuration).

The suEXEC process then becomes the target CGI script or SSI command and executes.

CONFIGURING AND INSTALLING SUEXEC

If you are interested in installing suEXEC support in Apache, run the `configure` (or `config.status`) script like this:

```
./configure --prefix=/path/to/apache \
            --enable-suexec \
            --suexec-caller=httpd \
            --suexec-userdir=public_html
            --suexec-uidmin=100 \
            --suexec-gidmin=100
            --suexec-safepath="/usr/local/bin:/usr/bin:/bin"
```

Here's the detailed explanation of this configuration:

◆ `--enable-suexec` enables suEXEC support.

◆ `--suexec-caller=httpd` changes *httpd* to the UID you use for the `User` directive in the Apache configuration file. This is the only user account permitted to run the suEXEC program.

◆ `--suexec-userdir=public_html` defines the subdirectory under users' home directories where suEXEC executables are kept. Change *public_html* to whatever you use as the value for the `UserDir` directive, which specifies the document `root` directory for a user's Web site.

◆ `--suexec-uidmin=100` defines the lowest UID permitted to run suEXEC-based CGI scripts. This means UIDs below this number can't run CGI or SSI commands via suEXEC. Look at your `/etc/passwd` file to make sure the range you chose doesn't include the system accounts that are usually lower than UIDs below 100.

◆ `--suexec-gidmin=100` defines the lowest GID permitted as a target group. This means GIDs below this number can't run CGI or SSI commands via suEXEC. Look at your `/etc/group` file to make sure that the range you chose doesn't include the system account groups that are usually lower than UIDs below 100.

♦ `--suexec-safepath="/usr/local/bin:/usr/bin:/bin"` defines the `PATH` environment variable that gets executed by suEXEC for CGI scripts and SSI commands.

ENABLING AND TESTING SUEXEC

After you install both the suEXEC wrapper and the new Apache executable in the proper location, restart Apache, which writes a message like this:

```
[notice] suEXEC mechanism enabled (wrapper: /usr/local/sbin/suexec)
```

This tells you that the suEXEC is active. Now, test suEXEC's functionality. In the `httpd.conf` file, add the following lines:

```
UserDir public_html
AddHandler cgi-script  .pl
```

`UserDir` sets the document `root` of a user's Web site as *~username/* `public_html`, where *username* can be any user on the system. The second directive associates the `cgi-script` handler with the `.pl` files. This runs Perl scripts with `.pl` extensions as CGI scripts. For this test, you need a user account. In this example, I use the host `wormhole.nitec.com` and a user called `kabir`. Try the script shown in Listing 15-4 in a file called `test.pl` and put it in a user's `public_html` directory. In my case, I put the file in the `~kabir/public_html` directory.

Listing 15-4: A CGI script to test suEXEC support

```perl
#!/usr/bin/perl
# Make sure the preceding line is pointing to the
# right location. Some people keep perl in
# /usr/local/bin.
my ($key,$value);
print "Content-type: text/html\n\n";
print "<h1>Test of  suEXEC<h1>";
foreach $key (sort keys %ENV){
    $value = $ENV{$key};
    print "$key = $value <br>";
    }
exit 0;
```

To access the script via a Web browser, I request the following URL:

```
http://wormhole.nitec.com/~kabir/test.pl
```

A CGI script is executed only after it passes all the security checks performed by suEXEC. suEXEC also logs the script request in its log file. The log entry for my request is

```
[200-03-07 16:00:22]: uid: (kabir/kabir) gid: (kabir/kabir) cmd: test.pl
```

If you are really interested in knowing that the script is running under the user's UID, insert a `sleep` command (such as `sleep(10);`) inside the `foreach` loop, which slows the execution and allows commands such as `top` or `ps` on your Web server console to find the UID of the process running `test.pl`. You also can change the ownership of the script using the `chown` command, try to access the script via your Web browser, and see the error message that suEXEC logs. For example, I get a server error when I change the ownership of the `test.pl` script in the `~kabir/public_html` directory as follows:

```
chown root test.pl
```

The log file shows the following line:

```
[200-03-07 16:00:22]: uid/gid (500/500) mismatch with directory (500/500) or
program (0/500)
```

Here, the program is owned by UID `0`, and the group is still `kabir` (500), so suEXEC refuses to run it, which means suEXEC is doing what it should do.

To ensure that suEXEC will run the `test.pl` program in other directories, I create a `cgi-bin` directory in `~kabir/public_html` and put `test.cgi` in that directory. After determining that the user and group ownership of the new directory and file are set to user ID `kabir` and group ID `kabir`, I access the script by using the following command:

```
http://wormhole.nitec.com/~kabir/cgi-bin/test.pl
```

If you have virtual hosts and want to run the CGI programs and/or SSI commands using suEXEC, use `User` and `Group` directives inside the `<VirtualHost . . .>` container. Set these directives to user and group IDs other than those the Apache server is currently using. If only one, or neither, of these directives is specified for a `<VirtualHost>` container, the server user ID or group ID is assumed.

For security and efficiency, all suEXEC requests must remain within either a top-level document `root` for virtual host requests or one top-level personal document `root` for `userdir` requests. For example, if you have four virtual hosts configured, structure all their document `roots` from one main Apache document hierarchy if you plan to use suEXEC for virtual hosts.

CGIWrap

CGIWrap is like the suEXEC program because it allows CGI scripts without compromising the security of the Web server. CGI programs are run with the file owner's permission. In addition, CGIWrap performs several security checks on the CGI script and isn't executed if any checks fail.

CGIWrap is written by Nathan Neulinger; the latest version of CGIWrap is available from the primary FTP site on `ftp://ftp.cc.umr.edu/pub/cgi/cgiwrap`. CGIWrap is used via a URL in an HTML document. As distributed, CGIWrap is configured to run user scripts that are located in the `~/public_html/cgi-bin/` directory.

CONFIGURING AND INSTALLING CGIWRAP

CGIWrap is distributed as a `gzip`-compressed `tar` file. You can uncompress it by using `gzip` and extract it by using the `tar` utility.

Run the `Configure` script, which prompts you with questions. Most of these questions are self-explanatory.

A feature in this wrapper differs from suEXEC. It enables `allow` and `deny` files that can restrict access to your CGI scripts. Both files have the same format, as shown in the following:

```
User ID
```

```
mailto:Username@subnet1/mask1,subnet2/mask2. . .
```

You can have

- ◆ A username (nonnumeric UID)

- ◆ A user `mailto:ID@subnet/mask` line where subnet/mask pairs can be defined

For example, if the following line is found in the `allow` file (you specify the filename),

```
mailto:Myuser@1.2.3.4/255.255.255.255
```

user `kabir`'s CGI scripts can be run by hosts that belong in the `192.168.1.0` network with netmask `255.255.255.0`.

After you run the `Configure` script, you must run the `make` utility to create the CGIWrap executable file.

ENABLING CGIWRAP

To use the wrapper application, copy the CGIWrap executable to the user's `cgi-bin` directory. This directory must match what you have specified in the configuration process. The simplest starting method is keeping the `~username/public_html/cgi-bin` type of directory structure for the CGI script directory.

1. After you copy the CGIWrap executable, change the ownership and permission bits like this:

   ```
   chown root CGIWrap
   chmod 4755 CGIWrap
   ```

2. Create three hard links or symbolic links called `nph-cgiwrap`, `nph-cgiwrapd`, and `cgiwrapd` to CGIWrap in the `cgi-bin` directory as follows:

```
ln [-s] CGIWrap cgiwrapd
ln [-s] CGIWrap nph-cgiwrap
ln [-s] CGIWrap nph-cgiwrapd
```

On my Apache server, I specified only the .cgi extension as a CGI script; therefore, I renamed my CGIWrap executable to `cgiwrap.cgi`. If you have similar restrictions, you may try this approach or make a link instead.

3. Execute a CGI script like this:

```
http://www.yourdomain.com/cgi-bin/cgiwrap/username/scriptname
```

To access user `kabir`'s CGI script, `test.cgi`, on the `wormhole.nitec.com` site, for example, I must use the following:

```
http://wormhole.nitec.com/cgi-bin/cgiwrap/kabir/test.cgi
```

4. To see debugging output for your CGI, specify `cgiwrapd` instead of `CGIWrap`, as in the following URL:

```
http://www.yourdomain.com/cgi-bin/cgiwrapd/username/
scriptname
```

5. If the script is an nph-style script, you must run it using the following URL:

```
http://www.yourdomain.com/cgi-bin/nph-
cgiwrap/username/scriptname
```

Hide clues about your CGI scripts

The fewer clues you provide about your system to potential vandals, the less likely your Web site is to be the next victim. Here's how you can hide some important CGI scripts:

◆ Use a nonstandard script alias.

Use of `cgi-bin` alias has become overwhelmingly popular. This alias is set using the `ScriptAlias` directive in `httpd.conf` for Apache as shown in this example:

```
ScriptAlias /cgi-bin/ "/path/to/real/cgi/directory/"
```

You can use nearly anything to create an alias like this. For example, try

```
ScriptAlias /apps/ "/path/to/real/cgi/directory/"
```

Now the apps in the URL serve the same purpose as `cgi-bin`. Thus, you can use something nonstandard like the following to confuse vandals:

```
ScriptAlias /dcon/ "/path/to/real/cgi/directory/"
```

 Many vandals use automated programs to scan Web sites for features and other clues. A nonstandard script alias such as the one in the preceding example usually isn't incorporated in any automated manner.

◆ **Use nonextension names for your CGI scripts.**

Many sites boldly showcase what type of CGI scripts they run, as in this example:

```
http://www.domain.com/cgi-bin/show-catalog.pl
```

The preceding URL provides two clues about the site: It supports CGI scripts, and it runs Perl scripts as CGI scripts.

If, instead, that site uses

```
http://www.domain.com/ext/show-catalog
```

then it becomes quite hard to determine anything from the URL. Avoid using the .pl and .cgi extensions.

 To change an existing script's name from a .pl, .cgi, or other risky extension type to a nonextension name, simply rename the script. You don't have to change or add any new Apache configuration to switch to nonextension names.

Reducing SSI Risks

SSI scripts pose a few security risks. If you run external applications using SSI commands such as exec, the security risk is virtually the same as with the CGI scripts. However, you can disable this command very easily under Apache, using the following Options directive:

```
<Directory />
  Options IncludesNOEXEC
</Directory>
```

This disables exec and includes SSI commands everywhere on your Web space. You can enable these commands whenever necessary by defining a directory container with narrower scope. See the following example:

```
<Directory />
  Options IncludesNOEXEC
</Directory>
<Directory "/ssi">
  Options +Include
</Directory>
```

This configuration segment disables the `exec` command everywhere but the `/ssi` directory.

 Avoid using the `printenv` command, which prints out a listing of all existing environment variables and their values, as in this example:

`<--#printenv -->`

This command displays all the environment variables available to the Web server — on a publicly accessible page — which certainly gives away clues to potential bad guys. Use this command only when you are debugging SSI calls, *never* in a production environment.

As shown, there are a great deal of configuration and policy decisions (what to allow and how to allow it) that you must make to ensure Web security. Many become frustrated after implementing a set of security measures, because they don't know what else is required. Once you have implemented a set of measures, such as controlled CGI and SSI requests as explained above, focus your efforts on logging.

Logging Everything

A good Web administrator closely monitors server logs, which provide clues to unusual access patterns. Apache can log access requests that are successful and that result in error in separate log files as shown in this example:

```
CustomLog /logs/access.log common
ErrorLog /logs/error.log
```

The first directive, `CustomLog`, logs each incoming request to your Web site, and the second directive, `ErrorLog`, records only the requests that generated an error condition. The error log is a good place to check problems that are reported by your Web server. You can use a robust log analysis program like Wusage (`www.boutell.com`) to routinely analyze and monitor log files. If you notice, for example, someone trying to supply unusual parameters to your CGI scripts, consider it a hostile attempt and investigate the matter immediately. Here's a process that you can use:

1. Get the complete URL used in trying to fool a CGI script.

2. If you didn't write the script, ask the script author about what happens when someone passes such URL (that is, parameters within the URL after ?) to the script. If there's a reason to worry, proceed forward or stop investigating at this point — but make a note of the IP address in a text file along with the URL and time and date stamp.

3. If the URL makes the script do something it shouldn't, consider taking the script offline until it's fixed so that the URL can't pose a threat to the system.

4. Use host to detect the hostname of the bad guy's IP address. Sometimes host can't find the hostname. In such a case, try traceroute and identify the ISP owning the IP address.

5. Do a whois domain lookup for the ISP and find the technical contact listed in the whois output. You may have to go to a domain register's Web site to perform the whois lookup if you don't have the whois program installed. Try locating an appropriate domain register from InterNIC at www.internic.net.

6. Send an e-mail to the technical contact address at the ISP regarding the incident and supply the log snippet for his review. Write your e-mail in a polite and friendly manner.

The ISP at the other end is your only line of defense at this point. Politely request a speedy resolution or response.

7. If you can't take the script offline because it's used too heavily by other users, you can decide to ban the bad guy from using it. Say you run your script under the script alias ext which is set up as follows:

```
ScriptAlias /ext/ "/some/path/to/cgi/scripts/"
```

Change the preceding line of code to the following:

```
Alias /ext/ "/some/path/to/cgi/scripts/"
```

Add the following lines after the above line:

```
<Location /ext>
    SetHandler cgi-script
    Options -Indexes +ExecCGI
    AllowOverride None
    Order allow,deny
    Allow from all
    Deny from 192.168.1.100
</Location>
```

Replace 192.168.1.100 with the IP address of the bad guy. This configuration runs your script as usual for everyone but the user on the IP address given in the Deny from line. However, if the bad guy's ISP uses dynamically allocated IP addresses for its customers, then locking the exact IP address isn't useful because the bad guy can come back with a different IP address next time. In such a case, you must consider locking the entire IP network. For example, if the ISP uses 192.168.1.0, then you must remove the 100 from the Deny from line to block the entire ISP. This is a drastic measure and may block a lot of innocent users at the ISP from using this script, so exercise caution when deciding to block.

8. Wait a few days for the technical contact to respond. If you don't hear from him, try to contact him through the Web site. If the problem persists, contact your legal department to determine what legal actions you can take to require action from the ISP.

Logs are great, but they're useless if the bad guys can modify them. Protect your log files. I recommend keeping log files in their own partition where no one but the root user has access to make any changes.

Make sure that the directories specified by ServerRoot, CustomLog, and ErrorLog directives aren't writable by anyone but the root user. Apache users and groups don't need read or write permission in log directories. Enabling anyone other than the root user to write files in the log directory can cause a major security hole. To ensure that only root user has access to the log files in a directory called /logs, do the following:

1. Change the ownership of the directory and all the files within it to root user and root group by using this command:

```
chown -R root:root /logs
```

2. Change the directory's permission by using this command:

```
chmod -R 750 /logs
```

Logging access requests can monitor and analyze who is requesting information from your Web site. Sometimes access to certain parts of your Web site must be restricted so that only authorized users or computers can access the contents.

Restricting Access to Sensitive Contents

You can restrict access by IP or hostname or use username/password authentication for sensitive information on your Web site. Apache can restrict access to certain sensitive contents using two methods:

◆ IP-based or hostname-based access control

◆ An HTTP authentication scheme

Using IP or hostname

In this authentication scheme, access is controlled by the hostname or the host's IP address. When a request for a certain resource arrives, the Web server checks whether the requesting host is allowed access to the resource; then it acts on the findings.

The standard Apache distribution includes a module called mod_access, which bases access control on the Internet hostname of a Web client. The hostname can be

◆ A fully qualified domain name

◆ An IP address

The module supports this type of access control by using the three Apache directives:

◆ allow

◆ deny

◆ order

The allow directive can define a list of hosts (containing hosts or IP addresses) that can access a directory. When more than one host or IP address is specified, they should be separated with space characters. Table 15-1 shows the possible values for the directive.

TABLE 15-1 POSSIBLE VALUES FOR THE ALLOW DIRECTIVE

Value	Example	Description
`all`	`allow from all`	This reserved word allows access for all hosts. The example shows this option.
A fully qualified domain name (FQDN) of a host	`allow from wormhole.nitec.com`	Only the host that has the specified FQDN is allowed access. The `allow` directive in the example allows access only to `wormhole.nitec.com`. This compares whole components; `toys.com` would not match `etoys.com`.
A partial domain name of a host	`allow from .mainoffice. nitec.com`	Only the hosts that match the partial hostname have access. The example permits all the hosts in the `.mainoffice.nitec.com` network access to the site. For example, `developer1.mainoffice. nitec.com` and `developer2. mainoffice.nitec.com` have access to the site. However, `developer3. baoffice.nitec.com` isn't allowed access.
A full IP address of a host	`allow from 192.168.1.100`	Only the specified IP address is allowed access. The example shows a full IP address (all four octets are present), 192.168.1.100, that is allowed access.
A partial IP address	`allow from 192.168.1` `allow from 130.86`	When not all four octets of an IP address are present in the `allow` directive, the partial IP address is matched from left to right, and hosts that have the matching IP address pattern (that is, it's part of the same subnet) have access. In the first example, all hosts with IP addresses in the range of 192.168.1.1 to 192.168.1.255 have access. In the second example, all hosts from the 130.86 network have access.

Continued

TABLE 15-1 POSSIBLE VALUES FOR THE ALLOW DIRECTIVE *(Continued)*

Value	Example	Description
A network/ netmask pair	allow from 192.168.1.0/ 255.255.255.0	This can specify a range of IP addresses by using the network and netmask addresses. The example allows only the hosts with IP addresses in the range of 192.168.1.1 to 192.168.1.254 to have access.
A network/n CIDR specification	allow 192. 168.1.0/24	This is like the previous entry, except the netmask consists of *n number of* high-order 1 bits. The example allows from 192.168.1.0/255.255.255.0. This feature is available in Apache 1.3 and later.

The deny directive is the exact opposite of the allow directive. It defines a list of hosts that can't access a specified directory. Like the allow directive, it can accept all the values shown in Table 15-1.

The order directive controls how Apache evaluates both allow and deny directives. For example:

```
<Directory "/mysite/myboss/rants">
    order deny, allow
    deny from myboss.mycompany.com
    allow from all
</Directory>
```

This example denies the host myboss.mycompany.com access and gives all other hosts access to the directory. The value for the order directive is a comma-separated list, which indicates which directive takes precedence. Typically, the one that affects all hosts (in the preceding example, the allow directive) is given lowest priority.

Although allow, deny and deny, allow are the most widely used values for the order directive, another value, mutual-failure, can indicate that only those hosts appearing on the allow list but not on the deny list are granted access.

In all cases, every allow and deny directive is evaluated.

If you are interested in blocking access to a specific HTTP request method, such as GET, POST, and PUT, the <Limit> container, you can do so as shown in this example:

```
<Location /cgi-bin>
   <Limit POST>
      order deny,allow
      deny from all
      allow from yourdomain.com
   </Limit>
</Location>
```

This example allows POST requests to the cgi-bin directory only if they are made by hosts in the yourdomain.com domain. This means if this site has some HTML forms that send user input data via the HTTP POST method, only the users in yourdomain.com can use these forms effectively. Typically, CGI applications are stored in the cgi-bin directory, and many sites feature HTML forms that dump data to CGI applications through the POST method. Using the preceding host-based access control configuration, a site can allow anyone to run a CGI script but allow only a certain site (in this case, yourdomain.com) to actually post data to CGI scripts. This gives the CGI access in such a site a bit of read-only character. Everyone can run applications that generate output without taking any user input, but only users of a certain domain can provide input.

Using an HTTP authentication scheme

Standard mod_auth module-based basic HTTP authentication confirms authentication with usernames, groups, and passwords stored in text files. This approach works well if you're dealing with a small number of users. However, if you have a lot of users (thousands or more), using mod_auth may exact a performance penalty — in which case, you can use something more advanced, such as DBM files, Berkeley DB files, or even a dedicated SQL database. The next section presents a few examples of basic HTTP authentication.

REQUIRING A USERNAME AND PASSWORD

This example creates a restricted directory that requires a username and a password for access. I assume the following are settings for a Web site called apache.nitec.com:

```
DocumentRoot   "/www/htdocs"
AccessFileName .htaccess
AllowOverride  All
```

Assume also that you want to restrict access to the following directory, such that only a user named reader with the password bought-it can access the directory:

```
/www/htdocs/readersonly
```

The following steps create the appropriately restricted access:

1. Create a user file by using `htpasswd`.

   A standard Apache distribution includes a utility called `htpasswd`, which creates the user file needed for the `AuthUserFile` directive. Use the program like this:

   ```
   htpasswd -c /www/secrets/.htpasswd reader
   ```

   The `htpasswd` utility asks for the password of `reader`. Enter **bought-it** and then reenter the password to confirm. After you reenter the password, the utility creates a file called `.htpasswd` in the `/www/secrets` directory. Note the following:

   - The `-c` option tells `htpasswd` that you want a new user file. If you already had the password file and wanted to add a new user, you would not want this option.

   - Place the user file outside the document `root` directory of the `apache.nitec.com` site, as you don't want anyone to download it via the Web.

   - Use a leading period (.) in the filename so it doesn't appear in the output on your Unix system. Doing so doesn't provide any real benefits but can help identify a Unix file because its use is a traditional Unix habit. Many configuration files in Unix systems have leading periods (`.login` and `.profile`).

2. Execute the following command:

   ```
   cat /www/secrets/.htpasswd
   ```

   This should show a line like the following (the password won't be exactly the same as this example):

   ```
   reader:hulR6FFh1sxK6
   ```

   This command confirms that you have a user called `reader` in the `.htpasswd` file. The password is encrypted by the `htpasswd` program, using the standard `crypt()` function.

3. Create an `.htaccess` file.

   Using a text editor, add the following lines to a file named `/www/htdocs/readersonly/.htaccess`:

   ```
   AuthName "Readers Only"
   AuthType  Basic
   AuthUserFile /www/secrets/.htpasswd
   require user reader
   ```

   The preceding code works this way:

- `AuthName` sets the realm of the authentication.

  This is really just a label that goes to the Web browser so that the user is provided with some clue about what she will access. In this case, the "Readers Only" string indicates that only readers can access this directory.

- `AuthType` specifies the type of authentication.

  Because only basic authentication is supported, `AuthType` is always `Basic`.

- `AuthUserFile` specifies the filename and path for the user file.

- require specifies that a user named reader is allowed access to this directory.

4. Set file permissions.

   After the `.htaccess` and `.htpasswd` files are created, make sure that only the `Apache` user can read the files.

 No users except the file owner and Apache should have access to these files.

5. Use a Web browser to access the following URL:

   `http://apache.nitec.com/readersonly`

   Apache sends the 401 status header and WWW-Authenticate response header to the browser with the realm (set in `AuthName`) and authentication-type (set in `AuthType`) information. The browser displays a pop-up dialog box that requests a username and password.

   Check whether a user can get in without a username or password — enter nothing in the entry boxes in the dialog box and click OK. This should result in an authentication failure and an error message. The browser receives the same authentication challenge again, so it displays another dialog box.

   Clicking Cancel results in the browser showing the standard `Authentication Required` error message from Apache.

   Clicking Reload or refresh in the browser requests the same URL again, and the browser receives the same authentication challenge from the server. This time enter **reader** as the username and **bought-it** as the password, and click OK. Apache now gives you directory access.

You can change the Authentication Required message if you want by using the ErrorDocument directive:

```
ErrorDocument 401 /nice_401message.html
```

Insert this line in your httpd.conf file and create a nice message in the nice_401message.html file to make your users happy.

ALLOWING A GROUP OF USERS TO ACCESS A DIRECTORY

Instead of allowing one user called reader to access the restricted area (as demonstrated in the previous example), try allowing anyone belonging to the group named smart_readers to access the same directory. Assume this group has two users: pikejb and bcaridad.

Follow these steps to give the users in the group smart_readers directory access.

1. Create a user file by using htpasswd.

   Using the htpasswd utility, create the users pikejb and bcaridad.

2. Create a group file.

   Using a text editor such as vi (available on most Unix systems), create a file named /www/secrets/.htgroup. This file has one line:

   ```
   smart_readers: pikejb bcaridad
   ```

3. Create an .htaccess file in /www/htdocs/readersonly.

   Using a text editor, add the following lines to a file called /data/web/apache/public/htdocs/readersonly/.htaccess:

   ```
   AuthName "Readers Only"
   AuthType  Basic
   AuthUserFile /www/secrets/.htpasswd
   AuthGroupFile /www/secrets/.htgroup
   require group  smart_readers
   ```

   This addition is almost the same configuration that I discussed in the previous example, with two changes:

   - A new directive, AuthGroupFile, points to the .htgroup group file created earlier.

   - The require directive line requires a group called smart_readers.

     This means Apache allows access to anyone that belongs to the group.

4. Make sure .htaccess, .htpasswd, and .htgroup files are readable only by Apache, and that no one but the owner has write access to the files.

MIXING HOST-BASED ACCESS CONTROL WITH HTTP AUTHENTICATION

In this example, you see how you can mix the host-based access control scheme with the basic HTTP authentication method found in Apache. Say you want to allow the `smart_readers` group access to the same directory as it has in the second preceding example, "Allowing a group of users to access a directory," and you want anyone coming from a domain called `classroom.nitec.com` without a username and password to have access to the same directory.

This means if a request for the URL `http://apache.nitec.com/readersonly` comes from a domain named `classroom.nitec.com`, the request is processed without HTTP authentication because you perform the following steps:

1. Modify the `.htaccess` file (from the preceding example) to look like this:

   ```
   AuthName "Readers Only"
   AuthType  Basic
   AuthUserFile /www/secrets/.htpasswd
   AuthGroupFile /www/secrets/.htgroup
   require group  smart_readers
   order deny, allow
   deny from all
   allow from classroom.nitec.com
   ```

   This adds three host-based access control directives (discussed in earlier sections).

   - The `order` directive tells Apache to evaluate the `deny` directive before it does the `allow` directive.

   - The `deny` directive tells Apache to refuse access from all hosts.

   - The `allow` directive tells Apache to allow access from `classroom.nitec.com`.

     This third directive effectively tells Apache that any hosts in the `classroom.nitec.com` domain are welcome to this directory.

2. Using a Web browser from a host called `user01.classroom.nitec.com`, if you try to access `http://apache.nitec.com/readersonly`, your browser displays the username and password authentication dialog box. This means you must authenticate yourself.

   This isn't what you want to happen. So what's going on? Apache assumes that both host-based and basic HTTP authentication are required for this directory — so it denies access to the directory unless it can pass both methods. A solution to this problem is the `satisfy` directive, which you can use like this:

   ```
   AuthName "Readers Only"
   AuthType  Basic
   ```

```
AuthUserFile /www/secrets/.htpasswd
AuthGroupFile /www/secrets/.htgroup
require group  smart_readers
order deny, allow
deny from all
allow from classroom.nitec.com
satisfy any
```

The satisfy directive takes either the all value or the any value. Because you want the basic HTTP authentication activated only if a request comes from any host other than the classroom.nitec.com domain, specify any for the satisfy directive. This effectively tells Apache to do the following:

```
IF (REMOTE_HOST NOT IN .classroom.nitec.com DOMAIN) THEN
   Basic HTTP authentication Required
ENDIF
```

 If you want only users of the classroom.nitec.com subdomain to access the directory with basic HTTP authentication, specify all for the satisfy directive; this tells Apache to enforce both authentication methods for all requests.

Controlling Web Robots

Your Web site isn't always accessed by human users. Many search engines index your Web site by using *Web robots* – programs that traverse Web sites for indexing purposes. These robots often index information they shouldn't – and sometimes don't index what they should. The following section examines ways to control (most) robot access to your Web site.

Frequently used search engines such as Yahoo!, AltaVista, Excite, and Infoseek use automated robot or spider programs that search Web sites and index their contents. This is usually desirable, but on occasion, you may find yourself wanting to stop these robots from accessing a certain part of your Web site.

If content in a section of your Web site frequently expires (daily, for example), you don't want the search robots to index it. When a user at the search-engine site clicks a link to the old content and finds that the link doesn't exist, she isn't happy. That user may then go to the next link without returning to your site.

Sometimes you may want to disable the indexing of your content (or part of it), because the robots can overwhelm Web sites by requesting too many documents too rapidly. Efforts are underway to create standards of behavior for Web robots. In the meantime, the Robot Exclusion Protocol enables Web site administrators to place a robots.txt file on their Web sites, indicating where robots shouldn't go.

For example, a large archive of bitmap images is useless to a robot that is trying to index HTML pages. Serving these files to the robot wastes resources on your server and at the robot's location.

This protocol is currently voluntary, and etiquette is still evolving for robot developers as they gain experience with Web robots. The most popular search engines, however, abide by the Robot Exclusion Protocol. Here is what a robot or spider program does:

1. When a compliant Web robot visits a site called `www.domain.com`, it first checks for the existence of the URL:

   ```
   http://www.domain.com/robots.txt
   ```

2. If this URL exists, the robot parses its contents for directives that instruct the robot to index the site. As a Web server administrator, you can create directives that make sense for your site. Only one `robots.txt` file may exist per site; this file contains records that may look like the following:

   ```
   User-agent: *
   Disallow: /cgi-bin/
   Disallow: /tmp/
   Disallow: /~kabir/
   ```

   In the preceding code

   - The first directive tells the robot that the following directives should be considered by any robots.

   - The following three directives (`Disallow`) tell the robot not to access the directories mentioned in the directives.

 TIP You need a separate `Disallow` line for every URL prefix you want to exclude. For example, your command line should not read like this:

```
Disallow: /cgi-bin/ /tmp/ /~kabir/
```

You should not have blank lines in a record. They delimit multiple records. Regular expressions aren't supported in the `User-agent` and `Disallow` lines. The asterisk in the `User-agent` field is a special value that means any robot. Specifically, you can't have lines like either of these:

```
Disallow: /tmp/*
Disallow: *.gif
```

Everything not explicitly disallowed is considered accessible by the robot (some examples follow).

To exclude all robots from the entire server, use the following configuration:

```
User-agent: *
Disallow: /
```

To permit all robots complete access, use the following configuration:

```
User-agent: *
Disallow:
```

You can create the same effect by deleting the robots.txt file. To exclude a single robot called WebCrawler, add these lines:

```
User-agent: WebCrawler
Disallow: /
```

To allow a single robot called WebCrawler to access the site, use the following configuration:

```
User-agent: WebCrawler
Disallow:
User-agent: *
Disallow: /
```

To forbid robots to index a single file called /daily/changes_to_often.html, use the following configuration:

```
User-agent: *
Disallow: /daily/changes_to_often.html
```

Content Publishing Guidelines

If you've applied the preceding steps, your Web site is reasonably fortified for security. Even so (as mentioned before), be sure to monitor log activities to detect unusual access. Remember, too, that the human components of your Web site (such as content publishers and script developers) need training for site security. Establish guidelines for them.

Content publishers and script developers should know and adhere to the following guidelines:

◆ Whenever storing a content file, such as an HTML file, image file, sound file, or video clip, the publisher must ensure that the file is readable by the Web server (that is, the username specified by the `User` directive). No one but the publisher user should have write access to the new file.

◆ Any file or directory that can't be displayed directly on the Web browser because it contains information indirectly accessed by using an application or script shouldn't be located under a `DocumentRoot`-specified directory. For example, if one of your scripts needs access to a data file that shouldn't be directly accessed from the Web, don't keep the data file inside the document tree. Keep the file outside the document tree and have your script access it from there.

◆ Any time a script needs a temporary file, the file should never be created inside the document tree. In other words, don't have a Web server writable directory within your document tree. All temporary files should be created in one subdirectory outside the document tree where only the Web server has write access. This ensures that a bug in a script doesn't accidentally write over any existing file in the document tree.

◆ To fully enforce copyright, include both visible and embedded copyright notices on the content pages. The embedded copyright message should be kept at the beginning of a document, if possible. For example, in an HTML file you can use a pair of comment tags to embed the copyright message at the beginning of the file. For example, `<!-- Copyright (c) 2000 by YourCompany; All rights reserved. -->` can be embedded in every page.

◆ If you have many images that you want to protect from copyright theft, look into *watermarking* technology. This technique invisibly embeds information in images to protect the copyright. The idea is that if you detect a site that's using your graphical contents without permission, you can verify the theft by looking at the hidden information. If the information matches your watermark ID, you can clearly identify the thief and proceed with legal action. (That's the idea, at least. I question the strength of currently available watermarking tools; many programs can easily remove the original copyright owner's watermarks. Watermark technology is worth investigating, however, if you worry about keeping control of your graphical content.)

Creating a policy is one thing and enforcing it is another. Once you create your own publishing policy, discuss this with the people you want to have using it. Get their feedback on each policy item — and, if necessary, refine your policy to make it useful.

Using Apache-SSL

I want to point out a common misunderstanding about Secure Sockets Layer (SSL). Many people are under the impression that having an SSL-enabled Web site automatically protects them from all security problems. Wrong! SSL protects data traffic only between the user's Web browser and the Web server. It ensures that data isn't altered during transit. It can't enhance your Web site's security in any other way.

Apache doesn't include an SSL module in the default distribution, but you can enable SSL for Apache by using the Apache-SSL source patch. The Apache-SSL source patch kit can be downloaded from www.apache-ssl.org. The Apache-SSL source patch kit turns Apache into a SSL server based on either SSLeay or OpenSSL.

In the following section, I assume that you have already learned to install OpenSSL (if not, see Chapter 11), and that you use OpenSSL here.

Compiling and installing Apache-SSL patches

As mentioned before, you need OpenSSL installed for Apache-SSL to work. I assume that you have done the following:

◆ Installed OpenSSL in the /usr/local/ssl directory as recommended in Chapter 11

◆ Extracted the Apache source tree into the /usr/src/redhat/SOURCES/apache_x.y.zz directory

  For example, the Apache source path for Apache 2.0.01 is /usr/src/ redhat/SOURCES/apache_2.0.01.

Here's how you can set up Apache for SSL support.

1. su to root.

2. Change the directory to the Apache source distribution (/usr/src/ redhat/SOURCES/apache_x.y.zz).

3. Copy the Apache-SSL patch kit (apache_x.y.zz+ssl_x.y.tar.gz) in the current directory and extract it by using the tar xvzf apache_x.y.zz+ssl_x.y.tar.gz command.

4. Run patch -p1 < SSLpatch to patch the source files.

5. Change the directory to src and edit the Configuration.tmpl file to have the following lines along with other unchanged lines.

```
SSL_BASE=/usr/local/ssl
SSL_APP_DIR= $(SSL_BASE)/bin
SSL_APP=/usr/local/ssl/bin/openssl
```

6. Change back your current directory to src by running the cd .. command.

7. Run the ./configure command with any command-line arguments that you typically use. For example, to install Apache in /usr/local/apache, run this script with the --prefix=/usr/local/apache option.

8. Run make and make install to compile and install Apache.

This compiles and installs both standard (httpd) and SSL-enabled (httpsd) Apache. Now you need a server certificate for Apache.

Creating a certificate for your Apache-SSL server

See Chapter 11 for details on creating a certificate for your Apache server. To create a temporary certificate to get going quickly, you can simply do the following:

1. Change directory to the src (for example, /usr/src/redhat/SOURCES/ apache_x.y.zz/src) subdirectory of your Apache source distribution.

2. Run the make certificate command to create a temporary certificate for testing purposes only. The make certificate command uses the /usr/local/ssl/bin/openssl program to create a server certificate for you. You are asked a few self-explanatory questions. Here's an example session of this command.

```
ps > /tmp/ssl-rand; date >> /tmp/ssl-rand; \
RANDFILE=/tmp/ssl-rand /usr/local/ssl/bin/openssl req -config
../SSLconf/conf/ssleay.cnf \
-new -x509 -nodes -out ../SSLconf/conf/httpsd.pem \
-keyout ../SSLconf/conf/httpsd.pem; \
ln -sf httpsd.pem ../SSLconf/conf/`/usr/local/ssl/bin/openssl
\
x509 -noout -hash < ../SSLconf/conf/httpsd.pem`.0; \
rm /tmp/ssl-rand
Using configuration from ../SSLconf/conf/ssleay.cnf
Generating a 1024 bit RSA private key
.................++++++
.............................................++++++
writing new private key to '../SSLconf/conf/httpsd.pem'
-----
You are about to be asked to enter information that will be
incorporated
into your certificate request.
What you are about to enter is what is called a Distinguished
Name or a DN.
```

```
There are quite a few fields but you can leave some blank
For some fields there will be a default value,
If you enter '.', the field will be left blank.
-----
Country Name (2 letter code) [GB]:US
State or Province Name (full name) [Some-State]:California
Locality Name (eg, city) []:Sacramento
Organization Name (eg, company; recommended) []:MyORG
Organizational Unit Name (eg, section) []:CS
server name (eg. ssl.domain.tld; required!!!)
[]:shea.intevo.com
Email Address []:kabir@intevo.com
```

The certificate called httpsd.pem is created in the SSLconf/conf subdirectory of your Apache source distribution. For example, if the path to the directory containing your Apache source distribution is /usr/src/redhat/SOURCES/ apache_x.xx, then the fully qualified path — which you use to configure Apache in the following section — is as follows:

/usr/src/redhat/SOURCES/apache_x.xx/SSLconf/conf/httpsd.pem

Now you can configure Apache.

Configuring Apache for SSL

When you ran make install in the "Compiling and installing Apache-SSL patches" section, you created an httpsd.conf file in the conf subdirectory of your Apache installation directory. For example, if you used --prefix=/usr/ local/apache to configure Apache, you find the httpsd.conf file in /usr/local/ apache/conf. Rename it to httpd.conf, using the following command:

mv /usr/local/apache/conf/httpsd.conf /usr/local/apache/conf/httpd.conf

 Make sure you replace /usr/local/apache/conf with appropriate pathname if you installed Apache in a different directory.

You have two choices when it comes to using SSL with Apache. You can either enable SSL for the main server or for virtual Web sites. Here I show you how you can enable SSL for your main Apache server. Modify the httpd.conf file as follows

1. By default, Web browsers send SSL requests to port 443 of your Web server, so if you want to turn the main Apache server into an SSL-enabled server, change the `Port` directive line to be

```
Port 443
```

2. Add the following lines to tell Apache how to generate random data needed for encrypting SSL connections:

```
SSLRandomFile file /dev/urandom 1024
SSLRandomFilePerConnection file /dev/urandom 1024
```

3. If you want to reject all requests but the secure requests, insert the following directive:

```
SSLRequireSSL
```

4. To enable SSL service, add the following directive:

```
SSLEnable
```

5. By default, the cache server used by SSL-enabled Apache is created in the `src/modules/ssl` directory of the Apache source distribution. Set this directory as shown below:

```
SSLCacheServerPath \
/path/to/apache_x.y.zz/src/modules/ssl/gcache
```

6. Add the following to enable the cache server port and cache timeout values:

```
SSLCacheServerPort logs/gcache_port
SSLSessionCacheTimeout 15
```

7. Tell Apache where you are keeping the server certificate file.

   - If you created the server certificate by using the instructions in Chapter 11, your server certificate should be in `/usr/local/ssl/certs`.

   - If you apply the test certificate now (using the `make certificate` command discussed earlier), then your test certificate is in `/path/to/apache_x.y.zz/SSLconf/conf`, and it's called `httpsd.pem`.

   Set the following directive to the fully qualified path of your server certificate as shown with the following code.

```
SSLCertificateFile \
/path/to/apache_x.y.zz/SSLconf/conf/httpsd.pem
```

8. Set the following directives as shown, and save the `httpd.conf` file.

```
SSLVerifyClient 3
SSLVerifyDepth 10
SSLFakeBasicAuth
SSLBanCipher NULL-MD5:NULL-SHA
```

TIP   To SSL-enable a virtual host called `myvhost.intevo.com` on port 443, use the following configuration:

```
Listen 443
<Virtualhost myvhost.intevo.com:443>
  SSLEnable
  SSLCertificateFile /path/to/myvhost.certificate.cert
</Virtualhost>
```

Now you can test your SSL-enabled Apache server.

Testing the SSL connection

If you have installed Apache in the `/usr/local/apache` directory, run the `/usr/local/apache/bin/httpsdctl start` command to start the SSL-enabled Apache server. If you get an error message, check the log file for details. A typo or a missing path in the `httpd.conf` file is the most common cause of errors. Once the server is started, you can access it by using the HTTPS protocol. For example, to access an SSL-enabled Apache server called `shea.intevo.com`, I can point a Web browser to `https://shea.intevo.com`. If you use the test certificate or a home-grown CA-signed certificate (see Chapter 11 for details) the Web browser displays a warning message stating that the certificate can't be verified. This is normal, because the certificate isn't signed by a known certificate authority.

Accept the certificate, and browse your SSL-enabled Web site.

Summary

Web servers are often the very first target of most hack attacks. By fortifying your Web server using techniques to reduce CGI and SSI risks and logging everything, you can ensure the security of your Web sites. Not allowing spiders and robots to index sensitive areas of your Web site and restricting access by username or IP address can be quite helpful in combating Web vandalism.

## Chapter 16

DNS Server Security

IN THIS CHAPTER

◆ Checking DNS configuration using Dlint

◆ Using Transaction Signatures (TSIG) to handle zone transfers

◆ Limiting DNS queries

◆ Creating a `chroot` jail for the DNS server

◆ Using DNSSEC for authentication

ACCORDING TO A RECENT *Men & Mice* Domain Health Survey, three out of four Internet domains have incorrect DNS configurations. Incorrect DNS configuration often leads to security break-ins. This chapter examines correcting, verifying, and securing DNS configuration using various techniques.

Understanding DNS Spoofing

DNS *spoofing* (attack by falsifying information) is a common DNS security problem. When a DNS server is tricked into accepting – and later using incorrect, nonauthoritative information from a malicious DNS server, the first DNS server has been spoofed. Spoofing attacks can cause serious security problems – like directing users to the wrong Internet sites or routing e-mail to unauthorized mail servers – for vulnerable DNS servers.

Hackers employ many methods to spoof a DNS server, including these two favorites:

◆ **Cache poisoning.** A malicious hacker manipulates DNS queries to insert data into an unprotected DNS server's cache. This poisoned data is later given out in response to client queries. Such data can direct clients to hosts that are running Trojan Web servers or mail servers, where the hackers may retrieve valuable information from users.

◆ **DNS ID prediction scheme.** Each DNS packet has a 16-bit ID number associated with it, which DNS servers use to determine what the original query was. A malicious hacker attacks DNS server A by placing a recursive query that makes server A perform queries on a remote DNS server, B, whose information will be spoofed. By performing a denial-of-service (DoS) attack and predicting the DNS ID sequence, the hacker can place query responses to A before the real server B can respond. This type of attack is hard but not impossible, because the ID space is only 16 bits, and DoS attack tools are common hackerware these days.

How can you protect your DNS server from spoofing attacks? Begin with the following two principles:

◆ Keep your DNS configuration secure and correct.

◆ Ensure that you are running the latest release version of DNS server software.

Running the latest stable DNS server software is as simple as getting the source or binary distribution of the software from the server vendor and installing it. Most people run the Berkeley Internet Name Domain (BIND) server. The latest version of BIND is at `www.isc.org/products/BIND`. Keeping your DNS configuration correct and secure is the challenge.

Checking DNS Configuring Using Dlint

Poorly configured DNS servers are great security risks because they're exploited easily. However, a free tool called Dlint can help you analyze any DNS zone and produce reports on many common configuration problems in the following listing:

◆ Hostnames that have A records must also have PTR records.

DNS configurations that have A records but no corresponding PTR records can't be verified by servers that want to perform reverse DNS lookup on a host. Dlint checks for missing PTR records for A records found in your in configuration.

◆ For each PTR record in the `in-addr.arpa` zone there should an equivalent A record. Dlint reports missing A records for PTR records.

◆ Dlint recursively traverses subdomains (subzones) and looks for configuration problems in them, too.

◆ Common typos or misplaced comments can create incorrect configuration; `Dlint` tries to catch such errors.

Getting Dlint

Here's how you can install Dlint on your system.

You can download Dlint from www.domtools.com/dns/dlint.shtml. As of this writing the latest version of Dlint is 1.4.0. You can also use an online version of Dlint at www.domtools.com/cgi-bin/dlint/nph-dlint.cgi. The online version has time restrictions, so I recommend it only for trying the tool.

Installing Dlint

Dlint requires DiG and Perl 5. DiG is a DNS query utility found in the BIND distribution. Most likely you have it installed. Run the dig localhost any command to find out. If you don't have it, you can get DiG from www.isc.org/bind.html. I assume that you have both DiG and Perl 5 installed on your Linux system.

To install Dlint do the following:

1. su to root.

2. Extract the Dlint source package using a suitable directory.

   I extracted the dlint1.4.0.tar package in the /usr/src/redhat/ SOURCES directory using the tar xvf dlint1.4.0.tar command. A new subdirectory gets created when you extract the source distribution.

 Change your current directory to the new directory, which in my case is dlint1.4.0. Make sure you substitute the appropriate Dlint version number (of the source distribution you downloaded) in all the instructions given here.

3. Run the which perl command to see where the Perl interpreter is installed.

4. Run the head -1 digparse command to see the very first line of the digparse Perl script used by Dlint. If the path shown after #! matches the path shown by the which perl command, don't change it. If the paths don't match, modify this file using a text editor, and replace the path after #! with the path of your Perl interpreter.

5. Run the make install command to install Dlint, which installs the dlint and digparse scripts in /usr/local/bin.

   Now you can run Dlint.

Running Dlint

The main script in the Dlint package is called `dlint`. You can run this script using the following command:

```
/usr/local/bin/dlint domain | in-addr.arpa-domain
```

For example, to run `dlint` for a domain called `intevo.com`, you can execute `/usr/local/bin/dlint intevo.com`. Listing 16-1 shows an example output.

Listing 16-1: Sample output from dlint

```
;; dlint version 1.4.0, Copyright (C) 1998 Paul A. Balyoz <pab@domtools.com>
;;     Dlint comes with ABSOLUTELY NO WARRANTY.
;;     This is free software, and you are welcome to redistribute it
;;     under certain conditions.  Type 'man dlint' for details.
;; command line: /usr/local/bin/dlint domain.com
;; flags: normal-domain recursive.
;; using dig version 8.2
;; run starting: Fri Dec 29 13:34:07 EST 2000
;; =============================================================
;; Now linting domain.com
;; Checking serial numbers per nameserver
;;     1997022700 ns2.domain.com.
;;     1997022700 ns1.domain.com.
;; All nameservers agree on the serial number.
;; Now caching whole zone (this could take a minute)
;; trying nameserver ns1.domain.com.
;; 3 A records found.
ERROR: "ns1.domain.com. A 172.20.15.1", but the PTR record for
        1.15.20.172.in-addr.arpa. is "k2.domain.com."
        One of the above two records are wrong unless the host is a name server
        or mail server.
        To have 2 names for 1 address on any other hosts, replace the A record
        with a CNAME record:
        ns1.domain.com. IN      CNAME   k2.domain.com.
ERROR: "ns2.domain.com. A 172.20.15.1", but the PTR record for
        1.15.20.172.in-addr.arpa. is "k2.domain.com."
 One of the above two records are wrong unless the host is a name server
 or mail server.
        To have 2 names for 1 address on any other hosts, replace the A record
        with a CNAME record:
        ns2.domain.com. IN      CNAME   k2.domain.com.
;; =============================================================
```

```
;; Now linting domain.com.
;; Checking serial numbers per nameserver
;;      1997022700 ns1.domain.com.
;;      1997022700 ns2.domain.com.
;; All nameservers agree on the serial number.
;; Now caching whole zone (this could take a minute)
;; trying nameserver ns1.domain.com.
;; 3 A records found.
ERROR: "ns1.domain.com. A 172.20.15.1", but the PTR record for
       1.15.20.172.in-addr.arpa. is "k2.domain.com."
       One of the above two records are wrong unless the host is a name
       server or mail server.
       To have 2 names for 1 address on any other hosts, replace the A record
       with a CNAME record:
       ns1.domain.com. IN      CNAME   k2.domain.com.
ERROR: "ns2.domain.com. A 172.20.15.1", but the PTR record for
       1.15.20.172.in-addr.arpa. is "k2.domain.com."
       One of the above two records are wrong unless the host is a name
       server or mail server.
       To have 2 names for 1 address on any other hosts, replace the A record
       with a CNAME record:
       ns2.domain.com. IN      CNAME   k2.domain.com.
;; no subzones found below domain.com., so no recursion will take place.
;; ============================================================
;; dlint of domain.com. run ending with errors.
;; run ending: Fri Dec 29 13:34:09 EST 2000
;; ============================================================
;; dlint of domain.com run ending with errors.
;; run ending: Fri Dec 29 13:34:09 EST 2000
```

As you can see, dlint is verbose. The lines that start with a semicolon are comments. All other lines are warnings or errors. Here domain.com has a set of problems. ns1.domain.com has an A record, but the PTR record points to k2.domain.com instead. Similarly, the ns2.domain.com host has the same problem. This means the domain.com configuration has the following lines:

```
ns1         IN      A       172.20.15.1
ns2         IN      A       172.20.15.1
k2          IN      A       172.20.15.1
```

The configuration also has the following PTR record:

```
1       IN      PTR     k2.intevo.com.
```

The `dlint` program suggests using `CNAME` records to resolve this problem. This means the configuration should be:

```
ns1        IN        A       172.20.15.1
ns2        IN        CNAME   ns1
k2         IN        CNAME   ns1
```

The PTR record should be:

```
1     IN     PTR     ns1.intevo.com.
```

After fixing the errors in the appropriate configuration DNS files for domain.com, the following output is produced by the `/usr/local/bin/dlint domain.com` command.

```
;; dlint version 1.4.0, Copyright (C) 1998 Paul A. Balyoz <pab@domtools.com>
;;      Dlint comes with ABSOLUTELY NO WARRANTY.
;;      This is free software, and you are welcome to redistribute it
;;      under certain conditions.  Type 'man dlint' for details.
;; command line: /usr/local/bin/dlint domain.com
;; flags: normal-domain recursive.
;; using dig version 8.2
;; run starting: Fri Dec 29 13:38:00 EST 2000
;; =============================================================
;; Now linting domain.com
;; Checking serial numbers per nameserver
;;      1997022700 ns2.domain.com.
;;      1997022700 ns1.domain.com.
;; All nameservers agree on the serial number.
;; Now caching whole zone (this could take a minute)
;; trying nameserver ns1.domain.com.
;; 1 A records found.
;; =============================================================
;; Now linting domain.com.
;; Checking serial numbers per nameserver
;;      1997022700 ns1.domain.com.
;;      1997022700 ns2.domain.com.
;; All nameservers agree on the serial number.
;; Now caching whole zone (this could take a minute)
;; trying nameserver ns1.domain.com.
;; 1 A records found.
;; no subzones found below domain.com., so no recursion will take place.
;; =============================================================
;; dlint of domain.com. run ending normally.
;; run ending: Fri Dec 29 13:38:01 EST 2000
```

```
;; ================================================================
;; dlint of domain.com run ending normally.
;; run ending: Fri Dec 29 13:38:01 EST 2000
```

As shown no error messages are reported. Of course, Dlint (dlint) can't catch all errors in your configuration, but it's a great tool to perform a level of quality control when you create, update, or remove DNS configuration information.

Securing BIND

BIND is the most widely used DNS server for Linux. BIND was recently overhauled for scalability and robustness. Many DNS experts consider earlier versions of BIND (prior to 9.0) to be mostly patchwork.

Fortunately BIND 9.0 is written by a large team of professional software developers to support the next generation of DNS protocol evolution. The new BIND supports back-end databases, authorization and transactional security features, SNMP-based management, and IPv6 capability. The code base of the new bind is audited and written in a manner that supports frequent audits by anyone who is interested.

The new BIND now supports the DNSSEC and TSIG standards.

Using Transaction Signatures (TSIG) for zone transfers

Transaction Signatures (TSIG) can authenticate and verify the DNS data exchange. This means you can use TSIG to control zone transfers for domains you manage.

Typically, zone transfers are from primary to secondary name servers. In the following named.conf segment of a primary name server the IP addresses listed in the access control list (acl) called dns-ip-list can transfer the zone information only for the yourdomain.com domain.

```
acl "dns-ip-list" {
        172.20.15.100;
        172.20.15.123;
};
zone "yourdomain.com" {
  type master;
  file "mydomain.dns";
  allow-query    { any; };
  allow-update   { none; };
  allow-transfer { dns-ip-list; };
};
```

Unfortunately, malicious hackers can use IP spoofing tricks to trick a DNS server into performing zone transfers. Avoid this by using Transaction Signatures. Let's say that you want to limit the zone transfer for a domain called `yourdomain.com` to two secondary name servers with IP addresses 172.20.15.100 (`ns1.yourdomain.com`) and 172.20.15.123 (`ns2.yourdomain.com`). Here's how you can use TSIG to ensure that IP spoofing tricks can't force a zone transfer between your DNS server and a hacker's DNS server.

 Make sure that the DNS servers involved in TSIG-based zone transfer authentication keep the same system time. You can create a `cron` job entry to synchronize each machine with a remote time server using `rdate` or `ntp` tools.

1. Generate a shared secret key to authenticate the zone transfer.

2. Change the directory to `/var/named`.

3. Use the `/usr/local/sbin/dnssec-keygen` command to generate a set of public and private keys as follows:

   ```
   dnssec-keygen -a hmac-md5 -b 128 -n HOST zone-xfr-key
   ```

   The public key file is called `Kzone-xfr-key.+157+08825.key`, and the private key file is `Kzone-xfr-key.+157+08825.private`. If you view the contents of the private key file, you see something like the following:

   ```
   Private-key-format: v1.2
   Algorithm: 157 (HMAC_MD5)
   Key: YH8Onz5xO/twQnvYPyh1qg==
   ```

4. Using the `key` string displayed by the preceding step, create the following statement in the `named.conf` file of both `ns1.yourdomain.com` and `ns2.yourdomain.com`.

   ```
   key zone-xfr-key {
     algorithm hmac-md5;
     secret "YH8Onz5xO/twQnvYPyh1qg==";
   };
   ```

Use the actual `key` string found in the file you generated. Don't use the key from this example.

5. Add the following statement in the `/etc/named.conf` file of the `ns1.yourdomain.com` **server:**

```
server 172.20.15.123 {
    keys { zone-xfr-key; };
};
```

6. Add the following statement in the `/etc/named.conf` file of the `ns2.yourdomain.com` **server:**

```
server 172.20.15.100 {
    keys { zone-xfr-key; };
};
```

7. The full `/etc/named.conf` configuration segment of the `yourdomain.com` zone for the primary DNS server `ns1.yourdomain.com` is shown in Listing 16-2.

Listing 16-2: yourdomain.com configuration for primary DNS server

```
acl "dns-ip-list" {
        172.20.15.100;
        172.20.15.123;

};

key zone-xfr-key {
  algorithm hmac-md5;
  secret "YH8Onz5xO/twQnvYPyh1qg==";
};
server 172.20.15.123 {
   keys { zone-xfr-key; };
};
zone "yourdomain.com" {
  type master;
  file "mydomain.dns";
  allow-query    { any; };
  allow-update   { none; };
  allow-transfer { dns-ip-list; };
};
```

8. The full /etc/named.conf configuration segment of the yourdomain.com zone for the secondary DNS server ns1.yourdomain.com is shown in Listing 16-3.

Listing 16-3: yourdomain.com configuration for secondary DNS server

```
acl "dns-ip-list" {
        172.20.15.100;
        172.20.15.123;

};


key zone-xfr-key {
  algorithm hmac-md5;
  secret "YH8Onz5xO/twQnvYPyh1qg==";
};
server 172.20.15.100 {
   keys { zone-xfr-key; };
};
zone "yourdomain.com" {
  type master;
  file "mydomain.dns";
  allow-query    { any; };
  allow-update   { none; };
  allow-transfer { dns-ip-list; };
};
```

9. Restart named on both systems.

The preceding steps ensures zone transfers between the given hosts occur in a secure manner. To test that a shared TSIG key is used for zone-transfer authentication, you can do the following:

♦ Delete the yourdomain.com domain's zone file on the secondary DNS server (ns2.yourdomain.com).

♦ Restart the secondary name server.

♦ The secondary DNS server should transfer the missing zone file from the primary DNS server. You should see the zone file created in the appropriate directory. If for some reason this file isn't created, look at /var/log/ messages for errors, fix the errors, and redo this verification process.

Watch for these problems:

◆ If you change the shared TSIG key in any of the two hosts by one character, the zone transfer isn't possible. You get an error message in /var/log/ messages that states that TSIG verification failed because of a bad key.

◆ Because the named.conf file on both machines now has a secret key, ensure that the file isn't readable by ordinary users.

TIP

If you want to dynamically updates of DNS configuration if the request is signed using a TSIG key, use the allow-update { key *keyname*; }; statement. For example, allow-update { key zone-xfr-key; }; statement allows dynamic updates between the hosts discussed here. If the public and private key files for a key named zone-xfr-key is in the /var/named/ keys directory, you can run /usr/local/bin/nsupdate -k/var/ named/keys:zone-xfr-key to update DNS zone information for the yourdomain.com domain.

Running BIND as a non-root user

On a Linux kernel 2.3.99 and later, you can run BIND as a non-root user using the -u option. For example, the /usr/local/sbin/named -u nobody command starts BIND as the nobody user.

Hiding the BIND version number

Because software bugs are associated with certain versions, the version information becomes a valuable piece of information for malicious hackers. By finding what version of BIND you run, a hacker can figure what exploits (if any) are there for it and try to break in. So it's wise not to give your version number willingly. You can simply override the version information given by BIND by adding the version statement in the options section. For example, the following configuration segment tells named to display Unsupported on this platform when version information is requested.

```
options {

    # other global options go here
        version "Unsupported on this platform";
};
```

TIP

As with the version number, you don't want to give your host information. In the sprit of making a potential attacker's job harder, I recommend that you don't use HINFO or TXT resource records in your DNS configuration files.

Limiting Queries

Anyone can perform a query with most DNS servers on the Internet. This is absolutely unacceptable for a secure environment. A DNS spoof attack usually relies on this fact, and an attacker can ask your DNS server to resolve a query for which it can't produce an authoritative answer. The spoof may ask your server to resolve a query that requires it to get data from the hacker's own DNS server. For example, a hacker runs a DNS server for the id10t.com domain, and your DNS server is authoritative for the yourdomain.com domain. Now, if you allow anyone to query your server for anything, the hacker can ask your server to resolve gotcha.id10t.com. Your DNS server gets data from the hacker's machine, and the hacker plays his spoofing tricks to poison your DNS cache.

Now, say that your network address is 168.192.1.0. The following statement makes sure that no one outside your network can query your DNS server for anything but the domains it manages.

```
options {
    allow-query { 168.192.1.0/24; };
};
```

The allow-query directive makes sure that all the hosts in the 168.192.1.0 network can query the DNS server. If your DNS server is authoritative for the yourdomain.com zone, you can have the following /etc/named.conf segment:

```
options {
  allow-query { 168.192.1.0/24; };
};
zone "yourdomain.com" {
      type master;
      file "yourdomain.com";
      allow-query { any; };
};
zone "1.168.192.in-addr.arpa" {
      type master;
      file "db.192.168.1";
      allow-query { any; };
};
```

This makes sure that anyone from anywhere can query the DNS server for your-domain.com but only the users in the 168.192.1.0 network can query the DNS server for anything.

 Don't allow anyone outside your network to perform recursive queries. To disable recursive queries for everyone but your network, add this line:

```
allow-recursion { 192.168.1.0/24; };
```

You can also disable recursion completely, for everyone, by using the following option in the global options section:

```
recursion no;
```

 You can't disable recursion on a name server if other name servers use it as a forwarder.

Ideally, you should set your authoritative name server(s) to perform no recursion. Only the name server(s) that are responsible for resolving DNS queries for your internal network should perform recursion. This type of setup is known as *split DNS configuration.*

For example, say that you have two name servers — ns1.yourdomain.com (primary) and ns2.yourdomain.com (secondary) — responsible for a single domain called yourdomain.com. At the same time you have a DNS server called ns3.your-domain.com, which is responsible for resolving DNS queries for your 192.168.1.0 network. In a split DNS configuration, you can set both ns1 and ns2 servers to use no recursion for any domain other than yourdomain.com and allow recursion on ns3 using the allow-recursion statement discussed earlier.

Turning off glue fetching

When a DNS server returns a name server record for a domain and doesn't have an A record for the name server record, it attempts to retrieve one. This is called *glue fetching,* which spoofing attackers can abuse. Turning off glue fetching is as simple as adding the following statement in the global options section of /etc/named. conf.

```
options no-fetch-glue
```

chrooting the DNS server

The 9.*x* version of BIND simplifies creating a `chroot` jail for the DNS server. Here's how you can create a `chroot` jail for BIND.

1. `su` to `root`.

2. Create a new user called `dns` by using the `useradd dns -d /home/dns` command.

3. Run the `mkdir -p /home/dns/var/log /home/dns/var/run /home/dns/var/named /home/dns/etc` command to create all the necessary directories.

4. Copy the `/etc/named.conf` file, using the `cp /etc/named.conf /home/dns/etc/` command.

5. Copy everything from `/var/named` to `/home/dns/var/named`, using the `cp -r /var/named/* /home/dns/var/named/` command.

6. Run the `chown -R dns:dns /home/dns` command to make sure that all files and directories needed by `named` are owned by user `dns` and its private group called `dns`.

 If you plan to run `named` as `root`, use `root:root` instead of `dns:dns` as the `username:groupname` in this command.

Now you can run the name server using the following command:

`/usr/local/sbin/named -t /home/dns -u dns`

If you plan to run `named` as `root`, don't specify the `-u dns` command.

Using DNSSEC (signed zones)

The DNS Security Extension (DNSSEC) is an authentication model based on public key cryptography. It introduces two new resource record types, `KEY` and `SIG`, to allow resolves and name servers to cryptographically authenticate the source of any DNS data. This means a DNS client can now prove that the response it received from a DNS server is authentic. Unfortunately, until DNSSEC is widespread, its benefit can't be fully realized. Here I show you how you can create the necessary DNSSEC configuration for a domain called `domain.com`.

1. Create a pair of public and private keys for the `domain.com` domain. From the `/var/named` directory, run the `/usr/local/sbin/dnssec-keygen -a DSA -b 768 -n ZONE domain.com` command.

   This command creates a 768-bit DSA-based private and public key pair. It creates a public key file called `Kdomain.com.+003+29462.key` and a private key file called `Kdomain.com.+003+29462.private`.

   The `29462` number is called a *key tag,* and it varies. Insert the public key in the zone file (`domain.com.db`) with a line like this at the beginning of the file:

   `$INCLUDE /var/named/Kdomain.com.+003+29462.key`

2. Create a key set using the `/usr/local/sbin/dnssec-makekeyset -t 3600 -e now+30 Kdomain.com.+003+29462` command.

   This command creates a key set with a time-to-live value of 3,600 seconds (1 hour) and expiring in 30 days. This command creates a file called `domain.com.keyset`.

3. Sign the key set, using the `/usr/local/sbin/dnssec-signkey domain.com.keyset  Kdomain.com.+003+29462` command.

   This command creates a signed key file called `domain.com.signedkey`.

4. Sign the zone file by using the `/usr/local/sbin/dnssec-signzone -o domain.com domain.db` command, where `domain.db` is the name of the zone file in the `/var/named` directory.

   This command creates a signed zone file called `domain.db.signed`.

5. Replace the zone filename for `domain.com` in the `/etc/named.conf` file.

   For example, the `/etc/named.conf` configuration segment in the following code shows the zone declaration for `domain.com`.

```
zone "domain.com" IN {
        type master;
        file "domain.db.signed";
        allow-update { none; };
};
```

Summary

Every Internet request (Web, FTP, email) requires at least one DNS query. Since BIND is the most widely used DNS server available today, it is very important that your BIND server is configured well for enhanced security. Checking the DNS configuration using Dlint, using transaction signatures for zone transfer, and using DNSSEC ensures that your DNS server is as secure as it can be.

Chapter 17

E-Mail Server Security

E-MAIL COMMUNICATION TAKES A leading role in today's business-to-business (B2B), business-to-consumer (B2C), and peer-to-peer (P2P) arenas. Many consider e-mail to be the "killer app" of the Internet era. I don't doubt it for a bit.

Today, over a billion e-mails are exchanged worldwide every day. Most of these e-mails are routed to their destinations by a select few Mail Transport Agents (MTAs). Sendmail, an MTA, has been around for many years and is usually the default MTA for most Unix and Unix-like distributions (which include Red Hat Linux).

Unfortunately, as e-mail use becomes more common, it's becomes a target for abuse and break-ins. The open-source and commercial software industries are responding to a real-world need for secure e-mail services by updating Sendmail. Among these updates are new MTAs especially designed for scalability and security. This chapter discusses e-mail-related security issues, focusing on popular MTAs and their roles in potential solutions.

What Is Open Mail Relay?

The biggest problem in the world of e-mail is unsolicited mail or *spam*. The underlying e-mail protocol, Simple Mail Transport Protocol (SMTP), is just that — simple. It is not designed to be secure. Accordingly, the biggest abuse of e-mail service is called *open mail relay*.

An MTA receives mail for the domain it's responsible for. It's also able to relay messages to other MTAs responsible for other domains. When you write an e-mail using an e-mail client like Pine, Netscape Messenger, or Outlook, the mail is delivered to your local MTA, which then relays the message to the appropriate MTA of the destination address. So mail sent to `kabir@nitec.com` from a user called `reader@her-isp.com` is delivered from the MTA of `her-isp.com` to the MTA for `nitec.com`.

Traditionally, each MTA also allows anyone to relay messages to another MTA. For example, only a few years ago you could have configured your e-mail program to point to the mail server for the `nitec.com` domain and sent a message to your friend at `someone@someplace-not-nitec.com`. This means you could have simply used my mail server to relay a message to your friend. What's wrong with that? Nothing – provided the relaying job doesn't do the following:

♦ Take system resources from the MTA used

♦ Send e-mail to people who don't want to receive it

Unfortunately, legitimate-opportunity seeking individuals and organizations weren't the only ones to realize the power of e-mail as a mass-delivery medium. Scam artists started spamming people around the globe, using any open-relay-capable MTA they could find. They simply figured that by using the open relaying capability built into the MTAs around the world, they could distribute their junk messages for profit without incurring any cost proportional to the distribution capacity.

As spamming became more prevalent and annoying, the Internet community became worried about the abuse. Some users formed blacklists of known spammers, some filed legal actions, and some resorted to fixing MTAs. Why bother? Here are some good reasons.

♦ **If an open mail-relay attack uses your MTA, your reputation can be tarnished.** Many people receiving the spam via your e-mail server automatically assign you as the faulty party and possibly publicize the matter on the Internet or even in public mediums. This can be a public relations disaster for an organization.

♦ **An open relay attack can cost you money.** If the spam attack is large, it may take your own e-mail service down. Your legitimate e-mail messages may get stuck in a queue, because the mail server is busy sending spam.

♦ **An open relay attack can mean legal action against your organization.** As legislators pass Internet-related laws, it is likely that soon open relays will become a legal liability.

♦ **You may be blacklisted.** People whose e-mail accounts are abused by a spammer using open mail relay can file your mail server information to be included in a blacklist. This can stop you from sending legitimate e-mail to domains that automatically check with blacklists such as the MAPS (Mail Abuse Prevention System) Realtime Blackhole List.

The MAPS RBL authority are quite reasonable about removing a black-listed server from their list once the server authority demonstrates that the server is no longer an open mail relay.

◆ Spammers use tools that search the Internet for open relays automatically.

If you want a secure, relatively hassle-free network, I recommend that you take action to stop open mail from relaying via your e-mail servers.

Is My Mail Server Vulnerable?

To find whether your mail server (or any mail server) is vulnerable to an open mail-relay attack, do the following test.

1. Log on to your Linux system (or any system that has `nslookup` and Telnet client tools).

2. **Run the** `nslookup -q=mx  domain.com` **command where** `domain.com` is the domain name for which you want to find the MX records.

   The MX records in a DNS database point to the mail servers of a domain. In this example, I use a fictitious domain called `openrelay-ok.com` as the example domain. Note the mail servers to which the MX records of the domain actually point. The domain should have at least one mail server configured for it. In this example, I assume the mail server pointed to by the MX record for the `openrelay-ok.com` domain is `mail.openrelay-ok.com`.

3. **Run the** `telnet` *mailserver-host* `25` **command, where** *mailserver-host* is a mail server hostname. I ran the `telnet mail.openrelay-ok.com 25` command to connect to port 25 (standard SMTP port) of the tested mail server.

4. **Once connected, enter the** `ehlo localhost` **command to say (sort of)** hello to the mail server. The mail server replies with a greeting message and waits for input.

5. **Enter the** `mail from:` *you@hotmail.com* **command to tell the mail server** that you want to send mail to a Hotmail address called *you@hotmail.com*. I recommend using any address outside your domain when replacing *you@hotmail.com*. The server acknowledges the sender address using a response such as `250 you@hotmail.com... Sender ok`.

   If the server responds with a different message, stating that the sender's e-mail address isn't acceptable, make sure you are entering the command correctly. If you still get a negative response, the server isn't accepting the e-mail destination, which is a sign that the server probably has special `MAIL FROM` checking. This means the server probably won't allow open relay at all. Most likely you get the okay message; if so, continue.

   At this point, you have instructed the mail server that you want to send an e-mail from *you@hotmail.com*.

6. Tell the server that you want to send it to *you@yahoo.com* using the `rcpt to:` *you@yahoo.com* command. If the server accepts it by sending a response such as `250 you@yahoo.com... Recipient ok`, then you have found an open mail relay. This is because the mail server accepted mail from `you@hotmail.com`, and agreed to send it to `you@yahoo.com`.

If you aren't performing this test on a `yahoo.com` mail server, then the mail server shouldn't accept mail from just anyone outside the domain to send to someone else outside the domain. It's an open mail relay; a spammer can use this mail server to send mail to people outside your domain, as shown in Listing 17-1.

Listing 17-1: Using an open mail relay

```
$ telnet mail.openrelay-ok.com 25
Trying 192.168.1.250...
Connected to mail.openrelay-ok.com.
Escape character is '^]'.
220 mail.openrelay-ok.com ESMTP Sendmail Pro-8.9.3/Pro-8.9.3;
Sun, 31 Dec 2000 11:04:33 -0800
EHLO localhost
250-mail.openrelay-ok.com Hello [192.168.1.250], pleased to
meet you
250-EXPN
250-VERB
250-8BITMIME
250-SIZE
250-DSN
250-ONEX
250-ETRN
250-XUSR
250 HELP
mail from: you@hotmail.com
250 you@hotmail.com... Sender ok
rcpt to: you@yahoo.com
250 you@yahoo.com... Recipient ok
data
354 Enter mail, end with "." on a line by itself
THIS MAIL SERVER CAN BE AN OPEN MAIL RELAY!
FUTURE SPAM WILL BE SERVED FROM HERE!
YOU NEED TO BLOCK THIS ASAP!
.
250 LAA15851 Message accepted for delivery
```

If you perform the preceding test on a mail server that doesn't allow open mail replay, the output looks very different. Here's an example Telnet session on port 25 of a mail server called `mail.safemta.com`, showing how the test does on a protected mail server; you get the following ouput:

```
[kabir@209 ~]$ telnet localhost 25
Trying 172.20.15.250...
Connected to mail.safemta.com.
Escape character is '^]'.
220 172.20.15.250 ESMTP Sendmail 8.11.0/8.11.0; Sun, 31 Dec 2000 14:07:15 -0500
ehlo localhost
250-172.20.15.250 Hello mail.safemta.com [172.20.15.250], pleased to meet you
250-ENHANCEDSTATUSCODES
250-8BITMIME
250-SIZE
250-DSN
250-ONEX
250-XUSR
250-AUTH DIGEST-MD5 CRAM-MD5
250 HELP
mail from: you@hotmail.com
250 2.1.0 you@hotmail.com... Sender ok
rcpt to: you@yahoo.com
550 5.7.1 you@yahoo.com... Relaying denied
```

The listing shows the mail server rejecting the recipient address given in the `rcpt to: you@yahoo.com` **command**.

 If your mail server doesn't reject open mail relay requests, secure it now!

Securing Sendmail

Sendmail is the most widely distributed MTA and currently the default choice for Red Hat Linux. Fortunately, by default the newer versions of Sendmail don't allow open relay functionality. Although this feature is available in the latest few versions, I recommend that you download and install the newest version of Sendmail from either an RPM mirror site or directly from the official open source Sendmail site at `www.sendmail.org`.

I strongly recommend that you download *both* the binary RPM version (from an RPM mirror site such as www.rpmfind.net) *and* the source distribution (from www.sendmail.org). Install the RPM version using the `rpm -ivh sendmail-version.rpm` command where *sendmail-version.rpm* is the latest binary RPM of Sendmail. Installing the binary RPM version ensures that the configuration files and directories are automatically created for you.

 You can decide not to install the binary RPM and simply compile and install the source distribution from scratch. The source distribution doesn't have a fancy installation program, so creating and making configuration files and directories are a lot of work. To avoid too many manual configurations, I simply install the binary distribution and then compile and install the source on top of it..

Also, extract the source-distribution tar ball in a suitable directory, such as /usr/src/redhat/SOURCES. Then follow the instructions in the top-level readme file to compile and install Sendmail. In the following section I discuss various Sendmail security and control features related to combating spam. To use these features, you must incorporate them in your Sendmail configuration file found in /etc/mail/sendmail.cf. However, don't directly modify this file. Instead, modify the *whatever*.mc file in the cf/cf directory where *whatever*.mc is the name of the macro file per the top-level readme file. When you modify the *whatever*.mc file, make sure you generate the /etc/mail/sendmail.cf file using the m4 /path/to/whatever.mc > /etc/mail/sendmail.cf command. Remember these rules:

◆ Back up your current /etc/mail/sendmail.cf file first.

◆ Run this command from the cf/cf subdirectory of your source distribution.

 I use the linux-dnsbl.mc configuration as the replacement for the whatever.mc file. The linux-dnsbl.mc file is in the source distribution of Sendmail, but it's extracted outside the subdirectory that the tar command creates when extracting Sendmail. To use it, copy it to the cf/cf subdirectory in the newly created Sendmail source distribution directory.

In the following section, when I mention a Sendmail feature using the FEATURE (featurename) syntax, add it to the appropriate *whatever*.mc file and recreate the /etc/mail/sendmail.cf file. In my example, I add it to /usr/src/redhat/SOURCES/sendmail-8.11.0/cf/cf/linux-dnsbl.mc, which is shown in Listing 17-2.

Listing 17-2: /usr/src/redhat/SOURCES/sendmail-8.11.0/cf/cf/linux-dnsbl.mc

```
divert(0)dnl
include(`../m4/cf.m4')dnl
VERSIONID(`$Id: Kitchen Sink  2000/08/09 ')
OSTYPE(linux)dnl
define(`confCON_EXPENSIVE', `true')dnl
define(`confDEF_USER_ID',`mail:mail')dnl
define(`confDONT_PROBE_INTERFACES',`true')dnl
define(`confPRIVACY_FLAGS',
`needmailhelo,noexpn,novrfy,restrictmailq,restrictqrun,noetrn,nobodyreturn')dnl
FEATURE(access_db)dnl
FEATURE(always_add_domain)dnl
FEATURE(blacklist_recipients)dnl
FEATURE(delay_checks)dnl
FEATURE(limited_masquerade)dnl
FEATURE(local_procmail)dnl
FEATURE(masquerade_entire_domain)dnl
FEATURE(relay_local_from_popip)dnl
FEATURE(redirect)dnl
FEATURE(relay_entire_domain)dnl
FEATURE(smrsh)dnl
FEATURE(use_ct_file)dnl
FEATURE(use_cw_file)dnl
FEATURE(domaintable)dnl
FEATURE(genericstable)dnl
FEATURE(mailertable)dnl
FEATURE(virtusertable)dnl
FEATURE(`dnsbl',`rbl.maps.vix.com')dnl
FEATURE(`dnsbl',`dul.maps.vix.com')dnl
FEATURE(`dnsbl',`relays.mail-abuse.org')dnl
dnl Remove to use orbs also
dnl FEATURE(`dnsbl',`relays.orbs.org')dnl
MAILER(smtp)dnl
MAILER(procmail)dnl
```

For example, if I recommend a feature called xyz using the FEATURE(xyz) notation, add the feature to the configuration file; then create the /etc/mail/sendmail.cf file, using the preceding command. The latest version of Sendmail gives you a high degree of control over the mail-relaying feature of your MTA.

Controlling mail relay

The latest version of Sendmail 8.11.2 allows you a high degree of control over the mail-relaying feature of your MTA. As mentioned before, mail relaying is disabled by default. Sendmail offers control of mail relay for legitimate uses. To enable the configuration controls discussed here, you need the following features in your m4 macro file to generate appropriate /etc/mail/sendmail.cf.

USING FEATURE(ACCESS_DB)

This feature enables the access-control database, which is stored in the /etc/mail/access file. The entries in this file have the following syntax:

LHS{tab}RHS

◆ Left-hand side (LHS) can be any item shown in Table 17-1

◆ {tab} is a tab character

◆ Right-hand side (RHS) can be any item shown in Table 17-2.

TABLE 17-1: LEFT SIDE OF AN ENTRY IN /ETC/MAIL/ACCESS

LHS	Meaning
user@host	An e-mail address
IP address	IP address of a mail server
Hostname or domain	Hostname of a mail server
From: user@host	Mail from an e-mail address called user@host
From: hostname or From:domain	Mail from a hostname or domain
To: user@host	Mail to an e-mail address called user@host
To: hostname or To:domain	Mail to a hostname or domain
Connect: hostname or Connect:domain	Connection from hostname or any host in the given domain name

---

TABLE 17-2: RIGHT-HAND SIDE OF AN ENTRY IN /ETC/MAIL/ACCESS

RHS	Meaning
RELAY	Enable mail relay for the host or domain named in the LHS
OK	Accept mail and ignore other rules
REJECT	Reject mail
DISCARD	Silently discard mail; don't display an error message
ERROR RFC821-CODE *text message*	Display RFC 821 error code and a text message
ERROR RFC1893-CODE *text message*	Display RFC 1893 error code and a text message

---

When you create, modify, or delete an entry in the /etc/mail/access file, remember these rules:

◆ Run the makemap hash /etc/mail/access < /etc/mail/ access command to create the database readable by Sendmail.

◆ Restart the server using the /rc.d/init.d/sendmail restart command.

REJECTING MAIL FROM AN ENTIRE DOMAIN OR HOST To reject a message from an entire domain (for example, from spamfactory.com), use the following command:

```
spamfactory.com          REJECT
```

To reject mail from a host called bad.scam-artist.com, use

```
bad.scam-artist.com      REJECT
```

The preceding configuration doesn't reject mail from other hosts.

REJECT MAIL FROM AN E-MAIL ADDRESS   To reject mail from an e-mail address called newsletter@fromhell.com, use

```
From:newsletter@fromhell.com    REJECT
```

You don't receive mail from the preceding address, but you can still send messages to the address.

RELAYING MAIL TO A DOMAIN OR HOST   To relay messages to a domain called busyrebooting.com, use

```
To:busyrebooting.com        RELAY
```

This command allows relaying messages to the busyrebooting.com domain, but Sendmail doesn't accept nonlocal messages from it; that is, Sendmail doesn't relay.

RELAYING MAIL FROM A DOMAIN OR HOST   To relay messages from a domain called imbuddies.com, use

```
Connect:imbuddies.com    RELAY
```

ACCEPTING A SELECTED E-MAIL ADDRESS FROM A DOMAIN   Sometimes you want to disallow e-mail from all users except for a few for a given domain. For example, to ban everyone but the e-mail addressees spy1@myfoe.net and spy2@myfoe.net for the myfoe.net domain, use

```
From:spy1@myfoe.net        OK
From:spy2@myfoe.net        OK
From:myfoe.net             REJECT
```

All e-mail except that from the first two addresses is rejected.

USING FEATURE(RELAY_ENTIRE_DOMAIN)

The database for this feature is stored in /etc/mail/relay-domains. Each line in this file lists one Internet domain. When this feature is set, it allows relaying of all hosts in one domain. For example, if your /etc/mail/relay-domain file looks like the following line, mail to and from kabirsfriends.com is allowed:

```
kabirsfriends.com
```

USING FEATURE(RELAY_HOSTS_ONLY)

If you don't want to enable open mail relay to and from an entire domain, you can use this feature to specify each host for which your server is allowed to act as a mail relay.

Enabling MAPS Realtime Blackhole List (RBL) support

MAPS RBL uses a set of modified DNS servers for access to a blacklist of alleged spammers, who are usually reported by spam victims.

The simplest way to start using the RBL to protect your mail relay is arranging for it to make a DNS query (of a stylized name) whenever you receive an incoming mail message from a host whose spam status you don't know.

When a remote mail server (say, 192.168.1.1) connects to your mail server, Sendmail checks for the existence of an address record (A) in the MAPS DNS server using a MAPS RBL rule set. Sendmail issues a DNS request for 1.1.168.192.blackholes.mail-abuse.org. If an address record (A) is found for 1.1.168.192.blackholes.mail-abuse.org, it is 127.0.0.2, which means that 192.168.1.1 is a blacklisted mail server. Your Sendmail server can then reject it.

To use the RBL add the following features to your configuration (mc) file, regenerate /etc/mail/sendmail.cf, and restart the server.

```
FEATURE(`dnsbl',`rbl.maps.vix.com')dnl
FEATURE(`dnsbl',`dul.maps.vix.com')dnl
FEATURE(`dnsbl',`relays.mail-abuse.org')dnl
```

To test your RBL configuration, run the /usr/sbin/sendmail -bt command. An interactive Sendmail test session is started as shown in the following listing:

```
ADDRESS TEST MODE (ruleset 3 NOT automatically invoked)
Enter <ruleset> <address>
> .D{client_addr}127.0.0.1
> Basic_check_relay <>
Basic_check_rela   input: < >
Basic_check_rela returns: OKSOFAR
```

Enter .D{client_addr}127.0.0.1, followed by Basic_check_relay <>, to check whether the address 127.0.0.1 is blacklisted. Because the address 127.0.0.1 is a special address (localhost) it's not blacklisted, as indicated by the message OKSOFAR.

Now test a blacklisted address: 127.0.0.2. You must enter the same sequence of input as shown in the following list:

```
> .D{client_addr}127.0.0.2
> Basic_check_relay <>
Basic_check_rela   input: < >
Basic_check_rela returns: $# error $@ 5.7.1 $: "550 Mail from " 127.0.0.2 "
refused by blackhole site rbl.maps.vix.com"
```

Here you can see that the address is blacklisted. Press Ctrl+Z to put the current process in the background, and then enter kill %1 to terminate the process.

The current version of Sendmail supports Simple Authentication and Security Layer (SASL), which can authenticate the user accounts that connect to it. Because a user must use authentication, spammers who (aren't likely to have user accounts on your system) can't use it as an open mail relay. (This new feature is not yet widely used.)

Before you can use the SASL-based authentication, however, install the Cyrus SASL library package (as shown in the next section).

COMPILING AND INSTALLING CYRUS SASL

Download the source distribution (cyrus-sasl-1.5.24.tar.gz or the latest version) from ftp://ftp.andrew.cmu.edu/pub/cyrus-mail. To compile and install the package, do the following:

When following these instructions, make sure you replace SASL version number 1.5.24 with the version number you download.

1. Extract the source into /usr/src/redhat/SOURCES, using the tar xvzf cyrus-sasl-1.5.24.tar.gz command. This creates a subdirectory called cyrus-sasl-1.5.24. Change directory to cyrus-sasl-1.5.24.

2. Run the ./configure --prefix=/usr command to configure the SASL source tree.

3. Run the make and make install to make and install the library.

If you change directory to /usr/lib and run the ls -l command, you see the SASL library files installed.

```
-rwxr-xr-x 1 root   root   685     Dec 31 04:45 libsasl.la
lrwxrwxrwx 1 root   root   16      Dec 31 04:45 libsasl.so -> libsasl.so.7.1.8
lrwxrwxrwx 1 root   root   16      Dec 31 04:45 libsasl.so.7 -> libsasl.so.7.1.8
-rwxr-xr-x 1 root   root   173755 Dec 31 04:45 libsasl.so.7.1.8
```

Now you can compile Sendmail with SASL support.

COMPILING AND INSTALLING SENDMAIL WITH SASL SUPPORT

If you already have a working Sendmail installation, you must back up all the necessary files using the following commands:

```
cp -r /etc/mail /etc/mail.bak
cp /usr/sbin/sendmail /usr/sbin/sendmail.bak
cp /usr/sbin/makemap /usr/sbin/makemap.bak
cp /usr/bin/newaliases /usr/bin/newaliases.bak
```

Download the latest Sendmail source from `www.sendmail.org`. I downloaded `sendmail.8.11.0.tar.gz`, the latest source as of this writing. Make sure you replace version information when completing the following instructions.

1. Extract the Sendmail source distribution using the `tar xvzf sendmail.8.11.0.tar.gz` command. This creates a subdirectory called `sendmail-8.11.0`. Change to this subdirectory.

2. Run the following commands to extract and install the Sendmail configuration files in the appropriate directories.

   ```
   mkdir -p /etc/mail
   cp etc.mail.tar.gz /etc/mail
   cp site.config.m4 sendmail-8.11.0/devtools/Site/
   cp sendmail.init /etc/rc.d/init.d/sendmail
   ```

3. Follow the instructions in the `INSTALL` file and build Sendmail as instructed.

4. Add the following lines in the `/usr/src/redhat/SOURCES/sendmail-8.11.0/devtools/Site/site.config.m4` file.

   ```
   APPENDDEF(`confENVDEF', `-DSASL')
   APPENDDEF(`conf_sendmail_LIBS', `-lsasl')
   APPENDDEF(`confLIBDIRS', `-L/usr/local/lib/sasl')
   APPENDDEF(`confINCDIRS', `-I/usr/local/include')
   ```

5. The `sendmail-8.11.0/devtools/Site/configu.m4` file is shown in Listing 17-3.

Listing 17-3: define(`confDEPEND_TYPE', `CC-M')

```
define(`confEBINDIR', `/usr/sbin')
define(`confFORCE_RMAIL')
define(`confLIBS', `-ldl')
define(`confLDOPTS_SO', `-shared')
define(`confMANROOT', `/usr/man/man')
define(`confMAPDEF',`-DNEWDB -DMAP_REGEX -DNIS -DTCP_WRAPPERS')
define(`confMTLDOPTS', `-lpthread')
define(`confOPTIMIZE',`${RPM_OPT_FLAGS}')
define(`confSTDIR', `/var/log')
APPENDDEF(`confLIBSEARCH', `crypt nsl wrap')
```

```
APPENDDEF(`confENVDEF', `-DSASL')
APPENDDEF(`conf_sendmail_LIBS', `-lsasl')
APPENDDEF(`confLIBDIRS', `-L/usr/local/lib/sasl')
APPENDDEF(`confINCDIRS', `-I/usr/local/include')
```

6. Change the directory to /usr/src/redhat/SOURCES/sendmail-
   8.11.0/sendmail and run the su Build -c command to rebuild
   Sendmail.

7. Run the sh Build install command to install the new Sendmail
   binaries.

8. Run the /usr/sbin/sendmail -d0.1 -bv root command to check
   whether you have SASL support built into your new Sendmail configuration. You should see output like the following:

```
Version 8.11.0
 Compiled with: MAP_REGEX LOG MATCHGECOS MIME7TO8 MIME8TO7
NAMED_BIND NETINET NETUNIX NEWDB NIS QUEUE SASL SCANF SMTP
USERDB XDEBUG
============ SYSTEM IDENTITY (after readcf) ============
      (short domain name) $w = 172
  (canonical domain name) $j = 172.20.15.1
         (subdomain name) $m = 20.15.1
              (node name) $k = 172.20.15.1
```

   As shown in bold, SASL is listed in the preceding output.

9. Run /usr/sbin/saslpasswd *username* to create the /etc/sasldb.db
   password file.

10. Run the /etc/rc.d/init.d/sendmail start command to start the
    Sendmail daemon.

11. Run the telnet localhost 25 command to connect to your newly com-
    piled Sendmail service. When connected enter the EHLO localhost com-
    mand. This displays output like the following.

```
220 209.63.178.15 ESMTP Sendmail 8.11.0/8.11.0; Sun, 31 Dec
2000 05:37:58 -0500
EHLO localhost
250-209.63.178.15 Hello root@localhost, pleased to meet you
250-ENHANCEDSTATUSCODES
250-8BITMIME
250-SIZE
250-DSN
```

```
250-ONEX
250-XUSR
250-AUTH DIGEST-MD5 CRAM-MD5
250 HELP
```

As shown, the newly built Sendmail now supports the SMTP AUTH command and offers DIGEST-MD5 CRAM-MD5 as an authentication mechanism.

The SMTP AUTH allows relaying for senders who successfully authenticate themselves. Such SMTP clients as Netscape Messenger and Microsoft Outlook can use SMTP authentication via SASL.

Sanitizing incoming e-mail using procmail

Most e-mail security incidents occur because users can attach all types of files to the messages. Attachments and embedded scripts are primary vehicles for such attacks as e-mail viruses and malicious macros. A filtering tool called procmail can help.

procmail can scan headers and the body of each message for patterns based on custom rules. It can take action when a certain rule matches. Here I show you how you can sanitize incoming e-mails using a procmail-based rule set.

You can download the procmail rule set (procmail-sanitizer.tar.gz) from www.impsec.org/email-tools/procmail-security.html.

Make sure that you have the following lines in your m4 macro file. (they generate the /etc/mail/sendmail.cf file):

```
FEATURE(local_procmail)dnl
MAILER(procmail)dnl
```

For reliable performance, take the following two measures:

◆ Install procmail from either

  ■ An RPM distribution on your Red Hat CD-ROM.

  ■ An RPM mirror site, such as http://www.rpmfind.net.

◆ Install the latest version of Perl on your system.

ESTABLISHING THE SANITIZER

Here's how you can set up the rule set for local delivery.

1. su to root.

2. Run the mkdir /etc/procmail command to create a subdirectory in /etc.

3. Run the chown -R root:root /etc/procmail command to change the ownership of the directory to root.

4. Copy the procmail-sanitizer.tar.gz file in /etc/procmail and extract it using the tar xvzf procmail-sanitizer.tar.gz command.

5. Create an /etc/procmailrc file as shown in Listing 17-4.

Listing 17-4: /etc/procmailrc

```
LOGFILE=$HOME/procmail.log
PATH="/usr/bin:$PATH:/usr/local/bin"
SHELL=/bin/sh
POISONED_EXECUTABLES=/etc/procmail/poisoned
SECURITY_NOTIFY="postmaster, security-dude"
SECURITY_NOTIFY_VERBOSE="virus-checker"
SECURITY_NOTIFY_SENDER=/etc/procmail/local-email-security-
policy.txt
SECRET="CHANGE THIS"
# this file must already exist, with
# proper permissions (rw--w--w-):
SECURITY_QUARANTINE=/var/spool/mail/quarantine
POISONED_SCORE=25
SCORE_HISTORY=/var/log/macro-scanner-scores
# Finished setting up, now run the sanitizer...
INCLUDERC=/etc/procmail/html-trap.procmail
# Reset some things to avoid leaking info to
# the users...
POISONED_EXECUTABLES=
SECURITY_NOTIFY=
SECURITY_NOTIFY_VERBOSE=
SECURITY_NOTIFY_SENDER=
SECURITY_QUARANTINE=
SECRET=
```

6. Run the touch /var/spool/mail/quarantine command to create the file. This file stores poisoned messages.

7. Run the touch /var/log/macro-scanner-scores command to create the file. This file stores historical scores for macros.

8. Change the permission for the /var/spool/mail/quarantine file using the chmod 622 /var/spool/mail/quarantine command.

The /etc/procmailrc file sets a number of control (environment) variables used to control the sanitizer and runs the sanitizer using the INCLUDERC setting. This resets the environment variables such that a user can't view the values of these variables by running setenv or set commands — a safer arrangement. These control variables are

◆ LOGFILE

Specifies the fully qualified path of the log. The default value allows the sanitizer to create a log file called procmail.log in a user's home directory.

The default value is $HOME/procmail.log.

◆ POISONED_EXECUTABLES

Specifies a fully qualified path of a filename, which lists the filenames and/or file extensions (with wild cards) that are considered poisoned if sent via attachment.

The default file contains a list of widely known poisoned attachment filenames. When a new poison attachment file name is released in public by CERT (or another security authority), add the name in this file.

The default value is /etc/procmail/poisoned.

◆ SECURITY_NOTIFY

Specifies a comma-separated list of e-mail addresses of people who should be notified when a poisoned e-mail is trapped by the sanitizer.

Only the header part of the trapped message goes to the e-mail list.

The default values are postmaster, security-dude.

◆ SECURITY_NOTIFY_VERBOSE

Specifies a comma-separated list of e-mail addresses of people who should be notified when a poisoned e-mail is trapped by the sanitizer.

In contrast to the SECURITY_NOTIFY variable, the trapped e-mail goes in its entirety to this list.

The default value is `virus-checker`.

◆ `SECURITY_NOTIFY_SENDER`

Specifies a filename whose contents are e-mailed to the sender of a poi-soned message. If the variable is a nonexistent file, a built-in message is sent instead.

 For this variable to take effect, the `SECURITY_NOTIFY` variable must be set to at least one e-mail address.

The default value is `/etc/procmail/local-email-security-policy.txt`.

◆ `SECURITY_NOTIFY_SENDER_POSTMASTER`

When set to a value such as `YES`, an e-mail goes to the violator's postmas-ter address.

◆ `SECURITY_NOTIFY_RECIPIENT`

When set to a filename, the intended recipient receives the contents of the file as a notice stating that an offending e-mail has been quarantined.

◆ `SECRET`

Specifies a random set of characters that are used internally to make it hard for a vandal to bypass the sanitizer rule set. Change the default to something in the 10- to 20-character range.

The default value is `CHANGE THIS`.

◆ `SECURITY_QUARANTINE`

Specifies the path of the file that quarantines the poisoned attachment.

The default value is `/var/spool/mail/quarantine`.

◆ `SECURITY_QUARANTINE_OPTIONAL`

■ When set to `YES`, a poisoned message is still sent to the intended recipient.

■ When set to `NO`, it is bounced.

◆ `POISONED_SCORE`

Specifies the *score* at which the sanitizer considers embedded Microsoft Office-related macros (found in such applications as Word and Excel) poisoned.

The sanitizer looks at the embedded macro and tries to match macro fragments with known poisoned macro-fragment code. As it finds questionable macro fragments, it keeps a growing score. When the score reaches the value specified by the variable, the macro is considered dangerous (that is, poisoned).

The default value is 25.

◆ MANGLE_EXTENSIONS

Contains a list of filename extensions to mangle and possibly poison. The built-in list of extensions should be sufficient for most installations.

◆ DISABLE_MACRO_CHECK

Disables scanning of Microsoft Office file attachments for dangerous macros.

■ The sanitizer contains a rudimentary scanner that checks Microsoft Office document attachments (such as Word documents, Excel spreadsheets, and PowerPoint presentations) for embedded Visual Basic Application (VBA) macros that appear to be modifying security settings, changing the Registry, or writing macros to the Standard Document template.

■ Documents are scanned for macros even if their extensions don't appear in the MANGLE_EXTENSIONS list. This means you can remove .doc and .xls extensions from the MANGLE_EXTENSIONS list to make your users happy, but still be protected by the scanner against macro-based attacks.

◆ SCORE_HISTORY

If you want to keep a history of macro scores for profiling to see whether your POISONED_SCORE is a reasonable value, set SCORE_HISTORY to the name of a file. The score of each scanned document is saved to this file.

The default value is /var/log/macro-scanner-scores.

◆ SCORE_ONLY

When this variable is set to YES, the sanitizer doesn't act when it detects a macro.

◆ SECURITY_STRIP_MSTNEF

Microsoft Outlook and Exchange support sending e-mail using a format called Outlook Rich Text. Among other things, this has the effect of bundling all file attachments, as well as other data, into a proprietary Microsoft-format attachment, usually with the name winmail.dat. This format is called *MS-TNEF* and isn't generally understandable by non-Microsoft mail programs.

- MS-TNEF attachments can't be scanned or sanitized and may contain hazardous content that the sanitizer can't detect. Microsoft recommends that MS-TNEF attachments are used only within your intranet, not the Internet.

- If you set `SECURITY_STRIP_MSTNEF` to any value, these attachments are stripped off the message, and it is delivered to the intended recipient with a notice that this happened. The message isn't poisoned.

◆ `DEFANG_WEBBUGS`

Disables inline images.

Web bugs are small images (typically only one pixel in size) that track an e-mail message. Identifying information is included in the image URL, and when an HTML-enabled mail program attempts to display the message, the location of the message can be tracked and logged. If you consider this a violation of your privacy, you can set `DEFANG_WEBBUGS` to any value, and the sanitizer mangles the image tag. You can still retrieve the URL from the message and decide whether to view the image.

◆ `SECURITY_TRUST_STYLE_TAGS`

Disables `<STYLE>` tag defanging.

- `<STYLE>` tags allow the author fine control over the appearance of the HTML content when it's displayed. It's used extensively by HTML-enabled mail programs, but it can be an attack vector – exploited by supplying scripting commands instead of appearance settings.

- By default, the sanitizer defangs `<STYLE>` tags, but this may leave an extra HTML end-comment tag (`-->1`) visible in the body of the message. You may want to trust `<STYLE>` tags on internally generated mail but defang them in mail received from the Internet.

◆ `DEBUG`

Enables output of some debugging information from the sanitizer.

◆ `DEBUG_VERBOSE`

Turns on verbose debugging of the sanitizer.

When the sanitizer runs, it creates a log file (default filename is `procmail.log` – set using the `LOGFILE` variable) that should be periodically reviewed and removed by the user. When attachments are poisoned, they are kept in a mailbox file called `/var/spool/mail/quarantine` (set by the `SECURITY_QUARANTINE` variable). You can the unmangle attachments fairly easily. For example, you can designate a workstation where you download mangled files from the quarantine mailbox, then disconnect the network cable before renaming and reading the emails with potentially dangerous attachments.

TREATING LOCAL MAIL DIFFERENTLY

The basic setup discussed here so far treats all mail equally, which isn't always what you want. For example, when user joe@yourdomain.com sends an e-mail with a Word or Excel attachment to jennifer@yourdomain.com, the attachment gets mangled and it probably shouldn't. Probably these two local users use virus-checking software and don't plan to harm each other. Don't mangle common document formats (such as Word and Excel) when the e-mail is initiated from within your own user domain. Just modify the /etc/procmailrc file like this:

1. Add the following lines before the INCLUDERC line in /etc/procmailrc.

```
:0
* ^From:.*<[a-z0-9]+@yourdomain.com>
* ^To:.*<[a-z0-9]+@yourdomain.com>
{
MANGLE_EXTENSIONS='html?|exe|com|cmd|bat|pif|sc[rt]|lnk|dll|o
cx|dot|xl[wt]|p[po]t|rtf|vb[se]?|hta|p[lm]|sh[bs]|hlp|chm|eml
|ws[cfh]|ad[ep]|jse?|md[abew]|ms[ip]|reg|asd|cil|pps|asx|wm[s
zd]' }
```

Enter the MANGLE_EXTENSIONS line in one line. Replace *yourdomain.com* with your domain name.

2. Save the file.

From now on, when MAIL FROM is set to user@yourdomain.com, **Word** (.doc) and Excel (.xls) attachments aren't mangled.

UNMANGLING ATTACHMENTS

To unmangle an attachment from the /var/spool/mail/quarantine mailbox file, do the following:

1. Edit the /var/spool/mail/quarantine file and locate the attachment.

2. You see that the sanitizer has added a set of Content-Type and Content-Security headers, followed by a security warning message just before the actual attachment data. Listing 17-5 shows an example of a poisoned (quarantined) attachment in this state.

Listing 17-5: Sample poisoned attachment segment

```
------=_NextPart_000_0027_01BF26F5.91230E60_
Content-Type: TEXT/PLAIN;
X-Content-Security: NOTIFY
X-Content-Security: REPORT: Trapped poisoned executable "cool.exe"
X-Content-Security: QUARANTINE
Content-Description: SECURITY WARNING
SECURITY WARNING!
The mail system has detected that the following
attachment may contain hazardous executable code,
is a suspicious file type or has a suspicious file name.
Contact your system administrator immediately!
Content-Type: application/octet-stream; name="cool.16920DEFANGED-
exe"
Content-Transfer-Encoding: base64
DxTaDxTaDxTaDxTaDxTaDxTaDxTaDxTaDxTaDxTaDxTaDxTaDxTaDxTaM
NATaNATaNATaNATaNATaNATaNATaNATaNATaNATaNATaNATaNATaNATaM
```

3. Now, locate the original Content-Type header, which usually has a value such as application/*something* (application/octet-stream in the preceding example).

4. Place the MIME boundary marker string (shown in bold in the preceding listing) just in front of the original Content-Type header. Remove everything above the marker string so that you end up with something like the Listing 17-6.

Listing 17-6: Sample of unmangled attachment segment

```
------=_NextPart_000_0027_01BF26F5.91230E60_
Content-Type: application/octet-stream; name="cool.16920DEFANGED-
exe"
Content-Transfer-Encoding: base64
DxTaDxTaDxTaDxTaDxTaDxTaDxTaDxTaDxTaDxTaDxTaDxTaDxTaDxTaM
NATaNATaNATaNATaNATaNATaNATaNATaNATaNATaNATaNATaNATaNATaM
```

5. Save the file; then load it (using a mail-user agent like Pine) and send it to the intended user.

The user still must rename the file because it is mangled. In the preceding example, the original filename was cool.exe, which was renamed to cool.16920DEFANGED-exe. The user must rename this file to cool.exe by removing the 16920DEFANGED string from the middle. If you change this in the Content-Type header during the previous step, the sanitizer catches it and quarantines it again. So let the user rename it, which is much safer because she can run her own virus checks on the attachment once she has saved the file to her system's hard drive.

Now you have a reasonably good tool for handling inbound attachments before they cause any real harm. Inbound mail is just half of the equation, though. When you send outbound e-mail from your network, make sure you and your users take all the necessary steps, such as virus-checking attachments and disabling potential embedded macros. Another helpful tool is the zip file. Compressing files and sending them in a zip file is better than sending them individually, because the zip file isn't executable and it gives the receiving end a chance to save and scan for viruses.

Outbound-only Sendmail

Often a Linux system is needed for sending outbound messages but not for receiving inbound mail. For example, machines designated as monitoring stations (which have no users receiving e-mail) have such a need. To meet it, you have to alter the standard Sendmail installation (which normally keeps the inbound door open).

Typically, Sendmail is run using the `/etc/rc.d/init.d/sendmail` script at start-up. This script starts the `sendmail` daemon using a command line such as:

```
/usr/sbin/sendmail -bd -q10m
```

Here the `-bd` option specifies that Sendmail run in the background in daemon mode (listening for a connection on port 25). The `-q10m` option specifies that the queue be run every ten minutes. This is fine for a full-blown Sendmail installation in which inbound and outbound e-mail are expected. In outbound-only mode, the `-bd` option isn't needed. Simply run Sendmail using `xinetd`. Here's how.

1. `su` to `root`.

2. Force Sendmail to run whenever a request to port 25 is detected.

   Do this by making `xinetd` listen for the connection and start a Sendmail daemon when one is detected. So create a `xinetd` configuration file called `/etc/xinetd.d/sendmail` for Sendmail, as shown following.

   ```
   service smtp
   {
           socket_type        = stream
           wait               = no
           user               = root
           server             = /usr/sbin/sendmail
           server_args        = -bs
           log_on_success     += DURATION USERID
           log_on_failure     += USERID
   ```

```
nice           = 10
disable        = no
only_from      = localhost
}
```

3. Run the queue every ten minutes so that outgoing mail is attempted for delivery six times per hour. For this, add a line in the /etc/crontab file as shown next:

```
10 * * * * /usr/sbin/sendmail -q
```

The only_from directive in the xinetd configuration file for Sendmail is set to localhost, which effectively tells xinetd not to start the Sendmail daemon for any request other than the local ones. The cron entry in /etc/crontab ensures that the mail submitted to the queue gets out.

Here xinetd helps us restrict access to the mail service from outside. But bear in mind that running Sendmail via xinetd requires that every time a new SMTP request is made, the xinetd daemon starts a Sendmail process. This can consume resources if you are planning to have a lot of STMP connections open simultaneously.

Running Sendmail without root privileges

If your site receives on an average a few hundred messages per hour, you are running a small mail server and should be fine using xinetd-based SMTP service. In fact, you can even enhance Sendmail security using xinetd by running it as a non-root process. Here I discuss how you can run Sendmail as a non-root user.

By default, the Sendmail daemon (sendmail) runs as a set-UID root process. This means that the root account can be compromised via Sendmail if the Sendmail daemon can be attacked with a buffer overflow attack or another innovative Sendmail exploit.

By running Sendmail as a xinetd-run SMTP service, you can demote it to an ordinary user. Here's how.

1. su to root.

2. Create a user called mail using the useradd mail -s /bin/false command.

3. Run the following commands to change permissions on files and directories used by Sendmail.

```
chown root:mail /var/spool/mail
chmod 1775 /var/spool/mail
chown -R :mail /var/spool/mail/*
chmod -R 660 /var/spool/mail/*
chown mail:mail /usr/sbin/sendmail
```

```
chmod 6555 /usr/sbin/sendmail
chown mail /var/spool/mqueue/*
chown -R mail:mail /etc/mail
chmod -R 664 /etc/mail
```

4. Create an /etc/xinetd.d/sendmail file like this:

```
service smtp
{
        socket_type         = stream
        wait                = no
        user                = mail
        group               = mail
        server              = /usr/sbin/sendmail
        server_args         = -bs
        log_on_success     += DURATION USERID
        log_on_failure     += USERID
        nice                = 10
        disable             = no
}
```

5. Modify the /etc/crontab file to have an entry like this:

```
10 * * * * mail /usr/sbin/sendmail -q
```

6. Modify the site.config.m4 file in your Sendmail distribution to include the following lines:

```
define(`confTEMP_FILE_MODE', `0660')dnl
define(`ALIAS_FILE', `/etc/mail/aliases')
```

7. Terminate the Sendmail daemon if it's currently running by the /etc/rc.d/init.d/sendmail stop or killall sendmail commands.

8. Restart xinetd using the killall -USR1 xinetd command.

9. Connect to Sendmail using the telnet localhost 25 command.

10. On another login session, run the ps aux | grep sendmail command to check whether Sendmail is running as the ordinary mail user. Here is sample output for this command:

```
mail 25274 0.0 0.7 4048 1808 ?     SN 04:11  0:00 sendmail:
server
root 25294 0.0 0.2 1520  592 ttyp0  S  04:15  0:00 grep
sendmail
```

As shown, Sendmail is run as the mail user. You can enter quit to exit the Telnet session to port 25. Now you have a Sendmail server that runs as an ordinary user.

Securing Postfix

As the new kid on the MTA block, Postfix has the luxury of built-in security features. It's a suite of programs instead of a single binary server like Sendmail.

Keeping out spam

Postfix offers a number of `main.cf` configuration options that can tackle spam.

FILTERING E-MAIL USING HEADER INFORMATION

You can use the standard e-mail headers such as `To:`, `From:`, `Subject:`, and `X-Mailer` to reject e-mail. For example, you can have the following configuration in `main.cf` file.

```
header_checks = regexp:/etc/postfix/reject-headers
```

It tells Postfix to read a file called `/etc/postfix/reject-headers`, which contains lines that have the following syntax:

```
regexp    REJECT
```

The left side (`regexp`) is basic regular expression. Here's an example of the `/etc/postfix/reject-headers` file:

```
/^To:   *you@xoom\.com$/              REJECT
/^From: mailer-daemon@myclient\.com$/ REJECT
/^Subject: Make money fast/           REJECT
```

All e-mail sent received with To: header containing at least the `you@xoom.com` string is rejected. Similarly, all e-mail sent from an account called `mailer-daemon@myclient.com` is rejected. The third regular expression states that any e-mail with the subject "`Make money fast`" is rejected.

You can also use *Perl-compatible regular expressions* (*PCREs*) for more advanced matches. For a file containing PCREs instead of basic regular expressions, simply use the following configuration in the `main.cf` file.

```
header_checks = pcre:/etc/postfix/reject-headers
```

 TIP PCRE statements can be complex. See Perl regular expression documentation for details.

REJECTING E-MAIL USING IP OR HOSTNAME

Often, an offending IP address or host must be blocked from using your email server. Here is how you can deny everyone but your computers:

1. In the `main.cf` configuration file, define your network addresses using the following line:

```
mynetworks = 192.168.1.0/24
```

2. To block access to your mail server by any host other than the ones in your network, add:

```
smtpd_client_restrictions = permit_mynetworks,\
                            reject_unknown_client
```

You can also use an access map file to reject or allow a single host or IP address. Here is how:

1. To use the access map for this purpose, add the following line:

```
smtpd_client_restrictions = hash:/etc/postfix/access
```

2. In the `/etc/postfix/access` file, you can add lines such as

```
Spammer-domain.com      REJECT
shannon.herisp.com      OK
herisp.com              REJECT
```

In the preceding code

- The first sample line in the access map states that all mail from a domain called `spammer-domain.com` should be rejected.

- The second line tells Postfix to allow connection from the `shannon.herisp.com` host but reject all other hosts in the `herisp.com` domain.

USING MAPS RBL

To use the MAPS RBL support you must define the following:

```
maps_rbl_domains = mail-abuse.org
smtpd_client_restrictions = reject_maps_rbl
```

The first line sets the hosts that need to be contacted to get the RBL list and the second line sets the restrictions that need to be applied.

Hiding internal e-mail addresses by masquerading

If you have a central mail server for outgoing mail on the network that services many hosts, there is a good chance that you must hide the hostname part of the e-mail address in the header. For example, if you have a user called joe on a host called pc-joe.yourcompany.com, when joe sends e-mail via the Postfix e-mail gateway machine, his address appears as joe@pc-joe.yourcompany.com. Not letting others know about your internal hostnames is a good security measure. You can enable the following options in main.cf.

```
masquerade_domains = $mydomain
masquerade_exceptions = root
```

In the preceding code

◆ The first line tells Postfix to enable address masquerading for your domain, set by the $mydomain variable.

This means joe@pc-joe.yourcompany.com appears as joe@yourcompany.com.

◆ The second line tells Postfix to leave the root user alone.

This means Sendmail doesn't masquerade for root.

Summary

An unprotected mail server is often an open mail relay, which allows spammers to send emails to people who do not want them. Such an abuse can waste resources and cause legal problems for companies that leave their email system open to such attacks. By controlling which hosts your mail server allows mail relay services, enabling the RBL rules, sanitizing incoming emails using procmail, and running Sendmail without root privileges, you can ensure the safety of your email service.

Chapter 18

FTP Server Security

IN THIS CHAPTER

- ◆ Securing WU-FTPD

- ◆ Restricting FTP access by username

- ◆ Building a chroot jail for FTP access

- ◆ Restricting access to sensitive files and directories

- ◆ Restricting upload privileges for anonymous FTP sites

- ◆ Using and securing ProFTPD

- ◆ Using PAM for ProFTPD authentication

- ◆ Creating a minimal anonymous FTP site

- ◆ Using Linux Capabilities with ProFTPD

AN FTP SERVER CAN be an important part of your Internet presence. Unfortunately, FTP servers have many security risks. Some of these risks depend on the server software; others are because of inappropriate server configuration. In this chapter you secure two widely used FTP servers: WU-FTPD and ProFTPD. I also show you how to control user access by using configuration options and directives provided by these FTP servers, create chroot jails to isolate FTP users into their own directory structure, and create anonymous FTP sites with security in mind.

Securing WU-FTPD

WU-FTPD is the default FTP server for Red Hat Linux. It's one of the most widely used FTP server packages. Recently, WU-FTPD (versions earlier than 2.6.1) was in the spotlight for security issues. However, all the known security holes have been patched in Red Hat Linux 7. Downloading the latest WU-FTPD source RPM package from an RPM finder site, such as http://www.rpmfind.net, and installing it as follows enhances security of your FTP service. The latest stable version is always the best candidate for a new FTP server installation.

1. Download the latest source RPM distribution.

2. Extract the source tar ball from the RPM package by using the `rpm -ivh filename` command, where `filename` is the name of the source RPM file (for example, `wu-ftpd-2.6.1.src.rpm`) in the `/usr/src/redhat/SOURCES` directory. You should now have a file called `wu-ftpd-version.tar.gz` (for example, `wu-ftpd-2.6.1.tar.gz`) in the `/usr/src/redhat/SOURCES` directory. Change your current directory to this directory.

3. Extract the `.tar` file by using the `tar xvzf filename` command.

   The file extracts itself to a new subdirectory named after the filename (with the filename in Step 2, for example, the directory would be named `wu-ftpd-2.6.1`).

4. Using the `cd directory_name` command, switch to the new subdirectory created in Step 3.

5. Consider using the security-related command-line options for the `configure` script, which I describe in Table 18-1. To do so, run the `./configure --option1 --option2` command, where `--option1` is the first option to use; `option2` is the second option and so on; you can have as many options as you want).

   For example, if you simply want to configure `WU-FTPD` with the `--enable-paranoid` option (yes, it's a real option), run the `./configure --enable-paranoid` command.

6. After you configure the source, install the binaries by running the `make` and `make install` commands.

TABLE 18-1: SECURITY-SPECIFIC COMMAND LINE OPTIONS FOR THE CONFIGURE SCRIPT

Option	What It Does	Why Use It?
`--enable-paranoid`	Enables paranoid mode, which disables features that are considered potential security risks, such as the nonstandard SITE commands, file-overwriting, and deletion.	This is the most restrictive way of running an FTP server, because users can't overwrite or delete any files.
`--disable-upload`	Disables the file-upload feature.	If you are sure that you don't need file uploads to the FTP server, this option is appropriate.

Option	What It Does	Why Use It?
--disable-overwrite	Disables the file-overwrite feature.	Using this option may make the FTP experience painful for your users, but it may be suitable for environments in which users are told that they can upload but not overwrite what they have uploaded.
--disable-anonymous	Disables the anonymous FTP server feature.	Unless you absolutely must run an anonymous FTP server, use this option. If you have only a few small files to offer, consider offering the files via your Web server.
--disable-virtual	Disables virtual FTP site support.	Virtual FTP service should be used only by organizations or ISPs that must provide a separate "virtual" FTP area for clients.
--disable-private	Disables the SITE GROUP and SITE GPASS commands that allow an already logged in FTP user to escalate his or her group privileges.	Allowing a user to change privilege level in an FTP session increases the risk of abuse. So consider using this option.

Restricting FTP access by username

The WU-FTPD server is a PAM-aware FTP service (see Chapter 10 for details on PAM). This means whenever a user connects to the FTP server, the authentication process is handled by PAM using the /etc/pam.d/ftp file. This file is shown in Listing 18-1.

Listing 18-1: /etc/pam.d/ftp

```
auth       required    /lib/security/pam_listfile.so item=user \
                   sense=deny file=/etc/ftpusers onerr=succeed
auth       required    /lib/security/pam_stack.so service=system-auth
auth       required    /lib/security/pam_shells.so
account    required    /lib/security/pam_stack.so service=system-auth
session    required    /lib/security/pam_stack.so service=system-auth
```

The first line in Listing 18-1 instructs PAM to load the `pam_listfile` module and read the `/etc/ftpusers` file. If the `/etc/ftpusers` file contains a line matching the username given at the FTP authentication, PAM uses the *sense* argument to determine how to handle the user's access request. Because this argument is set to deny, the user is denied access if the username is found in the `/etc/ftpusers` file.

DENYING A USER FTP ACCESS

To deny a particular user FTP access to your server, simply append the username in the `/etc/ftpusers` file. If a user to whom you've denied access tries to access the FTP server, the `/var/log/messages` file spits out error messages like the following:

```
Dec 12 15:21:16 k2 ftpd[1744]: PAM-listfile: Refused user kabir for service ftp
```

ALLOWING FTP ACCESS FOR A SELECT GROUP OF USERS

Instead of keeping a list of all the users that are denied access explicitly in `/etc/ftpusers`, you may want to consider denying access to everyone except certain users that are listed in a specific file. This method is preferred because it follows the well-known grand security scheme of denying everyone by default and allowing only those you must. This approach is superior to listing all the bad users in `/etc/ftpaccess`, because you can forget to include someone. Instead, you can turn this around and store only the authorized FTP usernames in `/etc/ftpaccess`. This way, everyone not mentioned in this file is denied by default. Here's how to implement this scheme:

1. Place a `#` in front of the `pam_listfile` line (the first line shown in Listing 18-1) in your `/etc/pam.d/ftp` configuration file. Doing so comments out the configuration.

2. Add the following configuration line as the first line in the file.

   ```
   auth required /lib/security/pam_listfile.so item=user \
   sense=allow file=/etc/userlist.ftp onerr=fail
   ```

3. Create a file called `/etc/userlist.ftp` that contains one username per line. Only the users named in this file have FTP access.

Run the `awk -F: '{print $1}' /etc/passwd > /etc/userlist.ftp` command if you want to create an initial version of the `/etc/userlist.ftp` file from the `/etc/passwd` file, which you can later edit to remove all users that you don't want to give FTP access.

Don't allow the `root` user or anyone in the `wheel` group to access your FTP server.

Setting default file permissions for FTP

In a multiuser environment, files created by one user may become accessible by another user if the permission settings are open. Setting default file permission is very handy for systems that act as Web and FTP servers for many different clients. If many of your users transfer their files on the FTP server, you can control the default `umask` for the FTP server so that one user's file isn't accessible by another.

You can learn about `umask` and file permissions in detail in Chapter 9.

For example, if you want permissions so only the user who created a particular file and his group can read the file uploaded on an FTP server, you can modify the `server_args` line in the `/etc/xinetd.d/wu-ftpd` file. By default, this line looks like

```
server_args          = -l -a
```

The following steps set a default `umask` for all files uploaded via FTP.

1. Add a `-u` argument with the appropriate `umask` value to the `-server_args` line. For example, to set the `640` (`rw- r-- ---`) permission for each file uploaded, you can set the `umask` value to `026` by changing the `-server_args` line like this:

   ```
   server_args              = -l -a -u026
   ```

2. Restart the `xinetd` server (`killall -USR1 xinetd`) and FTP a file via a user account to check whether the permissions are set as expected.

3. To disallow one client from seeing another client's files, use the `-u` option along with a special ownership setting. For example, say that you keep all your Web client files in the `/www` directory, where each client site has a subdirectory of its own (for example, `/www/myclient1`, `/www/myclient2`, and so on), and each client has an FTP account to upload files in these directories. To stop a client from seeing another's files:

- Use the -u option with the FTP server as described above.

- Reset the ownership of each client site like this:

  ```
  chown -R client:Web_server_user   /www/client_directory
  ```

If you run a Web server called httpd and have a client user called myclient1, then the command you use should look like this:

```
chown -R myclient1:httpd /www/myclient1
```

This command changes the ownership of the /www/myclient1 directory, along with all its subdirectories and files, to user myclient1 in group httpd. Doing so allows the user to

- Own, modify, and delete his or her files.

- Allow the Web server to read the files in the directory.

4. To disallow everyone else, change the permissions like this:

```
chmod -R 2750   /www/client_directory
```

For the current example, the actual command is

```
chmod -R 2750   /www/myclient1
```

This command sets all the files and subdirectory permissions for /www/myclient1 to 2750, which allows the files and directories to be readable, writable, and executable by the owner (myclient1) and only readable and executable by the Web server user (httpd). The set-GID value (2) in the preceding command ensures that when new files are created, their permissions allow the Web server user to read the file.

Using a chroot jail for FTP sessions

Typically, an ordinary user who logs in via an FTP connection can browse more files and directories than those he or she owns. This is because an FTP session is usually not restricted to a certain directory; a user can change directories and view files in /usr or / or /tmp or many other system-specific directories. Why is that so bad? Well, suppose this user is a bad guy who manages to get in via FTP – and now he can view the binaries you have on the system, possibly getting a close look at how you run your system. Suppose he decides to browse the /etc directory and download important configuration files. Not a happy thought, right? With WU-FTPD you can plug that hole by using a *chroot jail*.

BUILDING A CHROOT JAIL

A chroot jail limits what a user can see when he or she connects to your FTP server; it shows only a certain part of your filesystem. Typically, a chroot jail restricts a user's access to the home directory. To create a `chroot` jail, follow these steps.

1. Install the anonymous FTP RPM package from your Red Hat Linux CD-ROM or by downloading the `anon-ftp-version.rpm` package (for example, `anonftp-3.0-9.i386.rpm`) from an RPM-finder Web site such as `www.rpmfind.net`.

2. Install the package using the `rpm -ivh anon-ftp-version.rpm` command.

3. Run the `cp -r /home/ftp  /home/chroot` command. This copies everything from the home directory of the FTP user to `/home/chroot`. The files in `/home/chroot` are needed for a minimal execution environment for `chrooted` FTP sessions. After that, you can run the `rpm -e anon-ftp-version` command to delete the now-unneeded anonymous FTP package.

4. Install the `chrootusers.pl` script that you can find on the CD that came with this book (see the CD Appendix for info on where to find the script).

5. Run the `chmod 700 /usr/local/bin/chrootusers.pl` command to make sure the script can be run only by the `root` user.

6. Create a new group called `ftpusers` in the `/etc/group` file by using the `groupadd ftpusers` command.

7. Add a new line such as the following to the `/etc/ftpaccess` file.

   `guestgroup ftpusers`

8. You add users to your new `chroot` jail by running the `chrootusers.pl` script. If you run this script without any argument, you see the following output that shows all the options the script can use.

```
chrootusers.pl --start-uid=number --end-uid=number --chroot-group=group
              --update-ok
--start-uid=number where number is the starting UID value.
--end-uid=number where number is the ending UID value.
All the users with the UID in the starting and ending UID range
will be added (if update-ok is supplied).
--chroot-group=group specifies the name of the user group
where to add the users in the specfied range.
--update-ok specifies that this script should make the necessary
updates to /etc/group and /etc/passwd. By default, chrootusers.pl simply
writes a sh script in /tmp/chrootusers.pl.sh, which can be reviewed and run
by the super user using  the sh /tmp/chrootusers.pl.sh command.
```

As shown in the preceding output, the `--start-uid` and `--end-uid` options specify a range of user IDs; `--chroot-group` specifies the name of the group in `/etc/group`, and `--update-ok` commits all necessary changes to the `/etc/group` and `/etc/passwd` files. If you don't use `--update-ok`, the script writes a small `sh` shell script called `/tmp/chrootusers.pl.sh`, which you can review and run.

USING A UID RANGE TO THROW MULTIPLE USERS IN A CHROOT JAIL

The `chrootusers.pl` script makes it easy to add users (within a UID range) to `chroot` jails. Instead of typing many sensitive (and easily botched) commands repeatedly for each user that you want to place in `chroot` jail, you can use a simple script – which should reduce human error.

To configure each user account in a certain range of UIDs, run the `chrootusers.pl` script with the following command:

```
/usr/local/bin/chrootusers.pl --start-uid=lowest_ID --end-uid=highest_ID --chroot-group=ftpusers
```

In this command, *lowest_ID* is the lowest user ID number in the desired range, and *highest_ID* is the highest user ID number in the desired range. For example, if you want to configure each user account with UIDs between 100 and 999, *lowest_ID* is 100 and *highest_ID* is 999. If you run this command with `--start-uid=100` and `--end-uid=999`, it displays the following output:

```
Review the /tmp/chrootusers.pl.sh script.
```

If everything looks good run it as follows:

```
sh /tmp/chrootusers.pl.sh
```

If you choose, you can review the `/tmp/chrootusers.pl.sh` script using the `more /tmp/chrootusers.pl.sh` command or a text editor. Whether you review the file or not, finish by running the `sh /tmp/chrootusers.pl.sh` command to create the `chroot` jails for the users within the specified UID range.

WATCHING CHROOTUSERS.PL CREATE CHROOT JAILS

If you must know how the `chrootusers.pl` script works, this section is for you. In the following example, I configure each user account whose UID ranges between 100 and 999. If you have more than one user who falls under the range you provide using the `--start-uid` and `--end-uid` range, all of their accounts are configured for `chroot` jail. For this example, I have only one user (`sheila`) whose UID (501) falls between 100 and 999; only that user's account is chrooted. The process of creating a `chroot` jail looks like this:

1. Execute the `chrootusers.pl` script with the following command, which creates a `sh` script in the `/tmp` directory called `chrootusers.pl.sh.`:

   ```
   /usr/local/bin/chrootusers.pl --start-uid=100 \
                   --end-uid=999 \
                   --chroot-group=ftpusers
   ```

2. Run this `sh` script, using the `sh /tmp/chrootusers.pl.sh` command.

   If you want to avoid running the `sh` script manually, you can use the `-- update-ok` option with the command in Step 1, which tells the `chrootusers.pl` script to execute all the commands using the `sh` script. The `sh` script first adds `sheila`'s user account to the `ftpusers` group in `/etc/group` by executing the following command:

   ```
   /usr/sbin/usermod -G ftpusers sheila
   ```

3. User `sheila`'s home directory field is modified in `/etc/passwd` using the following command:

   ```
   /usr/sbin/usermod -d /home/sheila/./ sheila
   ```

   The user directory changes from `/home/sheila` to `/home/sheila/./`. When the `WU-FTPD` daemon reads home-directory entries like this one, it runs the `chroot("/home/sheila")` system call internally and then changes the directory to `"."` (which is the `root` (/) directory in the `chroot`ed environment).

4. The script copies the contents of the `/home/chroot` directory to `sheila`'s home directory using the following command:

   ```
   cd /home/chroot; /bin/tar cf - * | ( cd ~sheila; /bin/tar xf
   - )
   ```

   This ensures that the user account has all the necessary files to maintain `chroot`ed FTP sessions:

   - Command files (`/home/chroot/bin/*`)
   - Library files (`/home/chroot/lib/*`)
   - Configuration files (`/home/chroot/etc/*`)

5. The script adds entries for `sheila` to the `~sheila/etc/passwd` and `~sheila/etc/group` files by executing the following commands:

   ```
   /bin/echo "sheila:*:501:501::" >> /home/sheila/etc/passwd
   /bin/echo "sheila::501:"        >> /home/sheila/etc/group
   ```

Because the user sheila likely doesn't want to be called 501 (her user number), this entry allows commands like ls to display user and group names instead of user ID and group ID values when listing files and directories in an FTP session.

6. The script sets permissions for the copied files and directories so that user sheila can access them during FTP sessions.

```
cd /home/sheila; /bin/chown -R sheila:sheila bin etc lib pub
```

7. Repeat the preceding steps for each user whose UID falls in the range given in the chrootusers.pl script.

Securing WU-FTPD using options in /etc/ftpaccess

The default /etc/ftpaccess has a lot of room for modification in terms of security enhancement. In this section I show you how you can enhance WU-FTPD security by modifying this file.

LOGGING EVERYTHING

The more network traffic WU-FTPD logs the more you can trace back to the server. By default, WU-FTPD logs file transfers only to and from the server (inbound and outbound, respectively) for all defined user classes (anonymous, real, and guest). Following are all the log directives you can add to /etc/ftpaccess file.

◆ File transfers: Log file transfers if you want to see which files are being uploaded to or downloaded from the server by which user. Use the following directive in the /etc/ftpaccess file:

```
log transfers anonymous,real,guest inbound,outbound
```

◆ Security information: Enable logging of security violations for anonymous, guest, and real users by putting the following directives in the /etc/ftpaccess file:

```
log security anonymous,guest,real
log commands anonymous,guest,real
```

■ The first log directive tells WU-FTPD to enable logging of security violations for all default user classes.

■ The second log directive ensures that WU-FTPD logs all commands run by all default user classes.

RESTRICTING ACCESS TO SENSITIVE FILES AND DIRECTORIES

If you have decided against using a chroot jail for user accounts, you may want to consider restricting access to sensitive files and directories with the noretrieve directive in the /etc/ftpaccess file. Here are some sample uses of the noretrieve directive:

♦ To prohibit a file from being retrieved, the command syntax is

```
noretrieve file | dir [class=anonymous | real | guest]
```

♦ To prohibit anyone from retrieving any files from the sensitive /etc directory, you can add the following line in /etc/ftpaccess:

```
noretrieve /etc
```

♦ If you run an Apache Web server on the same system that runs your WU-FTPD server, you can add the following line in /etc/ftpaccess to ensure that directory-specific Apache configuration files (found in users' Web directories) can't be downloaded by anyone. Here's an example:

```
noretrieve .htaccess .htpasswd
```

If you decide to deny such privileges only to anonymous users, you can do so by using the following modified directive:

```
noretrieve .htaccess .htpasswd class=anonymous
```

♦ If you have set up a noretrieve for a certain directory but you want to allow users to download files from that directory, use the allow-retrieve file_extension directive. For example, allow-retrieve /etc/hosts allows users to download the /etc/hosts file even when noretrieve /etc is in effect.

RESTRICTING UPLOAD PRIVILEGES FOR ANONYMOUS FTP USERS

Many anonymous FTP servers that allow uploading can quickly become a swap meet for pirated software. If you must allow uploading of files as an anonymous WU-FTPD service, consider making it very hard for anonymous users to exploit your service. To tighten security for such an anonymous server, you can put the noretrieve, upload directives to work by following these steps:

1. Disable upload for all directories within your anonymous FTP account by using the upload directive like this:

```
upload /var/ftp * no
```

2. Create a directory in /var/ftp (substitute its name for the directory shown here) and explicitly open the upload permissions for this directory, like this:

```
upload /var/ftp/directory yes nobody ftp 0440 nodirs
```

For example, I can create a subdirectory called /var/ftp/incoming and add the following line in /etc/ftpaccess:

```
upload /var/ftp/incoming  yes nobody ftp 0440 nodirs
```

Here all the uploaded files in the /var/ftp/incoming directory would be owned by user nobody belonging to a group called ftp. The files have 0440 (-r--r-----) permission settings, and as such, anonymous FTP users who upload files in this directory cannot create any subdirectories.

3. Use the following directive to make all files in /var/ftp/*directory* non-retrievable:

```
noretrieve /var/ftp/directory
```

For the example, discussed in the previous step this directive is set as follows:

```
noretrieve /var/ftp/incoming
```

RESTRICTING ACCESS BY IP/NETWORK ADDRESSES

If you monitor your /var/log/secure log frequently and notice FTP connection attempts from unfamiliar IP addresses, consider investigating the attempts as potential security risks. You can use the /usr/bin/host *IP_address* command to resolve the IP addresses you are wondering about. Or, you can execute the /usr/sbin/traceroute *IP_address* command to trace the network path of the IP address. For example, if you have no users in Russia and your Traceroute output shows an IP address from Russia, you may want to simply block the IP from future FTP access attempts. In such a case, you can simply refuse FTP access to IP addresses – or even to an entire network – by using the deny directive. The syntax of the deny directive is

```
deny IP_address[/network mask] [fully_qualified_filename]
```

For example, to deny all the hosts in 192.168.1.0/24 (a Class C network,) you can add the following line in the /etc/ftpaccess file:

```
deny 192.168.1.0/24
```

TIP

To deny different IP addresses from multiple networks, simply list those IP addresses by separating them with single spaces. You can also specify a *fully qualified filename* — which lists all the IP addresses you want to deny — as in this example:

```
deny /etc/ftphosts.bad
```

Each line in this file can list one IP address or network in the CIDR format (for example, 192.168.1.0/24). Using an external file can keep your /etc/ftpaccess configuration file simpler to maintain, because it won't get cluttered by lots of IP addresses.

 To shut down FTP service temporarily, add an entry such as 0.0.0.0/0 to the /etc/ftphosts.bad file to disallow every IP address in the entire IP space. Remember to remove that entry once you are ready to re-enable the service.

In most cases, users don't need an explanation for access denial, but if your policy requires such civilized behavior, you can display the contents of a message file when denying access. For example, the following command shows everyone being denied access to the contents of the /etc/ftphosts.bad.msg file:

```
deny /etc/ftphosts.bad   /etc/ftphosts.bad.msg
```

Using ProFTPD

Earlier, this chapter demonstrated how to configure the WU-FTPD server to enhance FTP security. But WU-FTPD isn't the only FTP server you can get for Red Hat Linux; another FTP server called ProFTPD is now common — and as with the "cola wars," each server has its following (in this case, made up of administrators). Here are some of the benefits of ProFTPD:

◆ ProFTPD uses one Apache-like configuration file, which makes it easy to learn if you have configured Apache before.

 ProFTPD can also use an Apache-like optional feature that sets up per-directory configuration files, which can create a configuration specific to one directory.

◆ ProFTPD supports easy-to-configure virtual FTP sites.

◆ ProFTPD can control resources, such as how many instances of the server run at any given time to service simultaneous connections.

◆ ProFTPD can use Linux Capabilities (see Chapter 8 for details on Linux Capabilities).

Downloading, compiling, and installing ProFTPD

Before you can use ProFTPD, you must download and install the software. Here's how to acquire ProFTPD and get it running in the following list.

1. Download the latest stable ProFTPD source distribution (the filename should be proftpd-*version_number*.tar.gz or similar, where *version_number* is the version number in the filename, such as 1.2.2). You can download the ProFTPD source code from www.proftpd.net.

2. Become root (using the su command).

3. Extract the source distribution by running the following command:

   ```
   tar xvzf proftpd-version_number.tar.gz
   ```

   This creates a subdirectory of the in /usr/src/redhat/SOURCES directory called proftpd-*version_number* (for example, proftod-1.2.2). Change your current directory to the new subdirectory.

4. Run the ./configure --sysconfdir=/etc command to configure the source distribution for your system.

5. Run the make and make install commands to compile and install the binaries and default configuration files.

Configuring ProFTPD

The ProFTPD configuration file is /etc/proftpd.conf. The default copy of this file (without any comment lines) is shown in Listing 18-2.

Listing 18-2: Default copy of /etc/proftpd.conf

```
ServerName                   "ProFTPD Default Installation"
ServerType                   standalone
DefaultServer                on
Port                         21
Umask                        022
MaxInstances                 30
User                         nobody
Group                        nogroup
<Directory /*>
  AllowOverwrite             on
</Directory>
<Anonymous ~ftp>
  User                       ftp
  Group                      ftp
```

```
UserAlias                   anonymous ftp
MaxClients                  10
DisplayLogin                welcome.msg
DisplayFirstChdir           .message
<Limit WRITE>
  DenyAll
</Limit>
</Anonymous>
```

If you are familiar with Apache Web server configuration, you can see a couple of close similarities here:

♦ Single-line directives such as ServerName and ServerType

♦ Multiple-line container directives such as <Directory> and <Limit>

Before you configure ProFTPD, however, know the meaning of each directive for the configuration file. For a complete list of ProFTPD directives and their usage, read the ProFTPD user's guide online at the ProFTPD Web site, http://www.proftpd.net. Here I discuss only the directives shown in the default proftpd.conf file and the ones that have security and access control implications. They are as follows:

♦ **ServerName:** Gives your FTP server a name. Replace the default value, ProFTPD Default Installation, with something that doesn't state what type of FTP server it is. For example, you could use something like

```
ServerName      "FTP Server"
```

♦ **ServerType:** ProFTPD can run two ways:

  ▪ As a standalone service

    By default, the ServerType directive is set to standalone, which means that ProFTPD runs as a standalone service.

  ▪ As an xinetd-run (inetd) service

    Because ProFTPD is highly configurable using its own set of directives, there is no benefit from running under xinetd. Services that can't control their resource utilizations are better suited for xinetd, so I recommend that you leave the default alone. If you want to run it under xinetd anyway, I show you how in "Running ProFTPD as an xinetd-run service," later in this chapter.

♦ **DefaultServer:** ProFTPD supports virtual FTP servers, which means you have a main server (called the default server) and one or more virtual FTP servers. By default, the main server is enabled using the DefaultServer directive. If you plan on using only a set of virtual FTP servers and don't want any FTP request to default to the main server, turn it off by setting the DefaultServer directive to off.

Leave DefaultServer alone at least until you are completely familiar with all the directives and creating virtual FTP servers using ProFTPD.

- **Port:** Specifies the port that ProFTPD listens to for incoming connections. The default value of 21 should be left alone, or you must instruct your FTP users to change their FTP client software to connect to a different port on your FTP server.

- **Umask:** Specifies the default file and directory creation umask setting. The default value of 022 creates files or directories with 755 permissions, which is too relaxed. A value of 027 is recommended, and it ensures that only the owner and the group can access the file or directory.

- **MaxInstances:** Specifies how many ProFTPD instances are run simultaneously before refusing connections. This directive is effective only for the standalone mode of operation.

- **User:** Although the initial ProFTPD daemon must be run as root, for security ProFTPD switches to an ordinary user and group when the FTP service interacts with a client, thus reducing the risk of allowing a client process to interact with a privileged process. This directive simply tells ProFTPD which user to switch to.

- **Group:** Just as with the User directive, the Group directive specifies the user and group that run the ProFTPD server. Just as with the User directive, the initial ProFTPD daemon must be run as root.

 Although the default value of the User directive (nobody) is suitable for most Linux installations, the Group value (nogroup) is not. There's no nogroup in the default /etc/group file with Red Hat Linux. To solve this problem you can set the Group value to nobody (because there's a group called nobody in /etc/group that by default doesn't have any members). If you want to keep the default value for the Group directive for some reason, you can run the groupadd nogroup command to add a new group called nogroup.

- **<Directory_/*>:** Allows a set of directives that applies to a particular directory path. The default directory directive applies to /*, which is a wildcard path (meaning every file in every directory visible to ProFTPD). The AllowOverwrite directive, which is enclosed in the directory container, allows FTP clients to overwrite any file they want. This is a bad idea and should be set to off. Whenever one is trying to create a secure environment, the first step is to shut all doors and windows and only open those that are well guarded or a necessity.

 Setting AllowOverwrite to off in the /* directory context means you must create specific instances of AllowOverwrite on as needed. Yes, this may be a painful procedure, but it helps your security in the long run.

♦ **<Anonymous ~FTP>**: The final configuration segment of the default proftpd.conf file creates an anonymous FTP site. Unless you must have an anonymous FTP site, remove the entire anonymous FTP configuration segment.

If you follow the preceding recommendations, your modified /etc/proftpd.conf file looks like the one in Listing 18-3.

Listing 18-3: Modified /etc/proftpd.conf

```
ServerName              "FTP Server"
ServerType              standalone
DefaultServer           on
Port                    21
Umask                   027
MaxInstances            30
User                    nobody
Group                   nogroup
<Directory /*>
   AllowOverwrite       off
</Directory>
```

RUNNING PROFTPD AS A STANDALONE SERVICE
As mentioned before, you can run ProFTPD as a standalone service by setting the ServerType to standalone. Once you have set this directive, you can simply start the ProFTPD server while logged in as root using the /usr/local/sbin/proftpd command. However, starting ProFTPD manually in this manner isn't a reasonable system administration practice so do the following:

1. Become root by using the su command.

2. Install the `proftpd` script from the CD that comes with this book (see the CD Appendix for info on where to find the script) in your `/etc/rc.d/init.d` directory.

3. Add a new group called `nogroup` using the `groupadd nogroup` command.

4. Execute the following command:

```
ln -s /etc/rc.d/init.d/proftpd  /etc/rc.d/rc3.d/S95proftpd
```

This creates a symbolic link to the `/etc/rc.d/init.d/proftpd` script. Every time you start your system and it switches to run-level 3, the ProFTPD service starts automatically.

5. Run the following command:

```
ln -s /etc/rc.d/init.d/proftpd  /etc/rc.d/rc3.d/K95proftpd
```

Doing so creates a symbolic link to the `/etc/rc.d/init.d/proftpd` script. Every time you reboot or halt your system from run-level 3, the ProFTPD service stops automatically.

At any time (as `root`) you can run the `/etc/rc.d/init.d/proftpd start` command to start the ProFTPD service. If you make any configuration change in `/etc/proftpd.conf`, reload the configuration using the `/etc/rc.d/init.d/proftpd reload` command. Similarly, the `/etc/rc.d/init.d/proftpd stop` command can stop the service.

 To perform a scheduled shutdown of the FTP service you can also use the `/usr/local/sbin/ftpshut  HHMM` command. For example, the `/usr/local/sbin/ftpshut  0930` command stops the FTP service at 9:30 a.m. To prevent any connection before a certain time of the scheduled shutdown you can use the `-1  minute` option. By default, ProFTPD doesn't allow any new connections ten minutes before a scheduled shutdown. Remember to remove the `/etc/shutmsg` file when you want to enable the FTP service again.

RUNNING PROFTPD AS AN XINETD-RUN SERVICE

Although running ProFTPD in standalone mode is recommended, you may choose to run it using `xinetd`. For example, if you don't have a lot of user accounts that frequently must connect to your FTP server, running ProFTPD using `xinetd` is reasonable.

Before you configure ProFTPD as an xinetd-run service, first make sure that you aren't already running ProFTPD in standalone mode. Run the ps auxww | grep proftpd command to check whether any instances of ProFTPD are currently running. If necessary kill any running instances before following the steps below.

1. Add disable = yes in the /etc/xinetd.d/wu-ftpd file, which ensures that your WU-FTPD server isn't started by xinetd when a new FTP request comes.

2. Reload the xinetd configuration using the killall -USR1 xinetd command.

3. Modify the /etc/proftpd.conf file so that the ServerType directive is set to inetd instead of standalone.

4. Add a new group called nogroup by using the groupadd nogroup command.

5. Create a new xinetd configuration file called /etc/xinetd.d/proftpd with the following lines:

```
service ftp
{
        flags            = REUSE
        socket_type      = stream
        instances        = 30
        wait             = no
        user             = root
        server           = /usr/local/sbin/proftpd

        log_on_success   = HOST PID
        log_on_failure   = HOST RECORD
        disable          = no
}
```

6. Reload the xinetd configuration, using the killall -USR1 xinetd command.

7. Connect to the server from the local host, using the ftp localhost command. If your connection is refused, run the tail -f /var/log/messages command and try again. Notice the error messages that ProFTPD outputs; correct the problem(s) accordingly.

Monitoring ProFTPD

ProFTPD includes a few utilities that can help you monitor the service. For example, you can run ProFTP bundled utilities to count concurrent FTP connections or determine which users are connected to your server. In this section, I detail these utilities.

COUNTING FTP CONNECTIONS

To find how many people are connected to your FTP server, run the /usr/local/bin/ftpcount command. Here's an example of the output you get back:

```
Master proftpd process 8322:
  -   -        2 users
```

When you introduce a new FTP service, monitor it very closely for at least a few days. Typically, you should run commands like the preceding using the watch facility. For example, the watch -n 60 /usr/local/bin/ftpcount command can run on a terminal or xterm to display a count of FTP users every 60 seconds.

FINDING WHO IS FTP-CONNECTED

Run the /usr/local/bin/ftpwho command to see who is connected. Sample output follows:

```
Master proftpd process 8322:
 8387 0m1s   proftpd: sheila - reboot.intevo.com: IDLE
 8341 3m59s  proftpd: kabir  - k2.intevo.com: IDLE
   -   -        2 users
```

Here two users (sheila and kabir) are connected from two different machines on a LAN. The output shows:

- ♦ ProFTPD processes that service these users
- ♦ The master ProFTPD process ID

Securing ProFTPD

ProFTPD has a number of directives that you can use in the /etc/proftpd.conf file to create a secure and restrictive FTP service. In this section, I show you how you can use such directives to restrict FTP connections by remote IP addresses, enable PAM-based user authentication (see Chapter 10 for details on PAM itself), or create a chroot jail for FTP users.

RESTRICTING FTP CONNECTIONS BY IP ADDRESS

To restrict access to your FTP server by IP addresses, use the following configuration segment within the main server or a virtual server (within a `<VirtualHost>` container) or an anonymous FTP server (within an `<Anonymous>` container).

```
<Limit LOGIN>
  Order Allow, Deny
  Allow from goodIPaddr1, goodIPaddr2
  Deny from all
</Limit>
```

For example, to allow a host called `myhost.domain.com` access to your main FTP server, you can first find what the IP address is for `myhost.domain.com` by using the `host myhost.domain.com` command (or simply by running the `ping myhost.domain.com` command). For an IP address of 216.112.169.138, you create the following configuration in the `/etc/proftpd.conf` file:

```
<Limit LOGIN>
  Order Allow, Deny
  Allow from 216.112.169.138
  Deny from all
</Limit>
```

Doing so allows `myhost.domain.com` to connect to your FTP server. However, if `myhost.domain.com` doesn't have a static IP address, the user on that host probably can't connect the next time she gets a different IP address from her ISP. In this case, you may have to grant her entire network FTP-access privileges. For example, you can use:

```
Allow from 216.112.169.
```

 I don't recommend using hostnames in the `Allow` directive, because hostname lookups are slow and can reduce your server performance. Besides, hostnames are more likely to be spoofed than IP addresses.

USING PAM AS THE AUTHORITATIVE USER AUTHENTICATION METHOD

ProFTPD is a PAM-enabled application. (PAM is detailed in Chapter 10.) ProFTPD can use PAM to perform user authentication and any other type of access control that a PAM module can provide.

To use PAM with ProFTPD (that is, applying PAM for authentication), you can simply create a file called `/etc/pam.d/ftp` that contains the following lines:

```
%PAM-1.0
auth        required    /lib/security/pam_listfile.so item=user \
                        sense=deny file=/etc/ftpusers onerr=succeed
auth        required    /lib/security/pam_stack.so service=system-auth
auth        required    /lib/security/pam_shells.so
account     required    /lib/security/pam_stack.so service=system-auth
session     required    /lib/security/pam_stack.so service=system-auth
```

By default, ProFTPD enables PAM-based authentication, but it doesn't consider PAM as the ultimate authority in user authentication. Directives like AuthUserFile and AuthGroupFile can override an authentication failure reported by PAM. Because Red Hat Linux uses PAM-based authentication for just about all types of user access, PAM makes sense as the authoritative authentication scheme for ProFTPD. To establish it as such, add the following directives in the main server configuration in the /etc/proftpd.conf file:

```
AuthPAMAuthoritative on
AuthPAMConfig ftp
```

This makes sure ProFTPD obeys PAM as the ultimate user-authentication and authorization middleware; it tells ProFTPD to use the /etc/pam.d/ftp configuration for user authentication.

TIP If you want different virtual FTP sites to authenticate differently, you can use the preceding directives in a <VirtualHost> configuration.

USING A CHROOT JAIL FOR FTP USERS

ProFTPD makes using a chroot jail easy for FTP users. To create a chroot jail for users in their home directories, you can add the following directive to the main server configuration or to a virtual host configuration:

```
DefaultRoot "~"
```

This directive tells ProFTPD to chroot a user to his home directory (because ~ expands to the home directory of the user). To limit the jail to be a subdirectory of the home directory, you can use DefaultRoot "~/directory" instead. In contrast to WU-FTPD (discussed earlier in the chapter), you don't have to copy a lot of files to support the chroot jail for each user. You also don't need the chrootusers.pl script with ProFTPD.

You can limit the jail to a group of users, as shown in this example:

```
DefaultRoot "~" untrusted
```

Here only the users in the untrusted group in the /etc/group file are jailed. Similarly, if you want to jail all the users in a group called everyone but want to spare the users in a smaller group called buddies, you can use the same directive like this:

```
DefaultRoot "~" everyone, !buddies
```

The ! (bang) sign in front of the second group tells ProFTPD to exclude the users in the group from being chroot-jailed.

LIMITING FTP COMMAND PRIVILEGES

If you have a lot of directories on your server available via FTP, you may have different access-control requirements for some of them. You may want to prevent users from creating or deleting files and directories within a certain directory, or you may want to designate a sole upload directory for your users. This section demonstrates such configurations, using the <Limit> container directive.

Keep all your directives inside the /etc/proftpd.conf file.

DISABLING DIRECTORY CREATION-AND-DELETION PRIVILEGES To prevent all users from creating new directories (or removing existing ones) via FTP, use the following configuration:

```
<Directory /*>
  <Limit MKD RMD>
    DenyAll
  </Limit>
</Directory>
```

If you want to allow directory creation-and-deletion privileges to only a certain group called staff, you can use a modified version of the preceding configuration as shown next:

```
<Directory /*>
  <Limit MKD RMD>
    DenyAll
    AllowGroup staff
```

```
  </Limit>
</Directory>
```

Similarly, you can use the AllowUser directive to specify users to create and delete directories. If you want to deny these rights to only a few users, create a group (say, badusers) in /etc/group and use the following configuration to allow creation and deletion to everyone but the users in that group:

```
<Directory /*>
  <Limit MKD RMD>
     Order deny,allow
     DenyGroup badusers
     AllowAll
  </Limit>
</Directory>
```

ESTABLISHING AN UPLOAD-ONLY FTP SERVER   To allow only uploading of files to your FTP server, you can use the following configuration in the main server or a virtual-host container:

```
<Directory /*>
  <Limit RETR>
     DenyAll
  </Limit>
</Directory>
```

RESTRICTING ACCESS TO A SINGLE DIRECTORY   To keep users from poking around directories they shouldn't be in, you can limit all FTP users to a certain directory by using the following configuration:

```
<Directory /*>
  <Limit CWD>
     DenyAll
  </Limit>
</Directory>
```

With this configuration in place, users who FTP to the server can't change the directory. You can use DenyGroup groupname instead of the DenyALL to limit the scope of the configuration to one user group (groupname) defined in the /etc/group file.

SIMPLIFYING FILE TRANSFERS FOR NOVICE USERS   Many users get lost when they see too many directories or options available to them. Most users won't mind or know if you simplify their computer interactions. So if you have a group of users who must retrieve or store files in the FTP server on a regular basis, you may want to consider locking their access into one directory. For example, you have a group defined in /etc/group called novices, and you want to allow the users in this group to retrieve files from a directory called /files/download and upload files into a directory called /files/upload. The configuration you add to /etc/ proftpd.conf file to do the job looks like this:

```
<Directory /files/download>
  <Limit READ>
    AllowGroup novices
  </Limit>
  <Limit WRITE>
    DenyGroup novices
  </Limit>
</Directory>
<Directory /files/upload>
  <Limit READ>
    DenyGroup novices
  </Limit>
  <Limit WRITE>
    AllowGroup novices
  </Limit>
</Directory>
```

RESTRICTING DIRECTORY BROWSING PRIVILEGES   To limit directory-browsing privileges for a group of users, you can use the following configuration:

```
<Directory path>
  <Limit DIRS>
    DenyGroup group_name
  </Limit>
</Directory>
```

To limit directory-browsing privileges for a group called newfriends in a directory called /my/mp3s, use the following configuration. This prevents users in the newfriends group from getting listings of /my/mp3s directory:

```
<Directory /my/mp3s>
  <Limit DIRS>
    DenyGroup newfriends
  </Limit>
    </Directory>
```

CONTROLLING COMMAND BUFFER SIZE

Many "script kiddies" (novice hackers) try to attack a server by sending extremely long commands to them. They hope to cause some sort of buffer overflow, which can then be exploited. You can use the `CommandBufferSize` directive to control the length of the command sent by clients. Setting buffer size to 512 is sufficient for most scenarios. Set this in main server configuration.

KEEPING PRYING USERS AWAY FROM EACH OTHER

Usually when you access an FTP server on an ISP, you see more files than you should. Being able to peek and poke gives bad people ideas about what they can do to a system. So try to hide unnecessary files. Take a look at the following configuration segment:

```
DefaultRoot "/www"
<Directory /www>
   HideNoAccess on
   <Limit ALL>
      IgnoreHidden on
   </Limit>
</Directory>
```

This configuration allows a user to see only what you permit. When a user connects to a system with the preceding configuration, he sees only the files and directories in /www for which he has access privileges. This is true for every user who connects to this system. The `HideNoAccess` directive hides all the entries in the /www directory that a user cannot access. The `IgnoreHidden` directive tells ProFTPD to ignore any command from a user that is one of the hidden commands.

CREATING A MINIMAL ANONYMOUS FTP SITE

If people need to get only a few small files from your FTP server (say, a few kilobytes or a few megabytes), consider using a Web server rather than an anonymous FTP site. If you have a lot of files for download and want to allow uploading via an anonymous account, create an anonymous FTP server. The following /etc/proftpd.conf configuration shows an anonymous FTP server whose `incoming` directory allows users to upload files.

```
<Anonymous ~ftp>
User ftp
Group ftp
RequireValidShell off
UserAlias anonymous ftp
MaxClients 20
<Directory *>
   <Limit WRITE>
      DenyAll
```

```
    </Limit>
</Directory>
<Directory incoming>
    <Limit WRITE>
        AllowAll
    </Limit>
    <Limit READ>
        DenyAll
    </Limit>
</Directory>
</Anonymous>
```

ProFTPD automatically creates a chroot jail for any user logging in to an anonymous FTP site. The home directory of the ftp user is used as the root directory for the site.

The following list explains the purpose of the directives in the preceding configuration for an anonymous FTP site:

◆ User and Group: Both these directives ensure that all anonymous sessions are owned by User ftp and Group ftp.

◆ RequireValidShell: Because the built-in user FTP doesn't have a valid shell listed in /etc/passwd, this directive tells ProFTPD to still allow anonymous sessions for User ftp.

◆ UserAlias: This directive assigns anonymous to the FTP account so that anyone can log in to the anonymous FTP site, using either ftp and anonymous as the username.

◆ MaxClients: The preceding code example limits the number of anonymous connections to 20. You may have to change this setting as you find your system's load-tolerance levels.

◆ <Directory> containers: These assign various restrictions to named directories.

   ▪ The first directory container denies write privileges (upload, delete, modify) to everyone, for every directory.

   ▪ The next directory container gives the incoming subdirectory = write permissions for everyone.

   ▪ The final Limit directive ensures that users who upload files in the incoming directory cannot see or retrieve the files in that directory.

USING LINUX CAPABILITIES WITH PROFTPD

ProFTPD supports Linux Capabilities (see Chapter 8 to learn about Linux Capabilities in detail).

When a ProFTPD server with Linux Capabilities receives a client request, the ProFTP server launches a child server process to service the request. However, after a user authentication is successful, the child server process drops all the Linux Capabilities except cap_net_bind_service, which allows it to bind to a standard port defined in /etc/services. At this point, the child process can't return to root privileges. This makes ProFTPD very safe, because even if a hacker tricks it to run an external program, the new process that a ProFTPD creates can't perform any privileged operations because it doesn't have any Linux Capabilities – not even cap_net_bind_service.

To use Linux Capabilities, you must compile ProFTPD with a (still-unofficial) module called mod_linuxprivs. Here's how.

1. Become root using the su command.

2. Install the kernel source distribution from your Red Hat CD-ROM or download the source RPM from a suitable Web site, such as http://www.kernel.org.

   Make sure you install the source for the kernel you are currently running. For example, to install the source for the 2.4.1 kernel, you can run rpm -ivh kernel-source-2.4.1.i386.rpm command. The kernel source should be installed in /usr/src/linux-2.4.1 (your version number is likely to be different), and a symbolic link for /usr/src/linux points to the /usr/src/linux-2.4.1 directory.

3. Open the directory to which you extracted the ProFTPD source distribution earlier (when compiling it); then run the following command:

   ```
   ./configure --sysconfdir=/etc \
   --with-modules=mod_linuxprivs
   ```

4. Run the following command:

   ```
   ./configure --sysconfdir=/etc --with-modules=mod_linuxprivs
   ```

5. Run the make clean command to remove old binaries.

6. Run the make command followed by make install to install the new ProFTPD with the Linux Capabilities module.

To verify that the mod_linuxprivs is installed in your new ProFTPD binary, run the /usr/local/sbin/proftpd -l command, which shows a list like the following:

```
Compiled-in modules:
  mod_core.c
  mod_auth.c
  mod_xfer.c
  mod_site.c
```

```
mod_ls.c
mod_unixpw.c
mod_log.c
mod_pam.c
mod_linuxprivs.c
```

As shown in the preceding example, the mod_linuxprivs.c module is compiled, and ProFTPD now uses this module.

Summary

FTP servers are often the target of hackers who often trick the system to download password files or other secrets that they should not have access to. By restricting FTP access by username, setting default file permission, and using chroot jailed FTP service, you can protect against FTP server attacks.

Chapter 19

Samba and NFS Server Security

IN THIS CHAPTER

◆ Securing Samba Server

◆ Securing an NFS server

A LINUX SYSTEM IN a network often acts as a file server. To turn your Linux box into a file server you have two choices: Samba and NFS. In this chapter, I discuss how you can secure both of these services.

Securing Samba Server

This section discusses various security issues related to Samba Server.

Choosing an appropriate security level

Samba Server can use four different security levels. These security levels affect how client/server authentication takes place when Samba service is in use. When a Samba client initiates a connection to a Samba server, the server informs the client about the security level it operates under. The client then must adhere to the server-chosen security level.

The four security levels are as follows:

◆ Share

◆ User

◆ Server

◆ Domain

The security level is set using the `security` parameter in the `global` section in `/etc/samba/smb.conf` file.

USER-LEVEL SECURITY

When the `security` parameter is set to `user`, the Samba server operates using user-level security. In the latest Samba version, this is the default security level.

When a client connects to the server, the Samba server notifies it of the security level in use. In user-level security, the client sends a username and password pair to authenticate. The Samba server can authenticate the user only based on the given username and password pair or the client's host information. The server has no way to know which resource the client requests after authentication; therefore, it can't base acceptance or rejection of the request on any resource restriction.

Because Samba is a PAM-aware application, it uses PAM to authenticate the user, in particular the `/etc/pam.d/samba` configuration file. By default, this configuration file uses the `/etc/pam.d/system-auth` configuration with the `pam_stack` module. This means Samba authentication becomes synonymous with regular user-login authentication (which involves `/etc/shadow` or `/etc/passwd` files) under Linux. If you enable encrypted passwords in `/etc/samba/smb.conf`, the `/etc/samba/smbpasswd` file is used instead (see the "Avoiding plain-text passwords" section later in this chapter for details).

Once access is granted, the client can connect to any share without resupplying a password or a username/password pair. If a client successfully logs on to the Samba server as a user called `joe`, the server grants the client all the access privileges associated with `joe`; the client can access files owned by `joe.0`.

A client can maintain multiple user-authenticated sessions that use different username/password pairs. Thus, a client system can access a particular share by using the appropriate username/password pair — and access a whole different share by using a different username/password pair.

SHARE-LEVEL SECURITY

Share-level security is active when `/etc/samba/smb.conf` uses `security = share`. In share-level security, the client is expected to supply a password for each share it wants to access. However, unlike Windows 2000/NT, Samba doesn't use a share/password pair. In fact, when Samba receives a password for a given share access request, it simply tries to match the password with a previously given username and tries to authenticate the username/password pair against the standard Unix authentication scheme (using `/etc/shadow` or `/etc/passwd` files) or the encrypted Samba passwords (using the `/etc/samba/smbpasswd` file.)

If a username isn't found — and/or the requested share is accessible as a guest account (that is, one in which the `guest ok` parameter is set to `yes`) — the connection is made via the username found in the `guest account` parameter in the `/etc/samba/smb.conf` file.

One consequence of this security mode is that you don't have to make a Linux account for every Windows user you want to connect to your Samba server. For example, you can set the `guest account = myguest` parameter in the `/etc/samba/smb.conf` file and create a Linux user called `myguest` with its own password — and provide that password to Windows users who want to connect to shares where you've set the `guest ok` parameter to `yes`.

SERVER-LEVEL SECURITY

Server-level security is active when the `security = server` parameter is used in the `/etc/samba/smb.conf` file. In this mode, the Samba server informs the client that it is operating under user-level security, which forces the client to supply a username/password pair. The given username/password pair is then used to authenticate the client via an external password server whose NetBIOS name is set by using the `password server` parameter. The password server must be a Samba or Windows 2000/NT server, running under the user-level security mode.

If you have enabled encrypted passwords on the Samba server, also enable encrypted passwords on the password server. Typically, server-level security delegates authentication service to a Windows 2000/NT server.

A connection to the password server is maintained throughout the life of the Samba server.

DOMAIN-LEVEL SECURITY

Domain-level security is active when `security = domain` is used in the `/etc/samba/smb.conf` file. It is identical to server-level security with the following exceptions:

◆ The Samba server doesn't maintain a dedicated connection to the password server. It simply connects to the remote authentication server as needed and disconnects. This is good for the password server, because Windows 2000/NT licensing agreements are priced according to the number of connections.

◆ The Samba server can use Windows 2000/NT domain capabilities such as the trusted domain feature.

For example, say your Windows 2000 domain is called `SKINET` and your Samba server's NetBIOS name is `SMBSRV`. Your global configuration for domain-level security might look like this example:

```
netbios name     = SMBSRV
workgroup        = SKINET
password_server  = *
security         = domain
```

Whenever a client connects to the Samba server (`SMBSRV`) it uses the `SKINET` domain's primary domain controller as the password server and authenticates the client request.

Avoiding plain-text passwords

By default, Samba server expects plain-text passwords from a client system, which (to put it mildly) isn't ideal. You can change this behavior by *uncommenting* (removing the leading semicolon from) the following lines in the /etc/samba/ smb.conf file.

```
;  encrypt passwords = yes
;  smb passwd file = /etc/samba/smbpasswd
```

The preceding configuration tells Samba server to use encrypted passwords and authenticate users by using the /etc/samba/smbpasswd file when the security parameter is set to user.

When the preceding configuration is in use, the Samba server appends an eight-byte random value during the session-setup phase of the connection. This random value is stored in the Samba server as the *challenge*. The client then encrypts the challenge — using its user password — and sends the *response*. The server encrypts the challenge (using the hashed password stored in /etc/samba/smbpasswd) and checks whether the client-supplied response is the same as the one it calculated. If the responses match, then the server is satisfied that the client knows the appropriate user password; the authentication phase is complete. In this method of authentication, the actual password isn't transmitted over the network, which makes the process very secure. Also, the Samba server never stores the actual password in the /etc/samba/ smbpasswd file — only an encrypted, hashed version of the password is stored.

I highly recommend that you enable an encrypted password mode for authentication. Once you enable encrypted passwords, create an /etc/samba/smbpasswd file by converting the /etc/passwd like this:

1. su to root.

2. Generate a base /etc/samba/smbpasswd file, using the following command.

   ```
   cat /etc/passwd | /usr/bin/mksmbpasswd.sh > \
   /etc/samba/smbpasswd
   ```

3. Use the smbpasswd command to create passwords for the users. For example, the smbpasswd sheila command creates a password for an existing user called sheila in /etc/samba/smbpasswd file.

All users on your system can change their encrypted Samba passwords by using this command (without the argument).

Now your Samba server requires encrypted passwords for client access — which may be less convenient to users but is also vastly more secure.

Allowing access to users from trusted domains

If you use domain-level security, you can use the trusted domain feature of Windows 2000/NT. For example, say that you have a user called myuser in a Windows 2000/NT domain called ADMIN and your Samba server is part of a domain called ENGR. If the primary domain controllers for the both of these domains are set up such that there's a trust relationship, then myuser from ADMIN should be able to access the Samba server on the ENGR domain. You can do so by setting the following parameter in a global section of your /etc/samba/smb.conf file.

```
allow trusted domain = yes
```

When this parameter is set, users from trusted domains can access the Samba server – although they still need Linux user accounts on the Samba server. Add the following parameters in the global section of the /etc/samba/smb.conf file:

```
add user script = /usr/sbin/useradd %u -g smbusers
delete user script = /usr/sbin/userdel %u
```

With these parameters in place, when a user from a trusted domain attempts access on the Samba server (on a different domain) for the very first time, the Samba server performs domain-level security measures. It asks the primary domain controller (PDC) of its own domain to authenticate the user. Because you have already set up a trust relationship with the user's domain, the PDC for the Samba server can authenticate the user. The Samba server then creates a Linux user account and allows the user to access the requested resource.

When the allow trusted domain parameter is set to no, trust relationships are ignored.

Controlling Samba access by network interface

You can tell Samba to listen to one or more network interfaces of the Linux system. Say you are running Samba on a system with two network interfaces, eth0 (192.168.2.10) and eth1 (192.168.3.10), and want to restrict Samba service to eth0 only. In such a case, define the following parameters in the global section of your /etc/samba/smb.conf file.

```
interfaces = 192.168.2.10/24 127.0.0.1
bind interfaces only = yes
```

The first parameter, `interfaces`, defines the list of network interfaces that Samba listens to. The 192.168.1.10/24 network is tied to the `eth0` (`192.168.1.10`) interface and, hence, it is added in the interface list. The 127.0.0.1 interface is added because it is the local loopback interface and is used by `smbpasswd` to connect to the local Samba server. The next parameter, `bind interfaces only`, is set to `yes` to tell the Samba server to listen to only the interfaces listed in the `interfaces` parameter.

You can also use interface device names such as `eth0` and `eth1` with the `interfaces` parameter.

Controlling Samba access by hostname or IP addresses

You can tell the Samba server to only allow a set of hosts to access its resources. For example, the following restricts host access:

```
hosts deny = ALL
hosts allow = 192.168.1.0/24 127.0.0.1
```

In the preceding lines, access to Samba is restricted as follows:

◆ The first parameter disallows access to all hosts.

◆ The second parameter opens access to

▪ Hosts in the 192.168.1.0 network.

▪ The local host (127.0.0.1).

If you use `IP networks` as the value for the `hosts allow` parameter, you can exclude certain IP addresses too. For example, the following lines give all hosts in 192.168.1.0/24 network access to the Samba server except 192.168.1.100:

```
hosts deny = ALL
hosts allow = 192.168.1.0/24 EXCEPT 192.168.1.100
```

You can use hostnames instead of IP addresses. For example, the following allows access to three computers in the network:

```
hosts deny = ALL
hosts allow = kabirspc, lancespc, stevespc
```

Using pam_smb to authenticate all users via a Windows NT server

Typically, Linux is the newcomer in most organizations; if you have a Windows 2000/NT network where a Windows 2000/NT machine is used for authentication, usually management is easier if you can delegate Linux user authentication to the Windows 2000/NT server. Samba along with pam_smb can use a Windows 2000/NT server (or a Linux-based Samba server acting as a PDC) to authenticate users who want to log on to your Linux system via Telnet or SSH.

GETTING PAM_SMB
You can download the pam_smb source from the FTP site located at ftp://ftp. samba.org/pub/samba/pam_smb.

INSTALLING AND CONFIGURING PAM_SMB
To install and configure the pam_smb module do the following:

1. su to root.

2. Extract the pam_smb distribution file in a directory by using the tar xvzf *pam_smb.tar.gz* command. Change your current directory to the newly created directory called pam_smb.

3. Run the ./configure command to prepare the source distribution. To place the pamsmbd daemon somewhere other than default location (/usr/local/sbin), run the ./configure -- sbindir=*/path/to/pamsmbd* where */path/to/pamsmbd* is the path where you want to keep the daemon binary. To disable encrypted passwords you can run the configure script with the --disable-encrypt-pass option.

4. Run the make command. Copy the pam_smb_auth.so file to /lib/ security by using the cp pam_smb_auth.so /lib/security command.

5. Modify the /etc/pam.d/system-auth file as shown below:

```
#%PAM-1.0
# This file is auto-generated.
# User changes are destroyed the next time authconfig is run.
auth        sufficient    /lib/security/pam_smb_auth.so
#auth        sufficient     /lib/security/pam_unix.so likeauth nullok md5 shadow
auth        required      /lib/security/pam_deny.so
account     sufficient    /lib/security/pam_unix.so
account     required      /lib/security/pam_deny.so
password    required      /lib/security/pam_cracklib.so retry=3
password    sufficient    /lib/security/pam_unix.so nullok use_authtok md5
shadow
```

```
password    required    /lib/security/pam_deny.so
session     required    /lib/security/pam_limits.so
session     required    /lib/security/pam_unix.so
```

6. The configuration file is stored in /etc/pam_smb.conf, and it consists of three lines.

   ■ The first line is the NT logon domain name, which is to be used for authentication.

   ■ The second line is the primary domain controller name.

   ■ The third line is the secondary domain controller name.

 These don't have to be NT server machines — simply machines that can authenticate in the domain. For example, Listing 19-1 shows a sample version of /etc/pam_smb.conf. Here the first line, SKINET, is the domain name, the second line, PDCSRV, is the primary domain controller, and the last line, BDCSRV, is the secondary domain controller.

Listing 19-1: Sample version of /etc/pam_smb.conf

```
SKINET
PDCSRV
BDCSRV
```

7. If you installed pamsmbd in the /usr/local/sbin directory, add the following line in your /etc/rc.d/rc.local file so that the daemon is started automatically whenever your system is booted:

   /usr/local/sbin/pamsmbd

8. Run the /usr/local/sbin/pamsmbd command to start the daemon for the first time.

Now your Linux system performs user authentication by using the Windows NT domain controllers specified in /etc/pam_smb.conf. In the sample configuration file shown in Listing 19-1, the authentication process uses the PDCSRV machine in the SKINET domain. If PDCSRV is down, BDCSRV is used.

Are you mapping users between your Linux system and the Windows NT system performing the authentication? You can use the /etc/ntmap.db database created using the makemap command. See the ntmap.example file found in the source distribution for details. You can use the ntmap.sh script to convert ntmap.example to /etc/ntmap.sh.

Using OpenSSL with Samba

OpenSSL can secure your Samba service. Currently, only smbclient implements SSL communication with the Samba server. Because SSL is an established trusted protocol, new clients for both Linux and Windows are expected to be developed.

To use SSL with Samba service, install OpenSSL. See Chapter 11 for details on compiling and installing OpenSSL on your Linux system.

COMPILING SAMBA WITH SSL

Here I assume that you have installed OpenSSL in the default location (/usr/local/ssl). Download the Samba source code from www.samba.org or a Samba mirror site near you. Follow the instructions below to compile and install Samba with SSL:

1. su to root.

2. Extract the Samba source by using the tar xvzf samba-source.tar.gz command, where samba-source.tar.gz is the name of your source distribution, and change the directory to the newly created subdirectory.

3. Modify the makefile command by uncommenting the SSL_ROOT line.

4. Run make and make install to compile and install Samba binaries with SSL support.

5. Configure Samba to use SSL, as shown in the following section.

CONFIGURING SAMBA WITH SSL

Here's how you can configure Samba with SSL.

1. To enable SSL support in Samba, add the ssl = yes parameter in the global section of your /etc/samba/smb.conf file.

2. By default, when ssl = yes is set, Samba communicates only via SSL.

   - If you want SSL connections limited to a certain host or network, ssl hosts = hostname, IP-address, IP/mask parameter limits SSL connection to name hosts or IP addresses. For example, using ssl hosts = 192.168.1.0/24 in the global section of your

`/etc/samba/smb.conf` file limits SSL connection to 192.168.1.0/24 network.

- The `ssl hosts resign - hostname, IP-address, IP/mask` parameter disables SSL connection for only a certain number of hosts or IP addresses. For example, `ssl hosts resign = 192.168.1.10/24` disables SSL only for the 192.168.1.10 network, and all other clients must communicate via SSL.

3. The `ssl CA certDir = /usr/local/ssl/certs` parameter points to the directory in which certificate authority (CA) certificates are kept. You should have a file for each CA that the server trusts. Each filename must be the hash value over the Distinguished Name from the CA.

4. Use `ssl CA certFile = /usr/local/ssl/certs/trustedCAs.pem` to point to the file containing all server certificates.

   - If you use the `ssl CA certDir` parameter as shown in the preceding example, you don't need this parameter.

   - If you have only one CA certificate, use this instead of the `ssl CA certDir` parameter.

5. Use the `ssl server cert = /usr/local/ssl/certs/samba.pem` parameter to point to server's certificate.

   - Use the `ssl server key = /usr/local/ssl/private/samba.pem` parameter to point to the server's private key.

   - Use the `ssl client cert = /usr/local/ssl/certs/smbclient.pem` parameter to point to the certificate used by `smbclient`.

TIP This parameter is needed if the Samba server also requires a client certificate.

6. Use the `ssl client key = /usr/local/ssl/private/smbclient.pem` parameter to point to the private key file for smbclient.

7. Use the `ssl require clientcert = yes` parameter if the server rejects connections from a client without a valid client certificate. When a client submits the client certificate, the server verifies the certificate by using the authorized CA certificates found in the `ssl CA certFile` specified directory or the `ssl server cert` parameter specified file.

8. Use the `ssl require servercert = yes` parameter if server certificates are required when using `smbclient`.

Once you configure the `/etc/samba/smb.conf` file for SSL, you can run Samba with SSL support.

RUNNING SAMBA WITH SSL
Running Samba with SSL support is no different than running it without SSL support. However, if you used a pass phrase for the private key when you created it, you are asked for the pass phrase.

1. Using an encrypted (with a pass phrase) private key requires that you don't start Samba automatically from the `/etc/rc.d/rc3.d/Sxxsmb` (where *xx* is a number) symbolic link. It doesn't start and waits for the pass phrase.

2. If you must use a pass phrase for the private key, remove the symbolic link (`/etc/rc.d/rc3.d/Sxxsmb`) and always start the Samba server manually.

3. If you created an unencrypted private key, you can start the Samba server as usual. To manually start the server, run the `/etc/rc.d/init.d/smb start` command.

Samba is started as usual. The daemon asks for the private key's pass phrase before it goes to the background if the private key is encrypted. If you start `smbd` from `inetd`, this won't work. Therefore, you must not encrypt your private key if you run `smbd` from `inetd`.

Securing NFS Server

As with Samba, NFS servers are widely used as file servers. In this section, I discuss security issues related to the NFS server.

GRANTING READ-ONLY ACCESS TO THE EXPORTED DIRECTORY
To allow only read-only access to any directory or *filesystem* you export from your NFS server to the clients, you can use `ro` as the access option as shown in this example:

```
/apps   devpc.nitec.com(ro)
```

Here the `devpc.nitec.com` client system has read-only access to the `/apps` directory. I recommend using the `ro` option to export directories that store application binaries.

DISABLING ACCESS TO A CERTAIN DIRECTORY

When you export an entire filesystem or a directory, the subdirectories below the exported directory are automatically accessible using the same access options. However, this may not be always desirable. You may want to allow access to a directory called /pub but not a directory called /pub/staff-only. In such a case, use the noaccess access option like this:

```
/pub              weblab-??.nitec.com (ro)
/pub/staff-only   weblab-??.nitec.com (noaccess)
```

Here all the weblab-??.nitec.com (where ?? is any two characters) computers have read-only access to the /pub directory, but they can't access the /pub/staff-only directory because of the noaccess option in the next line.

MAPPING USERS BETWEEN THE NFS SERVER AND THE CLIENTS

After you set up an NFS server, one issue that quickly comes up is how to keep the user from mapping between the NFS server and the clients. For example, say that you are exporting a directory called /www that is owned by a user and group called webguru and webdev, respectively. The NFS client capable of mounting this directory must have a user called webguru or a webdev group for access. This isn't often desirable. In particular, don't give an NFS client root account privileges on the NFS-mounted directory. This is why the NFS server by default enforces an option called root_squash. This typically maps the root user (UID = 0) and root group (GID = 0) to user nobody on the client system. You can disable the default mapping of the root user and group to nobody by adding no_root_squash when defining your export lines, but I don't recommend it unless you have an extraordinary circumstance in which the NFS client and server are both in an isolated, trusted environment.

To map the root UID/GID pair to a particular UID/GID, you can use the anonuid and anongid access options as shown in the following example:

```
/proj    *.nitec.com (anonuid=500 anongid=666)
```

Here, anonuid and anongid are specified to allow root squashing to UID 500 and GID 666.

If you prefer to squash all the UID/GID pairs to an anonymous UID/GID pair, you can use the all_squash option as shown in this example:

```
/proj    *.nitec.com (anonuid=500 anongid=666 all_squash)
```

Here the /proj directory is exported to all hosts in the nitec.com domain, but all accesses are made as UID 500 and GID 666.

If you want a list of UIDs and GIDs that should be squashed using the anonymous UID/GID pair, you can use the squash_uids and squash_gids options as shown in this example:

```
/proj    *.nitec.com (anonuid=500 anongid=666 \
squash_uids=0-100 squash_gids=0-100)
```

Here all the UIDs and GIDs in the range 0–100 are squashed, using the anonymous UID 500 and GID 666.

An external map file can map NFS client–supplied UIDs and GIDs to any UID or GID you want. You can specify the map by using the `map_static` option as shown in this example:

```
/proj    *.nitec.com (map_static=/etc/nfs.map)
```

Here the /proj directory is exported to all the nitec.com hosts, but all NFS client–supplied UIDs and GIDs are mapped using the /etc/nfs.map file. An example of this map file is below:

```
uid  0-100  -  # squash all remote uids in the 0-100 range
gid  0-100  -  # squash all remote gids in the 0-100 range
uid  500    666 # map remove uid 500 to local uid 666
gid  500    777 # map remove gid 500 to local gid 777
```

Now you know all the frequently used options for creating the /etc/export file. Whenever the /etc/exports file is changed, however, the system has to let the NFS daemons know about this change. A script called `exportfs` can restart these daemons, like this:

```
/usr/sbin/exportfs
```

Now, to make sure both rpc.mountd and rpc.nfsd are running properly, run a program called rpcinfo like this:

```
rpcinfo -p
```

The output looks like this:

```
program vers proto  port
 100000   2   tcp   111   portmapper
 100000   2   udp   111   portmapper
 100021   1   udp   1024  nlockmgr
 100021   3   udp   1024  nlockmgr
 100024   1   udp   1025  status
 100024   1   tcp   1024  status
 100011   1   udp   728   rquotad
 100011   2   udp   728   rquotad
 100005   1   udp   1026  mountd
 100005   1   tcp   1025  mountd
 100005   2   udp   1026  mountd
```

```
100005   2   tcp   1025   mountd
100003   2   udp   2049   nfs
```

This shows that `mountd` and `nfsd` have announced their services and are working fine. At this point, the NFS server is fully set up.

SECURING PORTMAP

The `portmap` setting, in combination with `rpc.nfsd`, can be fooled — making files accessible on NFS servers without any privileges. Fortunately, the portmap Linux uses is relatively secure against attack; you can secure it further by adding the following line in the `/etc/hosts.deny` file:

```
portmap: ALL
```

The system denies `portmap` access for everyone. Now the `/etc/hosts.allow` file must be modified like this:

```
portmap: 192.168.1.0/255.255.255.0
```

This allows all hosts from the 192.168.1.0 network access to portmap-administered programs such as `nfsd` and `mountd`.

 Never use hostnames in the `portmap` line in `/etc/hosts.allow`, because use of hostname lookups can indirectly cause `portmap` activity, which triggers hostname lookups in a loop.

SQUASHING THE ROOT USER

Treating the `root` account on a client as `root` on the server is another security issue on the server side. By default, Linux prohibits `root` on the NFS client from being treated as `root` on the NFS server. This means an exported file owned by `root` on the server can't be modified by the client `root` user. To explicitly enforce this rule, modify the `/etc/exports` file like this:

```
/www www1.nitec.com(rw, root_squash)
```

Now, if a user with UID 0 (the `root` user) on the client attempts access (read, write, or delete) on the filesystem, the server substitutes the UID of the server's `nobody` account. This means the `root` user on the client can't access or change files that only the `root` on the server can access or change. To grant `root` access to an NFS, use the `no_root_squash` option instead.

USING THE NOSUID AND NOEXEC OPTIONS

You can disable `set-UID` programs from running off NFS using he `nosuid` option. For example, you can have a line like the following in the `/etc/exports` file:

```
/www www1.nitec.com(rw, root_squash, nosuid)
```

Here the `/www` directory is mountable on `www1.nitec.com`. Users on `www1.nitec.com` can read and write files and directories in `/www` but can't run `set-UID` programs from it.

You can also forbid execution of files on the mounted filesystem altogether by adding the the `noexec` option to the list of options.

Using Cryptographic Filesystems

In any modern business, many sensitive files live forever on the organization's LAN or WAN. Most reasonable organizations keep the sensitive files related to employee salary structure, payroll, accounting information, and strategic and competitive market research data in a secure network accessible to only the appropriate groups of users. Typically, though, system administrators are involved in managing such resources but are not related to them. In certain cases, you want a Linux guru to manage your LAN but not access certain files. Because the `root` user can change any permissions settings, a simple file permission doesn't stop the prying eyes of a inexperienced or unprofessional network administrator. So what can you do?

Typically, such files are protected using individual passwords at the application level. In other words, if a sensitive text document should reside in a Samba share, you simply password-protect the file and give the password to appropriate people who need access. This works, but management becomes very cumbersome because of all the password tracking.

The better solution is a *cryptographic filesystem,* such as TCFS. TCFS works in the kernel space, which helps improve performances and security. The dynamic encryption feature of TCFS allows a user to specify the encryption engine of choice used by TCFS. You can learn more about TCFS at `http://tcfs.dia.unisa.it`. You can also download TCFS from `ftp://tcfs.dia.unisa.it/pub/tcfs/`.

Summary

Samba and NFS are very important protocols for modern organizations. Many organizations use these services to share disks and printers among many users. Securing Samba and NFS service is, therefore, a very important step in enhancing your overall network security. By centralizing user authentication using a Samba or Windows 2000/NT based server, avoiding plain-text passwords, and restricting access via IP addresses you can ensure that your Samba service is as secure as it can be. Similarly, by enabling read-only access to NFS mounted directories, securing portmap service and squashing root access, and using non set-UID and non executable file settings, you can secure your NFS server.

Part V

Firewalls

Chapter 20

Firewalls, VPNs, and SSL Tunnels

IN THIS CHAPTER

- Using a packet-filtering firewall
- Using Squid as a firewall
- Using FreeS/Wan

A *FIREWALL* IS A device that implements your security policy by shielding your network from external threats. This device can take various forms — from dedicated, commercial hardware that you buy from a vendor to a Linux system with special software. This chapter covers turning your Linux system into various types of firewalls to implement your security policy and protect your network.

Because network security is big business, many classifications of firewalls exist; thanks to commercial computer security vendors, many firewall systems are really hybrids that perform diverse functions. Here I focus on two types of firewall — the packet filter and the proxy firewall — and examine how you can use virtual private networks (VPNs) to help implement secure access to your system.

Packet-Filtering Firewalls

A *packet filter* (sometimes called a *filtering gateway* or a *screening router*) is a firewall that analyzes all IP packets flowing through it and determines the fate of each packet according to rules that you create. A packet filter operates at the network and transport layer of the TCP/IP protocol stack. It examines every packet that enters the protocol stack. The network and the transport headers of a packet are examined for information on

- The protocol being used
- Source and destination addresses
- Source and destination ports
- Connection status

You can set a packet filter to use certain features of a packet as criteria for allowing or denying access:

♦ **Protocols.** A typical filter can identify the TCP, UDP, and ICMP protocols, so you can allow or deny packets that operate under these protocols.

♦ **Source/destination.** You can allow or deny packets that come from a particular source and/or are inbound to a particular destination (whether an IP address or port).

♦ **Status information.** You can specify field settings that either qualify or disqualify a packet for admission to your system. For example, if a TCP packet has the ACK field set to 0, you can deny the packet under a policy that does not allow incoming connection requests to your network.

Fortunately, Linux kernel 2.4.*x* comes with a highly configurable packet-filtering infrastructure called netfilter. The netfilter Web site is:

http://netfilter.filewatcher.org.

The netfilter subsystem of the Linux kernel 2.4 allows you to set up, maintain, and inspect the packet-filtering rules in the kernel itself. It is a brand new packet-filtering solution, more advanced than what was available to Linux kernel before 2.4.*x*; netfilter provides a number of improvements, and it has now become an even more mature and robust solution for protecting corporate networks.

However, don't think of netfilter as merely a new packet-filter implementation. It is a complete framework for manipulating packets as they traverse the parts of the kernel. netfilter includes

♦ Packet filtering, IP masquerading, and network-address translation (NAT).

♦ Support for *stateful inspection* of packets (in which the kernel keeps track of the packets' state and context).

♦ Support for the development of custom modules to perform specific functions.

Netfilter contains data structures called tables within the kernel to provide packet-filtering. Each table contains lists of rules called chains. There are three tables:

♦ filter

♦ nat

♦ mangle

Each rule contains a set of criteria and a target. When the criteria are met, the target is applied to the packet. For example, the filter table (which is the default table), contains the INPUT, FORWARD, and OUPUT chains. These function as follows:

- ◆ The `INPUT` chain within the `filter` table holds the rules for the packets that are meant for the system that is examining the packet.

- ◆ The `FORWARD` chain contains the rules for the packets that are passing through the system that is examining the packets.

- ◆ The `OUTPUT` chain holds the rules for packets that are created by the system itself (which is also examining the packets).

The following listing shows a way to visualize the relationship among tables, chains, and rules. For example, the filter table has INPUT, FORWARD, and OUTPUT chains where each of these chains can have 1 to N number of rules.

```
filter table
|
+---INPUT
|   |
|   +---input rule 1
|   +---input rule 2
|   +---input rule 3
|   |   ...
|   +---input rule N
|
+---FORWARD
|   |
|   +---forward rule 1
|   +---forward rule 2
|   +---forward rule 3
|   |   ...
|   +---forward rule N
|
+---OUTPUT
    |
    +---output rule 1
    +---output rule 2
    +---output rule 3
    |   ...
    +---output rule N
nat table
|
+---PREROUTING
|   |
|   +---pre routing rule 1
|   +---pre routing rule 2
|   +---pre routing rule 3
|   |   ...
|   +---pre routing rule N
|
```

```
+---OUTPUT
|   |
|   +---output rule 1
|   +---output rule 2
|   +---output rule 3
|   |   ...
|   +---output rule N
|
+---POSTROUTING
    |
    +---post routing rule 1
    +---post routing rule 2
    +---post routing rule 3
    |   ...
    +---post routing rule N
mangle table
|
+---PREROUTING
|   |
|   +---pre routing rule 1
|   +---pre routing rule 2
|   +---pre routing rule 3
|   |   ...
|   +---pre routing rule N
|
+---OUTPUT
    |
    +---output rule 1
    +---output rule 2
    +---output rule 3
    |   ...
    +---output rule N
```

When a packet enters the packet-filter-and-firewall system, the packet-filtering subsystem of netfilter determines whether the packet is for itself (INPUT) or is simply being forwarded through itself (FORWARD), or is being generated by itself (OUTPUT). In the case of an input packet, the rules in the INPUT chain are applied in order. The first rule to match the packet criteria wins. The target of the matched rule then becomes the action for the packet.

The mangle table is used to change or modify packets both before they are routed and after routing has been decided. The mangle table has two chains: PREROUTING and POSTROUTING to store rules that apply prior to routing and post of routing, respectively.

The third table, nat, is used for Network Address Translation (NAT), which is a process of substituting an Internet-routable IP address for (typically) private addresses in IP packets. This is also known as *IP masquerading*.

The target of a rule can vary according to the table – or even the chain – it occupies. Table 20-1 is a list of targets available in each table.

TABLE 20-1: TARGETS FOR RULES IN FILTER, MANGLE, AND NAT TABLES

Target	filter	mangle	nat	Description
REJECT	Yes	Yes	Yes	When this target is used for a matched packet, an error response is sent back to the system that created the packet.
DENY	Yes	Yes	Yes	The matched packet is simply dropped when this is the target of a rule. Unlike REJECT, no error response is sent to the system generating the packet.
ACCEPT	Yes	Yes	Yes	The matched packet is accepted when this target is in use.
TOS	No	Yes	No	This target allows you to set the Type Of Service (TOS) byte (8-bits) field in the IP header of the packet.
MIRROR	Yes	Yes	Yes	When this target is in use, the matched packet's source and destination addresses are reversed and the packet is retransmitted.
MARK	No	Yes	No	This target is used to set the mark field value of a packet. The marking of a packet can be used by routers to change the routing behavior for such packets.
MASQUERADE	No	No	Yes	This target is used to alter the source address of the matched packet. The source address is replaced with the IP address of the packet filter's interface, which the packet will go out from. This target is used for packet-filtering systems that use dynamic IP address to connect to another network (such as the Internet) and also acts as a gateway between the networks.

If you have static a IP address for the interface that connects to the outside network, use SNAT target instead. |

Continued

TABLE 20-1: TARGETS FOR RULES IN FILTER, MANGLE, AND NAT TABLES
(Continued)

Target	filter	mangle	nat	Description
DNAT	No	No	Yes	This target specifies that the destination address of the packet should be modified.
SNAT	No	No	Yes	This target specifies that the source address of the packet should be modified, including all future packets in this connection.
REDIRECT	No	No	Yes	Redirect is another special type of NAT. All incoming connections are mapped onto the incoming interface's address, causing the packets to come to the local machine instead of passing through. This is useful for transparent proxies.
LOG	Yes	Yes	Yes	This target allows you to log information regarding a matched IP packet.
TTL	No	Yes	No	This target is used to modify the Time To Live (TTL) field of a matched IP packet.

The `iptables` extended packet matching modules supply additional capabilities in the form of shared library add-ons and small kernel modules that provide additional functionality.

 The old ipchains and ipfwadm modules maintain backward compatibility. You can only load one of these two modules at a time. You can't have ipchains and iptables rules at the same time. I recommend upgrading to the latest, stable kernel so that you can use `iptables` of the `netfilter` subsystem.

Enabling netfilter in the kernel

To enable `netfilter` support you must ensure that you have enabled the `netfilter` support in the kernel itself. Here is how you can do that.

1. As `root`, run the `menu config` command from the `/usr/src/linux` directory.

I assume that you have downloaded and extracted the latest, stable Linux kernel from www.kernel.org or a geographically closer mirror site.

2. From the main menu select Networking options submenu. From the Networking options submenu select the Network packet filtering (replaces ipchains) option to enable netfilter support.

3. Enter the IP: Netfilter Configuration submenu that appears when you complete step 2. Select the following options to be included as modules as shown, using <M>.

```
<M> Connection tracking (required for masq/NAT)
<M>    FTP protocol support (NEW)
<M> Userspace queuing via NETLINK (EXPERIMENTAL)
<M> IP tables support (required for filtering/masq/NAT)
<M>    limit match support (NEW)
<M>    MAC address match support (NEW)
<M>    netfilter MARK match support (NEW)
<M>    Multiple port match support (NEW)
<M>    TOS match support (NEW)
<M>    Connection state match support (NEW)
<M>    Unclean match support (EXPERIMENTAL) (NEW)
<M>    Owner match support (EXPERIMENTAL) (NEW)
<M>    Packet filtering (NEW)
<M>      REJECT target support (NEW)
<M>      MIRROR target support (EXPERIMENTAL) (NEW)
<M>    Full NAT (NEW)
<M>      MASQUERADE target support (NEW)
<M>      REDIRECT target support (NEW)
<M>    Packet mangling (NEW)
<M>      TOS target support (NEW)
<M>      MARK target support (NEW)
<M>    LOG target support (NEW)
< > ipchains (2.2-style) support
< > ipfwadm (2.0-style) support
```

I don't recommend using ipchains and ipfwadm support; they are in Linux past and, therefore, let them stay there!

Don't select the Fast switching option; it's incompatible with packet-filtering support.

4. Compile, install, and boot up the new kernel.

When the kernel is installed and compiled, you can start creating your packet-filtering rules. The next section shows how to do so with use of `iptables`.

Creating Packet-Filtering Rules with iptables

The `iptables` program is used to administer packet-filtering rules under the `netfilter` infrastructure. Here I provide you with the basics of how you can use this tool, but I strongly encourage you to read the man pages for `iptables` after you read this section. Another reason to read the man pages is that the `iptables` program has many command-line switches, but only the common ones are discussed here.

Creating a default policy

You can create a default policy for a given chain using the following syntax:

```
/sbin/iptables -P chain_name target
```

For example:

```
/sbin/iptables -P input DENY
/sbin/iptables -P output REJECT
/sbin/iptables -P forward REJECT
```

This is often considered as a preferred default policy for the filter table. Here all packets are denied or rejected by default. All packets that are input to the firewall system are denied; all packets that are generated by the firewall system itself are rejected; all packets that are to be forwarded through the system are also rejected. This is called the "deny everything by default" policy. Security experts prefer the concept of locking all doors and windows down and then opening the ones that are needed. This default packet-filtering policy serves the same purpose and is recommended by me. This policy, created using the combination of these three rules, should be always part of your packet-filtering firewall policy.

Appending a rule

To append a new rule to a specific chain, the syntax is

```
/sbin/iptables -A chain_name  rule_parameters -j target
```

For example:

```
/sbin/iptables -A input -s 192.168.1.254 -j ACCEPT
/sbin/iptables -A input -s 192.168.1.0/24 -j DROP
```

Here both of the rules are appended to the input chain of the default table (filter). You can explicitly specify the filter table using the -t *table_name* option. For example, the following lines of code are exactly equivalent to the two rules mentioned earlier:

```
/sbin/iptables -A input -t filter -s 192.168.1.254 -j ACCEPT
/sbin/iptables -A input -t filter -s 192.168.1.0/24 -j DROP
```

The very first rule specifies that any packet destined for the system from another host whose IP address is 192.168.1.254 be accepted by the system. The second rule specifies that all IP packets from any host in the entire 192.168.1.0/24 network be dropped. Avid readers will notice that the first IP address 192.168.1.254 is within the 192.168.1.0/24 network. So the second rule drops it! However, since the first matching rule wins, all the packets from the 192.168.1.254 host are accepted even if the next rule says they should be dropped.

So the order of rules is crucial. One exception to *the first matching rule wins* is the default policy rule — any default policy rule, as in this example:

```
/sbin/iptables -P input DENY
/sbin/iptables -A input -t filter -s 192.168.1.254 -j ACCEPT
/sbin/iptables -A input -t filter -s 192.168.1.0/24 -j DROP
```

Here the very first rule denies all packets but since it is the default policy (denoted by the -P option) it still allows other rules to be examined. In other words, the position of a policy rule does not prohibit other rules from being evaluated.

TIP You can write chain names in upper case or lower case. For example, INPUT and input are both acceptable.

Listing the rules

To list all the rules in a chain, simply run /sbin/iptables -L chain_name. For example, /sbin/iptables -L input lists all the rules in the input chain of the default filter table.

Deleting a rule

To delete a rule from a chain, run `/sbin/iptables -D chain_name rule_number`. For example, `/sbin/iptables -D input 1` deletes the first rule in the input chain of the default filter table.

To delete all the rules from a given chain, run `/sbin/iptables -F chain_name`. For example, `/sbin/iptables -F input` flushes (that is, empties) all the rules in the input chain.

You can also delete a rule by replacing the `-A` (append) option with `-D` (delete) option in your rule specification. For example, say that you have added the following rule:

```
/sbin/iptables -A input -t filter -s 192.168.1.0/24 -j DROP
```

Now if you want to delete it without listing all rules and determining the rule number as discussed earlier, simply do the following:

```
/sbin/iptables -D input -t filter -s 192.168.1.0/24 -j DROP
```

This deletes this rule.

Inserting a new rule within a chain

To insert a new rule in a specific chain at a specific position, the syntax is

```
/sbin/iptables -I chain_name  rule_number rule_parameters -j target
```

For example:

```
/sbin/iptables -I input 1 -s 192.168.1.254 -j ACCEPT
```

This inserts the rule in the number one position in the input chain of the default filter table.

Replacing a rule within a chain

To replacing an existing rule in a specific chain at a specific position, the syntax is

```
/sbin/iptables -R chain_name  rule_number rule_parameters -j target
```

For example:

```
/sbin/iptables -R input 1 -s 192.168.1.254 -j ACCEPT
```

This replaces the rule in the number one position in the input chain of the default filter table with the new rule.

You can use the `iptables` program to create/modify/delete rules and policies in packet-filtering firewalls.

Creating SOHO Packet-Filtering Firewalls

The Small Office/Home Office (SOHO) is a common phenomenon in a working world that has more small-business owners and telecommuters than ever before. The emergence of Digital Subscriber Line (DSL) and cable based Internet connections in recent years have made it possible for a full-time Internet connection for even the smallest home office. The drop in PC hardware price has given many SOHO owners a real chance at creating multinode networks. In this section I discuss how a SOHO can create a simple firewall system to take protective measures against the outside world of people with way too much time for hacking.

Suppose that there are three machines on the network and all three of them have real, static IP addresses as shown. Here each machine has an IP address that can be routed on the Internet. Suppose also that you – as the SOHO administrator – decide to turn the Linux box into a firewall, as shown in Figure 20-1.

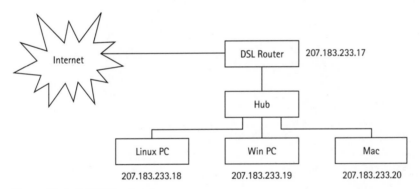

Figure 20-1: A SOHO network

Here the Linux PC has been set up with two Ethernet interfaces (eth0 and eth1). The eth0 is connected to the DSL router and it has a real IP address. The internal, private LAN interface of the Linux PC (eth1) has a private IP (192.168.1.254) and the two other systems in this LAN also have private IP addresses.

In this configuration, all outgoing packets from the private network flow through the Linux firewall machine to the outside world; similarly, all incoming packets from the Internet come to the private network via the firewall machine. This Linux PC must implement the following:

♦ IP forwarding to enable packet movement between eth0 and eth1

♦ IP masquerading to dynamically alter the private IP addresses of the private LAN to its own external interface (eth0) address for the outside world

♦ Packet-filtering rules to protect access to the private LAN

Enabling IP forwarding is quite easy. You can simply add the following command in the /etc/rc.d/rc.local script to enable IP forwarding when you boot up your Linux system.

```
/sbin/sysctl -w net.ipv4.conf.all.forwarding=1
```

You can also execute it from the shell to turn on IP forwarding at any time. Since you have already enabled the netfilter support in the kernel as discussed in the previous section, you can enable the masquerading and packet filtering using iptables, as shown in the script called soho-firewall.sh, Listing 20-1.

Listing 20-1: soho-firewall.sh

```
#!/bin/sh
# Path of the iptables program
IPTABLES=/sbin/iptables
# Private LAN address
INTERNAL_LAN="192.168.1.0/24"
# Private LAN Interface
INTERNAL_LAN_INTERFACE="eth1"
# Private LAN interface address
INTERNAL_LAN_INTERFACE_ADDR="192.168.1.254"
# External LAN Interface
EXTERNAL_LAN_INTERFACE="eth0"
# External LAN interface address
EXTERNAL_LAN_INTERFACE_ADDR="207.183.233.18"
# Flush all the current packet filtering rules
$IPTABLES -F
# Set default policy to deny everything
$IPTABLES -P input DENY
$IPTABLES -P output REJECT
$IPTABLES -P forward REJECT
# Enable local (loopback) interface
```

```
$IPTABLES -A input -i lo -j ACCEPT
$IPTABLES -A output -i lo -j ACCEPT
# Enable internal LAN access to the firewall's
# internal interface
$IPTABLES -A input -i $INTERNAL_LAN_INTERFACE \
         -s $INTERNAL_LAN -j ACCEPT
# Enable firewall generated packets destined for
# the internal LAN
$IPTABLES -A output -i $INTERNAL_LAN_INTERFACE \
         -d $INTERNAL_LAN -j ACCEPT
# Setup masquerading for everything not destined to
# the internal LAN
$IPTABLES -t nat -A POSTROUTING -o $ EXTERNAL_LAN_INTERFACE \
         -d ! $INTERNAL_LAN \
         -j MASQUERADE
# Only forward packets from internal LAN
$IPTABLES -A FORWARD -s $INTERNAL_LAN -j ACCEPT
$IPTABLES -A FORWARD -d $INTERNAL_LAN -j ACCEPT
```

This script allows you to change the necessary variables to make it work in a similar, real-world environment. When the script is executed as shown in Listing 20-1, it effectively creates the following packet-filtering rules.

```
/sbin/iptables -F
/sbin/iptables -P input DENY
/sbin/iptables -P output REJECT
/sbin/iptables -P forward REJECT
/sbin/iptables -A input -i lo -j ACCEPT
/sbin/iptables -A output -i lo -j ACCEPT
/sbin/iptables -A input -i eth1 -s 192.168.1.0/24 -j ACCEPT
/sbin/iptables -A output -i eth1 -d 192.168.1.0/24 -j ACCEPT
/sbin/iptables -t nat -A POSTROUTING -o eth0 -d ! 192.168.1.0/24 -j MASQUERADE
/sbin/iptables -A FORWARD -s 192.168.1.0/24 -j ACCEPT
/sbin/iptables -A FORWARD -d 192.168.1.0/24 -j ACCEPT
```

The script has these rules:

◆ The very first rule flushes all the existing rules in the filter table.

◆ The next three rules should be familiar to you since they are the default policy rules. These rules state that no packet can enter, leave, or be forwarded to/from this system. Basically, these three rules lock up the IP traffic completely.

◆ The next two rules enable traffic to and from the local loopback interface (lo) so that you can access other systems when logged onto the firewall machine itself.

◆ The next rule specifies that any packet with source IP residing in the 192.168.1.0/24 network be accepted on the eth1 interface. Remember that the eth1 interface in Figure 20-2 is the internal, private network interface of the firewall system. We want this interface to accept packets from other nodes (that is, hosts) in the private network.

◆ The next rule specifies that packets generated (that is, output) by the firewall itself for the 192.168.1.0/24 network be allowed.

◆ The next rule is the masquerading rule. It uses the nat table and the POSTROUTING chain. This rule states that all packets not destined for the 192.168.1.0/24 network be masqueraded. For example, if a packet from the Windows PC (192.168.1.1) system destined for an external system with IP address 207.183.233.200 is detected by the firewall machine, it changes the source address of this packet such that the 207.183.233.200 sees 207.183.233.18 (eth0) address as the source address. When response packet from 207.183.233.200 arrives at 207.183.233.18, the NAT facility retranslates the destination address to be 192.168.1.1.

At this point, what you have is a firewall system that forwards masqueraded IP traffic to the external interface (eth0) but no inbound packet can be seen from the outside world by the internal, private network. You need to now categorically open connectivity from external interface to the internal network.

Allowing users at private network access to external Web servers

In this case you want to do the following:

◆ Outbound traffic rule – Create a rule that allows the external interface of the firewall to send (that is, output) HTTP requests using the standard port 80.

◆ Inbound traffic rule – Create a rule that allows the external interface of the firewall to receive (that is, input) HTTP responses from outside Web servers.

Here is a rule that you can add to the soho-firewall.sh script to implement the outbound traffic rule:

```
$IPTABLES  -A output -i $EXTERNAL_LAN_INTERFACE -p tcp \
       -s $EXTERNAL_LAN_INTERFACE_ADDR 1024-65535 \
       -d 0/0 80 -j ACCEPT
```

This rule looks as follows when shell script variables are substituted for appropriate values:

```
/sbin/iptables -A output -i eth0 -p tcp \
        -s 207.183.233.18 1024-65535 \
        -d 0/0 80 -j ACCEPT
```

This rule allows the firewall to output HTTP packets on port 80 destined to any IP address using the external interface. The 1024–65535 range specifies that the Web browser can use any of the non-privileged ports (that is, ports greater than 0–1023) in the connection and, therefore, the firewall will not block packets with such a source port number.

Similarly, you need the following line in the script to accept HTTP response traffic destined for the external interface.

```
$IPTABLES  -A input  -i $EXTERNAL_LAN_INTERFACE -p tcp ! -y \
        -s 0/0 80 \
        -d $EXTERNAL_LAN_INTERFACE_ADDR 1024-65535 \
        -j ACCEPT
```

In this case, packets sent by outside Web servers to the external interface of the firewall via the external IP address of the firewall as the destination are accepted for any unprivileged port as long as the source port is HTTP (80).

As you can see, opening bi-directional connection requires that you know which port a particular service runs on. For example, suppose you want to allow the outside world access to your Web server in the private network.

Allowing external Web browsers access to a Web server on your firewall

Running a Web server on a firewall is not a good idea but might be necessary (resource wise) for a SOHO. In such case, you want to do the following:

◆ Create a rule that allows any IP address to connect to the HTTP port (80) on your firewall machine's external interface.

◆ Create a rule that allows the firewall/Web server to respond to unprivileged ports (which Web clients use for client-side connection) when source IP address is any IP and source port is HTTP (80).

The following lines can be added to the soho-firewall.sh script to implement these rules.

```
# Allow any IP to connect to firewall's external
# interface to send a HTTP request for the
```

```
# internal network
$IPTABLES  -A input -i $EXTERNAL_LAN_INTERFACE
           -p tcp ! -y \
           -s 0/0 1024-65535  \
           -d $EXTERNAL_LAN_INTERFACE_ADDR 80 \
           -j ACCEPT
# Allow internal HTTP response to go out to the
# world via the external interface of the firewall
$IPTABLES  -A output -i $EXTERNAL_LAN_INTERFACE
           -p tcp \
           -s $EXTERNAL_LAN_INTERFACE_ADDR 80  \
           -d 0/0 1024-65535 \
           -j ACCEPT
```

If you want to enable HTTPS (Secure HTTP) connections, add the following lines:

```
# Enable incoming HTTPS connections
$IPTABLES  -A input -i $EXTERNAL_LAN_INTERFACE
           -p tcp ! -y \
           -s 0/0 443  \
           -d $EXTERNAL_LAN_INTERFACE_ADDR 1024-65535 \
           -j ACCEPT
# Enable outgoing HTTPS connections
$IPTABLES  -A output -i $EXTERNAL_LAN_INTERFACE
           -p tcp \
           -s $EXTERNAL_LAN_INTERFACE_ADDR 1024-65535 \
           -d 0/0 443 \
           -j ACCEPT
```

In order to interact with the Internet, you are most likely to need a few other services enabled, such as DNS, SMTP, POP3, and SSH. In the following sections, I show you how.

DNS client and cache-only services

In a SOHO environment you are likely to use your ISP's name server for resolving DNS queries or you can use a caching only, local name server to boost your overall DNS related performance. First, suppose that you only want to enable access to the remote DNS server at your ISP network. Suppose that you have set up the following variable in the soho-firewall.sh script to point to the IP address of the name server.

```
NAMED_ADDR="207.183.233.100"
```

Now, to allow your private network to access the name server, you should add the following lines in the script.

```
# Allow packets from external interface of the
# firewall to access an outside named server
$IPTABLES  -A output -i $EXTERNAL_LAN_INTERFACE
           -p udp \
           -s $EXTERNAL_LAN_INTERFACE_ADDR 1024-65535  \
           -d $NAMED_ADDR 53 \
           -j ACCEPT
# Allow an external named to respond to internal
# request by delivering query response packets
# to external interface of the firewall
$IPTABLES  -A input -i $EXTERNAL_LAN_INTERFACE
           -p udp \
           -s $NAMED_ADDR 53 \
           -d $EXTERNAL_LAN_INTERFACE_ADDR 1024-65535  \
           -j ACCEPT
```

The very first rule ensures that the firewall allows outputting of DNS query packets on port 53 via the UDP protocol. The second rule ensures that the firewall allows DNS query response packets originating from the name server to be accepted.

Sometimes, when the DNS response is too large to fit in a UDP packet, a name server uses a TCP packet to respond. This occurs rarely unless you have systems in your internal network that want to perform DNS zone transfers, which are often large. If you want to ensure that rare large DNS responses are handled properly, add two more of the same rules as shown above except replace the -p udp protocol to -p tcp. Also use the ! -y option for the input rule.

Now if you run a DNS server internally on the private LAN or even on the firewall machine (not recommended), then you need to allow the caching server to perform DNS queries to your ISP's DNS server when it cannot resolve an internal request from the cache. In such case, add the following lines to the same script.

```
# Allow DNS resolver to connect to external
# name server on port 53
$IPTABLES  -A output -i $EXTERNAL_LAN_INTERFACE
           -p udp \
           -s $EXTERNAL_LAN_INTERFACE_ADDR 53  \
           -d $NAMED_ADDR 53 \
```

```
          -j ACCEPT
# Allow external name server to connect to firewall
# system's external interface in response to a
# resolver query
$IPTABLES  -A input -i $EXTERNAL_LAN_INTERFACE
          -p udp \
          -s $NAMED_ADDR 53 \
          -d $EXTERNAL_LAN_INTERFACE_ADDR 53 \
          -j ACCEPT
```

SMTP client service

To access SMTP mail server from the internal network, add the following lines in the soho-firewall.sh script

```
    # Change the SMTP server IP address as needed
    SMTP_SERVER_ADDR="1.2.3.4"
    # Enable outgoing SMTP connections
$IPTABLES  -A output -i $EXTERNAL_LAN_INTERFACE
          -p tcp \
          -s $EXTERNAL_LAN_INTERFACE_ADDR 1024-65535 \
          -d $SMTP_SERVER_ADDR 25 \
              -j ACCEPT
# Enable incoming SMTP responses from external SMTP
# server
$IPTABLES  -A input -i $EXTERNAL_LAN_INTERFACE
          -p tcp ! -y \
          -s $SMTP_SERVER_ADDR 25 \
          -d $EXTERNAL_LAN_INTERFACE_ADDR 1024-65535 \
          -j ACCEPT
```

POP3 client service

To access POP3 mail server from the internal network, add the following lines in the soho-firewall.sh script.

```
    # Change the POP3 server IP address as needed
    POP_SERVER_ADDR="1.2.3.4"
    # Enable outgoing POP3 connections
$IPTABLES  -A output -i $EXTERNAL_LAN_INTERFACE
          -p tcp ! -y \
          -s $EXTERNAL_LAN_INTERFACE_ADDR 1024-65535 \
          -d $POP_SERVER_ADDR 110 \
              -j ACCEPT
```

```
# Enable incoming POP3 responses from external POP3
# server
$IPTABLES  -A input -i $EXTERNAL_LAN_INTERFACE
          -p tcp ! -y \
          -s $POP_SERVER_ADDR 110 \
          -d $EXTERNAL_LAN_INTERFACE_ADDR 1024-65535  \
          -j ACCEPT
```

Passive-mode FTP client service

To access FTP server from the internal network, add the following lines in the soho-firewall.sh **script.**

```
# Change the FTP server IP address as needed
FTP_SERVER_ADDR="1.2.3.4"
# Enable outgoing FTP connections
$IPTABLES  -A output -i $EXTERNAL_LAN_INTERFACE
          -p tcp ! -y \
          -s $EXTERNAL_LAN_INTERFACE_ADDR 1024-65535  \
          -d $POP_SERVER_ADDR 21 \
               -j ACCEPT
# Enable incoming FTP command responses from
# external FTP server
$IPTABLES  -A input -i $EXTERNAL_LAN_INTERFACE
          -p tcp ! -y \
          -s $FTP_SERVER_ADDR 21 \
          -d $EXTERNAL_LAN_INTERFACE_ADDR 1024-65535  \
          -j ACCEPT
# Enable passive mode data connections
$IPTABLES  -A output -i $EXTERNAL_LAN_INTERFACE
          -p tcp ! -y \
          -s $EXTERNAL_LAN_INTERFACE_ADDR 1024-65535  \
          -d $POP_SERVER_ADDR 1024-65535 \
               -j ACCEPT
# Enable passive mode data response
$IPTABLES  -A input -i $EXTERNAL_LAN_INTERFACE
          -p tcp ! -y \
          -s $FTP_SERVER_ADDR 1024-65535  \
          -d $EXTERNAL_LAN_INTERFACE_ADDR 1024-65535  \
          -j ACCEPT
```

SSH client service

If you want to allow SSH client connection to an external SSH server, add the following lines in the soho-firewall.sh script.

```
# Set the IP address of your external SSH server
# here. A random IP address is used in this example
#
EXTERNAL_SSH_SERVER_ADDR="207.177.175.60"
# Allow the firewall to connect to SSH server
# for the masquerading nodes behind it that want
# to connect to the SSH server
$IPTABLES  -A output -i $EXTERNAL_LAN_INTERFACE
          -p tcp \
          -s $EXTERNAL_LAN_INTERFACE_ADDR 1020-65535  \
          -d $ EXTERNAL_SSH_SERVER_ADDR 22 \
          -j ACCEPT
# Allow an external SSH server to deliver SSH packets
# to the external interface of the firewall
$IPTABLES  -A input -i $EXTERNAL_LAN_INTERFACE
          -p tcp ! -y \
          -s $EXTERNAL_SSH_SERVER_ADDR 22 \
          -d $EXTERNAL_LAN_INTERFACE_ADDR 1020-65535  \
          -j ACCEPT
```

Note that SSH clients use 1020 or higher ports and, therefore, you need to use 1020-65535 range.

Other new client service

Once you have identified a new service that you want to control using the firewall, do the following:

1. Determine what server (SERVER_ADDR) you want to access from the internal network.

2. Determine what ports are going to be used in such connectivity. Most likely the service uses a port defined in /etc/services file. Find that port (ASSIGNED_PORT).

3. Determine what ports the client software uses for the client-side of the connection. Typically, the unassigned ports (1024-65535) are used.

4. Determine what protocol is being used, TCP or UDP.

   ■ For TCP protocol, use the -t tcp and ! -y options

   ■ for UDP, use -t udp option.

5. Create an output rule that allows the external interface of the firewall to send packets to the server.

Internal clients can access the internal interface of the firewall and their requests for the external service is automatically forwarded to the external interface. And this is why we create the output rule for the external interface. This rule appears as follows:

```
/sbin/iptables -A output -i external_interface \
               -p protocol_name \
               -s external_interface_address UNASSIGNED_PORTS \
               -d external_server_address ASSIGNED_PORT \
               -j ACCEPT
```

6. Create an input rule that allows the external server to respond with packets.

The rule looks like this:

```
/sbin/iptables -A input -i external_interface \
               -p protocol_name [ ! -y ] \
               -s external_server_address ASSIGNED_PORT \
               -d external_interface_address UNASSIGNED_PORTS \
               -j ACCEPT
```

Creating a Simple Firewall

There are times when I am asked to create a simple firewall. Yes, there are people who ask such questions. They want security, complete flexibility in everything, which reminds me of the phrase "have your cake and eat it too." In such cases, I simply create the following rules in a script called /etc/rc.d/firewall-dummy.sh:

```
#!/bin/sh
#
# Packet filtering firewall for dummies
#
IPTABLES=/sbin/iptables
# Drop all rules in the filter table
$IPTABLES -F FORWARD
$IPTABLES -F INPUT
$IPTABLES -F OUTPUT
# Create default drop-and-reject-everything policy
$IPTABLES -P input DENY
```

```
$IPTABLES -P output REJECT
$IPTABLES -P forward REJECT
# Enable loopback
$IPTABLES -A INPUT -i lo -p all -j ACCEPT
# Enable ICMP. Yes, even a dummy knows
# how to use ping these days!
$IPTABLES -A INPUT -p icmp -j ACCEPT
# Enable caching DNS
$IPTABLES -A INPUT -p tcp --dport 53 -j ACCEPT
$IPTABLES -A INPUT -p udp --dport 53 -j ACCEPT
# We do not want to allow new connection so
# accept only those incoming packets that do
# not have the SYN flag set. In other words,
# these packets are not new connection requests
$IPTABLES -A INPUT -p tcp ! --syn \
        --dport :1023 -j ACCEPT \
        -- syn -- dport :1023 -j ACCEPT
# Most everything that a Internet dummy does
# need unprivileged port access for both TCP and UDP
# so enable them
$IPTABLES -A INPUT -p tcp --dport 1024: -j ACCEPT
$IPTABLES -A INPUT -p udp --dport 1024: -j ACCEPT
```

Creating Transparent, proxy-arp Firewalls

Suppose that you have a small office where several Linux/Windows 9x/2K/NT machines are connected to the internet using a modem or DSL/cable/ISDN router. You want to allow the world access to the Web server in your network and also want to implement some of the packet-filtering rules you learned earlier.

Suppose your ISP provided you with an Internet connection via the network X.Y.Z.32/27.

You have each machine on the network use the X.Y.Z.35 address as its Internet gateway address – which allows each machine to send and receive packets to and from the outside world. Now you have two choices for your firewall:

- ◆ Set up a firewall machine between your LAN and the Internet feed (which is the typical place for a firewall).

The problem with the typical placement of a firewall is that if the firewall machine is down, the entire LAN is disconnected from the Internet. If Internet access is a big part of your business, that spells trouble — especially for a small company.

◆ Use a transparent `proxy-arp` firewall.

In this case, the firewall machine is less of a potential obstacle to your company's Internet connection. If the firewall machine is down, you can simply take out the network cable connected to eth0 on the firewall and reconnect it to the hub on the other side (eth1 side) and you should have full Internet connectivity. You might need to have your ISP refresh the arp cache and/or reboot some of your machines, but your network regains Internet access in a very short time.

The idea behind this setup is as follows: the Linux firewall machine has two network interfaces eth0 and eth1 set to the same IP address (X.Y.Z.50) and has APR proxying and IP forwarding turned on. This allows the machine to see all the packets that are either originated from your LAN or that are coming to your LAN from the outside world via the ISP feed. Therefore, you can use packet filtering on such packets like a regular firewall system.

The only real advantage is that if the firewall is down for upgrade, or other uncontrollable reasons, you can recover your connectivity in a much shorter time than if you had a regular firewall configuration where you had private IP addresses for your LAN and all the hosts were pointing to the firewall as their gateway to the Internet. In this configuration, the host machines don't even know that their packets are being scanned, forwarded by the man-in-the-middle type of transparent `proxy-arp` based firewall system. Assuming that you have a Linux system with two Ethernet network cards (eth0, eth1) installed, here is how you can create such as a setup.

1. As `root`, you need to create a custom kernel that supports netfilters.

   You can use the make menuconfig command to set this option from the `/usr/src/linux` directory. Select the `[ ] Network packet filtering (replaces ipchains)` from the `Networking options` submenu from the main menu and compile, install, and test your new kernel. For help in compiling, installing, and booting a new kernel, see Chapter 2.

2. Download and install the `iproute` package using RPM.

   For example, I installed the `iproute-2.2.4-10 rpm` package, which I downloaded from a RPM mirror site called `www.rpmfind.net`.

3. Set up both of the `/etc/sysconfig/network-scripts/ifcfg-eth0` and
   `/etc/sysconfig/network-scripts/ifcfg-eth1` to have the same

   - IP address

   - Network address

   - Network mask

4. Add the following lines in your `/etc/rc.d/rc.local` script to enable the
   `proxy_arp` feature for both of your Linux network interfaces.

   ```
   /sbin/sysctl net.ipv4.conf.eth0.proxy_arp=1
   /sbin/sysctl net.ipv4.conf.eth1.proxy_arp=1
   ```

5. Add the following line in `/etc/rc.d/rc.local` script to enable IP forwarding between the eth0 and eth1 interfaces.

   ```
   /sbin/sysctl -w net.ipv4.conf.all.forwarding=1
   ```

6. Add the following lines in your `/etc/rc.d/rc.local` script. Don't forget
   to replace the X.Y.Z.32/27, X.Y.Z.35 with appropriate network addresses.

   ```
   /sbin/ip route del X.Y.Z.32/27 dev eth0
   /sbin/ip route add X.Y.Z.35 dev eth0
   /sbin/ip route add X.Y.Z.32/27 dev eth1
   ```

   This tells the kernel that packets for the X.Y.Z.35 address (that is, the
   address of the router) is routed on eth0 and the rest of the network is
   available on eth1. Since you have enabled IP forwarding between the
   interfaces, any outside packet destined for an internal LAN host are seen
   by eth0 and forwarded onto eth1.

At this point, either you can wait awhile for the `arp` caches to expire or restart
your router. At that point you should be able to get back and forth between the
router and the other servers on the network. If you look at your `arp` cache on a
server, it will show the `mac` address of the router as the `mac` address of eth1 on your
Linux firewall. After you have this layer working, you can add your rules.

Creating Corporate Firewalls

A corporation that has a lot of day-to-day Internet interaction is likely to spend
quite a bit of resource in building a secure infrastructure. Here, I explore one such
infrastructure that you can build with a set of Linux-based packet-filtering firewalls. Note that a packet-filtering firewall is only *one* of the important components
in a high-grade security solution. As a rule of thumb, multiple (and redundant)
security measures ensure a higher degree of security. This section focuses only on

the packet-filtering aspect of the solution; later sections cover other security components that you can integrate with packet filtering to build a robust, well-secured environment for your organization.

A multiple-firewall environment, known as a *Demilitarized Zone (DMZ)*, keeps the corporate public servers such as the Web server (Apache server), FTP server, mail server, and DNS server (if any) behind the primary firewall. The internal network (consisting of employee workstations, and possibly internal-only servers) resides behind another, separate firewall. Each of these firewalls has a distinct purpose; an examination of each purpose follows.

Purpose of the internal firewall

The internal firewall protects the internal network from outside access. It forwards non-local traffic to the DMZ and restricts incoming traffic. This firewall should be configured to do the following:

♦ Implement the default deny-all-packets policy.

♦ Masquerade the internal traffic meant for the DMZ services or for the outside world.

♦ Allow only incoming traffic that has been generated in response to internal requests. Incoming packets to this firewall must not have SYN bit set.

♦ Limit the internal network's access to outside services

Purpose of the primary firewall

The external (primary) firewall protects the entire corporate network, but its main task is to do the following:

♦ Implement the default "deny all packets" policy.

♦ Allow access to the DMZ servers from the outside world.

♦ Masquerade the packets that are generated by the internal firewall (on behalf of internal nodes) to the outside world to make the packets appear to be coming from the primary firewall's external interface.

When the firewall is doing its job correctly, a typical scenario looks like this:

1. A user at a workstation in the internal LAN initiates a HTTP request for an outside domain via her Web browser.

2. The internal firewall masquerades her requests to its own external interface (the DMZ site).

3. The primary firewall sees this outgoing packet, masquerades it, and forwards to the outside world.

4. The Web server on the outside knows only that the external IP address of the primary firewall has requested access to an outside domain. Accordingly, the Web server sends response packets to the DMZ site, which ensures that outside systems do not know who the real user is — and (more importantly) can't get hold of the user-account information for unauthorized uses.

Note that you can decide to not masquerade outgoing packets on the internal firewall — the external firewall masquerades them anyway — but if you masquerade outgoing packets on the internal firewall, you can use simpler packet-filtering rules on the external (primary) firewall. When implemented consistently, such an arrangement can enhance performance without harming security. Because the primary firewall sees all packets from the internal network as coming from one address — that of the internal firewall's external interface — that one IP is the only one you have to deal with when you create access rules on the primary firewall.

 In this example, I use a DMZ network 192.168.1.0/24 (actually a private network) — but in the real world, you cannot access a non-routable, private network from the Internet. You have to use an Internet-routable, non-private network for your real-world DMZ. Ask your ISP to allocate a subnet to your company's use — and to route all packets addressed to the subnet to your firewall's external interface address instead. Then assign each server in your DMZ a real IP address to make them accessible from the outside world via the firewall. Note also that the external network address for the primary firewall is also assigned by your ISP; the example uses a random number that is routable on the Internet.

Implementing these firewalls for the given scenario is a distinct process. Note that when you follw the instructions in the next two subsections, you must change IP addresses to match those on your own network environment.

Setting up the internal firewall

To set up your internal firewall, follow these steps:

1. Create an sh script (called internal-firewall.sh) that defines the settings of the internal network as follows:

```
#!/bin/sh
IPTABLES=/sbin/iptables
INTERNAL_LAN="192.168.2.0/24"
```

```
INTERNAL_LAN_INTERFACE="eth1"
INTERNAL_LAN_INTERFACE_ADDR="192.168.2.254"
EXTERNAL_INTERFACE="eth0"
EXTERNAL_INTERFACE_ADDR="192.168.1.1"
```

2. Flush out all the rules in the `filter` table by appending the following lines to the script:

```
# Drop all rules in the filter table
$IPTABLES -F FORWARD
$IPTABLES -F INPUT
$IPTABLES -F OUTPUT
```

3. Implement the default policy by appending the following lines to the script:

```
# Create default drop and reject everything policy
$IPTABLES -P FORWARD DROP
$IPTABLES -P OUTPUT ACCEPT
$IPTABLES -P INPUT DROP
```

4. Enable the local loopback interface by appending these lines:

```
# Enable loopback
$IPTABLES -A INPUT -i lo -p all -j ACCEPT
```

5. Enable the Internet Control Message Protocol (ICMP) packets used by `ping` and other services:

```
$IPTABLES -A INPUT -p icmp -j ACCEPT
```

6. Allow internal LAN access to the firewall's internal interface by appending these lines:

```
$IPTABLES -A input -i $INTERNAL_LAN_INTERFACE \
          -s $INTERNAL_LAN -j ACCEPT
```

7. Allow access to firewall-generated packets destined for the internal LAN:

```
$IPTABLES -A output -i $INTERNAL_LAN_INTERFACE \
          -d $INTERNAL_LAN -j ACCEPT
```

8. Set up masquerading for everything not destined for the internal LAN:

```
$IPTABLES -t nat -A POSTROUTING -o $EXTERNAL_LAN_INTERFACE \
          -d ! $INTERNAL_LAN \
          -j MASQUERADE
```

9. Forward only those packets that come from the internal LAN by appending these lines:

```
$IPTABLES -A FORWARD -s $INTERNAL_LAN -j ACCEPT
$IPTABLES -A FORWARD -d $INTERNAL_LAN -j ACCEPT
```

At this point, you have a firewall that can masquerade internal traffic meant for outside servers. Now you have to decide what types of services your internal users may access — for example, HTTP, SMTP, POP3, DNS, and AUTH (part of `identd`) — and create specific firewall rules for each service.

Setting up the primary firewall

To set up your external (primary) firewall, create an `sh` script called `firewall-primary.sh` script, as shown in Listing 20-2.

Listing 20-2: Firewall-primary.sh

```
#!/bin/sh
IPTABLES=/sbin/iptables
DMZ_LAN="192.168.1.0/24"
DMZ_INTERFACE="eth1"
DMZ_INTERFACE_ADDR="192.168.1.254"
WORLD_INTERFACE="eth0"
WORLD_INTERFACE_ADDR="207.177.175.66"
INTERNAL_LAN="192.168.2.0/24"
DMZ_FTP_SERVER_ADDR="192.168.1.10"
DMZ_APACHE_SERVER_ADDR="192.168.1.20"
DMZ_MAIL_SERVER_ADDR="192.168.1.30"
DMZ_DNS_SERVER_ADDR="192.168.1.40"
# Drop all rules in the filter table
$IPTABLES -F FORWARD
$IPTABLES -F INPUT
$IPTABLES -F OUTPUT
# Create default drop and reject everything policy
$IPTABLES -P FORWARD DROP
$IPTABLES -P OUTPUT ACCEPT
$IPTABLES -P INPUT DROP
# Enable loopback
$IPTABLES -A INPUT -i lo -p all -j ACCEPT
# Enable the Internet Control Message Protocol (ICMP)
# packets that are used by ping and others
$IPTABLES -A INPUT -p icmp -j ACCEPT
# Enable DMZ LAN access to the firewall's
# internal interface
$IPTABLES -A input -i $DMZ_LAN_INTERFACE \
        -s $DMZ_LAN -j ACCEPT
# Enable firewall generated packets destined for
# the DMZ LAN
$IPTABLES -A output -i $DMZ_LAN_INTERFACE \
```

```
            -d $DMZ_LAN -j ACCEPT
# Setup masquerading for packets generated by the
# internal private LAN that is not meant for itself
$IPTABLES -t nat -A POSTROUTING -o $EXTERNAL_LAN_INTERFACE \
            -s $INTERNAL_LAN \
            -d ! $INTERNAL_LAN \
            -j MASQUERADE
# Forward packets from DMZ LAN
$IPTABLES -A FORWARD -s $DMZ_LAN -j ACCEPT
$IPTABLES -A FORWARD -d $DMZ_LAN -j ACCEPT
```

The next step is to add rules to enable the services offered in the DMZ.

ACCESSING FTP SERVERS IN YOUR DMZ

You want to allow FTP server access from the outside world, but you also want to regulate it to prevent FTP from becoming a security risk. The following code lays the foundation for such a policy:

```
# Enable incoming FTP connections from
# outside world
$IPTABLES   -A input -i $WORLD_INTERFACE
            -p tcp \
            -s 0/0 1024-65535  \
            -d $DMZ_FTP_SERVER_ADDR 21\
            -j ACCEPT
    # Enable outgoing FTP connections
$IPTABLES   -A output -i $WORLD_INTERFACE
            -p tcp ! -y \
            -s $DMZ_FTP_SERVER_ADDR 21  \
            -d 0/0 1024-65535  \
                -j ACCEPT
# Enable incoming FTP data channel connection from
# outside world
$IPTABLES   -A input -i $WORLD_INTERFACE
            -p tcp \
            -s 0/0 1024-65535  \
            -d $DMZ_FTP_SERVER_ADDR 1024-65535  \
            -j ACCEPT
# Enable outgoing FTP data connections
$IPTABLES   -A output -i $WORLD_INTERFACE
            -p tcp ! -y \
            -s $DMZ_FTP_SERVER_ADDR 1024-65535  \
            -d 0/0 1024-65535  \
                -j ACCEPT
```

ACCESSING APACHE SERVERS IN DMZ

You want to allow Apache server access from the outside world. Here is the script:

```
# Enable incoming HTTP requests from
# outside world
$IPTABLES  -A input -i $WORLD_INTERFACE
          -p tcp \
          -s 0/0 1024-65535 \
          -d $DMZ_APACHE_SERVER_ADDR 80\
          -j ACCEPT
# Enable outgoing HTTP responses
$IPTABLES  -A output -i $WORLD_INTERFACE
          -p tcp ! -y \
          -s $DMZ_APACHE_SERVER_ADDR 80  \
          -d 0/0 1024-65535 \
            -j ACCEPT
```

ACCESSING DNS SERVERS IN DMZ

You want to allow DNS server access from the outside world. Here is the script:

```
# Enable incoming client/server DNS requests from
# outside world
$IPTABLES  -A input -i $WORLD_INTERFACE
          -p udp \
          -s 0/0 1024-65535 \
          -d $DMZ_DNS_SERVER_ADDR 53\
          -j ACCEPT
    # Enable outgoing client/server DNS responses
$IPTABLES  -A output -i $WORLD_INTERFACE
          -p udp \
          -s $DMZ_DNS_SERVER_ADDR 53 \
          -d 0/0 1024-65535 \
          -j ACCEPT
# Enable incoming server/server DNS requests from
# outside world
$IPTABLES  -A input -i $WORLD_INTERFACE
          -p udp \
          -s 0/0 53 \
          -d $DMZ_DNS_SERVER_ADDR 53\
          -j ACCEPT
# Enable outgoing server/server DNS responses
$IPTABLES  -A output -i $WORLD_INTERFACE
          -p udp \
          -s $DMZ_DNS_SERVER_ADDR 53 \
          -d 0/0 53 \
          -j ACCEPT
```

ACCESSING IDENTD (AUTH) SERVERS IN DMZ

You want to allow identd server access from the outside world. The identd server is usually run on the mail server to provide user authentication service. I assume that you are running identd on DMZ_MAIL_SERVER. Here is the script:

```
# Enable incoming auth requests from
# outside world
$IPTABLES  -A input -i $WORLD_INTERFACE
           -p tcp \
           -s 0/0 1024-65535  \
           -d $DMZ_MAIL_SERVER_ADDR 113\
           -j ACCEPT
    # Enable outgoing auth responses
$IPTABLES  -A output -i $WORLD_INTERFACE
           -p tcp ! -y \
           -s $DMZ_MAIL_SERVER_ADDR 113  \
           -d 0/0 1024-65535  \
           -j ACCEPT
```

The following code enables auth client service for your mail server.

```
# Enable incoming auth response from
# outside world
$IPTABLES  -A input -i $WORLD_INTERFACE
           -p tcp \
           -s 0/0 113 \
           -d $DMZ_MAIL_SERVER_ADDR 1024-65535  \
           -j ACCEPT
# Enable outgoing auth requests from mail server
$IPTABLES  -A output -i $WORLD_INTERFACE
           -p tcp \
           -s $DMZ_MAIL_SERVER_ADDR 113  \
           -d 0/0 1024-65535  \
           -j ACCEPT
```

ACCESSING MAIL SERVERS IN DMZ

You want to allow mail server access from the outside world.

```
# Enable incoming SMTP requests from
# outside world
```

```
$IPTABLES  -A input -i $WORLD_INTERFACE
           -p tcp \
           -s 0/0 1024-65535  \
           -d $DMZ_MAIL_SERVER_ADDR 25 \
           -j ACCEPT
# Enable outgoing SMTP requests/responses
$IPTABLES  -A output -i $WORLD_INTERFACE
           -p tcp ! -y \
           -s $DMZ_MAIL_SERVER_ADDR 25  \
           -d 0/0 1024-65535  \
                -j ACCEPT
```

REDIRECTING PACKETS

Say you want to redirect all internal network (192.168.2.0/24) packets going to a specific Web site at IP address 193.1.1.193 and port 80 to be redirected to a Web server at IP address 193.1.1.195. You can add the following rule to the primary firewall rule file:

```
$IPTABLES -t nat -A POSTROUTING -s 192.168.2.0/24 \
          -d 193.1.1.193 \
          -p tcp --dport 80 \
          -j SNAT --to 193.1.1.195
```

LOGGING INFORMATION ABOUT PACKETS

You can use `netfilter`'s built-in logging support (`/var/log/messages`) to troubleshoot rule errors and monitor traffic. For example:

```
/sbin/iptables -A input -s 193.1.1.193 -j LOG
```

Whenever a packet from 193.1.1.193 machine enters the firewall, it's logged. To control the number of log entry, you can use the `-m limit --limit` *rate* options. For example:

```
/sbin/iptables -A input -s 193.1.1.193 -m limit --limit 10/second -j LOG
```

The above rule will log a maximum of 10 packets from 193.1.1.193 host. You can also use a prefix to identify a special IP address using the `--log-prefix` *prefix* option. For example:

```
/sbin/iptables -A input -s 193.1.1.193 -m limit \
               --limit 10/second \
               --log-prefix 'BAD GUY' -j LOG
```

The above rule will prefix the log entry for 193.1.1.193 using the words 'BAD GUY'.

SETTING TYPE OF SERVICE (TOS) IN IP PACKET

You can prioritize one type of traffic over another by setting the TOS value in the IP packet header. The TOS values can be one of the following:

- Minimize-Delay

- Maximize-Throughput

- Maximize-Reliability

- Minimize-Cost

- Normal-Service

For example, to provide interactive performance to telnet while using ftp at the same time:

```
/sbin/iptables -A PREROUTING -t mangle -p tcp \
             --sport telnet -j TOS \
             --set-tos Minimize-Delay
/sbin/iptables -A PREROUTING -t mangle -p tcp \
             --sport ftp -j TOS \
             --set-tos Minimize-Delay
/sbin/iptables -A PREROUTING -t mangle -p tcp \
             --sport ftp-data -j TOS \
             --set-tos Maximize-Throughput
```

STATEFUL INSPECTION

Netfilter provides the ability to associate all the packets of a particular connection to each other; packets that are not considered part of an existing connection can be denied or rejected. Packet-filtering rules can now be created to base their target on one of the following states:

- NEW: This packet is attempting to create a new connection.

- RELATED: This packet is related to the existing connection, and is passing in the original direction.

- INVALID: This packet doesn't match any existing connections.

- ESTABLISHED: This packet is part of an existing connection.

- RELATED+REPLY: This packet is not part of an existing connection, but is related to one. For example, if there is a FTP command connection (via port 21) to a host, then the ftp-data connection (via port 1024 or above) to the same host is related to the other connection.

For example, to accept packets that are part of an established connection, you can define a rule such as:

```
/sbin/iptables -A input -m state \
               -state ESTABLISHED -j ACCEPT
```

Or you can forward a packet from one interface to another if the packet is part of a related or established connection using the following rule:

```
/sbin/iptables -A forward -m state \
               -state ESTABLISHED, RELATED -j ACCEPT
```

NETWORK ADDRESS TRANSLATION (NAT) RULES

The NAT table in the Netfilter implementation allows you to masquerade, and redirect, and even load-balance packets. Specifically, the following NAT target options are currently available:

- ◆ DNAT: This target specifies that the destination address of the packet should be modified.

- ◆ SNAT: This target specifies that the source address of the packet should be modified, including all future packets in this connection.

- ◆ REDIRECT: This is a specialized case of DNAT that alters the destination IP address to send the packet to the machine itself.

When packets get their source or destination addresses translated due to a matching rule, these packets are retranslated back to normal source and/or destination addresses on the return path so that the packets are delivered back to the appropriate host.

Using the POSTROUTING chain in the NAT table, you can create a simple round-robin load-balancing environment. For example, to load-balance HTTP traffic for 192.168.1.1 to 192.168.1.20, 192.168.1.21, 192.168.1.22, you can create a rule as follows:

```
/sbin/iptables -t nat -A POSTROUTING \
               -s 192.168.1.1 \
               --to 192.168.1.20-192.168.1.22 \
               -j DNAT
```

TESTING PACKET-FILTERING RULES

First of all, you should list all your rules per chain using the /sbin/iptables -L chain_name [-t table_name] command. For example, to list all the rules in the input chain of the default filter table, run the /sbin/iptables -L input command.

To test an existing rule, simply replace the -A (if you appended the rule) or -I (if you inserted the rule) with -C and insert values for source and destination IP addresses. For example, say you have a rule such as the following:

```
/sbin/iptables -A input -i eth1 -p tcp \
               -s 0/0 \
               -d 192.168.1.100 \
               -dport 80 \
               -j REJECT
```

This rule states that a packet from any IP address (-s 0/0) destined to port 80 of IP address 192.168.1.100 on Ethernet interface eth1 is to be rejected. To test this rule, you can run the following code:

```
/sbin/iptables -C input -i eth1 -p tcp \
               -s 207.177.175.66 \
               -d 192.168.1.100 \
               -dport 80 \
               -j REJECT
```

You should see an output stating that the packet is rejected. If your rule calls for address translation, you should see a message stating that packet is masqueraded; similarly, if your rule calls for dropping the packet, you should see a message stating so.

PEER-TO-PEER SERVICES

Most people on the Internet (and almost everywhere else) have heard of Napster. I loved Napster in the beginning – but later, when I noticed Napster clients on the office network, I had to stop loving it (at least in the office). I could not allow users to run Napster (even before its legal imbroglio) because its peer-to-peer file-sharing software could have opened a security hole in our corporate network – exposing a treasure trove of sensitive data, intellectual properties, and client databases. So an addendum to our (normally very flexible) user policy had to exclude all peer-to-peer software in the office environment. However, the addendum also needed specific enforcement (junior engineers took it upon themselves to find a way to get around the restriction).

Peer-to-peer (P2P) networking is not new, but the availability of high-speed networking (such as DSL and cable) on the home front made P2P quickly popular. In my humble opinion, Napster brought P2P on the spotlight. Also, AOL Instant Messaging (AIM) became the dominant personal-networking tool of choice. These tools are great for personal use but since they are major security hazards, they are not welcome in the business environment just yet. Most of these network toys communicate using simple, clear-text protocols that are (for that reason) unsafe – and many of these tools access the hard disk of the computer they run on. Hard-drive access is exactly what we had to deny to Java applets if we were to keep it secure. Many of us were extremely reluctant to let these personal, social-networking tools get full access to sensitive private data. The following sections cover how you can block these services if you need to.

BLOCKING NAPSTER AND ITS FUTURE GENERATIONS   Napster client uses Napster servers to find music files. If you can block access to the Napster servers, you should be able to disable casual Napster users. Here's how:

1. Download the Napster client software on a PC, run it and use the `netstat -n` command to view which servers it connects to. You will notice that Napster servers are on 64.124.41.0 network. You can run `ping server.napster.com` a few times and find out that the `hostname` network mentioned earlier is load-balanced by using multiple IPs.

2. Add the following rules to drop all incoming and outgoing packets to and from the Napster network.

   ```
   /sbin/iptables -A input -s 64.124.41.0/24 -j DROP
   /sbin/iptables -A output -d 64.124.41.0/24 -j DROP
   ```

As mentioned before, this technique blocks the casual Napster user. If you have network-savvy users who have friends with Internet servers, you might still have a Napster problem in your network; troublemakers can still connect to Napster via a remote proxy server. In such a case, your only option is to pay a visit to the user's superior and report the issue. Of course, if you are dealing with a campus environment where students are bypassing your Napster blockade, your only hope is to figure out a way to reduce the bandwidth available to such activity.

 If the Napster users in your network are using open source Napster Servers (OpenNap), you have to block them individually as well. You can find a list of OpenNap servers at `www.napigator.com/list.php`.

Unfortunately, the next generation of Napster (called GnutellaNet) is a much harder beast to tame. P2P clients based on the Gnutella protocol form GnutellaNet — a network of computers without any central server. Therefore, the service is not easy to block. You can block the default port (6346) used by Gnutella-based P2P client software such as Gnotella and BearShare — but completely blocking these P2P programs is virtually impossible. Your best choice is to reduce the bandwidth available to these clients.

BLOCKING INSTANT MESSENGERS   AOL Instant Messenger (AIM) is a great personal communication tool — but it is also a potential security risk. To block AIM on your network, follow these steps:

1. Download AIM and use `netstat -n` to detect which server it connects to. Typically, AIM clients connect to the `login.oscar.aol.com` server on port 5190. Run `nslookup -q=a login.oscar.aol.com` from the command line to discover the IP addresses that are in the load-balancing pool. For example, when I ran the `nslookup` command mentioned earlier, I got

```
Name:     login.oscar.aol.com
Addresses:  152.163.241.128, 152.163.242.24, 152.163.242.28,
152.163.241.120
```

2. You can block all connection to each of the IP addresses for `login.oscar.aol.com` using a pair of rules such as the following:

```
/sbin/iptables -A input -s 152.163.241.128 DROP
/sbin/iptables -A output -d 152.163.241.128 DROP
```

After you have added this pair of rules for each IP address that points to this server, your system should effectively block AIM.

TIP   Don't forget to check for new IP addresses that might show up as AOL decides to add or drop servers in their load-balancing server pool.

Yahoo! Messenger can be blocked in a similar way, by blocking off outbound access to `msg.edit.yahoo.com`, `edit.messenger.yahoo.com`, `csa.yahoo.com`, `csb.yahoo.com`, and `csc.yahoo.com`. Each of the above host names resolves to multiple IP addresses — so you have to add each individual IP address to your list of those you want block. Of course, Yahoo! can always add new addresses at any time, making this an ongoing battle.

MSN Messenger can be blocked by blocking IP access to the Hotmail network 64.4.0.0 through 64.4.63.255.

Blocking MSN Messenger may or may not block access to Hotmail itself.

NOTE   These measures to block P2P file sharing and communication software are (at most) interim solutions. We must find better ways to allow/deny access to these interesting software in the corporate environment. There should be an initiative between the developers and the systems security experts to come to some common ground to allow both sides to be in a win-win situation. Until then, your best bet is to keep monitoring these software products and their vendors on an ongoing basis, staying ready to plug any security hole that opens.

Secure Virtual Private Network

Firewalls are typically deployed to protect an internal network from outside harm. But what if you wanted to communicate with two different networks that are geographically separated. For example, say you wanted to connect to the branch office in California from New York using Internet. In such a case, using firewalls at both end will make sure that both networks are protected from potentially harmful Internet traffic, but how can you make sure that the entire transport (that is, the path) between the networks is secure? In other words, what if you could create a tunnel that connects the two geographically disjoined networks. This is typically referred to as a *virtual private network (VPN)*.

Typically, a VPN is a private network over a public network such as the Internet. For example, say your company has a branch office in San Jose, California, and another one in Manhattan, New York. You can use a VPN to connect the private networks in California and New York over the Internet. All the traffic on the private network is only seen by the end networks; that is, the users in the San Jose office and the Manhattan office.

Just using a VPN does not guarantee that the virtual network established over the public network is safe. This is why I recommend the Free S/WAN solution, which uses an implementation of Internet Protocol Security (IPSEC) and IKE for Linux.

IPSEC uses strong cryptography to provide both authentication and encryption services. Secure authentication ensures that users are who they really are and encryption of data packets ensure that they are not altered in transit. Hence, IPSEC is most suitable for building secure tunnels through public, untrusted networks such as the Internet. By placing an IPSEC private-to-public-network gateway machine on each private network, you create a secure tunnel — a "virtually private" network. Such a VPN has one specific purpose: to ensure the privacy of its users, even though it includes machines at several different sites that are connected by the insecure Internet.

The standard IP packet (IPv4) consists of header and data bytes; the header contains the source and destination addresses among other information. A hacker can change the header to create a man-in-the-middle or spoof attack. Using IPSEC prevents such attacks because both the header byte and the data byte are digitally signed — therefore, any alteration while the packet is in transit causes the receiving IPSEC gateway machine to discard the packet. The Authentication Header (AH) and Encapsulating Security Payload (ESP) mechanism in IPSEC ensures the integrity and confidentially of both header and data.

In general, I recommend not using NAT when considering IPSEC based VPN technology. If you use Network Address Translation (NAT), then you might not be able to use IPSEC with AH protocol. NAT changes the source and/or destination of IP packets, which appears as an attack when IPSEC checks the packet header signature. IPSEC using the ESP in tunnel mode encapsulates the entire original packet into a new packet and the remote IPSEC gateway using the same ESP protocol in tunnel mode will only evaluate the original packet stored within the received packet. This ensures that the original packet is secured within the new packet and works with NAT.

Compiling and installing FreeS/WAN

To compile and install FreeS/WAN do the following:

1. As `root`, you must compile and install the latest Linux kernel from the kernel source distribution.

   See Chapter 2 for details on how to compile, install, and boot a new kernel. You must continue with the following instruction after you have successfully booted from a custom compiled kernel.

2. Download FreeS/WAN source distribution from the following site or its mirror sites:

   `ftp://ftp.xs4all.nl/pub/crypto/freeswan/`

   Extract the source into the `/usr/src` directory by copying the tar ball in that directory and running `tar xvzf freeswan-version.tar.gz` command. This will create a new subdirectory in `/usr/src`.

3. From the `freeswan` directory in `/usr/src`, run `make menugo`, which will run the `make menuconfig` command and also run other `freeswan` installation scripts to allow you customize kernel configuration, compile it and also create a pair of RSA authentication keys, which are stored in `/etc/ipsec.secret` file.

   When you see the menu-based kernel-configuration screen, you can customize anything you want — or simply save the configuration to let the `freeswan` installation continue. If any errors are detected during this process, you should review the `out.kbuild` or `out.kinstall` files to get the details on the errors you encounter.

The RSA keys generated by the `freeswan` configuration scripts are suitable only for authentication, not for encryption. IPSEC uses them only for authentication.

4. To install the kernel the easy way, from the FreeS/WAN directory run the `make kinstall` command to install the new kernel and any modules that are needed.

TIP

If you want to go through the standard kernel-building process instead of using FreeS/WAN, you can run the following commands:

```
make dep
make bzImage
make install
make modules
make modules_install
```

CAUTION

You should back up your existing kernel and modules and also create a LILO configuration that allows you to boot the old kernel in case the new kernel doesn't boot. (See Chapter 2 for details.)

5. Run the `/sbin/lilo` command to reconfigure LILO.

6. Reboot the system, using the `/sbin/shutdown -r now` command.

TIP

Look for boot messages stating that Kernel (code) Linux IP Security (KLIPS) is initializing and Pluto is starting. You can run `dmesg | grep -i KLIPS` and/or `dmesg | grep -i pluto` if you missed the boot messages.

Creating a VPN

Here I show you how you can create an IPSEC VPN using FreeS/WAN.

For my example, each of the unjoined local area networks — one in San Jose, California, and another one in New York City — has a FreeS/WAN gateway machine connected to the Internet. Creating a IPSEC VPN to exist between these two networks is (as you may expect) a two-part process unto itself.

CONFIGURING THE FIRST OF TWO LANS FOR A VPN

On the San Jose, CA FreeS/WAN gateway, do the following:

1. Make sure IP forwarding is turned on.

2. Make sure you have compiled the kernel with `netfilter` support; this configuration procedure uses packet-filtering rules to restrict access to the San Jose gateway.

3. Modify the `/etc/ipsec.conf` to have the lines shown in Listing 20-3.

Listing 20–3: /etc/ipsec.conf

```
config setup
  interfaces="ipsec0=eth0"
  klipsdebug=none
  plutodebug=none
  plutoload=%search
  plutostart=%search
conn %default
    keyingtries=0
    authby=rsasig
conn sjca-nyc
  left=207.177.175.60
  leftsubnet=192.168.1.0/24
  leftnexthop=207.177.175.1
  right=207.183.233.17
  rightsubnet=192.168.2.0/24
  rightnexthop=207.183.233.1
  auto=start
  leftid=@sjca.domain.com
  rightid=@nyc.domain.com
  leftrsasigkey=0x01035d3db6bdabeb8d9a62eb8d798d92a1
  rightrsasigkey=0x01032d2dbadfeeddead62eb8d798d92b2
```

Here the first line of the file tells KLIPS that you are describing a machine configuration. The next line defines the interfaces that FreeS/WAN should use. In the example just given, `interfaces="ipsec0=eth0"` tells the system to use eth0 interface as the first IPSEC (`ipsec0`) interface. In most cases, you can set `interfaces=%defaultroute`; the typical default route is also the default connection to the Internet.

TIP If you want to know which interface is considered for default route by FreeS/WAN, you can run the `ipsec showdefaults` command.

It is not necessary to use multiple interfaces to create multiple VPNs; for example `interfaces="ipsec0=eth0 ipsec1=eth1"` defines two IPSEC interfaces using eth0 and eth1 Ethernet interfaces.

- The `klipsdebug=none` line tells FreeS/WAN not to use debugging.

  If you want to enable debugging, set this to `all` instead.

- The `plutodebug=none` line disables debugging for the Pluto daemon that negotiates keys and connections in FreeS/WAN.

  To enable debugging, set this to `all` instead.

- The `plutoload` and the `plutostart` lines list connects that are to be loaded and negotiated by the Pluto daemon. You can set both of these to a quoted list of connection names.

  Here I have set them to `%search`, which tells Pluto to load only those connections that have `auto=add` or `add=start` in this file's connection definition. Setting up the VPN between two offices means both gateways are likely to be available most of the time; setting `plutostart=%search` and `auto=start` in `connection description` makes good sense. This way, whenever a connection is lost, it can be easily retried and restarted by Pluto. However, if this VPN were built for a different purpose (such as supporting a set of mobile systems that are likely to be offline most of the time), then the connection description should not include `auto=start`. Instead, it should include `auto=add` so the gateway does not retry connections automatically. In such a case, connection is only initiated when the mobile system starts the negotiations.

- The `conn %default` section defines the defaults for all the connections.

  In our example configuration, the `keyingtries` option is set to 0, which means that it forever retries key negotiations to establish connections. In other words, if a connection goes down, the FreeS/WAN server will retry again and again to reestablish the connection.

  The `authby` option specifies that we want to use RSA signature (`rsasig`) in the authentication process.

- The `conn sjca-nyc` section defines our VPN connection that we named `"sjca-nyc"` (short for *San Jose CA to New York City*). Always use meaningful names when defining connection names. It helps readability of your connection specifications.

  The left option is set to the interface address of the San Jose, CA office network gateway. This is the external interface of the gateway system called `sjca-gw.domain.com`. The `leftsubnet` is the private network that the left gateway is connecting to the right. Here it is 192.168.1.0/24. The leftnexthop defines the default route of the gateway machine. Since in our diagram the default route is set to the router with IP address 207.177.175.1, the leftnexthop is set to this address.

 Why specify the next hop address or default route for the gateway machine? The KLIPS does not use the default "default route" used by the normal network subsystem, so you must specify this. If the gateway machines are directly connected by themselves, you do not need to set this.

The `right`, `rightsubnet`, and `rightnexthop` are the right equivalent of `left`, `leftsubnet`, `leftnexthop`, respectively. The only difference is that the `right`, `rightsubnet`, and `rightnexthop` applies to the right side of the diagram and the left equivalents apply to the left side of the diagram.

- The `auto=start` option tells Pluto to initiate the connection every time it starts.

  You can also use `auto=add` instead if you want to start the connection manually.

- The `leftid` and `rightid` options create unique identifiers used in association with the RSA public key during two-way communication.

  These are the names the systems use to identify themselves during connection negotiation.

  When naming a system using the `leftid` or `rightid` option, the best option is to use `@FQDN` format, which stands for *fully qualified domain name* (as shown in this example configuration).

- The `leftrsasigkey` and `rightrsasigkey` options are set to the public key found in `/etc/ipsec.secret` file in the `pubkey` field.

3. Make sure the `/etc/ipsec.secret` file has the RSA key generated during the FreeS/WAN setup. If do not have a key, you can generate one using the `ipsec rsasigkey 1024 >> /tmp/rsakey.txt`. Once it's generated, you must place the key in the `/etc/ipsec.secret` file, as shown here:

```
: rsa {
#Insert contents of the /tmp/rsakey.txt file here
}
```

CONFIGURING THE SECOND OF TWO LANS FOR A VPN

On the New York City gateway in the example, follow the same steps as for the San Jose gateway to create the same configuration.

To enhance the security of a gateway system, create a script called /etc/rc.d/ipsec-gw.firewall.sh, as shown in Listing 20-4.

Listing 20-4: /etc/rc.d/ipsec-gw.firewall.sh

```
#!/bin/sh
IPTABLES=/sbin/iptables
# Make sure you change the following interface
# address and private LAN addresses for your
# network
WORLD_INTERFACE_ADDR="207.177.175.60"
PRIVATE_LAN="192.168.1.0/24"
# Drop all rules in the filter table
$IPTABLES -F FORWARD
$IPTABLES -F INPUT
$IPTABLES -F OUTPUT
# Default policies
$IPTABLES -P input DENY
$IPTABLES -P output REJECT
$IPTABLES -P forward REJECT
# Enable loopback
$IPTABLES -A INPUT -i lo -p all -j ACCEPT
# Enable ICMP. Yes, even a dummy knows
# how to use ping these days!
$IPTABLES -A INPUT -p icmp -j ACCEPT
# Only allow ipsec traffic, ESP(50) and AH(51) from and to
the Internet
$IPTABLES -A input -p udp\
        -d $WORLD_INTERFACE_ADDR 500 \
        -j ACCEPT
$IPTABLES -A input -p 50 \
        -d $WORLD_INTERFACE_ADDR  \
        -j ACCEPT
$IPTABLES -A input -p 51 \
        -d $WORLD_INTERFACE_ADDR  \
        -j ACCEPT
# Allows internal subnet access
$IPTABLES -A input -s $PRIVATE_LAN -j ACCEPT
# Allows traffic from and to internal LANs
$IPTABLES -A forward -b \
        -s $PRIVATE_LAN \
        -d $PRIVATE_LAN -j ACCEPT
```

Add `/etc/rc.d/ipsec-gw.firewall.sh` at the end of your `/etc/rc.d/rc.local` script to ensure that the gateway loads its packet-filtering rules whenever the system reboots. This script only allows IPSEC-specific traffic in and out of the gateway system.

When installing this script, make sure you change the `WORLD_INTERFACE_ADDR` and `PRIVATE_LAN` interface according to the gateway location. Set the script for the left side (San Jose, CA) to `WORLD_INTERFACE_ADDR="207.177.175.60"` and `PRIVATE_LAN="192.168.1.0/24"` (as shown in the listing); set the New York City side to `WORLD_INTERFACE_ADDR="207.183.233.17"` and `PRIVATE_LAN="192.168.2.0/24"` per our diagram.

Of course, you also use real IP and network addresses to create your configuration.

STARTING AND STOPPING A VPN CONNECTION
At this point, you are ready to bring up the gateways. The procedure looks like this:

1. Reboot both gateways.

2. Run the `ls -l /proc/net/ipsec_*` command on each gateway.

   You should see a list of files such as `ipsec_eroute`, `ipsec_spi`, `ipsec_spigrp`, `ipsec_spinew`, `ipsec_tncfg`, and `ipsec_version`.

3. `cat` the `/proc/net/ipsec_tncfg` to make sure the `ipsec0` interface is up and running and pointing to `eth0`.

4. On each gateway, start IPSEC by using the `ipsec auto --up` *name* command where *name* is the name of connection you want to bring up.

   In this example, the command is `ipsec auto --up sjca-nyc`.

5. After IPSEC is started, run the `ipsec look` command to see whether your connection is up and running. You should see a route indicated between the two private networks via the `ipsec0` interface.

6. To stop a connection, simply replace `--up` with the `--down` option.

   When you shut down a connection, make sure you shut it down from both gateways.

If you are setting up a VPN, test to make sure you can start a complete VPN connection from one gateway. The other gateway should start automatically, as soon as it recognizes a connection-negotiation request coming from the gateway that initiates the connection.

TESTING THE CONNECTION

From the private network on one side of the connection, `ping` a machine on the private network of the other side of the connection. For example, in our example, we can send `ping` requests from a machine in the San Jose, CA, office to a machine in the New York office. When testing, use a client machine on the private network instead of the gateways themselves. For example, in our current example, we can `ping` from a machine with IP address 192.168.1.10 on 192.168.1.0/24 to a machine on 192.168.2.50 on 192.168.2.0/24. If `ping` requests are answered by the machine on the other end, you have a working VPN connection. Now try other services such as `telnet` or `ssh`.

Stunnel: A Universal SSL Wrapper

Secure Socket Layer (SSL), developed by Netscape Corporation (now part of AOL), has become the de facto standard for secure online transaction. Although SSL was primarily developed for Web security, now you can use SSL for other services that are not even SSL capable themselves. Such services include IMAP, POP3, LDAP, etc., that are commonly used by all of us.

The magic solution is to use Stunnel, which can secure non-SSL services by providing the SSL layer without any modification to the code involved in the implementation of the service itself. In order to use Stunnel, you will need to install OpenSSL; see Using OpenSSL chapter for details. You can download Stunnel source code from the official Stunnel site (`www.stunnel.org`). The next step is to install Stunnel on your system.

Compiling and installing Stunnel

Download the Stunnel source distribution, `stunnel-version.tar.gz`, from the Web site mentioned earlier (or from another reliable mirror site).

1. As `root`, extract the source into `/usr/src`, using the `tar xvzf stunnel-version.tar.gz` command.

2. Run the `configure` script from the newly created `stunnel-version` directory.

3. Run the `make` and `make install` commands to install Stunnel.

Now you are ready to use Stunnel to wrap many popular services.

Securing IMAP

You have two ways of using Stunnel with the IMAP service on your system, depending on how it's configured. You can run the IMAP service directly via stunnel or run IMAP service as a xinetd managed service. The first method is only recommended if you have IMAP clients who do not use SSL protocol for connection.

RUNNING IMAPD DIRECTLY VIA STUNNEL

If you want to run a non-SSL version of `imapd` for clients that cannot use SSL to connect to the service, then do the following:

> Disable `imapd` as you run in the current method; instead run `imapd` using the following command from a startup script such as `/etc/rc.d/rc.local`:

```
/usr/sbin/stunnel -p /usr/local/ssl/certs/stunnel.pem \
                  -d 993 \
                  -r localhost:143
```

> This command runs `stunnel` using the specified certificate file on the IMAPS port (993) and proxy for the `imapd` daemon running on `localhost` port 143. The command also allows your non-SSL IMAP clients to connect on the standard IMAP port (143), and you can configure the SSL-capable IMAP clients to connect to port IMAPS (993) instead.

Alternatively, you can run the IMAP service as follows:

```
/usr/sbin/stunnel -p /usr/local/ssl/certs/stunnel.pem \
                  -d 993 \
                  -l /usr/sbin/imapd
```

This approach yields the same result by running the `imap` daemon (specified by `-l`) rather than connecting to a daemon that is already running on the IMAP port (143).

USING XINETD TO RUN SECURE IMAPD

If you use `xinetd` to run IMAP service, modify your `/etc/xinetd.d/imapd` configuration file as follows:

```
service imap
{
        disable         = no
        socket_type     = stream
        wait            = no
        user            = root
        port            = 143
        server          = /usr/sbin/stunnel
        server_args     = stunnel imapd -l /usr/sbin/imapd --imapd
        log_on_success   += USERID
        log_on_failure  += USERID
        #env            = VIRTDOMAIN=virtual.hostname
}
```

Don't forget to reload xinetd configuration using the `killall -USR1 xinetd` command.

Securing POP3

To connect to your POP3 mail server via SSL, reconfigure your /etc/xinetd.d/ pop3s configuration script as follows:

```
service pop3s
{
        disable          = no
        socket_type      = stream
        wait             = no
        user             = root
        server           = /usr/sbin/stunnel
        server_args      = stunnel pop3s -l /usr/sbin/ipop3d --ipop3d
        log_on_success   += USERID
        log_on_failure   += USERID
}
```

If you have POP3 client software that cannot use SSL, then you can use a POP3 redirector service as follows:

1. Set up a normal (that is, not using Stunnel) POP3 server on a system that uses the following /etc/xinetd.d/pop3 service configuration.

    ```
    service pop3
    {
            disable          = no
            socket_type      = stream
            wait             = no
            user             = root
            server           = /usr/sbin/stunnel
            server_args      = -c -r pop3server-using-
    stunnel:pop3s
            log_on_success   += USERID
            log_on_failure   += USERID
    }
    ```

2. Set up a POP3 server using stunnel, as shown in the first xinetd configuration example (/etc/xinetd.d/pop3s).

3. Change the *pop3server-using-stunnel* to the hostname of the POP3 server that is using Stunnel. This will allow non-SSL capable POP3 clients to connect to a host that uses stunnel to forward POP3 traffic to another server using SSL.

Securing SMTP for special scenarios

Say you run a SMTP server that allows your roaming, mobile employees to connect and send mail to many branches of your organization. If you want to keep your email transactions secure, you can use.

```
/usr/local/sbin/stunnel -d 25 \
                        -p /var/lib/ssl/certs/server.pem \
                        -r localhost:smtp
```

Note that you are securing SMTP delivery between the end-user and your mail server. If the mail is to be sent to another server outside your domain, it will not be secure. This special scenario is only applicable for situations for an organization where all mail is sent internally via the secure method and external mail goes through some other SMTP relay.

Summary

Packet filtering is a means to impose control on the types of traffic permitted to pass from one IP network to another. The packet filter examines the header of the packet and makes a determination of whether to pass or reject the packet based upon the contents of the header. Packet filtering capability found in the iptables allows you to make security rules for incoming and outgoing IP packets. On the other hand, security tools such as a VPN and stunnel allow you to secure two networks or various network services, respectively.

Chapter 21

Firewall Security Tools

IN THIS CHAPTER

- ◆ How to use various security assessment or audit tools
- ◆ How to use various port scanners
- ◆ How to use log monitoring tools
- ◆ How to use CGI scanners
- ◆ How to use password crackers
- ◆ How to use packet sniffers

IN THIS CHAPTER, I introduce you to various security tools that you can use to audit, monitor, and detect vulnerabilities in your individual Linux system or an entire network.

Using Security Assessment (Audit) Tools

It is a great idea to audit your system security periodically to ensure that your assessment of your system security is correct. In this section, I cover a few security assessment tools that can help you in this process.

Using SAINT to Perform a Security Audit

Periodic security audit is a standard procedure for a security administrator. Security Administrator's Integrated Network Tool (SAINT) can help you audit a single Linux system or an entire network.

SAINT is based on the infamous SATAN tool. SAINT probes user specified target systems for security vulnerabilities and produces analysis reports so that you can take appropriate action. Features include

- ◆ Scanning through a firewall
- ◆ Updated security checks from CERT and CIAC bulletins

- ◆ Four levels of severity (red, yellow, brown, and green)
- ◆ A feature-rich HTML interface

Make sure you have permission before using SAINT to audit a system or a network. If you let SAINT loose on a system or network that you don't have permission for, you may be in legal trouble — the owner may consider your audit an intrusion attempt!

SAINT can detect many vulnerabilities such as:

- ◆ Guessable read and write SNMP community strings
- ◆ SITE EXEC buffer overflows and others in FTP servers
- ◆ Problems within NFS configurations
- ◆ Mail servers that permit relaying
- ◆ Instances of FrontPage that may contain security flaws
- ◆ Root kits

For a full list of vulnerabilities that SAINT finds, check `http://www.wwdsi.com/cgi-bin/vulns.pl`.

GETTING STARTED WITH SAINT

Here is how you can get started with SAINT. (Make sure you have a Web browser, such as Navigator or Lynx, on the system to run SAINT.)

1. Download the latest source distribution from the official SAINT Web site at `http://www.wwdsi.com/saint`.

   The source distribution is usually called `saint-version.tar.gz` (e.g., `saint-3.1.2.tar.gz`).

2. As root, extract the source in `/usr/local/src` using the `tar xvzf saint-version.tar.gz` command. You should have a new subdirectory called saint-*version*. From this new subdirectory, run `./configure; make; make install` commands to install configure, compile, and install SAINT on your system.

To start, run `./saint` from the command-line. SAINT starts using a Web browser.

CONFIGURING AUDIT PARAMETERS

When you start SAINT using the `./saint` command from the installed directory, it displays a set of links such as the following:

```
SAINT home
WWDSI
SAINT Home
Data Management
Target Selection
Data Analysis
Configuration Management
SAINT Documentation
Troubleshooting
```

First, you should select the `Configuration Management` option to configure audit parameters. You see a page with many options that you can set. Most default options should work for you. However, the following option should be set according to your need level.

```
What probe level should I use?
    ( ) Light
    ( ) Normal
    (*) Heavy
    ( ) Heavy+
    ( ) Top 10 (scans specifically for SANS Top 10 Internet Security
Threats)
    ( ) Custom (Set up custom scan)
```

This option configures the probe level; the default is set to `Heavy`. For example, if you are aware of the SANS top 10 security threats (see `http://www.sans.org/topten.htm`) and want to check if your system exhibits such threats, select the `Top 10` option.

 When you make a change to any configuration options in this page, save the changes using the `Change the configuration file` link.

AUDITING A SINGLE SYSTEM OR NETWORK

Once you have configured SAINT, you can select a target host or network to audit using the Target Selection link found in the top page.

1. You have to enter one or more hostnames or IP addresses or subnet address to audit.

   For example, to scan a machine called `rhat.nitec.com`, I have entered the following information in the Target Selection page.

   ```
   Primary target selection
           Primary target host(s) or network, e.g. rhat.nitec.com
           May be a single host, space-separated list, IP range,
   or subnet:
           (*) rhat.nitec.com_____
           OR
           File containing list of target host(s):
           ( ) target_file_____
                   (*) Scan the target host(s) only. (Disables
   smurf check.)
                   ( ) Scan all hosts in the target hosts'
   subnet(s).
   ```

   - If you want to scan multiple hosts, you can enter their hostnames in the same line. Separate the names with a space.

   - If you have a file with hostnames, you can specify the path here and scan them.

TIP If you plan on using SAINT for a number of hosts on a regular basis, create a file with hostnames and use it here to save some typing and avoid errors.

NOTE The first time you start a scan in each SAINT session, it warns you about not connecting to external Web servers while using SAINT.

2. Select a scanning level from the following options:

   ```
   Scanning level selection
   Should SAINT do a light scan, a normal scan, or should it hit
   the (primary) target(s) at full blast?
           ( ) Light
           ( ) Normal (may be detected even with minimal
   logging)
   ```

```
        (*) Heavy (avoids WinNT ports that are known to crash
system)
        ( ) Heavy+ (doesn't avoid WinNT ports that are known
to crash system)
        ( ) Top 10 (scans specifically for SANS Top 10
Internet Security Threats)
        ( ) Custom (Set up custom scan)
```

 Scanning can temporarily take many resources from the target machine, so don't perform heavy scans on busy machines. Scan when the target system or network isn't heavily loaded with other work.

3. If you are behind a firewall, check the Firewall Support option from below.

```
Firewall Support
Is the host you are scanning behind a firewall? If it is, you
should enable firewall support, or your results might not be
accurate, or you might get no results at all.
        (*) No Firewall Support
        ( ) Firewall Support
```

 Only choose firewall support if SAINT isn't running on the target system itself or SAINT system and the target system or network has a firewall between them. Making SAINT aware of the firewall's presence allows for a more accurate scan.

4. Click Start.

Once the scan is complete you see a results screen. Here is an example result of running a heavy scan on a single host called rhat.nitec.com.

```
                SAINT data collection
```

```
    Data collection in progress...
    03/26/01-08:41:37 bin/timeout 60 bin/fping rhat.nitec.com
    03/26/01-08:41:37 bin/timeout 60 bin/tcpscan.saint

12754,15104,16660,20432,27665,33270,1-1525,1527-5404,5406-888
7,8889-9999 rhat.nitec.com
```

```
    03/26/01-08:41:37 bin/timeout 20 bin/ostype.saint
rhat.nitec.com
    03/26/01-08:41:37 bin/timeout 20 bin/finger.saint
rhat.nitec.com
    03/26/01-08:41:38 bin/timeout 20 bin/rpc.saint
rhat.nitec.com
    03/26/01-08:41:38 bin/timeout 20 bin/dns.saint
rhat.nitec.com
    03/26/01-08:41:38 bin/timeout 20 bin/ddos.saint
rhat.nitec.com
    03/26/01-08:41:39 bin/timeout 60 bin/udpscan.saint

19,53,69,111,137-139,161-162,177,8999,1-18,20-52,54-68,70-110
,112-136,140-160,163-176,178-176
    0,1763-2050,32767-33500 rhat.nitec.com
    03/26/01-08:42:22 bin/timeout 20 bin/ftp.saint
rhat.nitec.com
    03/26/01-08:42:22 bin/timeout 20 bin/relay.saint
rhat.nitec.com
    03/26/01-08:42:22 bin/timeout 20 bin/login.saint -o -u
root -p root telnet rhat.nitec.com
    03/26/01-08:42:22 bin/timeout 20 bin/sendmail.saint smtp
rhat.nitec.com
    03/26/01-08:42:22 bin/timeout 90 bin/http.saint 1263
rhat.nitec.com                                              '
    03/26/01-08:42:22 bin/timeout 20 bin/login.saint -r -u
wank -p wank telnet rhat.nitec.com
    03/26/01-08:42:24 bin/timeout 90 bin/http.saint http
rhat.nitec.com
    03/26/01-08:42:24 bin/timeout 20 bin/rlogin.saint
rhat.nitec.com
    03/26/01-08:42:24 bin/timeout 20 bin/rsh.saint -u root
rhat.nitec.com
    03/26/01-08:42:24 bin/timeout 20 bin/statd.saint Linux 7.0
rhat.nitec.com
    03/26/01-08:42:24 bin/timeout 20 bin/ssh.sara
rhat.nitec.com
    03/26/01-08:42:25 bin/timeout 20 bin/rsh.saint
rhat.nitec.com
    03/26/01-08:42:25 bin/timeout 60 bin/smb.saint
rhat.nitec.com
    03/26/01-08:42:27 bin/timeout 20 bin/mountd.sara
rhat.nitec.com
```

```
    03/26/01-08:42:27 bin/timeout 20 bin/printer.saint
rhat.nitec.com
    03/26/01-08:42:27 bin/timeout 20 bin/login.saint -r -u
rewt -p satori telnet rhat.nitec.com
    03/26/01-08:42:28 bin/timeout 20 bin/dns-chk.saint
rhat.nitec.com
    03/26/01-08:42:29 bin/timeout 20 bin/login.saint -o -u
root telnet rhat.nitec.com
    03/26/01-08:42:43 bin/timeout 20 bin/ftp_bounce.saint
rhat.nitec.com
    03/26/01-08:42:44 SAINT run completed
    Data collection completed (1 host(s) visited).
```

As you can see, a number of scans were run including UDP, TCP, DNS, HTTP, and RPC. SAINT also tries to detect the remote software platform and version.

5. Click Continue with report and analysis for a summary of your scan results.

ANALYZING THE SCAN RESULTS

You can analyze the data collected after a scan by either clicking on the Continue with report and analysis link or clicking on the Data Analysis link from the top page. Once you are in the Data Analysis page, you see the following options:

```
Table of contents
     Vulnerabilities

   * By Approximate Danger Level
   * By Type of Vulnerability
   * By Vulnerability Count

Host Information
   * By Class of Service
   * By System Type
   * By Internet Domain
   * By Subnet
   * By Host Name

Trust
   * Trusted Hosts
   * Trusting Hosts
```

You can analyze the gathered data in many ways. The first option allows you to analyze the data by approximating the danger level. An example of this analysis for rhat.nitec.com is shown below:

```
Vulnerabilities - Danger Levels


    Table of contents

    Critical Problems RED Denial of Service
        Areas of Concern YELLOW Information Gathering
        Potential Problems BROWN Possible vulnerabilities
        BROWN Limit Internet Access ?


    Note: hosts may appear in multiple categories.

RED Denial of Service
    * top-10 rhat.nitec.com: denial-of-service in BIND 8.2.2 (CVE 1999-0849
1999-0851)
YELLOW Information Gathering
* rhat.nitec.com: Excessive finger information (CVE 1999-0612)


BROWN Possible Vulnerabilities
* rhat.nitec.com: possible vulnerability in Linux lpd
    * top-10 rhat.nitec.com: rpc.statd is enabled and may be vulnerable (CVE
1999-0018 1999-0019
        1999-0210 1999-0493 2000-0666)


BROWN Limit Internet Access ?
Vulnerabilities - Danger Levels (p2 of 2)
    * rhat.nitec.com: rlogin is enabled
    * rhat.nitec.com: rshd is enabled
    * rhat.nitec.com: Sendmail command EXPN is enabled
    * rhat.nitec.com: Sendmail command VRFY is enabled
```

One critical problem (marked as RED) is detected for `rhat.nitec.com`.

```
top-10 rhat.nitec.com: denial-of-service in BIND 8.2.2 (CVE 1999-0849 1999-0851)
```

This problem, vulnerability in the DNS software (BIND 8.2.2), is listed as one of the top 10 security threads by SANS (`http://www.sans.org`).

A potential problem (marked as YELLOW) is detected:

```
rhat.nitec.com: Excessive finger information (CVE 1999-0612)
```

Here, SAINT reports that the `rhat.nitec.com` system allows for excessive finger information when finger service is used to find information on a user. This can potentially lead to other security risks.

Finally, it also lists some potential vulnerabilities (marked as BROWN), which are:

```
    rhat.nitec.com: possible vulnerability in Linux lpd
    top-10 rhat.nitec.com: rpc.statd is enabled and may be vulnerable (CVE
1999-0018 1999-0019
      1999-0210 1999-0493 2000-0666)
```

The printer daemon (lpd) and the Remote Procedure Call (RPC) stat daemon (rpc.statd) are enabled and may be associated with security issues.

Once you have identified vulnerabilities in a system or network, use the (Common Vulnerabilities and Exposures) CVE links to learn more about the problems. For example, to learn more about the DNS vulnerability detected in the scan for `rhat.nitec.com`, I can click on the (CVE 1999-0849 1999-0851) links listed in the analysis and find all the details.

The next step is to shut off the program or service that is vulnerable. This may not be possible if your business depends on this service or program. So I recommend that you find a fix as quickly as possible and replace the faulty program or service as soon as possible.

SARA

The original authors of SAINT wrote another security audit tool called Security Auditor's Research Assistant (SARA), which can be downloaded from `http://www-arc.com/sara`. SARA has a special firewall mode that allows detects hosts without using ping packets.

The source distribution can be installed as follows:

1. As root, extract the source distribution `sara-version.tar.gz` (e.g. `sara-3.3.5.tar.gz`) using `tar xvzf sara-version.tar.gz` command. This creates a new subdirectory called `sara-version` (e.g. `sara-3.3.5`). Change your current directory to this directory.

2. Run `make linux` to compile the source. A binary file called `sara` is created in the same directory.

3. Run the binary using `./sara` command.

   Using SARA is like using SAINT.

VetesCan

VetesCan is a bulk vulnerability scanner that you can download from `http://www.self-evident.com`. It contains many programs to check for network security exploits.

Once you have downloaded and extracted the source distribution, run the supplied `install` script from the source directory and the scanner is compiled and built. Running a scan on a host is as simple as running `./vetescan` *hostname* from the same directory.

Using Port Scanners

Hackers often scan networks for ports that are opened. They run programs that try to connect to ports and detect what server manages such ports. This information helps the hacker decide whether a machine is running a server software that has a known security vulnerability that can be exploited. This is known as port scanning. You can use port scanners to find which ports are open in your network before the hacker does. You want to make sure only the ports that you need for your organization are open. For example, if you only want the Web (HTTP) service to be accessed from the Internet, only make port 80 available. Here I discuss how you can use port scanners to find out what ports are opened for a given system.

Performing Footprint Analysis Using nmap

The nmap utility is a port scanner that can scan ports on a single host or a network of hosts. It can scan TCP, UDP, ICMP ports and also guess the operating system being used on the target system. Specifically, nmap supports the following scanning options:

- Vanilla TCP connect() scanning
- TCP SYN (half open) scanning
- TCP FIN, Xmas, or NULL (stealth) scanning
- TCP ftp proxy (bounce attack) scanning
- SYN/FIN scanning using IP fragments (bypasses some packet filters)
- TCP ACK and Window scanning
- UDP raw ICMP port unreachable scanning
- ICMP scanning (ping-sweep)

- ◆ TCP Ping scanning

- ◆ Direct (non portmapper) RPC scanning

- ◆ Remote OS Identification by TCP/IP Fingerprinting, and

- ◆ Reverse-ident scanning

GETTING STARTED WITH NMAP

You can download the latest nmap source tar ball from `http://www.insecure.org` and compile and install it as follows:

1. As root, extract the downloaded source in `/usr/src` using `tar xvzf nmap-version.tar.gz` command, then change directory to the newly created subdirectory.

2. Run `./configure; make; make install` to configure and install nmap.

 I had trouble compiling the latest version of nmap on Linux so I downloaded the binary RPM distribution from site and installed it using the following command:

`rpm -vhU http://www.insecure.org/nmap/dist/nmap-2.53-1.i386.rpm`

If you want to install as above, make sure you change the version number as appropriate.

SCANNING TCP PORTS AND GUESSING OS

To scan for open TCP ports on a target system and at the same time guess what operating system it's using, run the nmap program as follows:

`/usr/bin/nmap -sT -O hostname/32`

Replace the hostname with the target hostname. The /32 tells nmap to scan only the given host on the network. If you specify /24, it scans all the hosts on the class C network where the given host resides. If you specify /16, it scans the class B network and /8 scans the class A network.

If you don't know the hostname, you can use the IP address instead. For example:

`/usr/bin/nmap -sT -O 192.168.1.100/32`

This command tells nmap to scan the TCP ports (-sT) on the 192.168.1.100 host only and guess its operating system. The output of the preceding command is shown below:

```
Starting nmap V. 2.53 by fyodor@insecure.org ( www.insecure.org/nmap/ )
Interesting ports on ns.domain.com (192.168.1.100):
(The 1506 ports scanned but not shown below are in state: closed)
Port       State       Service
21/tcp     open        ftp
22/tcp     open        ssh
25/tcp     open        smtp
53/tcp     open        domain
80/tcp     open        http
111/tcp    open        sunrpc
113/tcp    open        auth
443/tcp    open        https
444/tcp    open        snpp
554/tcp    open        rtsp
635/tcp    open        unknown
2049/tcp   open        nfs
3306/tcp   open        mysql
5050/tcp   open        mmcc
8080/tcp   open        http-proxy
9090/tcp   open        zeus-admin
31337/tcp  filtered    Elite
TCP Sequence Prediction: Class=random positive increments
                        Difficulty=3130032 (Good luck!)
Remote operating system guess: Linux 2.1.122 - 2.2.14
Nmap run completed -- 1 IP address (1 host up) scanned in 18 seconds
```

As you can see it has detected several TCP ports that are open and also guessed the operating system of the machine responding to the 192.168.1.100 address.

SCANNING UDP PORTS ON A HOST

To scan for open UDP ports, run nmap with -sU option. For example:

```
/usr/bin/nmap -sU hostname/32
```

Here nmap scans the UDP ports for the specified host.

Using PortSentry to Monitor Connections

PortSentry is a TCP/IP port monitoring tool that is part of the Abacus Project suite of tools. It allows you to detect port scans (probes) on your host. You can download PortSentry from http://www.psionic.com/abacus/portsentry.

When PortSentry detects activity on a monitored port, it can report it and also perform a specified action, which can include denying further attempts to access your system. Typically, a hacker scans ports for weakness in a service connected to a port and then attacks the service. Since PortSentry can detect access attempts to multiple monitored ports, it can deny the hacker the time he needs to launch massive attacks to say create buffer overflow or other kinds of attacks. When it detects a port scan, the following action is taken:

◆ A log entry is made via syslog facility.

◆ The source of the trouble is automatically added to the /etc/hosts.deny file.

◆ The local host isn't allowed to send any packets to the scanner system. This is done by adding a dead route for the scanner system.

◆ The local host is configured to drop all packets from the scanner system by using packet filtering rule.

GETTING STARTED WITH PORTSENTRY
Once you have downloaded and extracted the source in a subdirectory, edit the portsentry.conf file to have the following lines:

```
TCP_PORTS="1,11,15,79,111,119,143,540,635,1080,1524,2000,5742,6667,12345,12346,2
0034,31337,32771,32772,327
73,32774,40421,49724,54320"
UDP_PORTS="1,7,9,69,161,162,513,635,640,641,700,32770,32771,32772,32773,32774,31
337,54321"
ADVANCED_PORTS_TCP="1023"
ADVANCED_PORTS_UDP="1023"
ADVANCED_EXCLUDE_TCP="113,139"
ADVANCED_EXCLUDE_UDP="520,138,137,67"
IGNORE_FILE="/usr/local/psionic/portsentry/portsentry.ignore"
HISTORY_FILE="/usr/local/psionic/portsentry/portsentry.history"
BLOCKED_FILE="/usr/local/psionic/portsentry/portsentry.blocked"
BLOCK_UDP="1"
BLOCK_TCP="1"
KILL_ROUTE="/sbin/iptables -I input -s $TARGET$ -j DROP -l"
KILL_HOSTS_DENY="ALL: $TARGET$"
KILL_RUN_CMD="/bin/echo Attack host: $TARGET$ port: $PORT$ >>
/var/log/attacks.log"
SCAN_TRIGGER="0"
```

Table 21-1 explains each of the options in this configuration file.

TABLE 21-1: PORTSENTRY CONFIGURATION OPTIONS

Option	Meaning
TCP_PORTS	A comma separated list of TCP ports you want PortSentry to listen to. This list can't have any spaces in it and the maximum number of ports that can be listed is 64.
	This list isn't used for the advanced stealth scan detection.
UDP_PORTS	The same as above, except for UDP ports. This list isn't used for the advanced stealth scan detection.
ADVANCED_PORTS_TCP	Advanced monitoring starts at the given port and monitors all ports below it.
ADVANCED_PORTS_UDP	Same as above, except for UDP.
ADVANCED_EXCLUDE_TCP	A comma separated list of TCP ports that you want to exclude from monitoring. Ports such as HTTPS (443) or AUTH (113) etc. are often accessed by mistake so you should not monitor them. For example, do you want to set an alarm if someone accesses https://www.yourdomain.com by mistake instead of http://www.yourdomain.com? Most likely not.
ADVANCED_EXCLUDE_UDP	Same as above, except for UDP.
IGNORE_FILE	A fully qualified path of a file that lists IP addresses of hosts that PortSentry ignores.
BLOCKED_FILE	A fully qualified path of a file that lists IP addresses of hosts that PortSentry denies access.
BLOCK_UDP	This option enables (1) or disables (0) all automatic responses to UDP scans.
BLOCK_TCP	Same as above, but for TCP.
KILL_ROUTE	This is set to a command that disables communication between the PortSentry system and the bad guy (target host of PortSentry). When an attack is detected, this command is executed. The macro $TARGET$ is substituted for the IP address of the offending target host and $PORT$ is expanded to the port used by the attacker.
	As shown in the preceding configuration, the iptables command is used to drop packets when an attack is detected.

Option	Meaning
KILL_HOSTS_DENY	This specifies the line that is appended to the /etc/hosts. deny file. The default configuration show above adds an ALL: $TARGET$ line where the macro $TARGET$ expands to the IP address of the attacker host. The /etc/hosts.deny file is used by TCP wrapper programs to decide if connection from a host is denied on any services. Since ALL is used, TCP wrappers reject every connection. You can also drop in any TCP wrapper escape codes here as well (such as %h or twist). The macro $PORT$ substitutes the port that was connected to by the attacker.
KILL_RUN_CMD	This specifies a command that is run before the KILL_ROUTE specified command is run. For example, the sample configuration shows that the echo command is run to write a log entry about an attack.
	Note that if you are thinking about running a counter attack script, simply don't. It isn't appropriate and not worth the trouble that you can get into legally or with resources.
SCAN_TRIGGER	Sets how fast PortSentry reacts to incoming port scans. Default setting of 0 makes it react immediately. For example, a setting of 3 allows a potential attacker perform scan on three ports. Leave the default as is.
PORT_BANNER	When PortSentry detects a scan, it can send a text banner message set with this option. The banner isn't displayed for advanced stealth mode operation.
	If you want to ignore a few hosts even if they connect to a monitored port, add their IP addresses in portsentry.ignore file.
	Now you can compile and install the source using the make linux && make install command. The binaries and configuration files are installed in /usr/local/psionic/ portsentry directory. If you want to change this location, modify the Makefile, portsentry.conf, and portsentry_config.h files before running the preceding make command.
	Before you can start PortSentry, you need to know which of the six modes to use as shown in Table 21-2.

TABLE 21-2: PORTSENTRY MODES

Mode	Meaning
-tcp	Basic port-bound TCP mode. PortSentry binds to all the ports listed in TCP_PORTS option in portsentry.conf file.
-udp	Basic port-bound UDP mode. PortSentry binds to all the ports listed in UDP_PORTS option in portsentry.conf file.
-stcp	Stealth TCP scan detection mode. PortSentry uses a raw socket to monitor all incoming packets. If an incoming packet is destined for a monitored port it reacts to block the host. This method detects connect() scans, SYN/half-open scans, and FIN scans.
-sudp	Stealth UDP scan detection mode. This operates the same as the preceding TCP stealth mode. UDP ports need to be listed and they are then monitored. This doesn't bind any sockets, and it reacts to any UDP packet.
-atcp	Advanced TCP stealth scan detection mode. PortSentry listens to all the ports under ADVANCED_PORTS_TCP option specified port number. Any host connecting to any port in this range that isn't excluded (in ADVANCED_EXCLUDE_TCP option) is blocked. This mode is the most sensitive and the most effective of all the protection options. Make sure you know which ports you need to exclude for this mode to work properly. For example, if you include the AUTH (113) port here, an outgoing FTP connection may be rejected by an external FTP server that sends a request to identd daemon on your system. PortSentry allows FTP servers to make a temporary data connection back to the client on a high (> 1024) port.
-audp	Advanced UDP stealth scan detection mode. This is a very advanced option and you stand a good chance of causing false alarms. PortSentry makes no distinction between broadcast and direct traffic. If you have a router on your local network putting out RIP broadcasts, then you probably block them. Use this option with extreme caution. Be sure you use exclusions in the ADVANCED_EXCLUDE_UDP option.

For example, to run PortSentry in standard TCP mode use usr/local/psionic/portsentry/portsentry -tcp command. To ensure that PortSentry is started properly, you can view the /var/log/messages file to see such lines as the following:

```
adminalert: Psionic PortSentry 1.0 is starting.
adminalert: Going into listen mode on TCP port: 1
adminalert: Going into listen mode on TCP port: 11
```

```
adminalert: Going into listen mode on TCP port: 15
adminalert: Going into listen mode on TCP port: 79
adminalert: ERROR: could not bind TCP socket: 79. Attempting to continue
adminalert: Going into listen mode on TCP port: 111
adminalert: ERROR: could not bind TCP socket: 111. Attempting to continue
adminalert: Going into listen mode on TCP port: 119
adminalert: Going into listen mode on TCP port: 143
adminalert: Going into listen mode on TCP port: 540
adminalert: Going into listen mode on TCP port: 635
adminalert: Going into listen mode on TCP port: 1080
adminalert: Going into listen mode on TCP port: 1524
adminalert: Going into listen mode on TCP port: 2000
adminalert: Going into listen mode on TCP port: 5742
adminalert: Going into listen mode on TCP port: 6667
adminalert: Going into listen mode on TCP port: 12345
adminalert: Going into listen mode on TCP port: 12346
adminalert: Going into listen mode on TCP port: 20034
adminalert: Going into listen mode on TCP port: 31337
adminalert: Going into listen mode on TCP port: 32771
adminalert: Going into listen mode on TCP port: 32772
adminalert: Going into listen mode on TCP port: 32773
adminalert: Going into listen mode on TCP port: 32774
adminalert: Going into listen mode on TCP port: 40421
adminalert: Going into listen mode on TCP port: 49724
adminalert: Going into listen mode on TCP port: 54320
adminalert: PortSentry is now active and listening.
```

The last line indicates that PortSentry is running. You should see all the ports you told it to watch in the log. If a port is used, PortSentry warns you that it couldn't bind to it and continues until all the other ports are bound. In the preceding sample log entries, finger port (79) and sunrpc port (111) couldn't be bound to PortSentry because other services are already bound to them.

 Note that for the advanced stealth scan detection mode PortSentry only lists the ports that it doesn't listen for. This is an inverse binding.

Now, to see what happens when another host tries to connect to a monitored port, do the following experiment:

1. Run `tail -f /var/log/messages` on the system running PortSentry.

2. From another host on your network that has not been in the `portsentry.ignore` list, connect to a monitored port and watch the log window on the

PortSentry machine. For example, I connected to the monitored system from a host called `nano.nitec.com` on a monitored port 54320. Here is what `/var/log/messages` showed:

```
attackalert: Connect from host: nano.nitec.com/207.183.233.19
to TCP port: 54320
attackalert: External command run for host: 207.183.233.19
using command: "/bin/echo Attack host: 207.183.233.19 port:
54320 >> /var/log/attacks.log"
attackalert: Host 207.183.233.19 has been blocked via
wrappers with string: "ALL: 207.183.233.19"
```

I didn't have the KILL_ROUTE option turned on in portsentry.conf, so the iptables command was not issued.

3. Repeated connection attempts generates logs such as the following:

```
attackalert: Connect from host: nano.nitec.com/207.183.233.19
to TCP port: 54320
attackalert: Host: 207.183.233.19 is already blocked.
Ignoring
```

4. For advanced mode, you can telnet to any port not excluded to trip an alarm. If you disconnect and try to telnet again, you should find that the target system is unreachable.

To make sure PortSentry starts up each time you boot the system, append the following line in `/etc/rc.d/rc.local` script. Don't forget to change the *mode* argument to one of the six possible modes.

`/usr/local/psionic/portsentry` *mode*

Using Nessus Security Scanner

The Nessus security scanner is a client/server security auditing tool.

- ◆ The server, nessusd, is in charge of the audits.
- ◆ The client, nessus, interferes with the user through X11/GTK+ interface or command line.

COMPILING AND INSTALLING NESSUS

Here is how you can install and run this scanner.

1. Become root. Download the latest version of four files: `nessus-libraries-version.tar.gz`, `libnasl-version.tar.gz`, `nessus-core.version.tar.gz`, and `nessus-plugins.version.tar.gz` from

http://www.nessus.org. You must compile them in this order. Extract each file using `tar xvzf `*`filename.tar.gz`* command. For example:

```
tar xvzf nessus-libraries-1.0.7a.tar.gz
tar xvzf libnasl-1.0.7a.tar.gz
tar xvzf nessus-core-1.0.7a.tar.gz
tar xvzf nessus-plugins-1.0.7a.tar.gz
```

These commands don't extract all the source code in nessus-libraries, libnasl, nessus-core, and nessus-plugins directories. Here the software version is 1.0.7a.

2. Compile the nessus-libraries by changing your current directory to nessus-libraries and running `./configure` and `make && make install` to install the libraries.

3. Add `/usr/local/lib` in `/etc/ld.so.conf` and run `ldconfig`.

4. Compile libnasl by changing your current directory to `libnasl` and running `./configure` and `make && make install` to install the libraries.

5. Compile nessus-core by changing your current directory to nessus-core and running `./configure` and `make && make install` to install the core.

 If you don't use The X Window System or you don't want the nessus client to use GTK, you can compile a stripped-down version of the client that works from the command-line. To do this, add the `--disable-gtk` option to configure while building nessus-core as follows: `./configure --disable-gtk ; make && make install`

---

6. Compile nessus-plugins by changing your current directory to nessus-plugins and running `./configure` and the `make` command. Then run `make install` to install the plugins.

At this point, you have the nessus built.

CONFIGURING NESSUS SERVER

The nessusd server has its own users database. Each user has a set of restrictions. This allows you to share a nessusd server for a whole network and different administrators who only test their part of the network. The utility `nessus-adduser` can create a new nessus user account. Here is a sample session using this command.

```
Addition of a new nessusd user
```

```
------------------------------
Login : renaud
Password : secret
Authentication type (cipher or plaintext) [cipher] : cipher
Now enter the rules for this user, and hit ctrl-D once you are done :
(the user can have an empty rule set)
^D
Login          : renaud
Password       : secret
Authentication : cipher
Rules          :
Is that ok (y/n) ? [y] y
user added.
```

The Nessus server configuration is stored in /usr/local/etc/nessus/nessusd. conf. You should take a look at it and see whether anything needs to be changed. Most likely, you can keep the defaults.

To start the Nessus server, run ./nessusd -D from the command-line as root.

USING NESSUS CLIENT TO SCAN

Follows these steps to configure the Nessus client:

1. Run nessus from the command line.

   By default, the Nessus client shows

   - The Nessus server hostname (local machine)

   - Default port 3001

   - Default encryption type

2. Use the username/password pair created earlier to login.

3. Select the security check plugins that you want to perform.

   To know more about a particular check, click on the plugin name and more information appears. You can select/un-select options at the plugin level. Some plugins may require that you enter additional information at the plugin level.

4. Click on the Scan option button, then enter

   - Range of ports to scan

   - Maximum process threads to use on the system (the more threads you use, the more resources are used on both local system and the target system)

- Path to CGI scripts on the target system

- Port scanner software to use

These actions are optional:

- A reverse DNS lookup on the IP address of the target host before scanning

- Optimizing the test

5. Define the target system by clicking on the Target section button. Enter either

- A single hostname, IP address, or IP address/CIDR

- A comma-separated list of hostnames or IP addresses

For example, you can enter 192.168.1.0/24 to scan the entire 192.168.1.0 network.

6. Click the Start the scan button to start the test.

To restrict the test using one or more rules, you can add rules using the User tab window to exclude one or more systems from a scan.

Once you have started the scan, you see a graphical status for each host showing. After the scan is complete, a report window appears showing all the findings. For each host, you have a detailed report, which also points out the potential solution and/or Common Vulnerability Exposure (CVE) identification number.

Using Strobe

Strobe is a high speed TCP port scanner. You can download it from `http://www.insecure.org/nmap/scanners`. Once you have downloaded the source distribution, you can extract it and run `make install` from the new strobe subdirectory. You can run strobe from this directory using the `./strobe` *hostname* `-f` command. For example:

```
strobe nano.nitec.com -f
```

The preceding command scans a host called `nano.nitec.com` in fast mode (`-f`). Here's a sample output:

```
strobe 1.03 (c) 1995 Julian Assange (proff@suburbia.net).
nano.nitec.com    echo            7/tcp Echo [95,JBP]
nano.nitec.com    discard         9/tcp Discard [94,JBP]
nano.nitec.com    daytime        13/tcp Daytime [93,JBP]
nano.nitec.com    qotd           17/tcp Quote of the Day [100,JBP]
nano.nitec.com    chargen        19/tcp ttytst source Character Generator
nano.nitec.com    ftp            21/tcp File Transfer [Control] [96,JBP]
nano.nitec.com    smtp           25/tcp Simple Mail Transfer [102,JBP]
nano.nitec.com    nameserver     42/tcp Host Name Server [99,JBP]
nano.nitec.com    domain         53/tcp Domain Name Server [81,95,PM1]
nano.nitec.com    kerberos       88/tcp Kerberos [BCN]
nano.nitec.com    loc-srv       135/tcp Location Service [JXP]
nano.nitec.com    netbios-ssn   139/tcp NETBIOS Session Service [JBP]
nano.nitec.com    ldap          389/tcp Lightweight Directory Access Protocol
nano.nitec.com    microsoft-ds  445/tcp
nano.nitec.com    printer       515/tcp spooler (lpd)
nano.nitec.com    nterm        1026/tcp remote_login network_terminal
nano.nitec.com    irc-serv     6666/tcp internet relay chat server
nano.nitec.com    afs3-bos     7007/tcp basic overseer process
```

You can also generate statistics on the scan by using the `-s` option.

Using Log Monitoring and Analysis Tools

Logs are very valuable in fighting security problems. Often a hacker makes many failed attempts before getting in. Sometimes I have seen failed attempts for days from hackers which led me to fix one or more security problems before anyone got it. So monitoring logs and using tools to analyze them is a great security measure. Here I will discuss log monitoring and analysis tools.

Using logcheck for detecting unusual log entries

You can use the logcheck tool to scan your system logs for unusual log activity caused by port scans or other attacks. Download the source distribution from http://www.psionic.com/abacus/logcheck. A typical logcheck-enabled system works as follows:

◆ Every hour logcheck script is run, which runs the logtail program.

◆ The logtail program finds the position in the log where logcheck finished last time (if any).

◆ The logcheck script performs keyword searches on the new log entries for

   ▪ Active system attacks

   ▪ Security violations

   ▪ Unusual system activity

◆ If there is anything to report, it sends an email to the administrator

INSTALLING LOGCHECK

To install logcheck from the source distribution do the following:

1. As `root` extract the source distribution using the `tar xvzf logcheck-version.tar.gz` command. Enter the newly created logceck-version subdirectory.

2. Run make linux to compile and install. The logcheck configuration files are stored in `/usr/local/etc` directory. The `logcheck.sh` script is also stored in `/usr/local/etc`. However the logtail program is stored in `/usr/local/bin`.

CONFIGURING LOGCHECK

The `logcheck.sh` is the main script. There are four configuration files:

◆ `logcheck.hacking`

   The `logcheck.hacking` file contains a list of keywords that logcheck scans for in the logs. When logcheck finds a keyword match in a log file it reports it under ACTIVE SYSTEM ATTACK title in the email message. Keywords are case insensitive.

◆ `logcheck.ignore`

   The `logcheck.ignore` file contains a list of keywords that you want logcheck to ignore. Anything that you don't specify here is reported in the email under Unusual System Activity. Keywords are case sensitive.

◆ `logcheck.violations`

   The `logcheck.violations` file contains a list of keywords that indicate a security violation. A keyword match from this file results in reporting the entry in Security Violation section of the email.

◆ `logcheck.violations.ignore`

To exclude a violation keyword from being reported, you can use the
`logcheck.violations.ignore` file. Any keyword that is found in
`logcheck.violations.ignore` isn't reported, even if `logcheck.`
`violations` includes it. Note that keywords searches for the ignore
file is insensitive.

Ideally, logcheck would like to scan a single log file such as `/var/log/`
`messages`, but that's not really a good idea from a system management point of
view. Therefore, logcheck actually creates temporary log files by combining `/var/`
`log/messages`, `/var/log/secure` and `/var/log/maillog` to a temporary file in
`/usr/local/tmp/check.PID`.

The default logcheck.sh script doesn't check the FTP transfer log `/var/`
`log/xferlog`. To check it, add `$LOGTAIL   /var/log/xferlog   >>`
`$TMPDIR/check.$$` in the section where you find the following lines:

```
$LOGTAIL /var/log/messages > $TMPDIR/check.$$
$LOGTAIL /var/log/secure >> $TMPDIR/check.$$
$LOGTAIL /var/log/maillog >> $TMPDIR/check.$$
```

By default, logcheck sends email to the root account on the localhost. If
you want to change that modify the logcheck.sh script by changing SYSADMIN=
root to SYSADMIN=*your@emailaddress,* where your@emailaddress is the email
address you want to use instead. For local users, simply specify username instead of
the full address.

Decide whether you want to run `logcheck.sh` on a hourly, daily, or weekly,
basis. I recommend that you run it on a hourly basis at the beginning, then switch
to a daily report. This allows you to weed out false alerts at the beginning quickly,
then get a daily report. To setup an hourly cron job, simply run the following command as root once:

```
ln -s /usr/local/etc/logcheck.sh  /etc/cron.hourly/logcheck.sh
```

Similarly, to run it every day, run:

```
ln -s /usr/local/etc/logcheck.sh  /etc/cron.daily/logcheck.sh
```

Once you have created one of these two symbolic links, cron daemon runs the
script on the schedule you choose.

If you want to run the logcheck script more frequently than once an hour, add
the script in `/etc/crontab` instead. For example:

```
00,15,30,45 * * * * /usr/local/etc/logcheck.sh
```

This line in /etc/crontab has crond daemon run the script every 15 minutes.

Swatch

This is a Perl-based system log (/var/log/message) monitoring script that can monitor system events and trigger alarms based on patterns stored in a configuration file. It has multiple alarm methods, (visual and event triggers). Here is how you can install and configure swatch.

1. Download the tar ball from http://www.stanford.edu/~atkins/ swatch/ and extract it as root in a directory. Change directory to the newly created subdirectory.

2. Run perl Makefile.PL ; make ; make test commands.

3. Modify the swatchrc.monitor or swatcher.personal configuration file to suit your needs. The configuration format is quite simple. For example:

```
watchfor    /keyword/
        echo bold
        bell 3
```

The preceding configuration tells swatch to echo the bell (character 0x7) three times if the keyword is seen in the /var/log/messages file. Rename your configuration file to .swatchrc and keep it in /root/ directory.

4. Run swatch using the /path/to/swatch/swatch --config-file=/ root/.swatchrc command on a xterm or shell window.

IPTraf

IPTraf is an ncurses-based IP LAN monitor that utilizes the built-in raw packet capture interface of the Linux kernel. It generates various network statistics, including

◆ Total, IP, TCP, UDP, ICMP, and non-IP byte counts

◆ TCP source and destination addresses and ports

◆ TCP packet and byte counts

◆ TCP flag statuses

◆ UDP source and destination information

◆ ICMP type information

◆ OSPF source and destination information

◆ TCP and UDP service statistics

◆ Interface packet counts

♦ Interface IP checksum error counts

♦ Interface activity indicators

♦ LAN station statistics

IPTraf can be used to monitor the load on an IP network, the most used types of network services, the proceedings of TCP connections, and others. You can download IPTraf from `http://cebu.mozcom.com/riker/iptraf`.

Using CGI Scanners

CGI scanners are used to scan a Web server for CGI script-related vulnerabilities. There are two scanners that I like.

Using cgichk.pl

This is a simple CGI scanner written in Perl. You can download the source from `http://www.packetstorm.securify.com` Web site. When run from the command line using `perl cgichk.pl` command, it asks you to enter a hostname for the Web server you want to scan and a port number (default 80). You can also choose to log the results in a file.

First, it checks the HTTP protocol version being used by the Web server. For example, the following sample session shows that we are scanning a machine called `rhat.nitec.com`.

```
CGI scanner [in Perl] v1.1
Host: rhat.nitec.com
HTTP Port [80]:
Log Session?(y/n)y
Log File [rhat.nitec.com.scan]:
Press [enter] to check the httpd version...
HTTP/1.1 200 OK
Date: Tue, 27 Mar 2001 04:50:47 GMT
Server: Apache/2.0.14 (Unix)
Last-Modified: Mon, 26 Mar 2001 20:23:13 GMT
ETag: "1ba42-1000-c65eee40"
Connection: close
Content-Type: text/html; charset=ISO-8859-1
```

Once it detects the protocol version, it asks you to press the enter key to start checking for CGI vulnerabilities. Following output shows a sample scan for CGI security issues on `rhat.nitec.com` Web server running Apache 2.0.

```
Searching for UnlG - backdoor   : Not Found
Searching for THC - backdoor    : Not Found
Searching for phf               : Not Found
Searching for Count.cgi         : Not Found
Searching for test-cgi          : Not Found
Searching for nph-test-cgi      : Not Found
Searching for nph-publish       : Not Found
Searching for php.cgi           : Not Found
Searching for handler           : Not Found
Searching for webgais           : Not Found
Searching for websendmail       : Not Found
Searching for webdist.cgi       : Not Found
Searching for faxsurvey         : Not Found
Searching for htmlscript        : Not Found
Searching for pfdisplay         : Not Found
Searching for perl.exe          : Not Found
Searching for wwwboard.pl       : Not Found
Searching for www-sql           : Not Found
Searching for view-source       : Not Found
Searching for campas            : Not Found
Searching for aglimpse          : Not Found
Searching for glimpse           : Not Found
Searching for man.sh            : Not Found
Searching for AT-admin.cgi      : Not Found
Searching for filemail.pl       : Not Found
Searching for maillist.pl       : Not Found
Searching for jj                : Not Found
Searching for info2www          : Not Found
Searching for files.pl          : Not Found
Searching for finger            : Not Found
Searching for bnbform.cgi       : Not Found
Searching for survey.cgi        : Not Found
Searching for AnyForm2          : Not Found
Searching for textcounter.pl    : Not Found
Searching for classifields.cgi  : Not Found
Searching for environ.cgi       : Not Found
Searching for wrap              : Not Found
Searching for cgiwrap           : Not Found
Searching for guestbook.cgi     : Not Found
Searching for edit.pl           : Not Found
Searching for perlshop.cgi      : Not Found
Searching for anyboard.cgi      : Not Found
Searching for webbbs.cgi        : Found!
Searching for environ.cgi       : Not Found
Searching for whois_raw.cgi     : Not Found
```

```
Searching for _vti_inf.html    : Not Found
Searching for service.pwd      : Not Found
Searching for users.pwd        : Not Found
Searching for authors.pwd      : Not Found
Searching for administrators   : Not Found
Searching for shtml.dll        : Not Found
Searching for shtml.exe        : Not Found
Searching for args.bat         : Not Found
Searching for uploader.exe     : Not Found
Searching for rguest.exe       : Not Found
Searching for wguest.exe       : Not Found
Searching for bdir - samples   : Not Found
Searching for CGImail.exe      : Not Found
Searching for newdsn.exe       : Not Found
Searching for fpcount.exe      : Not Found
Searching for counter.exe      : Not Found
Searching for visadmin.exe     : Not Found
Searching for openfile.cfm     : Not Found
Searching for exprcalc.cfm     : Not Found
Searching for dispopenedfile   : Not Found
Searching for sendmail.cfm     : Not Found
Searching for codebrws.asp     : Not Found
Searching for codebrws.asp 2   : Not Found
Searching for showcode.asp     : Not Found
Searching for search97.vts     : Not Found
Searching for carbo.dll        : Not Found
Server may have CGI vulnerabilities.
```

In the preceding code, the bold line is a potential CGI security risk. The webbbs.cgi script can be abused by script kiddies and wannabe hackers to break into the system. If your scan results one or more identified security risks, consider removing the scripts or updating them with appropriate fixes.

Using Whisker

Whisker is a Perl-based CGI scanner that I like a lot. You can download the source distribution from http://www.wiretrip.net/rfp. Once downloaded, extract the source in a directory and run the whisker.pl script as perl whisker.pl -h *host-name*. For example, perl whisker -h rhat.nitec.com command runs the scanner on the Apache Web server running on the named host. The result is:

```
= Host: rhat.nitec.com
= Server: Apache/2.0.14 (Unix)
+ 200 OK: HEAD /cgi-bin/webbbs.cgi
+ 200 OK: HEAD /manual/
+ 200 OK: HEAD /temp/
```

The scan output uses HTTP status code (such as 200, 303, 403, and 404) to indicate security risks. For example, the preceding scan result shows that there are three potential risks found (200) on the server. If you want more information, run whisker with `-i` and `-v` options. For example, the `perl whisker.pl -h www.domain.com -i -v` command runs it on www.domain.com. Here is a sample scan output:

```
= - = - = - = - = - =
= Host: www.domain.com
- Directory index: /
= Server: Apache/1.3.12 (Unix) mod_oas/5.1/
-  www.apache.org
+ 302 Found: GET /scripts/
+ 403 Forbidden: GET /cgi-bin/
+ 200 OK: HEAD /cgi-bin/upload.pl
+ 403 Forbidden: HEAD /~root/
+ 403 Forbidden: HEAD /apps/
+ 200 OK: HEAD /shop/
+ 200 OK: HEAD /store/
```

Notice that there are a few 200 OK lines, which means that the exploits exists. 403 states that access to exploitable resource is denied but it still exists – this is both good and bad. It's good because, as the server is configured, the exploit isn't accessible. If the configuration changes, the exploit may become available; that's why 403 in this case is bad news. The 302 lines indicate false positives. This is because many servers are configured to respond with a custom error message when a requested URL is missing and this generates a 302 HTTP status code.

You can also use `-I n` (where n = 0 to 9) option to enable evasive mode for evading Intrusion Detection System (IDS) on the Web server. So if you use any IDS solution, you can also test your IDS effectiveness. For example, if your IDS knows about /cgi-bin/phf (a known CGI risk), using `-I 1` attempts to trick your IDS using URL encoding so the /cgi-bin/phf request is sent in an encoded URL instead of directly using /cgi-bin/phf in the request. Similarly, `-I 2` tries to confuse an IDS using extra /./ pattern in the URL. For details, run whisker without any argument.

Using Malice

Malice is also another Perl-based CGI vulnerability scanner. It has anti-IDS evasion capabilities and a large list of checks.

Using Password Crackers

When a hacker gets a hold of a password file, he runs password cracker programs to detect weak passwords that are easy to guess or based on dictionary words. By using password crackers on your own password files you can detect guessable or weak passwords before the hacker does. Here I will discuss how you can use password crackers.

John The Ripper

This is a very popular password cracking tool that you can download from http://www.openwall.com/john. This is a good tool to use to try to crack your password file (/etc/passwd) so that you can find weak passwords.

 When using a cracker program, be sure that you are authorized to run crack programs. If you work for a company and aren't directly responsible for system administration, ask the boss for the permission or unnecessary legal trouble may find you.

To install john, do the following:

1. Download and extract the source distribution from the official Web site. Change your current directory to the src subdirectory under the newly created subdirectory called john-*version* (where version is the version number of your source distribution).

2. Run the make linux-x86-any-elf command to compile and install john in the run subdirectory in john-*version*/run.

To crack your password file, follow these steps:

1. If you are using shadow password, unshadow it by running the following command from the run subdirectory under john-*version* directory:

   ./unshadow /etc/passwd /etc/shadow > /etc/passwd.john

2. Run ./john /etc/passwd.john from the same subdirectory.

   Depending on how many passwords you have in the password file and their complexity, the cracking can take a very long time.

3. To get the cracked passwords, run ./john -show /tmp/passwd.john command from the run subdirectory.

4. To see if any root account (UID = 0) got cracked or not run ./john -show -users:0 /tmp/passwd.john command from the run subdirectory.

Cracking passwords takes a lot of system resources. Don't run john on a production server. If you must run on a busy system, consider using nice to lower priority. For example, `nice -n 20 /path/to/john /etc/passwd.txt &` command is nice to your system.

If you run john in the foreground (that is, you don't use & when running it), you can press control+c to abort it. You can also restore an aborted session by running john with only the `-restore` command-line option.

Crack

Like John the Ripper (john), you can use Crack to take a crack at cracking your passwords. Crack is the classic password cracker. It can be downloaded from `http://www.users.dircon.co.uk/~crypto`.

Using Intrusion Detection Tools

Intrusion detection tools are great when it comes to detecting security breaches in a computer system. Here are two such tools that can help you enhance your system security.

Tripwire

Tripwire Open Source Linux Edition, under the General Public License (GPL), is a file and directory integrity checker that creates a database of signatures for all files and directories and stores them in a single file. When Tripwire is run again, it computes new signatures for current files and directories, then compares them with the original signatures stored in the database. If there is a discrepancy, the file or directory name is reported with information about the discrepancy.

See the Using Tripwire Open Source, Linux Edition section in Chapter 9 for details on how to use Tripwire.

LIDS

The Linux Intrusion Detection System (LIDS) enhances security from within the kernel of the Linux operating system. In the LIDS security model, the subject, the object, and the access type are in the kernel, so it's called a reference monitor. The LIDS project Web site is `http://www.lids.org/about.html`. Chapter 8 describes this tool.

Using Packet Filters and Sniffers

Packet filtering is a technique that allows you to drop or reject unwanted IP packets. Similarly, packet sniffers allow you to detect dangerous payload within the packets. Tools that provide you with such powerful security techniques are discussed here.

Snort

This is a packet sniffer, packet logger, and network intrusion detection system that analyzes network traffic analysis and logs IP packets. Snort uses a flexible rules language and a detection engine that utilizes modular plugin architecture. Snort has a real-time alert capability that incorporates alert mechanisms for

◆ Syslog

◆ A user-specified file

◆ A UNIX socket

◆ Win Popup messages to Windows clients using Samba's smbclient.

You can download snort from `http://www.snort.org`.

If you use network switches instead of hubs, your switch must mirror traffic on the switched port for the machine running snort.

Snort uses the libpcap library. You must install libpcap library, which can be downloaded from `http://www.tcpdump.org`. It features rules based logging and can perform content searching/matching in addition to being used to detect a variety of other attacks and probes, such as

◆ Buffer overflows

◆ Stealth port scans

◆ CGI attacks

◆ SMB probes

Here is how you compile and install snort on your system:

1. Download snort source distribution from the official Web site. As `root`, extract the source using `tar xvzf snort-version.tar.gz` command. From the newly created subdirectory, run `./configure` to configure the

source. The `configure` script detects if you have supported database (such as MySQL and Postgres) and for files necessary for the database plugin.

 Although I had MySQL with appropriate header and library distributions, Snort couldn't compile because of an error. So I had to disable the MySQL related compilation by changing the CPPFLAGS =   -I/usr/include/mysql -DENABLE_MYSQL -I/usr/include/pgsql DENABLE_POSTGRESQL -I/usr/include -DENABLE_SSL line in Makefile to CPPFLAGS = -I/usr/include -DENABLE_SSL

2. Run `make && make install` to compile and install snort.

3. Configure Snort using the `snort.conf` file.

   ■ Set the HOME_NET variable in the file to your home network.

   ■ Optionally, you can set the DNS_SERVERS variable.

   ■ If you plan on creating new snort rules, consult the snort rule-writing guide found on the official Web site.

4. Save the configuration file changes.

5. Create the log directory for Snort by using `mkdir -p /var/log/snort`.

 When you run Snort on a specific network interface it's in promiscuous mode.

USING SNORT IN SNIFFER MODE

To sniff TCP/IP packets on the network, run the `/usr/local/bin/snort  -v` command. This prints TCP/IP packet headers, like this:

```
03/28-22:34:48.123739 207.183.233.19:1660 -> 207.183.233.20:22
TCP TTL:128 TOS:0x0 ID:37163 IpLen:20 DgmLen:40 DF
***A**** Seq: 0xA99ACDBA  Ack: 0xAE054C32  Win: 0x7F0  TcpLen: 20
=+=+=+=+=+=+=+=+=+=+=+=+=+=+=+=+=+=+=+=+=+=+=+=+=+=+=+=+=+=+=+=+
03/28-22:34:48.123810 207.183.233.19:1660 -> 207.183.233.20:22
TCP TTL:128 TOS:0x0 ID:37164 IpLen:20 DgmLen:40 DF
***A**** Seq: 0xA99ACDBA  Ack: 0xAE054E62  Win: 0x5C0  TcpLen: 20
=+=+=+=+=+=+=+=+=+=+=+=+=+=+=+=+=+=+=+=+=+=+=+=+=+=+=+=+=+=+=+=+
```

```
03/28-22:34:48.123879 207.183.233.19:1660 -> 207.183.233.20:22
TCP TTL:128 TOS:0x0 ID:37165 IpLen:20 DgmLen:40 DF
***A**** Seq: 0xA99ACDBA  Ack: 0xAE05508A  Win: 0x398  TcpLen: 20
=+=+=+=+=+=+=+=+=+=+=+=+=+=+=+=+=+=+=+=+=+=+=+=+=+=+=+=+=+=+=+=+
```

Snort prints packet header information until you stop it by pressing Control+C. When you abort Snort using such a key combination, it prints packet statistics, like this:

```
===============================================================================
Snort received 441 packets and dropped 0(0.000%) packets
Breakdown by protocol:              Action Stats:
     TCP: 438       (99.320%)       ALERTS: 0
     UDP: 0         (0.000%)        LOGGED: 0
    ICMP: 0         (0.000%)        PASSED: 0
     ARP: 0         (0.000%)
    IPv6: 0         (0.000%)
     IPX: 0         (0.000%)
   OTHER: 3         (0.680%)
 DISCARD: 0         (0.000%)
===============================================================================
Fragmentation Stats:
Fragmented IP Packets: 0            (0.000%)
   Rebuilt IP Packets: 0
   Frag elements used: 0
Discarded(incomplete): 0
   Discarded(timeout): 0
===============================================================================
TCP Stream Reassembly Stats:
   TCP Packets Used:      0         (0.000%)
 Reconstructed Packets: 0           (0.000%)
   Streams Reconstructed: 0
===============================================================================
```

If you want to see more than just the TCP/UDP/ICMP header information, such as application data in transit then do the following:

♦ Run /usr/local/bin/snort -vd. If you want more information such as the link layer headers, run snort with -vde options.

♦ If you want to log the packets to a log directory, run snort with -vde -l *path* options where path should be a suitable log directory.

♦ If you want to analyze the logged packets using a tcpdump format compatible analysis tool, you can use -l path -b options.

USING SNORT IN NETWORK INTRUSION DETECTION MODE

You need to have a rule file, such as `snort.conf`, to run in network intrusion detection mode. For example:

```
/usr/local/bin/snort -d -c snort.conf
```

Here, Snort applies all the rules in `snort.conf` file and log entries in `/var/log/snort` directory by default.

 TIP By default, Snort uses full alert mode (-A full), which may be a bit slow for a fast network. You can use -A fast instead. This ensures that Snort writes simple alert messages in the log file and logs packet data in tcpdump format.

GShield

GShield is an iptables firewall that you can download from `http://muse.linux-mafia.org/gshield.html`. It supports network address translations (NAT), demilitarized zone (DMZ), port forwarding, transparent proxy and many other cool features.

Useful Utilities for Security Administrators

There are many programs that a security conscious administrator needs frequently. Here I will discuss four such security utilities for such security emergencies.

Using Netcat

Netcat (nc) is a network utility that allows you to create raw socket connection to a port. Over a raw connection, data can be sent or received. It's a great network debugging and exploration tool that can act as a backend for another script that serves as a client or server using TCP or UDP protocols.

INSTALLING NETCAT

Here is how you can install Netcat on your system:

1. Download the Netcat RPM source from RPM sites, such as `http://www.rpmfind.net`.

   Simply enter `netcat` as the keyword for the search interface and you find both source and binary RPM distributions.

2. Download the netcat-*version*-src.rpm. Don't forget to replace version with appropriate version number.

3. As root, run **rpm -ivh netcat-version-src.rpm**. This installs a tar ball file in /usr/src/redhat/SOURCES directory. Run mkdir -p /usr/src/red-hat/SOURCES/netcat; mv /usr/src/redhat/SOURCES/nc*.tgz /usr/src/redhat/SOURCES/netcat commands to create a subdirectory called netcat in /usr/src/redhat/SOURCES and move the *ncversion*.tgz (for example, nc110.tgz) file in this directory.

4. Change your current directory to the newly created /usr/src/redhat/SOURCES/netcat directory. From this directory, run tar xvzf *ncversion*.tgz command to extract the source.

5. Once extracted, run make linux command to compile the source. If you have errors, try make nc instead. Either way, you end up with a new binary called nc in the current directory. Install the binary in a suitable directory, such as /usr/bin using cp nc /usr/bin; chmod 755 /usr/bin/nc commands.

Now you have Netcat binary nc installed on your system. You should be able to access it from anywhere as long as you have /usr/bin directory in your path.

> Telnet is a very limited TCP client. Using it in scripts is difficult due to its limitations. For example, telnet client doesn't allow you to send arbitrary binary data to the other side, because it interprets some of the byte sequences as its internal command options. Telnet also mixes network output with its own internal messages, which makes it difficult for keeping the raw output clean. It's also not capable of receiving connection requests nor can it use UDP packets. Netcat doesn't have any of these limitations and it's much smaller and faster than telnet and has many other advantages.

Netcat's major features are:

♦ TCP or UDP connection to and from any port

♦ Full DNS (forward/reverse) lookup capabilities

♦ Ability to use any local source port and network address

♦ Built-in port-scanning capabilities, with randomizer

♦ Built-in loose source-routing capability

- ◆ Slow-send mode, one line every N seconds

- ◆ Hex dump of transmitted and received data

- ◆ Optional ability to let another program service established connections

- ◆ Optional telnet-options responder

The simplest way to use Netcat is to run nc *hostname portnumber*. This makes a TCP connection to the named host on the given port. There are many command-line options that you can use. Run nc -h to find out about all the command-line options.

CREATING A SIMPLE CLIENT/SERVER USING NC

You can use Netcat (nc) to create a simple client/server solution.

1. Run the following command on one shell or xterm window:

```
/usr/bin/nc -l -p 9999  -v
```

This command tells Netcat (nc) to listen to port 9999 and be verbose (-v) about it. This is the server.

If you don't specify a port number using the -p option, nc automatically finds an unused port and uses it for the connection. Of course you must use -v option to have nc tell you what port it's using in this case or else you won't be able to connect to it from the client side. Also note that if you are using UDP mode (using -u option) instead of the default TCP mode, then you must provide port number using -p option.

2. Run the following command in another shell or xterm window:

```
/usr/bin/nc -v localhost 9999
```

This tells another instance of nc to run as a client and connect to local-host using port 9999. As soon as you make the connection using this preceding command, you see a message on the server window. For example, when the preceding commands are run on a host called rhat.nitec.com, the server window shows the following messages after the client connects.

```
listening on [any] 9999 ...
connect to [127.0.0.1] from rhat.nitec.com [127.0.0.1] 1407
```

Entering text on the client or the server gets the message sent to each side. This acts like a simple talk or chat client/server solution.

If you want to display a text message to anyone who connects to the nc server running on port 9999, you can modify the nc command used to startup in server mode as follows:

```
/usr/bin/nc -l -p 9999  -v  < /path/to/file
```

When you start the nc server using this command line, the /path/to/file is displayed whenever a new client connects to the server. To disconnect the client from the server, press Control+C.; the server automatically stops, too.

CREATING A HEX DUMP OF YOUR CONNECTION

It is often a good idea to get a hex dump of the entire network conversation so you can see what data is exactly being received or sent. Netcat allows you to do that using the -o filename option. For example:

```
/usr/bin/nc -v localhost 25 -o /tmp/smtp.hex
```

This command connects to the local SMTP server on port 25 and allows you to record all incoming and outgoing data in /tmp/smtp.hex in Hex format. For example, a sample short session for the preceding command is shown below:

```
220 rhat.nitec.com ESMTP Sendmail 8.11.0/8.11.0; Tue, 27 Mar 2001 10:50:57 -0800
helo domain.com
250 rhat.nitec.com Hello IDENT:kabir@rhat.nitec.com [127.0.0.1], pleased to meet
you
quit
221 2.0.0 rhat.nitec.com closing connection
```

After connecting to the local SMTP server via nc, I entered the helo command (spelled helo, not hello). The server responded with a greeting, then I entered the quit command to log out. The data collected in the /tmp/smtp.hex is shown below:

```
< 00000000 32 32 30 20 72 68 61 74 2e 6e 69 74 65 63 2e 63 # 220 rhat.nitec.c
< 00000010 6f 6d 20 45 53 4d 54 50 20 53 65 6e 64 6d 61 69 # om ESMTP Sendmai
< 00000020 6c 20 38 2e 31 31 2e 30 2f 38 2e 31 31 2e 30 3b # l 8.11.0/8.11.0;
< 00000030 20 54 75 65 2c 20 32 37 20 4d 61 72 20 32 30 30 #  Tue, 27 Mar 200
< 00000040 31 20 31 30 3a 35 30 3a 35 37 20 2d 30 38 30 30 # 1 10:50:57 -0800
< 00000050 0d 0a                                           # ..
> 00000000 68 65 6c 6f 20 64 6f 6d 61 69 6e 2e 63 6f 6d 0a # helo domain.com.
< 00000052 32 35 30 20 72 68 61 74 2e 6e 69 74 65 63 2e 63 # 250 rhat.nitec.c
< 00000062 6f 6d 20 48 65 6c 6c 6f 20 49 44 45 4e 54 3a 6b # om Hello IDENT:k
< 00000072 61 62 69 72 40 72 68 61 74 2e 6e 69 74 65 63 2e # abir@rhat.nitec.
< 00000082 63 6f 6d 20 5b 31 32 37 2e 30 2e 30 2e 31 5d 2c # com [127.0.0.1],
```

```
< 00000092 20 70 6c 65 61 73 65 64 20 74 6f 20 6d 65 65 74 # pleased to meet
< 000000a2 20 79 6f 75 0d 0a                               # you..
> 00000010 71 75 69 74 0a                                  # quit.
< 000000a8 32 32 31 20 32 2e 30 2e 30 20 72 68 61 74 2e 6e # 221 2.0.0 rhat.n
< 000000b8 69 74 65 63 2e 63 6f 6d 20 63 6c 6f 73 69 6e 67 # itec.com closing
< 000000c8 20 63 6f 6e 6e 65 63 74 69 6f 6e 0d 0a          # connection..
```

In the preceding code, I marked the data I entered via nc in bold face.

◆ Lines starting with the < character represent data received by nc from the remote server.

◆ Lines starting with the > character are generated by the local nc user (in this case, me).

CREATING A PORT SCANNER

You can use nc as a port scanner by running it as follows:

```
/usr/bin/nc -v -w 2 -z hostname port_range
```

In the preceding example,

◆ -w specifies timeout for connections and final network read.

◆ -z enables zero-I/O mode for scanning purposes, which prevents sending any data to a TCP connection and very limited probe data to a UDP connection.

◆ port_range is a numeric range of port. For example:

```
/usr/bin/nc -v -w 2 -z rhat.nitec.com 1-1024
```

This command does port scans for all ports ranging from 1 to 1024 on rhat.nitec.com system. Here's an example:

```
rhat.nitec.com [127.0.0.1] 1024 (?) open
rhat.nitec.com [127.0.0.1] 587 (?) open
rhat.nitec.com [127.0.0.1] 515 (printer) open
rhat.nitec.com [127.0.0.1] 514 (shell) open
rhat.nitec.com [127.0.0.1] 513 (login) open
rhat.nitec.com [127.0.0.1] 139 (netbios-ssn) open
rhat.nitec.com [127.0.0.1] 113 (auth) open
rhat.nitec.com [127.0.0.1] 111 (sunrpc) open
rhat.nitec.com [127.0.0.1] 80 (www) open
rhat.nitec.com [127.0.0.1] 79 (finger) open
rhat.nitec.com [127.0.0.1] 53 (domain) open
rhat.nitec.com [127.0.0.1] 25 (smtp) open
rhat.nitec.com [127.0.0.1] 23 (telnet) open
```

```
rhat.nitec.com [127.0.0.1] 22 (ssh) open
rhat.nitec.com [127.0.0.1] 21 (ftp) open
```

As you can see, nc shows a number of open ports. If you need to slow down the rate of scan, use the -i seconds option to delay each scan by specified number of seconds. Scanning is performed from highest ranging port to lowest. If you want to randomize the scanning of ports, use the -r option. You can also specify multiple ranges; for example, /usr/bin/nc -v -w 2 -z rhat.nitec.com 20-50 100-300 scans ports between 20 to 50 and 100 to 300 only.

CREATING A SIMPLE FILE TRANSFER SOLUTION

This example demonstrates how you can turn Netcat into a file transfer client server solution.

1. Run nc on the machine where you want to receive one or more files, as follows:

   ```
   /usr/bin/nc -l -p port_number | /bin/tar xvzfp -
   ```

2. Change the port_number to a real port number > 1024. For example:

   ```
   /usr/bin/nc -l -p 9999 | /bin/tar xvzfp -
   ```

   In this case, nc on the receiving host listens on local port 9999. Data received by nc is passed to the tar program, which uncompresses the data (due to the z flag) from STDIN (due to the - flag) and writes the files to disk.

3. On the sender machine, run the following command:

   ```
   /bin/tar cvzfp - path | /usr/bin/nc -w 3 receiver_host 9999
   ```

   Change the path to the fully qualified path name of the file or the directory you want to copy and the receiver_host to the host name that is listening for data. For example:

   ```
   /bin/tar cvzfp - /etc | /usr/bin/nc -w 3 rhat.nitec.com
   9999
   ```

   This command transfers all the files in /etc directory to the rhat.nitec. com system via port 9999.

Tcpdump

This is a powerful and popular network packet monitoring tool. It allows you to dump the network traffic on STDOUT or in a file. You can download it from http://www.tcpdump.org.

Tcpdump depends on libpcap, a system-independent interface for user-level packet capture library that must be installed on the system before you can compile tcpdump. The libpcap source distribution is available at the tcpdump site. You can download, extract, and install it by running `./configure && make install` command from the newly created subdirectory where the source distribution resides.

To install tcpdump on your system, follow these steps:

1. Download the source distribution from the official tcpdump site. Extract the source using `tar xvzf tcpdump-version.tar.gz` command and change directory to the newly created subdirectory.

2. Run `./configure` to configure the source, then run the `make && make install` command, which installs the binary in `/usr/local/sbin` directory.

Now you can run tcpdump to monitor network traffic between hosts. For example, to monitor traffic between a router called `router.nitec.com` and the local machine I can run:

```
/usr/local/sbin/tcpdump host router.nitec.com
```

If I `ping` the `router.nitec.com` from the local machine, tcpdump displays output such as the following:

```
23:36:58.794492 rhat.nitec.com > router.nitec.com: icmp: echo request
23:36:58.797811 router.nitec.com > rhat.nitec.com: icmp: echo reply
23:36:59.794478 rhat.nitec.com > router.nitec.com: icmp: echo request
23:36:59.798558 router.nitec.com > rhat.nitec.com: icmp: echo reply
23:37:00.794464 rhat.nitec.com > router.nitec.com: icmp: echo request
23:37:00.797777 router.nitec.com > rhat.nitec.com: icmp: echo reply
23:37:01.794465 rhat.nitec.com > router.nitec.com: icmp: echo request
23:37:01.797784 router.nitec.com > rhat.nitec.com: icmp: echo reply
```

Some tools for viewing and analyzing tcpdump trace files are available from the Internet Traffic Archive (http://www.acm.org/sigcomm/ITA/). You can also use a program called tcpslices (ftp://ftp.ee.lbl.gov/tcpslice.tar.Z) to analyze portions of tcpdump output.

LSOF

This is a very powerful diagnostic tool that allows you to associate open files with processes. It lists information about all files that are open by a process. You can download the source distribution from `ftp://vic.cc.purdue.edu/pub/tools/unix/lsof`. Here's how you compile and install it:

1. As `root`, extract the downloaded tar ball in a directory and change your current directory to the newly created subdirectory.

2. Run `./configure linux` to configure the source distribution. You are asked if you want to take an inventory of all the files in this distribution. Entering `no` will works in most situations. If you think you may have a damaged distribution, say `yes`.

3. You are asked to customize `machine.h` header file. Enter *y* to customize.

4. You are asked if you want to enable HASSECURITY. Entering *y* ensures that only root user can run lsof to examine all open files; other users may examine only the files that belong to them.

5. You are asked to enable or disable WARNINGSTATE. Leave the default as is — allowing lsof to display warnings is a good idea.

   By default, HASKERNIDCK is disabled. This option allows lsof to verify its own integrity in a way, but the process is slow. Keep the default unless you're paranoid (like me).

6. You are asked whether you want to backup the old `machine.h` to `machine.h.old` and use the new one. Enter *y* to indicate positively.

7. Run `make && make install` to compile and install lsof.

   The binary is installed in `/usr/sbin` directory.

FINDING PROCESSES ATTACHED TO AN OPEN FILE
You can find which processes are using a certain file. Run the following command:

```
/usr/sbin/lsof /path/to/filename
```

/path/to/filename is the fully qualified pathname of the file you want lsof to report on, like this:

```
/usr/sbin/lsof /var/log/messages
```

In this case, I want to know which process opened this log file. A typical output is

```
COMMAND PID USER   FD   TYPE DEVICE   SIZE  NODE NAME
syslogd 339 root    2w   REG    3,1 189003 50854 /var/log/messages
```

As you can see, only the Syslog daemon (syslogd) has opened this file, which is expected because this daemon writes to this file.

FINDING AN UNLINKED LOCALLY OPEN FILE

Sometimes, a file's directory entry can be removed while a process is writing to it. This creates a very big problem. For example, you may find that your /var partition is filling, yet you don't see a file getting bigger. The lsof tool can help you find such a culprit. Here's a simple example:

1. As `root`, change directory to `/tmp`.

2. Run `mkdir /tmp/test` and change your current directory to `/tmp/test`.

3. Run `yes AAAAAAAAAAAAAAAAAAAAA > /tmp/test/culprit.txt &`.

    This creates a file called `culprit.txt` in `/tmp/test` that grows — fast! The `yes` program constantly writes the string AAAAAAAAAAAAAAAAAAAAA.

4. Run `ls -l /tmp/test/culprit.txt` a few times to see the file size grow.

    Once it reaches a few megabytes, run `rm -f /tmp/test/culprit.txt` to delete the file. Now you have created a situation where the yes program is still writing the open file handled for `/tmp/test/culprit.txt`, which is now unlinked!

5. When you run `df`, you see that your /tmp partition (or the partition containing the /tmp directory) is losing space fast! This is when you need lsof.

6. Run `ps auxww | grep yes` to see if yes is still running, which it should.

7. Run `/usr/sbin/lsof +L1`

    You see an output similar to the following

    ```
    COMMAND PID USER   FD TYPE DEVICE     SIZE NLINK   NODE NAME
    yes      9148 root 1w REG  3,1    314163200     0   3447
    /tmp/test/culprit.txt (deleted)
    ```

    As you can see, the file is still growing even though it's deleted! In the preceding example, the file has grown to 31,416,320 bytes (~ 31 MB). The +L1 option tells lsof to display all files that have a maximum of 1 links associated with them. This limits the output to a single link or 0 linked (deleted) files.

    Signaling or terminating the program is the only course of action you can take. In this example case, you can run `killall yes` to terminate all instances of the yes command. You can also use `kill -9 PID` command to terminate the command using the PID shown in the lsof output.

You can limit lsof to report link counts on a single filesystem by using the `-a` option. For example, to limit the output to `/usr` partition, you can enter `/usr/sbin/lsof -a +L1 /usr`.

Remember these limitations:

- lsof can't always report link count.

  For example, it may not report link counts for First In First Out (FIFO) buffers, pipes, and sockets.

- The link count also doesn't work properly on NFS filesystem.

UNBLOCKING UMOUNT WITH LSOF

Sometimes you want to unmount a filesystem and run umount /filesystem and the program reports that the filesystem is busy. You need to know which files, programs, and users are still using it so you can politely tell the users to get off the filesystem. In such a case, you can run

```
/usr/sbin/lsof mountpoint
```

Here, mountpoint is the mount position. For example, `/usr/sbin/lsof /home` tells you all the files opened from /home partition. Note that sometimes lsof can't find any open files on a partition but it may still show busy status. In such a case the kernel has internal references to one or more files in the filesystem. The only solution in this case is to wait for the references to go away or commenting out the appropriate mount entry for the filesystem in `/etc/fstab` and reboot. Be careful when you comment out mount points in `/etc/fstab`, because a system may not boot happily if such filesystems as /, /usr, /home, /tmp (if any), and /var aren't available.

FINDING OPENED NETWORK CONNECTIONS

If you want to find out all the opened sockets on your system, you can run `/usr/sbin/lsof -i`.

Want to find all the network connections to a remote host with IP address 207.183.233.19? You can run

```
/usr/sbin/lsof -i@207.183.233.19
```

A typical output is

```
COMMAND  PID  USER TYPE NODE NAME
smbd     2630  root IPv4 TCP r.nitec.com:netbios-ssn->n.nitec.com:3230
(ESTABLISHED)
smbd     2630  root IPv4 TCP r.nitec.com:1032->n.nitec.com:netbios-ssn (CLOSE)
sshd     8013  root IPv4 TCP r.nitec.com:ssh->n.nitec.com:3886 (ESTABLISHED)
sshd     9185  root IPv4 TCP r.nitec.com:ssh->n.nitec.com:4121 (ESTABLISHED)
nc       9211 kabir IPv4 TCP r.nitec.com:9999->n.nitec.com:4131 (ESTABLISHED)
```

Here, lsof reports that several commands are connected to the 207.183.233.19 (n.nitec.com) address. smbd (Samba daemon), sshd (SSH daemon) and a nc command are connected to the given IP address. The last connection is suspicious because it offers the remote IP a connection on an odd (non standard) port 9999 and it's also run by a regular user. Therefore, it needs to be investigated further.

Typically, network administrators use netstat program to casually monitor network connection activity. However, netstat and lsof can work together to solve problems.

Here's a typical output from netstat:

```
Active Internet connections (w/o servers)
Proto Recv-Q Send-Q Local Address           Foreign Address        State
tcp       0      0 rhat.nitec.com:9999     nano.nitec.com:4174    ESTABLISHED
tcp       0      0 rhat.nitec.com:ssh      nano.nitec.com:4121    ESTABLISHED
tcp       0      0 rhat.nitec.com:ssh      nano.nitec.com:3886    ESTABLISHED
tcp       0      0 rhat.nitec.com:1032     nano.nitec.:netbios-ssn CLOSE
tcp       0      0 rhat.nitec.:netbios-ssn nano.nitec.com:3230    ESTABLISHED
```

Now you need to find out why a remote host, nano.nitec.com, is on port 9999 of your system. What process is serving this remote connection? Run /usr/sbin/lsof -iTCP@nano.nitec.com and you get the name of the process and its owner that is serving this port on the local system.

FINDING ALL THE FILES OPENED BY A PROGRAM

To know what files a particular program has opened, run the /usr/sbin/lsof -p *PID* command. For example, I ran ps auxw on my system and noticed a line such as the following:

```
kabir    9233  0.0  0.1  1552  652 pts/1     S     08:21   0:00 nc -l -p 9999
```

Now I want to know what files are opened by the nc command whose PID is 9233. So I ran /usr/sbin/lsof -p 9233. The following output appears:

```
COMMAND  PID USER   FD   TYPE DEVICE   SIZE   NODE NAME
nc      9233 kabir  cwd    DIR   3,1   4096  96578 /tmp
nc      9233 kabir  rtd    DIR   3,1   4096      2 /
nc      9233 kabir  txt    REG   3,3  17204 256103 /usr/sbin/nc
nc      9233 kabir  mem    REG   3,1 434945  80492 /lib/ld-2.1.92.so
nc      9233 kabir  mem    REG   3,1 4776568 80499 /lib/libc-2.1.92.so
nc      9233 kabir  mem    REG   3,1 234205  80522 /lib/libnss_files-2.1.92.so
nc      9233 kabir  mem    REG   3,1 290019  80528 /lib/libnss_nisplus-
2.1.92.so
nc      9233 kabir  mem    REG   3,1 380006  80508 /lib/libnsl-2.1.92.so
```

```
nc      9233 kabir  mem    REG   3,1 274024   80526 /lib/libnss_nis-2.1.92.so
nc      9233 kabir  1u     CHR 136,1              3 /dev/pts/1
nc      9233 kabir  2u     CHR 136,1              3 /dev/pts/1
nc      9233 kabir  4u     IPv4 329604              TCP rhat.nitec.com:9999-
>nano.nitec.com:4174 (ESTABLISHED)
```

This output shows all the files, devices, libraries, and network sockets that this program has currently opened. If you want to find all instances of a command and which files each have opened, run /usr/sbin/lsof -c *command_name*. For example, /usr/sbin/lsof -c sshd shows all instances of the sshd server and their opened files.

Ngrep

This is the grep for the network traffic. It uses the libpcap library access the network packet. This tool allows you to specify regular expressions to match against contents within TCP, UDP, and ICPM packets. You can download the source distribution from http://www.packetfactory.net/Projects/ngrep. To install it, do the following:

1. Download and as root extract the source in a directory. A new subdirectory is created. Make the new subdirectory your current directory.

2. Run ./configure && make install to configure, compile, and install the binaries and man pages. The ngrep binary is installed in /usr/bin directory.

   Here are a few examples:

   ```
   /usr/bin/ngrep -qd eth0 'yahoo' tcp port 80
   ```

   This command tells ngrep to monitor the eth0 interface for TCP packets on port 80 that contains the string 'yahoo'. On a host on the same sub-net, I can use a Web browser to create target network packets as follows: http://www.google.com/search?q=yahoo

   Since the packet generated by that host has the string 'yahoo' in the data, ngrep catches is as follows:

   ```
   T 207.183.233.19:2225 -> 216.239.37.100:80 [AP]
     GET /search?q=yahoo HTTP/1.1..Accept: image/gif, image/x-
   xbitmap, imag
     e/jpeg, image/pjpeg, application/vnd.ms-powerpoint,
   application/vnd.ms
     -excel, application/msword, */*..Referer:
   http://www.google.com/..Acce
     pt-Language: en-us..Accept-Encoding: gzip, deflate..User-
   Agent: Mozill
     a/4.0 (compatible; MSIE 5.5; Windows NT 5.0)..Host:
   www.google.com..Connection: Keep-Alive..Cookie:
   ```

```
PREF=ID=5b67841b6f7a913d:TM=982401088:LM
  =982401088....
/usr/bin/ngrep -qd eth0 'USER|PASS' tcp port 21
```

Here, ngrep is told to monitor interface eth0 for either 'USER' or 'PASS'
strings for TCP port 21, which is the command port for FTP connections.
If I connect to this host from another workstation on the same network,
I can get the username and password used for an FTP connection. A sample ngrep captured data is

```
T 207.183.233.19:2267 -> 207.183.233.20:21 [AP]
  USER kabir..
T 207.183.233.19:2267 -> 207.183.233.20:21 [AP]
```

Summary

Ensuring computer security is a hard job. Thankfully, there are many tools such as
security assessment or audit tools, port scanners, log monitoring and analyzing
tools, CGI scanners, password crackers, packet sniffers, and intrusion detection
tools that you can use to identify, detect, and possibly (and hopefully) eliminate
security holes. Ironically, these tools are also available to the hackers. Hopefully,
you will run them on your system to eliminate security vulnerability before they
know anything about it.

Appendix A

IP Network Address Classification

Currently, Ipv4 (32-bit IP) addresses are used on the Internet. A 32-bit IP address is divided into two parts: the network-prefix and the host-number. Traditionally, each IP address belongs to an IP class.

The class hierarchy is identified by a self-encoded key in each IP address:

◆ If the first bit of an IP address is 0, it is Class A.

◆ If the first two bits are 10, the address is Class B.

◆ If the first three bits are 110, the address is Class C.

Class A IP network addresses

Each Class A network address has these three elements (from left to right):

◆ The highest bit set to 0

◆ A 7-bit network number

◆ A 24-bit host-number

Class A networks are now referred as /8 networks.

Only the first eight bits are used in defining the network prefix; therefore, the maximum possible number of Class A (/8) networks is 128. However, only 126 ($2^7 - 2$) Class A (/8) networks are available. Two special addresses must be excluded from the list of valid Class A (/8) networks:

◆ 0.0.0.0 (the entire IP space or default route)

◆ 127.0.0.0 (loopback network).

Each Class A Network can have 16,777,214 ($2^{24} - 2$) possible hosts. We must exclude x.0.0.0 and x.1.1.1 host addresses where x is the 8-bit network-prefix with the first bit set to 0. The address with all 0s is considered the *network address*; the one with all 1s is considered the *broadcast address*.

Class B IP network addresses

Each Class B network address has its two highest-order bits set to 10. The network-prefix is 14 bits long and the host-number is 16 bits long. A Class B network is referred to as a /16 network. A total of 16,384 (2^{14}) networks are possible in Class B and each such network has 65,534 (2^{16} – 2) available hosts.

Class C IP network addresses

Each Class C network address has its three highest-order bits set to 110. The network-prefix is 21-bits long and the host-number is 8 bits long. A Class C network is referred to as a /24 network. A total of 2,097,152 (2^{21}) networks are possible in Class C; each such network has 254 (2^8 – 2) available hosts.

Table A-1 summarizes each of these classes.

TABLE A-1: IP CLASS NETWORKS

Address Class	Starting IP Address (in Decimal Dotted Notation)	Ending IP Address (in Decimal Dotted Notation)
A (/8)	1.xxx.xxx.xxx	126.xxx.xxx.xxx
B (/16)	128.0.xxx.xxx	191.255.xxx.xxx
C (/24)	192.0.0.xxx	223.255.255.xxx

Subnetting IP networks

Each of the IP classes (A, B, or C) can be subdivided into smaller networks called *subnets*. When you divide any of the IP classes into subnets, you gain two advantages:

◆ You help minimize the routing table for your outmost router.

◆ You hide the details of your networked organization.

For example, say you have a Class B network, 130.86.32.0. Your router to the Internet receives all IP packets for this entire network. After the packets enter your network, however, you might use several subnets to route the IP packets to different divisions of your organization. In the absence of subnetting, you would either use a large Class B network or multiple Class C networks to support the divisions of your organization. In the latter case, your router table would have to list a larger number of routes – which usually slows down the performance of the network.

To create a subnet, you divide the host-number portion of the IP class address into two components:

♦ Subnet number

♦ New host number

The old host number had two parts; the new subnet number has three; thus, subnetting shifts from a two-level class hierarchy to a three-level subnet hierarchy.

As an example of subnetting, consider a Class C network called 192.168.1.0. Say that we want to create six subnets for this network where the largest subnet has 20 hosts.

The very first step is to determine how many bits are necessary to create six subnets from the host-number part, which is 8-bit. Since each bit can be 1 or 0, we must subnet along binary boundaries and, therefore, the possible subnets are 2 (2^1), 4 (2^2), 8 (2^3), 16 (2^4), 32 (2^5), 64 (2^6), and 128 (2^7). Since we need six subnets, the best choice for us is 8 (2^3), which gives us 2 additional subnets for the future. If we use a 3-bit subnet number, there are five bits in the new host-number. So, the maximum subnet mask would be 255.255.255.224 — or (in binary) 11111111. 11111111. 11111111. 11100000. The last subnet mask 255.255.255.224 can be also represented as /27, which is called an *extended network-prefix*. At this point, a Class C (/24) network is subnetted using /27 (a 3-bit extended network prefix). Table A-2 shows all the subnets possible for this network.

TABLE A-2: SUBNETS OF 192.168.1.0/24 NETWORK

Network (Subnet)	Subnet Mask (Dotted-decimal notation)	Subnet Mask (Binary)	Maximum Hosts
192.168.1.0/27	255.255.255.0	11111111. 11111111. 11111111.00000000	30
192.168.1.32/27	255.255.1.32	11111111. 11111111. 11111111.00100000	30
192.168.1.64/27	255.255.1.64	11111111. 11111111. 11111111.01000000	30
192.168.1.96/27	255.255.1.96	11111111. 11111111. 11111111.01100000	30
192.168.1.128/27	255.255.1.128	11111111. 11111111. 11111111.10000000	30

Continued

TABLE A-2: SUBNETS OF 192.168.1.0/24 NETWORK *(Continued)*

Network (Subnet)	Subnet Mask (Dotted-decimal notation)	Subnet Mask (Binary)	Maximum Hosts
192.168.1.160/27	255.255.1.160	11111111. 11111111. 11111111.10100000	30
192.168.1.192/27	255.255.1.192	11111111. 11111111. 11111111.11000000	30
192.168.1.224/27	255.255.1.224	11111111. 11111111. 11111111.11100000	30

Appendix B

Common Linux Commands

MOST WORK WITH LINUX consists of entering commands one after another. The structure of each command follows an established rule commonly known as its command-line *syntax*. If you don't follow the syntax correctly, a command may execute incorrectly, and problems can result.

When you type a command, the entire on-screen line it occupies is the *command line*. Although normally you issue commands one at a time, you can type multiple commands on the command line if you separate your commands with semicolons. The system executes these commands as if they were one continuous command. For example, you can clear the screen and then list the contents of the current directory by typing the following command line:

```
clear; ls
```

When you enter a command, you type the name of the command, followed (if necessary) by other information. Items that follow the name of the command and modify how it works are *arguments*. For example, consider the following command line:

```
wc -l doc.txt
```

Two arguments appear in this example, the `-l` and the `doc.txt`. It's up to the program to determine how to use the arguments.

Two types of arguments exist: options and parameters. *Options* come right after the program name and are usually prefixed with a dash (minus-sign character). The *parameters* come after the options. From the preceding example, the `-l` is an option telling wc to count the number of lines; `doc.txt` is a parameter indicating which file to use.

When entering commands at the command line, remember the arguments are case sensitive just as filenames in Unix are. Overall, the general syntax of a Unix command is

```
command_name options parameters
```

Basics of wildcards

When you use directory and file commands, you can use special characters called *wildcards* to specify patterns in filenames—which identify what the command

must work on. For example, to list all the files in the current directory that end in
.c, use:

```
ls *.c
```

The asterisk is a wildcard. The shell interprets the pattern and replaces it with all
the filenames that end in .c. Table B-1 shows commonly used wildcards.

TABLE B-1: COMMONLY USED WILDCARD CHARACTERS

Wildcard	Meaning
*	Match any sequence of one or more characters.
?	Match any single character.
[ ]	Match one of the enclosed characters or range.

Table B-2 shows examples of wildcard usage in various locations within the
filename.

TABLE B-2: EXAMPLES OF WILDCARD USAGE

Example	Meaning
Jo*	Files that begin with Jo
Jo*y	Files that begin with Jo and end in y
Ut*1*s.c	Files that begin with Ut, contain an 1, and end in s.c
?.h	Files that begin with a single character followed by .h.
Doc[0-9].txt	Files with the names Doc0.txt, Doc1.txt, . . . , Doc9.txt
Doc0[A-Z].txt	Files with the names Doc0A.txt, Doc0B.txt, . . . , Doc0Z.txt

As you can see, using wildcards can make selecting multiple items easy.

Basics of regular expressions

Various Unix commands use *regular expressions*. They provide a convenient and consistent way of specifying patterns to be matched. Though similar to wildcards, regular expressions are much more powerful; they provide a wider scope of pattern selecting. Several different Unix commands use regular expressions, including ed, sed, awk, grep, and, to a limited extent, vi and emacs.

The special characters in Table B-3 are typical of regular expressions in general. Understand these special characters and you need to learn only a few variations as they arise.

TABLE B-3: SPECIAL CHARACTERS FOR REGULAR EXPRESSIONS

Symbol	Meaning
.	Match any single character except newline.
*	Match zero or more of the preceding characters.
^	Match the beginning of a line.
$	Match the end of a line.
\<	Match the beginning of a word.
\>	Match the end of a word.
[ ]	Match one of the enclosed characters or range of characters.
[^]	Match any characters not enclosed.
\	Take the following symbol literally.

Within a regular expression, any character that does not have a special meaning stands for itself. For example

◆ To search for lines that contain "foo" in the file data.txt, use

```
grep foo data.txt
```

◆ To search for only lines in data.txt that begin with the word foo, use

```
grep '^foo' data.txt
```

The use of single quotes tells the shell to leave these characters alone and to pass them to the program. Single quotes are necessary whenever using any of the special characters.

◆ The dollar sign indicates you want to match a pattern at the end of the line:

```
grep 'hello$' data.txt
```

Any lines ending with "hello" result in a match using the preceding regular expression.

◆ To look for a pattern that begins a word, use \<.

```
grep '\<ki' data.txt
```

The preceding expression searches for words that begin with ki in the file data.txt. To find the pattern wee, but only at the end of a word, use

```
grep 'wee\>' data.txt
```

From Table B-3, notice that the period matches any single character except new-line. This comes in handy if you are searching for all the lines that contain the letters "C" followed by two letters and end in "s"; here, the regular expression is:

```
grep 'C..s' data.txt
```

This expression matches patterns like: Cats, Cars, and Cris if they are in the file data.txt.

If you want to specify a range of characters, use a hyphen to separate the beginning and end of the range. When you specify the range, the order must be the same as in the ASCII code. For example, to search for all the lines that contain a "B" followed by any single lowercase letter, use:

```
grep 'B[a-z]' data.txt
```

It is also possible to specify more than one range of characters in the same pattern.

```
grep 'B[A-Za-z]' data.txt
```

The preceding example selects all lines that contain the letter *B* followed by an uppercase or lowercase letter.

How to Use Online man Pages

The online man (short for *manual*) pages are divided into eight major sections, as in Table B-4. Other sections may come with your particular version of Unix; most, if not all, contain eight major sections. Section 1 contains the description of the bulk of Unix commands. Most users can get by fine with only this section of the manual. Sections 2, 3, 4, and 5 of the Unix manual are of interest only to programmers. Section 8 is only for system administrators.

TABLE B-4: SECTIONS OF MAN PAGES

Section	Topic
1	Executable programs or shell commands
2	System calls (functions the kernel provides)
3	Library calls (functions within system libraries)
4	Special files (usually in `/dev`)
5	File formats (that is, `/etc/passd`)
6	Games
7	Miscellaneous information
8	Maintenance commands

Modern Unix systems provide much more detail than their ancestors; commonly their sections are broken into subsections. For instance, section 6 is a reference for games. However, you may find a section 6a (for adventure games), a section 6c (for classic games), and so on.

The `man` command allows you to view the online manuals. The syntax for this command is as follows:

```
man [-k] [section] keyword
```

The keyword is usually the name of the program, utility, or function. The default action is to search in all the available sections following a predefined order and to show only the first page found, even if the keyword exists in several sections.

Because commands may appear in several sections, the first page found might not be the `man` page you are looking for. The command `printf` is a good example.

Say you are writing a program and would like to know more about the ANSI C library function `printf ()`. Just by typing

```
man printf
```

you get information about `printf`. However, the `man` pages for this `printf` are for the shell command `printf`. Obviously, this is the wrong information. A reasonable solution is to list all the sections that cover `printf` (if it exists in multiple sections) and to select the correct one. You can search the keywords of the `man` pages with the `-f` option:

```
man -k printf
fprintf        printf (3b)    - formatted output conversion
```

```
fprintf        printf (3s)      - print formatted output
printf         printf (1)       - write formatted output
printf         printf (3b)      - formatted output conversion
printf         printf (3s)      - print formatted output
```

The printf in question here is a library function. It is in section 3 (from Table B-4) or, more specifically, in section 3b or 3s from the output. To specify a particular section of a man page, pass it to man at the command line:

```
man 3b printf
```

Now this is the correct information!

General File and Directory Commands

This section examines file- and directory-specific commands you are likely to use on a daily basis.

cat

Syntax:

```
cat   file   [>|>]   [destination file]
```

The cat command displays the contents of a file to stdout. It is often helpful to examine the contents of a file by using the cat command. The argument you pass to cat is the name of the file you want to view. To view the total content of a filename:

```
cat name
Kiwee
Joe
Ricardo
Charmaine
```

cat can also merge existing multiple files into one:

```
cat name1 name2 name3 > allnames
```

This example combines the files name1, name2, and name3 to produce the final file allnames. You establish the order of the merge by the order in which you enter the files at the command line.

Using `cat`, you can append a file to another file. For instance, if you forgot to add a `name4` in the previous command, you can still produce the same results by executing the following:

```
cat name4 >> allnames
```

chmod

Syntax:

```
chmod [-R] permission-mode  file or directory
```

You can use this command to change the permission mode of a file or directory. The permission mode is specified as a three- or four-digit octal number, as in this example:

```
chmod 755  myscript.pl
```

The preceding command changes the permission of a script called `myscript.pl` to 755 (`rwxr-xr-x`), which allows the file owner to read, write, and execute and allows only read and execute privileges for everyone else. Here is another example:

```
chmod -R 744 public_html
```

The preceding command changes the permissions of the `public_html` directory and all its contents (files and subdirectories) to 744 (`rwxr-r-`), which is a typical permission setting for personal Web directories you access using `http://server/~username` URLs under Apache Server. The `-R` option tells `chmod` to recursively change permissions for all files and directories under the named directory.

chown

Syntax:

```
chown [ -fhR ] Owner [ :Group ] { File . . . | Directory. . . }
```

The `chown` command changes the owner of the file the File parameter specifies to the user the *Owner* parameter specifies. The value of the *Owner* parameter can be a user ID or a login name in the `/etc/passwd` file. Optionally, you can also specify a group. The value of the *Group* parameter can be a group ID or a group name in the `/etc/group` file.

Only the `root` user can change the owner of a file. You can change the group of a file only if you are a `root` user or if you own the file. If you own the file but are not a `root` user, you can change the group only to a group of which you are a member. Table B-5 discusses the details of the `chown` options.

TABLE B-5: CHOWN OPTIONS

Option	Description
-f	Suppresses all error messages except usage messages.
-h	Changes the ownership of an encountered symbolic link but not that of the file or directory the symbolic link points to.
-R	Descends directories recursively, changing the ownership for each file. When a symbolic link is encountered and the link points to a directory, the ownership of that directory is changed, but the directory is not further traversed.

The following example changes ownership of the file from one user to another:

```
chown bert hisfile.txt
```

clear

Syntax:

```
clear
```

The clear command clears your terminal and returns the command line prompt to the top of the screen.

cmp

Syntax:

```
cmp [-ls] file 1 file2
```

This command compares the contents of two files. If the contents show no differences, cmp by default is silent.

To demonstrate, file1.txt contains

```
this is file 1
```

```
the quick brown fox jumps over the lazy dog.
```

and file2.txt contains

```
this is file 2
the quick brown fox jumps over the lazy dog.
```

The only difference between the two files is the first line, last character. In one file, the character is 1, and the other file has a 2, as shown here:

```
cmp file1.txt file2.txt
file1.txt file2.txt differ: char 14, line 1
```

The results of cmp correctly identify character 14, line 1 as the unequal character between the two files. The -l option prints the byte number and the differing byte values for each of the files.

```
cmp -l file1.txt file2.txt
14 61 62
```

The results of the preceding example show us that byte 14 is different in the first and second files; the first file has an octal 61 and the second file has an octal 62 in that position.

Finally, the -s option displays nothing. The -s option only returns an exit status indicating the similarities between the files. It returns 0 (zero) if the files are identical and 1 if the files are different. Last, the -s option returns a number >1 (greater than 1) when an error occurs.

cp

Syntax:

```
cp  [-R] source file or directory  file or directory
```

Use the cp command to make an exact copy of a file. The cp command requires at least two arguments: the name of the file or directory you want to copy, and the location (or filename) of the new file. If the second argument is a name for a directory that already exists, cp copies the source file into that directory. The command line looks like this:

```
cp main.c main.c.bak
```

The preceding example copies the existing file main.c and creates a new file called main.c.bak in the same directory. These two files are identical, bit for bit.

cut

Syntax:

```
cut  [-cdf list]  file
```

The cut command extracts columns of data. The data can be in bytes, charac-ters, or fields from each line in a file. For instance, a file called names contains information about a group of people. Each line contains data pertaining to one per-son, like this:

```
Fast   Freddy:Sacramento:CA:111-111-1111
Joe    Smoe:Los Angeles:CA:222-222-2222
Drake Snake:San Francisco:CA:333-333-3333
Bill   Steal:New York:NY:444-444-4444
```

To list the names and telephone numbers of all individuals in the file, the options -f and -d should suffice:

```
cut -f 1,4 -d : names
Fast   Freddy:111-111-1111
Joe    Some:222-222-2222
Drake Snake:333-333-3333
Bill   Steal:444-444-4444
```

The -f list option specifies the fields you elect to display. The -d options define each field. In the preceding example, -d : indicates that a colon separates each field. Using : as the field delimiter makes fields 1 and 4 into *name* and *phone num-ber* fields.

To display the contents of a particular column, use the -c list option.

```
cut -c 1-5 names
Fast
Joe
Drake
Bill
```

The preceding example shows how to list columns 1 through 5 in the names file — and nothing else.

diff

Syntax:

```
diff [-iqb] file1 file2
```

You can use the diff command to determine differences between files and/or directories. By default, diff does not produce any output if the files are identical.

The diff command is different from the cmp command in the way it compares the files. The diff command is used to report differences between two files, line by line. The cmp command reports differences between two files character by character, instead of line by line. As a result, it is more useful than diff for comparing binary files. For text files, cmp is useful mainly when you want to know only whether two files are identical.

Considering changes character by character entails practical differences from considering changes line by line. To illustrate, think of what happens if you add a single newline character to the beginning of a file. If you compare that file with an otherwise-identical file that lacks the newline at the beginning, diff reports that a blank line has been added to the file, and cmp reports that the two files differ in almost every character.

The normal output format consists of one or more hunks of differences; each hunk shows one area in which the files differ. Normal format hunks look like this:

```
change-command
< from-file-line
< from-file-line. . .
--
> to-file-line
> to-file-line. . .
```

Three types of change commands are possible. Each consists of a line number (or comma-separated range of lines) in the first file, a single character (indicating the kind of change to make), and a line number (or comma-separated range of lines) in the second file. All line numbers are the original line numbers in each file. The specific types of change commands are as follows:

◆ 'lar': Add the lines in range r of the second file after line l of the first file. For example, '8a12,15' means *append lines 12–15 of file 2 after line 8 of file 1* or (if you're changing file 2 into file 1) *delete lines 12–15 of file 2.*

◆ 'fct': Replace the lines in range f of the first file with lines in range t of the second file. This is like a combined add-and-delete but more compact. For example, '5,7c8,10' means *change lines 5–7 of file 1 to read the same as lines 8–10 of file 2* or (if changing file 2 into file 1) *change lines 8–10 of file 2 to read the same as lines 5–7 of file 1.*

◆ 'rdl': Delete the lines in range r from the first file; line l is where they would have appeared in the second file had they not been deleted. For example, '5,7d3' means *delete lines 5–7 of file 1* or (if changing file 2 into file 1) *append lines 5–7 of file 1 after line 3 of file 2.*

For example, if a.txt contains

```
a
b
c
```

```
d
e
```

and b.txt contains

```
c
d
e
f
g
```

the diff command produces the following output:

```
1,2d0
< a
< b
5a4,5
> f
> g
```

The diff command produces output that shows how the files are different and has to happen for the files to be identical. First, notice how c is the first common character between the two files. The first line reads 1,2d0. This is interpreted as deleting lines 1 and 2 of the first file, lines a and b. Next, the third line reads 5a4,6. The a signifies append. If we append lines 4 through 6 of the second file to line 5 of the first file, the files are identical.

The diff command has some common options. The -i option ignores changes in case. diff considers upper- and lowercase characters equivalent. The -q option summarizes information — in effect, the -q option reports if the files differ at all. A sample output looks like this:

```
diff -q a.txt b.txt
Files a.txt and b.txt differ
```

The -b option ignores changes in whitespace. The phrase "the foo" is equivalent to "the   foo" if you use the -b option.

du

Syntax:

```
du [-ask] filenames
```

This command summarizes disk usage. If you specify a directory, du reports the disk usage for that directory and any directories it contains. If you do not specify a filename or directory, du assumes the current directory. du -a breaks down the total and shows the size of each directory and file. The -s option will just print the total. Another useful option is the -k option. This option prints all file sizes in kilobytes. Here are some examples of the various options:

```
du -a
247      ./util-linux_2.9e-0.1.deb
130      ./libncurses4_4.2-2.deb
114      ./slang1_1.2.2-2.deb
492      .

du -s
492      .
```

emacs

The emacs program, a full-screen visual editor, is one of the best editors. It is known for its flexibility and power as well as for being a resource hog. The power of emacs is not easily obtained. There is a stiff learning curve that requires patience and even more patience. There can be as many as four sequential key combinations to perform certain actions.

However, emacs can do just about anything. Aside from the basic editing features, emacs supports the following: syntax highlighting, macros, editing multiple files at the same time, spell checking, mail, FTP, and many other features.

When reading about emacs, you'll often see words like meta-Key and C-x. The meta key is the meta key on your keyboard (if you have one) or most commonly the Esc key. C-x is the syntax for Ctrl plus the X key. Any "C-" combination refers to the Ctrl key.

The two most important key combinations to a new emacs user are the C-x C-c and C-h C-h combinations. The first combination exits emacs. You'd be surprised to know how many people give up on emacs just because they cannot exit the program the first time they use it. Also, C-h C-h displays online help, where you can follow the tutorial or get detailed information about a command. Table B-6 shows emacs's most commonly used commands:

TABLE B-6: COMMON EMACS COMMANDS

Commands	Effects
C-v	Move forward one screenful.
M-v	Move backward one screenful.
C-p	Move the cursor to the previous line.

Continued

TABLE B-6: COMMON EMACS COMMANDS *(Continued)*

Commands	Effects
C-n	Move the cursor to the next line.
C-f	Move the cursor right one position.
C-b	Move the cursor left one position.
M-f	Move forward a word.
M-b	Move backward a word.
C-a	Move to beginning of line.
C-e	Move to end of line.
M-a	Move back to beginning of sentence.
M-e	Move forward to end of sentence.
<Delete>	Delete the character just before the cursor.
C-d	Delete the next character after the cursor.
M-<Delete>	Kill the word immediately before the cursor.
M-d	Kill the next word after the cursor.
C-k	Kill from the cursor position to end of line.
M-k	Kill to the end of the current sentence.
C-x	Undo the previous command.
C-x C-f	Open another file.
C-x C-s	Save the current file.
C-x C-w	Save the current file as another name.
C-x s	Save all the buffers that have recently changed.
C-x C-c	Exit emacs.

fgrep

The fgrep command is designed to be a faster-searching program (as opposed to grep). However, it can search only for exact characters, not for general specifications. The name fgrep stands for "fixed character grep." These days, computers and memory are so fast that there is rarely a need for fgrep.

file

Syntax:

```
file filename
```

The `file` command determines the file's type. If the file is not a regular file, this command identifies its file type. It identifies the file types directory, FIFO, block special, and character special as such. If the file is a regular file and the file is zero-length, this command identifies it as an empty file.

If the file appears to be a text file, `file` examines the first 512 bytes and tries to determine its programming language. If the file is an executable a.out, `file` prints the version stamp, provided it is greater than 0.

```
file main.C
main.C:          c program text
```

find

Syntax:
```
find [path] [-type fd1] [-name pattern] [-atime [+-]number of days] [-exec
command {} \;] [-empty]
```

The `find` command finds files and directories, as in this example:

```
find  .  -type d
```

The `find` command returns all subdirectory names under the current directory. The `-type` option is typically set to `d` (for directory) or `f` (for file) or `l` (for links).

```
find  .  -type f -name "*.txt"
```

This command finds all text files (ending with .txt extension) in the current directory, including all its subdirectories.

```
find  .  -type f -name "*.txt" -exec grep -l 'magic' {} \;
```

This command searches all text files (ending with the .txt extension) in the current directory, including all its subdirectories for the keyword "magic," and returns their names (because `-l` is used with grep).

```
find . -name "*.gif" -atime -1 -exec ls -l {} \;
```

This command finds all GIF files that have been accessed in the past 24 hours (one day) and displays their details using the `ls -l` command.

```
find . -type f -empty
```

This displays all empty files in the current directory hierarchy.

grep

Syntax:

```
grep [-viw] pattern file(s)
```

The `grep` command allows you to search for one or more files for particular character patterns. Every line of each file that contains the pattern is displayed at the terminal. The `grep` command is useful when you have lots of files and you want to find out which ones contain words or phrases.

Using the `-v` option, you can display the inverse of a pattern. Perhaps you want to select the lines in `data.txt` that do not contain the word "the":

```
grep -vw 'the' data.txt
```

If you do not specify the `-w` option, any word containing "the" matches, such as "toge[the]r." The `-w` option specifies that the pattern must be a whole word. Finally, the `-i` option ignores the difference between upper and lowercase letters when searching for the pattern.

Much of the flexibility of `grep` comes from the fact that you can specify not only exact characters but also a more general search pattern. To do this, use what you describe as "regular expressions."

head

Syntax:

```
head [-count | -n number] filename
```

This command displays the first few lines of a file. By default, it displays the first 10 lines of a file. However, you can use the preceding options to specify a different number of lines.

```
head -2 doc.txt
# Outline of future projects
# Last modified:  02/02/99
```

The preceding example illustrates how to view the first two lines of the text file `doc.txt`.

ln

Syntax:

```
ln [-s] sourcefile target
```

ln creates two types of links: hard and soft. Think of a link as two names for the same file. Once you create a link, it's indistinguishable from the original file. You cannot remove a file that has hard links from the hard disk until you remove all links. You create hard links without the -s option.

```
ln ./www ./public_html
```

However, a hard link does have limitations. A hard link cannot link to another directory, and a hard link cannot link to a file on another file system. Using the -s option, you can create a soft link, which eliminates these restrictions.

```
ln -s /dev/fs02/jack/www /dev/fs01/foo/public_html
```

This command creates a soft link between the directory www on file system 2 and a newly created file public_html on file system 1.

locate

Syntax:

```
locate keyword
```

The locate command finds the path of a particular file or command. locate finds an exact or substring match, as in this example:

```
locate foo
/usr/lib/texmf/tex/latex/misc/footnpag.sty
/usr/share/automake/footer.am
/usr/share/games/fortunes/food
/usr/share/games/fortunes/food.dat
/usr/share/gimp/patterns/moonfoot.pat
```

The output locate produces contains the keyword "foo" in the absolute path or does not have any output.

ls

Syntax:

```
ls [-laRl] file or directory
```

The ls command allows you to list files (and subdirectories) in a directory. It is one of the most popular programs. When you use it with the -1 option, it displays only the file and directory names in the current directory; when you use the -1 option, a long listing containing file/directory permission information, size, modification date, and so on is displayed; the -a option allows you to view all files and directories (including the ones that have a leading period in their names) within the current directory; the -R option allows the command to recursively display contents of the subdirectories (if any).

mkdir

Syntax:

```
mkdir directory . . .
```

To make a directory, use the mkdir command. You have only two restrictions when choosing a directory name: (1) File names can be up to 255 characters long, and (2) directory names can contain any character except the /.

```
mkdir dir1 dir2 dir3
```

The preceding example creates three sub-directories in the current directory.

mv

Syntax:

```
mv [-if]sourcefile targetfile
```

Use the mv command to move or rename directories and files. The command performs a move or rename depending on whether the targetfile is an existing directory. To illustrate, suppose you give a directory called foo the new name of foobar.

```
mv foo foobar
```

Because foobar does not already exist as a directory, foo becomes foobar. If you issue the following command,

```
mv doc.txt foobar
```

and foobar is an existing directory, you peform a move. The file doc.txt now resides in the directory foobar.

The -f option removes existing destination files and never prompts the user. The -i option prompts the user whether to overwrite each destination file that exists. If the response does not begin with "y" or "Y," the file is skipped.

pico

Syntax:

```
pico [filename]
```

This full-screen text editor is very user-friendly and highly suitable for users who migrate from a Windows or DOS environment.

pwd

Syntax:

```
pwd
```

This command prints the current working directory. The directories displayed are the absolute path. None of the directories displayed are hard or soft symbolic links.

```
pwd
/home/usr/charmaine
```

rm

Syntax:

```
rm [-rif] directory/file
```

To remove a file or directory, use the rm command. Here are some examples:

```
rm doc.txt
rm ~/doc.txt
rm /tmp/foobar.txt
```

To remove multiple files with rm, you can use wildcards or type each file individually. For example

```
rm doc1.txt doc2.txt doc3.txt
```

is equivalent to:

```
rm doc[1-3].txt
```

rm is a powerful command that can cause chaos if used incorrectly. For instance, you have your thesis that you've worked so hard on for the last six months. You decide to rm all your docs, thinking you are in another directory. After finding out a backup file does not exist (and you are no longer in denial), you wonder if there were any ways to have prevented this.

The rm command has the -i option that allows rm to be interactive. This tells rm to ask your permission before removing each file. For example, if you entered:

```
rm -i *.doc
rm: remove thesis.doc (yes/no)? n
```

The -i option gives you a parachute. It's up to you to either pull the cord (answer no) or suffer the consequences (answer yes). The -f option is completely the opposite. The -f (force) option tells rm to remove all the files you specify, regardless of the file permissions. Use the -f option only when you are 100 percent sure you are removing the correct file(s).

To remove a directory and all files and directories within it, use the -r option. rm -r will remove an entire subtree.

```
rm -r documents
```

If you are not sure what you are doing, combine the -r option with the -i option:

```
rm -ri documents
```

The preceding example asks for your permission before it removes every file and directory.

sort

Syntax:

```
sort [-rndu] [-o outfile] [infile/sortedfile]
```

The obvious task this command performs is to sort. However, sort also merges files. The sort command reads files that contain previously sorted data and merges them into one large, sorted file.

The simplest way to use sort is to sort a single file and display the results on your screen. If a.txt contains:

```
b
c
a
d
```

to sort a.txt and display the results to the screen:

```
sort a.txt
a
b
c
d
```

To save sorted results, use the -o option: sort -o sorted.txt a.txt saves the sorted a.txt file in sorted.txt. To use sort to merge existing sorted files and to save the output in sorted.txt, use:

```
sort -o sorted.txt a.txt b.txt c.txt
```

The -r option for this command reverses the sort order. Therefore, a file that contains the letters of the alphabet on a line is sorted from z to a if you use the -r option.

The -d option sorts files based on dictionary order. The sort command considers only letters, numerals, and spaces and ignores other characters.

The -u option looks for identical lines and suppresses all but one. Therefore, sort produces only unique lines.

stat

Syntax:

```
stat file
```

This program displays various statistics on a file or directory, as in this example:

```
stat foo.txt
```

This command displays the following output:

```
File: "foo.txt"
Size: 4447232       Filetype: Regular File
Mode: (0644/-rw-r—r—) Uid: ( 0/root)  Gid: (0/root)
Device: 3,0   Inode: 16332     Links: 1
Access: Mon Mar  1 21:39:43 1999(00000.02:32:30)
Modify: Mon Mar  1 22:14:26 1999(00000.01:57:47)
Change: Mon Mar  1 22:14:26 1999(00000.01:57:47
```

You can see the following displayed: file access, modification, change date, size, owner and group information, permission mode, and so on.

strings

Syntax:

```
strings filename
```

The `strings` command prints character sequences at least four characters long. You use this utility mainly to describe the contents of nontext files.

tail

Syntax:

```
tail [-count | -fr] filename
```

The `tail` command displays the end of a file. By default, `tail` displays the last 10 lines of a file. To display the last 50 lines of the file `doc.txt`, issue the command:

```
tail -50 doc.txt
```

The `-r` option displays the output in reverse order. By default, `-r` displays all lines in the file, not just 10 lines. For instance, to display the entire contents of the file `doc.txt` in reverse order, use:

```
tail -r doc.txt
```

To display the last 10 lines of the file `doc.txt` in reverse order, use:

```
tail -10r doc.txt
```

Finally, the `-f` option is useful when you are monitoring a file. With this option, `tail` waits for new data to be written to the file by some other program. As new data are added to the file by some other program, tail displays the data on the screen. To stop tail from monitoring a file, press Ctrl+C (the intr key) because the `tail` command does not stop on its own.

touch

Syntax:

```
touch file or directory
```

This command updates the timestamp of a file or directory. If the named file does not exist, this command creates it as an empty file.

umask

See the section on default file permissions for users in Chapter 4.

uniq

Syntax:

```
uniq [-c] filename
```

The `uniq` command compares adjacent lines and displays only one unique line. When used with the `-c` option, `uniq` counts the number of occurrences. A file that has the contents:

```
a
a
a
b
a
```

produces the following result when you use it with `uniq`:

```
uniq test.txt
a
b
a
```

Notice that the adjacent a's are removed—but not all a's in the file. This is an important detail to remember when using `uniq`. If you would like to find all the unique lines in a file called `test.txt`, you can run the following command:

```
sort  test.txt  | uniq
```

This command sorts the `test.txt` file and puts all similar lines next to each other, allowing `uniq` to display only unique lines. For example, say that you want to find quickly how many unique visitors come to your Web site; you can run the following command:

```
awk '{print $1}' access.log | sort | uniq
```

This displays the unique IP addresses in a CLF log file, which is what Apache web server uses.

vi

The vi program is a powerful full-screen text editor you can find on almost all Unix systems because of its size and capabilities. The vi editor does not require much in the way of resources to utilize its features. In addition to the basic edit functions, vi can search, replace, and concatenate files, and it has its own macro language, as well as a number of other features.

vi has two modes: input and command. When vi is in *input mode*, you can enter, insert, or append text in a document. When vi is in *command mode*, you tell vi what to do from the command line—move within the document, merge lines, search, and so on. You can carry out all vi functions from command mode except the entering of text. You can enter text only in input mode.

A typical vi newbie assumes he is in input mode and begins typing his document. He expects to see his newly inputted text, but what he really sees is his current document mangled because he is in command mode.

When vi starts, it is in command mode. You can go from command mode to input mode by using one of the following commands: [aAiIoOcCsSR]. To return to command mode, press the Esc key for normal exit, or press Interrupt (the Ctrl+C key sequence) to end abnormally.

Table B-7 shows a summary of common vi commands and their effects in command mode.

TABLE B-7: SUMMARY OF COMMON VI COMMANDS

Keys	Effects
Ctrl+D	Moves window down by half a screen.
Ctrl+U	Moves window up by half a screen.
Ctrl+F	Moves window forward by a screen.
Ctrl+B	Moves window back by a screen.
k or up arrow	Moves cursor up one line.
j or down arrow	Moves cursor down one line.
l or right arrow	Moves cursor right one character.
h or left arrow	Moves cursor left one character.
Return	Moves cursor to beginning of next line.
- (minus)	Moves cursor to beginning of previous line.
w	Moves cursor to beginning of next word.
b	Moves cursor to beginning of previous word.

Commands	Effects
^ or 0	Moves cursor to beginning of current line.
$	Moves cursor to end of current line.
A	Inserts text immediately after the cursor.
o	Opens a new line immediately after the current line.
O	Opens a new line immediately before the current line. Note this is an uppercase letter o, not a zero.
x	Deletes character under the cursor.
dw	Deletes a word (including space after it).
D or d	Deletes from the cursor until the end of line.
d^	(d caret) Deletes from the beginning of the line to the space or character to the left of the cursor.
dd	Deletes the current line.
U	Undoes last change. Note that 2 undos will undo the undo (nothing changes).
:w	Writes the changes for the current file and continues editing.
:q!	Quits vi without saving any changes.
:ZZ	Saves current file and exits vi.

wc

Syntax:

```
wc [-lwc] filename
```

The wc (word count) command counts lines, characters, and words. If you use the wc command without any options, the output displays all statistics of the file. The file test.txt contains the following text:

```
the quick brown fox jumps over the lazy dog
. wc test.txt
      1       9      44 test.txt
```

The results tell us there is one line with nine words containing 44 characters in the file test.txt. To display only the number of lines, use the -l option. The -w option displays only the number of words. Finally, the -c option displays only the total number of characters.

whatis

Syntax:

```
whatis keyword
```

This command displays a one-line description for the keyword entered in the command line. The whatis command is identical to typing man -f. For instance, if you want to display the time but you are not sure whether to use the time or date command, enter:

```
whatis time date
time          time (1)        - time a simple command
date          date (1)        - print the date and time
```

Looking at the results, you can see that the command you want is date. The time command actually measures how long it takes for a program or command to execute.

whereis

The whereis command locates source/binary and manuals sections for specified files. The command first strips the supplied names of leading pathname components and any (single) character file extension, such as .c, .h, and so on. Prefixes of s. resulting from use of source code control are also dealt with.

```
whereis ls
ls: /bin/ls /usr/man/man1/ls.1.gz
```

The preceding example indicates the location of the command in question. The ls command is in the /bin directory, and its corresponding man pages are at /usr/man/man1/ls.1.gz.

which

Syntax:

```
which command
```

The which command displays the path and aliases of any valid, executable command.

```
which df
/usr/bin/df
```

The preceding example shows us that the df command is in the /usr/bin directory. which also displays information about shell commands.

```
which setenv
setenv: shell built-in command.
```

File Compression and Archive-Specific Commands

The commands in this section compress, archive, and package files.

compress

Syntax:

```
compress [-v] file(s)
```

The compress command attempts to reduce the size of a file using the adaptive Lempel-Ziv coding algorithm. A file with a .Z extension replaces a compressed file. Using any type of compression for files is significant because smaller file sizes increase the amount of available disk space. Also, transferring smaller files across networks reduces network congestion.

The -v (verbose) option displays the percentage of reduction for each file you compress and tells you the name of the new file. Here is an example of how to use the compress command:

```
ls -alF inbox
-rw----    1 username cscstd    194261 Feb 23 20:12 inbox
compress -v inbox
inbox: Compression: 37.20%—replaced with inbox.Z
ls -alF inbox.Z
-rw----    1 username cscstd    121983 Feb 23 20:12 inbox.Z
```

gunzip

Syntax:

```
gunzip [-v] file(s)
```

To decompress files to their original form, use the `gunzip` command. `gunzip` attempts to decompress files ending with the following extensions: `.gz`, `-gz`, `.z`, `-z`, `_z`, `.Z`, or `tgz`.

The `-v` option displays a verbose output when decompressing a file.

```
gunzip -v README.txt.gz
README.txt.gz:          65.0%-replaced with README.txt
```

gzip

Syntax:

```
gzip [-rv9] file(s)
```

The `gzip` command is another compression program. It is known for having one of the best compression ratios but for a price. It can be considerably slow. Files compressed with `gzip` are replaced by files with a `.gz` extension.

The -9 option yields the best compression sacrificing speed. The `-v` option is the verbose option. The size, total, and compression ratios are listed for each file. Also, the `-r` option recursively traverses each directory compressing all the files along the way.

```
ls -alF README.txt
-rw-r-r-  1 root     root          16213 Oct 14 13:55 README.txt
gzip -9v README.txt
README.txt:             65.0%-replaced with README.txt.gz
ls -alF README.txt.gz
-rw-r-r-  1 root     root          5691 Oct 14 13:55 README.txt.gz
```

rpm

Syntax:

```
rpm -[ivhqladefUV] [-force] [-nodeps] [-oldpackage] package list
```

This is the Red Hat Package Manager program. It allows you to manage RPM packages, making it very easy to install and uninstall software.

To install a new RPM package called `precious-software-1.0.i386.rpm`, run:

```
rpm -i precious-software-1.0.i386.rpm
```

You can make `rpm` a bit more verbose by using `-ivh` instead of just the `-i` option. If you have installed the package and for some reason would like to install it again, you need to use the `--force` option to force rpm.

If you are upgrading a software package, you should use the `-U` option, as in this example:

```
rpm -Uvh precious-software-2.0.i386.rpm
```

This command upgrades the previous version of the precious-software package to version 2.0. However, if you have installed a newer version and want to go back to the previous version, `rpm` detects this condition and displays an error message saying that the installed version is newer than the one you are trying to install. In such a case, should you decide to proceed anyway, use the `--oldpackage` option with the `-U` option to force `rpm` to downgrade your software.

To find a list of all available packages installed on your system, run:

```
rpm -qa
```

To find out which package a program such as sendmail belongs to, run:

```
rpm -q sendmail
```

This returns the RPM package name you use to install sendmail. To find out which package a specific file such as `/bin/tcsh` belongs to, run:

```
rpm -qf /bin/tcsh
```

This displays the package name of the named file. If you are interested in finding the documentation that comes with a file, use the `-d` option along with the `-qf` options. To list all files associated with a program or package, such as sendmail, use the `-l` option, as shown here:

```
rpm -ql sendmail
```

To ensure that an installed package is not modified in any way, you can use the `-V` option. For example, to verify that all installed packages are in their original state, run the following:

```
rpm -Va
```

This option becomes very useful if you learn that you or someone else could have damaged one or more packages.

To uninstall a package such as sendmail, run:

```
rpm -e sendmail
```

If you find that removing a package or program breaks other programs because they depend on it or its files, you have to decide if you want to break these programs or not. If you decide to remove the package or the program, you can use the --nodeps option with the -e option to force rpm to uninstall the package.

tar

Syntax:

```
tar [c] [x] [v] [z] [f filename]  file or directory names
```

The tar command allows you to archive multiple files and directories into a single .tar file. It also allows you to extract files and directories from such an archive file, as in this example:

```
tar cf source.tar *.c
```

This command creates a tar file called source.tar, which contains all C source files (ending with extension .c) in the current directory.

```
tar cvf source.tar *.c
```

Here the v option allows you to see which files are being archived by tar.

```
tar cvzf backup.tar.gz  important_dir
```

Here all the files and subdirectories of the directory called important_dir are archived in a file called backup.tar.gz. Notice that the z option is compressing this file; hence, give the resulting file a .gz extension. Often, the .tar.gz extension is shortened by many users to be .tgz as well.

To extract an archive file, backup.tar, you can run:

```
tar xf backup.tar
```

To extract a compressed tar file (such as backup.tgz or backup.tar.gz), you can run:

```
tar xzf backup.tgz
```

uncompress

Syntax:

```
uncompress [-v] file(s)
```

When you use the compress command to compress a file, the file is no longer in its original form. To return a compressed file to its original form, use the uncompress command.

The uncompress command expects to find a file with a .Z extension, so the command line "uncompress inbox" is equivalent to "uncompress inbox.Z."

The -v option produces verbose output.

```
uncompress -v inbox.Z
inbox.Z: —replaced with inbox
```

unzip

Syntax:

```
unzip file(s)
```

This command decompresses files with the .zip extension. You can compress these files with the unzip command, Phil Katz's PKZIP, or any other PKZIP-compatible program.

uudecode

Syntax:

```
uudecode file
```

The uudecode command transforms a uuencoded file into its original form. uudecode creates the file by using the "target_name" the uuencode command specifies, which you can also identify on the first line of a uuencoded file.

To convert our uuencoded file from the following entry back to its original form:

```
uudecode a.out.txt
```

As a result, you create the executable file a.out from the text file a.out.txt.

uuencode

Syntax:

```
uuencode in_file target_name
```

The uuencode command translates a binary file into readable form. You can do so by converting the binary file into ASCII printable characters. One of the many uses of uuencode is transmitting a binary file through e-mail. A uuencoded file appears as a large e-mail message. The recipient can then save the message and use the uudecode command to retrieve its binary form.

The target_name is the name of the binary file created when you use the uuencode.

This example uuencodes the executable program a.out. The target name that uudecode creates is b.out. Save the uuencoded version of a.out in the file a.out.txt.

```
uuencode a.out b.out > a.out.txt
```

zip

Syntax:

```
zip [-ACDe9] file(s)
```

This compression utility compresses files in a more popular format, enabling compatibility with systems such as VMS, MS-DOS, OS/2, Windows NT, Minix, Atari, Macintosh, Amiga, and Acorn RISC OS. This is mainly because of zip's compatibility with Phil Katz's PKZIP program. Files compressed with zip have the .zip extension.

The zip command has an array of options that are toggled by its switches. This command can create self-extracting files, add comments to ZIP files, remove files from an archive, and password-protect the archive.

These are a few of the features zip supports. For a more detailed description, see your local man page.

File Systems — Specific Commands

The commands in this section deal with file systems.

dd

Syntax:

```
dd if=input file [conv=conversion type] of=output file [obs=output block size]
```

This program allows you to convert file formats, as in this example:

```
dd if=/tmp/uppercase.txt   conv=lcase of=/tmp/lowercase.txt
```

This command takes the /tmp/upppercase.txt file and writes a new file called /tmp/lowercase.txt and converts all characters to lowercase (lcase). To do the reverse, you can use conv=ucase option. However, dd is most widely used to write a boot image file to a floppy disk that has a file system that mkfs has already created. For example:

```
dd if=/some/boot.img  conv=lcase of=/dev/fd0 obs=16k
```

This command writes the /some/boot.image file to the first floppy disk (/dev/fd0) in 16KB blocks.

df

Syntax:

```
df  [-k] FileSystem | File
```

The df command summarizes the free disk space for the drives mounted on the system. Hard disk space is a vital (and often scarce) resource in a computer; monitor it carefully. Mismanagement of hard disk space can cause a computer to crawl on its knees and can cause some unhappy users.

```
df
```

Filesystem	512-blocks	Free	%Used	Iused	%Iused	Mounted on
/dev/hd4	49152	25872	48%	2257	19%	/
/dev/hd2	1351680	243936	82%	19091	12%	/usr
/dev/hd9var	49152	12224	76%	2917	48%	/var
/dev/hd3	57344	52272	9%	125	2%	/tmp
/dev/lv00	57344	55176	4%	19	1%	/tftpboot
/dev/hd1	163840	16976	90%	1140	6%	/home
/dev/fs01	8192000	6381920	23%	20963	3%	/home/fs01
/dev/fs02	8192000	1873432	78%	72	1%	/home/fs02

To view the disk space summary for the current file system:

```
df .
```

Filesystem	512-blocks	Free	%Used	Iused	%Iused	Mounted on
/dev/fs01	8192000	6381920	23%	20963	3%	/home/fs01

Notice that the db output is printed in 512-byte blocks. It may seem odd to think of blocks with this size if you are used to 1K blocks or more precisely 1,024-byte blocks. The -k option displays the summary with 1,024-byte blocks instead:

```
df -k .
Filesystem     1024-blocks     Free %Used    Iused %Iused Mounted on
/dev/fs01          4096000   3190960   23%    20963     3% /home/fs01
```

With the -k option in mind, the results are very different. If you interpret the output incorrectly, you may run out of disk space sooner than you think.

edquota

See the section on assigning disk quotas to users in Chapter 7 for details.

fdformat

Syntax:

```
fdformat  floppy-device
```

This program does a low-level format on a floppy device, as in this example:

```
fdformat /dev/fd0H1440
```

This formats the first floppy disk (/dev/fd0) as a high-density 1.44MB disk.

fdisk

mkfs

Syntax:

```
mkfs [-t fstype] [-cv] device-or-mount-point [blocks]
```

This command allows you to make a new file system, as in this example:

```
mkfs -t ext2  /dev/hda3
```

The preceding command creates an ext2-type file system on the /dev/hda3 partition of the first IDE hard disk. The -c option allows you to instruct mkfs to check bad blocks before building the file system; the -v option produces verbose output.

mount

Syntax:

```
mount -a [-t fstype] [-o options] device  directory
```

This command mounts a file system. Typically, the mount options for commonly used file systems are stored in /etc/fstab, as in this example:

```
/dev/hda6  /intranet  ext2  defaults 1 2
```

If the preceding line is in /etc/fstab, you can mount the file system stored in partition /dev/hda6 as follows:

```
mount  /intranet
```

You can also mount the same file system as follows:

```
mount  -t ext2 /dev/hda6 /intranet
```

Use the -t option to specify file system type. To mount all the file systems specified in the /etc/fstab, use the -a option, as in this example:

```
mount  -a -t ext2
```

The preceding command mounts all ext2 file systems. Commonly used options for -o option are ro (read-only) and rw (read/write), as in this example:

```
mount  -t ext2 -o ro /dev/hda6 /secured
```

The preceding command mounts /dev/hda6 on /secured as a read-only file system.

quota

See the section on monitoring disk usage in Chapter 7 for details.

quotaon

See the section on configuring your system to support disk quotas in Chapter 7 for details.

swapoff

Syntax:

```
swapoff -a
```

This command allows you to disable swap devices. The -a option allows you to disable all swap partitions specified in /etc/fstab.

swapon

Syntax:

```
swapon -a
```

This command allows you to enable swap devices. The -a option allows you to enable all swap partitions specified in /etc/fstab.

umount

Syntax:

```
umount  -a [-t fstype]
```

This command unmounts a file system from the current system, as in this example:

```
umount  /cdrom
```

The preceding command unmounts a file system whose mount point is /cdrom and the details of whose mount point are specified in /etc/fstab.

The -a option allows you to unmount all file systems (except for the proc file system) specified in the /etc/fstab file. You can also use the -t option to specify a particular file system type to unmount, as in this example:

```
umount  -a -t iso9660
```

This command unmounts all iso9660-type file systems, which are typically CD-ROMs.

DOS-Compatible Commands

If you need access to MS-DOS files from your Linux system, you need to install the Mtools package. Mtools is shipped with Red Hat as an RPM package, so installing it is quite simple. See the rpm command for details on how to install an RPM package.

Mtools is a collection of utilities that allow you to read, write, and move around MS-DOS files. It also supports Windows 95–style long filenames, OS/2 Xdf disks, and 2m disks. The following section covers the common utilities in the Mtools package.

mcopy

Syntax:

```
mcopy [-tm] source-file-or-directory  destination-file-or-directory
```

Use the mcopy utility to copy MS-DOS files to and from Linux, as in this example:

```
mcopy  /tmp/readme.txt   b:
```

The preceding command copies the readme.txt file from the /tmp directory to the b: drive. The -t option enables you to automatically translate carriage return/ line feed pairs in MS-DOS text files into new line feeds. The -m option allows you to preserve file modification time.

mdel

Syntax:

```
mdel msdosfile
```

This utility allows you to delete files on an MS-DOS file system.

mdir

Syntax:

```
mdir [-/] msdos-file-or-directory
```

This utility allows you to view an MS-DOS directory. The -/ option allows you to view all the subdirectories as well.

mformat

Syntax:

```
mformat [-t cylinders] [-h heads] [-s sectors]
```

This utility allows you to format a floppy disk to hold a minimal MS-DOS file system. I find it much easier to format a disk by using an MS-DOS machine than to specify cylinders, heads, sectors, and so on.

mlabel

Syntax:

```
mlabel [-vcs] drive:[new label]
```

This utility displays the current volume label (if any) of the name drive and prompts for the new label if you do not enter it after the drive: in the command line. The -v option prints a hex dump of the boot sector of the named drive; the -c option clears the existing volume label, and the -s shows the existing label of the drive.

System Status – Specific Commands

The commands in this section deal with status information on system resources.

dmesg

Syntax:

```
dmesg
```

This program prints the status messages the kernel displays during bootup.

free

Syntax:

```
free
```

This program displays memory usage statistics. An example of output looks like this:

```
                  total    used    free    shared  buffers  cached

Mem:            127776   124596  3180    30740    2904     107504
-/+ buffers/cache: 14188    113588
Swap:           129900   84      129816
```

shutdown

Syntax:

```
shutdown [-r] [-h] [-c] [-k]  [-t seconds] time [message]
```

This command allows a superuser or an ordinary user listed in the /etc/ shutdown.allow file to shut the system down for a reboot or halt. To reboot the computer now, run:

```
shutdown -r now
```

To halt the system after the shutdown, replace the -r with -h. The -k option allows you to simulate a shutdown event, as in this example:

```
shutdown -r -k now System going down for maintenance
```

This command sends a fake shutdown message to all users. The -t option allows you to specify a delay in seconds between the warning message and the actual shutdown event. In such a case, if you decide to abort the shutdown, run shutdown again with the -c option to cancel it.

Note that you can use the HH:MM format to specify the time, as in this example:

```
shutdown -r 12:55
```

This reboots the system at 12:55. You can also use *+minutes* to specify time, as in this example:

```
shutdown -r +5
```

This starts the shutdown process five minutes after you print the warning message.

uname

Syntax:

```
uname [-m] [-n] [-r] [-s] [-v] [-a]
```

This command displays information about the current system, as in this example:

```
uname -a
```

This command displays a line such as the following:

```
Linux picaso.nitec.com 2.0.36 #1 Tue Oct 13 22:17:11 EDT 1998 i586 unknown
```

The -m option displays the system architecture (for instance, i586); the -n option displays the host name (for instance, picaso.nitec.com); the -r option displays the release version of the operating system (for instance, 2.0.36); the -s option displays the operating system name (for instance, Linux); and the -v option displays the local build version of the operating system (for instance, #1 Tue Oct 13 22:17:11 EDT 1998).

uptime

Syntax:

```
uptime
```

This command displays current time, how long the system has been up since the last reboot, how many users are connected to the server, and the system load in the last 1, 5, and 15 minutes.

User Administration Commands

The commands in this section deal with user administration.

chfn

See the section on modifying an existing user account in Chapter 7.

chsh

See the section on modifying an existing user account in Chapter 7.

groupadd

See the section on creating a new group in Chapter 7.

groupmod

See the section on modifying an existing group in Chapter 7.

groups

Syntax:

```
groups [username]
```

This command displays the list of group(s) the named user currently belongs to. If no username is specified, this command displays the current user's groups.

last

Syntax:

`last [-number] [username]  [reboot]`

This command displays a list of users who have logged in since `/var/log/wtmp` was created, as in this example:

`last julie`

This command shows the number of times user julie has logged in since the last time `/var/log/wtmp` was created.

`last -10 julie`

This command shows only the last 10 logins by julie.

`last reboot`

This displays the number of times the system has been rebooted since `/var/log/wtmp` file was created.

passwd

Syntax:

`passwd username`

This command allows you to change a user's password. Only a superuser can specify a username; everyone else must type `passwd` without any argument, which allows the user to change his or her password. A superuser can change anyone's password using this program.

su

Syntax:

`su  [-]  [username]`

You can use the `su` command to change into another user, as in this example:

`su john`

This command allows you to be the user john as long as you know john's password, and this account exists on the server you use.

The most common use of this command is to become root. For example, if you run this command without any username argument, it assumes that you want to be root and prompts you for the root password. If you enter the correct root password, su runs a shell by using the root's UID (0) and GID (0). This allows you effectively to become the root user and to perform administrative tasks. This command is very useful if you have only Telnet access to the server. You can telnet into the server as a regular user and use it to become root to perform system administrative tasks. If you supply the - option, the new shell is marked as the login shell. Once you become the root user, you can su to other users without entering any password.

useradd

See the section on creating new user account in Chapter 7.

userdel

See the section on deleting or disabling a user account in Chapter 7.

usermod

See the section on modifying an existing user account in Chapter 7.

who

Syntax:

```
who
```

This command displays information about the users who are currently logged in to a system. You can also use the w command for the same purpose.

whoami

Syntax:

```
whoami
```

This command displays your current username.

User Commands for Accessing Network Services

The commands in this section allow you to access various network services.

finger

Syntax:

```
finger user@host
```

This program allows you to query a `finger` daemon at the named host, as in this example:

```
finger kabir@blackhole.integrationlogic.com
```

This command requests a `finger` connection to the `finger` daemon running on the `blackhole.integrationlogic.com` server. If the named host does not allow `finger` connections, this attempt fails. On success, the `finger` request displays information about the named user. If the user has a `.plan` file in the home directory, most traditional `finger` daemons display this file. Because `finger` has been used by hackers to cause security problems, most system administrators disable `finger` service outside their domains.

ftp

Syntax:

```
ftp ftp hostname or IP address
```

This is the default FTP client program. You can use this to FTP to an FTP server, as in this example:

```
ftp  ftp.cdrom.com
```

This opens an FTP connection to `ftp.cdrom.com` and prompts you to enter a username and a password. If you know the username and password, you can log in to the FTP server and upload or download files. Once you are at the FTP prompt, you can enter `help` or ? to get help on FTP commands.

lynx

Syntax:

```
lynx [-dump] [-head] [URL]
```

This is the most popular interactive text-based Web browser, as in this example:

```
lynx http://www.integrationlogic.com/
```

This command displays the top page of the site. It is a very handy program to have. For example, say you want to quickly find what kind of Web server the site uses without asking the Webmaster. You can run the following command:

```
lynx -head http://www.integrationlogic.com/
```

This displays the HTTP header the lynx browser receives from the Web server. An example of output is shown here:

```
HTTP/1.1 302 Moved
Date: Tue, 02 Mar 1999 06:47:27 GMT
Server: Apache/1.3.3 (Unix)
Location: http://www.integrationlogic.com/index.shtml
Connection: close
Content-Type: text/html
```

As you can see, this header shows that www.integrationlogic.com runs on the Apache 1.3.3 Web server on a Unix platform. Note that not all Web sites give their Web server platform information, but most do. If you would like to avoid the interactive mode, you can use the -dump option to dump the page on the screen (stdout). For example,

```
lynx -dump -head http://www.integrationlogic.com/
```

This dumps the header to stdout. The -dump feature can be quite handy, as in this example:

```
lynx -dump -head http://webserver/new.gif > new.gif
```

This allows you to save new.gif on the Web server host on a local file called new.gif.

The interactive mode allows you to browse sites that are compatible with text-only browsers.

mail

Syntax:

```
mail user@host [-s subject] [< filename]
```

This is the default SMTP mail client program. You can use this program to send or receive mail from your system. For example, if you run this program without any argument, it displays an ampersand (&) prompt and shows you the currently unread mail by arranging the messages in a numbered list. To read a message, enter the index number, and the mail is displayed. To learn more about mail, use the ? command once you are at the & prompt.

To send a message to a user called kabir@integrationlogic.com with the subject header About your Red Hat book, you can run the following command:

```
mail  kabir@integrationlogic.com  -s "About your Red Hat book"
```

You can then enter your mail message and press Ctrl+D to end the message. You can switch to your default text editor by entering ~v at the beginning of a line while you are in compose mode.

If you have already prepared a mail message in a file, you can send it using a command such as

```
mail  kabir@nitec.com  -s "About your Red Hat book" << feedback.txt
```

This sends a message with the given subject line; the message consists of the contents of the feedback.txt file.

pine

Syntax:

```
pine
```

This is a full-screen SMTP mail client that is quite user-friendly. If you typically use mail clients via telnet, you should definitely try this program. Because of its user-friendly interfaces, it is suitable for your Linux users who are not yet friends with Linux.

rlogin

Syntax:

```
rlogin [-l username] host
```

This command allows you to log remotely into a host. For example, to log in to a host called shell.myhost.com, you can run:

```
rlogin shell.myhost.com
```

Because rlogin is not safe, I recommend that you use it *only* in a closed LAN environment.

The -l option allows you to specify a username to use for authentication. If you would like to log remotely into a host without entering a password, create a .rhosts file in the user's home directory. Add the hostname or IP address of the computer you use to issue the rlogin request. Again, because many consider this a security risk, I do not recommend wide use of rlogin.

talk

Syntax:

```
talk username tty
```

If you need to send a message to another user, e-mail works just fine. But if you need to communicate with another user in real time (as in a telephone conversation), use the talk command.

To talk to another user who is logged in:

```
talk ronak@csus.edu
```

The user you request has to accept your talk request. Once the user accepts your talk request, you can begin talking (or typing) to each other. The talk program terminates when either party executes Ctrl+C (the intr key combination).

telnet

Syntax:

```
telnet hostname or IP address [port]
```

This is the default Telnet client program. You can use this program to connect to a Telnet server, as in this example:

```
telnet  shell.myportal.com
```

This command opens a Telnet connection to the shell.myportal.com system if the named host runs a Telnet server. Once a connection is opened, the command prompts you for username and password and, on successful login, allows you to access a local user account on the Telnet server.

wall

Syntax:

```
wall
```

This command allows you to send a text message to every terminal whose user has not disabled write access to the TTY via the `mesg n` command. Once you type `wall`, you can enter a single or multiline message; you can send it by pressing Ctrl+D.

Network Administrator's Commands

The commands in this section allow you to gather information on network services and on the network itself.

host

Syntax:

```
host [-a] host IP address
```

By default, this program allows you to check the IP address of a host quickly. If you use the `-a` option, it returns various sorts of DNS information about the named host or IP address.

hostname

Syntax:

```
me
```

s program displays the host name of a system.

nfig

ux:

```
fig [interface] [up | down] [netmask mask]
```

This program allows you to configure a network interface. You can also see the state of an interface using this program. For example, if you have configured your Red Hat Linux for networking and have a preconfigured network interface device, eth0, you can run

```
ifconfig eth0
```

and see output similar to the following:

```
eth0 Link encap:Ethernet  HWaddr 00:C0:F6:98:37:37
inet addr:206.171.50.50  Bcast:206.171.50.63 Mask:255.255.255.240
UP BROADCAST RUNNING MULTICAST  MTU:1500  Metric:1
RX packets:9470 errors:0 dropped:0 overruns:0 frame:0
TX packets:7578 errors:0 dropped:0 overruns:0 carrier:0 collisions:0
Interrupt:5 Base address:0x340
```

Here ifconfig reports that network interface device eth0 has an Internet address (inet addr) 206.171.50.50, a broadcast address (Bcast) 206.171.50.63, and network mask (Mask) 255.255.255.240. The rest of the information shows the following: how many packets this interface has received (RX packets); how many packets this interface has transmitted (TX packets); how many errors of different types have occurred so far; what interrupt address line this device is using; what I/O address base is being used; and so on.

You can run ifconfig without any arguments to get the full list of all the up network devices.

You can use ifconfig to bring an interface up, as in this example:

```
ifconfig eth0 206.171.50.50 netmask 255.255.255.240 \
broadcast 206.171.50.63
```

The preceding command starts eth0 with IP address 206.171.50.50. You can also quickly take an interface down by using the ifconfig command, as in this example:

```
ifconfig eth0 down
```

This command takes the eth0 interface down.

netcfg

See the section on using netcfg to configure a network interface card in Chapter 9.

netstat

Syntax:

```
netstat [-r] [-a] [-c] [-i]
```

This program displays the status of the network connections, both to and from the local system, as in this example:

```
netstat -a
```

This command displays all the network connections on the local system. To display the routing table, use the `-r` option. To display network connection status on a continuous basis, use the `-c` option. To display information on all network interfaces, use the `-i` option.

nslookup

Syntax:

```
nslookup [-query=DNS record type] [hostname or IP] [name server]
```

This command allows you to perform DNS queries. You can choose to query a DNS server in an interactive fashion or just look up information immediately, as in this example:

```
nslookup -query=mx integrationlogic.com
```

This command immediately returns the MX records for the `integrationlogic.com` domain.

```
nslookup -query=mx integrationlogic.com ns.nitec.com
```

This command does the same, but instead of using the default name server specified in the `/etc/resolv.conf` file, it uses `ns.nitec.com` as the name server. You can also use `-q` instead of `-query`, as in this example:

```
nslookup -q=a  www.formtrack.com
```

This command returns the IP address (Address record) for the named hostname. You can run `nslookup` in interactive mode as well. Just run the command without any parameters, and you will see the `nslookup` prompt. At the `nslookup` prompt, you can enter "?" to get help. If you are planning on performing multiple DNS queries at a time, interactive mode can be very helpful. For example, to query the NS records for multiple domains such as `ad-engine.com` and `classifiedworks.com`, you can just enter the following command:

```
set query=ns
```

Once you set the query type to `ns`, you can simply type `ad-engine.com` and wait for the reply; once you get the reply, you can try the next domain name; and so on. If you would like to change the name server while at the `nslookup` prompt, use the `server` command, as in this example:

```
server ns.ad-engine.com
```

This will make `nslookup` use `ns.ad-engine.com` as the name server. To quit interactive mode and return to your shell prompt, enter exit at the `nslookup` prompt.

ping

Syntax:

```
ping [-c count] [-s packet size] [-I interface]
```

This is one of the programs network administrators use most widely. You can use it to see whether a remote computer is reachable via the TCP/IP protocol. Technically, this program sends an Internet Control Message Protocol (ICMP) echo request to the remote host. Because the protocol requires a response to an echo request, the remote host is bound to send an echo response. This allows the `ping` program to calculate the amount of time it takes to send a packet to a remote host, as in this example:

```
ping blackhole.nitec.com
```

This command sends `ping` messages to the `blackhole.nitec.com` host on a continuous basis. To stop the `ping` program, you press Ctrl+C, which causes the program to display a set of statistics. Here is an example of output of the `ping` requests the preceding command generates:

```
PING blackhole.nitec.com (209.63.178.15): 56 data bytes
64 bytes from 209.63.178.15: icmp_seq=0 ttl=53 time=141.5 ms
64 bytes from 209.63.178.15: icmp_seq=1 ttl=53 time=162.6 ms
64 bytes from 209.63.178.15: icmp_seq=2 ttl=53 time=121.4 ms
64 bytes from 209.63.178.15: icmp_seq=3 ttl=53 time=156.0 ms
64 bytes from 209.63.178.15: icmp_seq=4 ttl=53 time=126.4 ms
64 bytes from 209.63.178.15: icmp_seq=5 ttl=53 time=101.5 ms
64 bytes from 209.63.178.15: icmp_seq=6 ttl=53 time=98.7 ms
64 bytes from 209.63.178.15: icmp_seq=7 ttl=53 time=180.9 ms
64 bytes from 209.63.178.15: icmp_seq=8 ttl=53 time=126.2 ms
64 bytes from 209.63.178.15: icmp_seq=9 ttl=53 time=122.3 ms
64 bytes from 209.63.178.15: icmp_seq=10 ttl=53 time=127.1 ms
-- blackhole.nitec.com ping statistics--
11 packets transmitted, 11 packets received, 0% packet loss
round-trip min/avg/max = 98.7/133.1/180.9 ms
```

The preceding output shows 10 `ping` requests to the `blackhole.nitec.com` host. Because the program is interrupted after the 11th request, the statistics show that ping has transmitted 11 packets and has also received all the packets, and therefore no packet loss has occurred. This is good in that packet loss is a sign of poor networking between the ping requester and the ping responder. The other interesting statistics are the round-trip minimum (min) time, the average (avg) time, and the maximum (max) time. The lower these numbers are, the better the routing is between the involved hosts. For example, if you ping a host on the same LAN, you should see the round-trip numbers in the one-millisecond range.

If you would like to have ping automatically stop after transmitting a number of packets, use the -c option, as in this example:

```
ping -c 10 blackhole.nitec.com
```

This sends 10 ping requests to the named host. By default, ping sends a 64-byte (56 data bytes + 8 header bytes) packet. If you are also interested in controlling the size of the packet sent, use the -s option, as in this example:

```
ping -c 1024 -s 1016 reboot.nitec.com
```

This command sends a packet 1,024 (1016 + 8) bytes long to the remote host.

By sending large packets to a remote host running weak operating systems (you know what they are), you might cause the host to become very unusable to the user(s) on the remote host. This could be considered as an attack by many system administrators and therefore is very likely to be illegal in most parts of the world. So be very careful when you start experimenting with ping and someone else's computer.

route

Syntax:

```
route add -net network address netmask dev device
route add -host hostname or IP dev device
route add default gw hostname or IP
```

This command allows you to control routing to and from your computer. For example, to create a default route for your network, use the route command as follows:

```
route add -net network address netmask    device
```

For example, to create a default route for 206.171.50.48 network with a 255.255.255.240 netmask and eth0 as the interface, you can run:

```
route add -net 206.171.50.48 255.255.255.240 eth0
```

To set the default gateway, you can run the route command as follows:

```
route add  default gw gateway address device
```

For example, to set the default gateway address to 206.171.50.49, you can run the following command:

```
route add  default gw 206.171.50.49 eth0
```

You can verify that your network route and default gateway are properly set up in the routing table by using the following command:

```
route -n
```

Here is an example of output of the preceding command:

```
Kernel IP routing table
Destination    Gateway Genmask        Flags Metric Ref Use Iface
206.171.50.48 0.0.0.0 255.255.255.240 U     0      0   6   eth0
127.0.0.0      0.0.0.0 255.0.0.0       U     0      0   5   lo
0.0.0.0        206.171.50.49  0.0.0.0 UG     0      0   17  eth0
```

 TIP Make sure you have IP forwarding turned on in `/etc/sysconfig/network` and also in the kernel to allow routing packets between two different network interfaces.

tcpdump

Syntax:

```
tcpdump expression
```

This is a great network debugging tool. For example, to trace all the packets between two hosts brat.nitec.com and reboot.nitec.com, you can use the following command:

```
tcpdump host brat.nitec.com and reboot.nitec.com
```

This command makes `tcpdump` listen for packets between these two computers. If `reboot.nitec.com` starts sending `ping` requests to `brat.nitec.com`, the output looks something like the following:

```
tcpdump: listening on eth0
09:21:14.720000 reboot.nitec.com> brat.nitec.com: icmp: echo request
09:21:14.720000 brat.nitec.com> reboot.nitec.com: icmp: echo reply
09:21:15.720000 reboot.nitec.com> brat.nitec.com: icmp: echo request
09:21:15.720000 brat.nitec.com> reboot.nitec.com: icmp: echo reply
09:21:16.720000 reboot.nitec.com> brat.nitec.com: icmp: echo request
09:21:16.720000 brat.nitec.com> reboot.nitec.com: icmp: echo reply
09:21:17.730000 reboot.nitec.com> brat.nitec.com: icmp: echo request
09:21:17.730000 brat.nitec.com> reboot.nitec.com: icmp: echo reply
```

If you are having a problem connecting to an FTP server, you can use `tcpdump` on your LAN gateway system to see what is going on, as in this example:

```
tcpdump port ftp or ftp-data
```

This displays the FTP-related packets originating and arriving in your network.

As you can see, this allows you to debug a network problem at a low level. If you are experiencing a problem in using a service between two hosts, you can use `tcpdump` to identify the problem.

traceroute

Syntax:

```
traceroute host or IP address
```

This program allows you to locate network routing problems. It displays the routes between two hosts by tricking the gateways between the hosts into responding to an `ICMP TIME_EXCEEDED` request. Here is an example of `traceroute` output that shows the route from my local system to the `blackhole.nitec.com` host:

```
traceroute to blackhole.nitec.com (209.63.178.15), 30 hops max, 40 byte packets
 1 router (206.171.50.49)  4.137 ms   3.995 ms   4.738 ms
 2 PM3-001.v1.NET (206.171.48.10) 32.683 ms   33.295 ms   33.255 ms
 3 HQ-CS001.v1.NET (206.171.48.1) 42.263 ms   44.237 ms   36.784 ms
 4 ix.pxbi.net (206.13.15.97) 106.785 ms   63.585 ms   101.277 ms
 5 ix.pxbi.net (206.13.31.8) 86.283 ms   64.246 ms   69.749 ms
 6 ca.us.ixbm.net (165.87.22.10) 71.415 ms   72.319 ms   85.183 ms
 7 mae.elxi.net (198.32.136.128) 101.863 ms   80.257 ms   67.323 ms
 8 y.exli.net (207.173.113.146) 71.323 ms   104.685 ms   110.935 ms
 9 z.exli.net (207.173.113.217) 69.964 ms   137.858 ms   85.326 ms
```

```
10 z1.exli.net (207.173.112.251) 81.257 ms   107.575 ms   78.453 ms
11 209.210.249.50 (209.210.249.50) 90.701 ms   91.116 ms   109.491 ms
12 209.63.178.15 (209.63.178.15)  83.052 ms   76.604 ms   85.406 ms
```

Each line represents a hop; the more hops there are, the worse the route usually is. In other words, if you have only a few gateways between the source and the destination, chances are that packets between these two hosts are going to be transferred at a reasonably fast pace. However, this won't be true all the time because it takes only a single, slow gateway to mess up delivery time. Using traceroute, you can locate where your packets are going and where they are perhaps getting stuck. Once you locate a problem point, you can contact the appropriate authorities to resolve the routing problem.

Process Management Commands

The commands in this section show you how to manage processes (that is, the running programs in your system).

bg

Syntax:

bg

This built-in shell command is found in popular shells. This command allows you to put a suspended process into background. For example, say that you decide to run du -a / | sort -rn > /tmp/du.sorted to list all the files and directories in your system according to the disk usage (size) order and to put the result in a file called /tmp/du.sorted. Depending on the number of files you have on your system, this can take a while. In such a case, you can simply suspend the command line by using Ctrl+Z and type bg to send all commands in the command line to the background, bringing your shell prompt back on-screen for other use.

 TIP If you want to run a command in the background from the start, you can simply append & to the end of the command line.

To find out what commands are running in the background, enter jobs and you see the list of background command lines. To bring a command from the background, use the fg command.

fg

Syntax:

```
fg [%job-number]
```

This built-in shell command is found in popular shells. This command allows you to put a background process into foreground. If you run this command without any argument, it brings up the last command you put in the background. If you have multiple commands running in the background, you can use the `jobs` command to find the job number and can supply this number as an argument for `fg` to bring it to the foreground. For example, if `jobs` shows that you have two commands in the background, you can bring up the first command you put in the background by using:

```
fg %1
```

jobs

Syntax:

```
jobs
```

This built-in shell command is found in popular shells. This command allows you to view the list of processes running in the background or currently suspended.

Task Automation Commands

The commands in this section show you how to run unattended tasks.

Productivity Commands

The commands in this section help you increase your productivity.

bc

Syntax:

```
bc
```

This is an interactive calculator that implements a calculator-specific language as well. Personally, I am not all that interested in learning the language, but I find this tool very useful for doing quick calculations. When you run the command without any arguments, it takes your input and interprets it as calculator-programming statements. For example, to multiply 1,024 by 4, you can simply enter 1024*4 and the result is displayed. You can reuse the current result by using the period character.

cal

Syntax:

```
cal [month] [year]
```

This nifty program displays a nicely formatted calendar for the month or year specified in the command line. If you do not specify anything as an argument, the calendar for the current month is displayed. To see the calendar for an entire year, enter the (Western calendar) year in the 1–9999 range, as in this example:

```
cal 2000
```

This command displays the following calendar for the year 2000:

```
                             2000

        January                February                March
Su Mo Tu We Th Fr Sa    Su Mo Tu We Th Fr Sa    Su Mo Tu We Th Fr Sa
                  1            1  2  3  4  5              1  2  3  4
 2  3  4  5  6  7  8     6  7  8  9 10 11 12     5  6  7  8  9 10 11
 9 10 11 12 13 14 15    13 14 15 16 17 18 19    12 13 14 15 16 17 18
16 17 18 19 20 21 22    20 21 22 23 24 25 26    19 20 21 22 23 24 25
23 24 25 26 27 28 29    27 28 29                26 27 28 29 30 31
30 31
         April                  May                    June
Su Mo Tu We Th Fr Sa    Su Mo Tu We Th Fr Sa    Su Mo Tu We Th Fr Sa
                  1        1  2  3  4  5  6              1  2  3
 2  3  4  5  6  7  8     7  8  9 10 11 12 13     4  5  6  7  8  9 10
 9 10 11 12 13 14 15    14 15 16 17 18 19 20    11 12 13 14 15 16 17
16 17 18 19 20 21 22    21 22 23 24 25 26 27    18 19 20 21 22 23 24
23 24 25 26 27 28 29    28 29 30 31             25 26 27 28 29 30
30
          July                 August               September
Su Mo Tu We Th Fr Sa    Su Mo Tu We Th Fr Sa    Su Mo Tu We Th Fr Sa
                  1           1  2  3  4  5              1  2
 2  3  4  5  6  7  8     6  7  8  9 10 11 12     3  4  5  6  7  8  9
 9 10 11 12 13 14 15    13 14 15 16 17 18 19    10 11 12 13 14 15 16
16 17 18 19 20 21 22    20 21 22 23 24 25 26    17 18 19 20 21 22 23
23 24 25 26 27 28 29    27 28 29 30 31          24 25 26 27 28 29 30
30 31
```

```
        October                 November                December
Su Mo Tu We Th Fr Sa    Su Mo Tu We Th Fr Sa    Su Mo Tu We Th Fr Sa
 1  2  3  4  5  6  7              1  2  3  4                    1  2
 8  9 10 11 12 13 14     5  6  7  8  9 10 11     3  4  5  6  7  8  9
15 16 17 18 19 20 21    12 13 14 15 16 17 18    10 11 12 13 14 15 16
22 23 24 25 26 27 28    19 20 21 22 23 24 25    17 18 19 20 21 22 23
29 30 31               26 27 28 29 30           24 25 26 27 28 29 30
                                                31
```

ispell

Syntax:

```
ispell filename
```

This program allows you to correct spelling mistakes in a text file in an interactive fashion. If you have a misspelling in the file, the program suggests a spelling and gives you options to replace it with a correctly spelled word. This is the spell checker for text files.

mesg

Syntax:

```
mesg [y | n]
```

This program allows you to enable or disable public write access to your terminal, as in this example:

```
mesg y
```

The preceding command enables write access to your terminal so that another user on the same system can use the write command to write text messages to you. The n option allows you to disable write access. If you do not want to be bothered by anyone at any time, you can add mesg n to your login script (.login) file.

write

Syntax:

```
write username tty
```

This program allows you to write text messages to the named user, provided the user has not disabled write access to his or her TTY, as in this example:

```
write  shoeman
```

This command allows you to type a text message on screen, and when you finish the message by pressing Ctrl+D, the message is displayed on the user shoeman's terminal. If the user is logged in more than once, you have to specify the terminal name as well, as in this example:

```
write  shoeman ttyp0
```

This allows you to write to shoeman and to display the message on terminal ttyp0. If someone has multiple terminals open, you might want to run the w or who command to see which TTY is most suitable.

Shell Commands

In this section, you will find some very basic shell commands.

alias

Syntax:

```
alias   name of the alias = command
```

This is a built-in shell command available in most popular shells. This command lets you create aliases for commands, as in this example:

```
alias dir  ls -l
```

This command creates an alias called dir for the ls -l command. To see the entire alias list, run alias without any argument.

history

Syntax:

```
history
```

This is a built-in shell command available in most popular shells. This command displays a list of commands you have recently entered at the command line. The number of commands that the history command displays is limited by an environment variable, also called history. For example, if you add set history =

100 to your .login file, whenever you log in, you allow the history command to remember up to 100 command lines. You can easily rerun the commands you see in the history by entering their index number with a "!" sign. For example, say that when you enter the history command, you see the following listings:

```
1  10:25   vi irc-bot.h
2  10:25   vi irc-bot.c
3  10:26   which make
```

To run the vi irc-bot.c command again, you can simply enter !2 in the command line.

set

Syntax:

```
set var = value
```

This is a built-in shell command available in most popular shells. It allows you to set environment variables with specific values, as in this example:

```
set foo = bar
```

Here a new environment variable foo is set to have bar as the value. To see the list of all environment variables, run set by itself. To view the value of a specific environment variable, such as path, run:

```
echo $path
```

This shows you the value of the named environment variable. If you use this command quite often to set a few special environment variables, you can add it to .login or .profile or to your shell's dot file so that the special environment variables are automatically set when you log in.

source

Syntax:

```
source filename
```

This is a built-in shell command available in most popular shells. This command lets you read and execute commands from the named file in the current shell environment.

unalias

Syntax:

```
unalias   name of the alias
```

This is a built-in shell command available in most popular shells. This command lets you remove an alias for a command, as in this example:

```
unalias dir
```

This command removes an alias called dir. To remove all aliases, use the * wild-card as the argument.

Printing-Specific Commands

This section discusses commands that help you print from your Linux system.

lpq

Syntax:

```
lpq [-al] [-P printer]
```

The lpq command lists the status of the printers. If you enter lpq without any arguments, information about the default printer is displayed.

```
lpq
 Printer: lp@rembrandt  'Generic dot-matrix printer entry'
 Queue: no printable jobs in queue
 Status: server finished at 21:11:33
```

The -P option specifies information about a particular printer. The -a option returns the status of all printers.

With the -l option, lpq reports the job identification number, the user name that requests the print job, the originating host, the rank in queue, the job description, and the size of the job.

lpr

Syntax:

```
lpr [-i indentcols] [-P printer] [filename]
```

This command sends a file to the print spool to be printed. If you give no filename, data from standard input is assumed.

The -i option allows the option of starting the printing at a specific column. To specify a particular printer, you can use the -P printer option.

```
lpr main.c
```

The preceding example attempts to print the file main.c.

lprm

Syntax:

```
lprm [-a] [jobid] [all]
```

The lprm command sends a request to lpd to remove an item from the print queue. You can specify the print jobs the job ID or username is to remove, or they can include all items.

To remove all jobs in all print queues:

```
lprm -a all
```

To remove all jobs for the user "kiwee" on the printer "p1":

```
lprm -Pp1 kiwee
```

Appendix C

Internet Resources

THIS APPENDIX PROVIDES YOU with a list of Linux resources. Many Linux-oriented newsgroups, mailing lists, and Web sites are available on the Internet. Although you are likely to discover many more new Linux resources as time passes and as Linux's popularity increases, the following resources are likely to remain in good health at all times. I use these resources on an almost daily basis.

Usenet Newsgroups

The following Usenet newsgroups can be a great place to learn about advances in Linux, to engage in Linux-specific discussions, and also to find answers to questions you might have.

The comp.os.linux hierarchy

Linux has its own hierarchy of Usenet newsgroups. These groups are strictly Linux only. Before you post an article or a question in any of these newsgroups (or any Usenet newsgroup), make sure you know the charter of the group. In particular, when you are looking for answers to questions or solutions to problems, make sure you have read the available frequently asked questions, man pages, and how-to documentation. If you post a question that has been answered in a FAQ or a how-to document, chances are that some people who participate in that group might not take it kindly. Also, be careful when you post the same question in multiple groups (known as cross-posting) in the hope that you are increasing your chances of getting answers. As long as your post is relevant to the group, it is okay.

COMP.OS.LINUX.ADVOCACY (UNMODERATED)
This newsgroup is intended for discussions of the benefits of Linux compared with other operating systems.

COMP.OS.LINUX.ANNOUNCE (MODERATED)
This newsgroup is intended for all Linux-specific announcements. You will find information on new Linux software, bug and security alerts, and user group information here.

COMP.OS.LINUX.ANSWERS (MODERATED)

The Linux FAQ, how-to, readme, and other documents are posted in this news-group. If you have a question about Linux, check this newsgroup before posting your question in any Linux newsgroup.

COMP.OS.LINUX.DEVELOPMENT.APPS (UNMODERATED)

This newsgroup is intended for Linux developers who want to discuss development issues with others.

COMP.OS.LINUX.HARDWARE (UNMODERATED)

This newsgroup is intended for hardware-specific discussions. If you have a question about a piece of hardware you are trying to use with Linux, look for help here.

COMP.OS.LINUX.M68K (UNMODERATED)

This newsgroup is for Motorola 68K architecture-specific Linux development.

COMP.OS.LINUX.ALPHA (UNMODERATED)

This newsgroup is for Compaq/Digital Alpha architecture-specific discussions.

COMP.OS.LINUX.NETWORKING (UNMODERATED)

This newsgroup is intended for networking-related discussions.

COMP.OS.LINUX.X (UNMODERATED)

This newsgroup is intended for discussions relating to the X Window System, version 11, and compatible software such as servers, clients, libraries, and fonts running under Linux.

COMP.OS.LINUX.DEVELOPMENT.SYSTEM (UNMODERATED)

This newsgroup is intended for kernel hackers and module developers. Here you will find ongoing discussions on the development of the Linux operating system proper: kernel, device drivers, loadable modules, and so forth.

COMP.OS.LINUX.SETUP (UNMODERATED)

This newsgroup is intended for discussions on installation and system administration issues.

COMP.OS.LINUX.MISC (UNMODERATED)

This is the bit-bucket for the comp.os.linux hierarchy. Any topics not suitable for the other newsgroups in this hierarchy are discussed here.

Miscellaneous Linux newsgroups

The following newsgroups are mainstream Linux newsgroups. Most of these groups are geographically oriented and typically used for local Linux-related announcements for Linux user group meetings and events.

- ◆ alt.fan.linus-torvalds
- ◆ alt.uu.comp.os.linux.questions
- ◆ aus.computers.linux
- ◆ dc.org.linux-users
- ◆ de.alt.sources.linux.patches
- ◆ de.comp.os.linux.hardware
- ◆ de.comp.os.linux.misc
- ◆ de.comp.os.linux.networking
- ◆ de.comp.os.x
- ◆ ed.linux
- ◆ fido.linux-ger
- ◆ fj.os.linux
- ◆ fr.comp.os.linux
- ◆ han.sys.linux
- ◆ hannet.ml.linux.680x0
- ◆ it.comp.linux.pluto
- ◆ maus.os.linux
- ◆ maus.os.linux68k
- ◆ no.linux
- ◆ okinawa.os.linux
- ◆ tn.linux
- ◆ tw.bbs.comp.linux
- ◆ ucb.os.linux
- ◆ uiuc.sw.linux
- ◆ umich.linux

Unix security newsgroups

The following newsgroups are mainstream Unix security newsgroups. They often discuss current security matters that might also apply to Linux.

- ◆ `comp.security.announce`

- ◆ `comp.security.misc`

- ◆ `comp.security.pgp.announce`

- ◆ `comp.security.ssh`

- ◆ `comp.security.unix`

Mailing Lists

Mailing lists provide a good way of getting information directly to your e-mail account. If you are interested in Linux news, announcements, and other discussions, mailing lists can be quite helpful. This is especially true of mailing lists that provide a digest option. Such mailing lists send a digest of all daily or weekly messages to your e-mail address.

General lists

The following Linux mailing lists are general. They provide good general discussions of Linux news and helpful information for beginning Linux users.

LINUX-ANNOUNCE
Subscribe to Linux-Announce by sending e-mail to `linux-announce-request@ redhat.com` with the word **subscribe** in the subject line of the message.

LINUX-LIST
To subscribe, send e-mail to `linux-list-request@ssc.com` with the word **subscribe** in the body of your message.

LINUX-NEWBIE
To subscribe, send e-mail to `majordomo@vger.rutgers.edu` with the words **subscribe linux-newbie** in the body of your message.

LINUXUSERS
To subscribe, send e-mail to `majordomo@dmu.ac.uk` with the words **subscribe linux users** in the body of your message.

Security alert lists

The following mailing lists deal with Linux and computer-security issues. I strongly recommend that you subscribe to the BugTraq mailing list immediately.

BUGTRAQ

Although BugTraq is not specific to Linux, it is a great bug alert resource. To subscribe, send e-mail to `listserv@netspace.org` with the following as the body of the message: SUBSCRIBE **bugtraq your-firstname your-lastname**.

LINUX-SECURITY

Red Hat Software, Inc. hosts this mailing list. To subscribe, send e-mail to `linux-security-request@redhat.com` with the words **subscribe linux-security** in your subject line.

Special lists

The following mailing lists deal with two issues: Linux as a server platform and Linux as a desktop platform.

SERVER-LINUX

To subscribe, send e-mail to `listserv@netspace.org` with the words **subscribe SERVER-LINUX** in your subject line.

WORKSTATION-LINUX

To subscribe, send e-mail to `listserv@netspace.org` with the words **subscribe WORKSTATION-LINUX** in your subject line.

Web Sites

Many Web sites provide Linux-oriented information. Here are a few good ones.

General resources

The following Web sites are general. Most of these sites act as portal sites:

- ◆ `www.redhat.com/`
- ◆ `www.linux.com/`
- ◆ `www.linuxresources.com/`
- ◆ `http://linuxcentral.com/`
- ◆ `www.linuxcare.com/`

Publications

The following Web sites are official Web sites for various Linux publications:

◆ www.linuxgazette.com/

◆ www.linuxjournal.com/

◆ www.linuxworld.com/

Software stores

The following Web sites offer commercial Linux software:

◆ www.cheapbytes.com/

◆ www.linuxmall.com/

◆ www.lsl.com/

Security resources

The following Web sites deal with computer security:

◆ www.cert.org/

◆ www.securityfocus.com/

◆ www.replay.com/redhat/

◆ www.rootshell.com/

User Groups

A local Linux user group could be just the help you need for finding information on Linux. You can locate or even register a new user group of your own in your area by using the following URL: www.linuxresources.com/glue/index.html.

Appendix D

Dealing with Compromised Systems

SYSTEM ADMINISTRATORS INEVITABLY FIND themselves addressing computers that have been hacked. When you do, remember these simple steps.

Unplug the system's network cable

Keeping a compromised connection to the outside network (i.e. Internet) is the most risky thing to do and it is highly recommended that you take it off the network immediately. This advice is hard to follow if the compromised system is critical to your business operations. You must consider the following:

◆ Although you might have discovered that your system has been compromised, you might not know the full extent of how the attacker got into your system and, therefore, it is likely that he or she can return to do further damage.

◆ By keeping a compromised system on the network you might be aiding the attacker in launching attacks on other networks, which can result in legal complications and even fines against your organization.

◆ If you have valuable customer data in your compromised system, it might still be available to the attacker(s).

Hopefully, the above are reasons enough to unplug your system. Document when and how you have taken the system off the network.

Notify Appropriate Authorities

Contact your organization's management and inform them about the incident at hand. Have your management team formulate a plan of action in terms of legal and law enforcement involvement. Many companies shy away from reporting incidents in the fear of bad PR. This might be something that you need the management to sort out.

Most likely, you will be asked to answer three essential questions:

- ◆ **When did this take place?** You will have to wait until you perform the first analysis to answer this question. You might not ever find out when it actually took place.

- ◆ **How bad is the situation?** This one you can answer when you have looked at all your data and compared them against a clean set.

- ◆ **Can you stop it?** Well, by taking the system off the network, you have stopped the attack, and to stop the same attacker in the future you will need to know what happened and take appropriate action.

Create a Backup Copy of Everything

Once you have unplugged the system from your network, back up your data. Hook up a monitor and a keyboard to your now-isolated system so you can access it without putting other network components at risk. Then back up all contents of tapes or other media.

You must not change anything before you have made a verifiable backup.

Consider performing a low-level disk-copy operation if possible. For example, if you have a disk available that matches the specifications of your system disk, use the dd command to copy the entire system disk to the identical disk (which you have to attach to the system first). Make sure you verify the backup or disk copy separately (on another system, if possible).

Ideally, if you can backup the system and data disks into identical disks and boot them up on another stand-alone system, you can perform all your investigative analysis in that second machine and leave the actual compromised system alone for legal reasons.

Analyze the Compromised System Data

Once you have a verified backup copy of all data on the compromised system, you can start your analysis. If you used Tripwire (as advised in this book), you should be able to detect the modified files and directories quite easily by comparing the read-only database with the compromised files and directories.

1. Check the password file (/etc/passwd, /etc/shadow) for any unusual entries in these files.

TIP Look especially for UID 0 and GID 0 lines. If any user other than root is assigned to UID or GID, you may have a lead. You can run grep ':0:' /etc/passwd to detect such entries.

2. Look for log entries in /var/log/messages, /var/log/secure, or any other log files relevant to your system.

   For example, if you detected the intrusion because someone reported that your Web site was defaced, look through the Web server log to see what IP addresses have recently visited your Web site. Look for any unusual activity.

3. Boot up the system in normal mode (possibly multiuser run-level 3) and run the lsof > /tmp/lsof.out command to see what files are opened in the system.

   Review the /tmp/lsof.out file and see if you see any unusual program opening any file or any unusual file being opened by an innocent-looking program.

   Unfortunately, detecting such activity requires a lot of past experience in looking at lsof output of running systems. Novice users (or the victims of a clever attacker) may not find this technique effective.

4. Run the top program on a shell to see what programs are running on your system. You can also examine a ps auxww output, looking for any unusual program currently running. Typically, attackers create a backdoor to the system by leaving a Trojan horse program or a network daemon running.

5. Run the watch netstat -p command to see what programs are connecting (or trying to connect in your case) to the outside world. See if you see anything unusual.

Restoring the system

The best step to take in the aftermath of a system compromise is to completely reformat your hard disks – *after* you have made sure to back up all valuable data and made all the copies needed to satisfy any legal requirements (which you should find out from your legal counsel).

Completely redo the system to ensure that no trace of any Trojan program is left on the system and also implement all the security measures discussed in this book.

If you were successful in identifying the actual time of the incident when attackers got into your system, restore from backup tapes that pre-date that time (if possible). When restoring your system, do the following:

♦ **Do not use the same passwords as before.** Change everyone's password and also change any database passwords that were used in any database that were hosted in the system.

♦ **If you know how the attack was performed, make sure you fix the problem.** One way to test your solution is to try out the same attack on your system after you fix it.

♦ **Inform CERT about your incident.** You should also inform CERT (www.cert.org) about this incident. Visit their official Web site to find out who to call (and how to contact them via Web or e-mail).

Appendix E

What's On the CD-ROM?

THE CD-ROM THAT ACCOMPANIES this book contains many great security software programs and files that will save you a lot of time. To navigate the CD-ROM quickly, use a file browser program such as File Manager under the X Window System systems or Windows Explorer under Windows systems.

To view the contents of the CD-ROM, Red Hat Linux users must mount the CD-ROM using the `mount` command.

The following sections describe what you can find on the CD.

Book Chapters in Searchable PDF Format

All the chapters of the book are included on the CD in PDF format so that you can search and print information from it for your own use only. We have included Acrobat Reader 5.0 for Windows platforms in the CD for your convenience.

Unix/Linux users must use the Adobe Acrobat Reader for their systems. Other PDF readers may not work with searchable PDF documents.

Sample Book Scripts in Text Format

All sample scripts developed by the author are included on the CD in text format. Copy each script from appropriate directory and modify as you need to.

Make sure you turn on execute permission for scripts to run.

- **Tripwire.** Tripwire Open Source, Linux edition is a data/network integrity software. You can learn more about Tripwire at `http://www.tripwire.com/products/linux`.

- **OpenSSL.** OpenSSL is the open-source implementation of the Secure Socket Layer (SSL) protocol. Many programs, such as Apache-SSL and OpenSSH, need the OpenSSL source distribution.

 The CD-ROM that accompanies this book includes software developed by Ben Laurie for use in the Apache-SSL HTTP server project.

- **OpenSSH.** OpenSSH is a secure shell program that uses OpenSSL technology to encrypt all network traffic. You can learn more about OpenSSH at `http://www.openssh.org`.

- **John The Ripper.** John the Ripper is a password cracker, which detects weak passwords. You can learn more about this software at `http://www.openwall.com/john/`.

- **Netcat.** Netcat is a network utility program that allows a system administrator to debug and explore network security issues. It works with TCP and UDP protocols.

- **gShield.** gShield is an iptables firewall. You can learn more about gShield at `http://muse.linuxmafia.org/gshield.html`.

- **cgichk.pl.** cgichk.pl is a Perl script that acts as a simple CGI script scanner, which looks for known vulnerabilities in Perl-based CGI scripts.

- **Postfix.** Postfix is a Sendmail alternative SMTP mail server. You can learn about Postfix at `http://www.postfix.org`.

- **SARA.** Security Auditor's Research Assistant (SARA) is security analysis tool, which is based on the famous security assessment tool called SATAN. To learn more about SARA, visit `http://www-arc.com/sara`.

- **PortSentry.** PortSentry is a port scan detection tool. You can learn about this tool at `http://www.psionic.com/abacus/portsentry/`.

- **Whisker.** Whisker is a CGI vulnerability scanner, which detects known CGI vulnerabilities in CGI scripts.

- **SAINT.** Security Administrator's Integrated Network Tool (SAINT) is a security assessment tool, which has been derived from the famous security assessment tool called SATAN. You can learn more about SAINT at `http://www.wwdsi.com/saint/`.

- ◆ **Swatch.** Swatch monitors log entries in log files and has the ability to trigger alarms or events in case of security breaches. You can learn more about Swatch at http://www.stanford.edu/~atkins/swatch/.

- ◆ **tcpdump.** tcpdump is a network packet dump and monitoring tool. You can monitor specifics of each packet traveling via a network interface using this tool. To learn more about this tool, visit http://www.tcpdump.org.

- ◆ **Perl.** The source distribution of the Perl scripting language is included on the CD. To install Perl on your Red Hat Linux system, extract the source distribution in a directory such as /usr/local/src on your hard disk and read the INSTALL file for details.

- ◆ **Nessus.** Nessus is a network security audit client/server tool. You can learn about Nessus at http://www.nessus.org.

- ◆ **LIDS.** Linux Intrusion Detection System (LIDS) is a kernel-level intrusion detection and protection system for Linux. You can learn more about LIDS at http://www.turbolinux.com.cn/lids/. This software is included in the CD.

- ◆ **LSOF.** LSOF shows the list of files opened by processes. You can learn more about LSOF at ftp://vic.cc.purdue.edu/pub/tools/unix/lsof/.

- ◆ **Nmap.** Network Mapper (Nmap) is a network scanner and security auditing utility. To learn more about Nmap visit http://www.insecure.org/nmap/.

- ◆ **Vetescan.** Vetescan is a suite of security vulnerability scanner and exploit detection programs. You can learn about Vetescan at http://www.self-evident.com.

- ◆ **ngrep.** ngrep is a network traffic equivalent of the famous Unix utility called grep. It allows you to use regular expressions to match data within an IP packet. To learn more about ngrep visit http://www.packetfactory.net/Projects/ngrep.

- ◆ **Apache Web Server.** The latest release version of the Apache server source distribution is included on the CD.

The CD-ROM that accompanies this book includes software developed by the Apache Software Foundation (http://www.apache.org).

Troubleshooting

If you have difficulty installing or using any of the materials on the companion CD, try the following solutions:

◆ **Turn off any anti-virus software that you may have running.** Installers sometimes mimic virus activity and can make your computer incorrectly believe that it is being infected by a virus. (Be sure to turn the anti-virus software back on later.)

◆ **Close all running programs.** The more programs you're running, the less memory is available to other programs. Installers also typically update files and programs; if you keep other programs running, installation may not work properly.

◆ **Reference the ReadMe:** Please refer to the ReadMe file located at the root of the CD-ROM for the latest product information at the time of publication.

If you still have trouble with the CD, please call the Hungry Minds Customer Care phone number: (800) 762-2974. Outside the United States, call 1 (317) 572-3994. You can also contact Hungry Minds Customer Service by e-mail at techsupdum@hungryminds.com. Hungry Minds will provide technical support only for installation and other general quality control items; for technical support on the applications themselves, consult the program's vendor or author.

Index

A

continued

continued

GNU General Public License

Version 2, June 1991
Copyright © 1989, 1991 Free Software Foundation, Inc.
59 Temple Place, Suite 330, Boston, MA 02111-1307, USA
Everyone is permitted to copy and distribute verbatim copies of this license
document, but changing it is not allowed.

Preamble

The licenses for most software are designed to take away your freedom to share
and change it. By contrast, the GNU General Public License is intended to guarantee your freedom to share and change free software – to make sure the software is
free for all its users. This General Public License applies to most of the Free
Software Foundation's software and to any other program whose authors commit
to using it. (Some other Free Software Foundation software is covered by the GNU
Library General Public License instead.) You can apply it to your programs, too.

When we speak of free software, we are referring to freedom, not price. Our
General Public Licenses are designed to make sure that you have the freedom to
distribute copies of free software (and charge for this service if you wish), that you
receive source code or can get it if you want it, that you can change the software or
use pieces of it in new free programs; and that you know you can do these things.

To protect your rights, we need to make restrictions that forbid anyone to deny
you these rights or to ask you to surrender the rights. These restrictions translate to
certain responsibilities for you if you distribute copies of the software, or if you
modify it.

For example, if you distribute copies of such a program, whether gratis or for a
fee, you must give the recipients all the rights that you have. You must make sure
that they, too, receive or can get the source code. And you must show them these
terms so they know their rights.

We protect your rights with two steps: (1) copyright the software, and (2) offer
you this license which gives you legal permission to copy, distribute and/or modify
the software.

Also, for each author's protection and ours, we want to make certain that everyone understands that there is no warranty for this free software. If the software is
modified by someone else and passed on, we want its recipients to know that what
they have is not the original, so that any problems introduced by others will not
reflect on the original authors' reputations.

Finally, any free program is threatened constantly by software patents. We wish to avoid the danger that redistributors of a free program will individually obtain patent licenses, in effect making the program proprietary. To prevent this, we have made it clear that any patent must be licensed for everyone's free use or not licensed at all.

The precise terms and conditions for copying, distribution and modification follow.

Terms and Conditions for Copying, Distribution, and Modification

0. This License applies to any program or other work which contains a notice placed by the copyright holder saying it may be distributed under the terms of this General Public License. The "Program", below, refers to any such program or work, and a "work based on the Program" means either the Program or any derivative work under copyright law: that is to say, a work containing the Program or a portion of it, either verbatim or with modifications and/or translated into another language. (Hereinafter, translation is included without limitation in the term "modification".) Each licensee is addressed as "you".

   Activities other than copying, distribution and modification are not covered by this License; they are outside its scope. The act of running the Program is not restricted, and the output from the Program is covered only if its contents constitute a work based on the Program (independent of having been made by running the Program). Whether that is true depends on what the Program does.

1. You may copy and distribute verbatim copies of the Program's source code as you receive it, in any medium, provided that you conspicuously and appropriately publish on each copy an appropriate copyright notice and disclaimer of warranty; keep intact all the notices that refer to this License and to the absence of any warranty; and give any other recipients of the Program a copy of this License along with the Program.

   You may charge a fee for the physical act of transferring a copy, and you may at your option offer warranty protection in exchange for a fee.

2. You may modify your copy or copies of the Program or any portion of it, thus forming a work based on the Program, and copy and distribute such modifications or work under the terms of Section 1 above, provided that you also meet all of these conditions:

   a) You must cause the modified files to carry prominent notices stating that you changed the files and the date of any change.

b) You must cause any work that you distribute or publish, that in whole or in part contains or is derived from the Program or any part thereof, to be licensed as a whole at no charge to all third parties under the terms of this License.

c) If the modified program normally reads commands interactively when run, you must cause it, when started running for such interactive use in the most ordinary way, to print or display an announcement including an appropriate copyright notice and a notice that there is no warranty (or else, saying that you provide a warranty) and that users may redistribute the program under these conditions, and telling the user how to view a copy of this License. (Exception: if the Program itself is interactive but does not normally print such an announcement, your work based on the Program is not required to print an announcement.)

These requirements apply to the modified work as a whole. If identifiable sections of that work are not derived from the Program, and can be reasonably considered independent and separate works in themselves, then this License, and its terms, do not apply to those sections when you distribute them as separate works. But when you distribute the same sections as part of a whole which is a work based on the Program, the distribution of the whole must be on the terms of this License, whose permissions for other licensees extend to the entire whole, and thus to each and every part regardless of who wrote it.

Thus, it is not the intent of this section to claim rights or contest your rights to work written entirely by you; rather, the intent is to exercise the right to control the distribution of derivative or collective works based on the Program.

In addition, mere aggregation of another work not based on the Program with the Program (or with a work based on the Program) on a volume of a storage or distribution medium does not bring the other work under the scope of this License.

3. You may copy and distribute the Program (or a work based on it, under Section 2) in object code or executable form under the terms of Sections 1 and 2 above provided that you also do one of the following:

a) Accompany it with the complete corresponding machine-readable source code, which must be distributed under the terms of Sections 1 and 2 above on a medium customarily used for software interchange; or,

b) Accompany it with a written offer, valid for at least three years, to give any third party, for a charge no more than your cost of physically performing source distribution, a complete machine-readable copy of the corresponding source code, to be distributed under the terms of Sections 1 and 2 above on a medium customarily used for software interchange; or,

c) Accompany it with the information you received as to the offer to distribute corresponding source code. (This alternative is allowed only for noncommercial distribution and only if you received the program in object code or executable form with such an offer, in accord with Subsection b above.)

The source code for a work means the preferred form of the work for making modifications to it. For an executable work, complete source code means all the source code for all modules it contains, plus any associated interface definition files, plus the scripts used to control compilation and installation of the executable. However, as a special exception, the source code distributed need not include anything that is normally distributed (in either source or binary form) with the major components (compiler, kernel, and so on) of the operating system on which the executable runs, unless that component itself accompanies the executable.

If distribution of executable or object code is made by offering access to copy from a designated place, then offering equivalent access to copy the source code from the same place counts as distribution of the source code, even though third parties are not compelled to copy the source along with the object code.

4. You may not copy, modify, sublicense, or distribute the Program except as expressly provided under this License. Any attempt otherwise to copy, modify, sublicense or distribute the Program is void, and will automatically terminate your rights under this License. However, parties who have received copies, or rights, from you under this License will not have their licenses terminated so long as such parties remain in full compliance.

5. You are not required to accept this License, since you have not signed it. However, nothing else grants you permission to modify or distribute the Program or its derivative works. These actions are prohibited by law if you do not accept this License. Therefore, by modifying or distributing the Program (or any work based on the Program), you indicate your acceptance of this License to do so, and all its terms and conditions for copying, distributing or modifying the Program or works based on it.

6. Each time you redistribute the Program (or any work based on the Program), the recipient automatically receives a license from the original licensor to copy, distribute or modify the Program subject to these terms and conditions. You may not impose any further restrictions on the recipients' exercise of the rights granted herein. You are not responsible for enforcing compliance by third parties to this License.

7. If, as a consequence of a court judgment or allegation of patent infringement or for any other reason (not limited to patent issues), conditions are imposed on you (whether by court order, agreement or otherwise) that contradict the conditions of this License, they do not excuse you from the

conditions of this License. If you cannot distribute so as to satisfy simultaneously your obligations under this License and any other pertinent obligations, then as a consequence you may not distribute the Program at all. For example, if a patent license would not permit royalty-free redistribution of the Program by all those who receive copies directly or indirectly through you, then the only way you could satisfy both it and this License would be to refrain entirely from distribution of the Program.

If any portion of this section is held invalid or unenforceable under any particular circumstance, the balance of the section is intended to apply and the section as a whole is intended to apply in other circumstances.

It is not the purpose of this section to induce you to infringe any patents or other property right claims or to contest validity of any such claims; this section has the sole purpose of protecting the integrity of the free software distribution system, which is implemented by public license practices. Many people have made generous contributions to the wide range of software distributed through that system in reliance on consistent application of that system; it is up to the author/donor to decide if he or she is willing to distribute software through any other system and a licensee cannot impose that choice.

This section is intended to make thoroughly clear what is believed to be a consequence of the rest of this License.

8. If the distribution and/or use of the Program is restricted in certain countries either by patents or by copyrighted interfaces, the original copyright holder who places the Program under this License may add an explicit geographical distribution limitation excluding those countries, so that distribution is permitted only in or among countries not thus excluded. In such case, this License incorporates the limitation as if written in the body of this License.

9. The Free Software Foundation may publish revised and/or new versions of the General Public License from time to time. Such new versions will be similar in spirit to the present version, but may differ in detail to address new problems or concerns.

Each version is given a distinguishing version number. If the Program specifies a version number of this License which applies to it and "any later version", you have the option of following the terms and conditions either of that version or of any later version published by the Free Software Foundation. If the Program does not specify a version number of this License, you may choose any version ever published by the Free Software Foundation.

10. If you wish to incorporate parts of the Program into other free programs whose distribution conditions are different, write to the author to ask for permission. For software which is copyrighted by the Free Software Foundation, write to the Free Software Foundation; we sometimes make exceptions for this. Our decision will be guided by the two goals of preserving the free status of all derivatives of our free software and of promoting the sharing and reuse of software generally.

No Warranty

11. BECAUSE THE PROGRAM IS LICENSED FREE OF CHARGE, THERE IS NO WARRANTY FOR THE PROGRAM, TO THE EXTENT PERMITTED BY APPLICABLE LAW. EXCEPT WHEN OTHERWISE STATED IN WRITING THE COPYRIGHT HOLDERS AND/OR OTHER PARTIES PROVIDE THE PROGRAM "AS IS" WITHOUT WARRANTY OF ANY KIND, EITHER EXPRESSED OR IMPLIED, INCLUDING, BUT NOT LIMITED TO, THE IMPLIED WARRANTIES OF MERCHANTABILITY AND FITNESS FOR A PARTICULAR PURPOSE. THE ENTIRE RISK AS TO THE QUALITY AND PERFORMANCE OF THE PROGRAM IS WITH YOU. SHOULD THE PROGRAM PROVE DEFECTIVE, YOU ASSUME THE COST OF ALL NECESSARY SERVICING, REPAIR OR CORRECTION.

12. IN NO EVENT UNLESS REQUIRED BY APPLICABLE LAW OR AGREED TO IN WRITING WILL ANY COPYRIGHT HOLDER, OR ANY OTHER PARTY WHO MAY MODIFY AND/OR REDISTRIBUTE THE PROGRAM AS PERMITTED ABOVE, BE LIABLE TO YOU FOR DAMAGES, INCLUDING ANY GENERAL, SPECIAL, INCIDENTAL OR CONSEQUENTIAL DAMAGES ARISING OUT OF THE USE OR INABILITY TO USE THE PROGRAM (INCLUDING BUT NOT LIMITED TO LOSS OF DATA OR DATA BEING RENDERED INACCURATE OR LOSSES SUSTAINED BY YOU OR THIRD PARTIES OR A FAILURE OF THE PROGRAM TO OPERATE WITH ANY OTHER PROGRAMS), EVEN IF SUCH HOLDER OR OTHER PARTY HAS BEEN ADVISED OF THE POSSIBILITY OF SUCH DAMAGES.

End Of Terms And Conditions

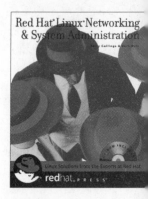